UNCHARTED

UNCHARTED

A
COUPLE'S EPIC
EMPTY-NEST
ADVENTURE
SAILING FROM
ONE LIFE TO
ANOTHER

KIM BROWN SEELY

SASQUATCH BOOKS
SEATTLE

Printed in the United States of America

SASQUATCH BOOKS with colophon is a registered trademark of Penguin Random House LLC

23 22 21 20 19   9 8 7 6 5 4 3 2 1

Editor: Gary Luke | Production editor: Jill Saginario
Design and cover illustration: Tony Ong
Map illustrations: Elizabeth Person
Interior photographs: Kim Brown Seely

Library of Congress Cataloging-in-Publication Data is available.

ISBN: 978-1-63217-255-6

Sasquatch Books
1904 Third Avenue, Suite 710
Seattle, WA 98101

SasquatchBooks.com

FOR JEFF
and for our sons,
Sam and James

CONTENTS

PART THREE

AUTHOR'S NOTE

To write this book I pulled out my sailing journals, researched history and facts when I could, compared notes with people who appear in the book, and called upon my own memory. I have tinkered with the chronology of a few events for the sake of narrative flow. I've changed the names of some, but not all, of the people because not everyone I've written about knew they were going to be characters in a book. That said, there are no composite characters in this book. These changes aside, this is a true story, constructed from memory.

STRAIT OF GEORGIA

VANCOUVER

NANAIMO

WALLACE I.

GALIANO I.

SALT SPRING I.

BEDWELL HARBOUR

SOUTH PENDER I.

SAN JUAN ISLANDS

FRIDAY HARBOR

LOPEZ I.

VANCOUVER ISLAND

VICTORIA

CANADA USA

CANADA USA

SALISH SEA

STRAIT OF JUAN DE FUCA

WHIDBEY I.

PUGET SOUND

OLYMPIC PENINSULA

LAKE WASHINGTON

BAINBRIDGE I.

SEATTLE ELLIOTT BAY

N

PROLOGUE

The wind beat upon the white canvas, blowing an anthem like freedom. The sun was out, always a pleasant surprise in northern Canada; the sails were high, and we were higher, flying across a cold blue sea. Minutes before, we'd been enjoying a long crossing, the boat heeled over, humming along. Now it was time to start the engine, bring in the sails, and motor through a maze of small rock islands. But when we turned the key, nothing. There was no charge, no reassuring rumble of safety. I took a deep breath and held it.

We hadn't left time to tack, hadn't planned on having to turn our big boat, and now we were barreling toward a rocky islet, me at the helm and my husband, Jeff, down below, banging a wrench on the starter. I stood at the sailboat's wheel, twisting a tiny metal key in the ignition—praying that the solenoid he was hammering would engage.

The key was pathetic. The island loomed closer. We weren't going to make it.

Jeff shot up, released a line, and we slammed the boat hard to windward, coming about. I let out my breath, stunned.

We were alone together and had courted this chaos. We were grown-ups and people's parents. We'd raised two sons together, battled cancer together, and lived on both coasts of North America together. When our sons left home, we'd found ourselves on one of those coasts with a window of time, and so we'd launched ourselves into it. But now, with a boat whose moods changed as mercurially as our own, we were wrestling with forces larger than ourselves, and sometimes, paying a price.

We were immersed in a world that was brand-new for both of us—it felt immediate yet eternal. I loved the rhythm of waves lapping at our boat; it seemed like a long-lost friend. We all have ocean in our veins. Back home at our house just outside Seattle, we'd been dreaming of exploring this world for a while. I'd first heard of it from a sailor I'd met at a dinner; he was ferrying a well-known *National Geographic* photographer to a rarely visited part of British Columbia's coast to shoot wildlife photos.

When the story came out a year later, I was slayed: on the cover of *National Geographic* there was an image of a white bear. There was something strange about the bear: it had fur the color of a yellow Lab. Even though it was a white bear or so-called spirit bear, it wasn't Arctic white like a polar bear, nor was it cinnamon brown like a grizzly. It was some weird vanilla-white in between. It reminded me of a mythical creature—like what you might get if you crossed a bear with a dog. Its snout was brown and its paws were brown, but its claws were translucent. Across its shoulder blades matted tufts of fur stood up like they'd been dipped in orange marmalade.

"What's that?"

"A *spirit bear*," I told my husband, when he found me that fateful day frozen in front of our coffee table, staring at the yellow-bordered cover. It trumpeted, "The Wildest Place in North America: Land of the Spirit Bear."

The spirit bear, I learned, was, in fact, a black bear born with a double-recessive gene causing white fur. It was a walking contradiction: a *white* black bear. Also known as the Kermode bear, it was rare—more rare than the giant panda. I pictured fur and forest, rain and sea; bold explorers sailing off to distant wilderness islands and hiking through giant trees; Paul Nicklen, the *National Geographic* photographer, waiting in the woods for days and then weeks until the singular moment when he came upon this strange creature climbing a cedar.

This particular spirit bear had been photographed in British Columbia's Great Bear Rainforest, part of planet Earth's largest intact coastal temperate rainforest, at the far edge of the North American continent. More than thirteen thousand years before, humans lived alongside these bears. But now the region, which stretched from north of Vancouver Island to south of the Alaska Panhandle—a rugged and complex maze of islands and fjords where vast swaths of cedar and spruce met the North Pacific—was about as remote as you can get in this world.

I have a weakness for *remote*. Never in my life have I wanted anything as much as I wanted to sail off in search of that spirit bear.

Our sons were leaving the nest, the economy was in free fall, our jobs were stagnant, and it seemed my husband and I had come to the edge of something: we could live safe, small lives or try something totally new by launching into the unknown. And so, the year before our second son left for college, we bought a gently worn sailboat.

The boat that turned out to be the best deal at the time was an enormous, fifty-four-foot, cutter-rigged sailboat—a ridiculous amount of boat for two people with no prior sailing experience together to learn how to sail. Our friends all thought we were nuts. No one we knew had ever been to Canada's Great Bear Rainforest. And oh, by the way, didn't we know it rained up there all the time?

But our plan didn't seem all that far-fetched to me. My husband and I had always dreamed of doing something like this. Up until then, we'd spent the majority of our lives together as many couples do: trying to be decent parents and good friends and engaged and informed citizens and thoughtful sons and daughters, all while making a living. Now, with our boys leaving home, we had an opening.

It was a time of transience: one son in college, another on his way; our small family, after years of intense and close living, was dispersing. Also, my husband had survived a recent cancer scare. We were suddenly acutely aware of the impermanence of things and imagined a sailing adventure would create space in which to share something true and lasting together. After a decade of the roller coaster of working hard and raising a family, my husband and I hoped we'd come to rest for a few weeks at sea. (How little did we know.)

Here, we told ourselves, was where we would begin again.

In setting off on our sailboat, first the four of us, then just the two of us, we'd pay attention to the shape of the journey. After we said goodbye to our sons, we'd embrace these weeks of adventure, putting all our chips on wildness. We figured a sailing expedition would allow us the time and distance to sort out our lives at this juncture, and we looked forward to the quiet and solitude of sailboat living over the modern world's noise and clamor.

Coming from a long line of campers and covered-wagon crossers, pilgrims, and pioneers, it was staying put in our home near Seattle and driving the same circles day after day—becoming prisoners to the known—that seemed unthinkable. If you want to create a larger life, I reasoned, you expand the size of your universe. That is, you come to the edge and step (or sail) over.

I knew our boys, resilient and smart, would survive wherever they were. And I hoped they'd still like us enough by then to come sail around from time to time. I imagined a snug cabin caulked against storms. A teapot whistling on the stove. Shelves lined with the best books. Somewhere small to live well in a world filled with uncertainty. This is the story, then, about how my husband and I (and occasionally our kids) lived simply and boldly during that time in a place that was both immense and contained: immense in the sheer expansiveness of sea and possibility; contained in that our boat felt as compact as a shell, and we existed in a world of our own design, a world that stood outside time as we knew it.

Returning home, our house felt strangely quiet, and another journey began. This is also the story of the interlude before that journey— of moving from one life to another, and the passages in between.

PART ONE

And once for all, let me tell thee and assure thee, young man, it's better to sail with a moody good captain than a laughing bad one.

—HERMAN MELVILLE

Moby Dick

MIGRATIONS

I'd always known Empty-Nesting would be uncharted territory.

My mother had told me how it had gone for her: "The house was so different when you left," she confided one day out of the blue. I was practically thirty.

"It was?" I said, startled. We were having lunch near my office in midtown Manhattan, where I'd worked for a decade. My mother was visiting from California. I was suddenly flooded with guilt: I'd never even *thought* about how it had been for my parents once I'd left for college.

"You were away at school, and we missed you but didn't want to bother you—you were a freshman!" my mom said, as if that explained everything. She took a sip of water, refolded her napkin. "But by the time your sister left for college, I realized I'd fallen into a kind of depression."

"You did? Why didn't you ever say anything?!"

"Well, that's why I'm telling you now . . . in case you ever feel like you might be dealing with depression," she said, smiling brightly.

"Well, how are you? Are you okay now?" I was stunned. I had a hundred questions . . . Like many young girls growing up in the 1960s and '70s, my sister and I had been encouraged to follow our dreams—to be whatever we wanted to be. Our parents had always pushed us to excel, to be independent, to venture as far from home as possible. Also, our parents were young. They were hip. I was proud of them, and it had never occurred to me, even remotely, that in pleasing them we were hurting them—and that my mom, especially, would so fiercely, deeply miss us. That she'd be sad once she'd launched us on our way.

My mother, a fine-boned woman—with chic bobbed hair, china-blue eyes, and the metabolism of a hummingbird—said she was better. And anyway, she didn't want to dwell on the past. Since then, her career as a photographer had taken off, had given her new purpose. Indeed, she'd go on to create a serious artist's life in the space after kids, with her work hanging in major museum collections and several critically acclaimed photography books to her name. As we were leaving the restaurant, however, she said, "I'm taking some medication now—it helps." And then, "Do I seem any different to you?"

~~~~~~~~~

Another thing I'd noticed, watching my parents' generation, was divorce. It was as if kids had been magnets holding these couples together—almost like they'd mostly stayed together *because* of their kids. But once children no longer factored into the equation, legions of seventies parents woke up and discovered they didn't have that much in common. You could count the couples splitting up along the Southern California cul-de-sacs where we'd grown up. *Sproing! Sproing! Sproing!* They bounced apart like atoms released from ionic bonds; without those kid-fusing electrons, there wasn't much to fuse them in place. But my parents stayed together, supportive of each other.

I suppose it was with this in mind then—wary of depression, watching divorces *still* springing up, as rampant as gray hairs, hearing girlfriends say, "I feel like everyone's leaving! Our kids are leaving, our parents are leaving!"—that I'd hit on the vague idea of some kind of shared project, something my husband and I could take up together as novice empty nesters.

We'd had shared projects before. My husband, Jeff, worked on Wall Street when we first met, but he lived in a rent-controlled apartment on Manhattan's Upper West Side. Shortly after I fell in love with him and agreed to give up my downtown artist-garret to move uptown to his place, he bought an old farmhouse in Connecticut. And so we began spending weekends there, fixing it up. In retrospect, the project was ideal training for the enormous, irrational leap of faith required to take on a sailboat years later. The difference, however, was that in Connecticut we'd also inherited several wooded acres, fruit trees, a two-hundred-year-old house in need of a new furnace, and a tumbledown barn.

We couldn't afford to fix the furnace or hire any kind of help, so we wore multiple layers of clothing inside the house and worked like dogs outside. If we had weekend guests, we'd con them into a group project like tarpapering the roof of the shed or whitewashing the fence. Then we'd cook up a big dinner—mixed grill with flank steak and sausage, or herb-crusted lamb with roast potatoes and a green salad with the garlicky vinaigrette out of *The Silver Palate Cookbook*—strip the sheets off the beds the next morning, drive all the laundry back to our apartment, wash the sheets in the basement, go to work all week, and do it all over again the next weekend.

We were married in the backyard of that house in a late-September wedding with about a hundred friends, our families, and a Jersey Shore band that drove up from Asbury Park. Two years later, when our first son, Sam, was born, we retreated to the farm when he was only three days old. The quiet and solitude of those Connecticut weekends held us together as a fledgling family. But there were also lonely days. Days when I experienced the paralyzing isolation that comes from feeling trapped, as a young mother, in a house with a white picket fence.

More than once I found myself alone in that house on a Saturday afternoon, with a baby in one arm and a flower vase in the other. And I understood viscerally what Betty Friedan had so brilliantly warned middle-class white women of more than twenty years before. I felt overwhelmed, isolated, and stuck. To be clear, this was a first world kind of stuck, and yet there I was—standing on two-hundred-year-old tulip-wood floors on a bright spring weekend, wanting to wing a ceramic vase through a plateglass window and break out of there. A house is a haven. But it can also be a cage.

Decades later my understanding would shift, part of growing into adulthood, and I'd remember the farm as a key chapter, but an odd chapter for someone who craved a less settled existence. I'd think of all the choices that go into making a life—the decisions people make, individual and combined. Drops of water, incalculable, collecting in a pool. It takes years sometimes to recognize when it's time to make a few ripples.

My husband loved the house. But we were also trapped by it and could never afford to do the things needed to maintain it. When a job opportunity in Seattle offered to move us all west in the dot-com 1990s, we packed up our apartment, sold the farm, and threw a massive goodbye party for our friends. We knew almost no one in Seattle but started a new chapter there. One of the art directors at the magazine where I worked in Midtown Manhattan said to me on my way out the door: "It's a healthy thing to repot yourself every few years."

I prayed he was right.

~~~~~~

Twenty years later: We had worked all our lives and had never taken more than two weeks off to travel—even though I was a professional travel writer, having spent decades working in publishing. Jeff had simultaneously built up a company in Seattle and sold it, agreed to run another and sold *it*—the last while battling prostate cancer. Now he was a cancer survivor, and our kids would soon be heading off. We had diligently squirreled away savings since our first jobs, setting money aside for years.

Also, we'd been lucky. There was paying for college, but somehow our boys had both been awarded academic scholarships, which helped. *What were we waiting for?* we wondered. True, we loved to work, but the world, its oceans and continents, lay right outside the front door. Life in all its complexity—and even more so with this window of good health—seemed worth celebrating.

We were in this dangerously vulnerable state then, looking for some sort of project, a new shared adventure, when my husband came up with the idea of buying a used boat off the internet.

"Hey, honey, check this out," he said one night, fingers tapping on his laptop.

"It's a Moody 54, bank owned."

I peered at the screen.

"Isn't it cool?" he continued, tap-tapping.

"Kind of," I replied. "Where is it?"

"Rhode Island."

"Hmm . . . ," I said warily. "Well, that's convenient."

Three weeks later my husband flew to Rhode Island to check out the boat. It was snowing, and the temperature was fifteen degrees. His best friend, a college buddy from Boston, drove down to meet him, and they called in a third party, a local boat surveyor.

"I think we should get her," my husband said, clicking through boat photos on his laptop the night he got home.

Uh-oh. It had already become *her.*

"I know it takes vision to imagine having cocktails in this frozen cockpit," he went on, "but . . ."

"It's covered in ice!" I protested, interrupting while squinting at the big blue hull. The foredeck was frosted over and the cockpit, even more forlorn, caked with almost a foot of snow. The bilges inside the hull were frozen solid with brown scum water; a riot of mildewed cushions and plastic parts lay strewn around inside the cabin. I peered at an image of Jeff and his compadre, also named Jeff, shivering inside the sad-looking cabin, grinning sheepishly at the camera in their down parkas, ski caps, and leather gloves.

"Trust me, she's a screaming deal," my husband said happily. "Plus, at this price, we can afford to move her across the country and put some work into her."

All I could think was: *It's fifty-four feet! A fifty-four-foot money pit!* And, *I don't even know how to sail!*

I looked at my husband, already obsessed with the complexities of this new nautical project.

Had he actually just said, *Move her across the country?*

I pictured how the boat would look once it got here: the huge hull with its seventy-five-foot mast, a giant flagpole announcing to the entire world that someone on board was having a midlife crisis.

But then I considered all the places we could go: the San Juan Islands, the Gulf Islands and the Queen Charlotte Islands off the Canadian coast, Alaska . . . Heck, maybe we'd even learn enough someday to cruise south to Mexico or cross the Pacific. It was thrilling. But it was also 2009, a year when sane people were not out shopping for sailboats, even used ones: The economy was a mess. Daily headlines screamed "Record Layoffs!" "Housing Foreclosures!" "Bankruptcy!" Millions of people were looking for work.

And then a wild idea hit me: *If the world turned upside down and everything went under, we could live aboard the boat.*

We'd have the ideal survival capsule. This notion, ridiculous as it was, calmed me. And so, caught up in the idea of it all I said, "Okay, in addition to saving for the boys' college educations, we'd better start an Empty-Nest Fund." I let myself imagine how it would feel, to have a boat, and all the food we'd need for months on her. To be able to go anywhere we wanted—maybe even sail halfway around the world!

Ever since our friends' kids had begun heading off, I'd been noticing the ways many of those friends' lives shape-shifted. It seemed to be a time when fierce, almost biological empty-nesting patterns emerged. Downsizing—putting the family home on the market and moving into a simpler, smaller place—was a familiar refrain. Another common trend was getting a new dog to fill the void. But that wasn't always a shared project; the wives seemed to do most of the dog walking.

As I watched my friends downsize, simplifying their nests; or stay in their homes but spend the next years refinishing the floors; or troll rescue-dog sites, looking for abandoned canines to love and be loved by and fill those empty rooms, I began to wonder if unknown to ourselves, we each had an image buried somewhere deep inside that was a new chapter, an image that outwardly was of a place or a thing but was actually of ourselves. Maybe it was ourselves, our new selves, that we were attempting to define as we cleaned out our drawers, and repainted our children's rooms, and adopted yellow Labs and big-eared collies and mixed retrievers.

What does it take to sustain a long-term relationship when the most shared common ground (in our case, the kids) shifts? What do we need to define and continue to define in order to sail ourselves into the unknown? To shape ourselves alongside another person for the duration?

As the idea of our boat grew real, and we began making plans to move her across the country and rename her, and wash the grit from her decks, revealing the weathered weave of her bones beneath—I realized it was ourselves that we were slowly shaping, it was ourselves that we were putting into a kind of order, it was yet another life that we were creating.

TEST FLIGHTS

~~~~~~

On a rare warm Saturday afternoon in June, when the white flanks of Mount Rainier were looming above Lake Washington, I drove through downtown Seattle, where everyone was strolling past Pike Place Market carrying bunches of flowers or standing on street corners sipping iced Americanos. I wanted a coffee desperately, but resisted the temptation to join them and continued on toward the marina at Elliott Bay. I had a date with a giant sailboat.

I knew little about boats—not even that cruising boats when they aren't cruising have unwieldy power cords that must be uncoiled and dragged down the dock and plugged in to shore power. But what I did know thrilled me. *Heron* had arrived in Seattle a few weeks earlier after her long overland journey from Rhode Island. She'd spent several weeks in a local shipyard on Lake Union being righted and reassembled, and was now—after many frozen months onshore and being trucked across the country—finally ready for a test sail. I'd been down to the shipyard, but it wasn't until I walked out to her new slip on the bay and saw her lofty mast, as long and thin as a heron's neck, soaring skyward over a sea of boats, that I realized I was both captivated—and terrified.

We'd been in the market for a smaller boat, something easier to handle. With *Heron*'s prior owner sadly losing her to a bank, and the bank wanting only to rid itself of the big blue sailboat on its books, she'd cost less than her forty-seven-foot siblings. We learned we could have her for a song if we were willing to put some work into her.

Hesitating at her size, we'd called a friend of a friend who captained a fifty-four-foot sailboat. Sure, his Halberg-Rassy was a lot of boat to maintain, he'd said. Sort of like running a small city, mechanically speaking.

But I hadn't focused on that. All I'd heard was a deep, melodious voice describing *all the adventures he'd had*. I was sold. And with fifty-four feet, I thought, you could really get somewhere. With the whole family!

But now that she was here, I realized how casually we'd made our decision. How would we ever dock her, just the two of us? She was a beast.

She was tied stern in, with her new name, *Heron*, displayed in discreet white lettering across her wide navy-blue transom. Her side rails, spanning sixteen feet across at her ample waist, floated somewhere around my ribs as I stood on the dock. I felt the frailness of my bones, and now that the moment was upon me, upon us all, discovered within myself a shocking depth of naïveté. I'd never been a practical person. I had a way of falling in love with ideas—romantic notions of places, concepts of things. Even worse, I craved contemplation but had never really gotten into the habit of deep introspection; I'd been too busy, and much preferred searching out other people's motives to examining my own.

Now as I stood there, I felt in my core a blind, nearly comical degree of faith. Faith in what? All I knew was that it was a reflexive, almost genetically predisposed kind of faith, the strain that has doomed legions of seekers and explorers but also driven and saved a few of the lucky ones. Faith in the journey. Faith that we'd somehow figure it out.

Dwarfed, I placed my left foot up on the boat, grabbed the thick metal stanchions on either side of the gate, and swung myself aboard.

Jeff and one of our closest friends, Dave, were already there, readying the lines.

"I've gotta hand it to you, Jeff. Most people would go out and find themselves a thirty-foot boat, maybe test the waters," Dave was saying, eyeing the towering rig overhead. "But not you. You go out and jump right in. I mean, this is a *serious sled*."

"Hey, Dave. Hi, Chet," I said. "Chet" was the nickname our oldest East Coast friends and I used for Jeff. When several people had volunteered to help take *Heron* out for the first time, we'd gratefully taken them up on it. First up was Dave, who'd signed on for this spontaneous day sail only hours ago. A fit guy in his late forties, Dave and I had been classmates in college. His wife, Laura, was one of my closest friends. We'd all overlapped for a few years in New York City.

"You don't have to entertain me," Dave said and grinned, perhaps calculating he'd be entertained anyway, while Jeff and I sat staring glumly at *Heron*'s schoonerlike bow. "Let's just practice docking this thing. Wouldn't you feel better if you had more hours under your belt getting her in and out of the slip? It's got to be just like parallel parking."

So that's what we did. Jeff eased the capacious *Heron* out of her slip, her saurian rig at rest with no apparent wind, while Dave and I raced around tying and untying lines to her sturdy cleats, raising and lowering her bulky sausage-shaped fenders, and leaping from *Heron*'s broad haunches to the dock, where we'd scramble to lash her down before her massive bow bit into the even bigger white-fiberglass yacht beside us.

After an hour or so of this, all of us imagining our fellow dock mates watching the newbies sweat through dock drills, we decided we'd had enough practice.

"Okay, let's get out of here and put the sails up so you can relax, Jeff," Dave suggested helpfully.

～～～～～

It was a golden summer evening. The sun blazed in the sky and the wind, what little there was, felt like a warm sigh. We motored *Heron* out of the marina and set a course straight across Puget Sound's Elliott Bay. Looking up, I could see the mast, struts, and halyards slicing the wide blue sky into triangles. Now that we were moving, the boat really did feel like a long-necked seabird, and I was thinking how *Heron* was the perfect name for our giant avian offspring. (The boat naming had been a family affair—we'd considered constellation names and names of stars; names drawn from Greek myths; music names, Northwest names, indigenous names; all kinds of nature names. But in the end, our boat was stately and blue and long necked—like a great blue heron. So *Heron* she became.)

It was time to raise the mainsail.

Dave and I cleared the lines and grabbed a winch handle. I don't remember which of us cranked out the mainsail; it's a two-person job: one cranking out sail, the other (Jeff in this case), at the helm, where there is a button that simultaneously unfurls the sail from the mast. When the sail was three-quarters of the way out, it jammed in the furler, like a massive cloth caught in a zipper.

"F*ck! How did that happen?!" Jeff cried. The three of us stood with our heads tilted back, staring up at the mast. *Heron's* huge white mainsail rippled from it but wouldn't budge up or down.

"Maybe try pulling it back in some?" Dave suggested. Jeff tried the button for the supposedly self-furling automatic furler again. *Grrrr . . . Grrrr . . . Grrr . . .* the furler growled audibly. The enormous sail stretched tighter and tighter. It was stuck. We tried letting it out again, pushing the button the other way.

"F*cker!" yelled my husband the captain.

Raised in New Jersey, toughened on Wall Street, my husband was somehow unleashed out on the water, unbound by rules or conventions. Especially as he confronted the physical realities of our stately new bird of a boat, with her confounding mechanical systems.

"Shoot," I said, trying to get into the swing of things. "What now?!"

Indigo clouds began massing over Bainbridge Island to the west. A bolt of lightning cracked the sky.

We tried tacking to pull the sail loose, a tough order in light wind.

We tried the self-furler again. "Come on! Come on!" Jeff muttered.

"Guys, it's starting to rain," I pointed out. We were exposed on the wide plane of water that fronted the city. What if lightning hit the rig?

Finally, as if nothing out of the ordinary had happened, the sail began sliding back in, rolled up, and disappeared inside the mast.

There's something so infuriatingly temperamental about boats. It's one of the things that make them almost human—you have to really know a boat, its quirks, ins and outs. And each one is different in its own mechanical way—especially a big sailboat such as ours. But *Heron* was new to us; indeed, she was the only Moody 54 in the Northwest. We'd never met her prior owners, and we were only *beginning* to get acquainted with her particular idiosyncrasies.

It was the kind of moment that called for a high-five, but there wasn't time. With the rain picking up, Jeff and Dave encouraged me to take the helm, which I did, barely avoiding a collision with a 450-foot-long ferry. We motored back toward the marina, thoroughly chastised. *Heron* was not only a big girl—she had a mind of her own.

FLOATING NEST

~~~~~~~

"Did you know that seven hundred people *die each year* from boating accidents in America?" asked James.

"I swear, James just loves that shit," said his older brother, Sam.

Our boys were up, shuffling their lanky six-foot frames into jeans and fleece a few feet away. They swore a lot on the boat. *Too late to do much about that now*, I thought, turning a page in my book.

James was seventeen. The kind of kid who would skim the various Worst-Case Scenario handbooks, then quiz me on what to do if we were attacked by a wolf pack, or maybe hit by a tsunami on the way to school. Never mind that when we weren't sailing we lived in the suburbs of Seattle, where both of these scenarios were highly unlikely. Next he handed me a travel magazine with a story titled: "One Rogue Wave: A Fishing Trip Goes Horribly Wrong."

"Oh great, just what we need!" said Sam, then nearly twenty and home from college for the summer, with mock exasperation.

"How 'bout some eggs and hash browns?" my husband asked expectantly. There was a moment of silence, then everyone burst out laughing, and I flung my book across the sailboat's galley table. "Eggs and hash browns" had become the new definition around our house for the sorry lengths that I would go to as our last child was about to leave the nest.

"Yeah, man, you really missed the boat on the eggs and hash browns," James said, sitting up straighter.

Sam, famously easygoing, just grinned and said, "Dude? You mean Mom actually gets up and cooks you breakfast before school?"

"*Dude*, you barely had time to grab a Pop-Tart. It must really suck being the older brother," my husband teased, a few feet away.

And so it went. The back-and-forth banter of boys and men. I loved it.

And I would miss it.

It's pathetic, but true: a friend of ours had mentioned that his wife—a woman I admired—was getting up early every morning to cook her son scrambled eggs and a pile of hash browns—and before I could help myself, I'd asked James if he'd like that.

Of course he'd said, "Yes."

Dang.

So now at home when my alarm went off in the dark at 6:25 a.m., that's what it was for: time for me to get up, grind the coffee, and start two skillets sizzling. It's absurd, I know, to pamper your kids like this. But when James shuffled into the kitchen, poured ketchup on a mound of hash browns so professional they could have been fried up by a short-order cook, headed for the door in his hoodie a few minutes later, and actually called out "I love you, Mom!" I fell for it every time. Even the act of cooking had become a way to secure a place in my son's heart. I was sending him out the door with a piece of me.

After James left, Jeff and I would sit at the kitchen counter and read the *New York Times* before work.

"He'll always remember the year his mom made him eggs and hash browns for breakfast," my husband might say sweetly.

"Thanks, honey," I'd reply, wondering what on earth would get us out of bed the next year when both the boys were gone.

<hr />

My husband and I were young when we married. I was twenty-six, Jeff thirty-two. The decades since have been busy. When you are fresh faced and in the reproductive years, you have a lot of energy. But still. How did we all do it? Even thinking about it exhausts me. Looking back, I feel time shrinking. It's as if I can reach out and tap the shoulder of that girl sitting at her desk in Midtown Manhattan and turn her swivel chair away from her Rolodex and sharpened pencils and black leather boots and point her west. I wish I could tell that worker-bee girl with her shoulder pads and daily to-do list that life is long. I wish I could tell her she won't always be this tired.

Some facts: Jeff and I met at a beach house on the Jersey Shore. We'd fallen for each other the moment we met; were inseparable after a few weeks; spent almost every night together after our first date; married two years later and lived in a rambling apartment on the Upper West Side. Both of our sons were born in Manhattan. It was the eighties. Jeff worked in finance; I worked in publishing. We were obsessed with those jobs. I loved my career as a young editor so much that when my paycheck landed on my desk twice a month, it felt like a surprise every time. We toiled long hours, traveled for business, and on city weekends—even though we employed a nanny during the week—sometimes argued over who would take the kids to the park and who would catch up at the office. We did not have what today is called work-life balance.

But we did have luck. Jeff worked on the sixty-second floor of the South Tower of the World Trade Center. And on the day of the first bombing, the 1993 truck bombing, he was not in the tower because he was in Vermont. We'd snuck away for a long winter weekend. He was on a pay phone, checking in with his boss, when a twelve-hundred-pound truck-bomb detonated in the parking garage beneath the towers. His boss, who'd been headed down to the garage when Jeff called, heard a muffled thud and said, "Hang on a minute." No one knew yet what had happened. The call ran late, which spared Jeff's boss from being in his SUV at that exact moment, as planned. Months later, when they identified pieces of the Jeep Grand Cherokee, they determined it had been less than a hundred feet from the blast.

~~~~~~~~

Fast-forward fifteen years. From the cockpit I spied my husband on *Heron*'s stern deck. It was summer in the Northwest, and he was wearing old chinos and a plaid flannel shirt. A gust of wind across the water caught his hair, which was more salt than pepper. Fog coated the cove, the surrounding evergreens swirled in mist. A rigging knife rested easily in one hand. A line of rope in the other.

So, he was splicing line. I took a long sip of coffee. A pair of binoculars sat at my side. A new book I couldn't wait to start lay on the table. I was supposed to be practicing knots and line tying but had some sort of mental block against the nautical arts.

When did my husband learn to splice line? I wondered. Who was this person? How could it be that even after twenty-some years of marriage, there were still pockets, holdover skills from earlier lives I didn't know?

We did not need knots to run our house on land just outside Seattle. But here in our new water life, the minute a rope left the store and landed on your boat it was never *a rope* again. It was *a line*. Lines and knots are ancient technology, and even in our digital age, they're indispensable—but up until that year, I'd never tied much more than my shoelaces.

Evidently, there is only one way to tie knots and cleat lines and coil them, Sam and James and I were learning—*the right way*, unless you wanted to look like a landlubber. In addition, the minute you take ownership of a boat, you are fighting the elements: wind, water, mildew, mold, rust, decay. A shipshape boat is a matter of character. In our case it was also two people trying to hedge their bets against chaos, disintegration, and disaster.

My husband and I were in this battle with the elements together. But he was the one with the original hands-on skills. He'd learned how to sail during summers growing up at the Jersey Shore. For years before we met, he also crewed aboard a fifty-one-foot boat named *Gannet* that raced weekends in Long Island Sound and every two years to Bermuda.

He completed an end splice on a new dock line so it wouldn't unravel. *This is good!* I thought—brushing off Boy Scout skills, these tangible, handheld remnants of maritime culture in Seattle, the city of virtual reality. And although I was a reluctant learner, I vowed to become a decent line coiler and cleater—just the basics—without feeling too threatened by the seamanship gap that loomed as wide as an ocean in our relationship.

Because if I dwelled on that, I figured, we'd never go anywhere.

～～～～～～

It was morning again aboard *Heron*. A slice of crisp dawn air slipped through the hatch above our bed. We liked to keep the cabin cold at night and slept buried beneath a comforter and worn cotton sheets. But that made the first step out of bed a tough one. And so we burrowed deeper.

Trying to wake under these circumstances wasn't easy. In addition to the scent of briny air, like opium for sleeping, there was also the gentle rocking—the *lap, lap, lap*—of water brushing against the hull. The effect was similar to being an infant rocked in a cradle. Or what I imagined it might be like to be an infant rocked in a cradle. I was a rather large infant, now in my late forties and curled next to my husband, who was in his early fifties. Our New York City days felt lifetimes ago.

How did we get here? Two middle-aged people naked as oysters, floating in a fifty-four-foot shell of a sailboat while the Northwest tried to warm a new day on the Salish Sea. A girlfriend had texted me while we were still in cell phone range, a few days' sail north of Seattle: "But where will you sleep?!"

Now this message was frozen on my phone, a relic from the world of connectivity . . . There had been no others since.

Where *would* we sleep? I opened my eyes, feeling guilty. *Heron*, or *Mighty Heron*, as our friends had nicknamed her, was not only a large, seaworthy sailboat, she was a comfortable sailboat. There was honey-colored wood all around—the raised floor beside my berth, the cabinets that wrapped past my ear, the wall at the foot of the bed. Our bed was, in fact, an actual mattress tucked into a wood frame, and beyond the bed, which dominated the boat's rear cabin like a small island, everything was burnished cherry veneer—the walls, the built-in drawers with their stainless spring-release knobs, even the two slim hanging lockers.

It was like waking up inside a chestnut, I thought, *or maybe a cello case—if the case were made of the same lustrous wood and had the same amplified resinous scent as the cello. No,* I thought, drifting off again with the gentle *rock, splash . . . rock, splash . . .* of the hull: *It was like waking up inside a cello itself. A cello afloat on a lake, under a sky as vast as the sea.*

And so, we drifted and dreamed. By the time I dragged myself out of bed and walked the four steps from the sailboat's aft-sleeping cabin to the main salon, Jeff—who was a morning person with the energy of armies, as well as chief underwriter, oil-filter changer, hull cleaner, macerator fixer, ham-radio operator, DJ, and I'll admit it, captain of this unlikely ark—had already showered and made a pot of coffee.

"Here, your *latte* is ready," he said with a wink, handing me a cup.

He sat down a foot away, beside the VHF radio, tuning in the marine weather forecast. He was wearing old jeans with a hole worn through the left-rear pocket, a flannel shirt, leather Top-Siders detaching from their soles. He had skin the color of a brown olive, crow's-feet that wrinkled beside startling blue eyes, dark hair starting to silver at the temples, cropped short. At the crown of his head his hair stood straight up, the kid he once was still mischievously present. We'd been married twenty-five years, not all of them easy, but he's the kind of man who has a grouchiness that's surprisingly winning, and the stories he tells still slay me, even though—and here's the key: I'd heard most of them about a million times before. I sipped my coffee, watched him dial in the VHF.

A disembodied voice intoned, "Winds moderate, northwest ten to fifteen."

"Probably a good day to cross the Strait of Georgia," my husband said.

"Sounds great!" I exclaimed, already buzzed on coffee.

It was Day Four of our Maiden Voyage—a fun two-week family trip that would forever be remembered as the Disastrous Maiden Voyage or the Infamous Maiden Voyage. We were anchored off British Columbia's Salt Spring Island, and it was still cold on the boat, too cold to do much more than pull on flannel pajamas and slide into my command post on the built-in green leather couch that wraps the dining table and take a quick survey. Past the table—which anchors our twelve-by-fourteen-foot living space and serves as ground zero on *Heron*—nearly everything we'd need to survive was within arm's reach. The galley, big enough for one cook at a time, was tucked into an alcove directly across from me. Next to that was another, shorter fir-green leather couch, also built in. That was the extent of our furniture. There were some cherry-veneer cabinets on either side of the small couch: one held shatterproof wineglasses; the other, crucial life-sustaining foods—almonds, dried apricots, potato chips, chocolate chip cookies. Between them was an oblong porthole flanked by two antique-brass ship's lanterns my husband had carted around since lifting them from his parents' basement in the seventies, and a few feet of books we planned to read in all our spare time.

"It's not a boat, it's a library!" my husband had quipped a few days earlier, eyeing the books, many of them heavy hardbacks, including a Merriam-Webster dictionary for Scrabble, an exploration section (biographies of Captain James Cook and Joseph Banks and Richard Henry Dana's *Two Years Before the Mast*), lots of current fiction, some classic fiction (we're a family obsessed with *Moby Dick*), and a little history and nonfiction and poetry wedged beneath the portholes so the books wouldn't tumble too far when *Heron* was heeled on her side in a stiff wind.

To my right was a two-foot passage leading to the forward berth, a head, and a tiny paneled office with a fold-down bunk. Our world below, in terms of physical space, consisted of four snug rooms, a warren of concealed lockers, and an engine compartment. But our world, in terms of created space, felt like a free-floating cabin adrift at just the right distance from the shore's information overload and nonstop pace.

Next to the companionway, a wall with a built-in bookshelf crammed with the kinds of books you tend to collect when you're all hope, heading out for your first season on the water: *Chapman Piloting & Seamanship*; a *Waggoner Cruising Guide*, billed as "the Bible for Northwest Cruising"; the daunting *Current Atlas: Juan de Fuca Strait to Strait of Georgia*, which opened to pages of tables for calculating the Northwest's strong currents; and the true bible for Northwest waters, *Ports and Passes*, an annual volume in which tide and current information is listed on a page for each day of the year, including high and low tide. Next to these were guides to the night sky and its constellations (we'd finally learn the stars!), and the pocket-sized *Audubon Field Guide to the Pacific Northwest*, with its illustrations of sponges and sea anemones, mollusks and snails, jellyfish, oysters, barnacles, crabs and sea stars; working up to all the

Northwest seabirds: the loons, the grebes and pelicans, graceful cormorants and egrets. Even the words describing the things we hoped to learn in our new floating world sounded lovely and strange.

Across from the books was the navigation table, one of *Heron's* best places: a built-in desk with a green leather bench and a desktop that lifted to reveal all kinds of useful stuff stashed within. A mess of charts for plotting your course. Notebooks, pens, rulers, tide charts. On the wall adjacent to the nav table was an electrical control panel as complex as a pilot's, blanketed with marine radios and gauges, and a daunting thirty-seven switches. The switches were labeled: Sockets. Immersion Heater. Engine Battery Charger. Auxiliary Battery Charger. Air Con Pump. Fresh Water Pump. Gray Water Pump. Macerator . . . All the things that controlled the complex world that made up *Mighty Heron's* many systems. Most of them were completely baffling to me.

As Jeff liked to joke, "If you really want to scare yourself, just lift up one of these floor panels." Then he'd pry up one of *Heron's* floorboards for an unsuspecting visitor and cry "Aaaaahhhh! What is all that down there?" before slamming the panel back in place. Just a glimpse of the dark bilges, with their subterranean tangle of snaking hoses and pipes and dank filters, was enough to make you think about heading straight for land.

~~~~~~

Jeff and I had sailed dinghies together before *Heron*, but neither of us had ever captained anything close to the forty-eight thousand pounds of teak and fiberglass we now commanded, for better or worse. While I fell in love with the notion of the boat as a sort of floating cottage, my husband fell for the very boatness of *Heron*, her classic lines (to a sailor's eye), perfectly proportioned to a seventy-five-foot mast and technical rig, the big Yanmar diesel engine, the quiet Kohler generator—and most of all, the way she handled, what she felt like with eighteen knots of wind off the stern quarter. "Not too different from a runaway freight train," he'd say, only half joking.

So when we found ourselves about to cross the Strait of Georgia, the 135-mile-long, 20-mile-wide waterway, actually a small sea in its own right, separating Vancouver Island from mainland British Columbia, for the first time, we were all acutely aware—even the boys—how vulnerable we were, how seriously out of our element.

We were still learning a new language: the very words we used, even words for basic directions, were different. It was never "right" or "left" on the water but instead "starboard" or "port." Similarly, the front of the boat was always the "foredeck" or "bow"; the back was "aft," or the "stern." There were words for parts of the boat we rarely saw, subterranean places where frightening things happened if you weren't diligent: the bilges (where water could collect), the keel (which could scrape rock or grow barnacles). While we were seated in the center cockpit, our heads were covered from the elements most days by a length of canvas stretched tight called a bimini. The canvas that provided shelter from wind and rain pummeling the bow was the dodger.

"Let's raise the main!" one of us had suggested. Finally, we had enough room to point *Heron* on a beam reach (when the wind comes across the boat at a right angle), and raise and trim the mainsail.

"Wahoo! It's blowing seven and a half!" I'd yelped, making light of the Northwest's notoriously fickle wind.

"Okay, load up the winch!" Jeff called out.

One of us grabbed a metal winch handle and fit it into one of two stainless-steel winches, gleaming bright as shiny hubcaps atop the cabin.

"Let's go!" urged my husband, who—used to the competitive intensity of Big Yacht Racing, having crewed in open-water races to Bermuda, grinding winches in the midnight rain—was not impressed by his clueless, lackadaisical crew.

And for good reason.

"Uh, which one is it again?" I asked, eyeing the eight lines arrayed atop the cabin.

"Which one do you think it is? The one that says *Outhaul*!" snapped the captain.

I took over the helm while Jeff showed the boys how to wrap the thick blue outhaul line around the winch. Then Sam and James started cranking the handle, which in turn began wrapping the outhaul, pulling the clew of the sixty-foot-tall mainsail out of the mast.

"Okay, honey, raise the mainsail!" Jeff yelled back to me at the helm.

"From here?" I said, frozen.

"Push the frickin' button!"

I stared at a half dozen black switches to the right of the helm. They all looked alike. Which one was it? One had a white symbol like a sail on it, but so did another.

"JESUS! Push the Goddamn button! Sam, you do it!"

Sam hustled back, managed to find the right switch, pushed it, and the leading edge of the mainsail began emerging from the mast and sliding out along the boom. We all stared up, watching the enormous white sail fill the space above our heads.

"Okay, that's it!" Jeff called out.

James clamped down the lever securing the outhaul, cleared the winch, and *Heron* heeled over on her side, slicing through small crescent waves, picking up speed.

I sat numbly. Clearly, the captain and I had *a lot* to learn together.

But there was no time for hurt feelings. It was thrilling to ghost across the strait, electrifying! I *would*, I told myself, learn this and become spectacular at it, even though it wasn't going to be easy. "What do you think?" I said casually. "Put up the jenny?"

"Mom's the boss," Jeff said, eyeing me.

It was blowing an easy ten. The jenny, also called a genoa, is a large foresail, (fuller than a jib) that sweeps back past the mast. I took the helm again while Sam and James got the lines ready and Jeff loaded up a third, smaller winch, which would sustain even more force; it sat farther back, on the edge of the cockpit, with its twin on the opposite side. Once everything was loaded up, Sam began pulling out the genoa . . . all 830 square feet of her.

"Whoa," James said.

We were really moving—the sun bouncing off all that canvas, now *two* enormous shimmering wings stretched taut—hurtling through our first open-water crossing. *Heron* heeled farther and farther to the right; we cut the engine.

Perfect silence: as we sped along there was only the rhythmic beating of waves splashing one-two, one-two, against the hull, the powerful hum of wind filling big sails a faster staccato—one-two, one-two, one-two, one-two—in a deep blue sky. All that space and stillness and the hum of the boat made me think, for some reason, of God.

"*Dude*, wanna put up the staysail?" Sam ventured.

The staysail is our third sail, a small sail, compact enough that in a light wind you can pull it in and out by hand, just by tugging a line. On a cutter rig like *Heron*'s it's designed to direct the wind more efficiently between the two big sails.

"Sure, let's go for it," someone said.

"We are *hauling ass*!" noted the captain, putting appreciative heft into each word.

We were now shredding the water, heeled over on one side, truly clueless as to how much power we'd harnessed, how much sail we'd raised . . . It took your breath away, flying along on that big blue boat, dependent upon nothing but wind. I loved speeding through the crisp sea air, salty and bracing. Loved all that canvas. Loved having every sail up, the engine silenced. It felt like life itself. Chaotic, true . . . but *alive*!

Naturally, what goes up must come down. And now every sail, every line—and there were so many of them—was under hundreds of pounds of pressure. Only one of us had the slightest idea what he was doing out there, understood how much force was actually on those lines, what would happen if one of them caught an unsuspecting finger in a winch under five thousand pounds of pressure or flew loose, cracking faster than a whip and took out an eye. And, evidently, Jeff was also under too much pressure . . .

We lost our wind ghosting behind the uninhabited hump of Texada Island, which rises menacingly on the far side of the Strait of Georgia. It was time to bring in the jib. "How many times do I have to tell you where the jib furlers are?!"

We chugged our way across the far side of the Strait of Georgia as the sun lowered; edged our way up BC's southern Sunshine Coast; then tired, and spent, attempted to anchor the *Mighty Heron* in a narrow, shallow inlet that grew narrower and more shallow the farther in we ventured.

"I wouldn't do that if I were you!" a wiry bearded man hollered ominously from his ramshackle dock, warning us away from the inner harbor. Evidently, our chart didn't show just how shallow things got. We managed to maneuver our way around and get the hell out of there, beating a lumbering retreat. Exhausted, we next tried anchoring in a cove at the inlet's entrance, but our anchor dragged on the shale bottom. Grouchy and hungry, we then motored on to Thormanby Island, where we found eighty-five feet of water and finally anchored off this improbably lovely place called Gill Beach.

After we cut the engine the four of us sat there in the silence, numb. The wild, luminous beauty of the place stood in sharp contrast to all the heavy tensions of the day. Before crossing the strait, we'd tied up for gas at a wharf in busy Nanaimo, a harbor city where Captain Jeff, fully grasping for the first time how spectacularly clueless his crew was, had lost his cool when we'd tied the fenders on incorrectly. He'd then lost it again when the boys failed to snap to and leap off the boat quickly enough to secure the dock lines. The odd dynamic was that the boys and I were bonding, forming an eyeball-rolling, wisecracking team in opposition to Jeff the Boat Nazi.

"Mom, you've really got to get these fenders down," James had whispered at the Nanaimo dock, demonstrating the clove hitch again. "Here, like this."

Sam dutifully trudged into town with me to help with the grocery shopping. Anything to get off the boat . . .

But back on board, tempers soon grew short again. There was just too much boat, too much to do. Now, sitting in the stillness, our trip seemed utterly overwhelming. Not to mention the fact that my husband and I were planning to spend a lot of time together on this boat without the boys once they moved on in their own lives. How would we manage just the two of us? *What on earth were we thinking?*

A tear slipped from the corner of my left eye and traced its way down my windblown cheek.

The boys were dumbfounded. "What's wrong? What's the matter, Mom?"

"*Nobody liiikes me,*" I sobbed idiotically, completely undone by the day. Even worse, our first big crossing, and Jeff and I had already turned into a caricature of the clichéd boating couple: out of control, screaming at each other.

My husband was flabbergasted. "Of course we like you!" he said. "We love you, honey. It's just that, jeez, you know—it's a lot out here. It's all new! You're doing a great job. It's going to be great. Here, Sam, take a picture of your mom and me." And he'd handed the camera to Sam.

"Mom, you're so emo," Sam had joked, trying to lighten the mood as I brushed away errant tears with the back of my hand. Then he snapped a portrait of Jeff and me standing on *Heron*'s stern, facing the camera. Jeff has his arm around me. He is wearing a red fleece. I am wearing a white fleece. Behind us is a beautiful, shallow bay, Buccaneer Bay—and behind that, barely visible, the low isthmus of a driftwood-strewn beach connecting the two halves of British Columbia's Thormanby Island. You can see some of Thormanby's steep cliffs rising to the left of the frame, and scraggly fir and pine trees in the darkening light. Overhead is a magnificent sky streaked with purple clouds. I am smiling a toothy white grin. Jeff looks rugged and handsome.

It stuns me now to see this portrait: the image, in fact, that graces the leather-bound cover of the book we made in the months after that first trip. You see a smiling couple in a postcard setting. What you don't see are the invisible currents and blustery seas we'd just waded into. It's strange, how we capture so many family moments this way: squeeze people into a frame and click the photo. It's our way of making memories. But what you rarely see in so many family portraits is what's actually happening. And what a shame! The stuff we lash down—the painful parts, messy as sea slime and scary as eels—is, in retrospect, more real.

It took me years to realize that each of us would eventually find our footing on that big blue boat. To be the capable crew we envisioned: a team, whether two person, or four. To move easily, with skill and intention, across its decks and to understand its many systems. That damn boat would challenge us and push us, throw us and teach us. So many times along the way I would want things to be different than they were! The wanting was an ocean, and even though my husband and I were in it together, I had to find my own way across its blustery seas. It took us years to get there. But I liked the freedom: the thrill of being out on the water, surrounded by vastness and the pure bracing air that was the essence of the North Pacific. I was looking for something but wasn't sure where I'd find it until I arrived. It was the wildest place I'd ever been. A place called the Great Bear Rainforest.

PART TWO

The oyster bed, as the tide of life ebbed and the children went away to school, college, marriage or careers, was left high and dry. A most uncomfortable stage followed. . . . In bleak honesty it can only be called "the abandoned shell." Plenty of solitude, and a sudden panic at how to fill it, characterize this period.

—ANNE MORROW LINDBERGH

Gift from the Sea

CASTING OFF

~~~~~~~~

Day one of the big trip, under a milky dawn sky on the first morning of August, James drove us down to the boat.

"Don't forget to set your alarm. You don't want to be late for work," I told my youngest son, who had a job managing a kayak center on Seattle's Lake Washington before heading east to college in three weeks.

"Okay, got it." James yawned as he steered my Volvo SUV, crammed with one last load of gear. (His older brother, Sam, who was far more levelheaded than his parents, had an internship in San Francisco and was living there for the summer.)

"He'll be *fine*," Jeff said from the passenger seat, glancing at James. "After all, he's eighteen."

"Exactly!" I said from where I sat in the back seat, my mind reeling as I imagined the raging party about to transpire in our living room, word of which had no doubt gone viral on Facebook the second we'd pulled out of the driveway.

But as we sped across the 520 Bridge, which spans Lake Washington and links the suburbs east of the city (where we live) with Seattle, leaving our eighteen-year-old home to fend for himself for a week or so was the least of my worries. That August morning Jeff and I would be casting off for two months alone together aboard *Heron*. And although the boys would eventually join us for fourteen days, after twenty-some years of married life, spending this much time on the boat, *just the two of us*, was a first. We'd be moving from a land-based world grounded by kids, friends, and jobs—a world where each of us could jump in the car if needed, or take a walk—to a water-based world. A world where we'd be together twenty-four hours a day in a very small space.

Trying something like this had been the whole goal of buying the boat to begin with, and by god, here we were! This trip—our so-called Empty-Nesting Adventure—was a culmination of sorts. Our sailing trip with the boys the previous summer, our weekends and over-nights and day sails up and down Elliott Bay had all been dry runs, or wet runs, as it were. This was it, but the idea of the adventure had somehow grown bigger than the boat itself. I thought back to when we were first considering boating. I'd read a magazine article about a sailor who was on his fifth circumnavigation of the world. He'd summed up centuries of philosophy with his simple life motto: "Live while you're alive!" And it had seemed to me then that when you find yourself at a particular life juncture, you can allow your hopes and dreams to fade—or you can create new ones.

Damn.

And there had been the cover of *National Geographic*, with its cover line that leaped out and grabbed me and sold me so thoroughly I'd immediately turned around and sold Jeff.

The Great Bear Rainforest, according to *National Geographic*, was "the planet's last large expanse of coastal temperate rain forest." At eight million acres it was nine times the size of Olympic National Park, five times the size of Banff, twice the size of the Serengeti.

This forest possessed the rarest of all environmental qualities: critical mass. It was a place that was still utterly wild and not only out there—but *out there*, out there. Standing in our family room after showing the article to Jeff, I closed the magazine and gazed at its front cover—a leafy green thicket framing a surreal-looking black bear with vanilla-white fur—then declared with stupefying naïveté that we would sail north! Not just north to the San Juan Islands, or the Canadian Gulf Islands, or to Desolation Sound, but north around Cape Caution and north farther still—north to the Great Bear Rainforest in search of the spirit bear.

The spirit bear wasn't real to me then. It was an idea, ghostlike and vague, rich with strangeness and mystery that resonated perfectly with my hopelessly optimistic and impractical explorer's gene—handed down, I'm convinced, on both sides of my family (but more on that later). Wanderlust stirred within me as I studied our maps of coastal BC, and plotted out the distances we'd journey—like Jacques Cousteau on the *Calypso*!—to the Great Bear Rainforest.

To my husband's credit, he signed on to the quixotic quest immediately: sure, we could go north, even *way* north, why not? We'd set off in search of the mystical spirit bear, we agreed, just because the idea of it seemed cool. We'd go because spirit bears are revered and rare creatures; they're what the Gitga'at First Nation, whose traditional territory includes the islands where the bears live, call *mooksgm'ol*, a walking contradiction—a *white* black bear. We'd go because searching for a spirit bear would give us something to point ourselves toward and serve as a sort of distraction once the boys left—and it was just the two of us aboard *Heron*—in the wilds of British Columbia.

Neither albino nor polar bear, the spirit bear is a white variant of the black bear, or American bear. And it's found almost exclusively in the Great Bear Rainforest, a place as ecologically distinct as the Amazon and the Great Barrier Reef, a place so remote you can practically only get there by boat. We'd go because there were maybe only a thousand of these rare white black bears (some estimates put the number closer to between one hundred and four hundred, making them more rare than the giant panda). The bears existed almost entirely on two uninhabited, densely forested islands—Princess Royal Island and Gribbell Island—islands that were about five hundred nautical miles from our home in Seattle. We decided that if we were lucky, and the weather held, we could get there and back in two months' time, before the Northwest's bone-chilling cold and damp arrived and the end-of-season fog, known as Arctic sea smoke, swept in, settling down and swaddling the mist-shrouded fjords like a wool blanket.

We'd spent July consumed by trip prep: fitting out our fifty-four-foot, oceangoing cutter rig (a boat with two headsails that can be tacked simultaneously) for two months at sea. I'd devoted the previous weeks to creating lists and more lists, making trips to Trader Joe's, crossing things off the lists, then remembering other things and making additional trips. We'd stored our dry provisions in piles around our dining room, which began to resemble a food bank. One night I carried all the chicken and pork chops and flank steak I'd procured to the kitchen, and Jeff and I spent the next hour or so dividing it all into smaller portions, wrapping those in plastic, then wrapping the plastic tight in white freezer paper. Each slim white package was taped and labeled with a Sharpie pen. Our freezer was soon stacked with neat white bricks of protein, like a butcher's.

A week before our departure I filled insulated freezer bags with the frozen food and began hauling those down to the boat. There were bags of Trader Joe's frozen side dishes—risotto with asparagus tips, garlic potatoes, and country potatoes. There were desserts: pound cake and lemon bars and a cumbersome frozen carrot cake, which I planned to defrost in the middle of nowhere and present as a minor miracle. All this I drove across the 520 Bridge and through the city and out to the dock, unloaded into a handcart, wheeled out to the boat, unloaded onto the boat, eased down the companionway-ladder and into the cabin, unpacked, then repacked in layers in the freezer. There were bags of almonds and walnuts, and salted pistachios, and dried apricots. These were laid in the big, wide drawer that pulls out from beneath the settee and has to be wedged with an orange plastic doorstop in a gale, since the latch is broken and the drawer is so heavy it flies open. There were cans of Diet Coke and cans of Heineken and many bottles of wine. These were all stored either in the hatch beneath the forward bunk or in the boat's astonishing number of cubbies and hiding spots, such as the single floorboard that pulls up between the main salon and the forward berth and has room beneath it to lay in six bottles. When I was done I collapsed on the settee, knocked out from all my exertions, and then remembered another thing: Coffee! And balsamic vinegar! Time to start another list.

We'd found a young couple to house-sit for our dog and ancient cat. (James would stay behind to finish his last week at work, then fly up on a small floatplane with Sam to meet us on the boat.) We'd put a stop to the newspapers and mail, figured what to do, more or less, with incoming bills. With two boys now in college, it felt like a typhoon of back-to-back tuition waves were rolling at us; somehow these had to be paid. Jeff was selling the remnants of the last company he'd been running; in addition to finalizing the sale, he aimed to rent out the office space, tie up loose ends, and fold up shop in time to leave the dock on August 1. I was a freelance writer; we wouldn't be scrounging up much tuition from that during our sail, unfortunately, but there were still articles to file, deadlines to meet. Boxes of college supplies for James needed to be packed and shipped. Flights had to be booked.

How had our simple empty-nest adventure grown so complicated? Overwhelmed by the endless logistics, I'd wander into the backyard where the summer garden was in full bloom, pick as much lettuce as I could, then stake the young dahlias so they wouldn't sprout up, topple over, and crush everything come fall.

In addition to selling the business, Jeff had been focused on readying the boat. For Jeff, *Heron* was not only the realization of a lifelong dream but also his reward for selling his first company and, to a lesser extent, surviving the sale of the second. The first company, an online brokerage, provided investors a way to make automatic purchases of stock online. Jeff had built the business from a handful of employees to nearly two hundred when he sold it nine years later. After the sale he'd stepped aside, but he had also earned enough money that for the first time in his life he could afford to slow down a little if he chose. And this was when he learned, three months after selling the company, that he had aggressive prostate cancer. It seemed unbelievably unfair. He signed on to run the second company, a business that needed a new leader at the helm, as it were, while simultaneously navigating and recovering from prostate cancer surgery. "I can't just sit at home all day having cancer," he'd rationalized.

But the second business barely survived the recession when it hit. *Heron* was docked a short drive from Jeff's office in downtown Seattle, close enough that he could drive to Fisheries Supply at noon, pick up a handful of washers or a bilge pump, whip by the boat, and be back for a meeting before two o'clock in the afternoon. As the economy drifted south and Jeff grew increasingly frustrated trying to turn the business around, the boat by comparison was a tangible entity he could deal with. Where the business was virtual—information and services—the boat was actual, a physical object made of real working parts, parts that could be fixed. It was a beautiful thing, with wood that needed refinishing and canvas that needed cleaning and electronics that needed understanding and a thousand tasks that needed tending. Jeff threw himself into readying the boat, and as the economy worsened, it became a refuge. With the realization that we'd no longer have to be home all the time once James left for college, the prospect of taking the boat on some sort of extended journey grew more and more appealing.

A boat being a boat, there were an infinite number of things to fix. The whole sailboat had been dismantled, everything abovedeck stripped off to truck the boat across the country. So that first season, everything had to be put back on: the winches, the stanchions for the lifelines, the railings, the windshield, the stainless cowl vents and dorade boxes, the davits in the back, the bimini top, and of course, the mast, boom, standing rigging and running rigging (all the lines used to hoist and control the sails). We put in a new generator. We put in a new water pump. We replaced one whole bank of batteries. We stripped, sanded, and varnished the teak. We buffed the navy fiberglass hull, and Jeff had pumped up the dinghy and rigged a system of lines to hang it from the stern. Sweetest of all was the Seely Step: a portable teak step Jeff had designed, with two-inch legs that fit squarely into the teak cockpit grating behind the wheel. I could easily pull out the step, secure it in place, and actually see over the boat's canvas dodger when I took the helm. (The makers of the mighty Moody 54 evidently hadn't taken into account the possibility of a five-foot-four woman at the helm.)

Leaning forward from the back seat while James drove us to the dock for our departure, I stared at the two guys up front—they were talking about surfing. "I don't want you going down to Westport while we're gone," Jeff was saying.

"Why not?" James replied.

"It's more than a two-hour drive each way, and paddling out in those swells is *not* an option when we aren't home. Got it?"

"Yeah. Okay," James said with a shrug.

We'd allowed our second son to take more physical risks than most parents we knew: driving with a friend down to the Washington coast to surf when he was sixteen and a half. They'd camp on the beach or roll out sleeping bags in the back of James's ancient Volvo wagon, cook up cans of chili for dinner, wake early, and pull on their wetsuits. The Zen surfing life appealed to James, but now that we were heading off on our own Zen journey, we wanted him safe at home.

As for Sam, I'd just spent a rare mother-son weekend with him in San Francisco. He'd proudly shown me the 1930s streetcar he rode to his summer job each morning, taken me to the Ferry Building farmers market (which he thoughtfully guessed I'd like), then on to vintage-clothes shopping and pawing through vinyl LPs and used books together (which he knew we'd both like) in the Haight. We'd had a wonderful visit, and I realized this exciting thing: knowing your kids as grown-ups is a whole new world. But now that Jeff and I would be setting sail for weeks on end, we'd all be living distant lives.

Landing in Seattle after the visit with Sam, I'd wheeled my carry-on past a woman wrestling with a toddler. He was trying to climb atop a bench, then atop a trash can; she was putting on a brave face while he went on thrashing. I smiled to myself, remembering nightmare flights with the boys at that age. There was the time a woman approached me at baggage claim and said, "I heard you all on the plane and just wanted to tell you, it gets better." She was right. It *does* get better! So much better. There's a darn good reason most women don't have kids in their fifties.

My mind was awhirl with images: James's lacrosse team winning the state championship his senior year after beating its longtime rivals; the screaming fans, the trophy cup, the team party at our house afterward, which Sam skillfully orchestrated on the fly when the cops busted the first party and the kids had nowhere to go. Senior prom, with the guys in their tuxes, the girls in their clingy, thigh-skimming, sherbet-colored dresses. James's graduation, where he had played the guitar and sung a duet, the song "Falling Slowly" from the film *Once*, in front of hundreds of people. Although James spent hours in his room composing lyrics and belting out songs that he recorded on an 8-track, when he'd auditioned for graduation and been chosen to perform at the main event, we were stunned. This would be the first time he'd played in front of more than a handful of people. As he stepped up to the front of the gym in his long blue gown, placed his guitar across his knees, and looked out at the bleachers to find his older brother, his longtime confidant, for encouragement, I prayed silently that he'd just get through the song. But he did more than that—he played it beautifully.

I thought now about the chorus:

Take this sinking boat and point it home
We've still got time . . .

Now, as we neared the boat on that August day when we set out, I was once again a bundle of nerves, apprehensive and anxious. My lifelong wanderlust had, for years, carried me off on writing assignments around the globe. But this felt different somehow, more like a permanent departure, since one of my favorite parts of travel-ing—the coming home—would be different. Sam and James would be gone. Jeff and I would return, eventually, to an empty house. My worst fears about myself—among them, that I just wasn't ready to handle domestic life à deux—might soon prove true.

I had wanted to sail north, I now realized, to take time to move slowly from the life we were leaving toward the new life we knew nothing about. But as we turned into the parking lot next to the docks at Elliott Bay and went off in search of a handcart to wheel our duffel bags down to the boat, half of me wanted desperately to say: *Um, you know what, guys? Maybe this isn't such a good idea after all. How about we go grab some breakfast and call it a day?* But I couldn't let myself go there. Jeff and James knew me too well. We'd been planning this trip for months now. They'd hear the hesitation and uncertainty in my voice. They'd sense I had no idea what I'd gotten us into. And I didn't. But the more I stewed over all this as we unpacked our final provisions, the more I came to see how failure in this endeavor was not an option. This was a turning point and I knew it.

TAKING THE HELM

~~~~~~~

"Want to back her out?" my husband asked the instant we had the boat packed, bounding back aboard from the dock where he'd fast-walked toward the stern and, in a second, unplugged *Heron*'s shore power.

"What?" I said, horrified. "*Are you kidding me?*"

"Now's as good a time as any," he replied, leaping down to the cockpit and landing with a little sinking motion that he steadied with a hand on the wheel.

James and I exchanged meaningful glances, the three of us now standing in the mighty blue sailboat's teak-and-fiberglass cockpit. "Go for it, Mom," he said. I raised my eyebrows, considering. Tentatively, I stepped up to the helm. *Am I really going to do this?* I faced the three-foot-wide wheel and panel of instruments alongside it, not at all sure this was a good idea.

Jeff stood beside me and went through the gears while James watched intently, no doubt hoping someday he'd be next: neutral, forward, reverse. We reviewed how the bow thruster works. (A bow thruster is a propulsion device built into the bow to make a boat more maneuverable.)

"Mom, this is big," James said encouragingly, at my right shoulder.

"I know," I replied, giving him a sidelong glance.

"Okay—ready, honey? Let's do it!" Jeff called from the dock. Without any warning or ceremony whatsoever, he'd jumped back off the boat and was crouched beside the forward cleat, ready to untie our bowline. It all happened really fast.

Imagine that you are learning to back out of a parking spot for the first time, but your car is fifty-four feet long and leaves no room for error: screw up a foot to the right, and you'll inflict thousands of dollars' worth of damage; back out six inches too far, and you'll ram the big boys moored behind you. I was petrified but also knew this was a test of sorts—and that I had to rise to the occasion if I was ever going to be an equal partner in this boating thing. I'd also heard that women are inherently better than men at the finer points of helmsmanship—although docking is something almost every woman I've met on the water says was initially way beyond her comfort zone.

Without time to think about what was actually happening, I turned and gave James a quick hug.

"James, get the stern line!" Jeff called.

"Got it," James said, scrambling over the lifelines to the dock. Alone on the boat, I put *Heron* in reverse and began inching all twenty-four tons of her back out of the slip. At what seemed like the last possible second, Jeff clambered back aboard while I was waving with one hand to James standing on the long finger dock, my other hand on the wheel. I called out, "Bye, James! Bye!"

"Don't look at him—watch your bow!" barked Skipper Jeff. "Turn the wheel hard to the right. *Now!*"

And with that we barely cleared the boat tied to our right, the wooden dock inches to our left, the power cruisers parked a few feet behind us. And then we were gliding out alongside the long rock jetty, which pointed like a crooked finger into Puget Sound.

"Not bad, Mom!" James yelled after us.

I looked over my shoulder and grinned, then unpeeled my fingers from the wheel and glanced back for a final little victory wave as James turned and traipsed up the dock, pulling an empty handcart behind him.

"Nicely done. I knew you could do it," Jeff said.

"Um, that was stressful," I said, gripping the wheel again.

"It was perfect!" Jeff countered, delighted with himself. "I planned it weeks ago as a distraction, realizing we'd be leaving our son behind."

"Really?" I said, feeling humbled but also empowered at the helm, steering the big boat around the jetty's final turn.

"Look, the heron!" Jeff cried. And sure enough, the great blue heron that sometimes stands sentry at the tip of the rock jetty was there, with his taut long legs and hefty gray-blue girth and prehistoric resilience. We swung the boat to the northwest and sped out into the lead-blue sea.

~~~~~~~~~~

We motored out of Elliott Bay, the body of water that fronts the city, the Seattle skyline receding behind us. Low gray clouds blanketed the sky. The water was still as glass, the wind a whisper at just three and a half knots. I pointed the boat upwind to a heading of 349° north, my left hand resting lightly on the wheel and my right hand on the throttle. I pushed the throttle forward until we reached a speed of seven knots. There would be no use putting the sails up until we had more wind. Behind us in Seattle the Space Needle stood to the left of and slightly apart from the city, its flying-saucer-shaped dome piercing the clouds. Bainbridge Island stretched long and low before us, pressed between the gleam of the silvery bay and the gloom of an overcast sky. Along the island's spine, a fringe of evergreens brushed low clouds as soft as fleece.

While Jeff went below to mark our bearings and chart a course, I took one last look at the city and everything we were leaving behind, then turned and studied the panel of electronic instruments arrayed across the top of *Heron*'s companionway, about eight feet in front of me.

Our plan was to head north, threading through Washington State's San Juan Islands and British Columbia's Gulf Islands up the Inside Passage through the many archipelagos, then sail past the northern tip of Vancouver Island, and on up around Cape Caution to the wild, exposed Spider Islands. We would sail farther still to the seldom-visited native settlements of Bella Bella and Klemtu, then continue to the native village of Hartley Bay and neighboring Gribbell Island. The latter was one of the homes of the elusive spirit bear. We'd circumnavigate Gribbell Island, about a hundred miles south of the Alaska border, then point *Heron* south and head home again, another five hundred nautical miles, in mid-September. We'd be one of the last cruising boats that far north come fall. The days would be turning colder and growing shorter, the Pacific Northwest Coast's fog settling into the long sinuous fjords, making navigation in an area notorious for challenging navigation even trickier.

These electronic instruments would be our touchstones. At least, as a nontechnical person, that's how I thought of them. I knew I had to become as familiar with them, as comfortable, say, as with the apps on my iPhone.

I studied them from left to right: first came the wind indicator, which showed the apparent wind angle and wind speed (in sailing, the *apparent* wind is the wind direction and speed you feel while a boat is *moving*; it differs from true wind, which is the wind direction and speed you feel when your vessel is standing still). Next came the compass (with a sliding digital bar across the bottom, representing the rudder's position); then, the GPS: the Garmin Marine Autopilot, which lets you set and maintain a specific course without having to steer manually; and finally, my favorite: digital readouts for boat speed (in knots), water temperature (a chilly 56.9 degrees Fahrenheit, that August morning), and water depth (an astounding 591 feet).

Right then they made my head throb. But I knew that by the end of the summer they'd be as familiar as the dashboard of my SUV, or at least I hoped they'd be. Plus, they were exciting; they represented something fiercely real, something we're increasingly insulated from in our modern climate-controlled lives: the elements. Wind. Water. The boat's physical location on the water, and the wind's force on *Heron*'s sails, propelling the boat. For the next two months navigating this hazard-strewn coast, our survival would depend on the physical elements. We would need to *pay attention*, and that in itself was thrilling.

Peering out over the canvas bimini, past *Heron*'s bow toward the water, I had the feeling that we were forgetting something. I gazed out at all the gray-blueness, our watery new world, and felt lighter. I sipped some coffee from the metal cup I'd brought up from below and began to feel a tingling between my shoulders. And suddenly I was smiling. It was the first time I remembered smiling since we'd begun working through our long departure list weeks before.

I blinked and squinted, staring out at the cold blue eye of the water. It stared straight back, riffled only slightly by the morning's breath of wind. Something was missing: fear. The fear I'd carried around for years, lodged like ballast deep in my chest, was suddenly gone. The fear I never admitted to, though it had been my center of gravity since the boys were young; the anxiety that Jeff and I would somehow get something wrong, screw things up, not keep them safe—the fear that had been with me since the day each of them was born—had momentarily vanished. I hadn't known it was there until it was gone.

The lightness in my chest blossomed and grew. Soon my entire body felt as if it were humming. I felt stronger—and at the same time lighter, as though I could simply lift my arms above my head and will my toes to rise off the boat. I took a deep breath and tilted my head back at the sky.

Keep them safe, keep them safe, keep all my boys safe, I intoned silently to the clouds. Of all the things that had convinced me that Jeff and I should undertake this journey, the fact of our boys leaving was the thing that made me believe most deeply in our quest: There was nothing more we could do for them. They were now part of the larger world, soon to be launched on their own life journeys.

Jeff climbed back up to take over the helm, and I gave him a Mona Lisa smile before switching places and stepping down to the nav station to check our GPS position. A screen above the wooden desk showed where we were in relation to every inch of the mapped coastline. Using the system, we could chart our course from waypoint to waypoint. We still carried paper charts for navigating the intricate coast, but we were growing spoiled by modern electronics—and so we used the charts less and less. Our position as we cruised out of Elliott Bay was latitude 47.80° north by longitude 122.46° west.

I went back up to the cockpit, thinking about latitude and longitude. When was the last time we'd had to remember which was which—grade school? I stared at the compass, a relic from the distant past, with its 360 degrees, the four cardinal directions and the ninety degrees between each of them: north corresponding to 0 degrees, east to 90 degrees, south to 180, and west to 270. After years of navigating family life and professional life, I was shocked to think that in all that time we'd never needed to navigate where we were, literally, on the planet. But now we did. Exhilarated, I gave Jeff a hug, and he turned to kiss me before I could sit down to shelter out of the wind.

Jeff and I took our positions on either side of the cockpit. After weeks of provisioning, boat chores, the long hours at work, goodbyes to friends, not to mention managing the shifting logistics of our eighteen- and twenty-one-year-olds' lives, we were exhausted. We fought the urge to check our digital devices. Instead, we sat adjusting to the cool Pacific Northwest air—not quite sixty degrees on the water—and took in our new world.

Gazing past the instruments, I let my eyes rest on the bow of the boat, our front-porch view for the next eight weeks: teak, water, sky. *Heron*'s teak decks had weathered to a soft silver-gray. At the point where the port and starboard decks met like a pair of ribs at the bow, they were the color of driftwood and bleached as bone. Beyond the bow, water stretched on until it met the dome of the sky.

The stillness was almost shocking. I closed my eyes and listened. I could hear the wind dimpling the water. I could hear the water dancing off *Heron*'s hull. I could hear the low drone of the motor.

It's surprising how the human ear responds to man-made sounds: speech, traffic, telephones. I suppose an absence of those is what we call silence. Maybe in the suburbs it really is quiet once all the leaf blowers stop. But in that particular moment on the water, I was struck by how full a silence could be—and we didn't even have enough wind yet to raise the sails and turn off the motor.

"We're riding the tide now," Jeff said. "We're moving nine and a half knots over the bottom with a two-knot current."

This was a good thing—we'd hoped to catch one of the Northwest's strong tides that first day. Our goal was to make it to San Juan Island's Friday Harbor (about sixty miles) by dusk, but that wouldn't happen battling a current. It felt wonderful to be riding the tide together, the *Mighty Heron* coasting up Puget Sound, leaving behind the busy world with its incessant demands.

Jeff went below to unpack, and I sat on watch, thinking how sailing is like meditation during an age of *distraction*: 24/7 instantaneous news, Facebook updates, Instagram pics, tweets, texts, email; how the more ways we have to connect, the more many of us seem desperate to unplug—and how, like teenagers, we've gone from knowing little about the world to knowing too much overnight, to feeling full and empty at the same time. Boat travel feels deep and elemental, in part, I suspect, because boats are among the most ancient forms of human transport, in there with traveling on foot. Archaeologists have found fragments of boats estimated to be eight thousand years old.

The month before we'd departed, while I was working on a Microsoft project involving digital identity, I'd heard the average American spends at least eight and a half hours a day in front of a screen. And the average American teenager sends or receives seventy-five text messages a day. *Should I check my texts to make sure James made it home okay?* I thought.

But there wasn't time.

An eight-hundred-foot-long Evergreen container ship was approaching in the distance. I reached for the binoculars: *EVER-GREEN* emblazoned in Jolly Green Giant–sized block letters across a forest-green hull as long as two football fields. The waters of Puget Sound contain some of the busiest shipping lanes in the world. Nearly five thousand oceangoing ships enter the Strait of Juan de Fuca every year; now one of them was passing us to port, and it was close enough that I could see the rust stains dripping down its looming bow. This was no big deal: Pleasure boats and tankers share the shipping lanes, but since a sailboat (which normally has right of way) gives way to a megavessel, I veered off to starboard to give the big boy plenty of room. It wasn't any larger than any other behemoth container ship, but for some reason it threw up a mammoth wake—maybe eight to ten feet high . . .

"Holy crap, look at those waves!" Jeff cried out, dashing up on deck from below.

Unfortunately, we couldn't do anything *but* "look."

We each reached for a winch and hung on tight as a wave of murky green water crashed over the bow, and *Heron* dove into the trough behind the huge wake.

"Watch out!" Jeff yelled.

A poolful of seawater washed toward us over the foredeck, slammed into the windscreen, and sloshed back, funneling down the deck drains. We braced ourselves, in shock. It was all over in seconds.

"That was *intense*!" I said. "Was I too close?"

"No, you were fine. If we'd had more time, we could have tried to steer away—, that was a monster wake . . ."

But then Jeff realized he'd left *Heron*'s hatches open a crack.

Big mistake.

Cold saltwater was still pouring like a stream through the cabin hatches, raining down, and sloshing back and forth on the wooden desk, puddling atop the front stateroom comforter, soaking the banquette, and dripping off the teak dining table onto the cabin's honey-colored teak floor.

"What the—!" bellowed the skipper.

"*Uh-oh*," breathed the chief mate.

~~~~~~~~~

We spent the next fifteen minutes on our hands and knees, cursing, using up every fresh-laundered towel we had to mop up the mess. By two o'clock, striped towels were hanging off *Heron*'s every rail, drying in the sun; the boat looked like it had been commandeered by pirates.

"I should have immediately throttled down, what a dumb shit," Jeff said when we finally returned to the open cockpit.

"I'm just glad *you're* the one who left the hatches open," I said.

CROSSING OVER

~~~~~~

When I told a friend that my husband and I were thinking of sailing around for a while when our sons left for college, he raised his eyebrows, then said: "Ah, boating! Where good marriages go to die."

"Have you ever sailed before?" my best friends inquired. Or more to the point: "But you've never *really* sailed before!"

"Of course I've sailed before!" I said indignantly.

But I hadn't. Not even in sailing camp. I'd grown up windsurfing on the bays near my family's home in Southern California, that was it. Standing on a surfboard while hauling a sail out of the water, pointing it into the wind and muscling a teak wishbone boom around to harness a gust, then hanging on with all my might whenever a steady breeze kicked in.

Everything I knew about sailing I'd learned from a weekend or two spent with East Coast friends on their C&C 36, and a seven-pound doorstop of a book called *Chapman Piloting & Seamanship*, by Elbert S. Maloney.

The *Chapman* had been a Valentine's Day present the year before. Valentine's had fallen on a Saturday that year. Since it was a Saturday during the height of the recession, we'd stayed in and cooked: grilled steaks, new potatoes roasted with rosemary and olive oil, spinach sautéed with lemon and garlic. It was a rainy night. Thousands of tiny drops beat upon the roof while I lit the candles in the dining room. As a splurge, Jeff opened a special bottle of wine, a coveted Washington cabernet sauvignon. In the past we might have gone out for dinner and traded Valentine's Day cards. But this year, the year after the prostate cancer surgery, the stress of everyone trying to keep their businesses above water, of downsizing, of Jeff's having to let good people go, realizing how that would affect them, their families; of watching magazines I loved writing for—*National Geographic Adventure* and *Parenting* and, inconceivably, *Gourmet* lay off talented staff and shut down after years, or in some cases, decades of publishing, or shrink their editions until the once fat-and-glossy magazines were as thin as brochures . . . Having endured all that, something different and almost defiant seemed in order. Something that said, *We are still here and deliberately, intentionally, trying to take charge of our destiny during these uncertain times*, if just for a while; something that demonstrated each of us believed in the other, in the world we could create together, even when the world outside was shitty. I gave Jeff a pair of tickets to hear what was then an up-and-coming local indie band, the Fleet Foxes, a favorite of his. Jeff loved new music, was up on all the emerging artists and bands. The Fleet Foxes had just appeared on the Seattle music scene then, and they were gaining national attention with their soaring melodies and retro harmonies. Their music was fresh and wide-eyed. Hopeful. Jeff presented me with a red-foil-wrapped brick, heavy as a concrete block.

"What *is* this?" I'd laughed, incredulous, paper and tape tumbling to the floor.

"It's the most unromantic present of all time—it's *Chapman*!" he'd said with a grin, reaching over to refill my wineglass. "The classic seaman's bible, encyclopedia, and übermanual all rolled into one."

"Wow," I'd murmured. *Chapman Piloting & Seamanship* weighed in at a bicep-busting 927 pages, with 1,500 illustrations and diagrams. Then in its sixty-sixth edition, it was still considered the leading reference book for power and sailboats, and has been since it was first published in 1917. "It's pretty heavy—does this go on the boat?

"Sure, why not," Jeff said with a shrug. "You're the least likely person on the planet to open a book like *Chapman*."

Oh yeah? I sipped my wine, listening to rain lash the windows. It was true: you couldn't find a less-likely candidate to sign up for this sailing thing. I am petite; hate to be wet; don't do well in cold; have arms as thin as toothpicks and the mechanical aptitude of a houseplant. I turned the book's pages tentatively. They laid out a whole new world, a physical world—navigation, sail trim, tides, currents, electronics, radio communication, knots, weather. I studied a diagram of a sailboat, its graceful outline illustrating the physics of standing rigging, each line labeled like the borders of a triangular country. If it was a world that could be learned partly through books, there might be hope, I thought, brightening.

~~~~~~~~~

In March of James's senior year of high school, I'd signed up for a weekend sailing course taught by the American Sailing Association. It offered four classes: Basic Keelboat Sailing, Basic Coastal Cruising, Bareboat Chartering, and one on Coastal Navigation. Those of us who had signed up for Basic Keelboat Sailing met around a conference table in the basement of a small marina in Kirkland, Washington, east of Seattle. The instructor, Ed, turned out to be a wiry retiree with the infinite patience of an Eagle Scout.

"*Squirrel comes up out of the hole, looks around, goes behind the tree, and back down the hole,*" Ed recited, demonstrating a bowline with a yard of practice rope.

My classmates, Mark and Tyler, a father and his fifteen-year-old son, nailed the bowline after a couple of tries.

"*Squirrel comes out of the hole . . . looks around . . .*" I recited dutifully, then got stuck holding my squirrel end of the rope frozen in midair. Which way was the hole again?

Ed stood next to me demonstrating how to tie the knot in slow motion. "*Squirrel comes out of the hole . . . ,*" we recited together. After ten or so tries, I finally got it, grateful there were only two classmates to witness what was probably the worst case of rope-tying dyslexia Ed had ever encountered.

Next we memorized Rules of Right-Away. There was a riddle to remember these by. Ed wrote it out on the whiteboard: *Only New Reels Catch Fish So Purchase Some Often.*

"*O* equals an Overtaken boat," he explained. "An Overtaken boat has right of way over *N*, which stands for Not Under Command.

Sailboats have right of way over Powerboats, I scribbled in my notebook. *But boats with Restricted Maneuverability (Cargo ships! Tankers!) have right of way over Sail!*

We covered additional useful safety tips, including the proper way to use an air horn: five short blasts means *danger*.

And the 50/50/50 rule, which pretty much speaks for itself: if you're in 50-degree water (Puget Sound) for 50 minutes, you have a 50 percent chance of surviving.

Out on the water, we practiced tacking the school's J/22 under a grim spring sky. Ed taught us to call out when captaining:

"Ready about!"

"Ready!" the well-trained crew chirped.

And, "Prepare to jibe!"

"Ready!" we'd confirm.

"Jibe ho!" we'd shout, executing the jibe.

It was cold on Lake Washington that weekend. Gunmetal-gray clouds closed in over the lake, like a lid on a pot. The four of us huddled in the J-boat's fiberglass cockpit taking turns at the tiller, and I tried to imagine myself captaining *Heron*, calling out to my wisecracking crew: "Jibe ho!"

I knew the word "ho" would set off Jeff and the boys immediately, like a pack of wiseass jackals.

No, sailing a boat the size of *Mighty Heron*, which made tacking more of a major team commitment than a flick of the tiller, would not involve saucy sea commands. But I'd skimmed my Basic Keelboat Sailing book and somehow managed to ace the multiple-choice test Ed handed out at the end of the day . . . *Yes!*

The sense of accomplishment was familiar: like earning a Girl Scout badge for something you've barely tried. An A for showing up and getting your toes wet. I telephoned to sign up for the next class in the series, Coastal Cruising. The guy who picked up the phone was more helpful than he knew.

"Not to discourage you from paying to take this class, but we don't have one scheduled right now," he admitted. "But honestly? If you have a boat you can cruise on, just get out there and do it. You'll learn, believe me—trial by fire."

~~~~~~~

And so here Jeff and I were a few months later, just the two of us, trial by fire.

I glanced up from *Heron*'s cockpit, where we sat dressed for summer in the Northwest—jeans, nubby sweaters, fleece vests, jackets, ski caps, wool socks, suede sneakers. We were motoring past the west side of Whidbey Island, thirty-five miles north of Seattle. The island stretched long and thin as a string bean, rising at its westernmost flank to chalky cliffs. A trail I knew traced the wind-scoured cliff edge there, bookended by a beautiful forest of Douglas fir, alder, spruce, and red-barked madrone. I reached for the binoculars, scanned the cliff face, and spotted a group of hikers, tiny as ants, marching single-file against the sky.

Were we ready for this trip? I had no idea, but how can you tell until you try? From land we must have appeared even smaller than the hiker-ants, I thought. I am petite, compact. My face is narrow and feral-looking, with myopic blue eyes framed by an untamable wedge of wavy brown hair. Jeff is taller, a darkly handsome, scowling misanthrope who had met his match: a complicated man captaining a complicated boat.

Given our differences, the connection between us has always been surprising. I spent the first twenty years of my life in sunny California. There were four of us, my parents, younger sister, and me. We lived in a suburban ranch house on a street named Wavecrest and then a cedar house perched on a cliff with a distant view of the Pacific. My parents both come from pioneer families, and sometimes I think it's destiny that generations later the descendants of those who had journeyed on pilgrim ships and wagon trains would end up as far west as they could get, clinging to a cliff, staring out to sea.

My energy derives from movement. When I was a girl we'd drive our Volkswagen camper van through the West each summer. In Southern California the dry flats of the Owens Valley rose to meet the rugged foothills of the Sierras, and here the pioneers—and even some of our ancestors—had settled, hauling water by mule-drawn wagon between California towns with names like Big Pine and Lone Pine. Once my parents, ten-year-old sister, Kristen, and I, then thirteen, drove to Bodie, a ghost town east of the Sierra Nevada, and went exploring. We walked through silver-gray sagebrush, looking for the place where our great-great-grandfather had lived. I pretended we were archaeologists. The coarse desert scrub crunched beneath our feet, and the air smelled like juniper. It was so dry my frizzy 1970s hair hung straight.

We never did find my great-great-grandfather's house, although we found imprints in the dust where foundations of houses dating from the 1800s had stood. The few buildings remaining had unpainted porches and wood bleached to a silvery white. The wood was the same color as the dust. Above, the sky shone so clean and blue it made my scalp tingle.

Typically, we would drive up the California coast from our home south of Los Angeles, or brave the hairpin turns of the Sierras' steep flanks, park the van, load up our packs, and hike for days. After miles of switchbacking up a peak, we'd camp near a clear, cold alpine lake or a stream. My sister and I would pull off our boots, tape moleskin over our blisters, and head off to explore. Sometimes we would read, or write in our journals. Each new campsite felt like our own private realm.

In the late afternoons my father would rig up fishing poles, and we'd hurl salmon eggs into mountain lakes, bent on hooking rainbow trout. As night fell my mother would panfry the fish we'd caught. We learned how to fork the tender flesh from the bones and to ignore the fish heads with their gaping mouths and eyes cooked to pearls. Among the many qualities we absorbed in the California wilderness, one of the most useful, it seemed to me, was to be unflinching but feminine: a pioneer woman's trait, as disarming in the Mojave as it is in Manhattan.

After dinner we'd build a fire and sit around it, toasting the soles of our boots. We slept side by side on the ground, sleeping bags unfurled right under the stars. My sister and I were never afraid—except for the time we awoke with our mother whispering, "How big is it?" We sat up and stared straight into three pairs of eyes glowing like yellow embers in the dark. My father crawled out of his bag, swearing and banging a pair of Sierra cups together, and he finally drove off a mother black bear and her two cubs. Then he built a fire and kept watch while the three of us played dead, trying to will ourselves to disappear into the earth itself. Lying there, my heart cartwheeling against my ribs, I'd never felt more terrified or alive.

My family wasn't religious, but I had a hunch about God. The mountains seemed created for our worship. There were high granite peaks, an expansive sky, and cottony white clouds. Each day was long and hard and grand. Stitched together, the hiking days made a sort of pilgrimage. Even during the drive to a distant trailhead, I felt like I was exactly where I wanted to be: perched between my young parents and gazing out the window to take everything in, my strong-willed little sister splayed on the bench in the back. The road stretched endlessly ahead of us and behind us, so we were suspended in time and place as well. I liked moving through that expansive landscape. I liked the feeling of being between one place and another. As the towns spread farther apart, the sense of time diminished, and we each became lost in a mythical landscape that was as much internal as it was external. We were a family.

When you are a child learning the world, your parents help shape your perceptions. When you are a parent introducing your own children to the world, you discover those perceptions—things you had almost forgotten—resurfacing, as if hardwired to your DNA. These memories in me of our family's wandering through the West were so deep that as soon as my own boys were old enough, all I wanted to do was take them exploring.

Luckily, my husband was willing to come along.

By contrast, Jeff is an East Coast boy. He and his two sisters grew up in a modest ranch house like I did, but on a cul-de-sac in southern New Jersey. He spent summers fishing and surfing and learning to sail on the Jersey Shore, where his parents rented a series of small beach houses, then finally bought one in Beach Haven township two blocks from the Atlantic. Rather than ramble around mountain ranges, living out of camper vans and backpacks like we did, his family established summer traditions, returning to the same shore like migrating birds, putting down roots.

Looking back on the early years of our marriage, I think of all the influences shaping not just us but any two people committed to making a new life together. In our case there were cultural differences: East versus West; tradition versus freedom. Jeff had been raised Catholic; my family questioned organized religion. He was a Republican when we first met; I was a Democrat. Out here, the waters of the Pacific Northwest Coast were terra incognita for both of us, and even though we were sun and moon, East Coast and West Coast, they beckoned like Oz.

~~~~~~

We hoped to make some distance the first night and checked the *Current Atlas*, although the water lay still as glass. We'd be riding across the strait as water rushed back out of Puget Sound toward the sea; calculating the distance, and the speed of the current, we figured this should take us about six hours at *Heron*'s cruising (motoring) speed, just over seven knots. After drying out from our run-in with the container ship, we'd had all three sails—the mainsail, staysail, and jib—up briefly, but no sooner had we raised them than the wind disappeared and *Heron* slowed from cruising to crawling, barely making two knots.

"Shit—if we go any slower, we'll be moving backward!" Jeff had said.

So we'd furled the big jib, brought in the staysail, wrapped the mainsail, and turned the key: *Heron*'s engine chugged to life, and now we were motoring north, making good time.

The Garmin VHF radio crackled. Jeff picked it up, wielding the black handheld with its spiraling black cord like a cop on some nautical sitcom. What is it with guys and radios?

"This is Victoria Coast Guard Radio," the dispatcher said. "A heart attack has been reported on a forty-six-foot blue-hulled motor vessel off Cypress Island with two passengers aboard. Over. Any boats in the immediate vicinity of Cypress Island available to help are requested to radio Victoria Coast Guard. I repeat, any vessels in the immediate vicinity available to help are requested to radio Victoria Coast Guard."

Just as suddenly as it sprang to life, channel 16 went silent.

"Jesus, that would be scary," Jeff said.

"I know, scary as hell," I said, imagining a couple, maybe twenty-five years older than us, floating off Cypress Island thirty miles to the north—one of them struggling to keep the other alive. Or maybe it was two friends, fishing buddies. Or a father and son. We didn't know, never would because we weren't in the immediate vicinity and couldn't speed to their assistance. All we knew was that life changes in an instant.

That's the thing, I thought. *You never know when your moment will be, when that instant will come—but it will, as sure as the wind now raking the water into small, hysterical waves.*

"Life is short," Jeff said, reading my mind.

"Aye, that it is," I said, stepping up from the cockpit to the wide, flat stern deck directly behind for a 360-degree view of Puget Sound and its fir-trimmed islands. I stretched my arms wide, reaching into what felt like a dizzying amount of space, and gulped in clean crisp air. "So what if it's a cliché. We've got to grab it while we can, Chet, don't you think?"

"We do, Brownie."

And that's how we passed the first morning, alone at sea together aboard *Heron*, nearly drowned by a cargo tanker, totally skunked by the wind, but at least out there and tasting the salt in the sea air, adjusting to the bracing chill over the water, feeling the lightness and freedom of almost being empty nesters, of going for it, wherever *it* might be.

~~~~~~~

After turkey and avocado sandwiches for lunch and a hard ration of one chocolate chip cookie each, we rounded Partridge Point, the westernmost elbow of Whidbey Island. Our Garmin Canadian Hydrographic navigation software, with maps and weather loaded into *Heron*'s nav system, showed we'd just crossed into the Strait of Juan de Fuca. Standing in the open-air cockpit at the wheel, peering at the GPS chart plotter mounted at the helm, we could make out a computerized version of *Heron*, a black boat symbol swimming steadily over a white computerized sea, trailing a dotted line. These were our "tracks," the first nascent miles of our journey. *We're doing this!* I thought. *We're finally truly doing this! We're headed north—aboard Heron! We're finally sailing off for a while!*

Only we weren't sailing.

There was no wind.

~~~~~~~

The Strait of Juan de Fuca, a roughly hundred-mile-long, ten- to eighteen-mile-wide stretch of sea, leads from the open Pacific on the west to the San Juan Islands on the east. It is banded by Vancouver Island to the north and the Olympic Peninsula to the south, and can be flat calm or extremely rough, depending on the wind and current. The typical summer pattern, according to our *Waggoner Cruising Guide*, another indispensable onboard reference, calls for "calm mornings, with a westerly sea breeze rising by mid-day," I read aloud. "Increasing to 30 knots or more in the late afternoon."

"*Hmmpph*," Skipper Jeff snorted. "Barely five knots, more like it."

We chugged on, the low drone of the engine like a drug. I fought to keep my eyes open; it wasn't easy. There was something about being on that boat, the sway of the hull, regardless of whether you were underway or anchored: if you let yourself drift off, you slipped into a coma, a sleep so profound it was almost physically impossible to open your eyes.

In real life what woman ever lies down in the middle of the day? Take a nap? Preposterous! Well, maybe once every two years on a Sunday . . . But typically? For most of us parents, especially women, there's so much to keep track of, so many interruptions, so many pressing things to do—work-work to catch up on, or mom tasks to take care of, or phone calls to return, or meals to start, or deadlines to meet, or a sick friend to check in on, or someone to pick up in fifteen minutes—that the concept of lying down and closing your eyes at two in the afternoon is not only ludicrous but virtually impossible, like a small cyclone allowing itself to stop spinning in the midst of forces that demand it whirl on.

But aboard *Heron* the afternoon stretched lazily ahead. Jeff seemed fine at the helm, so I lay down along one of two teak benches rimming the cockpit, each padded with a four-inch-thick cushion. The low drone of the motor and the postlunch haze after all the stress of departing were deadly; watching fair-weather clouds drift overhead, I allowed myself to close my eyes just for a moment, then fell into an utter stupor, the sleep to end all sleep. All the concerns and busyness of the past few weeks fell away, left behind in Seattle.

"Ah, the narcolepsy effect," Jeff said, when I regained consciousness nearly two hours later. Someone had covered me with a Pendleton blanket. "How'd you sleep, Bug?"

"Umm, good . . . but I can't . . . keep my eyes open," I mumbled, my eyelids heavy as lead weights.

I'd come to just before Cattle Pass, the narrow channel between Lopez Island and San Juan Island. If you're entering the San Juan Islands from the south, Cattle Pass marks your arrival in the storied archipelago. A fresh odor came from the faster current, the smell of cold purity that is the essence of the North Pacific. Late-afternoon light had broken through the clouds, and although the air temperature was still brisk, maybe almost sixty degrees, the water glowed with coppery warmth, reflecting the sun.

~~~~~~~~

"Cool, whale!" Jeff suddenly exclaimed, leaping up. "Close! Maybe only thirty yards off!"

"Where?!" I bolted upright, instantly awake, every cell in my body charged with adrenaline.

"There!" Jeff pointed hurriedly toward three o'clock off the starboard beam. "It was small . . . maybe a minke."

We both stared, fixated on the spot where the slender minke whale, a thirty-five-foot cousin of the much larger humpback, was—but we didn't see him again.

But now that we were looking, there was so much more. We grabbed the binoculars and passed them back and forth. Clusters of glaucous gulls swooped and dove and whirled, feeding raucously on upswells of marine life kicked up by the Cattle Pass chop. Small black terns with slender bills darted by with rapid wing flaps. Two pelagic cormorants flew north, their heads and long necks stretched forward, like worried commuters. When the wheeling gulls spotted an appetizing morsel, they all started chanting at once, louder and louder: *Caw-wok! Caw-wak! Caw-waak! Caw-waaak!* They were as noisy as frat boys at a party, trying to outdo one another before diving in for the tangy feast.

We'd only left James and our suburban life outside Seattle a few hours earlier, but already it felt as if we'd crossed over into another realm: a world with ancient rhythms. And indeed, we had.

Puget Sound and the Strait of Juan de Fuca are deep basins, glacial troughs gouged out of bedrock by a lobe of the Cordilleran Ice Sheet during the last ice age, about fifteen thousand years ago. As the ice retreated, it scoured the land, gouging deep sounds and sculpting the San Juan Islands at the convergence of Puget Sound and the Strait of Juan de Fuca. The channels beneath us, which dropped away a dizzying 800, 1,200, even 1,600 feet beneath the boat, are bathed in upswells of super nutrient-rich particles, a sort of nutrient soup that supports a rich stew of invertebrates and algae, which in turn feeds an incredible diversity of predators and grazers.

Jeff and I were riveted—everything, the shimmering prisms of late-afternoon light dancing on the current; the insistent wavelets lapping at *Heron*'s hull; the smell of the ocean and salt air—it all felt so alive, as if there were a pulsing life force deep beneath the boat, thousands of feet below us, rising and surfacing. Roxy Music's *Avalon* was playing on the iPod Jeff had brought up to the cockpit table, the stylized anthem "Avalon" surging from a portable speaker.

The 1980s British pop soundtrack should have been a weird pairing with our watery surroundings, but the soaring, sea-drenched melodies matched the elation of the moment. Staring out at the wild sparkling scene, we passed the binoculars back and forth, sweeping the water.

"Look, what's that?" I pointed. A pair of Dall's porpoises, their backs shiny black, their triangular-tipped dorsal fins neatly slicing the sea, were leaping alongside *Heron*'s hull like curved commas. I trained the binoculars on them. A moment later a gang of harbor seals with doglike muzzles and comical whiskers floated by, only their heads visible above water. They looked like curious sentries checking out the boat.

"Hi, seals! Hi, porpoises!" I called.

<hr>

We rounded Turn Island, the small, forested marine park that marks the southern entrance to San Juan Island's Friday Harbor, and motored up to the end of a wooden dock. A tall, long-limbed man in faded red shorts and a navy-blue T-shirt emblazoned with *Work Less* on the back climbed off his sailboat and came over to catch our bowline.

"Ah, full service. Thanks!" I said, tossing the line to him before jumping from the boat to the dock with the spring line and hurriedly threading it through a wooden beam, lashing the boat to the dock, then running back to catch the stern line, which Jeff jumped down and secured. After all the lines were tied, we climbed back to the cockpit, turned the key, and shut down the engine. Ah, stillness. We both grinned, acting nonchalant, like we did this every day. But then we climbed into the cabin below, switched off all the nav instruments—and, filled with utter relief, did an exaggerated high-five. We had arrived.

CANADA'S AMAZON

~~~~~~

It was one thing to dream about the Great Bear Rainforest. It was another thing to get there. The Great Bear Rainforest—or GBR, as I began calling it—is fantastically remote. The region is *way* beyond the end of the road. It is miles and miles of epic wilderness, a far-flung place so far past the end of the road, there *are* no roads— no roads, no cars, and very few people. The landscape is boat- or floatplane-access only, and most spectacular, the forest is one of the last places on the planet where wild land still meets wild ocean.

Warmed by the Pacific and fed by the rain, the Great Bear Rainforest spans a 250-mile swath of evergreen-cloaked fjords and rocky, forested islands that include most of British Columbia's central and north coast. Sometimes known as Canada's Amazon, the Great Bear covers an area the size of Ireland and contains one-fourth of the world's remaining intact temperate rainforest—the operative word being *rain*.

I was worried about the rain. Precipitation falls eight, ten, some-times twelve months a year here—cumulative rainfall measuring 78 to 117 inches annually. Why would anyone living in Seattle, one of the world's wettest places, averaging 38 inches of rain each year, even consider spending their hard-earned summer in a place that's even wetter? I'd ordered a video, a National Geographic documentary about the Great Bear Rainforest, and set up a screening for Jeff and the boys one night in the winter before we set sail.

"*Fifteen feet of precipitation can fall in this place each year!*" the dramatic narrator intoned. "But the wolves and bears seem to shrug off the downpour. *Everything* here must shrug off the rain. Aboard the *Achiever* [the film's sturdy-looking research vessel], there is a soggy sense of exhilaration . . ."

The boys looked on in disbelief while the *Achiever*'s hardy crew pulled on Gore-Tex pants and hooded slickers, then motored toward shore hunched in an inflatable dinghy, rain skewering their backs.

"Looks like fun," Jeff said sarcastically.

The next scene featured a crazed wolf biologist scuttling around the soaking wet woods on his hands and knees collecting wolf scat. Rain dripped off his eyebrows and puddled along his collarbone as he carefully scooped fresh wolf poop into a vial.

The wolf man sniffed the wolf scat and smiled contentedly, as if he'd discovered a fine wine.

"He's nuts!" Sam said.

"Poop man," James said.

But incredibly, none of the three questioned our Great Bear plans. I hoped maybe the Nat Geo crew had sailed in early spring, the wettest season, and that by the time *Heron* made it that far north in late August and early September, we'd catch the Great Bear's eight-week "dry" season, when it still rains but less. Months before, we'd pulled out our charts and traced a route from Seattle to Princess Royal and Gribbell Islands, the uninhabited "mother islands of the white bear," in the heart of the Great Bear Rainforest. We'd added up the nautical miles and the days, calculating we could make it there and back in the two-month window we'd have before the Northwest coast weather turned from long summer days and golden autumn light to winter.

To get there we'd cruise north from Seattle to Desolation Sound, a section of the BC coastline riddled with deep inlets, islands, and coastal mountains at the northern end of the Strait of Georgia. We'd then head north again, navigating a series of treacherous tidal rapids, braving the stomach-churning Johnstone Strait, and rounding the aptly named Cape Caution before making our way north farther still. Our *Waggoner Cruising Guide* warned:

> North of Desolation Sound you'll find colder water, harsher weather, fewer services, and a greater number of rocks, reefs, and tidal rapids . . . Careful planning is paramount. You need to know the times of slack water at each rapid, and you need to know how long it will take to get to each rapid. You must have complete and up-to-date charts on board, and a copy of *Ports and Passes*. You must be comfortable calculating the times of slack water at the various rapids. For transiting shallow channels, you must also calculate the times and heights of tides.

These warnings intimidated me, as was their intention. The challenges, along with the greater distances, rain, and colder weather, are the very real reasons why so few cruising boats head north from Desolation Sound or round Cape Caution beyond that. As I tidied up that first August afternoon at Friday Harbor—putting the *Waggoner* and our charts back in the bookshelf, cleaning the galley, stowing the binoculars—I hoped we weren't in over our heads. Then, while Jeff hosed down the boat to get the salt off and puttered about, his way of relaxing, I pulled on a pair of running tights, dug out my running shoes from the depths of the drawer beneath the aft cabin bed, climbed the companionway to the cockpit, and stood slowly, stretching my arms and legs after my first day in the cockpit.

"Bye, honey!" I waved, loping up the aluminum ramp leading to shore from the finger piers where *Heron* was secured in a quiet corner of the harbor. I passed eight or ten other boats tied for the night; they ranged from thirty- to fifty-foot sailboats, to a lovely 1920s wooden launch, to several white-fiberglass power cruisers, top-heavy as floating appliances. One of these, an immense chunk of floating white plastic, was fittingly called *Cream Cheese. At least they have a sense of humor*, I thought, grinning; even the round life preserver hanging off the stern was named *Bagel*.

At the top of the ramp I turned and began trotting along the shoulder of a two-lane wooded road rimming the island. My legs felt wobbly, as if the dirt path etched into the grassy shoulder was mysteriously rising and falling. There were very few cars. When a driver passed, maybe once every five or ten minutes, he or she would give a little wave.

I emerged from the woods to a clearing where fields of dry grass swept toward the San Juans—in August the islands lay like brown bears sprouting fir forests on their backs. There was a certain certainness of late-afternoon light here; it glinted off the yellow-gold fields exuberantly by midsummer, shafting itself around each blade of grass so that everything appeared almost illuminated from within. As I picked up speed, my heart leaped a little at the island's sunlit air and the sensation of being off the boat after only a day. In the weeks to come there would be fewer and fewer opportunities to walk, let alone run, once we reached the rocky, forested, bear-populated islands to the north.

The road entered the woods again, a tangle of fir and alder and cinnamon-barked madrone, and I descended a long hill toward the Sound. Suddenly, the scrub parted and a tawny brown doe stepped out, maybe twenty feet in front of me, and delicately crossed the road. I kept going, nearly colliding with the spotted fawn that skittered out of the dense foliage after its mother. At the base of the hill the road rounded a wide curve with waterfront homes built on a low bank opening onto San Juan Channel. In the distance beyond I could see the shining white glacier peak of Mount Baker rising over the sea, still capped with snow. Now I was breathing hard. I knew my friend Pete's house was around the next bend, so I kept going. Pete had died suddenly a few years before; not only had he left his young wife behind, but the grief was compounded because he had been one of those irrepressible souls whose tragic absence in his early fifties left a gaping hole in our world. Doubled over at what had been the entrance to his long forested driveway, I whispered, "We miss you, Pete. Damn you and your hilarious self . . ." I stood. Listened. The leaves on the tall trees stirred slightly, but otherwise, everything was silent as eternity.

When I turned to start back, my heart filled with the sad acceptance that Pete was no longer here, coupled with my wondering whether, in some ways, he was. By then evening shadows were advancing. *Thank you for watching over us*, I prayed in silence.

The air was cooling off. *Uh-oh*, I thought. *Jeff will be worried.*

Then I spied a flash of movement up ahead, and a small gray fox darted across the section of road I was running toward—the silver tip of its tail like a flag, as if to say: *I heard you, I'm here.*

I froze, my heart full. I'd never seen a fox in the wild before. They are shy, secretive creatures, and it is very rare to encounter one.

Then, dead sure that Pete had in fact heard me, that maybe this was a sign, I smiled at the notion that his spirit could be with us, watching over *Heron*—even though he hadn't known much about boats—and hightailed it back to the dock.

~~~~~~~

We awoke at dawn the next morning but couldn't bring ourselves to get out of bed—it was so darn cold in the cabin. So we lingered beneath the sheets while the sun warmed *Heron*. It was weird waking up without kids down the hall and pets underfoot.

"I feel honored to be in a room with such beauty," Jeff said, starting to laugh, gazing at me in my hideous turquoise-and-orange-flowered flannel pajamas.

"Hmm, that's generous of you," I said apologetically, though I was laughing too. "I know they're terrible, but they're part of my strategy!" I'd wrestled the pj's on under the covers, and after all those contortions wasn't about to take them off. My plan was to leap directly from bed into a pair of Ugg slippers, then wrap a terry-cloth robe on top of the flannel. After that we'd drink coffee until we were warm enough to shed the flannel for jeans, long-sleeved T-shirts, and fleece or wool sweaters, it being August and all.

I took four steps from the aft cabin to the main salon, where Jeff was dialing in the day's marine weather forecast, and turtled my head out of the hatch. It was a sunny, dewy morning.

"Ah, breakfast with Bug!" Jeff grinned, looking up.

I grimaced. "Still not looking so hot, though."

"Yes, but it's there. Your beauty is *emerging*."

By eight thirty we'd wiped our bowls clean of every last speck of oatmeal and brown sugar, untied the lines from the cleats, and pushed off from Friday Harbor. I took *Heron*'s helm while Jeff went to record notes in the log. Our GPS position was N 48° 35', W 123° 03'. The depth was 469 feet beneath the hull, the water temperature a chilly fifty-four degrees. The air temperature, according to the thumb-sized thermometer affixed to the helm, was sixty-six, but it felt more like sixty coming off the sea, glimmering like a million shards of glass beneath the cold morning sun.

I guided *Heron* up San Juan Channel, which runs between the northeast flank of San Juan Island and neighboring Shaw Island. I was feeling experienced in a way I hadn't the day before, left hand on the wheel, right hand lightly dangling a pair of binoculars. To my left (or *port*) side, San Juan Island's waterfront estates, all cedar and fir and tasteful glass construction, poked through the trees; to my right (or *starboard*), Shaw Island looked like a forest of evergreen, but I knew it had bigger properties—some of the islands' most beautiful—tucked among the firs. We motored past the wild, low-lying Wasp Islands and on toward Spieden Island. Tumbled clouds filled the sky and a faint breeze from the west ruffled the water. There wasn't enough wind to put up the sails, but no matter; we wouldn't have room to sail anyway, navigating the narrow channels.

"Check out Spieden up ahead," Jeff said, taking over the wheel. "It looks sort of like a velvet lion." He took the binoculars and we both stared at the island's tawny flanks and close-cropped yellow grass. One of the driest of the San Juan Islands, five-hundred-acre Spieden is privately owned by Jim Jannard, the Californian who founded Oakley sunglasses. In 1969 prior owners had imported exotic animals such as Corsican sheep and Asian fallow deer to the island, attempting to turn it into a big-game hunting operation. Public backlash from San Juan Island locals soon shut them down. As we passed the island a free-ranging herd, a remnant from that experiment, grazed on the slopes alongside us.

A violent splashing interrupted our surreal wildlife count.

"Someone just got eaten," I said.

"Yup. Good morning for that seal, bad morning for some fish being ripped apart," my husband replied.

In our time afloat we'd come to recognize certain signs: noisy thrashing and *slap-thwop*ping sending up a riot of white water meant a seal or a sea lion tearing into lunch. I liked a Sunday morning marked by nature's violence. I considered the seal, its belly full. I considered the fish, submitting to the seal. I thought how many months it had been since we'd seen this kind of *Wild Kingdom* moment play out in real time, months when a more typical weekend interruption might be the disembodied telephone voice of Rachel: "Hi, this is Rachel from Cardholder Services . . . contact us concerning your eligibility for lowering your interest rates." But for the next eight weeks we'd be free of annoying telemarketers. Out of range and released from all those electronic pests that are now part of global society, a universal plague for those who crave solitude.

~~~~~~~~~

By a quarter to ten we were across Boundary Pass, the liquid boundary line between Washington State and British Columbia. At first nothing seemed different.

"Hello, Canada!" I called out to no one in particular as we putt-putted along, a trace of wind now dead on the nose. Just ahead the Gulf Islands—the Canadian continuation of the San Juans—were spread out. I peered through the binoculars. The Gulf Islands looked rockier, wilder, and slightly scruffier than the San Juans.

At Bedwell Harbor, on South Pender Island, we idled around, then tied up once a boat-length spot cleared at the customs dock. Jeff jumped off the boat with our passports, strode up the pier, and called in our arrival on a courtesy phone nailed to a piling, declaring our wine cellar—thirteen bottles. A boat's crew is required to stay on board while the skipper clears customs, so I sat in the cockpit and tried to look nonchalant, even though I'd just staged my own minirebellion. With apples, blueberries, peaches, nectarines, plums, cherries, potatoes, and corn on the cob not allowed to cross the border into Canada, I'd busied myself earlier burying contraband. I'd squirreled away our apples, oranges, nectarines, lemons, and a precious lime in a tote stuffed behind the robe in my narrow closet. Then, just to be extra safe, I'd stashed the produce bin's avocados and vine-ripened tomatoes deep in the toes of my wool socks. *Hope I remember where I've hid everything*, I thought, imagining the grisly discovery of an oozing, overripe avocado weeks down the road.

Thirsty after crawling around finding such creative hiding places for our fruit and vegetables, I swung past the galley, opened the waist-high fridge, grabbed a water bottle, and took a slug while simultaneously pulling myself up into the cockpit with a jaunty pirate swagger.

What the *hell?* My lips were on fire. Holding in a gulp of the smoky-tasting liquid, I lowered myself back down the steps like a spastic fire-eater straight out of a Fellini-esque circus, spitting what I hadn't swallowed into the galley sink.

"Christ, did you fill the water bottles with booze?" I sputtered as Jeff reboarded the boat.

"Just one bottle. Straight gin. Ha! Nothing like a slug of booze at ten in the morning. That'll put the Bug in a good mood."

"Jeez, maybe you could warn me next time?"

"Puts hair on your chest."

"I don't want hair on my chest." I grimaced, still panting. "So how did customs go, we're clear?"

"For thirteen bottles of wine we paid as much in duty as it cost us to buy them," Jeff said. "But at least we're legal."

"Ouch," I said as I untied the stern, untied the bow, and—with Captain Jeff easing *Heron*'s hull from the dock—pulled myself aboard.

～～～～～～

Unlike the San Juan Islands—where environmental regulations and a kind of Northwest reverse snobbishness dictate that multimillion-dollar retreats peeked from between the trees to preserve the natural landscape—homes here perched boldly. Pender Island's steep cliffs rose to bald banks capped by spyglass-view homes. We motored out of Bedwell Harbor, then ghosted past the long string-bean island of Galiano to starboard.

After we stern-tied in a narrow finger of a cove at Wallace Island Marine Provincial Park—a maneuver that required nosing *Heron* through a lineup of a dozen other boats, calculating where to drop anchor with enough room for the boat to swing, then backing up, rowing a dinghy to shore with a piece of line spooling out from *Heron*'s stern, jumping off the dinghy, wrapping the line around a tree, rowing the dinghy back, then wrapping the end of that line around a stern cleat with enough length to allow for the tide's rising or falling but not so much that we'd swing into our neighbors—I realized we were having a new and different, very concrete kind of fun. Nosing the fifty-four-foot *Heron* into the cove was no small feat, but it was intensely absorbing. In the moments after we'd completed this drill, actually dropping fifty feet of chain without any shouting (we'd developed a series of handsignals: one finger for fifty feet of chain, two fingers for a hundred feet, thumbs up for anchor set and holding), I looked up and noticed the wonder that surrounded us. There were rocky outcroppings layered like baklava leaves, and in the channel beyond them were rock piles blanketed by noisy seals and sea lions and their sausagelike pups. If you ventured too close to the harem, a big-nosed sea lion would poke abruptly from the water, deliver an outraged thunderous burp, and sink.

We spent the rest of the afternoon reading on either side of the cockpit. I don't remember what pages Jeff was turning; in honor of Salt Spring, the fertile island rising just to our west, I had *High Endeavours: The Extraordinary Life and Adventures of Miles & Beryl Smeeton* aboard. Brigadier Miles Smeeton and his wife, Beryl, were a famously daunting couple who settled on Salt Spring Island between their round-the-world adventures in the 1950s and '60s. I'd tracked down a copy of *Once Is Enough*—Miles's account of their six-thousand-mile passage across the Southern Ocean, and subsequent pitchpoling and dismasting in a violent storm a thousand miles west of Cape Horn. In his understated way Miles invites you to vicariously step aboard their ketch *Tzu Hang* and right into their warm, sturdy marriage, with their mutual admiration for each other and lust for big waves, as well as long doses of undiluted solitude on the seas. As British novelist Nevil Shute wrote in his introduction to the book: "What can one say of a woman who, catapulted from the cockpit of a somersaulting yacht into the sea and recovered on board with a broken collarbone and a deep scalp cut, worked manually like a man with her broken bone and did not wash the blood from her hair and forehead for three weeks, judging that injuries left severely alone heal themselves best?"

Heck, I didn't know what to say about that except that Beryl was obviously a remarkable woman. Beautiful too. Inspired by their partnership and by Beryl's adventuring, her willingness to think outside the box and buck every convention of her time, I'd adopted them and their romantic quest for hazardous adventure as role models of sorts. Not so much for the sailing feats they'd survived but for Beryl's zest for life, her spirit. As Miles himself, forever self-deprecating, once observed: "If a flying-saucer landed in front of us and an insect hand beckoned us on board, she would step inside without hesitation, while I, distrustful and suspicious behind the nearest bush, would watch the door close and Beryl take off for infinity."

If I were honest with myself, I knew I was more tentative, like Miles. But I tried to keep an image of Beryl—of both of them, actually—in mind.

Jeff and I had a code we'd use when things got rough: "What would the Smeetons do?" we'd say.

TIDAL TIME

The thing about sailing to the Great Bear Rainforest that was so profound to me that summer—and yet also, so very simple—was how pared down life aboard *Heron* was and yet how rich each moment felt as a result. How there were so few choices to make. Jeans or shorts? Sails up or down? Our job most days was simply to move on, to skim over the surface of the water, to get ourselves safely from point A to point B. Our focus was on calculating the tides and currents, on watching the weather. Our intent was to pay attention. We'd worried we might grow bored, but as we learned to navigate our new world, the hours, strangely, felt more full. In all marriages there is struggle, and ours was no different. But the anxiety I'd had about being alone as empty nesters began to dissipate as we learned to see each other anew. We were finding new ways to communicate, from shared hand signals to shared silences.

On the fourth day we awoke to a sparkling morning, hauled up the anchor, and headed out to cross the Strait of Georgia. The wind was blowing a steady sixteen knots, and the air had "warmed" to sixty-eight degrees. The water waltzed with light chop. Nursing a cup of coffee in the cockpit, I squinted up at a cornflower-blue sky streaked with high cirrus clouds, noted the cool wind on my face. It all felt delicious, especially with the sun caressing my back, despite the bright red Mustang Survival inflatable life vest cinched around me. I felt capable and, frankly, pretty badass.

"Jeff, you'd better get your life vest on . . . *now!*" I barked. "I'm raising the main."

"Who are you and what have you done with my wife?!" Jeff said. He laughed, dropping the bottle of Lexol he'd been using to polish the side rails and snapping to attention with mock exaggeration. "Jesus!"

Then Jeff mimed a lazy-ass sailor, yawning, reluctantly turning his attention to the cockpit packed with its winches and lines.

"Yeah, well the wind's up, and it's just right. You'd better get ready, bud."

We raised the mainsail. Then Jeff cleared all the lines for the jib, and we brought it out, followed by the staysail. Soon we were heeled over thirty degrees, humming along on a perfect close reach. *Heron* loves this point of sail, feels like she's doing what she's designed to do, her big hull rushing through the water with a determined sort of leaping, bounding over waves with clean rapidity. Hanging on to the helm, hands wide on the wheel, is the same sensation of speed and power you might have astride a sure-footed horse galloping across an open field. Except on the water, the steed is the magnificent *Heron*, the field as wide and blue as the sky.

Out of nowhere our VHF radio crackled to life. "*Heron*, calling the sailing vessel *Heron*. Over."

Jeff and I looked at each other. *Huh?*

"*Heron*, sailing vessel *Heron*. Over."

He reached for the radio clipped to the wheel stem. I hung on to the wheel. The port rail now angled precipitously toward the water, and I wedged my feet wide in the cockpit for balance. White spray flew past . . .

"This is *Heron*," Jeff said, then listened. "Well, thank you," he went on, brightening. "That's nice of you to radio over. It's a Moody. A Moody 54."

There was only one other boat within sight, a sapphire-blue-hulled motor yacht; it had been approaching us for miles and was now passing to starboard in the opposite direction. Its captain had made the effort to radio and say how awesome *Heron* looked, all sails up on this tack, heeled over, displaying her white waterline stripes and fresh coat of red bottom paint. *Gorgeous*, he'd said.

"Gosh, that was nice," I said, after the call. "Well, she *is* gorgeous!"

~~~~~~~~~

By the morning of the fifth day, we'd forgotten what day of the week it was.

"So it's Thursday. Just in case you were wondering," Jeff said. "August fifth."

"It is?" I replied.

We were way outside normal time now. We'd crossed over into Tidal Time: a state of mind where time is determined more by the sun and the moon and the tide than anyone's wristwatch, cell phone, or calendar. It had taken us four days of hard motoring north into BC waters to get here, plus a few days of shifting our physical and emotional states after that, letting go of the outside world with its system of engagement.

There was no place we had to be. We felt light as mist. We felt giddy . . . free! We'd docked the night before in Pender Harbour, home to a community of artists and retirees drawn to the hilly coves and islands of BC's Sechelt Peninsula. Now we were skimming across a bay in *Heron*'s inflatable dinghy, looking for the grocery store. Since the boys would be joining us three days hence, it seemed like a good idea to stock up on fruit and chips and maybe some Kokanee, a Canadian beer. (The drinking age in Canada is eighteen, so we let the boys drink on the boat—even though James wasn't twenty-one, the drinking age in Washington State.)

But that was the only place we had to be: meeting the boys' floatplane on a dock at Cortes Island on August 8.

That was our sole agenda.

~~~~~~~~~

We finally shoved off around one o'clock that day, motoring up Agamemnon Channel toward Jervis Inlet—one of the many great fjords and the deepest, dropping away to 2,402 feet beneath us—that cut into the BC interior. As I surveyed the land, more mountainous here but also defined by these dramatic fjords, I realized we'd come far enough by then that the terrain had begun to change. The landscape around us was still dark forest-green, but the towering conifers blanketed entire mountains instead of capping rockbound islands. Occasionally, we'd spy an outpost of a cabin clamped hard as a barnacle to rock in a cleared section of trees. But mostly, to both port and starboard, rugged hillsides cloaked in aromatic cedar, spruce, and hemlock rose straight out of the water. There was no beach between forest and sea; the trees simply took over where the water stopped. Beyond them an infinity of mountains extended into the distance.

With the sun warming the day to temperatures in the low seventies, we shed our fleece, layer by layer. Off came the baseball caps and Gore-Tex. Out came the sunscreen. The water was glassy, its surface taut as cellophane. Before long we were stripped down to nothing but T-shirts and jeans, munching lunch from plates balanced on our laps: mixed-greens salad topped with chopped apple and hazelnuts. We put *Heron* on autopilot and kicked back in the cockpit, feeling like we had everything we needed stowed aboard and could just keep going—cruise to Alaska and then cross the Pacific maybe, no problem.

"Nectarine?" I asked, grandly. "Chocolate chip cookie?"

"Sure, why not?" Jeff grinned. "How about *both*?"

After about nine miles we reached the junction of Agamemnon Channel and Jervis Inlet, turning west into Jervis's wide mouth. We then not only left *Heron* on autopilot but also—since the water was so deep and the fjord nearly half a mile wide—both left the cockpit, each of us riding one of the boat's burnished teak seats that together form a pair of perches mounted on opposite sides of the stern. We were pointed toward the distant peaks of Vancouver Island, and beyond that, the Pacific rolling all the way to Japan. With fifty-four feet of *Heron* floating before me, I felt powerful riding into the sun, sort of like an Egyptian queen being ferried down the Nile.

"I love this!" I shouted across to Jeff, spreading my arms.

"This is where all civilization breaks down!" he shouted back, smiling.

As it turned out, he wasn't that far off. Since we'd pretty much left civilization behind already, all that was left now was the breakdown.

ETCH-A-SKETCHED
IN BLIND BAY

~~~~~

Small stunted pines sprouted from the islands and their windswept escarpments. We motored through them slowly, checking depths, noting the other boats already anchored, debating where a good spot for *Mighty Heron* might be. Like we did most days, we'd considered the various anchoring options described in our cruising guides, calculated distances, checked our charts, and decided together beforehand where we'd go. We were prepared. Descriptions of the forty-two-acre Hardy Island Marine Provincial Park sounded alluring: "Provides a small protected anchorage . . . The warm, clean and green waters surrounding the area are reminiscent of a more tropical place."

Perhaps we were distracted by the concept of *a more tropical place*; maybe we were worn out after five hours of motoring without any real wind, or just getting overconfident. But whatever the reason, we failed to note that the Hardy Island guide also warned: "Mariners should use caution when anchoring, as there is a rocky bottom."

If there's one lesson I've learned—whether in boating or in life—it's that the minute you grow the least bit complacent, nature and circumstance conspire to correct you, reaching up to grab an ankle, shake you hard, and remind you of the natural order of things and who, in fact, is boss.

Which is exactly what happened as we attempted to anchor in Hardy Island Marine Park in the aptly named Blind Bay.

Well over two dozen boats had beaten us to Blind Bay and were anchored with their lines stern-tied around the few graceful red-barked madrone trees clinging to the shore's granite cliffs. Beside the cliffs the bay dropped away precipitously; we realized we'd have to anchor deep—in sixty to seventy feet of water. On top of that, with our roundabout detour up Agamemnon Channel and lazy start to the day, we'd arrived late: there was little room to maneuver, and our mariner neighbors were eyeing us warily. Already well into evening cocktails, they were wondering who'd be the "lucky ones" to wind up with us anchored too close next door.

Circling round we finally found enough room between boats to drop anchor, back in, and stern-tie to a cliff. I walked up to the foredeck, crouched down, lifted the lid to the chain locker, and reached in for the small handheld remote that runs *Heron*'s anchor windlass. When I pushed the button that should trigger the electric windlass so the heavy anchor chain begins unspooling, lowering the anchor from the bow of the boat to the water, nothing happened. The windlass's clutch plate spun but without moving any chain. I tried again. No dice. Again. Nada. Instead of the plate's teeth grabbing the chain and lowering *Heron*'s fifty-five-pound anchor, the mechanical windlass just spun and spun.

"It's not working!" I called, turning back to Jeff. He was at the helm, driving the boat behind the dodger and windscreen, and he couldn't hear a word I was saying.

"Drop the anchor!" he called up.

"It's not working! It's not doing anything!"

I tried the windlass again.

"What are you *doing*? Drop the anchor!" Jeff shouted back, exasperated.

I pointed to the useless remote, gave a shrug.

"Just pull some chain out—drop it by hand!"

Hmm, okay. I yanked a few feet of chain from the windlass onto the foredeck, stepped forward keeping my feet clear, and shoved the huge anchor over. But instead of dropping a few feet, the anchor began pulling chain from the windlass and, as the weight tipped the balance, picking up speed. Jeff left the helm and rushed up just as the windlass, freewheeling wildly, began spewing close to four hundred feet—*six hundred pounds*—of heavy three-eighths-inch-thick galvanized-steel chain straight off the bow and into Blind Bay.

"Take the helm!" Jeff shouted, at my shoulder in a flash and ripping the remote from my hands.

We switched places, and I hustled back to the wheel, leaving Jeff on the bow to wrestle with the windlass. "Put it in neutral!" he hollered.

Shit. I'd driven the boat before—but only forward. I had no idea which click on the lever's rotation was neutral. Plus, wasn't it already *in* neutral?

Before our arrival Blind Bay had been blissfully silent. Now it sounded like a symphony of jackhammers had gone off, thanks to us, the noisy chain reverberating over the water and echoing off the cliffs: *Clankity, clankity, clankity, clankity-clankity, CLANKITY-CLANKITY-CLANK* . . . The racket was accelerating, growing louder and louder as the weight of the anchor pulled what chain was left out of the boat.

But that wasn't the worst of it. I looked up just as Jeff sprang forward in his leather Top-Siders and jumped on the violently spewing chain. I shrieked involuntarily, knowing how dangerous this was, how any attempt to stop that avalanche of metal could mangle a foot or sever an ankle. But my husband's first instinct was to stop the anchor and chain from flying off the boat. So he jumped—managing to halt the thing without losing his feet. Then, still standing on the hefty chain, he reached down, grabbed the steel-bit anchor lock, and shoved it through the remaining links, securing them seconds before the last hundred feet shot off the boat.

Unfortunately, this heroic effort was too late—we'd already sent nearly three hundred feet and nearly five hundred pounds of chain freewheeling over the bow. And so, thanks to this colossal screwup, most of our anchor chain lay on the bottom of Blind Bay, useless as piles of spaghetti.

Once the heavy-metal explosion ceased, the cove was dead silent.

I could hear someone clear his throat on the boat where he was standing, watching, thirty yards away. I was mortified. I felt like I was going to pass out. I stood at the helm, wanting to disappear, every ounce of me aching to melt into the deck—but I knew I had no choice but to stay there and ride the thing out.

"Christ, you could have lost both feet!" I hissed to Jeff, who'd just walked back to me at the helm. *"What was that?"*

"A shit storm, that's what," he said, nodding toward the bow. "Don't worry. I analyzed it and figured if I jumped hard enough, it wouldn't break my legs."

"*Great*. What a nightmare," I muttered under my breath.

"We've got to get that chain back on board."

"I know, but how?"

While we were trying to figure out what to do, a dinghy motored across Blind Bay in our direction and idled up to the side of the boat.

"Um, *hoop* you won't mind my asking, having a little trouble with your windlass?" our neighbor, a concerned Canadian, maybe midforties, said, his raised *o*'s and laid-back delivery the epitome of understatement.

We admitted that yes, we were, as a matter of fact, having "a little trouble" with our windlass.

"*Hoommm.* Did yeh check yeh clutch plate?" our new friend wanted to know.

Jeff and I looked at each other. Had we what?

"Yeh, clutch plate . . . on the windlass. They looooosen up some-times, eh?"

Jeff and I raised our eyebrows, traded a you-learn-something-new-every-day-out-here glance.

"Hmmm," Jeff said, "maybe it loosened when we were crossing the strait?"

"Yup," he concurred, bobbing alongside us. "It happens."

While the kind Canadian hung to *Heron's* side rail, we dragged out a tool kit.

"That oughta do it," Jeff said, tapping down the tightened wind-lass with a winch handle. "It was great of you to come over, thanks. Can we offer you a beer at least?"

"Guess it's about that time of day, isn't it?" Our new friend grinned as we handed a beer over the side of the hull to him. "So what'll yeh do now?"

Jeff and I looked at each other, assured him we'd be fine, and he paddled off. But damn, the windlass wasn't the half of it: now we had a ton of chain to crank back onto the boat.

~~~~~~

I thought my nightmare was almost over, but no. Ten minutes later it had morphed into a full-blown fiasco. I was back at the helm; Jeff was back on the bow. But this time Captain Jeff was leaning over the rail, staring into the murky depths and trying to follow the chain's trail to where, apparently, it was snagged on Blind Bay's rocky bottom.

"Reverse! *Reverse!*" he was shouting. *Shit.* I put the boat in reverse, I hoped, and was indeed backing *Heron*, closer and closer, dangerously close to the cliff we'd originally planned to stern-tie to. I'd never even backed *Heron* until leaving the dock in Seattle four days before. I focused on trying to keep the stern straight in these close quarters.

"Now forward. *Forward!*" Jeff hollered.

I pushed the throttle forward again while my husband simultaneously tried to troubleshoot the chain and keep us floating in the desired spot.

"Is it in gear? *Forward!*" he shouted back.

Get me out of here! I thought. I tried to adopt a cool-as-a-cucumber-I-drive-this-boat-all-the-time stance, but I couldn't help sneaking a glance at the boats around us. God, people had come up and were actually standing on their sterns like prairie dogs, all heads turned our way, enjoying the drama. Each of them had probably been here before, I told myself, but tonight was our special night. A few hours earlier we'd been floating along on top of the world. Then suddenly we were completely screwed. *Why did I sign up for this?* I wondered.

Jeff and I moved forward and back, forward and back, hovering over the chain pile, slowly pulling steel up with our now-working windlass, until the chain remaining over the bow suddenly stretched tight as piano wire.

Oh no. What was *this*?!

Try as we might, moving backward and forward, we couldn't loosen it. With all our gyrations, we'd managed to wrap ourselves around one of Blind Bay's notorious bottom rocks. *Arrgghhhhh!* I rubbed my head with both hands, feeling a killer migraine coming on.

Jeff set down the remote, strolled back to me at the helm again.

"Now what?" I asked, massaging my temples.

We looked at each other. We were in this together.

"Well, we're not going anywhere," Jeff said, sitting down and gazing gloomily toward the bow. "You don't even need a stern tie. You've got a hundred or so feet of chain and a fifty-five-ton anchor down there now—it's called a rock."

~~~~~~~~~

We switched off the engine, lowered ourselves into the cabin, and shut the hatch—disappearing like Butch and Sundance after a hairy shoot-out into the safety of our secret lair. It was an indescribable relief to be alone together. Jeff hurled himself onto the settee. I sank to the small green leather couch on the opposite side of the cabin, shaken and embarrassed, insanely glad to be off that helm and out of sight.

Then we both looked at each other . . . and burst out laughing.

"Oh my god! Oh my god!" I kept saying. "What a fiasco! A total fiasco! That was the *worst!*"

"Worst *ever*," Jeff concurred. "What a shit show. I had no idea the clutch plate could come loose."

"Well, now we know. Seriously, I'm just so relieved you didn't lose any toes out there!"

"Or *feet*," Jeff said.

"Or your legs, you big fat idiot."

"At least I'm not so bad looking, for such a big fat idiot," my husband tossed back with his most winsome grin. "Let's have a beer and regroup, figure this thing out."

"*That* is a brilliant idea," I said, brightening.

So we stole two of the boys' cans of Kokanee beer from the fridge and popped the tops, out of commission but at least safe for the moment. It was a new kind of moment, but it was a tense moment: darkness was coming and we had to figure this thing out together *fast*. We were becoming a culture of two. When was the last time we'd faced a challenge like this together? It felt like us against the world, or the rock, as it were.

～～～～～

There was a groaning. We listened. Every few seconds, a horrible, tortured, plate-tectonics-shifting kind of groaning noise would reverberate through *Heron*'s floorboards. We could literally *feel* the sound. It came up through the bilges and floor and fed straight through our feet.

I looked at Jeff.

He looked at me.

"We're out of here," he said.

The noise was just the sound of chain dragging across rock, but we had no idea what had really happened down below, how much chain was wrapped around how much rock in which direction, or how solid our hold was. Our chart plotter, a screen display that integrates GPS data with an electronic navigational chart, showed a web of chain circling round and round in tighter loops, then backward and forward—our entire anchoring debacle mapped out like the trail of an insane sea snail.

"That's hilarious!" Jeff said, peering over the nav table at the image. "In fact, I think someone needs to take a picture of this right now." He whipped out his iPhone and pointed it at the screen.

We both stared at the absurd trail we'd unwittingly Etch-A-Sketched in Blind Bay. We knew we'd never sleep—we'd be up all night worrying about the boat, that it might work itself loose and drift too close to the rocks or one of our neighbors. Retreat, as late in the day as it was, started to seem like our best option. Within ten minutes we'd calculated how long it would take to return to Pender Harbour (where we'd *started* the day twelve hours earlier), tied a buoy to the chain, and tossed the whole thing—all the remaining chain and anchor—overboard. We figured we could mark the spot on our GPS and come back the next day to salvage the pieces.

"You're not leaving, are you?" a young husband and wife anchored on a pretty little ketch called out as we motored past, tails between our legs.

"Yep, can you believe it? After all that!" I said. We waved back jauntily, trying to look casual.

HERE'S TO FINGERS
AND TOES

~~~~~~~~

We left Blind Bay and turned south, heading into Malaspina Strait, the wide body of water that would have been the more direct route that morning. I took the helm from Jeff and checked my watch while he went below to plot our course. It was already seven o'clock at night, and it would take us about two hours to reach Pender at our cruising speed.

Jeff brought up the portable speakers and plugged in the iPod.

I didn't mind driving, I was so tremendously relieved just to be *out of there.*

I looked out and surveyed the still, windless sea, chagrined.

Then, realizing we'd never been underway together this late in the day, I looked up at the sky. It shone silver and pink, like the inside of a mussel shell. Everything was illuminated by the setting sun. And although there was nothing but the smell of ozone and salt and we were in the middle of the darkening sea after acting like the

Northwest's two biggest oafs afloat, there was also so much: purple sea beneath us, mountains in all directions, the vast sky shining and then fading to black as the stars emerged overhead.

We were so tired. Bone tired. My stomach growled . . .

But at the same time it struck me we weren't home just standing in the kitchen and cooking the same thing for dinner again, or driving the boys around in the same old suburban circles, or sitting in our office cubicles staring at screens. We were outside on what felt like the edge of the earth, seeing it again for what seemed like the first time in a long time. I blinked. I felt so small suspended over the surface of the sea beneath that sky. But as *Heron* slid on through the twilight, and the sky began to deepen, a new moon, thin as a sliver of ice, rose.

Gazing up, my hands on the wheel, I felt powerful. As I looked out at the limitless seas of the stars, really looked at them, a feeling of calm came over me. I had a conscious realization of what it feels like to be intensely alive. And I felt gratitude not only for being alive but also for being part of something larger and so much more mysterious. Suddenly, the distance between *Heron* and the stars seemed to disappear. I was out in the middle of the sea, on the edge of a darkening night, but felt expansive, entirely safe.

"I love you, Chet," I said.

He looked at me like I was crazy. Even though the past few hours had been ridiculously traumatizing, the worst imaginable, we'd somehow come through them—and come through them together.

"You're okay, Bug," Jeff said as I drove on into the dark. He wrapped his arm around me. In the damp cold I was intensely aware of the warmth of his body against mine. "You're turning out to be one heck of a chief mate, you know. Tough as hell. Who'd have figured?"

I laughed, shivering with pleasure. "That's nice of you to say."

It was one heck of a compliment coming from my husband.

And as I squinted deeper into the night, it occurred to me that maybe it might even be true.

Two hours later, in total darkness, which heightened the spicy smell of the surrounding forest and sun-warmed odor of rock wafting off land, we floated up to the same dock we'd left eight hours earlier. Unbelievably, there was fifty-four feet left.

"Just like the Flying Dutchman!" a fellow boater called out as we limped in for a port-side tie, utterly spent.

I was ready to scarf down some Cheerios and call it a night, but my husband declared he was going to cook us dinner, and he did. It was nearly ten o'clock at night when we sat down to grilled prawns, fresh that morning, piled atop linguine, and a bottle of Galardi Terra di Lavoro 2004, pulled from the stash beneath the floorboards.

"Here's to fiascos!" Chet said, raising his glass.

"Here's to fingers and toes," I added.

～～～～

The next morning, our sixth day afloat, we awoke in the exact same place we'd started the day before. Except that carefree, easy feeling, the giddy freedom we'd spent nearly a week to gain, was gone. We would meet the boys in less than two days! And not only were we groggy from drinking too much red wine the night before, we no longer had an anchor or chain. And without an anchor or chain, we'd be unable to anchor in all the remote coves and bays we'd planned to explore with the boys. How had we gone from being capable adults to such complete idiots in less than a week?

We sat in the cabin with a stack of cruising guides and a pot of strong coffee between us, assessing our situation. We located three local divers and dialed them all: Bruno, Andy, and Fig. I was eager to meet a guy named Fig, but only Andy picked up when we called. It turned out Andy also ran the local water taxi, so he could meet us in Blind Bay.

By nine o'clock in the morning, we'd hired him and were headed all the way back north. After nearly two hours motoring along the exact same coast we'd just traversed the night before, nothing looked beautiful. The sea was choppy and grim. The damp sky sagged. When we finally pulled into Blind Bay, it was deserted. All the boats from the day before had pulled up anchor by then and left.

In the middle of the bay, a pathetic little buoy bobbed . . .

Our anchor float! Which marked the spot where we'd dropped the chain.

We turned off the engine and drifted over, hoping Andy would show.

"Having fun now, Chet?" I asked.

He sighed, looking weary.

"It's not so bad, we'll figure it out," I said, softening.

"Well, we'd better. We don't have any choice."

The quiet was calming. A red-tailed hawk circled overhead. Finally, after twenty minutes or so, an aluminum skiff rounded the corner. Our relief at the sight of the guy at the wheel was enormous.

"Howdy!" he called out with a wave. "You the folks who called about a diver?"

The maneuver turned out to be tricky with just the three of us. We decided Andy would bring his boat alongside *Heron*, and I'd jump aboard to help him into his dry suit. Jeff would stay with *Heron* since it was impossible for us to anchor—without, um, an anchor on board.

It was choppy in the bay, and a long jump . . .

"Hi," I said, landing in the bottom of the bobbing skiff with a thud.

"Hi," Andy said. He was about my age, late forties or early fifties, freckled, doughy. He took off his boots. Pulled down his jeans. Peeled off his socks. I looked the other way.

"Could you zip my suit up?" he asked.

I turned back around. "Sure, happy to," I said. "We were so glad you could come out this morning!" I babbled, zipping the back of the thick black neoprene carefully, like a mom packing a two-hundred-pound toddler into a snowsuit six sizes too small, careful not to catch any skin in the zipper. "There you go," I breathed.

Andy put on his flippers and mask, lowered himself to the skiff's transom. I didn't envy his having to slide into the murky depths of Blind Bay.

"Here goes nothing," he said a few minutes later, treading water then sinking out of sight.

I stood watching the spot where Andy had been. Pallid bubbles rose in a ring. The wind blew, ruffling the restless surface of the water. I looked over at Jeff floating on *Heron*, about two hundred feet away. Gave a little wave. Minutes ticked by . . .

Finally, a riot of bubbles shot to the top and Andy resurfaced.

I helped haul him into the skiff. "That's some rock you managed to lasso," he said, dripping, climbing aboard. "Wrapped your chain round a boulder the size of a car."

"No kidding," I said. "So, what do you think?"

Andy said he'd been able to free most of the chain so that we could crank it back on board. But he hadn't managed to get it all.

Ten minutes later, Andy had anchored his skiff and we'd both climbed back aboard *Heron*. I was stationed at the helm, an expert on the stick by now, trying to keep the boat idling in neutral and the bow centered over the spot where the anchor and chain were looped tight as a noose, we now knew, beneath a Volkswagen-sized boulder.

Jeff and Andy were standing on the bow, scheming.

In the end here's what they did: pulled the end of the chain with the anchor attached back on board by rigging up a pulley system, removed the anchor, attached that end of the chain to the windlass and wrapped in as much as they could, about half, until they reached the section stuck under the boulder. We'd have to somehow cut the rest loose and leave it behind. But how?

I watched the two of them, bonding through physics and the laws of motion. The sun had warmed the chill off the morning, and they sat in shorts on the bow, dripping sweat, chain stretched taut, trying to figure out what to do next. We were lashed to a boulder seventy-five feet down by a chain with links the size of limes. I shook my head. The situation seemed hopeless.

"We can't give up now, Jeff!" Andy was saying, "This is man against nature!"

"Maybe we can cut through it," Jeff said.

"I don't know, that's one monster chain," Andy said doubtfully.

"Hang on a sec," Jeff said, disappearing below. He reemerged with a pair of monster bolt cutters.

"Where'd you get those?" I asked as he clambered by.

Then Jeff went back up to the bow and, holding the heavy-duty cutters in both hands while Andy pulled the chain taut, tried to cut through the galvanized steel. He may as well have been trying to sever a branch with a pair of fingernail scissors. I held my breath . . .

Clank. With enough pressure the cut passed through the chain, which snapped in half and dropped in two pieces to the deck.

It was a miracle!

All three of us stood there under the bright noon sun in the middle of nowhere, whooping and cheering and high-fiving.

"I can't believe you had that bolt cutter aboard," Andy said with respect.

"Way to go, Chet!" I enthused.

"It's no big deal," Jeff said with a hangdog look, although I knew how psyched he really was. "With my luck?" he added. "I figure you never know when you'll have to cut yourself loose, so you might as well be prepared."

BOYS

~~~~~~~

"I can't believe the boys will be here in a few hours," I keep saying, sipping my coffee in the cockpit.

"Yeah, our last morning before the hyenas land," Jeff mutters, raising his mug in a mock halfhearted salute, then reading me the quote printed on its side: *Every Dog Has His Day.*

Heron has four of these indestructible mugs. You also stand a good chance of getting *Wake Up Sleepyhead, Wake Up and Smell the Coffee,* or *Rise and Shine.* I've got *Rise and Shine* and, strangely, the morning feels that way, rising and shining and kind of miraculous: that we've made it this far, and that we're docked at Cortes Island in Desolation Sound (after an unplanned detour to Powell River, a mill town where we'd managed to find a marine store and 220 feet of three-eighths-inch-thick braided nylon rope, which Jeff wove to the 120 remaining feet of anchor chain, solving that problem). Soon the boys' floatplane from Seattle will appear over the bluff, circling like a stiff-legged cormorant before splashing down in Cortes Bay.

In honor of their arrival—Sam all the way from San Francisco, where he has a week off from his summer internship; and James, who has just finished his last day managing the kayak center in Seattle before heading east to college—we are making *Heron* family ready. It doesn't take long. Jeff sprays the salt off the dark blue hull and scrubs the deck. I fold down the bunk that turns the starboard office into a berth, climb up, and lie down testing it out. Hmmm . . . It's hard as a board and barely six feet long. The boys will have to figure out who gets the sleeping shelf (which I attempt to disguise by tucking a Therm-a-Rest pad beneath striped sheets), and who gets the double forward berth. But oh well—someone can always camp on deck.

Next I pull on a pair of yellow rubber gloves and attack the forward head. I hate cleaning. But the head is so compact, even I can handle it—and it's strangely satisfying, making everything *shipshape*. I discover I can clean the whole thing, including the teak floor, sink, and toilet (known as the head since the days of early wooden sailing ships, when a ship's toilet was placed at the *head* of a vessel, where splashing water served to clean it naturally), with a tiny sponge. This takes maybe five minutes. Ten if I go big and shine up the stainless.

The galley is already in order, so I hang a fresh striped towel from the gimbaled stove (which swings from a pivot point and stays level so you can boil water for tea, for example, when the boat is heeled over on its side), and dig out some plums for the fruit bowl. There's a lot to be said for the simplicity of living in a small space. *It's ironic*, I think. *No sooner do we obtain our dream houses than the urge to downsize sets in—much like a hermit crab longs to shed its shell.* Boat space is pared-down space. And the new shell? Boundless freedom.

Still, *Heron* is downright luxurious compared with the floating summer home of Desolation Sound's most storied mom, Muriel Wylie Blanchet. With the boat in order, Jeff and I are free to relax while we wait. My husband strikes up a conversation with a couple on a boat down the dock. I reach for Blanchet's memoir *The Curve of Time*, a remarkable tale by a woman who, left a widow in 1927, rents out her home to earn extra money, packs her five children onto a twenty-five-foot motor launch, and cruises the coastal waters of British Columbia for fifteen years. Blanchet's account of their unstructured days exploring Desolation Sound reads almost like fiction, but her adventures are all very real: single-handedly, she acts as skipper, navigator, engineer, and mum, steering her crew through encounters with tides, storms, rapids, cougars, and bears. Blanchet's voice is so understated and matter-of-fact, however, that what you take away from the story isn't the notable accomplishment of her basic survival (and how unusual her adventures were for that time) but instead the quiet self-assurance of a woman teaching her children the wonders of the natural world.

One of my favorite parts of the book is when she describes the family's twenty-five-foot cruiser, *Caprice*: "At times we longed for a larger boat," she writes, "for each summer, as the children grew bigger, the boat seemed to grow smaller, and it became a problem how to fit everyone in. She was only twenty-five feet long with a beam of six and a half feet, and until later, when the two oldest girls went East to school, she had to hold six human beings and sometimes a dog as well."

As author Timothy Egan, a Seattle native, explains in his intro to *The Curve of Time*'s most recent edition: "They were six people and a dog on a boat of no more than a hundred and fifty square feet. Imagine being crammed into a medium-sized bathroom with your family, and you have some idea what the floating quarters were like." But he also underscores the book's lovely, lyrical quality, adding: "Ah, but the *Caprice* was merely a vehicle to the larger world."

~~~~~~~~~

The boys call us to say their flight from Seattle is delayed, so I turn next to British author Jonathan Raban's description of life aboard the first ship associated with these waters, the *HMS Discovery*, captained by British navigation legend Captain George Vancouver in 1792.

"*Discovery* was a few inches short of one hundred feet long," Raban writes in his terrific *Passage to Juneau*, describing his solo journey retracing Vancouver's route up the Inside Passage. Raban continues:

> Cramped and smelly at the best of times . . . the quarter-deck—an area reserved for gentlemen of all ranks—was roughly 28 x 30; it was also the ship's farmyard. One could hardly take a step without tripping over a piglet or a chicken, or colliding with a bony goat. This cluttered and constricted space had been made even smaller by the addition . . . [of] a glass greenhouse, 8 x 12 feet, in which newly discovered plants could be returned, alive, to England . . . With five commissioned officers, a dozen or so animals, and the greenhouse, the quarterdeck was already overloaded. But *Discovery* had taken on an unprecedented number of young gentlemen, aged from 16 to 22.

Yikes! I think, marking the passage in case there are ever any grumblings of mutiny from our own young gentlemen. *How ridiculously lucky we are, how fortunate to have been born in the twentieth century not the eighteenth century*, I tell myself, imagining the cramped and reeking *Discovery* inching its way between these then uncharted islands, crammed with miserable livestock. Even worse, Captain Vancouver sailed the *Discovery* and his company's smaller ship, the *Chatham*, into the area on an unseasonably dark and rainy night in 1792. Both ships felt their way through these waters in a very unpleasant navigation, as if blindfolded while trying to anchor, according to Vancouver. He and his crew of 170 men were astonished to find the water incredibly deep even close to shore. What they had no way of knowing is that Desolation Sound has the most dramatic drop in altitude from mountain peak to ocean floor in all North America, with fjords dropping away to depths of up to six hundred meters, nearly two thousand feet.

Finally, nearing midnight, they anchored off what is now Kinghorn Island in the middle of Desolation Sound. Vancouver and his crew then spent a drizzly three weeks charting the region in rowboats. Our little "adventure" with the boys, regardless what happened, would be a pleasure cruise by comparison.

~~~~~~~~~

While getting there is slightly easier than it was two hundred years ago, what makes Desolation Sound so storied is that it has hardly changed at all: it is still a wild and undeveloped coastline dotted with islands and islets, coves, lagoons, towering cliffs and granite outcroppings, all framed by thick coniferous forest that ranges almost to the snowy peaks of the Coast Mountains. Each summer, the area receives a two-month population boost as swarms of boaters flock to the region in powerboats, yachts, sailboats, and kayaks; it's not uncommon for a hundred boats to share a small anchorage. But since the nearest road is twenty miles south, where the Pan-American Highway comes to an unceremonious stop in the tiny fishing village of Lund, the area remains largely protected and pristine.

Anyone who spends time in Desolation Sound will bump into Captain Vancouver. He was under orders of the United Kingdom's Royal Navy to chart the entire northwest coast of North America and find the secret, undiscovered waterway known as the Northwest Passage. The *Discovery* and her sister ship, the *Chatham*, had already been at sea for more than two years, painstakingly fulfilling orders to survey parts of the New Zealand, Australian, Hawaiian, and North American coastlines. Finally reaching British Columbia in 1792, Vancouver and his crew explored, surveyed, and charted the entire coast, naming practically every island and channel. Today, more than two hundred years later, every bay sailors anchor in, every shore they tie to, the captain and his lieutenants were there first.

George Vancouver was desperate to live up to his predecessor, Captain James Cook, the British explorer, navigator, and cartographer.

(Cook had an impeccable reputation as a brilliant captain who was well liked by his crew. His long list of maritime achievements were legendary, including the first recorded European contact with the Hawaiian Islands, the first circumnavigation of New Zealand, and sailing thousands of miles across largely uncharted areas of the globe.) But Vancouver had been battling a mysterious illness for much of his maiden voyage as captain, and by the time the *Discovery* reached North America, he was prone to violent fits of rage followed by long bouts of depression. He drove his lieutenants relentlessly, often accompanying his men as they rowed the lengths of the fjords and rounded the islands from dawn to well past dusk. Needless to say, Vancouver was not well liked by his men. But he was so driven, thorough, and exacting that his charts of the North American northwest coast served as the key reference for coastal navigation, and they were still being used well into the 1900s.

In his frustration at hitting a maze of dead ends in the deep, dark, and winding fjords of coastal British Columbia, Vancouver's anger and depression engulfed him. Sunk in gloom and staring up at a wall of seemingly impassable mountains, Vancouver christened the place Desolation Sound. Since no roads have ever been built in the area, the name fits to this day.

~~~~~~~~

Finally, at about three o'clock, we hear engines and look up to see a sturdy, yellow-and-white de Havilland Beaver floatplane chugging through pale blue sky. It circles once, splashes down, and motors up to the dock. The pilot steps onto the pontoon, lashes the plane to a dock cleat, and all of a sudden there are Sam and James! They unfold their lanky selves from the seven-passenger plane, grab their duffels, and lope toward us in jeans and fleece jackets, then embrace us in bear hugs. Jeff gets a dude!-how's-it-going kind of hug. I get a mom hug, each long-legged boy bending down and folding over me like a crane.

"Hey, Momma!" they say in unison. Then, "Hey, Dad. You guys made it! How's life been on *Heron*?"

"Oh, it's an adventure," I say. Adding mysteriously, "We've got a few good stories for you."

"Yeah?" James says. "So you were swamped the first day?!"

"Mom's doing a helluva job," Jeff says.

I just laugh and say, "Thank god the *real* crew is here!" I take them both in, drunk with the sight of them, feeling a combination of anticipation over the things we'll share in the coming days and relief that after the whole anchor-chain fiasco and attendant delays, we no longer have to get ourselves here. With pride and excitement, as if *Heron* were a new family member—which, in a way she is—we lead the boys to the gleaming hulk.

Within an hour the brothers' gear is stowed, they've worked out who's scored the forward berth, who's stuck on the sleeping shelf— and we're all in swimsuits, diving off the stern into Cortes Bay. Had I forgotten in just two weeks how big they both are? Or did they just *seem* bigger with the four of us all together within the confines of the boat?

They're both over six feet—sinewy, broad shouldered, and olive skinned, with dark brows framing blue eyes. There's a transformation in young men, a time when they have a kid's face still, but with that sharp nascent handsomeness lurking around the cheekbones. Both boys have passed through that phase, I notice, and are now, unmistakably, *men*. Men with chest hair. And beards!

"The days are long but the years are short," people say about the early years of child rearing. I remember some days being almost calcified in their slowness when Sam was a baby. Home alone in our Upper West Side apartment, I had never experienced time so minutely. Exhausted on the bed with him after a night of breast-feeding, strapping him into his Snugli infant carrier—each trip to the corner deli as complex as a polar expedition—clipping his tiny translucent fingernails. Time moved as though through sand.

And then, seemingly overnight, *two* babies, with the arrival of James just twenty-eight months after his brother, and it sped up! People were right, the years *were* short. Each stage of parenthood was interesting: time leaped along as legs grew longer and voices deepened and character formed, and the current stage was equally fascinating: these new adult people. They would have been irresistible to girls, had there been any lurking in the general environs. *Too bad*, I think, while we sit around on the stern deck wrapped in towels, drip-drying. *They're trapped in the middle of nowhere, without friends, or cars, or working cell phones, or females for miles in any direction.* There would soon be girlfriends, serious girlfriends, welcomed aboard. But this last week as a family we'd have them all to ourselves.

~~~~~~~~~

The two great tidal streams of the Northwest coast meet just south of Desolation Sound: one of them flows around the northern tip of Vancouver Island and down Johnstone Strait; the other around the south end of the Strait of Georgia. This is what keeps the waters around Desolation Sound warm, warm enough in summer for *swimming*—a terrible idea (without a wetsuit) almost anywhere north of Portland, where the water hovers between a chilly fifty-two and fifty-four degrees. But even with the novelty of a Northwest swim—of being able to dive headfirst off *Heron* with Jeff and both boys, kick around her big blue hull in the bracing clean water, then float on our backs like otters—none of us can stay in for long. The water, about sixty-eight, just isn't that warm.

To prolong what I know will be one of our last family moments like this for a while, I gaze up at the sky while we're sitting on the stern deck wrapped in towels, and I see great white cumulus clouds, like a fleet of puffed-out sails racing past. I love when the Northwest's low clouds lift; on *Heron*, the sky feels like a vast room where the furniture is constantly changing—whether it's scrolled clouds, or shreds of cloud, or feathered cirrus clouds, or searingly blue sky, the drama makes you feel very much like you're on a planet, part of the larger universe.

We share a dinner of grilled flank steak in the cockpit. Jeff opens a bottle of wine. The night is unusually mild, and as the sun dips behind the tops of the trees, a lantern is lit. It casts a warm glow over our long-limbed, permascruffed bunch, together again for one last week before Sam heads back to work in San Francisco and James leaves for college. We have our issues, God knows. But I want to drink it all in, inhale every atom of this moment anyway—the salty, sometimes sweet, other times foul-mouthed, milk-and beer-swilling, volatile but essentially good and warmhearted, and always funny gang that's been for these last years, my crew—before we all go our separate ways and the day-to-day texture of what we've known together as a family is permanently altered.

I make a vow to pay close attention, to not take any of it for granted while I've got it, even the moments I'd probably rather forget—our squabbling and inevitable screwups afloat. Then I do something I do sometimes when I want to remind myself where I am in my life: I look around and take a kind of basic metaphysical inventory:

"Thank you for this planet," I whisper to myself. "And for the sky."

"Thank you for this family, which is able to have dinner together tonight under the sky."

"Thank you for being—we are lucky to be here."

"Thank you for this time. I'm glad we were able to get ourselves here without drowning."

~~~~~~~~~

Family has always felt like an actual place to me, as if it weren't a group of individuals but a room we could retreat to, no matter how bad the day has been. A place where you can gather the wagons, so to speak, light a fire, have a drink, sit down to a meal, share a moment of the day, and where each of us can be who we really are. Part of what I love about being a parent is creating that place, and up until now that place had always been *home*. But the past seven days on *Heron* had changed that. Family wasn't a room at home anymore, I realized, but anywhere we were all together in the whole wide world. And now we were exploring that world, inhabiting it together in an entirely new way.

While the boys cleared the table, passing plates and forks down the steep companionway, I sat gazing up at the stars and thinking about how these would be our last family dinners for a while, just the four of us. I remembered James turning in his final assignment for AP Literature a few weeks earlier. The assignment had been to write an essay based on NPR's *This I Believe* series. He'd been struggling to find his topic. "Start with a simple idea, something concrete," I'd suggested.

So he'd begun an essay with the title: "I Believe in Water."

"How's your water essay coming?" I'd asked the next day. It seemed like such a natural for a surfing, sailing, kayaking, river-guiding kid.

"I decided on a different topic."

"Really? You're not writing about water?"

"No. I came up with a better idea: 'I Believe in Family Dinner.'"

〜〜〜〜〜〜

There was a little pang. A quick, sharp stab in the soft part of the chest. You hadn't seen it coming. It was one of those casual moments of parenting when your son or daughter does something out of the blue that let's you know that somehow you have, by the grace of God, done an okay job. That maybe you weren't such a terrible mom after all.

"Wow, that's a great idea," you said, trying not to sound overly enthusiastic. "I love it!"

You were dying to read the essay, of course. But you never did get to see it.

You wondered what it said about family, about family dinners. Was it about the food or the people gathering around the table? Was it about the conversation? The flare-ups and fights?

In our family each of us always sat in the same spot until Sam left for college, and then there was the Empty Chair. I figured that was what James would have written about: "The Empty Chair."

The little pang had started its ache again, rising from your chest to your throat, where it lodged itself awhile. Then it occurred to you that as a parent you can't expect to do everything well. To be effective you have to pick the few things you really care about—and then you realize that your son had somehow nailed it; he'd hit upon one of the things you most believe in, even though you'd never articulated it. You and your husband might have missed half the Little League games, you might have been lax in signing up for parent groups. Hell, you were a *horrible* volunteer, had been late to nine out of ten school pickups, but you rarely missed, in fact truly excelled at, Family Dinner.

No matter how stressful things were, the bulk of your parenting had probably taken place around the dinner table. It was a place where you and your husband lingered most nights, and drank far too much wine. Maybe you should have encouraged the boys to eat faster, excuse themselves sooner, get back to their homework. Instead, you'd spent hours sitting and talking. Talking about books, music, movies, school, work, the world. Or sometimes it was just silly banter, the guys trying out new band names on each other, or telling off-color jokes.

No, you weren't at all disciplined, far from it. But no matter how terrible a day had been, or how sick of your jobs you and your husband were, or how boring or unfair a day at school might have seemed, the dinner table was the one place you'd come together for the feeling that everything would be all right, if only for a moment.

"Chet," I said, raising my now empty wineglass one more time on the boat, with the boys down below doing dishes, "here's a toast to you and me and to the first of these last dinners with the boys. We should acknowledge how fleeting this time is, don't you think?"

"I do, Bug—we should be grateful. For our health, and for the guys even wanting to be on board with us."

I laughed. No doubt the boys would be counting down the days, eager to get back to their wheels, to their cell phones, to their friends and jobs and own lives. That's what we'd been preparing them for all these years, after all. Our real work, any parent's real work, is readying your kids for the world.

The night air began to chill and a big harbor seal popped his head out of the water, looking for all the world like a bald bewhiskered uncle, his face round as the moon. Sending Sam and James off to college—where they'd wake in dorms with new roommates, make their own choices, have the opportunity to reinvent their stories—would give them space to be themselves. They'd find out more about who they were, and we'd do the same. We needed that for us, but we needed it more for them. They needed to know we could float on our own, and that when the time came, they really were free to go.

"Hey, guys? Are you coming down to play Scrabble, or what?" came Sam's nightly summons from below.

Jeff poked his head down the main hatch and said heartily, as he dropped out of sight, "Ah, I see you've set up the board so I can *whip your asses* again!"

"Well, good luck with that, Dad," I could hear Sam say. The year before, Sam had beaten us every time.

"Can we try to use a few other words tonight, please?" I asked, descending. "Maybe clean it up a little?"

"You've got it, Momma," Sam said.

"Make way for the queen," Jeff said. And with that we all squeezed in together around the cabin's teak table, and spread out the tiles.

RAPIDS

~~~~~

The Yuculta Rapids form a natural barrier, a sort of watery gauntlet guarding the BC coast's wilder, less-traveled wilderness, and early the next morning we set off for our first time through. Jeff, Sam, and I were up just after dawn, pushing *Heron* off the dock, and by seven o'clock in the morning, Sam was back on the sleeping shelf, unconscious. James, who'd scored the front stateroom, hadn't even woken up.

While *Heron* slipped quietly out of Cortes Bay, Jeff and I sat hunched in the cockpit. The sky over Desolation Sound's massive peaks glowed with a soft dawn light, all orange and silver-pink. But we were both heads down, checking and rechecking our calculations: the maze of channels above Desolation are notorious for their rapids and violent whirlpools; they're the most powerful tidal rapids in the Northern Hemisphere. The first five rapids, known collectively as the Yucultas, lay dead ahead. They had our full attention.

When you examine a map of this section of the BC coast, the Strait of Georgia and Queen Charlotte Strait resemble the ends of an hourglass squeezing in to form an elongated, mountain-clad, watery maze between them. The tidal currents of the Strait of Georgia (the vast inland strait we'd crossed a few days earlier) flow north, where they bump into Queen Charlotte Strait's colder currents flowing south. The currents are like stationary waves, producing a maximum inflow and outflow three hours before high tide and three hours before low tide. They're generally weak, except when they crash into one another in the intricate waterway's long "waist" section, the web of passes and narrows you must thread your way through to reach the wild, remote places farther north where we longed to go. The trick is to time your passage so that you reach each of the half dozen rapids during slack tide, the thirty minutes or so twice a day when all the water pushing through goes still.

It was day two of week two for us, well into summer—the second week of August—but Calendar Time suddenly seemed far less relevant than Tidal Time. With the help of other boaters we'd met on the docks at Cortes Bay, we'd worked through the August dates in *Canadian Tide and Current Tables, Volume 6* and determined that if the Yucultas' five sets of rapids—Yuculta Rapids, Gillard Passage Rapids, Dent Rapids, Greene Point Rapids, and Whirlpool Rapids— were turning to slack at ten thirty in the morning today, we'd better be well on our way by seven o'clock to reach the first rapids in time to ride through safely.

"It's hard to believe we were baking in swim trunks at Cortes yesterday," Jeff said, revving the engine's speed slightly as he looked out at the water. It was rippled with light winds from the southeast. The air temperature was cool, fifty-five degrees. He zipped his jacket.

"I know," I said, warming my hands on a metal cup of mint tea. I blew on it, let the steam drift up to warm my cheeks while we went over the times and tide tables again. Once we both agreed we'd done the right math and could do no more calculations, we pushed on, with plenty of time to reflect, nervously, on all the things that were new to us: In the miles between Georgia Strait and Queen Charlotte Strait, we'd need to pay close attention to not only the tides and currents but also the weather. Once we passed through the Yucultas' gauntlet of rapids, we'd continue up Johnstone Strait, a tunnel-like wind funnel notorious for its pounding side swells when the weather picks up. But there would be time enough to watch the Weather. Meanwhile, the more interesting factor was the Tide, something we never considered in our hyperconnected modern lives.

"Hey, did you know that on a worldwide scale, the tide typically rises and falls less than about three feet, each day?" I asked, reading aloud from a cruising guide. "But in the Pacific Northwest we're talking tides of twelve to thirteen feet? That's nuts!"

"No shit," Jeff said. "Why do you think we're always checking the tide charts and watching our depth meter so closely?"

"Yeah, I get that. But do you know what causes the tides?"

"Of course I know what causes the tides—the pull of the moon."

"But I bet you'd sort of forgotten," I said.

"Never. It also has something to do with barometric pressure, since pressure changes also affect tides—and fishing."

It could be infuriating, sometimes, being with someone who was almost always right. And even when he wasn't, wasn't even close, Jeff had the confidence to assert he was. On the other hand, knowledge out here equaled survival; without my husband's nautical baseline there was no way we'd consider cruising all the way to the Great Bear Rainforest on our own. I was proud to be out there, the two of us. Yet I still wished I could be a salty motherf*cker and dish it right back.

"Oh, come on, Chet, admit it," I pressed again. "The tides aren't something you think about when you're checking, say, Google Calendar."

"You've got that right, Starbuck."

Then, since the boys were sound asleep, I punched him lightly and said with affection, "You're such an asshole, Ahab."

There are so many ways we manage, through all our differences, throughout all our years together, to say: *I'm crazy about you, just crazy about you.*

~~~~~~~

Even on the first weekday of the second week of August, we could feel a new edge of cool in the air. Fall comes early along the Pacific Northwest Coast. We were motoring only a few miles north of Desolation Sound's tall summits and deep fjords, but we could already sense how their steep-shouldered, long-fingered topography held the water, warming it. Masses of mist and cloud hugged Desolation's peaks, shouldering up behind us in the receding distance. Within an hour it was raining softly. We zipped *Heron*'s canvas and heavy plastic rain shield over the cockpit, then pulled on our ski caps. The air temperature was fifty-eight degrees, the wind from the southeast light, the water rippled. But it felt colder, way colder, on the water.

In one of the wettest parts of the world—ranging from 60 inches of rain each year in Desolation Sound to as much as 180 inches annually in the northern reaches of the Great Bear Rainforest—the indigenous people spoke of two broad categories of rain: male and female. "A 'she rain' is gentle, caressing, clinging, persistent," the American photographer Edward S. Curtis explained in a letter to his daughter Florence in 1914, while he was documenting the indigenous people of the Pacific Northwest Coast. "A 'he rain' is quite the opposite in all ways but that of persistence." I thought about that as I watched our first real rain. It was a "she rain," and we'd better get used to it.

"I think I'll put on my foul-weather gear," Jeff said.

"*Really*," I said. This was a first. "*Okay*, then. I've got the wheel."

Within the hour we'd both pulled on our foul-weather gear: stiff bright red jumpsuits over fleece sweaters, and red Gore-Tex jackets on top of that. Shortly after we'd agreed to buy the boat and ship her across country, Jeff had also talked me into joining him on a

Saturday afternoon "date" at a place called Fisheries Supply in the thick of Seattle's maritime industry. Picture a hardware store on steroids. When I said I'd go along, he was as delighted as I'd have been if he'd agreed to go shoe shopping at Bergdorf's with me. Wisely, he'd steered me away from the shelves of fasteners, lines, pumps, and epoxies (one with the worrisome name Gluzilla!) and straight for the racks of rubber-soled boat shoes and, um, clothes. It had been a long road from my years as a downtown New York City girl dressed in leather and vintage, to Seattle jeans, boots, and cozy sweaters—but you have to draw the line somewhere: Sperry Top-Siders and yacht-club logo-wear was a place I never, ever wanted to go.

Fortunately, my husband had other ideas. So we tried on foul-weather gear: bright red bib overalls with matching hooded Gore-Tex storm jackets that secured with so many Velcro strips you'd be more likely to succumb from suffocation before rain, wind, or weather. Velcroed and zipped into my Musto offshore foul-weather gear, I felt like an America's Cup racer. Or an astronaut. Small and fierce. Impermeable. Sexy and kind of badass.

Even better were the Xtratuf boots: black rubber, with thick-tread soles topped by a red stripe, rounded toes, and neoprene liners. You could wear them beneath your foul-weather gear or pull them on over jeans for an adventure-chic look that was also practical when clambering across slippery decks.

~~~~~~~~~

At around nine thirty, new acquaintances from the Cortes docks passed us in their big motor yacht. They looked annoyingly comfortable inside.

We waved. We could see their silhouettes and then their hands inside the toasty-looking, wind- and rainproof capsule, waving back.

"I hate them," I grumbled.

The VHF radio crackled to life: "It looks like you're making good time there, *Heron*."

Jeff picked up the receiver and switched to a local channel. "Thanks, *Overstory*, bet you guys are a little warmer than we are."

"Don't worry . . . we'll save you a spot at the docks!"

Gee thanks, I thought, watching them round the forested bend ahead of us, leave a frothy white wake, and disappear from sight.

~~~~~~~~~~

No sooner had the "she rain" started than she stopped. *Heron* was riding along on an immense amount of water, and as the channels narrowed and the tide began to still, the water's rain-pocked surface smoothed, then braided into long sinewy strands. Where Stuart, Sonora, and Dent Islands crowd up against the British Columbia mainland, they form a narrow Y-valve through which nearly all the water in Desolation Sound has to pass on its way to and from the sea. To the northeast of us, Bute Inlet—a deep fjord that reaches more than thirty miles into the BC interior and falls to depths of two thousand feet—drains on the ebb tide. When this happens twice a day, two rivers of water crash into each other in a cauldronlike basin of angry whirlpools and violent rips before they shoot together through the mother of all rapids, Dent Rapids.

All the rapids, Yuculta and Arran, Gillard Passage, and Dent, are famous for catching and swallowing canoes, fishing boats, barges, and tugs, and for fatalities because the currents are swift and the water deep. At any time other than slack water—a fifteen- to thirty-minute calm in the turbulence—each of these rapids can gulp down even a large vessel. Which is why we'd nervously checked and rechecked our calculations before setting off.

The boys began stirring just as we reached the entrance to Yuculta Rapids five minutes before slack. In the cycle of Tidal Time, it was a relatively tame moment; *Heron* enjoyed a fast and easy run through, her big blue hull grabbing a little in the current but still taking her first set of rapids in stride, which gave us confidence.

"Go, Chet!" I called, encouragingly. "All right, *Team Heron*!" And then as a joke, and because I was high on adrenaline, I stretched out my arms to their bony fingertips, flapped them up and down, wide, and squawked like a great blue heron, "*Rok-rok! . . . Rok-rok! Rok-rok!*"

The boys looked on disbelievingly.

"You're such a dork," Jeff said.

"That's pretty good, Mom," Sam said.

"Yeah, good one, Mom," James echoed.

~~~~~~

By eleven thirty Team Heron had conquered its first set of rapids and was rounding Stuart Island. The docks of Dent Island Lodge came into view, and we all let out a collective sigh of relief. We'd made it! After days at anchor we were looking forward to being a little spoiled at Dent Island. Restaurants and accommodations become fewer and farther between, and then nonexistent, as one moves north into the Great Bear Rainforest. We nosed *Heron* in alongside one of two concrete docks as a young man and woman in khaki pants and dark green polo shirts cheerfully caught our lines.

We introduced ourselves, then clambered off the boat to explore the lodge, a series of rustic cedar structures with green metal roofs, all connected by paths winding through the woods. Although Dent Island Lodge looks about as relaxed as a summer camp, that impression is deceiving: people come from all over the world to fish for the BC coast's legendary salmon. From May through September four species of salmon—coho, pink, chum, and the mighty king—run here; king salmon, also known as tyee or Chinook salmon, can weigh in at thirty pounds or more. We passed a chalkboard listing names of guests who had joined the honorary "Tyee Club" that summer by landing monster fish—30, 36, 38, and a whopping 42 pounds; an aluminum ramp led up to the main lodge. Inside was a reception area set with a tray of coffee and tea. There was also a game room with a stone fireplace, and an outdoor porch perched over the rapids of Canoe Pass, reversing tidal rapids, which are remarkable to watch: water roaring like a river at twelve knots in one direction, then slackening before roaring at twelve knots again in the opposite direction. The lodge is owned by two brothers from Seattle and their mom. We knew one of the brothers, Dan, and his wife, Amy; two of their three sons grew up with Sam and James.

Our boys, Jeff, and I explored the lodge's winding paths and soaked in the cedar hot tub overlooking the narrow tidal cut of crazy Canoe Pass. At dusk Jeff and I settled in to enjoy cocktails on *Heron*'s stern. Sam and James set up a game of backgammon in the cockpit. As we looked out at the surrounding wilderness, the scene felt like something we'd earned: the water now flat and still and shining. Above us bald eagles the size of small dogs perched on branches in clumps of raggedy pine and fir, while their neighbor, a magnificent great blue heron, stood stoically, his pterodactyl wings folded against his sides, the long bones of his outsized feet extending and retracting as he contemplated the water's edge. How *do* herons manage to stand for so long? I wondered, hoping our own *Heron* would prove to be as resilient.

"I'm making your mother a rum and tonic," Jeff said.

"Amen, brother," Sam replied, rolling the dice. "Wanna play, Dad?"

"Sure."

Soon we were all lounging in the cockpit under a warm evening sky, Jeff and Sam playing backgammon; James and I reading by the Northwest's long-lasting summer light.

"Lucky rolls," Sam said as Jeff got the first move.

"Ooooh, you son of a mongrel sheep! I'm getting *pasted*!" Jeff exclaimed a few minutes later.

"Guess that doesn't say much about you, Dad," James said, looking up from his book.

"I make 'em up as I go," Jeff replied.

THE REAL WORLD

~~~~~~

"So now you're going to enter the *Realll Worrrld . . .*" said our friend Dan, clowning around, drawing out the last two words with enough weight to sink a freighter.

Dan had grown up in the 1970s and '80s, exploring the channels, fishing the rivers, and hiking the watery mountainous wilderness that separates Vancouver Island from the Canadian mainland. In the 1970s, when land was cheap, his father bought an overgrown property with a rundown old cabin and a dock on remote Dent Island, set in the maze of islands and fjords east of Vancouver Island. His rationale was that the island was strategically placed for launching annual summer sailing trips to Alaska. When Dan didn't show enough interest in going to college, his dad flew him up to the island, dropped him off, and left him there in the middle of the BC wilderness with instructions to get rid of all the junk—the piles of moldy mattresses and old rusting appliances dusted with mouse poop—in the place. What he'd failed to mention was the guy who'd been living in the cabin for years. Dan was going to have to get rid of him too. As Dan recalls it, his dad and the man had it out, then Dan's dad stormed down the dock and flew off without saying a word to Dan, who was left there holding his duffel bag.

"Best thing that could have happened to me at that age!" Dan recalled. "It was brutal! I couldn't *wait* to get to college after that." After decades of sprucing up, that run-down old cabin in the middle of nowhere has evolved, with several lovely building additions, to become the award-winning Dent Island Lodge.

<hr>

We'd invited Dan and his wife, Amy, back to *Heron* for a nightcap. The four of us were sprawled on the fir-green leather couches in the main cabin, the kerosene lantern casting its amber glow over our impromptu party while the kids prowled around.

It had been a good day: we'd gone spin casting for "humpies"; these adult pink salmon grow a pronounced hump on their backs during fall migration, a morphological change to make them look bigger and badder (much as humans drive sports cars or big dumb boats and male peacocks have long tail feathers). We'd pulled on waders and boots, piling into a flat-bottom skiff and jet-boating up a river so shallow and clear you could see its bottom a few inches below. Everything felt wild and grand, and we felt small but exhilarated at the base of this evergreen mountain range. It was humbling, picturing it extending from the southwest Yukon through the Alaskan Panhandle and along the entire BC coast, sprouting a forest of fir and hemlock and spruce across its backs, capped by a collar of peaks sharp as incisors. Above them stretched a sky so blue it made anything seem possible.

We'd stood thigh-deep in the Southgate River, pulling salmon out, all nine of us, with Dan and Amy and their three boys plus ours, in a row. The pools at our feet were a riot of fish making their final journey home. It was a cinch to hook them—there were so many fish in the water it didn't even seem fair. Pinks jumping all around us and the boys high-fiving each other as they landed them, fish sailing through the air. It had been an epic day. But we would soon leave our friends and push on toward the Great Bear Rainforest miles and miles to the north—a place no one we knew, not even longtime locals like Dan, seemed to go.

To get there we'd have to pull ourselves away from the outdoor soaking tub and hot showers and dining room at the lodge and time our departure to make it through the gaping boils and boat-sucking maw of Dent Rapids around the corner, then pound our way up Johnstone Strait, the sixty-eight-mile-long, three-mile-wide channel separating the northeast coast of Vancouver Island from the mainland British Columbia coast.

"Those books behind you?" Dan was saying, he nodded at the shelf at my back. "In the *real world* they'll be on the floor. Those wineglasses hanging in the galley?"

Jeff and I glanced warily at the cabinet from which eight wineglasses hung suspended in rows from their feet, like bats.

"Forget about 'em—pieces of broken glass," Dan went on.

Everyone laughed. Jeff and I, a little uneasily.

"Seriously! That's why most people never head north from here!" Dan said emphatically, gesturing in the very direction we planned to go the next day: *north*.

The five boys were off exploring or rather, as we'd learn later, ordering drinks for themselves (and being served) up at the bar. No wonder they loved Canada.

～～～～～

We pushed off from Dent at dusk the next day, timing our departure to cross Dent Rapids during its brief window of slack, which was at 6:20 p.m. Having seen the water, a raging maelstrom, from the safety of the lodge, we were all on edge. As *Heron* approached the wide rapid, it was eerily calm. The four of us were uncharacteristically quiet on deck as the boat nosed into a bend where, for most of the day, angry boils raged and swirled. But during this brief window twice a day, an uneasy stillness hung over the pallid surface of the water. Gazing down as the current tugged at *Heron*'s hull, jerking it unnaturally, I couldn't help but to think of all the boats it had gulped down over the decades. Centuries, even. In 1792 the Spanish expeditions of Galiano and Valdes put them among the first to explore the passes. The indigenous people guided them through, explaining how during a few minutes each day they could transit when the standing waves and violent whirlpools quieted and became navigable.

Some fifteen thousand years ago, ages before the Spanish, the earliest people to migrate to North America from Russia were Paleo-Indians: they made their way across the Bering Sea to Alaska and from there traveled down the Inside Passage and through this cut between the Coast Mountains and Vancouver Island Ranges. How many had perished? In 2009 a fisherman had been thrown from a lurching boat into Dent Rapids. His body was pulled under, popped up like a log, and they say the last thing his friends saw was his hand reaching up, circling in the whirlpool, before even it disappeared. He was never seen again. We passed through, imagining swirling bones beneath us in the dull water, dark watery graves.

Minutes after making it through Dent Rapids, we saw a splash ahead. And then another. Dolphins!

I sighed with relief and grabbed the binoculars, handing them to Sam. James grabbed the camera, and the three of us rushed up to the bow and leaned over the lifelines . . . Dead ahead of the boat we saw them: three, four, *five* Pacific white-sided dolphins, leaping in breakneck arcs! Their smooth shiny grayness caught the light.

They sped straight for us, all muscle. "Wow!" one of the boys said. Then they disappeared and it was quiet again.

"Where are they?" Sam said, watching intently. "Under the boat?"

Soon they resurfaced, their powerful dark forms curving out of the water, like kids surfing both sides of the bow.

"That's the closest dolphins have ever been to us, not even five feet off the boat!" Jeff said.

"That was way cool," James added. "Those dolphins, the way they came straight at us, then divided flanks?"

They felt like young escorts, an unexpected welcoming committee from the wild, and just when we needed it most. Jeff and the boys hadn't been sure at all about heading on—leaving Desolation Sound's warm, inviting water, dashing the prospect of bumping into more friends and having more fun. But now, I hoped, after the excitement of sighting the dolphins, the prospect of exploring these more adventurous waters would be thrill enough.

<hr />

Somehow, we all noticed it. Everything felt different, as if Dent were *the dividing line* between north and south, wild and sheltered, the Real World and the idyllic. The weather was cooler. There was a sharpness to the air. The water darker. The surface was glassy now, surrounding us, reflecting the hillsides with their thick stands of fir, hemlock, cedar, and pine. Even the evergreens seemed greener. Long wisps of vapor clung to the channels, and a thick white blanket of cloud caressed the water's surface.

And there were so many birds! Bald eagles perched in the fir trees, their sharp eyes peering down from enormous snow-white heads. Small flocks of white gulls scattered like snowflakes across the dark sea. And hundreds of plump brown murrelets bobbed beside us, diving deep in search of fish, essentially "flying" underwater, using their muscular wings as flippers and their feet for steering, as *Heron* neared.

With a cockpit open to the sky, we could watch all the weather unfold, and feel it too. There might be water shining with clouds high above, backlit so that their centers looked gray and their outlines electrified, with windows of blue opening and closing between them. Or furrowed seas with a sharp wind whipping up spray as we hunkered behind the windscreen. Or we might have no wind but want wind, and instead sit staring up, cursing a clear blue sky that looked painted in, or a pale blue sky with numinous clouds drifting across its open face. We might lift our chins toward the blue and feel mist light as air whisper at our cheekbones, or the warmth of the sun.

You might look out and spot a mew gull, white with gray wings, surfing a log through the current. Or you might see delicate snow-white birds with carrot-orange legs skittering low. Or a fish jump clear out of the water. Or a seal splash. And splash again. Or two seals slapping the surface of the sea with their flippers. You might hear the *slap-slap, slap-slap* of seal on water and look up just in time to catch it: a shiny-wet brown body sinking, its splash flying up like a fountain.

One of the things you realize once you strip everything else away—the timeless unspooling of information and entertainment in a 24/7 media world—is that so many of us seem to hover, paralyzed by distraction. Believe me, I know. This hovering in a perpetual state of anxiety over stuff and the inequities induced by our commercial, capitalist culture may be part of the modern condition. But once you turn off everything and listen, really listen, the answer to all our wanting is so simple it's shocking.

And I think it's this: worldly failure is less of a soul killer than the failure to find clarity and grace, to be astonished by wonder, wherever it might occur.

~~~~~~~~~

When we finally turned into Blind Channel, fifteen nautical miles and two and a half hours later, it was almost dark. Tensions were high. We were tired and hungry and anxious about docking there for the first time in the near dark. We careened into a cove between two hulking islands of black forest, East Thurlow and West Thurlow. The current is so swift and strong there that as we approached Blind Channel—a humble boaters' resort with weathered wooden docks leading up to a little store with a single head of lettuce (which I bought) and a restaurant that's been run by the same family for two generations—a nasty side current pushed us too fast toward the docks.

On top of this James wasn't feeling well. At first we thought it was a hangover from Boys' Night Out, but eventually we realized it must have been some sort of intestinal bug. He hadn't complained, not once—but on every level, he wasn't himself. He was sleeping more than a typical teen, if that's even physically possible. He was suddenly not as engaged in the trip. Or if he was, he was joking around with his older brother, the two of them goofing off on the bow. Unfortunately, at the very moment we were entering this tense docking situation with its mean three-knot crosscurrent pushing *Heron*'s shiny blue hull too hard and too fast toward the wooden dock pilings, James dissolved in a fit of defiant giggles instead of helping secure the fenders and bow lines.

The more ticked off Skipper Jeff got, the funnier it all seemed to James. He couldn't recover—was, in fact, *way* beyond recovery . . . He was standing in his gray sweats and black-and-white wool plaid shirt, high on *Heron*'s bow as it swept through the dark over the blackening water, doubled over, derisive peals of laughter ricocheting back over the cockpit and toward the Blind Channel docks—which were full.

This didn't go down well with Skipper Jeff. Not well at all . . .

"Just shut the f*ck up!" Jeff shouted, exploding, not understanding yet on this inaugural trip just how efficiently sound carries over water.

It was too late: the F-word blasted out, echoing over the water and spreading like a toxic stench across everything.

The boys fell silent.

Everyone on the docks fell silent.

Bloody hell, I thought.

We made an epic entrance: slamming into the dock, the crosscurrent scraping *Heron* up against the big wooden pilings, Sam and I jumping off but not being able to lash the boat to the wooden dock rails in time to stop it, while Skipper Jeff scowled, barking directions. We were a disaster. By the time we were secured and the engine shut down, not one of us was speaking—we were just standing there, shaking. Plus, all our stomachs were growling—it was after eight, and dinner was no further along than a dripping bag of defrosted chicken thighs.

Feeding people is my strategy for resolving most tensions, even extreme family tensions in a small space. (Good music is Jeff's strategy.) I put the boys to work setting the galley table, had them put on some mordant but calming Randy Newman ballads, and then, utterly exhausted, we all finally sat down to our grilled chicken and rice.

<hr />

After dinner (and a family come-to-Jesus meeting on how, "We all have to pull together, guys, figure this stuff out together!"), Sam dutifully did the dishes. James asked to be excused since he still wasn't feeling well. Jeff and I sat down with *Ports and Passes* and attempted to calculate what time Greene Point Rapids, around the corner, and scary-sounding Whirlpool Rapids an hour beyond, turned slack. We figured that if we got up at five thirty the next morning, pushing off from the docks at six, we'd hit the first rapid at slack. Then we'd just have to take our chances on the next one, since we'd hit it *after* slack water. But from what Jeff had gleaned from his dockside intelligence gathering, Whirlpool wouldn't be that bad.

But we were worried about James.

We tuned in the marine weather forecast to check conditions for Johnstone Strait, the long channel we'd enter after the rapids. You don't want to be there in a summer swell.

"Winds twenty to thirty knots. Increasing to thirty to forty knots by late afternoon. Gale force warning in effect," the disembodied voice of Environment Canada's marine forecast intoned over the VHF radio.

"Having fun yet?" Jeff scowled.

"Yeah, in a sick kind of way," I confessed with a shrug. Deep in my bones, I loved this. Being in nature. Traveling through it. Contending with all her moods. Even the extreme ones. Even when my husband morphed into whacko Skipper Jeff. *What is wrong with me?* I wondered.

〜〜〜〜〜

The two of us awoke at five thirty in the morning, dressed in the dark, put on a pot of French press, and tuned in the marine forecast. With the challenge of a new adventure ahead, it was like we were somehow aligned again. Sails trimmed for the same tack. You can push them, stretch the canvas so far that every fiber is taut, but they won't rip. Instead, they create forward motion—sometimes it's only an imperceptible drift—but they're moving you incrementally forward nonetheless.

With the boys still asleep, we pushed off from the dock in the dim morning light. The water was silvered. Lightly choppy with curlicues of current diminishing. We rode toward the slack. Small waves danced at the boat, lapping against the hull. The sky was filled with gunmetal-gray clouds, brightening to pearly luminescence with the rising sun. The air was bracing, fifty-five degrees. It felt crisp and clean and smelled like mint and cold. A flock of terns wheeled overhead, mewling and swooping. I felt the morning on my face, the dawn and the sharp wind and the swoop of birds, the warm fingers of the sun just beginning to break through high cloud. Everything felt polished by fresh air.

Gripping mugs of coffee, Jeff and I hit Greene Pointe Rapids just as the current was turning to flood and flew through at five knots. *Heron* was shooting over the bottom at eleven and a half knots. Sailing along like a sled.

"We're flying!" Jeff said, impressed.

The boys were still asleep when we passed East and West Thurlow Islands just off the port beam, their humps rising up behind a thick curtain of vaulting fir trees. The trees grew right down to the water's edge, where low branches were shaved straight across, as if by a giant razor blade. The ruler-sharp line spoke to one thing: water. The rise of it and fall of it. The current. Its tremendous force.

We also saw our first clear-cuts: bald patches so raw and bare against the green, the contrast was shocking. We stared. So few people passed through this wilderness without roads that there weren't many witnesses. A tug pulled a long float of just-felled logs. Bark and splinter. The sad, rough brown load making its slow way south.

Eagles peered and swooped from the trees, soared elliptically through the sky.

"Many, many bald eagles," Jeff pronounced, the breath from his words hanging in the opaque morning light.

We watched a lone eagle head up the strait. He flew northwest, his ample shadow sliding over the boat like a blanket.

We were gaining confidence as we swept along, making speed on the current, soaring past fir-green islands. Then we were through the last of the rapids and could hear the wind whipping down Johnstone Strait. We rounded a bend and the cold hit the boat, muscling its way into the cockpit. It was August, but nevertheless there was a deep chill in the air. A gang of gulls went by, all whirry and chatty. And then a flock of smaller white birds. Gulls? Terns? They looked unnaturally white, those birds, skittering low over the water.

Until then I hadn't really paid attention, I thought. Hadn't even known how fresh and alive the world could be until we were moving through it at eleven and a half knots an hour. Which by any other measure would be slow. But here, in the Real World, it was fast. And yet there was also the opposite of *fast*, the rare intimacy we'd begun to have with the wild landscape, and with one another, afloat.

At home time so often passed in a blur with things that, in the end, really didn't matter. Racing through tasks each day without intention, or being stuck in traffic, could feel like death by annoyance. Like we weren't making much progress—and even worse, like the world wasn't making much progress. Like no matter how much we recycled and bought local, we'd still see trees being cut down, and fish being farmed, and beauty being destroyed, wiped out by greed. At the same time the world's remaining beauty and humanity is the reason we have hope. And what comforts us, what allows us to breathe a little easier, are moments like these, when every so often we allow ourselves time to contemplate, briefly, just being here. Now.

We were only beginning to discover how powerful it could be, sharing these moments. Contending with nature, you begin to recognize there is flow everywhere in the natural world—that the deep channels are actually tracks left by glaciers that moved really, really slowly, or that even a murmuration of starlings is made up of a mass of single birds that are part of a dynamic system—and you also come to realize that this same flow is in each of us. It is centering and empowering. I realized we could do this. We could trust ourselves to do this crazy thing together.

The swells picked up in Johnstone Strait. They came at us from the northwest, lead-gray rollers cresting. It was blowing twenty-five knots. Gusting thirty into an outgoing northbound tide. The swells were two feet. Three off the bow. Those waves would be nothing on an open sea. Mere furrows. But in Johnstone Strait, where the waves rose up and met a ripping chop, they were plenty.

We saw no other boats (they were tucked in safe harbors). But *Heron* crushed the furlers. Her heavy hull was built for oceans, and she rode each swell, pounded through, greeted the next.

Being on the sea is, in many ways, like navigating real life, I thought as our boat bashed through the swells. You will always have the elements against you. You will always suffer and struggle. And then you will have moments of pleasure. Maybe that's why people are drawn to the sea. To feel something both vast and intimate, something real. I was feeling the real acutely now: in the tips of my fingers. In my toes. Jeff and I hunkered down in the cockpit behind the windscreen.

The cold was fierce. I'd been sitting so long that even the tips of my hair had begun to freeze in the raw cold.

Which is when I began dreaming of pleasure.

~~~~~~~~~

I vanished, dropping like a vole in a hole, out of sight into the main cabin. I turned on the gas, stepped down, and secured myself in the little galley. Lit a blue flame and stood warming my hands over the burner.

Somehow, the boys slept on, with *Heron* smashing through the swells, pitching up and over each one, the slap of the side swell reverberating like the blows of a sledgehammer. James was on the forward berth. Sam on the side bunk. I wedged myself into the galley, rummaged around in the half fridge, pulled out butter, bacon, milk, blueberries, syrup. Stepped up, took three steps, stepped down, reached into the pilot-berth pantry for pancake mix. Found it. Stepped up, stepped down again into the galley. By then James was up.

"Making breakfast, Mom?"

"Yep, thought I might," I answered. "Feeling better?"

He disappeared to pull on jeans and his flannel shirt, then staggered across the pitching teak, where he landed on the settee a foot from the gimbaled stove, which was swinging like a monkey.

"Think so," he yawned. "How ya gonna cook the bacon?"

"Um, in a pan?"

"You should try a pot. We did it that way on the river—it turns out great."

Okay. I braced myself, dug out the big pot from the stacked pans that fit barely to the right of the swinging stove.

Together we set the bacon to fry. A delicious sizzle and pop filled the cabin. James had spent the previous summer working as a river guide, rowing a raft full of gear down the Salmon River in Idaho. He was, at seventeen, years younger than the rest of the crew. Needless to say, he learned a lot. Strange skills, like how to cook bacon in a pot, kept cropping up. It took teamwork to make that bacon on a boat; James took the lead.

"You can fit the whole pack in one pot," he explained. "Just stir all the strips together instead of laying them out one by one. It makes a ton more that way, see?"

"Momma is that bacon?" Sam called out from the side bunk.

Together in the pitching cabin, we cooked up the bacon, made pancake batter, pulled out the sauté pan, started the stove again, melted butter, ladled circles of batter. When the batter started to sizzle, we dropped on blueberries, then flipped the cakes.

I passed a plate up through the hatch to Jeff, who was still out there taking *Mighty Heron* through the pounding chill. Wisps of steam rose off the plate: hot blueberry pancakes with maple syrup, a stack of bacon, knife and fork wrapped in a napkin. You'd have thought the plate was piled with caviar.

"*Get out of here!*" Jeff exclaimed. "Pancakes and bacon?!"

"Better eat 'em while they're hot," I grinned, climbing up with my own plate.

The salty warmth of the bacon, crisp in the brisk morning air, the surprise of the sweet blueberries, each an exploding delight with a forkful of cake, was a simple meal that, given its unlikely setting, stood out. You endure. And then life's small pleasures leap out at you . . . Amidst the damp chill, we felt our spirits rising with the steam off the plates.

THE LUXURY OF SLOWNESS

You know you've settled into the luxury of slowness when, after lunch, everyone just finds a spot on the boat and drifts into a long afternoon nap. After making it through Johnstone Strait, we'd anchored in the Broughton Islands, a dreamlike archipelago of rock-bound, forest-capped islands at the strait's northern reaches. When I finally came to, James was stretched on the opposite settee, Sam was sprawled out on the forward berth, and Jeff was sitting in the cockpit, camera trained on a great blue heron.

The heron stood like a granite statue framed by funereal hemlock and spruce, its slate-blue feathers blown smooth. A wind stirred from the west, bearing salt off the sea.

"How long have you been sitting here?" I asked.

"Me?" my husband asked without turning his head, his eye melded to the camera perched on his knee. "About forty-five minutes. I'm waiting for this heron to fly so I can get an action shot," he said sardonically.

I stifled a guffaw. My husband, who rarely sits still, had definitely crossed over. There's a moment on any long journey when you can feel a physical change. If you've traveled far enough from home, and the journey has taken days—and especially if you stay away from the phone and the internet, which is not easy to do—there's a moment when you can *feel* different: it's the feeling of time expanding.

It's not only time itself that's different—the measurable fact that your hours are no longer defined by quantifiable calendar time—it's the *quality of the time*. It's richer, fuller, time you can taste. And if you pay attention, you'll notice one day that you're inhabiting that time. The heron peered at us with its tiny yellow eyes, not quizzically like a raven or a gull, but with a heron's stoic silence. I imagined then that this bird too must know something about time that we don't, and that our audience of trees and rocks and mosses and clouds know it—and that the sky, certainly, has always known it.

The heron opened its wings and lifted off, away from us. Its huge wings flapped like an old elephant's ears, and its long sinewy legs trailed behind. We watched him until he faded into the sky, disappearing like smoke.

~~~~~~~~

The next morning we docked in Port McNeill, a logging and fishing town on the northeast tip of Vancouver Island that's so bare bones it makes Seattle look like Manhattan. We then packed our duffels and made one last boat breakfast. We toasted our last slices of bread as well as the two bagels at the bottom of the bag. We scrambled the last eight eggs, shredded and sautéed all the potatoes for hash browns, fried up the rest of the bacon and sausages, drank the last of the juice. We did all the dishes, wiped down the galley, put away the cups and plates one last time, made up the bunks, then lifted our duffels up and out the companionway and into the cockpit, latched *Heron*'s hatches, and locked the main hatch.

It seemed odd, leaving *Heron* all alone in Port McNeill on the northern tip of Vancouver Island. But it was time for Sam to return to San Francisco and for James to head to college in upstate New York. Jeff and I would fly east with him, then fly straight back to the boat to resume our journey and travel north hundreds of miles into the Great Bear Rainforest.

The daily floatplane landed at noon off the end of the Port McNeill fuel dock. We walked fifty feet from the boat to the plane, presented our passports to the pilot, lifted our duffels into the back seats, and climbed aboard. The floatplane, a sturdy ten-seater, was a yellow-and-white de Havilland Otter. The model is called the workhorse of the Northwest because it was instrumental in mapping and survey work from Alaska all the way south to Chile; in Alaska it is still the ultimate bush aircraft. We picked up a few more passengers, touching down at ramshackle floating fishing lodges in the Broughton Islands. (One woman climbed aboard with a yellow hound named Laila; the dog was such a frequent flier that she just sprawled on the aisle floor between the seats.) We then flew over all the islands and forests and channels and fjords and straits and seas we'd just sailed past and struggled through. It was utterly amazing to me, gazing down from the little plane, to see all those islands and channels and fir-and-spruce-clad mountains and fjords—then the harbors with more and more boats moored in them as we went south—and to realize, with pride, that we had come to know this geography. In less than two and a half hours we covered the distance it had taken us two weeks to travel by boat, and landed at the northern end of Lake Washington. Twenty miles from downtown Seattle we sat on the curb like castaways, surrounded by a mountain of gear, and waited for a cab.

THE BIG DROP-OFF

August 20—a date I'd both eagerly anticipated and dreaded. It was time for James to leave home for college in upstate New York. Jeff and I would both tag along for the Big Drop-Off, then celebrate our Empty Nesthood by heading straight back to *Heron* and resume sailing north to the Great Bear Rainforest. A taxi waited in front of our house to drive the three of us to the airport; a pile of duffel bags sat by the front door.

James's room, upstairs, was the cleanest it had been in about eighteen years. It was strangely unsettling to walk past and see an expanse of oatmeal-colored Berber carpet where the erupted volcano of T-shirts, jeans, and hooded sweatshirts usually loomed over its messy landscape. A few days before, his last as the youngest son living at home, he'd washed and folded his shirts. He'd cleaned and packed his lacrosse gear. He'd straightened the stuff on his shelves and thrown away the spiral-bound notebooks and crumpled homework assignments that had been crammed in the dark corners of his desk for ages. *Who are you?* I felt like saying to this weirdly efficient new person.

I didn't know it yet, not consciously, but I felt it: my son had begun to *act* himself into adulthood. Watching him, I couldn't help but feel chagrined. (*Hmmm?* The kid had obviously been capable of putting his laundry away all along.) But I also felt a sense of pride. And this pride was inseparable from a piercing sense of loss. I understood suddenly that even though my youngest son was standing there in front of me—stuffing stacks of T-shirts into a duffel bag, familiar, mundane—he was also already leaving. The thought was frightening because as soon as it came to me, I knew it was true. Although the leaving was yet to begin in any actual way, we were moving toward it. It was inevitable.

I'd carefully not considered the prospect of saying goodbye, of launching our youngest into his own life. Returning from three weeks at sea (one of them with Sam and James), and preparing for another month, I had writing assignments to follow up on, and Jeff had a business to sell; we had bills to pay, pets to tend to, phone calls to make, goodbyes to say. The week was lost to errands and tying up loose ends.

But the significance of what was happening surfaced in other ways, without warning: a friend sending her youngest daughter off to college, and simultaneously struggling with an aging parent, blacked out driving home from Bed Bath & Beyond. The stress of so many conflicting emotions caused her to momentarily forget who and where she was *while driving on the freeway*. She picked up her cell phone and got her mother-in-law.

"I don't know where I am!" she shouted. "I can't remember how I got here!"

Her mother-in-law talked her off the road. Her husband rushed home from work. At the hospital they ran a battery of tests, the results of which were inconclusive. The ordeal was frightening. The doctors couldn't explain it—but my friend's sudden and total sense of dislocation, given the timing, made perfect sense to me. I wouldn't have understood it, even a year before, but at the time I got it—completely.

~~~~~~~

The packing-list items James and I had stockpiled—towels, extralong sheets, shower flip-flops, hangers, winter coats and boots, a medicine kit—had been boxed up, addressed, and shipped to the wilds of upstate New York. All that remained to tend to were the few personal and precious things he'd take with him on the plane—his laptop, his lacrosse gear, his duffel bag, his guitar.

"Well," Jeff said ceremoniously, opening the front door for all of us to exit, "I guess this is it."

"Are you sure you've got everything?" I said to James, my high, strangled voice betraying my own uncertainty.

"Yep . . . let's *go*," James said. At over six feet, in jeans and a plaid flannel shirt, he looked so tall and confident to me then, and at the same time, gangly and vulnerable, and so *young*.

James took one last look around the front hall of the house, patted our golden retriever, McCoy, goodbye, and stepped out the front door. The finality of his leaving felt like a kind of vortex we were all leaping into, blindly but hopefully. In mid-May a phone call from the lacrosse coach at St. Lawrence University had given him the confidence to accept the academic scholarship he'd been offered there.

"So, you want to come all the way out here and try out to play division three lacrosse for the Saints?" the coach had said. "Well, okay then."

So instead of enrolling at Santa Clara University in Northern California with his older brother—his original plan—he'd be 2,846 miles away at St. Lawrence. To get there, he could fly from Seattle to Syracuse (changing planes at Chicago's O'Hare), and then catch a two-hour shuttle van north, or fly to Ottawa, in Ontario, Canada, and catch a shuttle van south. Out of curiosity, James and I had

Google-mapped the route: it stretched all the way across the continent of North America, unspooling from the far upper-left corner of the map to the upper right like a thick blue worm, its head nearly reaching the Canadian border. It would take forty-five hours to make it across all those rivers and plains and mountain ranges by car, without stopping.

"Maybe I'll drive to school my sophomore year," he'd said.

"Great idea!" I said, playing up the adventure.

"Are you kidding me? His car would never survive the trip," said Jeff, always the realist. "That baby's got a hundred and sixty-two thousand miles on it."

"Maybe I'll have saved enough for a new one by then," James protested.

"Better start saving, bud," Jeff said, laughing.

~~~~~~~~~

The Big College Drop-Off, the culmination of the separation process that all of us, as parents, have to endure, had started many years earlier for my husband and me. The New York City Montessori preschool our sons attended on the Upper West Side took a hard line on the beginning of that process, even holding a "what to expect on the first day of school" training session for clueless parents. Separating from your children will be easier in the long run, the school's administrators suggested, if parents said goodbye to their kids *outside the school.* "Whatever you do, don't enter the classroom," we were advised in a pre-orientation. "*Once you cross that line, there will be no, we repeat, no turning back!*"

The Montessori method, developed more than a century ago by an Italian physician and educator named Maria Montessori, contends that given enough freedom—and an optimal environment—very young children (specifically, kids two and a half to six years old) are capable of self-directed learning. Parents, the theory goes, disturb the optimal learning environment. There was a very Montessori-like ritual at our sons' school's front gate, where the headmistress would greet each diaper-clad student by name ("Good morning, Sam," Ms. DeAlwis would say, pronouncing the name of our oldest son, Sam, as *Sahm*, in her clipped Sri Lankan accent—and even bending down to shake his pint-sized three-year-old hand). Then Sam's teacher, Mrs. Marikar, would smile and take Sam's other hand, leading him from West Ninety-Eighth Street on Manhattan's Upper West Side through the school's front gate, the two of them disappearing inside the building.

What the teachers failed to explain was that while it might be easier on three-year-olds (not to mention the school's narrow entryway, lined with cubbies as orderly as a ship's) if parents didn't cross the school's perimeter the first day, this first "goodbye" could be heartrending—even *traumatic* for some of the kids and most of the parents no matter where it transpired.

Sure enough, although several of the preschoolers took Mrs. Marikar's hand gamely, others clung to their parents as tightly as barnacles, wailing hysterically until they had to be peeled off limb by limb. Sam, independent by nature, was one of those toddlers who allowed himself to be led down the path and straight into the building. In his brown corduroys and navy-blue Patagonia jacket, he looked like a little man with a large coconut head on his way to work. The only giveaway was the diapers.

"How do you like that? Your son didn't even look back!" a dad we'd never met said to Jeff.

That was it? I felt numb, but also relieved in a way at how seamlessly our child had separated from us. But then we saw Anne, a mom we knew, standing on the sidewalk weeping, her husband's arm around her in a sort of helpless surrender. Her sorrow was contagious, and I realized with a sudden shock that watching our son disappear was simply the beginning. It was only the first step in what would be a long string of separations, some as ritualized as this one, and some as seemingly casual, though symbolic, as handing over the car keys for the first time.

Moms stood on the sidewalk afterward, trying to compose themselves and dabbing their eyes, while the dads smiled bravely. Then, since it was New York City, pretty much everyone rushed off to work. Jeff and I caught the No. 2 subway together. (He'd take it all the way to Chambers Street, then get off and catch a series of elevators to the sixty-second floor of the World Trade Center.) "Bye, Bug," he said, giving me a peck on the cheek as I jumped off the No. 2 at Times Square. The shiny doors slid shut, and the train sped off down the tunnel. I walked across town to my office at *Travel & Leisure* magazine. A mix of emotions—excitement for Sam, a bittersweet sadness about time passing, and a visceral need to know what was going on in that Montessori room, even though it was Sam's world now, separate from Jeff's and mine—left me feeling ill at ease and twitchy all over.

~~~~~~~

Flying east eighteen years later to take *James*, not Sam, to his freshman year at college, I find myself worrying more about me than about him. I sip tomato juice and watch our plane's path on the in-flight monitor as the three of us speed farther and farther away from home, passing over Canadian outposts with names like Moose Jaw and Winnipeg, Saskatoon and Thunder Bay. James will be one of the few students in his class from west of the Mississippi, but he's a confident kid I tell myself—he'll be fine.

Jeff, earbuds in place, looks utterly relaxed. I, on the other hand, have a familiar unease: it's a prickly sort of distractedness, like a mean case of hives mixed with PMS, the specific physical sensation I've come to recognize precedes each major life separation from our boys.

I'm a cool Seattleite now, I tell myself. I've trained myself not to be a maternal embarrassment to my sons. I don't allow myself to think about the impending Big Drop-Off. I don't even think about the precise moment when James and I will give each other that last hug and casually say "Goodbye," much the way his older brother stepped into his first school, when he was three. But it isn't easy sending your kids off to college, facing the empty nest for the first, or even the second or third time. Fortunately, lots of my friends are packing their sons and daughters off too, which has given me some sense of perspective, even some small comfort.

I thought some of us parents, especially the mothers in the mix, might be celebrating—happily pushing our demanding teens out the door, looking forward to reconnecting with our spouses, and our own lives, perhaps our careers too. But mostly what I hear is wistfulness, regret: "I can't believe our family will never be the same again!" "He's gone." "Her room is so quiet!" "I miss him terribly." "I can't help thinking of all the things I haven't taught them yet." "Where did the time go?"

My beloved friend Ellen (who somehow manages to be chic and wise at the same time), having sent two kids to college and launched a new career, had emailed me a few days before our flight: "Are you sad? Don't forget to have a good cry! You'll feel better afterward. Remember—this is what we WANT for them!"

"I cried yesterday from eight thirty to two thirty," my friend Janet, a former software executive, had confessed a few days earlier before taking her twins to college.

"See this?" her husband had chimed in, holding up a small notepad. "We call this the cry counter."

"You don't," I'd stammered in disbelief.

"Oh, but we do," her husband had said, smiling.

"Did you cry?" is the first thing moms ask other moms who've survived the Big Drop-Off.

I didn't cry when we took our older son, Sam, to college in Northern California. And though my friend's advice seemed sound, I wasn't sure I wanted to cry this time either—or even could.

With Sam we'd been sad anticipating his leaving home, and how different it would be having an empty chair at the dinner table—but the actual delivery of our first son to college turned out to be a festive occasion.

On the morning of move-in day we drove onto the Santa Clara campus just outside San Jose. A long line of SUVs snaked toward the main freshman dorm, an eleven-story tower in front of which families were parked and unloading what looked to be entire households: BarcaLoungers, beanbag chairs, couches, coffee tables, rugs, shelves, mirrors, refrigerators, microwaves, blenders, electric guitars, amplifiers—and to our clueless astonishment, complete entertainment systems: Nintendo Wiis, Sony PlayStations, Xboxes.

After Sam unpacked his one duffel and made up one of two narrow beds in his dorm room, we watched, transfixed, while the parents across the hall unwrapped a flat-screen as big as a Volkswagen. Outside, upperclassmen in shorts and flip-flops directed traffic while parties swung into gear in stucco bungalows across the street. Music blared. Beer-pong tournaments bounced. Girls in bikini tops lounged.

It was maybe eleven o'clock in the morning.

By the time we left our firstborn a few hours later, he was busy bonding with his dorm mates and clearly didn't need us moping around. Jeff and I had an hour or so to kill before heading to the airport, so we casually said goodbye, then strolled around campus until we found a small courtyard, where we lay down on the grass, faces up, like we'd been shot.

"It's funny, isn't it?" Jeff said, shielding his eyes from the sun. "It's kind of like that first goodbye, at Montessori. It sucks when they cling too much, and it sucks when they hardly notice you're gone."

Dropping off our youngest child, our last one at home, however, was a different story.

The day before the Big Drop-Off the three of us woke up in Ottawa, Ontario, and drove to Bed Bath & Beyond, a place so predictable, so generic it defies any specific notion of place and time. Parents and their teens prowled the store's wide aisles, staring and disoriented, shopping for college. Everyone looked vaguely shell-shocked. The hunt for pillows and comforters should be fun, even comforting. But I was contemplating a Great Wall of mattress pads, feeling panicky. White bundles individually wrapped in plastic towered overhead.

Twin. Twin. Twin, I read, scanning labels. I tilted my head back and squinted. Queen. Queen. King.

Where are the extralong twins?

"No use buying any of that bulky stuff in advance," Jeff had pointed out a few weeks before, skimming the pack list St. Lawrence, had sent. "We'll just pick it up in Canada, on our way to dropping him off in upstate New York. It'll probably be cheaper there anyway."

So Jeff, James, and I were on the loose in Ottawa at a Bed Bath & Beyond in search of the unwieldy: a desk lamp, a shower tote, storage bins. And those infernal extralong twin sheets, the universal bed standard for college dorms coast to coast, and something only a family of NBA players might happen to stock at home.

Where were the extralong twins?! Stacked even higher, where I couldn't see them? An infomercial blared from a shelf-side TV. It was chirping on about bedbugs—bedbugs were evidently on the rise in college dorms. "You can protect your child by investing in an entomologist-tested, impermeable mattress protector," an insistent stranger proclaimed.

I found a metal ladder chained to the shelves and began dragging it over to the mattress pads. It wouldn't reach. The infomercial was driving me insane. It's as if the bedbugs were inside my head. I glared at the screen: *If I bash it in and make it stop, maybe I'll be able to hear myself think.* Instead, I found a switch and turned off the TV.

"Are you okay, Mom?"

It was James, back with a cart.

"I'm going to kill your father!" I hissed. "I *knew* we should have ordered a mattress pad in advance. *They're out of extralongs!*"

"Let me just ask the saleslady," James said, suddenly the grown-up.

I always figure that in dealing with the unknown, you can't be too prepared. What if we had to leave our youngest three thousand miles from home sleeping on a bare mattress? Chances are he wouldn't even notice—like most teenagers he never made his bed anyway—but just the thought made me feel like my head might explode.

"Here you are," a well-coiffed saleslady said, appearing from nowhere with a mattress pad. I stared: it was an extralong twin.

"Can I help you with anything else?" she asked smoothly, reaching up to restart the TV.

What I wanted to ask her was whether BB&B happened to stock any Xanax this time of the year, but instead I said, "Nope, we're all set!" I then waved cheerfully, and pushed the cart down the aisle.

~~~~~~~~

Upstate New York, that third week in August, was *not* sunny California. The three of us drove our rental car south across the Canadian border toward Canton, New York. The air was humid and thick. The landscape was boggy and flat; fields of potatoes surrounded farmhouses with sagging porches and peeling clapboard. Dairy cows stood ankle-deep in the mud.

Upstate New York is old-world, as opposed to California's shiny new one, but we were excited for James. For a West Coast kid, this would be East Coast total immersion. We pulled into Canton, a rural community dating back more than two hundred years, with a three-block Main Street; we had just enough time to tour the St. Lawrence campus and get a good night's sleep at a local guesthouse before James moved into his dorm the next morning. Before heading to bed the three of us sat up in the room Jeff and I shared, watching old *Seinfeld* reruns while James downloaded the latest version of Skype onto his laptop; it would enable him to connect in real time with us (we hoped) and, more importantly to him, with friends who were simultaneously moving into freshman dorms coast to coast. The scale of it, when you considered the thousands of kids leaving for school that August and September (not to mention the staggering cost of tuition, plus room and board), began to feel more like a military deployment than a seasonal rite of passage.

"Night, James!" we called as he finally closed his laptop and traipsed down the hall to his room in the old guesthouse.

Jeff had booked the rooms at St. Lawrence's alumni house, a two-story white-clapboard structure, built in the late 1800s that had been restored for returning alums. The university left a key for us near the front porch. You let yourself in, signed a register, and were free to make yourself at home amidst the hallways hung with prints of legendary North Country snowstorms, a 1940s-era yellow kitchen with an empty fridge, and a formal living room stacked with piles of leather-bound yearbooks.

Our room was comfortable—and *extremely* traditional. A garden of red cabbage roses and trailing green ivy crept up the papered walls; the bed, blanketed with a matching cabbage-rose comforter, anchored the rest of the space, which featured spindle-legged, cherry side tables and floral upholstery. It was a lovely place. We were lucky to be there. And yet, pulling back the covers and crawling beneath those cabbage roses couldn't have felt more alien: in addition to the fact that we were about to leave our son in a tiny, landlocked town thousands of miles from home, I felt like we'd traveled back in time 150 years.

Around two in the morning, Jeff whispered, "Are you awake?"

"*Uh-huh.* I don't feel well," I replied.

That was putting it mildly. Usually a world-class sleeper, I'd been tossing for hours in a fit of anxiety over the big day ahead.

"My skin feels like it's crawling," I said.

"I'll turn on the 'air-conditioning,'" Jeff said, getting up.

The soothing hum of the wall fan came on. Jeff got back into bed.

"You can have a cry if you want," my husband said sweetly. Was he on the verge of a breakdown too? "Um, do you want a tissue? I'd better get a washcloth," he said.

I curled into a ball and let out a few muffled sobs. *Here it is,* I guessed, *the Big Cry.* Jeff got up, walked to the bathroom, and returned with a soft white terry square. He pressed the washcloth into my hand. I began to cry harder and let myself think about what was really happening: we'd flown all this way to leave our son on the opposite side of the country and formally cut the umbilical cord. He might come home for a summer or two—or, god forbid, longer if he couldn't find a job after graduating! But our roles as day-to-day parents would never be the same.

It was a long time before I could stop crying. I was transfixed with dread thinking about the dawn, and overcome with grief as I wept for the past, our lost past together as a family. I dabbed my eyes and nose with the washcloth while my husband rubbed my back.

Jeff wasn't crying, but he couldn't sleep either, evidently.

"It's a big moment. We could have another if you want."

"No we can't, you dope!" I blurted, although I knew this was only a husbandly offering, like suggesting we get a new puppy. *"Are you nuts?* This is it!"

The cool fan and its reassuring whir hummed.

I cried some more. It felt good to cry, to just let everything— heartache, regret, years we couldn't reclaim—well up, roll down my face, and soak the pillow.

Something about the feel of the washcloth, the way I was clutch- ing it, and the weave of the unfamiliar bed's cotton blanket reminded me of another place long ago. I let myself burrow deep and far away from the present, drifting back to that place: the hospital bed (two, actually) in Manhattan at Mount Sinai, where each of my sons was born. And where, in the blissed-out high following each of their births, I dozed, exhausted and ecstatic, cradling each tiny baby wrapped tight as a bean in the hospital's worn cotton receiving blankets.

I didn't wish for those days back, not at all. And yet . . .

I lay there in that strange room the night before Jeff and I were to leave our son and found myself longing for our first apartment on

West Ninety-Second Street in New York City, for the yellow-painted kitchen where we washed every dish, fork, and spoon by hand—and it still seemed such a luxury to even have a kitchen. I longed for summer nights on the Upper West Side when I'd come home from work and walk the boys to the corner pizzeria in their pajamas for Italian ices. I longed for the drafty old farmhouse in Connecticut, for the boys' upstairs bedroom with twin maple beds tucked under the eaves, and their wooden Brio train set under eternal construction on a green shag rug. I longed for another weekend, for a chance to read the boys stories without hurrying, or to sit with them on the floor and actually play with those trains instead of thinking about all the other things Jeff and I thought we should be doing. I longed for winter nights when Jeff would push back his chair after dinner and exclaim, "I know, let's go night-sledding!" I longed for the Flexible Flyer and the toboggan, and even for the dripping snow boots lined up on a mat.

Most of all I longed for the sense of possibility we had then—for the years ahead, and for the sense of discovery that on the best days would turn even the most ordinary moment into a shared memory: the kids standing on kitchen stools dying Easter eggs turquoise and yellow in spring; the barn with its smells of hay and horse manure and sweat in summer; the antique cider press that mashed crisp apples into juice each fall; and in winter, the night-sledding. I longed for the kerosene lanterns staked out on our dark hill, their glittery snow trail illuminating the night like stars.

I thought about all these things, lying in bed next to my husband of twenty-five years, in that old frame guesthouse, letting long-shelved memories pop up like balloons, hang suspended for a bit, then float away. I realized that the wonder of it was that any of these things were ours to begin with; because, of course, they weren't ours, not really. I knew that our sons, like everything—the snow, the stars, the seasons—had their own journeys. Our job, with luck, was to shepherd them along their way, to get them to this point—really, the start of that journey.

I let the past push against the walls of my heart until the present stepped in. *Get a grip! You need to be there for James in a few hours!* As the sun was coming up I finally fell asleep, exhausted.

~~~~~~~~

The alarm went off with a loud beep at seven. Jeff peered out the window and said, "Not very nice weather for Move-In Day, I'm afraid." At seven thirty I could hear Ford Explorers and Grand Cherokees, and I watched cars with roof boxes crammed with gear rolling past. By nine the three of us had packed up and were making our way toward campus in sticky late-summer rain. It was the worst weather imaginable for a college Move-In Day—the picture they never show you in the application brochure: an utter deluge, a fiasco.

Upperclassmen in St. Lawrence T-shirts stood forlornly on strategic street corners, pointing the way. A few of the lucky ones had umbrellas; most were soaked to the skin, as if they'd just swum across one of the North Country's many rivers or lakes fully clothed.

We found James's dorm, pulled our rented SUV up front, then all hopped out and began sprinting back and forth through ankle-deep water, thinking that if we ran fast enough, we might keep dry. But sprinting didn't make the least bit of difference. None of us had thought to bring a raincoat, because it was August—well, maybe Jeff had a raincoat, but that's Jeff, always planning ahead. I was wearing my favorite sandals, jeans, and a wrap sweater. James had on shorts. In less than ten minutes we were soaked to the skin, hair plastered to scalps, shoes squelching.

Jeff and I stood around in James's room, dripping, then helped him unpack his things and mop the puddles up off the linoleum. Since everyone else was bolting in and out of the storm as intently as we were, no one felt particularly friendly. The mood was tense. The only good thing that happened was the dad who rushed in carrying a heavy stereo speaker, began to slip on the wet floor, and then caught himself just before his feet slid out from under him.

"Man, that would have sucked," James whispered.

"No kidding. They haven't made speakers like those since nineteen seventy-six!" quipped Jeff, appreciatively.

We made a trip to Walmart for a minifridge; had lunch with a bunch of other drenched, anxious-seeming parents and their teens in the student center; and then it was time for Jeff and me to leave. Like many colleges dealing with the latest wave of superinvolved parents, St. Lawrence had wisely instituted a schedule for incoming freshman. The schedule makes it explicitly clear when parents should literally say goodbye. In our case the Velcro-parents' unsticking hour was four o'clock in the afternoon, after the president's welcome ceremony. But we'd decided to hit the road by three o'clock to drive back to Ottawa, catch a flight across Canada to Vancouver, and get back to *Heron*.

James hadn't met anyone yet, not even a roommate; somehow he'd wound up with a single. And he confessed that the giardia symptoms he'd contracted by accidentally gulping water while river kayaking earlier that summer (and which we only then realized probably linked to the intestinal illness he'd had on the boat) had suddenly returned. Did we maybe have any Imodium?

"*What?*" Jeff howled. "Are you *serious?*"

After a quick huddle the three of us decided that Jeff would find a drugstore, I would stay behind in James's dorm room to keep the door from locking, and James would join the rest of his dorm mates for the freshman welcome ceremony. When Jeff returned we'd leave the medicine in James's new room for him and dash to make our flight.

"Bye, Mom, I love you," James said, bending over to give me a great big bear hug. My boys are so tall, such men. I felt absurdly small and tears welled from my eyes, but I knew it was time, and that he'd really, truly be okay. "Bye, James, have fun settling in. It's going to be great!"

"Bye, son, I'm proud of you. We'll call you tomorrow," Jeff said.

And then suddenly lots of jittery freshmen were gathering at the end of the hall. Jeff rushed off in search of James's medicine, and James walked out to meet the other students. I sat in James's room at his new desk, which faced the window, and watched as he and his dorm mates ambled—maybe fifty or sixty of them in shorts and flip-flops, impervious to the rain—up the long, grassy slope leading away from the building.

As they grew smaller and smaller I could still pick out my son— his broad shoulders, easy relaxed gait. He was chatting with a girl to his left. They reached the crest of the hill and vanished.

Thank god he's rid of us! I thought. *That poor kid must be so relieved we've all finally said our goodbyes.*

And I realized with a little start that everything leading up to the Big Drop-Off—the countdown, the preparation, the anticipation of saying goodbye—had been worse than the goodbye itself. It had all felt bewildering, and yet perhaps this was what it felt like to be an empty nester.

I didn't know. I only knew that this was exactly what was supposed to happen—our sons and daughters were meant to walk off into their own lives.

And I knew it was time to go. When Jeff came back with the pills, we shut the door to James's room behind us and, feeling relieved that we'd done all we could, stepped out into the rain.

PART THREE

We always talk about the spacecraft as being a child, maybe a teenager. There was absolutely nothing anybody on the operations team could do, just to trust that we had prepared it well to set off on its journey on its own.

—ALICE BOWMAN, mission operations manager
NASA's New Horizons mission to Pluto

TRUE NORTH

~~~

The first thing I saw, back on the boat, was the boys' guitar case lying on the forward berth. The first thing Jeff saw was the boat. "She looks good—like we left here a few minutes ago, not a week ago," he said.

In the past twenty-four hours we'd skipped the St. Lawrence parents' welcome (where they basically tell the most hopeless helicopter parents *it's time to leave*), flown back across Canada to Vancouver, spent the night at an airport hotel, and risen at dawn to catch a small plane full of fishermen to the northern tip of Vancouver Island, where a teenaged driver in flip-flops met us at the one-room airport and ferried us in a Dodge Ram to Port McNeill. As we crested the forested hill and coasted down the long road toward the harbor, we could see a tall white mast soaring above the whale-watching boats.

"There's *Heron*!" we both cried, relieved.

Stepping out of the taxi truck and walking down to the docks, we noticed the weather had turned. While we were gone a wedge of cold had brought a new scent—the smell of sockeye salmon, of coming rain, of animal fur, of old conifers. Although it was late August, September was in the air, Port McNeill's handful of stores already advertising back-to-school sales. The school banners didn't make us melancholy—they just caught us off guard. While it was strange not to be in back-to-school, back-to-work mode, we discovered we had plenty to do.

We walked to town and raided the grocery store, stocking up on everything we'd need for the next month at sea: a mountain of produce, milk, eggs, hummus, cheese, bacon, meat, bread, more wine.

After reprovisioning, we walked with our laptops to Mugz Coffee and logged on to the free Wi-Fi. We wrapped up stray business and, most of all, let people know that as we headed north—into the wild and the Great Bear Rainforest—we might be out of both cell and email range.

~~~~~~~~

Lugging our laptops back to the dock, both lost in our growing unease about the days and weeks ahead, my core ached. It was as if I'd been punched in the gut. I felt utterly adrift and extremely unwell—waves of shock and dislocation washed over me.

I exclaimed out of the blue, "I don't like this, it's not right!"

The tide had gone out, leaving a wide mudflat between the two of us and the boats. A great blue heron on one leg surveyed the bleak expanse, still as a lawn ornament in the muck. "It feels so *off-balance* having James this far away, and Sam back on his own in San Francisco . . . like one of my arms has been accidentally misplaced, or a leg chopped off!"

"I know. I think we're both grieving," Jeff said, sweetly.

"Do you feel bad too?" I asked him, surprised. "Physically bad?"

"I do, Bug," he said.

I was caught off guard that my husband would feel the sense of loss so acutely as well. But of course he would. He's an emotional guy, a terrific dad, and as the boys had grown into young men themselves, he'd had a pair of compadres around the house. I thought of all the character traits he'd modeled for them—integrity; smarts, ingenuity, intellectual curiosity; a great sense of humor; loyalty, empathy, and even I had to admit, a highly evolved emotional IQ (for a guy). I thought of the eclectic passions he'd shared with the boys: their love of music, film, surfing—not exactly the easiest sport to learn in Pacific Northwest waters—and sailing.

"Well, it sucks," I said, reeling from the magnitude of it all, trying to fathom what this meant for all of us, moving forward.

My husband and I walked down the dock ramp in silence, past the seaplanes, the charter boats, the marine research vessels. I felt like our hearts had been ripped out of our chests and were floating along the dock in front of us.

We turned toward the wooden finger pier where *Heron* was tied.

"I don't like this," I said again in a sort of strangled voice. It was all I could think of to say.

"I know you don't," Jeff said. "I don't like it either."

By that afternoon it was raining hard. The rain pelted the roof of the cabin with a steady *drubdrubdrub*, and we cranked up the heater while making dinner: jasmine rice, cioppino, Caesar salad. Jeff pulled out a bottle of Burgundy. The late-summer light dimmed, then it was dark. *Abbey Road* was playing on the iPod, a good choice, those Beatles, for a nostalgic evening. I set two mats on the table, two place settings, two glasses, and I lit one candle. There were four pillows on the banquette, so now we each got two. Still, when dinner was ready and we slid in, those pillows weren't enough to bolster us. Not even close. It felt like we were swimming in space, adrift in quiet.

"This is harder than I thought it would be," I said, "having the guys gone so suddenly. I feel sad, don't you? Physically sad."

"It's going to take some time," Jeff said. "But I know this is the best thing, especially for James—he needs this. It's going to be great for him to be torn from his comfort zone in every way."

We sat hunched over the one candle, poking at our cioppino. "And, I also keep reminding myself what a ripping good time he's going to have, *must already be* having," he added, grinning.

"Well, that's true," I said, brightening.

"I remember so clearly when my parents left me at college—that feeling of *freedom*."

"I know. Me too . . ."

"It was the first time in my life I could do whatever I wanted—that I felt like my life was *mine*."

He was right, of course. This was exactly the way it was supposed to be, the way parents *want* it to be. Still, the wine tasted thin, the cioppino like filler. We sat side by side, taking in the new normal: *just the two of us.*

Then, out of the blue, my phone rang, a rarity aboard *Heron*, where we're often out of cell range. I walked over, glanced at the screen: it was Sam!

"Hi, Mom," he said.

"Sam, it's so good to hear from you!" I exclaimed, my heart flooded with a fizzy champagne feeling; it was such a rush of pleasure hearing his voice.

We placed the phone on the table, stood it up like a little person, and put it on speaker.

"You're back on the boat, right? How is it?"

"It's good!" I chirped, which wasn't at all true. "Although it's pretty quiet without you guys."

"Yeah? How'd *Heron* make out while we were gone?"

"She's in good shape," Jeff said. "Like we left just yesterday."

"Wow," Sam said. "That's gotta be a relief." He updated us on his job in San Francisco and on our friends who had returned from vacation and were, though never having met Sam, letting him live with them until his internship was over.

"Have the Hendricksons adopted you yet?" Jeff wanted to know.

Sam laughed. After all, he was going through an adjustment too: his brother on the East Coast, his parents on a sailboat headed god knows where, and him navigating an adventure of his own: new city, new job, and a new family.

"So how'd it go at St. Lawrence?" he asked.

We filled him in on the Big Drop-Off: James's room, the cute girl down the hall, the two hundred streakers who supposedly dashed naked through freshman orientation, a longstanding senior tradition.

"Really?" Sam said, clearly interested. "I'd better give him a call."

~~~~~~~

After talking with Sam, both Jeff and I felt better—and I realized the whole family was grieving in a way. How much sadder it would be, I thought, if we were *glad to be separated*, if there was nothing to grieve. From the instant they learn to roll over, every move a kid makes is one away from us. Crawling, cruising, walking, running, driving. I'd always understood, deep down, that our personal gauge of success as parents would be how far, how brazenly, the kids ventured into the world—coming back to us with their own discoveries as we'd look forward to returning to them. Maybe that's why I'd taken so many pictures of the boys side by side walking away from me: because part of me had always known that their futures would be walking out of my arms and into the world, and the knowledge broke my heart and filled it up at the same time. But none of that made the first nights of empty-nesting any easier.

Jeff stepped to the nav station and switched the iPod to dish-washing music while the sink filled with water. This usually meant cranking up J. Geils, or Talking Heads; instead, Kool & the Gang came on . . .

He was doing dishes to "Ladies Night"?

I had to laugh. The song was so darn cheesy, so seventies, so . . .

Discoing two steps back toward the galley where he was supposed to be *doing dishes*, my goofy husband grabbed my hand instead. *Uh-oh*, I could see where this was going; he dragged me up from the settee, danced me around the ten-foot-wide cabin. I tried out a few moves—not feeling particularly lithe in jeans and Ugg slippers, with less than six square feet for the two of us on the wooden raised floor. Still, we pranced forward and back, shook it, spun around like one of those little plastic couples twirling in endless circles atop a wedding cake.

"You can bet they aren't doing this on those other boats out there!" I shouted over the music, doing a faux boogie back across the four-foot sisal rug.

"*Come on*," Jeff quipped. "You don't think they're getting down on that hundred-fifty-foot Russian icebreaker?" He moved his hips in an exaggerated slow grind, then pranced forward and back, holding one hand in the air over his head, palm out, like a flag. "Get *down*, girl!"

"Uh, *no*, I don't," I laughed, grinning at how much funk my husband had always had for a white guy from New Jersey.

"What about the Aussies over there on *Polar Bear*?"

"Well . . . *maybe* the Aussies," I admitted. "But probably not to 'Ladies Night.' Frankly? I don't think there's much discoing down goin' on here in Port McNeill . . ."

"Shake it, girl!" my husband crowed. We pranced and shimmied, just because we could, *Heron*'s curtains drawn tight. It was as if we'd reached a sort of finish line and, having crossed it, got to be kids again while our kids had to figure out how to be adults. And although I was still feeling down, missing my sons keenly, after a while I also began to feel something else: an odd sense of lightness. It was as if I'd begun to recover a part of my being that was floating. Not floating as in wanting, but as in free. And with this new sense of buoyancy came another unexpected experience—I began to feel sexy again. It had been a while.

Jeff must have felt the same way. We stared at each other, dancing like fools who didn't give a damn on the rotting docks beside the mudflats in the middle of nowhere in the night, and said at the same time: "*Damn*, we can do whatever we want!"

"You should take your top off, Brown!" my husband suggested, shimmying by.

"My top?"

"Sure, why not?"

Well, it is getting kind of warm in here, I thought. *Why not?* So I pulled my sweater off, then flung my bra over my head. Now Curtis Mayfield's "Super Fly" was playing, the booming funk amplified by *Heron*'s snug interior, the beat bouncing off all that wood—and I felt great flinging my hair back and forth to the beat.

"Yeah, now we're talkin'!" my husband crowed.

Next up: the Commodores' "Brick House," an absurd song to be dancing to topless when you're as bird-breasted as yours truly, but you can't *not* dance to "Brick House" on a boat with those acoustics. Percy Sledge's "When a Man Loves a Woman" followed, then James Brown's "I Got You," and the Isley Brothers' funk classic "Fight the Power."

~~~~~~~~

In some ways the re-entry into life after kids feels like swimming around in a fishbowl that's suddenly been flipped on its side, spilling into an ocean of open water: you don't immediately realize you're set free. But as the two of us danced and pranced and shimmied around on that boat, just us on a night that, years hence, we'd always remember as the Floating Funkathon Dance Party (me in no more than Levi's and bare feet, feeling risqué, and my rakish husband wearing old jeans and a worn-in K2 ski T-shirt, his sexy, comic confidence mixed in with the smell of sweat and salt), we started to get it. All our internal hand-wringing and worrying began to fall away . . .

"You know what?" I said, finally collapsing on the settee, catching my breath. "We don't have to be so damn good all the time anymore!"

It was as if after all those years of being responsible parents, we had the mutual realization that not only had we crossed a sort of finish line: *We didn't have to set an example twenty-four hours a day.* We didn't have to be appropriate. And most of all? *We felt like we didn't have to worry.*

~~~~~~~~~

Maybe that's what the sense of lightness was about. We didn't have to wait up at night until we heard the back door click open. We could run around naked. We could eat dinner in our underwear. We could skip dinner. We could have sex any time of day, wherever we wanted. We could disco down to cheesy seventies music. We could boogie to James Brown like no one was watching. We could stay up late devouring reruns of *Game of Thrones*. We could stay up even later, watch an entire season's worth of *The Crown*. We could cuss and swear and fight. We could lock the door and turn out the lights and pretend no one was home on Halloween. We could invite our friends out for martinis on Monday. We could sleep late on Tuesday. We could stop making those goddamn hash browns. We could stop signing piles of permission slips. We could take off in September when everyone else was back to school. We could feed the dog steak at the dinner table. We could rest our elbows on the dinner table. We could put our feet up on the dinner table. We could smoke pot if we felt like it, which we never do, but it was an option now that it was legal in Washington State. We could learn a new language. Take up a new instrument. Play it badly. We could spend all Saturday reading in bed, even when the sun was shining. We could be utterly, exceptionally, brilliantly irresponsible. We could be bad . . .

"Prepare yourself for pleasure!" I called out.

The next morning we both overslept. I awoke finally, groggy and disoriented. But the memory of all the things we did together with such playful abandon didn't linger long.

James is on the opposite side of the country was the dull reality radiating from my core, eclipsing everything else, even the sultry fun my husband had instigated. I felt punched in the gut, leaden, as if the weight of this fact anchored me to the bed. Who were we if we were no longer day-to-day parents? We finally managed to get up and turn on the cabin heaters. Then we started a pot of coffee, pulled up our electronic charts, and tuned in to the VHF weather channel.

Where to go from here? Against everyone's advice we still wanted to sail north, embark on our empty-nest pilgrimage, even though it was late in the season and all the other boats were heading south. But now that we finally had a wide window of time, our plan seemed insane.

I pulled out our *Waggoner Cruising Guide* and reread the section on waters north of Vancouver Island: "Most cruisers limit their voyages to the waters south of a line that runs between [. . .] Port Hardy on Vancouver Island. North of this line the northern part of Queen Charlotte Sound is a natural barrier. It takes time, a strong boat, and good navigation skills to proceed farther up the coast."

Great, I thought.

But then, maybe we were not "most cruisers" . . .

We had time. We had a shared sense of purpose and a strong boat, and most important, our navigation skills were getting better every day.

"Bring cash," the cruising guide continued. "You'll still have telephone service, but not as often. Telus has the best cell phone coverage, although it's gone shortly after Port Hardy and doesn't re-emerge until Chatham Sound."

Huh—where the heck is Chatham Sound? I wondered, but there was no time to look that up. Jeff was already up on deck unplugging the power cords, readying *Heron* so I could untie the dock lines and clamber aboard as we pushed off.

Just then, as if on cue, my cell phone rang. It was James! I answered it, climbed the companionway, balancing the phone on the top step and putting it on speaker. Jeff and I both huddled in close.

"Hey, how are you guys?" we heard him say.

"We're good. How are you?"

"Great. The rain stopped yesterday, and now it's really hot and muggy."

James told us about the kids he'd met in his dorm at St. Lawrence—East Coast kids from New Hampshire and Connecticut and Maine—the classes he'd signed up for, the upperclassmen back on campus. He sounded good. He was anxious for classes to start. We asked him a bunch of questions. Told him we'd just found out we might not have any cell coverage for the next week or so, unfortunately, but that we'd check in with him as soon as we did.

"You won't have any cell?" he said.

"Well, we're not sure," I admitted, trying to sound calm. "We just read there aren't any cell towers north of here for a while, not until we get to someplace called Chatham Sound, but we're not sure how far that is . . . If you need something and can't reach us, call Grandpa Bart."

"Okay. Bye, Mom, bye, Dad. Love you guys."

After that, after just hearing both my sons' voices in the twenty-four hours before we set sail, I felt better.

The boys were engaging in their own lives, as they should be. It was fantastic for them. And good for us too. We'd get through this. We pushed off from the dock with two deep blasts from the bow thruster, feeling rusty with the whole process after a week away—pulling up the dripping fenders, then coiling and stowing the long bow and stern lines.

"We're headed north, just like you wanted," Jeff said as we cleared the harbor.

"I know," I said, looking up Chatham Sound. I had to pull out a new volume, *Exploring the North Coast of British Columbia*, to do it. I found Chatham Sound listed, turned to a page toward the back, and studied the map. My heart sank: *That* was it? *Way up there?*

Chatham Sound turned out to be the body of water just south of Prince Rupert, BC, running alongside the Alaska–British Columbia border. *Shit.* I'd realized we'd be isolated in these remote waters, but it had never occurred to me we'd be completely cut off, out of cell range for days, weeks even.

"You're not gonna believe this, but there's no cell until Prince Rupert!" I winced, shooting a beseeching look at my husband. "How can there be no cell between here and Alaska?"

We stared at each other for a long moment, and this was when I realized that our quest to sail north to the interior of the Great Bear Rainforest in hopes of seeing this near-mythic creature, the white bear, was no small thing. I sighed and realized that, like all true quests, this was a journey of the heart. A huge leap of faith.

And I also understood at last, truly understood, that this journey was a physical leaving behind of the world we once knew, in the hopes of glimpsing something magical before returning home. I wanted to be able to look back in ten years and think *I can't believe we did that!*—think it in a good way, a wondrously astounded way. I wanted to live joyfully, without regrets. I knew in my bones it was entirely too late to turn back—we'd already 100 percent committed to doing this thing—cell phones be damned.

HUMPBACKS

~~~~~

Queen Charlotte Strait, despite all the warnings about its being a lengthy crossing that exposes mariners to the full fury of the open Pacific, was still and calm; the wind was a murmur at 4.4 knots, the water glassy, spreading into gentle ovoids the size of hula hoops. The sky and strait extending behind us were a vast pale blue, round as an eye. Off *Heron*'s stern, gray and white bands of clouds stretched over the sea. One small cloud, cast out by the herd, drifted off to the west. Before us, the sky was darker, but more dramatic too. To the sides the Coast Range's dark brown peaks, some glazed with icy-white snow patches, were silhouettes against the darkening sky. We passed a few fishing boats headed in the opposite direction. Then, no one.

"There aren't any other boats," Jeff said.

"I know. It'll be okay," I said.

We texted Sam, reminded him we were heading north and would be out of cell range for a while. We also called my dad, Bart, in

California. As we spoke he pulled out his iPad and linked to Google Maps, zooming in on Queen Charlotte Strait.

"We just found out we probably won't have any cell service until Alaska!" I shouted. "So if the boys need anything, or someone needs to reach us in an emergency, well . . ." My voice trailed off as I imagined worst-case scenarios. "Can you be the boys' first point of contact if they need anything?" I finally managed.

"Of course I will," my dad agreed, always a dad.

"Okay, thanks!" I yelled into the phone, feeling slightly less panicked. "Thanks, Dad! We really appreciate it—I love you!" Then I unexpectedly teared up. My father is exceptional, the sort of man who stays steady and calm. I adored him.

Who does this? I thought. I remembered an amusing newspaper article I'd read before the Big Drop-Off; it advised parents not to worry if their college-aged kids didn't return their texts. It described real-life helicopter parents telephoning the dean's office in a panic when they were unable to reach their kids.

But what if the situation was reversed: *What if your kids can't reach you?* I wondered. What if they need to reach you but can't because you're out of cell range? What if they can't reach you for, say, seven or ten or twelve days? This hadn't come up in the article. It hadn't come up in the article because no responsible twenty-first-century parent would drop their kid off at college and then float off the face of the earth the very next day.

But the dilemma could not be helped. As with any true expedition, isolation came with the territory. Ahead in the distance were low-lying rock islands with wistful names: Wishart Island, Desertas Island, McLeod Island, Ghost Island. I peered at them through the binoculars. They looked like brown skipping stones scattered on an endless, impenetrable sea. Eventually, we neared and then threaded our way between them. The strait was vast and tidal. It seemed to stretch forever to the northwest, rising and falling like a breathing thing. I watched strands of languid kelp lift with the swells.

I shot one last quick text to the boys while we could: "Grandpa Bart says to text him if u need anything! We love you, have fun! Xo Mom"

Well, that's one way to cut the cord, I thought.

Jeff was down below, refining our course. I was up at the helm alone, surrounded by vastness: water and sky rimmed on the distant edges by dark mountains. Except before me there were no mountains, only a thin horizon line where silver water met a sky piled with gray clouds. So much space. So much seeming emptiness when all we had now was silence and each other's company. Was it nothing or was it everything? I stared and listened. There was only the sound of water riffling off the hull and the drone of the engine. I lifted my chin skyward and looked up, and after a long while heard the buzz of a floatplane stuttering across the sky.

We passed the last small rocky island.

We passed the point where the last bar on my cell phone shrank and disappeared.

I peered out beyond the wheel. *I'm glad to be alone*, I thought. *Sitting and listening and staring.* I felt drained. Emptied. As if all the energy and effort of the past twenty-some years of raising kids had seeped out of me. I zipped my coat tighter and sank deep inside myself; a small, hard nut, willing my heart not to hurt. But it did.

I thought of my girlfriends. Their doubt. *Why would you leave for* eight weeks *alone with your husband?* they'd questioned, incredulous. Maybe they were right. I missed my sister. I wished I'd called her before we left Port McNeill, but it was too late now.

Why are we doing this? I wondered. I let my doubt carry me up and out of the boat until I was utterly disassociated, mind wandering, lost, not even paying attention to the compass, the wheel, our GPS heading. I felt like the physical embodiment of absence. I missed the boys. The missing throbbed; a dull ache in my heart. I resented the ache, and I resented the fact that I couldn't seem to lift myself above it. I turned and watched *Heron*'s wake. The water spooled behind us like something the boat was secreting, yards and yards of blue ribbon. The distance between us and the boys lengthened, and as it did, separated us from that life as if it were time.

Why are we doing this? I wondered again.

Suddenly, as if in response, I heard—coming from the seemingly limitless space—a breath. A single exhalation so loud I could hear it, the air and force and timbre of it, floating across the water and landing on my head.

Huh?

Phhhuuuuuphhhhh.

There it was again: *Phhhuuuuuphhhhh,* I glanced up, the sound pulling me from my uneasy interior world. Oh! There, hanging less than two hundred yards off the starboard bow, was a plume of white mist—a whale spout—rising up. The air vibrated. Thrummed! I watched the mist hang in the air, suspended for a moment.

Then out of nowhere, maybe fifty feet from the whale spout, an enormous thing as big as a bus shot straight up out of the water—its titanic bulk a rocket, a jumbo jet fuselage, a building, impossibly vertical—then came crashing back down with a boom loud as a cannon blast, sending up a violent explosion of water.

"Jeff! Jeff!" I shouted toward the companionway. "Jeff, *whales!*"

And they came again. *Two* of them off the starboard bow, closer this time. A pair of gray giants exploded out of the sea, defied gravity for the briefest moment, then came crashing down, sending up a splash so massive I could feel its salty spray all over my upturned face. It was like I could feel the sea and the sky and the whales and the bracing air we were all breathing, the whole world of it on my skin.

"Jeff!" I yelled, laughing, incredulous. "Jeff, get up here— humpbacks!"

By the time he heard me and rushed up, he caught only their tails. They were good ones, though: shiny-wet black and big as steam shovels, surprisingly graceful, disappearing with a pair of slow-motion waves, and remarkably fluid for something so epic. As the hump-backs' mammoth gray girths went down, diving deep into the ancient ocean, their tails rose in a final salute, water streaming off.

Jeff and I watched together: surveyors of a newfound world. The whales, the wonder of them, cracked open my chest.

"Oh my *god*! Oh my *god*!" I kept saying, over and over.

~~~~~~~~~~

Sometimes I think you are able to keep going because you aren't really yourself anymore. Something shakes you to your core, an instant so charged, so astounding, you open yourself to every atom of it—as if you've escaped your own skin and let your soul spread forth. That is what the whales were like for me. They took my breath, grabbed me and shook me, startling me awake with a jolt so mighty I could feel my listless interior world shatter and something immediate and mysterious and vital usher me into the present one.

"Everything is so alive here," I whispered to Jeff.

And in that instant with the pair of humpbacks breaching right beside me, I also knew that Sam and James were fine. It's as if the two whales had signaled: We are here! We are with you! You might feel lost, but everything is with you, by the way: the sea, and the birds moving fluidly across it, and the whales swimming silently beneath it, and hundreds and thousands of miles away, your boys, Sam and James. We are all with you, but we are also free. And in between there are hundreds of millions of other living things—all connected. *That is the wonder of the world*—how you can know it, and as much of it as your heart can handle, both intimately and broadly.

And I do believe I met my boys there somehow in that instant. Not their souls but some greater portion of themselves, boundlessly present. Their spirit. It's like Einstein's theory that the only real time is that of the observer, who carries his or her own time and space. Or the ancient intuition that all matter, all "reality," is simply energy. On the boat that day I think the boys must've lent me some of their spirit because the hope and energy I felt then was as big as the sky. It was like a fiery blue space opening up inside you that makes you want to breathe in everything deep. I didn't tell Jeff about this; I didn't see how I could even begin to explain it, so all I said was, "Get the camera!"

He rushed down to grab the good Canon, but by the time he returned the whales were gone.

"Well, that was a game changer," I said. "Humpbacks! Humpbacks right off the bow!"

"*That* was insanely cool," Jeff replied. "Did you read that guy's story in *Cruising World*? The one about the humpback that breached and came down on the deck of his sailboat, crushing his mast?"

"No," I laughed. "But if those humpbacks had landed and taken me out? Well, it would be hard to think of a cooler way to go. Crushed by a humpback!" I grinned jauntily.

"*That* would be a horrible death," Skipper Jeff said, always the realist. "But I can see you're back in the game."

Then, even though my phone showed no bars, a text chimed through: James, 2:25 p.m.

"Just hung out with the Ultimate Lax Bro! Haha but ok call me when you get service, love you"

"You did?? We just saw two HUGE humpbacks breach out of the water. Xo Mom" I typed and hit Send, thumbs flying.

It sent!

"Haha cool! Talk to you soon."

But of course we wouldn't talk soon since our phones didn't work, and they wouldn't for a long time.

But not talking felt okay.

There was a northwest wind blowing 9.7 knots off the starboard beam, and a sky filled with scrolled white clouds, so Jeff and I got to it and raised the main.

SKULL COVE

When we reached the far side of the strait a few hours later and ghosted into a small protected anchorage, *Heron* was the only boat.

But what might have felt spooky or lonely only a day before now felt electrifying.

There had been something profound about seeing those humpbacks, the way the very air around them vibrated and tingled. And the sensation lasted, so that by the time we'd made our way through the cove's narrow entrance, threading *Heron* carefully between thirty-foot-high walls of granite worn smooth by thousands of years of rising and falling tides, checked the cove's depths, and lowered the anchor, we still had that feeling: it was the feeling of being spectacularly alive.

We shut down the engine and simply stood, taking in our surroundings. The cove, named Skull Cove on our charts, was haunting, still, luminous, green. Everywhere you turned—along the sides of small rock islets that floated around us, around the edges of the cove itself—vertical fingers of sculpted sand-brown granite pushed straight up out of the water. The water, which was ink black, reflected the rock, and above that, branches of tall, ancient-looking hemlocks and gnarled red cedar reached out as if to grab more air, more light, their limbs draped with moss.

A pair of loons yodeled loudly, winging their way overhead, their long gray necks pointed south.

"Loons!" we both called out like a pair of giant toddlers with a new word, looking up.

Then we just stood gazing west, where through a dip in the trees you could make out the northern tip of Vancouver Island thirty miles away and the sun sinking behind it.

We had the view entirely to ourselves.

But what felt even more striking was the intimacy of the setting, the feeling of being completely cut off from the outside world— anchored safely, just the two of us held by the forest, its arms encircling us. It was as if this place ringed with evergreens was a reward for having set out and crossed this much of the strait.

~~~~~~~~

It was lovely and eerie and strange that next night of empty-nesting.

It was like a second honeymoon, sort of.

Jeff set some crab traps—we had high hopes for Dungeness here. We watched the sun vanish behind the trees, saw eagles and herons and ospreys splash down in the stillness, shared cocktails while some ridiculously unlikely music blared (more James Brown, I think), made dinner together, went to bed and—passed out.

It's hard to define the essence of any long-term relationship, what elements bind two different people together over decades of time. But one aspect, I think, was symbolized for me by that intimate cove. It felt womblike, as if we'd sailed not only into a safe harbor but a shell, and there was nothing beyond the two of us. It was as if we carried everything we needed on that boat, and emotionally too, carried our world within us. There is satisfaction in needing nothing beyond your own making.

And so there you are, just the two of you, feeling you need nothing else, no one else. But then you look up and notice the trees. The whole world out there: whether it's friends, or community, or religion, or art, or politics, or saving the planet, or watching baseball games, or concerts, or just spending time with people you care about—or showing up for all those things—you bring more to them because you are together. These external things, these interests outside the two of you are, I believe, essential to marriages.

At least that's how it was for us.

Except when we awoke the next morning and peered up and out of the boat, the first thing we saw, *literally*, was trees.

Hundreds and hundreds of trees. You could smell them: the bristling clumps of cedars, their tarry-resiny reek mingling with the fresh, cold scent of the sea. The mossy-shaggy dignity of the huge ancient hemlocks. The tall, proud Sitka spruces. Ferns that had grown so capaciously they'd swallowed entire tree stumps. The sheer jungle energy of all these plants and trees clinging stubbornly to the rocks was palpable. It was as if all this rain-drenched and sea-washed fecundity had its own life force.

And then it hit us: since leaving Seattle we'd sailed past hundreds, thousands, tens of thousands of trees. We'd passed shores fringed emerald green with trees, houses peeking coyly between them, as we'd made our way up through the San Juans and Canadian Gulf Islands. We'd passed entire hillsides blanketed green pounding our way up Johnstone Strait. And we'd poked around the edges of the Great Bear Rainforest in the Broughton Islands.

But by crossing forty miles of Queen Charlotte Strait, *we'd finally entered the Great Bear Rainforest itself*—and this forest, with these trees, was unlike anything either of us had ever experienced. The impressive thing, the thing that was almost beyond words, was the sheer fertility of the surrounding forest. It was a rustling, pulsing, forest—but at the same time, a forest with an *ancient-feeling* presence: silent, dark, and deep. This was the kind of forest that could mystify you with its wildness.

It was thrilling to be discovering this whole new world for the first time together, a world thick and spooky as dreams. We felt young and a bit reckless. Every bird that whipped past the stern made my heart beat faster. Peering out at the wild forest, picturing the cove where *Heron* floated surrounded by trees upon trees, I hoped this would be a good place to land, the first days of empty-nesting.

HAKAI

~~~

When we awoke that next morning, *Heron* was still the only boat in the cove. Jeff pulled on his storm pants and sped off in the dinghy to pull a crab pot he'd set the night before. I tuned in the VHF weather channel and started a pot of French press. The forecast was unsettling. "Marine forecast for Pacific waters issued by Environment Canada: gale force warning in effect, Hecate Strait . . . Queen Charlotte Sound, wind southwest ten to twenty knots, increasing to southwest fifteen to twenty-five Monday afternoon. Chance of showers tonight. Seas, one meter," the now-familiar radio voice intoned.

Gale warnings are issued when wind speeds of thirty-four to forty-seven knots, excluding gusts, are forecast. Although we'd be well inside Hecate Strait transiting Queen Charlotte Sound, just hearing the words "gale force warning" made me sit up and lean in to the radio, my chest tightening, to make out exactly what the forecaster was saying, since we were new to this territory.

Should we stay or should we go? This was a big day: we'd be rounding Cape Caution, so named because the mainland cape is exposed to swells off the open Pacific as they roll in north of Vancouver Island and the sea floor shallows up dramatically; that means you get significant waves and currents in any kind of a blow. Beyond that, Cape Caution stands as a sort of psychological dividing line for boaters. This was the fateful place where Captain George Vancouver narrowly escaped disaster twice when both his ships, the *HMS Discovery* and *Chatham* ran up on rocks in the fog. Winds whipping up to twenty-five knots would be rough here, but at least we'd come to know the weather patterns: mornings were typically gentler, with forecasted winds increasing by afternoon. In Skull Cove, in fact, all was temporarily calm. I climbed into the cockpit and gazed out at water so still and dark you couldn't tell where it ended and the land began. It would be tempting to stay, to put off Cape Caution and the unknown open water, but I was also antsy to go.

~~~~~~~~~

Soon the stillness was broken by the whine of an outboard.

"A good day! I'm feeling fresh crab for lunch, baby!" Jeff called out over the engine, circling back to the boat.

I sighed and scrambled to the stern, then helped my husband heave the cumbersome wire crab trap, full of snapping claws, onto the boat.

He'd hauled up a rock crab and four Dungeness—three males and a female. The males, big with bright red-orange shells and meaty claws were keepers. The smaller female we tossed back to breed. We hurriedly put on a pot of water to boil, then went through the dance that was now almost routine: started the engine, turned on the navigation system, pulled up the anchor, checked our depths, and slipped out of Skull Cove. It was now or never if we hoped to get a jump on the weather. As we left a heron squawked and flew past, flapping wings wide as tattered flags over the water, and an enormous eagle screeched from a tree; both were good auguries, we thought.

No sooner had we nosed out of safe Skull Cove and set a northwesterly course of about 315 degrees, however, than we were surrounded by a thick blanket of fog. With visibility less than half a mile, we couldn't see the coast (or rocks) to starboard, nor could we make out anything more than half a mile to port. And most ominous, a cloud dense as a snow bank was creeping in from the sea.

"That must be the cold front," I said, dismally. It began to rain.

"The trick to staying warm is not to get cold," my husband replied, disappearing for a minute, then climbing back into the open cockpit having morphed into Captain Jeff: red Musto storm coat, red foul-weather storm pants, heavy sailing gloves, and a blue wool cap.

"Wow—that's some look for August," I said. But the truth was, he looked dashing. *A good thing*, I thought, *because with all this fog moving in, there isn't much else to look at.*

I, on the other hand, didn't look so hot. Down below, donning my own foul-weather gear, I noticed that an hour or so of pitching over five-foot side swells had turned my complexion a waxy gray green. I scowled and rummaged for a wool cap to cover my fog-drenched hair. Unfortunately, this wasn't a good look either—the cap only accentuated my angular face, which was turning greener the longer I stayed below. *Oh well, it is what it is*, I thought, pulling on thick wool socks and rubber boots.

When I reemerged in my own bright red foul-weather overalls, zipped snug over a thick black fleece, Captain Jeff howled and teased, "Your ass looks like a bag of potatoes!"

I smiled demurely and said, "Screw you, buddy!" Fact was, my foul-weather gear felt great. Just putting it on gave me a psychological boost: I wasn't a mom as much as a mom transformed into an astronaut, an Arctic explorer, or one of those badass Alaskan crab fishermen on the boys' favorite reality TV show, *Deadliest Catch*. I hip-bumped Captain Jeff off the wheel and noted our latitude: N 51°

10' 57". I knew that standing at the helm, staring out at the horizon and taking charge of the boat, was by far the best place to be if you feel queasy. The swells increased as a strong northwest wind kicked up. A deep chill settled in over the cockpit.

I can do this, I can do this, I thought . . .

I prayed I could.

While *Heron* slogged through the side swell, we brewed up ginger tea to keep our stomachs settled, sipped it from stainless storm cups. Jeff scrolled through his iPod, blasting some of the best albums of all time to keep us awake: Nirvana's *Nevermind*, Bob Dylan's *Blood on the Tracks*, *Exile on Main Street* by the Rolling Stones, *Stop Making Sense* by the Talking Heads, Paul Simon's *Graceland*, Jeff Buckley's *Grace*.

The chill and fog finally began to lift as we approached Cape Caution. We could see now that there were birds everywhere. Pigeon guillemots, common murres, pink-footed shearwaters, storm petrels. They rose and fell in the air over the waves, settled on the water, and rode up and down the crests, diving for fish, then flying again. We motored past Egg Island, which sits in spectacular isolation at the entrance to Fitz Hugh Sound from Queen Charlotte Sound, its red-roofed lighthouse exposed to the full sweep of the Pacific. Then, finally, mercifully, we were around the cape and waltzing up Fitz Hugh Sound, a wide channel protected by the cliffs of Calvert Island. The swells subsided and the fog dissipated, revealing bright blue sky.

The wind picked up, along with our spirits. We'd made it! We raised the main and sped along, harnessing a light breeze.

<hr>

An unreal quality attended those first few days, just the two of us. The dawning awareness that this was a new stage of life. Each small thing—the weather clearing! Rounding Cape Caution!—seemed outsized. Before, so much of our relationship had been kid focused. Work focused. Days conceived—and lived—as to-do lists. And now this: something wacky and worthy, just us. It was heady, yes, but also daunting, this uncharted territory together.

It turned out to be a dazzling, sunny afternoon. A few hours later we took down the sail and motored into Pruth Bay, a glacier-carved channel where scrappy windblown spruces clung to crevasses in steep rock walls. Around us, low cliffs, and salmon the size of fireplace logs leaping clear out of the water. "Toaster fish!" we exclaimed, watching the silly fish eject themselves into the air with startling enthusiasm.

We set the anchor and took in our surroundings. A low tombolo separated Pruth Bay from the open Pacific, and on that stretch of land sat a large red-roofed lodge and a series of cabins; according to our sailing guides, the enterprise had once been a fishing lodge but was now the site of an unusual undertaking called the Hakai Institute. Impressive docks fronted the place; a small Nordic tug was the only other boat anchored in the harbor.

I'd read in *Cruising the Secret Coast: Unexplored Anchorages* about a beautiful, deserted white-sand beach that sat on the opposite side of the lodge, facing the Pacific. But unlike sailors cruising the Caribbean or sailing the coast of Mexico, we wouldn't be strolling many deserted white-sand beaches in the Great Bear Rainforest. The fact that one existed here at all was so miraculous it was the main thing that kept me going that long day, hunkered down at the helm in my storm gear. I couldn't wait to take the dinghy over and walk on white sand.

In five minutes we'd peeled off our foul-weather gear, lowered ourselves into the dinghy, and motored across to the lodge. Two speedy-looking red-trimmed aluminum research vessels were tied to the docks; the *Hakai Express* and the *Hakai Spirit*. We lashed our dinghy to one of the sturdy concrete docks and walked up the ramp to land, where a small sign welcomed visitors to follow a rainforest trail to the beach. It felt wonderful to stretch our legs after the seven-hour crossing that day. Along the way we passed well-kept gardens planted with shrub roses and lavender, the red-roofed lodge, and several cabins; we then crossed a log bridge leading into the forest. The trail wound through ferns and salal (a sturdy Pacific Northwest Coast evergreen shrub with dark green lustrous leaves) and silver snags of ancient spruce trunks here and there, and then back into trees again—madrone, cedar, Sitka spruce. Then the minty, cedary scent of the forest shifted, and you could smell the beach before you saw it: driftwood and salt air. In the distance, the rhythm and rumble of surf.

Suddenly, we came out of the forest and there was the beach: a long, white-sand spit at low tide, glowing in late-afternoon light. It was so improbable, such a dramatic contrast, it was like stepping out of a dark tunnel and emerging on the other side of the earth in a different hemisphere—a warm, balmy, beachy hemisphere, Polynesia perhaps.

"Ahhh!" We both exhaled, taking in the tumble of small waves lapping the spit, the hiss and sizzle as the leading edge of the tide melted into the beach, the sweep of soft sand curving away left and right; most intriguingly, beyond the surf there were wind-scoured rock islets sprouting handfuls of trees that looked as ancient and bent as old men. We pulled off our boots, rolled up our jeans, sank our toes in the sand.

"This is outrageous," Jeff said. "Awesome."

Clearly, we'd arrived at a stunning and sacred place.

I twirled around, arms outstretched, then, when my husband turned and started walking left, I took off jogging to the right.

"See ya!" I called over my shoulder. It felt fantastic to be off the boat, moving my arms and legs, bare feet sinking into the tide and brisk water. It also felt good to be more than two feet apart from each other, all that fresh, tangy air and empty space filling the widening gap between us. I ran all the way to the other end of the beach, breathing hard, huffing in big breaths of emphatic freshness, pure, cold oxygen filling my lungs. Then I turned and ambled back, making prints in the smooth sand. There were no other human prints, just the delicate scratchings of sea creatures and shorebirds. Tiny birds the size of my thumb scattered before me, running in herky-jerky streams, and flocks of sandpipers and gulls waded in the shore break. Strands of sea kelp and piles of ochre-brown bull kelp lay strewn about like ribbons. Where the sand met the forest, decades-old driftwood and bleached cedar formed a weathered bulkhead.

I thought about how soothing the sound of surf can be. How primordial. As each foot-high wave rolled in, the soft rumble gently massaged my spin—and then, as it receded, the sound washed down its length, bathing me like embryonic fluid.

When I reached Jeff, we sat side by side on a huge log, watching gulls wheel overhead.

"Our own deserted beach," I said. "It's like a second honeymoon."

"Except it's not," Jeff said.

I gave Captain Jeff's arm a squeeze and smiled to myself, thinking about the prospect of our night ahead as I stared out at the sun-streaked water with its little islands and trees. Jeff got up and grabbed a long bleached stick and began poking at a pile of storm-swept timber, causing explosions of splinter and dust. Nobody had any idea where we were. *We're on a wild beach on the exposed Pacific on the very edge of the Great Bear Rainforest*, I thought with a kind of wonder. I felt lit up by being back in the world. And by the prospect of going farther still. It seemed a preposterous place for us to be, disconnected from our kids and friends and family as we were at this crucial time, each dressed in our one pair of jeans, pant legs rolled up, bare feet in the sand, our hair wild as that of unkempt dogs. But our perch on the beach was so heart-stirringly beautiful.

I pulled out my phone to take a picture of the storm-lashed islands, which looked like something out of a Japanese landscape, ospreys circling overhead.

Big mistake: no bars.

My heart sank at the sight of the little screen. The message was clear: *No Service.*

I simply hadn't anticipated what it would feel like to be so far removed on our sailing journey north of Port McNeill, the last outpost of civilization. I'd wanted a true adventure: weeks without the exterior noise of the fraught world, days as uncharted as blank paper. But that prospect was hard, having just left the boys. I had the sickening feeling Jeff and I would just have to go with it. There was nothing we could do about it now. I put the phone back in my pocket, zipped the pocket shut, and stared out at the otherworldly islands again.

A minute before, the sight of them had made me ecstatic. But now they seemed lonely, each its own tiny continent, heightening that sense of my own disconnectedness from the kids.

We dusted the sand off our toes and, in silence, hiked the trail back through the forest to the boat. I felt a sad unease. I knew Jeff was missing his virile youth. And I was missing my boys—but didn't know if it was for the life we used to have or for our life together on *Heron. What is Sam reading now*, I wondered. How were the final weeks of his summer job going? Jeff and I would be back on the boat and headed farther into the Great Bear Rainforest in the morning, even farther out of cell phone range—missing James's reports on his first college classes, friends, lacrosse practices.

But Jeff and I will be exploring a new place together, I reminded myself. *Exploring the Great Bear Rainforest and maybe even seeing a spirit bear.* And then we'd return to cell range and beloved voices— heading home to life not as it always had been but as it would be.

SERPENT ISLANDS

~~~~~~~

"Jesus, I didn't see that rock last night," Jeff says, alarmed, peering toward shore the next morning from the cockpit, where we're sipping coffee and eating peanut butter toast. "Holy shit!"

I scan the shore. Sure enough: the bald brown head of a rock—no, almost a small island—has emerged at the end of the long, narrow cove where we'd anchored the night before. As the tide receded the rock revealed itself: ten to twelve feet across, barnacle encrusted—"a total nightmare" as the boys would say—lying in wait just beneath the surface. If we'd anchored forty feet closer, it could have ripped a hole in *Heron*'s hull.

"Was that thing marked on the charts?" I say, putting down my coffee in disbelief.

"It wasn't. Damn. I'm not gonna lie—that thing could've sunk this entire boat."

"Damn," I say too.

"And here we'd be, two fools screwed in the middle of goddamn nowhere."

"Christ," I whisper.

We both stare some more at the rock island, then a gull wheels by and lands on it. He cocks his head and stares at us quizzically, not like he's wondering if we have any fish but like he can't believe what idiots humans can be.

Jeff and I have been taking more chances. The day before we'd pulled anchor and cut north through a cut on Calvert Island, then headed west into Hakai Pass, a wildly alive and exposed channel surrounded by hundreds of smaller islands and islets and fjords teeming with fish and wildlife. We'd raised the staysail just for grins and then cut west toward the open Pacific. Hakai's waters are legendary, known for some of the biggest Chinook salmon anywhere on the planet. Not just twenty- or thirty-pound salmon, but Really Big Salmon, forty-plus pounders. Small guided fishing boats bobbed in the chop along the edges of the cut. We'd heard that anglers had pulled in seventy-pound fish here, and that the all-time record stood at a monster 124-pound Chinook. Imagine, a salmon the size of a teenager! But we weren't there to fish.

We blew by the fishermen and continued motoring and sailing out toward the Spider Islands, a maze of deserted islands and waterways bordering Queen Charlotte Sound. We'd read that the water here was complex, the scenery astonishing—and that there were rarely any boats.

And once we left the fishing skiffs in our wake, all that appeared to be true. Threading our way (staysail still raised) between a narrow cut in a chain of completely exposed, serrated islands and islets— swells from the open Pacific pounding the rocks and exploding in sprays of white—I was suddenly aware that we just might be in over our heads. This wilderness sailing could be dangerous: it was something I *knew* but had never really *felt* before.

"Do you think we're okay here, Chet?" I wondered aloud. The narrow cut, the giant rocky outcroppings like the spine of the world poking out of the ocean, the force of the water—all those things sent a wave of fear through me. I sat up straight, trying to gauge our distance from the dark rocks looming to both port and starboard, the push of the current versus our power under motor and sail.

"Yep, we're good," Jeff said. "Just keep an eye out for rocks." His tone, focused and calm, contrasted with my own growing panic.

I glanced around wildly. Heck, there were rocks everywhere! "Yeah? I'm not sure about this," I squeaked as spray crashed over the bow and an osprey rowed through the air alongside the mast.

~~~~~~~

Making it through that rocky cut marked a turning point for the two of us. Pushing ourselves to take that kind of chance on *Heron* might have shaken me, but I realized the boat could handle it. And more importantly, *we*—Jeff and I together—could handle it. Jeff was a terrific boatman: fast thinking, responsive, logical, careful. A quick study. As his confidence in his skill and in *Heron*'s seaworthiness grew, my faith in him, in *Heron*, in just the two of us together—and in myself too—deepened. We were getting good at this and at the same time—by taking calculated risks—also learning our limits.

Once we'd made it through the exposed rock cut, we spied a pod of orcas feeding in the Pacific and raced out to see them. Herring gulls and Caspian terns and Arctic terns were everywhere; from below they looked like white kites soaring against the piercing blue sky. We could see puffs of white vapor shooting up from the sea—orca spray! By the time we reached the white mist, whales were gliding all around us, gorgeous torpedoes shining black but for that surprise yin-yang patch of white, their wet dorsal fins slicing through the water like scimitars. High on whales, we didn't want to be intrusive and chase them; instead, we'd backtracked and anchored off the Serpent Islands, a cluster of three uninhabited islands framing a small lagoon and pocket of white-sand beach. We'd read about the Serpents in our *Cruising the Secret Coast* guide. The only thing was that *Heron* was too big to anchor safely in the Serpents' tiny bay, so we anchored out farther and dinghied in, abandoning *Heron* to a falling tide. Speeding in for our wet landing and scrambling ashore on a deserted wild beach felt thrilling—like we'd morphed into castaways, my ultimate romantic travel fantasy come true. I shed my life jacket and was burying my toes in the sand, imagining myself rolling around in it with my Indiana Jones of a husband, when I looked down at my feet and froze . . .

Uh-oh. Prints. *Big* prints.

Prints with long tapered claws, each tipped by a sharp nail, were etched all over the beach.

What was it?!

Bear? Wolf? Cougar?

Large dog in need of a nail clipping?

We snapped a photo of the prints, which we were later told were from a wolverine (the largest member of the weasel family as well as a fierce and muscular carnivore). Except that, hilariously, they weren't from an elusive wolverine but instead from a frat party of sea otters. We went on to explore the rest of the beach. Past a small cut it opened onto exposed rocks and tide pools, bare now at low tide, facing the Pacific. Piles of bleached driftwood lay stacked along the high side of the beach, against low cliffs. We sat awhile, our backs against the driftwood, but it wasn't long before the hair on our necks began standing on end as we wondered what the sharp-clawed beast lurking above us in the cliffs could be. So much for my wild island fantasies . . .

We got up and explored tide pools instead, both of us feeling safer on two feet. Sea stars the size of hubcaps were glued to the rocks, and ginormous strands of bull kelp—which grows a remarkable seven inches a day, like seaweed on steroids, and whose bulb, resembling a small weird onion, is filled with carbon monoxide gas—lay strewn about everywhere. The database for seaweeds has identified about six hundred species and twelve thousand different Canadian seaweed specimens by DNA analysis, we'd read.

"I wish we had our pocket plankton book with us," I said, eyeing some bright green strands of surfgrass and leaves of eggplant-colored winged kelp. "I bet a lot of this stuff is edible. Seaweed's packed with nutrients, you know."

"It's all I can do to keep myself from getting down on my hands and knees and scarfing it down, it looks so good," Jeff deadpanned.

After that, sun sinking, we began looking for a place to anchor and ended up at the head of a long, forested finger cove—Leckie Bay. We were tired, on edge from pushing ourselves and the boat. But pushing ourselves further continued to serve up surprises. It was hard to imagine a day more intense or surreal: huge salmon leaped around Jeff as he dinghied out to drop the crab pot. Then, once the pot was set, he looked up, and there at the head of the cove stood a lone wolf, watching. I know because I was sitting in the stern, mesmerized by the airborne fish catapulting themselves around us, all iridescence and instinct. Concerned that Jeff was sitting in the middle of a flying fish storm, I'd peered past him to the head of the cove. And that's when I saw her: a wolf, female we assumed, with long legs and a silvery-brown coat. She stood, for a long time, watching us. Curious. It's possible that we were the first people she'd ever seen in the wild. Minutes passed. Jeff and I stayed very still, and the wolf did too. Then she turned and vanished into the forest.

When Jeff got back to the boat, he was pumped.

"Did you see that?!"

"I did. What a beauty . . ."

"I know, and what a cool encounter . . . the way she stood there, watching us. And these fish! I swear these damn fish think they're birds."

We'd heard about the wolves of the Great Bear Rainforest, knew the remote coast was home to some of the world's most mysterious and iconic wildlife. But we had no idea we'd be lucky enough to see a wild sea wolf. Genetically distinct from their inland cousins, indeed from wolves in any other part of the world, coastal wolves are rare. They're a unique subspecies of wolf that roam the estuaries, fish like bears, and swim like otters. That's right, these wolves *swim*—for miles between uninhabited islands, searching for salmon, black-tailed deer, intertidal crustaceans to eat. Smaller than gray wolves, which populate western Canada and now Yellowstone again, sea wolves are highly elusive and fiercely intelligent; the coastal wolves endure as fragile symbols of this rugged coastline, although not much is known about them outside of British Columbia.

Little did we know how rare our wolf encounter was.

In later seasons, exploring these same waters, we never again saw a wolf. It was only after years had passed—as we watched for wolves but never, ever, saw one—that we began to fully appreciate how singular and rare that encounter had been. Perhaps for the wolf too.

After a few days in *Heron* time we'd gone from feeling lost and adrift and punched in the gut to feeling as alive and attuned to the world as either of us had felt in years. There was the Frisson of Fear, shooting through that exposed rocky cut, followed by the Intense Euphoria of our own orca whale sighting and the mysterious print of an unknown paw, and then the quiet gaze of a lone wolf. Each encounter had brought a sense of elation tied to nothing but the moment.

"Where the hell *are* we?" Jeff had said in bed as we'd drifted off to sleep that night of the wolf encounter. "We're in some unbelievably remote cove. No one knows where we are . . ."

"That's the whole point," I'd said, reaching out to riffle my fingers through his hair.

"Yeah, it is. I'm liking this, this taking a little time between kids and returning home."

"You are?"

"I am. You know what I'm going to tell all my friends from here on out? I'm going to tell them, once you take your kids to college? Or once your kids leave? Whatever you do, *do not* go straight home! *Do not* rush right back to work—even though that tuition is terrifying. Take some time, even if it's just a few days. Go somewhere, anywhere. Rent an RV. Hit the road. Try van life. Get lost for a while! I think it's important, just taking this time. It makes more sense, really, than a honeymoon."

As we settled into our sailing-trip version of "it," our shared goals grew. We wanted to make it to the far reaches of the Great Bear Rainforest. We wanted to witness something rare and beautiful. We wanted to somehow try to see a spirit bear, a wondrous creature that exists only on this one corner of the planet (a corner that's ridiculously difficult to get to but happens to be almost in our own backyard). The spirit bear had started to assume a Holy Grail feel for us both. Sitting there in Leckie Bay that next morning, realizing how close we'd come to disaster with the uncharted rock, we realized that if our luck held, we could push ourselves and the boat in the gunkholing department—seeking out smaller coves and deserted inlets even farther off the beaten track.

In our first months cruising *Heron* with the boys, our instinct had been to follow the herd, pointing ourselves toward places described in the cruising guides. But it didn't take long for those places to lose their appeal in favor of the Pacific Northwest Coast's rich wilderness of serene anchorages in the wild. That's when we also began to think seriously about trying to find a long-lost native longhouse Jeff had heard about. It seemed preposterous: like trying to find a splinter in a forest. But it also felt like something that was a part of a larger journey to these strange, faraway, mythical-seeming, nobody-we-know-has-ever-been-there kinds of places. And we had a rough idea where to look.

Jeff had heard about a native settlement, an ancient longhouse said to be partly standing in the Great Bear Rainforest. There was word of its potentially being named a World Heritage Site. He'd met a pilot—a cool, long-haired, thirty-five-year-old who flew a 1948 Grumman Goose around the islands up there—and asked him about it. The pilot, who flew a vintage amphibious aircraft originally designed for reconnaissance because he loved flying over uncharted waters in the same way we hoped to explore them, told Jeff he'd heard of the longhouse—but that it was so mysterious it wasn't on any maps, or in any books, and there were no pictures.

"But here's roughly where I think it's supposed to be," he said, describing the terrain to Jeff.

"Wouldn't it be cool," Jeff thought, "to try and find it? Just because?" I had my doubts. All we knew was that the longhouse, if it existed, might be somewhere on the largest island along BC's northern coast, an island that was an almost nine-hundred-square-mile, densely forested, steeply mountainous wilderness with no maintained roads or permanent residents.

The pilot had described the rocky coastline and long fjords, the thickly treed cliffs. The site was so remote, the coastline so rugged, you could only reach it by boat, and then on foot. Jeff had pulled out his iPad loaded with electronic sailing charts and pinned the part of the island where the pilot thought it might be. But it was an enormous island and a tiny pin. The territory might as well have been a mark on a child's hand-drawn map.

～～～～～

Now we had a boat, we had time, and the site where the longhouse supposedly stood would be en route to Princess Royal and Gribbell Islands, the islands that were home to the legendary white spirit bear.

"What do you think about trying to find that ancient long-house as well?" Jeff mused as we headed up Hunter Channel the next afternoon.

My heart froze. I'd seen enough of the Great Bear Rainforest these past days to know how dense, how inaccessible it was. How you could be twenty paces from shore and become totally disoriented. There are no straight lines in a forest. My husband might as well have been asking: *Hey, want to see if we can find a place where we can anchor in an exposed channel in the middle of nowhere, then bushwhack around and see if we can see anything?*

I pictured us on a pointless, hopeless quest, hacking through the forest primeval, eyes peeled for some rotting cedar beams in an endless sea of pines and hemlocks. I could already see us stumbling, tripping over an ankle-twisting tangle of roots and branches, blocked by moss-covered walls of fallen trees, sinking into spongy forest floor carpeted in centuries of pine needles and mulching rot. What about bears?! What if we got lost?! What about trespassing? What if we did manage to find the longhouse but realized we were not only trespassing but also cursed because it was a culturally sensitive site? Or what if—and this was much more likely—we not only couldn't find anything close to the long-lost longhouse but couldn't find our way back to the boat?!

But in the spirit of adventure, and since the ancient longhouse would be Jeff's thing much as the spirit bear had been mine, I said, "Sure, why not?"

SHEARWATER

~~~~~~~~~

We were headed to Shearwater Marina, the last jumping off point before miles and miles of mostly uninhabited Great Bear Rainforest. Shearwater was said to have good moorage, a restaurant, laundromat, fuel dock, small grocery, and maybe even a pay phone—both an artifact and minor miracle! Shearwater did not have fresh water for public use, though, so we stopped en route at Bella Bella, a small First Nations community situated on the east side of Campbell Island, overlooking Lama Passage. We nudged *Heron* into a snug spot along Bella Bella's ramshackle wooden dock, found a hose with good fresh water, and ran the hose down to the boat. While Jeff took a shift topping off our water, I walked up the dock to explore the town.

Bella Bella is home to the Heiltsuk First Nation, which traditionally occupied thirteen thousand square miles of land and sea. But like many small communities along this remote coast, Bella Bella (with a population of about fifteen hundred today), has had a precarious existence since the closing of the region's canneries and collapse of the salmon fishery. Heavy industry like logging and mining no longer seems profitable or sustainable. Consequently, unemployment is high, the economy is fragile, attendant social problems are ongoing, and you feel all that. Walking the muddy stray-dog-filled streets toward the band store (which serves as the tribal community's only grocery store, liquor store, and post office), I thought Bella Bella felt like one of the bleakest places I'd ever been. At the base of the wooden band store building, however, there was a door overhung by a small sign: Koeye Cafe.

My heart leaped! A café? *Here?*

I opened the door and stepped into a small, inviting room. There were shelves filled with used books; random threadbare rugs, two worn leather armchairs nestled between wooden side tables set with reading lamps; a display case stacked with baskets of glass trading beads and artifacts; a counter where you could buy espresso. It was so unexpected, this oasis of warmth. I ordered a latte, my hands practically shaking with the thrill of it, then sipped my illicit coffee while scanning the spines of the lightly used books lining the walls: botany, birds, insects, natural history, anthropology, history of the Northwest coast, an entire shelf of ethnobotany, Canadian contemporary fiction, literary nonfiction.

It was a wonderful collection. Thrillingly so . . .

Here—in Bella Bella, where the muddy streets and ramshackle buildings and yards overflowing with debris revealed a hardscrabble existence.

"Excuse me, are these books . . . for sale?" I asked the young dark-haired woman behind the counter.

"No, I'm sorry. It's a reading library," she replied.

A reading library, I thought. *Even better.*

Another woman, a young girl really, wearing a chunky orange-and-pink sweater, was seated at a nearby computer; she was picking up books from boxes piled on the floor and inputting data. "What's a narrative?" she asked the dark-haired woman.

What is this place? I thought, intrigued, but didn't want to interrupt their work.

Bella Bella, I learned soon after, is the largest of twenty-three reserves set aside in 1913 for the Heiltsuk. Now the village is home to an amalgamation of tribes that originally occupied large winter and spring villages spread throughout their traditional territory. Canada's First Nations people have had centuries of injustices inflicted on them—dispossession of native lands and forced relocation onto desolate plots called reserves, the systematic relocation to residential schools where young children suffered decades of abuse, the destruction of traditional language, culture, and ways of living—just as America's Native Americans have. As I would soon learn, the Heiltsuk were facing another injustice as grave as all the others combined.

Hanging above the library's tasteful framed prints of northern BC's whales and schooners and rugged islands were large hand-lettered posters declaring: Solidarity of Nations, NO to Tankers, NO to ENBRIDGE! and Don't Waste 10,000 Years!

STAND UP FOR THE COAST: FIGHT ENBRIDGE! proclaimed a banner strung across one corner.

"What's *Enbridge?*" I asked the young woman behind the counter, who turned out to be Jess Housty, a twenty-five-year-old force of nature who would soon be elected to the Heiltsuk Tribal Council as its youngest member. An accomplished poet who had created Bella Bella's first and only library while she was still a teenager, Housty explained that Enbridge was one of Canada's largest exporters of western Canadian oil and that there had once been a plan to ram through one of the most contentious new pieces of fossil fuel infrastructure in North America: the proposed Northern Gateway Pipeline.

Bella Bella did not sit directly on the planned oil pipeline's route (that was 125 miles farther north), but its Pacific Ocean waters lay in the treacherous path the oil tankers would have taken en route to loading up with diluted tar sands oil. Housty, with her library as command central, had helped galvanize the local community's engagement before a review panel created by the Canadian government.

The plan to ship crude oil and bitumen through the Great Bear Sea along the northern coast of British Columbia was insane, but it took people from all walks of life working together in resistance for the Canadian government to finally introduce legislation in 2017 formally banning oil tankers from the Great Bear Sea. The ban was the direct result of thousands of people speaking up, a movement led by coastal First Nations like the Heiltsuk, which were forced to put enormous time and energy into justifying why the project could never go ahead. Individuals like Jess Housty had led the fight—and won that battle. But I had a sinking feeling there would be more.

"How was town?" Jeff asked twenty minutes later when I marched back to the fuel dock.

"There's a wonderful library and a café—can you believe it?" I asked, handing my cup over as proof. "Do you want a latte? It's a rare chance . . ."

"Nah, this place is rough—let's get out of here."

It *was* rough, not just the town but the dock, with sport fishermen and a steel-hulled charter schooner both jockeying for space at two splintery finger piers, and the reek of rot and fish guts, fuel and slime. Unlike marinas down south where there always seemed to be someone offering to catch a line as we kissed *Mighty Heron* up to the dock, here it was every boat for itself. We were expecting this and, having come this far, were ready for it. Still, as a boatload of fishermen watched, I felt self-conscious as I untied our bow line, tossed it over the rails, raced back along the dock to untie our stern, heaved it aboard, then hustled back to midships and casually, I hoped, pulled myself aboard.

Rough as Bella Bella was, there was so much more going on beneath the surface.

Buzzed on caffeine, energized by just being in a roomful of books, I felt my spirits lifting like the weathered gulls blasting off the docks and careening past our furled sails. Bella Bella was our first foray into a Canadian First Nations village, and something about it had not only gotten under my skin but also touched me.

<hr>

As we continued up the channel to Shearwater Marina, I couldn't stop thinking about Jess Housty's reading library. There was something powerful there in this unlikely corner of the wilderness, and in the physical fact of that collection of books and regional histories and ideas celebrating such a remote part of the world—and also in the presence of the two young women working together. I was at home there. I didn't know why and I didn't ask. But I think it had something to do with the realization that even in a place as isolated as Bella Bella, there were people whose innate spirit, energy, and belief make an incalculable difference—one book at a time.

Even so, the fact that pipelines like Enbridge's were *still* threatening the planet—and that a recently proposed liquid natural gas project involving supertankers was looming on the Great Bear Sea's horizon, even after plans for the Northern Gateway Pipeline were dashed—horrified me.

But the tiny library gave me a kind of hope.

<hr>

A few days later we were tied up at Shearwater Marina, listening to Coast Guard Radio Canada's continuous weather forecast: "Frontal system located over Haida Gwai . . . Visibility less than one mile. Gale warning in effect, wind southwest fifteen to twenty-five, increasing to twenty to thirty, then twenty-five to thirty-five this afternoon . . . Rain ending Wednesday morning."

We'd learned a lot, hanging around the Shearwater docks while waiting for the weather to clear. We'd met the green steel-hulled

Achiever's Captain Brian, whom we instantly recognized from the National Geographic film on the Great Bear Rainforest; he was doing laundry in the marina's communal laundry room.

"Hey, it's Captain Brian!" Jeff had said heartily by way of introduction, and I swear Captain Brian blushed from head to toe, all six-foot-four of him.

Then the three of us had stood around amiably folding T-shirts and boxer shorts on a massive twenty-foot-long table carved from a single cedar plank. The table was a thing of beauty, polished to a honeyed luster. I tried to hold Captain Brian's gaze casually, like the no-bullshit-don't-give-a-damn kind of chief mate I aspired to be, while folding my underthings. We talked about the film crews and biologists he'd had aboard his sloop, and the surfers he'd ferry to the outer coast of the Great Bear Rainforest in the fall to shoot a documentary.

The international film crews and surfers, it turned out, were all coming to draw attention to this remote corner of the world, to raise international awareness for its fragility.

~~~~~~~~~

We'd also tracked down Marven Robinson, one of the top spirit bear guides in BC, who lived in Hartley Bay, home of the Gitga'at First Nations community. With the realization that finding a spirit bear would be even less likely than finding Jeff's ancient longhouse in this impenetrable forest, I'd logged on to the intermittent Wi-Fi at Shearwater and looked up wildlife guides I'd read about in the *National Geographic* spirit bear article. Only one name kept popping up: Marven Robinson. I kept sleuthing and tracked down his phone number. Then, bolstered by a glass of wine, I called him from the pay phone inside the restaurant bar at the Shearwater Marina.

He picked up on the second ring. "Hey, Marven Robinson," he said.

I couldn't believe it. He'd actually answered; I had Marven Robinson on the line . . . ! I was nearly speechless with astonishment.

"Marven, uh . . . !" I said, stammering. "I'm headed your way on a sailboat. My husband and I are very interested in spirit bears. We've come all this way from Seattle, with the goal of trying to see one. I was wondering if we could possibly, um, hire you to guide us?"

"Sure," he said, easily. "They're not easy to see, and there's no guarantee. There's a small window of time when the bears are feeding, but you're in luck—this is a really good time of year for them. There's a white bear who was feeding just last week along a river inlet on Princess Royal Island. Where did you say you are now?"

And then we calculated the number of days and nights it would take us to make it all the way to Hartley Bay.

Marven wasn't actually *in* Hartley Bay. He was in Calgary buying a new truck. But, *miraculously*, he'd be back in Hartley Bay by the time we got there.

"Just call me when you get here," he said.

"Really? That would be fantastic!" I exclaimed, hardly able to believe our luck, that I'd just called from a pay phone and tracked down one of Canada's top wildlife guides: Marven Robinson, on his cell.

Thank you, thank you, I breathed to whatever gods must be crazy, clearly listening out there in the water, mountains, rain, and endless trees. And then I swaggered back to our table in the Shearwater pub and told Jeff he'd never believe what had just happened: I'd found us a Spirit Bear Guide.

And not just any bear guide: if we could make it all the way to Hartley Bay, we'd meet Marven Robinson himself.

~~~~~~~~

Shearwater turned out to be a sort of hub for everyone who cruised these cold rain-swept waters, its marine shop the only place within hundreds of miles for haul-outs, parts, and serious repairs; its docks and pub a wealth of local knowledge. There was a welcome-aboard, join-our-table sort of joie de vivre: if you'd gotten yourself this far, you were part of the club.

One afternoon there was a rap on *Heron's* hull. I looked out the window—and saw ankles on the dock. Who could it be? I poked my head out the hatch, and there stood a man who introduced himself as Richard Ying, smiling. "Join us for cocktails?" he asked.

And that was how Jeff and I found ourselves, an hour later, gathered around the galley table on Richard and his wife Jill's exquisite 1930s wooden motor yacht with our friend Pat Freeny and local marine biologists Ken and Edith Cripps, having a discussion about the secret of life. Richard was quick-witted and kind, a Chinese American who had retired early in his fifties after founding a software company and now exuded the easy confidence of a man who had found the time and space in which to even consider topics such as the secret of life. Jill, his wife, was petite and as exotic as a rare bird in these parts: pale white skin, dark brown hair piled beneath a wide-brimmed sun hat (even indoors at night), dramatic penciled-in eyebrows and wine-red lips. Pat was wiry, polite and patient, with a stealth wisdom playing in his eyes and an air of competent self-containment; he was an audiologist, a PhD and physician who taught at the University of Washington in Seattle, and for the past six summers he had been exploring the northern BC coast aboard his forty-eight-foot custom-designed sailboat, *Nirvana*. Hipster Ken was bearded and barrel-chested, with wire-rimmed glasses, quick eyes, and a black wool cap; he was a marine biologist who had sailed extensively. His wife, Edith, was blonde and outdoorsy; she exuded the complete confidence of a woman who had sailed herself around the world and now had two young daughters aboard her boat for summer cruising.

"I once asked the chairman of Wells Fargo what *he* thought the secret of life was," Richard said with a sly wink. "And you know what he said?"

We all waited, expectant.

"Yogurt."

"*Yogurt?*" Ken barked. Everyone chuckled.

Jill rolled her eyes; she'd evidently heard this one before.

"I think," Pat Freeny chimed in, "it's like that James Taylor song—'The secret of life is enjoying the passage of time.'"

We all nodded conspiratorially, sipped our whiskey or wine.

It was great to see Pat. He was, in fact, one of the first people we'd ever heard mention the Great Bear Rainforest. He was the person I'd originally met at the dinner who'd been spending his summers hosting *National Geographic* photographers aboard his boat. He'd had the good fortune to accompany Paul Nicklen, the photographer who had taken the astonishing spirit bear photos we'd seen, on those shoots, day after day. Now he was helping Paul photograph a new story about the last of the rare, wild coastal wolves. We told Pat about the mysterious wolf we'd encountered, and how unafraid she'd been.

"That's because the BC coast is one of the last places on the planet where wolves live relatively undisturbed by humans," Pat said.

Everyone nodded again, then drifted back to the topic of Time. Sailors, more than any other group of people I've met, have a different relationship with Time, understand how sailing is so much about settling into, getting comfortable with, accepting that different relationship with Time. And with Silence.

"When we were down off the coast of Ushuaia, and later exploring Antarctica? There were days when Ken and I realized we barely knew what month it was," Edith said wistfully.

I didn't say anything. Just sat listening, thinking how much I liked all these people—all but one of whom we'd only just met, but who were kindred spirits—and also how inexperienced I suddenly felt by comparison. One of the things I was beginning to understand about boating, and life in general, was that no matter how far you think you've traveled and how much you think you've seen—there are always those who have gone farther, who have lived more and seen more. I was *in awe* that Ken and Edith had sailed themselves to Antarctica. And yet I also got the sense that Edith's life now, this chapter, raising two young daughters on an island off the BC coast, was also an adventure, just in a different way.

Maybe that *is the secret of life*, I thought. Fully inhabiting it, *being in it*, embracing each chapter; recognizing that life, for most of us, isn't smooth sailing during which we can alter our course whenever we choose, but instead full of uncertainty, and more of a long slog through bumpy seas, with waves tossed at us and tossing us around. Sometimes, the waves are so high and come so fast it's hard, really hard, to just stay afloat.

And at the same time, I knew, have always known, that you can't discover new oceans unless you learn to live with that uncertainty and dare leave the shore. It was strange and energizing, meeting these new people in the middle of nowhere. Yet I already ached for the long, dreamy afternoons and evenings afloat, for the solitude.

Ken picked up a pen, drew a few lines on a napkin, and slid the napkin across the table toward us. It was the harbor at Hartley Bay, where we hoped to meet Marven Robinson in a week. He'd drawn the floatplane dock, the ferry dock, and the community dock. "Here's Hartley Bay," he said. "It's a small harbor, shallows up quick."

Jeff and I stared at the napkin.

"You don't want to block the floatplane dock, just head in and raft up to one of the fishing boats." He pointed with the tip of the pen, then drew a few *X*'s along the dock. "Marven's dad's purse seiner hasn't been out in years, just tie up to that."

"He won't mind?"

"Everybody does it up there—it's no problem."

"Hartley Bay's *great*," Jill and Pat chimed in.

"Oh, and look up Wally Bolton," Ken added, printing WALLY BOLTON on the napkin in neat block letters.

"Yeah, who's he?" Jeff asked.

"Just look him up," Ken answered, sliding the napkin toward us like a treasure map. "You won't be sorry."

KLEMTU

~~~~~~

Headed north again on our way to circumnavigate Princess Royal Island—and hopefully see a spirit bear—we were riding high. The wind and rain and angry gray storm clouds that had held us captive the past few days had decamped south, leaving a lightening sky in their wake. We were at the point of the journey where we didn't know what day it was, and more importantly, it didn't matter. It was late August, a glorious time to be northbound this late in the season when the few other cruising boats we encountered were all pointed south.

We'd been able to put calls through to the boys from the pay phone at Shearwater, and just hearing their voices reassured us all was well. Making our way up Seaforth Channel, it was as if the universe had freed up space—there was room to contemplate something larger. Just then, a violent splash. Jeff and I both looked up hurriedly. Humpbacks again! One was breaching in the distance, its white spray highlighted against dark mountains. And to starboard there were more whales lazily feeding.

"They're in slow mo," Jeff said, riveted. We watched them, a pair of humpbacks this time, their backs arching slowly through the water followed by the sensuous *flash . . . splash, flash . . . splash* of two forked tails. We were so close we could smell them. A big cloud of rank whale breath hung in the air; a fishy, planktonic smell like mounds of krill gone bad. But the thing that was most captivating was the *sound* of humpback breath. We could hear it—big breathy exhales, slow and drawn out; blowing sharply, then exhaling slowly. We listened, mesmerized, waiting for the whales' wet-black humps to resurface, then slide back down.

Wow! I felt like I had eyes all over my head. Like the two of us were twelve years old, so excited. I raced up to the foredeck with the good camera.

"I wouldn't get that close if I were you!" Jeff hollered.

But I couldn't help myself. I wrapped myself around the forestay and waited for the whales to resurface. It was riveting. *How could something so gargantuan be so gentle?*

Although as the whales came up and arched their backs, breathed in, blew out, went under and disappeared again, I began to feel older—not twelve, not fifty, but more like eighty—and overcome with sadness. It wasn't resignation; it was just plain old sadness, a mother's knowing-but-not-wanting-to-know kind of sorrow. I understood intuitively that just as whales can be both powerful and gentle, humans can be both greedy and shortsighted. We were so flawed, so painfully stupid sometimes, so, well, *human.* It was, I knew, our nature, and the pipeline and supertanker battles would rage on. If not here, nearby—risking calamitous oil spills. How ironic, given that more than half the oxygen in each breath we take comes from the plants and algae in the sea.

The cruising guides had very little information on Klemtu, the Kitasoo native village we reached late that afternoon after rounding Ivory Island and heading up Milbanke Sound, six- to ten-foot swells rolling in off the Pacific. There wasn't room to put up the mainsail with all the rocks, and even after securing things belowdecks, there was much crashing and bashing—books strewn about, the banquette drawer flinging itself in and out. I braced myself, went down to secure things, didn't stay down long. But *Heron* took it in stride, riding the swells, relishing them even.

As I said, however, our cruising guides had very little information on Klemtu. We'd found only a short paragraph, with basic info on the fuel dock, pay phone, Kitasoo band store—nothing about the community itself. Perhaps that was because cruising guides cater to, well, *cruisers*, and Klemtu has only one small dock with very little room to tie up, and no public marina. Prior to meeting Ken and Edith in Shearwater, we had heard from a sailing friend that Klemtu was a pit, basically "a garbage dump with a town."

But Ken, who worked with the coast's native villages, had insisted it was "great," that we should simply tie up at the fuel dock or raft to one of the fishing trawlers. Still, we were intimidated approaching the harbor. It was small, surrounded by mountains that shouldered up behind a ring of modest houses whose windows all gazed out at the water like pairs of unblinking eyes.

As we made our way up the narrow channel, we took turns squinting at Klemtu through the binoculars.

"That must be the dock," I said.

"Yep," Jeff replied.

"Do you think we can fit in on the port side? Do a starboard tie?"

"Just barely."

"Okay, give me a sec to ready the lines . . ."

We entered Klemtu's bay and floated in neutral, the only sail-boat, all fifty-four feet of us as obvious as an ostrich in a puddle, *Heron*'s seventy-five-foot mast and red-white-and-blue flag flying off the stern signaling: *Hi, everyone, the Americans are here!*

I secured the fenders, readied the bow and stern lines, then tied a short line around a midship cleat. (I'd figured out by then how to use leverage to my advantage, jumping off and lashing *Heron* to each dock with a quick side tie that stopped her forward motion.) Jeff maneuvered us slowly toward the splintered wooden dock while I leaned against the side of the cabin, line in hand and ready to leap. Since it was everyone for themselves up here, I was surprised when two young men in T-shirts, sneakers, and jeans stepped off a big black-hulled purse seiner with a sweeping bow that was tied to the other side of the dock, and offered to catch our lines.

"Thanks!" I said gratefully. "That was nice of you guys." It turned out they both worked on the purse seiner, the *Pacific Marl*, a fishing boat out of Vancouver. One of them looked to be in his twenties, the other no more than a boy, fourteen or fifteen. Both had thick dark hair and shy smiles. A slope-shouldered, balding man in a wool plaid shirt climbed down from the back of the purse seiner and strolled over to introduce himself.

"Hi, I'm Bob Black," he said. "This is my wife, Kathy." He motioned up at a friendly-looking woman in a green sweatshirt who was waving down from the fishing boat. The *Pacific Marl*, we learned, was one of the last remaining wooden-hulled fishing boats on the coast. Captain Black and Kathy were heading home to Vancouver after a summer of salmon fishing out of Prince Rupert. Bob said it had been Kathy's idea for the boys, their crew, to come over and help with our lines.

I smiled up at her and waved while salmon jumped around us in the harbor. We'd seen fish jumping up here, but these fish were fanatics—shooting clear out of the water, flinging their muscular fish selves with abandon around the bay.

"Heck, I've never seen anything like those fish jumping," Jeff said. "Are they feeding?"

Bob said Klemtu is one of the places where fresh water mingles with Pacific current; nirvana evidently, if you're a fish making a marathon swim.

"They're jumping because they're happy—happy they've made it home," the older of the two young crewmen said matter-of-factly.

~~~~~~~~

Klemtu turned out to be a small, remote village—the only one on Swindle Island and home to about 420 people. The residents consist of two indigenous cultural linguistic groups: the Kitasoo, from the outer coast, and the Xai'xais, from the inner coast. The village encircles the harbor, and a wide walking path runs from one end of the harbor's bay to the other, like a communal front porch for the whole town.

Jeff and I decided to take a walk along the path. A single paved road ran alongside it, and the majority of Klemtu's houses sat off this road, facing the bay. The water was still full of crazy jumping salmon, and soon a Great Pyrenees as big as a bear appeared out of nowhere and began following us. Then we noticed the ravens: enormous glossy birds with curved black beaks sat everywhere—on trees, atop phone wires, along the boardwalk railing. They didn't fly off as we passed them but, oddly, kept on sitting right where they were, cackling, like brazen old men and women on a park bench, checking us out.

At first we felt somewhat intimidated and self-conscious. We couldn't be more conspicuous, just off the boat, but everyone we passed (including kids with fishing poles, Kitasoo and Xai'xais moms pushing strollers, even surly teens) said "Hi." And everyone who drove by waved. Everyone was so friendly it was almost creepy. We continued along in this manner, waving back as we passed yards scattered with plastic toys, bikes, and broken-down fishing boats.

As we rounded the south end of the cove, a lanky, long-limbed man wearing jeans and a dark blue fleece stepped out of a wooden house as if he was going somewhere at the end of the day, "Hello, enjoying the beauty?" he said.

"Uh, yes," we both said, startled. "Yes! Yes we are."

Then, instead of hurrying off down the boardwalk like an American would have, the man just stood there with us, laptop bag slung over his shoulder, gazing out at the bay.

"Just visiting Klemtu?" he asked.

We nodded.

"You're on the sailboat, then?" he went on, glancing out at *Heron*.

She was hard to miss, and it dawned on me, chagrined, that *all* Klemtu knew we were here. We were the people on the sailboat. We laughed, asked if he lived in Klemtu.

"No," he said, going on to explain that he worked with the community as a therapist once a month.

"Really? What kind of therapist?" I asked.

"Neurolinguistic. I do Time Line Therapy," he said. Then Richard Hunt introduced himself and went on to explain about neurolinguistic Time Line Therapy, which has to do with memory and how it's formed—how when an experience happens, our subconscious assigns a texture or a mood to it: happy, sad, anxious . . .

An incredible calmness emanated from Richard Hunt. He appeared to be going somewhere but instead stood rooted to the ground, as if he had all the time in the world. We'd only just met, but he seemed so fully present; there was a solidness to him that put you immediately at ease. It was one of those encounters that instantly forms your impression of a place. And for me, my impression of Klemtu was the aspect of Richard Hunt: friendly but mysterious; spiritual, deep, fully inhabiting the place.

Then he explained in the most astonishing way how our earliest memories shape us.

And how our reactions to those earliest memories, according to indigenous beliefs, are based on our earlier spirits.

The spirits of our ancestors.

"Wow," Jeff and I both said. It was a lot to take in.

The three of us stood there in the road, looking out at the bay some more. Richard told us he lived in Alert Bay, near Port McNeill. He wondered whether we'd stopped there.

"*No*, but I wanted to!" I burst out, glaring at Jeff. Alert Bay was famed for its indigenous cultural center, the largest collection of First Nations masks and artifacts in all Canada. But we hadn't stopped. That day had been a long one and I couldn't talk Jeff into it.

Richard Hunt smiled and said that he'd picked up from our conversation that Jeff probably felt "some tension" about *not* stopping at Alert Bay. That Alert Bay now resonated for us with a significance created by our shared memory of my wanting to stop and Jeff's not wanting to stop, and our not stopping.

We had to laugh. "Wow," I said again, conspiratorially.

"Well, that pretty much nails it," Jeff said.

We stood watching the delirious fish continue to jump in circles, and Richard Hunt, apropos of nothing, launched further into the metaphysical, into a conversation you'd never have in the States with someone you'd met only minutes before but that made perfect sense here: "In our culture, we believe that spirit never dies," he explained. "That when you die your spirit is released to continue its journey into the next life . . . It's a form of reincarnation, if you will. So you may contain many earlier spirits."

~~~~~~~

One thing I've come to learn as a traveler is that if your journey is long enough someplace, it changes you a little while you are there. It's a subtle shift that, given enough time and space, might even surface in your dreams. Usually, it creeps up on you so gradually you're not even aware of the moment you've crossed over. But as Jeff and I walked back to the boat, I felt not only that *I* was different somehow but that *we* were different somehow. We could have gone on for a long time, standing there and talking with Richard Hunt about Time and Memory and Spirits. But instead, when the conversation came to its natural end, we bid Richard Hunt goodbye and ambled back to the boat, both of us lost in thought.

Here in this wild landscape hurled through with fish and birds, everything felt so blown open by wind, and rain, and sky. I felt blown open, and I could tell Jeff felt something like that too. I was thinking about Native American culture and First Nations culture and also people I'd encountered on assignment in the Himalayas, and Africa, and the Amazon; their "religions" wildly different, but all with a profound spiritual sense.

And although we'd only just arrived, I felt the same thing in the village of Klemtu: Spirit.

It's remarkable by comparison how divorced our sped-up Western culture is from the spiritual. We're big on religion, of course, but small on spirit—a casualty of our collapsed sense of time. We worship speed, but on an island in the middle of a rain-drenched forest on the edge of the sea—an island that had taken hours and days and weeks to reach—we'd met someone who had mastered the art of slow. Maybe part of our quest to glimpse the spirit bear, I realized, wasn't really about the bear itself but about the journey.

Back on the boat we did chores and grilled up dinner. I was rereading *The Snow Leopard*, Peter Matthiesen's classic account of his 1973 trek to Nepal in search of the rare and elusive snow leopard, and came across a particular Rilke quote I've encountered from time to time: "That is at bottom the only courage that is demanded of us: to have courage for the most strange, the most singular and the most inexplicable that we may encounter. That mankind has in this sense been cowardly has done life endless harm; the experiences that are called 'visions,' the whole so-called 'spirit-world,' death, all those things that are so closely akin to us, have by daily parrying been so crowded out of life that the senses with which we could have grasped them are atrophied. To say nothing of God."

It seemed so strange, almost uncanny, that we'd walked into that moment with Richard Hunt, had that conversation on the street in Klemtu. I wished those moments would happen more often: experiences when you are lifted outside your life, separated from ego, freed from particularity, where there is no time or space. But, I think, when one does happen, the singularity of the moment is proof that you're where you're meant to be.

〜〜〜〜〜

What did it mean? Jeff and I had sailed and fought our way through currents, and motored through driving rainstorms, and flown across straits with all the sails raised, and soared together, and sank together, and struggled, and awoke in the mornings and faced each other and done it all over again, for years, really, days of grinding tedium and days of bright triumph, days of sorrow and sadness, others made up of quiet small moments that meant everything but I couldn't see past them. And now the boys, with both of them leaving, had turned our lives upside down; their presence had become, after a rocky start, the wind in our sails; their departure blowing away our moorings as effortlessly as a wind shakes leaves from a tree, scattering everything we thought we knew, leaving an emptiness unlike any I'd ever known, waiting to be filled.

With what? I wondered. I didn't know.

I didn't know what next, what there could possibly be that would invest our lives with as much meaning. All I knew was that we were mysteriously here: a place where the past felt as distant as the boat's long-dispersed wake, the future only as pressing as tomorrow, and there was a healing immediacy to this moment. We were both standing together outside ourselves; no one knew us or cared what we did, what successes we'd had, what failures. What we'd *achieved* with the instincts of two salmon fighting our way upstream mattered not one wit. We were vulnerable, stripped of all pretense and defense.

We were facing a question: What now?

But the answer seemed less urgent once we'd allowed ourselves to ask.

~~~~~~~~~~

We sat around the small table in the main cabin, curtains drawn, eating a late dinner of grilled chicken. A knock came at the hull. Jeff turtled his head out, and there stood one of the two deckhands off *Pacific Marl*. Did we want to walk over and see the longhouse with them, he wanted to know? His cousin was the caretaker and had a key. Of course we did. Klemtu longhouse is revered as one of the most beautiful re-created longhouses—a type of long, proportionally narrow, single-room building representing the earliest form of permanent structure in many cultures—on the entire Pacific Northwest Coast. We'd been admiring the cedar facade with its striking red-and-black eagle, raven, wolf, and rare double-finned blackfish (orca) crests overlooking the harbor all afternoon. We leaped up from the table, left our plates, laced up our shoes.

It was a warm late-summer night, still light at a quarter to nine. All Klemtu seemed to be outside after dinner—either pushing a stroller slowly along the cedar-planked boardwalk, or leaning over its rail to drop a line in the cove.

Near the longhouse a round-faced beefy man in a worn T-shirt stopped to introduce himself. "Joe Robinson," he said, inquiring where we were from.

"Seattle," we said.

"You're on the sailboat?"

We nodded.

"When I first stepped inside the new big house and saw it, I cried," he offered, unbidden, his eyes the color of stones. "I thought: *This is Klemtu?* I couldn't believe it."

Then he turned quickly and entered a ground-floor unit in a yellow prefab structure, its yard strewn with plastic toys, and shut the door.

Another Robinson, Gary Robinson (our deckhand friend's cousin), met us at the longhouse, unlocked the door, and let us inside. I'd had no clue why the first Robinson, Joe, would have cried when he first stepped inside the big house, but standing there with Jeff, I got it. Everything smelled of rich, fragrant cedar, heightened by the pleasant, pungent scent of ash and cinders. Two massive cedar logs, each about four feet in diameter, ran the length of the longhouse. They supported a soaring cedar roof; the scale dwarfed us, but the space felt intimate too. It had a honeyed glow. Soft sand covered the floor, and seven rows of gleaming cedar bleachers climbed cedar walls. We sat gingerly in the bleacher seating, spoke softly. At either end of the house stood winged totems, mythical creatures carved from larger-than-life cedar logs. Representing the four family clans—eagle, raven, wolf, orca—they loomed toward a small opening in the cedar ceiling that let in a sliver of light.

It was a magnificent structure, completed in 2002 in the style of a traditional west coast big house. Until then Klemtu (indeed, most of the remaining First Nations communities) had been without any sort of traditional gathering places. But this building, in homage to the traditional big houses of the Tsimshian First Nations, created a space where for the first time in decades they could begin reconnecting with their past, drawing from their oral culture. Since then they had been trying to bring some of the ancient language, stories, music, and myths back to life.

We sat rapt while Gary, understated, bristly haired, wearing blue jeans and a blue windbreaker, talked of his family and his father, ancestors and potlatches, the traditions of Klemtu. Then Gary led us to the small "museum" shed next to the longhouse, where artifacts donated to the Kitasoo nation in honor of the new longhouse were being temporarily stored. The treasures included exquisite old coppers used in ceremonial potlatches (elaborate gift-giving feasts practiced by indigenous peoples of the Pacific Northwest Coast, among whom it was the primary economic system); button blankets; carved masks, including an ornate "bear" mask with a hinged jaw, flat copper nose, and copper eyes.

~~~~~~~~~

When I got into bed later and closed my eyes, there was not only the bear mask sprung to life as a live bear crossing a stream but also whales like birds leaping through the sky. It had been years, sadly, since I'd even remembered my dreams. I'd feared that maybe with all the distracted busyness of working life and mom life and wife life, I'd stopped dreaming altogether. But when I awoke the next morning before dawn at a thump on the stern and a crazy fish hitting *Heron* in midair, I realized I had, in fact, been dreaming . . .

It was a dream of a bear fording a stream, of sails filled with wind, and of whales like birds floating through sky.

The sky was an ocean, the stars were fish, the sails white wings.

In the midst of it all there floated a shimmery white whale. And I understood it was something I hadn't encountered since I was a small child who dreamed I could, and therefore believed I could, fly—it was my soul, my innermost spirit—me.

MEYERS NARROWS

~~~~~~~~

The barometric pressure had dropped and the wind, colder now, howled. We awoke to epic rain: sheets of water lashing the cabin, steamed-up windows, and a persistent *drip, drip, drip*: leaks. The cabin was freezing. It felt about forty-five degrees. I scuttled into the galley and swapped out the dish towel we'd been using to soak up rainwater that had begun seeping in through a seam in the starboard window. Jeff had sealed and resealed and sealed that edge again. But the seal refused to hold. And now when it rained, a thin slick of water coursed down the galley to the right of the gimbaled stove, puddling in a fist-sized pond on the cherry-wood shelf.

It had rained hard all night. So hard that for the first time *Heron* had sprung several leaks: there was not only water puddling on the shelf and behind the settee but also water dripping in through the snack cupboard, water slipping through one of the deck's stainless dorade boxes and splashing down, disconcertingly, a few inches from my head in the stern berth, where I slept. I wrung out the wet dish towel, hung it from a ceiling rail to dry, and spread out more towels to catch the new leaks. The situation was disheartening. Jeff revved up the generator and got the floor heaters going, along with a strong pot of coffee.

It would have been tempting to stay hunkered down in Klemtu, waiting out the weather. But once we dialed in the Garmin's electronic weather map, it showed the storm moving east. We were headed northwest—so when the rain stopped momentarily around eight that morning, we untied our lines and, beneath dark gray skies, slipped out of friendly Klemtu.

"Everywhere I look I see a fish jump," Jeff said wistfully, and it was crazy-true. With salmon leaping in determined circles, their rings widening around us in the fresh cold water, we headed north again.

~~~~~~~

The Inside Passage north of Klemtu is all humps of forest and rock, dark-treed islands schooled like furry whales in narrow channels. Ominous deadheads (submerged tree trunks and even treetops) and stray logs rode the outgoing tide, their tangle of roots and limbs lurking beneath the surface. Whole islands of kelp floated and swirled in the mist. The wind was blowing ten knots from the southeast, the barometer read 29.9 and falling, the rain started up again. There was no room in this watery maze to put up the mainsail, so we Velcroed our foul-weather gear tight and motored on past Swindle Island. It was work enough, just guiding *Heron* through all the logs and tangles; each log a potential spear lying in wait to puncture the hull, the kelp strands inches from strangling the propeller.

Up ahead were more swirling currents. Serious rapids. And Meyers Narrows—a dogleg channel that cut from the inside of Swindle Island to the outside. We'd have to time our passage, riding a flood tide to the channel's entrance, transiting the narrows on a high tide, then letting an ebb tide push us through. We'd known nothing of flood tides and ebb tides, currents and current tables, high tides and low in our other life. But in *Heron* life, even in its worst moments, we have absorbed and been absorbed by these things. Even puttering along in the rain, life felt thicker somehow, more immediate, the barriers between us and the world paper-thin.

We took turns: one at the helm peering from beneath the plastic rain shield through the binoculars, watching for swirling debris; the other standing scout on the bow. It was cold, but our foul-weather gear was snug. The hours were long. We settled into them and, in this way, passed the morning, mountains looming in the distance like gods.

~~~~~~~~~~

Because we moved so slowly on *Heron*, I felt the wide curve of the ocean beneath her hull and understood, if only instinctively, the vast healing immensity of the world. It was reassuring, reminding me of all that endures while so much else changes. I began to feel braver, bolder. I wanted to claim the sea—all of it: sky, cloud, light, wind, water—and have it claim us. The deck would be wet with spray, and suddenly we'd see a solitary humpback as big as a bus. The rain would be slipping and sliding down the shrouds, and I'd try to think about things that might be glad for this much rain, which wasn't always easy. *Moss*, I'd think. *Slugs. Trees. Fungi. Ferns* . . .

On days like this Jeff and I didn't talk much. It was a huge relief, having time and space to settle into separate solitudes. Jeff busy in his, fiddling with the single sideband radio, splicing a line, polishing a winch, fixing the long list of things on *Heron* that needed fixing, thinking while doing. Me more or less useless in that department, but expert at daydreaming . . .

I might think about the dual nature of marriage, the proximity, the intensity, of fury and love. Even on the calmest boat days, potential disaster lurked around every corner. Granted, Jeff and I had advanced leagues on the boat; we'd grown pretty smooth, the two of us, and were proud of it. But there were still inevitable screwups and flare-ups in such close quarters. The night I'd inadvertently spilled a whole glass of milk on the just refinished cherry-wood table and Jeff had barked: "You f*ck! You f*ck-up!" in front of the boys while milk pooled between the Scrabble tiles and dripped through the table hinges onto the teak floor, and we went to bed without speaking. The time we got into a screaming match over whether to put up the mainsail in Fitz Hugh Sound because Jeff was convinced the wind would die, but I flipped him the bird and put it up anyway—and then, relishing the wind, went on to raise the jib thinking *F*ck you, Skipper Jeff!* But I forgot to release the jib cleat, nearly ripping the whole side off the boat. The night we got into a fight about I couldn't even remember what later and were so fed up with each other we stormed off to opposite ends of the boat—there was no place else to go—and stayed there: one of us sleeping in the bow, the other in the stern.

I might think about the middle years of a sustained marriage: how they can be long and hard. What happens when you're long past the burning desire of your early days? Some of us crave new love, fall into the age-old game of shedding one relationship for another like caterpillars shed skins. Some of us crave stability. Others, and I'd put myself in this camp—with a husband, who was fearless and loyal enough to play along—crave adventure. Instead of collecting shoes, we lust after experiences. On days like this, even with sheets of rain in my face, I hoped our lives would be fuller, richer, by being out on the far edges of the earth. I wanted to look back in ten or twenty years and think *That was the trip of a lifetime!* in a grateful way, an astounded way. Mostly, I didn't want to wait and wait *for the right moment* only to realize that not only is it never the perfect time but that your window of time can pass.

We all have our own ways of making it through the world. But as *Heron* threaded her way through the channels and over the sea, I came to realize that people are together for reasons that are almost impossible to explain; it's hard to define why certain people are right for each other. I've always believed that opposites attract, that when you have two people with very different temperaments, they are often drawn to one another. The difficulties make you stronger—if you survive them. There's a lot to be said, I think, for warmth and steadfastness and the exhilarating sense that, even after decades, your marriage is still a work in progress.

~~~~~~~~~

By early afternoon we'd made it through Meyers Narrows: entering on a flood tide, leaving on an ebb tide. Making our way past thick forests of cedar and hemlock lining the passage, we veered slowly from starboard to port, mindful of the bottom; Meyers was a minefield studded with rocks. The water was deep enough, though, with a midday high tide, that we'd be fine if we paid attention. No sooner had we traversed the narrows, however, than the water opened up and the sky darkened, shading from gray to purple-black. By the time our ramen noodles were ready, we had to eat lunch beneath a dripping plastic bimini. We hadn't seen a single boat all day, not even a fishing boat or a kayaker, and as we ghosted our way north past ragged hemlock jungles beneath a purpling sky, the day felt dark and menacing.

We emerged at Laredo Channel, its wide mouth open to swells rolling off the Pacific, and were astonished to see the sky ahead begin to lighten. Dramatic patches of lilac and blue were opening and closing and then, out of nowhere, a sun as bright as a flame broke out to the west and burned through. We dared unzip our foul-weather gear a little, but not enough to jinx it—sailors are superstitious. The chance of blue sky, the mere possibility that better weather lay ahead, seemed unbelievable, miraculous really, given the way the day had begun.

As the green-fringed shoulders of Princess Royal Island hove into view, we faced a sudden decision: Should we try to find the ancient longhouse that Jeff had heard about? The site sounded extraordinary, but the prospect had seemed unthinkable an hour before; we'd put it out of mind entirely with the wind-lashed rain, even though we knew we were nearing the side of the island where Jeff had pinned the rough location. But Princess Royal is a massive place.

We pulled up our iPad's Garmin BlueChart and calculated we might just be able to make it across the mouth of the channel in about two hours. We'd explore the coastline, looking to see if there was anything like a break in the trees—a cove, a bay, an inlet—and if so, we'd also check for a remote chance of anchoring safely, then somehow scour the shore for a place where the longhouse might be before continuing on our way and anchoring for the night. It seemed ludicrous, like hunting for treasure with only the vaguest X marking the spot, but life doesn't offer up much unexpected in these days of GPS locators and trackers and mapping devices and even our own cell phones broadcasting our paths, inch by inch, like snails' trails.

We peered ahead at the impenetrable shore: nothing but trees and more trees and a thin band of rock where trees met sea. Even knowing where to look, chances were we'd never find the longhouse.

There were many things that could go wildly wrong. We could get lost. The boat could float away. We were way beyond cell range. What if we went ashore and ran into trouble? Then what?

My mind raced while we plowed on through the swells: Princess Royal is immense; how would we find a mostly disintegrated ruin in all those trees? At 869 square miles, the island is the fourth largest in British Columbia; it is located in an extremely remote area, accessible only by boat or air, utterly uninhabited.

"Aside from the Tsimshiam tribe," I'd read, which once kept a coastal village on the island but no longer live there, "almost no one has entered the inland rainforest of Princess Royal Island."

An air of mystery pervades the place. As the island grew closer, I could see its gleaming base, a fawn shimmer of rock dropping into a cold dark sea and flocks of seabirds wheeling by. There was no beach. Ancient spruce and lacy cedar, toes dug deep between rocks, towered up from the sea and clung there, not only impervious to storms blowing in but thriving; the spruce growing even and tall, the cedars' branches hung with beard lichen breathing in the Pacific's pure streaming air.

Of course, Princess Royal does have wildlife. It is perhaps best known as being one of only two islands (the other is Gribbell Island) that are home to the spirit bear. I took heart from this. We were in range of black bears, grizzly bears, wolves, and wolverines, and finally, after all this, the mythical white bear. Whether we'd see one or not, the fact that we'd made it all this way—*that we'd made this happen, on* Heron, *just the two of us here now*—filled my heart with a kind of wild, amazing disbelief.

LOOKING FOR A LONGHOUSE

Motoring along the massive curve of Princess Royal Island after crossing the channel, we peered at the trees, iPad in hand. I didn't have high hopes. But Jeff was on a mission.

"What do you think?" he said after a few hours, holding the iPad map alongside *Heron's* chart plotter.

I stared at the iPad.

Looked back at the chart plotter.

Stared at the iPad map again.

Peered ahead.

We were approaching a place where the coastline deviated from the norm. A narrow-waisted peninsula extended slightly into the sound like a thumb, interrupting the island's endless scrim of trees. Now that we were here, we could see that the spot Jeff had marked with the pilot's help sat on the inner curve of a small promontory. It was a place we would have ordinarily passed by, a place we would never have noticed. Most of all, it was a place we would never, in our wildest imaginations, have considered going ashore.

"Jesus, you think we can make it in there?" I asked doubtfully.

A rocky spit pummeled with threatening waves rolling in off the channel's open jaw to the Pacific rose just off the starboard bow. We'd have to round it, see what was on the other side . . .

"Let's at least try," Jeff said after a moment. "The tide's in our favor."

I didn't know what to say. As we rounded the tip of the point and pointed *Heron* toward shore, our chart plotter went blank: the water here was evidently completely uncharted. We'd have no way of knowing what was beneath us—how quickly the shallows shallowed up, or worse, where a hulking rock might lie in wait. Waves of spray burst over the jetty. But none of this would deter us. Dead ahead we could just make out, tucked inside the arm's inner crook, a long glimmering crescent of white-sand beach.

Now this was something. A beach this far north was miraculous by any measure. But this one, so hidden, felt like a mystery.

We both had a feeling we'd arrived someplace charged, somehow out of the ordinary.

"I think this might be it!" Jeff said.

"Do you really think we should go in?" I said.

I wanted to, but I didn't want to. Maybe this place, so hidden, was meant to remain unseen. And since it was uncharted, we had no way of knowing whether there would be two hundred feet of water—or two feet—beneath us. *Heron* needed six feet to clear. We hadn't seen another boat in a day.

We took in the cove: its inky-blue water, quarter-mile-long beach, white spray crashing on the rocks, backlit by sun. The sun seemed a good omen.

"We're here, aren't we?" Jeff said decisively. I knew what he was thinking: *We've made it all this way.* It was the spirit of the thing, *the quest*, but still . . . "It's risky for sure, but we've *got to* go check it out."

I took a deep breath, held it, unsure.

And when I could hold my breath no longer, I said simply, "Okay," and went up to the bow to watch for rocks while we slid gingerly over the water.

It was an hour before high tide, which was good, but that meant we had an hour at most to get in and out of there, which was bad.

Halfway into the cove, we anchored in twelve feet of water.

Even today that part of my husband remains a mystery to me: What kind of man takes a risk like that in the middle of nowhere? What kind of man let's a pin on an iPad lead him into some of the wildest, most remote waters on Earth? What kind of man sails five hundred miles, says "We're here, aren't we?"—risking not only himself but you and, let's face it, the boat that's his pride and joy—and then dinghies ashore?

We've been married nearly three decades, raised and launched two sons who are now men, and parts of my husband still surprise me.

Jeff is charming but in a prickly way, like a porcupine with a sentimental stripe. He's a grinch with heart, beneath quills that keep you on your toes. He's also loyal, upstanding as an old-growth tree, with the same two best friends since college. He's a talker. A storyteller. A whiskey and wine drinker. He's the type who keeps up with the latest rock music but also reads the *New Yorker* every week. He can be stylish, and outrageous. He's a man of character. He's someone who's got your back. He's the kind of guy who has worn the same pair of leather Top-Siders for fifteen years, socks poking out of holes in the toes, but he can't throw them away because he's steadfast. Instead, he buys a needle and leather thread and, sitting on the stern, stitches up the holes.

He was twenty-nine years old when we met; now he was nearly sixty, weathered, fit, his middle slightly thickened by time. I watched him, wearing his sailing bibs and boots—there was no time to change out of them—lower the dinghy, jump in, and steady the rubber raft while I clambered aboard. Then, just before I pushed off, he said, "Wait!" He scrambled out, disappeared, and then climbed back in clutching the handheld VHF radio. He hurriedly tucked it into his front bib with one hand, revved the outboard with the other, and we were off.

I was so thrilled, I could feel the blood fizzing though my veins. It was maybe fifty-four degrees out, but the sky had turned a bright sapphire blue, sunlight skittering on the water as we sped in toward shore. I watched *Heron* recede in the distance until it looked like a toy sailboat bobbing on a bathtub sea. And then it dawned on me: my husband was doing this for us. He'd made the decision to go ashore here, taken a calculated risk partly because he wanted to but mostly because he knew we needed this. Seeing this long-lost place was for us going forward, and for our marriage—which now, with the boys launched, would consist of shared experiences just the two of us.

Assuming we made it to the longhouse and back, it would be a gift.

And if we didn't make it, it would be a nightmare: the two of us stranded on this huge, wet deserted island in the middle of nowhere, the opening scenes of some twisted reality show: *Deadliest Catch* meets *Lost*.

The quest was very sweet. *And I am very lucky*, I should have been thinking. But I wasn't thinking—there was no time for that; instead, I peeled my eyes from *Heron* and watched the beach, which was coming up quickly. The bay shallowed beneath us, Jeff throttled down, and when we were in a foot or so of water I jumped out, waded in with the line, then turned and pulled Jeff and the raft in toward the sand. We tied the raft hurriedly around a log, hearts pounding, then went to find an ancient longhouse hidden in the forest. We didn't stop for anything. Soon the sun would be setting and the tide peaking and falling, leaving us and the boat dangerously exposed.

It's an odd feeling, searching for something you don't ever expect to find. The beach was maybe a quarter of a mile long and fifty feet wide. I was happy enough just to be off the boat, my sailing boots sinking into the sand.

But Jeff was like Indiana Jones on speed; he was striding ahead, intensely focused, eyes raking the forest a few feet to his left. I smiled to myself. He was still lean and handsome and bold, I thought. The kind of man who looks straight ahead but stays open to a good time. He was about thirty feet ahead of me when he suddenly stopped, turned at a lone stick standing straight up in the sand like a marker, and veered off into the forest. *Oh, Jesus, here we go.*

I knew about the sheer jungle energy of the trees and plants in the Great Bear Rainforest by now. How from the beach you can see far, but that once you enter this coastal forest, just twenty paces from shore you can become totally disoriented. The trail of a person, or the path to an ancient longhouse, can be easily lost.

I wasn't liking this experience so far, was jogging to the place where the stick stood, where Jeff had turned and headed into the trees, when I heard him yell . . .

~~~~~

When I reached the place where he'd gone in, I saw there was actually an opening in the trees, and a faint path between them. Most coastal forests are claustrophobic; there are ankle-twisting tangles of roots and vines, and every few feet or so your way is blocked by moss-coated trunks of fallen trees, with ferns and lichen and younger trees sprouting out of them. Most coastal forests are dark, thick, and wet. You have the feeling that if you lose your way, you could be grown over and swallowed up by the steady, ancient riot of growth.

But this forest was different. It was huge and eternal feeling, but instead of being dense and dark, it was airy and light. The air was intensely aromatic. The pine-needled path was soft and spongy underfoot, muting our passage, and when I looked up, shafts of sunlight were piercing the trees. It was like a silent, branched and needled cathedral, an awesome place to behold.

The trees, mostly Sitka spruces, were tall and slender, and Jeff was standing among them in his red Musto sailing bibs, beaming.

"You're not going to believe this!" he shouted. His face was lit up with the thrill of the hunt. "Hurry, it's insanely cool."

He turned, I followed him a short distance into the woods, and then I saw it: before us, the skeletal frame of an entire longhouse leaped out from the trees. It was preserved in the hush of the forest, like the bones of an ancient fallen-down Chartres. Massive cedar posts, five feet in diameter, stood in two corners, and on all four sides cedar-log beams—two suspended in midair, the others half fallen, all wrapped in a cloak of soft moss—outlined the structure of a Kitasoo longhouse. It looked strong and weathered and sacred. It looked like something from another century. It looked like time itself. I stood staring at the site, and the silence was so profound that I felt like I could hear for miles and miles, every sound off the water, every leaf stirring in the breeze, every twig, crackling and distinct.

But most astonishing: as my eyes settled upon the site, I could see the remnants of what was at one time tiered seating, like bleachers, descending into the earth. Now the tiers rimmed a sort of sunken garden filled with leafy salal and salmonberry, and fallen logs and entire continents of lichen, and thin saplings and hundreds upon hundreds of ferns. The wind blew from the west, bearing the salt of the sea and the perfume of ferns and the herby scent of hemlocks. The whole structure seemed to occupy its own space, one of silence and oblivion, protected from the beat of time. The forest, naturally, was reclaiming the site, but the space, as mystical as a medieval church, felt charged. I was transfixed. There was something magical and powerful in the sheer jungle energy of the leafy wilderness, in the quiet watchful witness of its unseen long-gone inhabitants. There was something sacred here.

Twenty minutes had passed, and we knew we didn't have much time. We needed to get back to the boat. There was much we could say—we'd somehow managed to find the ruins of the longhouse in the middle of all this wildness, a place where vanishing cultures once gathered, where people told stories to one another in languages now almost forgotten—but we were afraid to speak. We both knew that speaking here would be like dashing some very delicate bond to pieces, like kicking a cedar log into a thousand splinters—the papery, sinewy length of it scattering in the wind.

So instead, we stood there for a moment wondering at this place, claiming it as an intense and shared memory while the light beamed down through the trees and illuminated the fragile cedar bones. Then we turned and raced back to the boat.

BLACK BEAR

~~~

People ask me if I'm ever afraid on the boat. We've taken our fair share of risks for sure. We've done some treacherous things, like anchoring *Heron* off that wildly remote beach on a rising tide when we wanted to find the ancient longhouse, then threading our way through Philip Narrows, a cut that resembled the eye of a needle, a few hours later. Philip was one of the trickiest passages we'd ever attempted: only thirty feet wide and twenty-two feet deep, with submerged rocks to port and a huge mapped rock lurking dead ahead. But it was the only way to reach Kent Inlet, a series of hidden bays gracing the southwest coast of Princess Royal Island. We'd read about Kent Inlet and how this nearly landlocked chain of bays could, in fact, be entered through Philip Narrows at slack tide. Newly emboldened, we decided they looked worth the risk. With *Heron*'s sixteen-foot beam, we had to hug this shore, then that, to avoid this rock or the next—all fine, except there was so little maneuvering room to begin with.

"Oh hell. Don't tell me *that's* the way in?" Jeff said when we first spied the opening.

But it *was* the way in: a channel so narrow I instinctively sprinted to the bow; once stationed there I could barely breathe, I was so intent on willing us not to hit rock. I wrapped one arm around the headstay, gripped the bow rail with the other, and leaned out, peering into the dark green water. One of us always does this in tricky spots, although it feels futile, staring down at an impenetrable sea, watching for rocks. The water was almost black from my vantage; it was impossible to see through it at all. I stood there squinting anyway, watching the hull slice through the murk, praying that if we hit or, god forbid, *scraped* something, it wouldn't be on my watch. Finally, after ten or so tense minutes, we were through—then gliding among a string of one, then two, then three completely enclosed, forest-rimmed bays; each secluded body of water opening to the next. It was like entering a country of quiet—a place where our awareness suddenly shifted. We held our breath as we passed silently from one large body of water to the next in the late-afternoon light: not a single boat. Was it possible that we had this whole secret realm to ourselves?

We did.
We set the anchor.
Shut down the engine.
Shed our foul-weather gear.
Grinned in disbelief, then . . .
Slipped a kayak over the side.

~~~~~~~~~

The inlet's third and innermost bay, like so many on Princess Royal Island, was oblong and edged by Sitka spruce forest. Where the soil ran out at the shore's edge, trees teetered on rock. At its head, not far from where we'd anchored, a small waterfall tumbled. *Heron* floated maybe a hundred yards from the falls, so close you could hear the water chattering as it pooled over rock and watch salmon as big as your arm catapulting themselves toward the river. This, I knew, was precisely the kind of place you might be lucky enough to spot serious wildlife fishing for dinner: black bears, grizzlies, wolves.

I couldn't believe that finally, after days and weeks beating our way north toward the Great Bear Rainforest, we'd found the ancient longhouse and landed within range of the spirit bear—both on the same day.

Jeff, tired and elated, climbed into the dinghy and motored off to set a crab pot.

Alone on the boat, I noticed the pace of everything took on a delicious strangeness, as if I were watching things in slow motion. I lowered myself carefully, in jeans and bare feet, into one of two kayaks we kept lashed to *Heron*'s bow. Slim and light, the kayaks were a splurge. But in the weeks since we'd picked them up on Vancouver Island, they'd paid for themselves time and again. Our bodies ached from so many hours afloat. The kayaks, in addition to being beautiful, proved crucial: allowing us to not only get off the boat and get some exercise but also to have a bit of independence. One of the key things, we'd learned quickly, about surviving for long stretches in remote places, was the necessity of being able to take a much-needed break from each other. I grabbed a paddle, sliced through the water with light, even strokes, and glided toward the head of the cove. It was late afternoon, the hour when the angle of the sun was heading toward the ocean, and there was an odd clarity to the blue-gold light, the rinsed air illuminating the spruce trees sharply. At the base of the falls I sat and floated, listening. There was the riffling of water on rock, the splash of froth tumbling over boulders, the rhythm of the water, its steady patter massaging my spine.

I sat gulping in lungfuls of crisp air, while silver fat salmon flew past my head like jumbo jets. The salmon, crash-landing, sent up plumes of white. The mournful wail of a loon echoed overhead: *Where-are-you? Where-are-you?* Such a plaintive, wistful call.

The sun on the water was lit up, incandescent, the surface glittering and the concentric rings left by the salmon perfect and particular, even as they widened and dispersed, washed by the light.

I sat and floated and made myself very still, barely breathing, just watching and listening . . . There was the creek endlessly clattering, and the forest smelling of rain and moss and fern. There was the scent of damp earth and sun. The rising of mist, and the burning off of mist. The ravens in the trees, the bald eagles in the trees, the glossy sheen of their backs. I thought about the interminable boat chores, both large and small, that endlessly occupied us. Above us, the black night sky splashed with stars bright as knife points. The cacophony of birds at dawn.

I knew it couldn't be sustained, this intense awareness. But for the short time that Jeff was off on the distant shore, the exquisite solitude felt glorious. It was like a gift to myself, and I tried to memorize these moments in the wilderness and the silence of the longhouse in an effort to keep all these things inside me so I could rearrange them, and later tell the boys about them—and after that carry them around with me to create my own peacefulness when I was home, perhaps stuck in traffic. I was thinking all this, watching the falls, utterly transfixed, when I sensed a quick movement off my left shoulder.

I looked up and froze: an enormous black bear was standing onshore, maybe fifteen feet away, watching me.

How long has he been here?!

He was on all fours, snorfling up salmon in a gravel bed just past my ear, and he took a step forward, watching me watch him. He had a big salmon clenched in his teeth, and he was chewing. Bits of salmon and blood and river water streamed from his jaws. He had a massive square head. He was so close I could see one huge rib flex slightly beneath the black tips of his fur.

I was so shocked I pivoted and paddled away as fast as I could from him, putting a little distance between us. He was only interested in the salmon, of course, but he kept watching me, and was probably—let's face it—even more apprehensive than I was.

When I stopped paddling and turned to look back, he was still standing there, chewing. Our eyes met, both of us silent, curious. He lowered his ponderous head—he had huge jaws—picked another fish off the ground, ate it, eyed me. Was I food to him? *No, I am just here*, I thought. Part of the coastal forest. Maybe like kelp or a log.

I didn't move and the bear didn't move. He just stood there, gorging on salmon. Then he stepped into the stream, took a look at me over his shoulder, trundled out onto a wide flat rock, and fished his paw around in the water. He moved onto the next rock, then the next—and in this way he made his way back up the river. At one point he turned his whole body, so I could see him in perfect profile from snout to stub tail, as distinct as a black shadow against the river's white foam. Then he galloped off into the brush, splashing water up and making the rocks clatter even more loudly than the clattering falls.

My body had frozen and my fingertips beat. I felt as light as air, frail as an insect; a tiny, two-legged, human fly afloat in a fake fiberglass shell. The breeze tingled on every inch of my arms, my neck, my scalp, like I had antennae all over my head.

"A bear! I saw a bear!" I kept saying to myself, looking around wildly so I could tell Jeff. But by then he was a speck on the distant shore.

I couldn't believe this had happened: that in a single day that started out so darkly Jeff and I had, in fact, managed to find the longhouse, and I'd had this intense solo encounter with a black bear. I began paddling back to the boat, and with each stroke became happier and happier. I was filled with an ineffable joy, a magical lightness of being. By the time I reached the transom and heaved myself out of the kayak, then lay sprawled like a beached porpoise on the stern deck, I was absolutely elated.

"You'll never believe what happened!" I hollered at Jeff when he circled back in the dinghy.

KENT INLET

〜〜〜

Was it Wednesday or Thursday? Jeff and I were in time beyond time. Tidal time. After our intense push from Klemtu to this hidden inlet, a broad bay overhung with deep green spruce and cedar—relishing our intense luck to have this place all to ourselves—we'd decided to take a day. Miraculously, the sun had stayed with us and the sky was a passionate blue. Cloudless. Catching up on boat chores in shorts and flip-flops during the morning, we were aware of the sun warming *Heron*'s decks and our limbs, and were also attuned to the moon's pull—the rising and falling of the rapids feeding into the inlet, as well as the shifts in the tidal rapids and current marking the far end of the bay.

Our world was reduced to *Heron*, water, forest, rock, sky. The sound of the waterfall spilling from the woods just off the bow. The splash of the occasional salmon leaping, lazy now. The idea of bears, the mystery of them—the mythical white bear; all the bears unseen in the forest; even my own private black bear. That was all. And yet . . . How could a day feel so full?

To live successfully on a boat, one must take a conscious step backward in time. A lot of things don't work, or work only intermittently, or are forever on the verge of breaking and not working—and you can drive yourself nuts if you don't come to terms with all that. Along most of the northern coast we had no cell service; internet required finding a port with Wi-Fi, and even those signals were spotty at best. Learning the ways of living aboard *Heron*—where Facebook friends were traded for books, and twenty-four-hour news feeds were replaced by days that stretched into ages—had begun to change all that. Jeff and I had begun to move with the rhythms of this more exacting, but also simpler, way of living. Although there was no gym or yoga or jogging, it was a more physical way of living, with our bodies stretched by moving in ways they weren't used to—and where light and wind and weather dictated the day's routine.

Thinking about time and how nature used to be the theater of life for all our ancestors, I tried to imagine the people who carved and carried the big cedar poles of the ancient Kitasoo longhouse we'd found the day before. Although these islands are now wildly uninhabited, just two hundred years ago, some sixty thousand residents lived in tribal clusters along this sumptuous coast: Tlingits, Tsimshians, Haidas, Bella Bellas, Bella Coolas, Nootkas, Kwakiutls . . . The forests were once full of First Nations' ceremonial longhouses, massive cedar structures that are almost entirely gone now. The Kitasoo are one of fourteen tribes of the Tsimshian people, who now inhabit, along with the Xai'xais people (of Heiltsuk ethnic affiliation), the village of Klemtu. The name Kitasoo derives from the Tshimshian word *Gidestsu*, from *git-* (people of) and *disdzuu*, which refers to a large, tiered house depression, like the ancient longhouse.

Unlike our forebears, these First People, who dug rows of tiered seating into the cool forest floor long before climate change and global warming, saw nature as a whole to which they belonged rather than an unlimited resource to tame. Their numbers however, were small, and their impact on the environment could be sustained. They must have come by cedar canoe, hauled those canoes up onto the beach, gathered in the longhouse. It would have been a hard, cold life with endless hours spent foraging, but nature for them meant both spirit and sustenance.

Later, as Jeff and I became more proficient sailors, we would make more trips to Klemtu and Tsimshian territory, also sailing across Hecate Strait to the islands of Haida Gwaii. We learned that the ancient longhouse had stood in the forest for maybe five hundred years and was central in Kitasoo/ Xai'xais history and stories. They weren't always happy stories. In one, told to us by a shy fourteen-year-old girl in the Klemtu big house, the Haida came to the village of Klemtu, kidnapped the women and children while the men were out hunting, and made them slaves. The refrain of the story (which is also sung) was how, while traveling on the long canoe back to the islands of Haida Gwaii, the children were thirsty and there was no water.

We also learned that the longhouse had been the most sacred meeting place of all the tribal chiefs. During the almost seventy years that potlatch ceremonies were banned by the Canadian government, chiefs would meet there secretly in winter, making the arduous trek by canoe. One winter one of the canoes capsized and a chief was killed. Eventually, they stopped making the trip. It was too dangerous. Years later we retraced our journey, making it far enough north for a return visit. Scanning the shoreline through binoculars, I couldn't find the entrance, even knowing where it was located. It didn't matter. We couldn't imagine going in. Seeing the ancient longhouse once had been a gift.

~~~~~~~~

I was still reading Peter Matthiessen's *The Snow Leopard.* Although Matthiessen wrote the book in the 1970s—detailing his Himalayan trek with wildlife biologist George Schaller to the remote Dolpo region of Nepal, where they hoped to glimpse the elusive snow leopard—the book's spirit resonated here in the solitary reaches of the Great Bear, the planet's last large expanse of coastal temperate rainforest. I'd always loved *The Snow Leopard*, the simplicity of it, with its biblical cadences, taut and spare sentences. Haunting clarity. Although Matthiessen was on a quest to glimpse a snow leopard, the book, to my mind, is mostly about getting lost, about extending the boundaries of oneself into unknown territory.

Now and then I set the book down and picked up the binoculars. I peered through them from the cockpit, scanned the shore. A beautiful brown-and-white osprey soared hunting for fish, salmon flung themselves at the rocks and lay there silvering in the sun, but the black bear didn't come again. Jeff went fishing in the dinghy for sockeye, the loops lifting from his rod like a spell cast over the water.

Our boat sat alone in an ink-blue inlet on an uninhabited island. There were no other boats or people or roads for miles. I expanded this emptiness, thinking how to the west was the endless ocean, and then Japan. I felt a delicious surrender, lost to the world, as if we'd stripped away all the past trappings of our lives together, like shedding winter coats. All the being and doing and worrying and planning had evaporated, and I felt an expansive sense of calm. Even though I couldn't see it, encircled as we were here by a protective rim of trees, I could feel the horizon.

Surrounded by this forest and these steep walls of glacier-carved granite, knowing that no other boats could enter until the next tide cycle, cut off from the outside world, I wanted to stay on *Heron* forever. Lulled by the breeze and the sun, I felt completely unfamiliar to myself, almost unreal, as if parts of me had dissolved, were dissolving. The Buddhist ideal that there is no real self seemed spot-on here. At the heart of my emerging understanding was the conviction that nature holds the secret to balance and unity, not outside us but inside us, no separation. There was solace here. The boys were in their brand-new lives, where they should be, and somehow Jeff and

I had crossed a threshold of experience and exhaustion and were suspended in this new inner place.

The trick, I realized, lay in letting go. Though I dreaded the moment when both Sam and James would leave, I also saw how ready they were. For them, letting go of one family configuration meant making room to grab hold of an entire universe. I felt strangely light, as if I'd come to the end of something and passed through it. But I didn't know what it was.

~~~~~~~~~

We ate lunch in the cockpit, tearing into the pink flesh of fresh Dungeness crab, which we'd pulled into the boat that morning. It was delicious, made even more so because we'd caught the crabs ourselves. I stirred together a sauce: mayo, lemon, mustard. Sliced up a green apple. We crunched the pink claws with our teeth, sucked the sweet flesh from them. Everything tasted clean and fresh and had the subtle flavor of something that had just come hours ago from the sea.

No boats came in on the afternoon slack. We still had all Kent Inlet, this whole private realm of water, rock, trees, and sky, completely to ourselves—and would for the next twelve hours! The late-afternoon light bounced off the water, a sparkling indigo blue. We dinghied out in our muck boots and shorts and sprawled bare legged on flat barnacled rocks in the warm sun near a stream tumbling into the far side of the inlet, watching for spirit bears since here on Princess Royal Island we were finally in range of the rare places they inhabit. We sat and watched for a long time. We were so used to the quiet now, to one another's presence when the only other sound was a whispering breeze, that we could have just stayed indefinitely. After all, we had nowhere else to be. It was a lovely feeling, the stripping away of everything external. But sitting on barnacles hurts. After a while we looked at each other and grimaced. We were beyond language now, beyond words. So we both stood up at the exact same time.

~~~~~~~~~

By the time we got back to the boat at five o'clock, it was seventy degrees and the sun was shining, almost bikini weather. This kind of warmth, in the far northern reaches of the BC coast, was ridiculous, unheard-of! I couldn't believe our luck. Were the spirits taking pity on us? Trying, in no uncertain terms, to tell us something? We both stripped down to shorts and T-shirts. After days of wearing the same layers—jeans and thick socks and plaid-flannel shirts and fleece pull-overs—the warm rays of late-afternoon sun felt delicious on bare skin. Jeff went back out to check the traps.

I decided it was time for naked cocktails. I popped my head out the cockpit and peered at my husband of twenty-five years speeding across the water in his old T-shirt and ripped khaki shorts and neoprene boots and sinewy brown legs. Then I peeled off my shorts and climbed back up on deck wearing only a blue-and-white-striped French cotton T-shirt with a tease of laces down the back. Settling into one of two low-slung wooden folding chairs on the stern deck, toes tapping on *Heron*'s sun-warmed teak, I sat and waited, scissoring my thighs open and closed, like a bird's wings.

"You're not wearing anything under that!" Jeff said when he got back to the boat and, standing on the swim deck, found himself eye-level with my legs scissoring slowly open and shut, open and shut.

"Do you like it?" I smiled.

"I love it!" My husband grinned. "I'll have whatever you're having."

And that is how we found ourselves sipping rum and tonics, reclined on *Heron*, outside on a rare late-summer afternoon that felt like the sunniest day that ever was in the wilds of Canada.

"When was the last time we did it outside? Do you even remember?" I asked.

"Sometime in the eighties?" Jeff mused, laughing.

And so I took my husband by the hand and pushed him to the far side of the cockpit. "Sit down," I commanded. He obeyed for once, like an eager dog that suddenly remembers he might get a treat. I stood there for a moment, savoring the power surge I felt. Then I leaned forward and tugged off his boots and wool socks, one by one. And because we're such neat freaks on the boat, I didn't fling them over my shoulder, but lined them up side by side and tucked each sock into its boot. Next I unclasped his belt and tugged off his frayed khaki shorts.

And then, because this was where we had come after so many years, our desire still stretching before us but into what felt like a new kind of time, we took our time mapping this moment on one another's bodies. It was indescribably lovely: just being naked together outside, two souls that knew each other so well, but were surprised at the newness of finding ourselves here, playing outside on a Wednesday or maybe Thursday afternoon.

We switched places. Jeff knelt before me, and I closed my eyes. I felt everything, the sigh of the wind through the trees, the patter of the waterfall, the brush of breeze on my thighs, the warmth of the sun radiating up and down and then suddenly exploding like a star. I knelt before him, and he leaned back and gripped the stainless bars of the bimini while I watched him, his eyes closed: all of him fifty-eight years old and still crazy-sexy, although he didn't always think so—especially after the prostate cancer surgery, which for men, I think, is like losing themselves at first. Still, he's funny, and comfortable with himself, which is the sexiest thing you can ever be. I thought about making love to Jeff, his hips arrowing into me. Then I eased myself down on him and wrapped my legs around him, pulling him all the way up to my heart.

PRINCESS ROYAL ISLAND—AT LAST

Princess Royal Island loomed and vanished in the grays. To the west was the gaping expanse of the wild North Pacific; to the east an infinity of mountains. Here the Great Bear Rainforest felt like a world unto itself, completely cut off from the rest of North America by the Coast Mountains, whose jagged peaks gleam with snow, even in summer and fall.

I scanned the banks for bears. Nothing. We were finally here, circumnavigating Princess Royal Island, and in the neighborhood of *Ursus americanus kermodei*, the spirit bear! I leaned past the windscreen and gulped in big breaths of fresh, chilly, salty air.

Princess Royal Island is the largest island on the north coast of British Columbia, but its western shore was flatter than I'd imagined: low dusky hills, forested at the line just above where they met a thin, driftwood-strewn shore. Jeff and I took turns peering through the binoculars at the long string of rocky beaches—each a tumble of boulders rounded by centuries of storms off the Pacific, piles of driftwood, and ancient tree trunks worn silver. Above them gnarled red cedar, straggly spruce, and windblown hemlock grew straight up from the rock.

The sea beneath us was deep: eight hundred to a thousand feet. A red-and-black tug towing a container barge passed midmorning; otherwise, there were no vessels. Once home to a tiny mining outpost and small cannery, Princess Royal is now entirely uninhabited, and except for patches on its north end where clear-cutters once worked, the island feels forgotten, untouched, pristine. The nearest communities are the remote outposts of Klemtu to the south and Hartley Bay to the north. In one day's sail we were a century away.

We motored on, and I continued to scan the shore, looking for spirit bears. But every "bear" I thought I saw turned out to be a bone-white tree trunk . . . or a big white rock. Small things are hard to find in big country. Even something as dazzling as a white bear is easy to miss in wilderness this immense. You can spend days and weeks, months even, exploring remote places and not see much of anything wild. *Will the spirit bear guide, Marven Robinson, even remember we're coming?* I wondered.

As Jeff and I navigated these uncharted waters—still getting used to the way life felt without the boys in our midst and trying to learn to sail *Mighty Heron* alone together—we'd seized upon the spirit bear (for me) and the ancient longhouse (for Jeff) as beacons to point ourselves and the boat toward. Without kids, friends, and family—without the structure of jobs out here—we needed a new kind of goal. For us it became about trying to see something meaningful and beautiful. And the farther we ventured during that trip-of-a-lifetime summer, the more grateful we grew for these rare wonders of the Pacific Northwest Coast: Kermode bears and silent longhouses, and all the other wild creatures we came to know along the way— humpback whales, fin whales, and orca whales; mysterious coastal wolves and curious sea otters; bald eagles and ravens and great blue herons with their stoic patience and capacious wings; pairs of pigeon guillemots with their bright red feet; schools of salmon jumping and big flocks of brilliant white terns floating, their wings flashing across the sea. All these things, plus giant kelp that grew an astonishing two feet a day, and some of the world's biggest cedar trees, and entire universes of lichen and moss, thrived in our own stunningly wild and extremely hard to reach backyard—and all were remarkable. The farther we went the greater the distance grew between where we hoped we were going and all we'd left behind. And the sighting of these incredible places, along with the wolf, the whales, the wilderness, to my mind became centered on that one white bear.

A holdover from the last ice age, this subspecies of black bear inhabits only Princess Royal Island and a few surrounding islands and areas on the mainland. Its coat ranges from creamy white to a marmalade-caramel, but the bear is not an albino. Rather, scientists think this white phase of the black bear results from occasional manifestations of a double recessive gene and that it has an evolutionary advantage. (Providing camouflage against a cloudy sky when the bear pursues fish during late summer and fall salmon runs.) In the past decade the spirit bear has become a sort of "poster bear," a symbol for saving the world's last expanse of coastal temperate rainforest from logging and supertankers.

I thought about how time had dissolved while I watched that black bear from the kayak at the head of Kent Inlet. The past and the future, and all the weight bears carry—the weight of wilderness and wildness—had compressed into one clear, infinite moment. Everything else had fallen away, blown like scattering leaves.

~~~~~~

In Whale Channel, a stretch of silver-gray water between Princess Royal and Gil Island, we were suddenly surrounded by whales. *Humpbacks all around!* I scribbled in my sailing journal. We were both riveted by the massive shapes sliding up from the depths. They were so majestic, so *other*: the initial mist-drift of their spout, the slow-motion arch of each black back emerging from the water, and finally, the flip of the fluke, as individual as a fingerprint and graceful as a flag, before disappearing below.

But soon after this thrilling display, we reached the opening to Wright Sound, a complex starfish-shaped body of water that leads into six different channels, each stretching into a maze of intricate forested waterways. There was *finally* enough wind to put the sails up.

We raised the mainsail easily and flew over the late-afternoon seas on a beam reach. It was blowing fifteen to twenty knots, a strong northwesterly, serious business on a sled the size of *Heron*, her navy hull heeled over in the sparkling chop. Up went the small staysail. Easy. But when it was time to unfurl the big jib, Jeff was impatient and then furious when I hesitated—momentarily unsure about which line was the jib-furling line.

"*Figure it out! You* put it up!" he shouted.

Granted, I should have had it down by then. It was our second month on *Heron*, after all, but there was so little wind in these waters that we'd put up the jib only four or five times before, and the boys had been aboard on most of those occasions. Sam had been in charge of the jib furler. I stared at the web of lines and blocks and cleat— and froze.

"What do you need to do?" snapped Skipper Jeff, a rage brewing. "*Figure it out!*"

"I am!" I say.

"Well then, do it!"

"*I am!*" I shouted, staring at the mess of lines.

Things went downhill from there . . .

~~~~~~~~

It was a shit storm, exacerbated by Jeff's adrenaline and his fearing how on the edge we were out here, with wolves and whales for company and the days shortening since it was now September, a month when most Northwest boaters were far south, safely past Klemtu and

Bella Bella and Shearwater and Hakai Pass and Johnstone Strait and all the waters we'd need to navigate again on our long return home; how far from any other vessels or people or inhabited anything, and how out of control things could feel on this big boat on the rare occasion that we had enough wind to raise all the canvas. We were tired, which made everything worse. And it was clear that after two seasons, having learned so much and come so far, we still didn't always know what we were doing.

This kind of trial-by-fire, berating, verbal shit not good for any marriage, I scribbled in my sailing journal. We were steaming along now, no longer speaking. *Especially when you're hundreds of miles from home, surrounded by fog, cold, and freezing water. And the deck isn't a level playing field yet. Why would anyone sign up for this?? Our nerves are raw. We're both ground down. Tired. Barely speaking. But I understand the mechanics of the jib now. It is up. All three sails are up . . . and they are fucking BEAUTIFUL.*

I married my husband because he's my favorite person in the world. When given the choice of where to spend my time, I will always, always choose to be with him. But what happens when you are three decades into a relationship and you reach a crossroads, a place where you realize you could, in fact, each choose different directions? What happens when you are physically exhausted and rip-shit mad and done with each other, but you can't stomp off to the other end of the house because your home happens to be a goddamn sailboat? What happens when your children—who have been not only your planets and stars but also a distinct gravitational force buffering the differences between you—are suddenly launched into their own distant orbits?

I stared at my husband backlit by purple sky and angry clouds and huge white sails like the wings of a cormorant, which in that searing instant looked like a cross nailed to the sky, and thought:

My marriage could end. It could end right here in the middle-of-nowhere Whale Channel. It could end with me saying: *You're my favorite person in the world but you're impossible, you impatient jerk!*

And my funny, practical, always-prepared-for-the-worst-case-scenario husband could, with very good reason, fling his own accusations back at me: *If you spent even* half as much time *studying sail trim and knot-tying as you do watching for whales and bears and clouds and* scribbling in that damn notebook, *you might be a half-decent sailor!*

But there wasn't time for any of this because next, right then in the middle of Wright Sound, for no apparent reason, the wind died.

Skipper Jeff spat out a litany of curses. "*God damn it!* Why does the wind have to die when we finally get the sails up? Because it's the friggin' Pacific Northwest, that's why!" The hollering continued, scattering flocks of gulls in our midst.

"*Well, this is just great, Captain,*" I hissed. "You can't take it, can you? You can't take it because you're *losing it,* and you don't have the emotional toughness to *survive* this far out on the edge!"

We floated in silence, sails flapping.

～～～～～～

I couldn't raise all the sails on my own at the time, but I vowed then and there to master each and every one of them. And I did. My heart felt like it was lifting out of my chest that day in Wright Sound. I felt everything on my face that afternoon, the salt and the wet wind, and the cry of birds, and the searing fingers of the sun in its furious indigo sky. I could see the steep green mountains rising up, topped by equally dramatic cumulus clouds: purple-gray beneath, sunlit above. The hulk of Gil Island to port loomed an angry black. Shafts of late-afternoon light, luminous with fall, hit the boat.

I realized Jeff had a point. I was an exceptional first mate, but I sucked at sailing. I had to become not only more proficient at sailing but more proficient at sailing *Heron.* It was a matter of survival, for both of us.

I sketched a picture in my notebook to remember the jib and labeled the parts: jib furler, jib sheets for windward and leeward, cleat for jib-furling line. And then I labeled the steps. I would refer to this sketch several more times until I had all of it down cold and could raise that jib solo. Or tack it twenty-two times in a single day, as we did a few years later in a race off the wild west coast of Vancouver Island. Or raise all three sails, harden them up, and soar for eight hours on a wild reach across forbidding Hecate Strait, as we've done en route to explore the archipelago of Haida Gwaii.

But for now, here we were: Skipper Jeff and me, his enthusiastic but appallingly green first mate. We'd made it this far, damn it. All this way, nearly seven hundred nautical miles of wilderness sailing—with no one but us handling everything on this too-big boat in our new world of two.

CLOVE HITCH

Docking the boat in the small harbor tucked behind the stone break-water at Hartley Bay, a tiny aboriginal village that in addition to being the apex of our trip was home to Marven Robinson, didn't go any better. The wooden docks were lined with fishing boats and aluminum outboards. Squinting through the binoculars, we tried to tell whether there might be an empty space at the fuel dock. It was full. We pulled out Ken's napkin map: floatplane dock, fuel dock, shore, three finger piers.

"Everyone rafts in Hartley Bay," Ken had said. "You can tie up to Marven's dad's purse seiner—it hasn't moved in years."

But the rusted hulk of Marven's dad's fishing boat, the *Crystal-Gene*, loomed five feet above our decks when we managed to move *Heron* alongside—way more than the two of us were ready to handle, with me as sole leaper and line tier.

With little room to maneuver *Mighty Heron* in the shallow harbor, we panicked.

A sturdy-looking couple cleaning fish on the back deck of a battered cabin cruiser called out, "We'll move!" They dropped their fish knives and dragged their boat farther up the fuel dock.

Snapping at one another as violently as two crabs in a trap, we finally squeezed *Heron* in behind them, tied her up, and shut her down. The sun was starting to set. We were tired, cold, numb, short-tempered. Utterly spent, I was relieved we'd made it all the way to Hartley Bay, the northernmost point of our journey and a First Nations village so isolated it's accessible only by air and water. But Jeff was still worked up about the stern line, which I hadn't tied in a proper clove hitch, evidently.

I'd tied a half hitch. Not a clove hitch. *Sigh.*

So now he was redoing it and complaining loudly. I understood that he was doing this because he was exploding with nerves, having just half circumnavigated super-remote Princess Royal Island in a single shitty day and jockeyed ourselves into this tiny harbor. But this particular raw nerve, and my utter inability after all these weeks at sea to tie the proper knot, seemed emblematic of our strained relationship at this point: Was it coming untied as well?

"God *damn* it! *This won't hold. This* will!"

~~~~~~~~

Jeff had a point: it was ridiculous that I still hadn't mastered the perfect clove hitch. But I happen to know many highly intelligent knot-challenged humans.

I could definitely have been way better at this, but instead I ignored him and walked back to thank the couple that had moved their boat for us. Clad in blood-streaked yellow storm bibs (him) and a dull blue apron (her), they were cleaning an enormous eighty-five-pound halibut and exuded good-natured capability. They explained in thick Russian accents that they lived in Kitimat, a fishing and logging town about fifty miles inland and northeast, toward the BC-Alaska border. It had taken them all day to reel in the fish, they said, beaming. I offered to take their picture, and they posed on either side of the huge dripping halibut as adoringly as if it were a child. Meanwhile, men aboard the sturdy powerboat tied off *Heron*'s stern took pity on us and tossed a whole coho they'd caught down to the dock. "A small one!" they laughed, teasingly. "Just enough for two!"

It was embarrassing. Damn. We hadn't caught a fish today or any other day. We were pathetic, but we weren't complete idiots—we took the salmon.

Back on the boat we sidestepped one another in silence. I was numb with exhaustion, nerves long past frayed. It felt like my inner self had separated from my body and floated straight up out of the boat—a white tern hovering overhead or a dark raven sitting on one of the halyards, watching from a safe distance. As the evening chilled, the docks grew damp. A thick mist settled in over the harbor, enveloping the cedar pilings surrounded by metal crab traps and oblong buoys, plastic fishing buckets and thick rubber hoses. There was the sound of halyards slapping and ravens chortling, the smell of bird shit mixed with the sharp clean scent of the sea. Jeff was clearly pushed past his breaking point as well. *Please*, I thought, *just let this day be over.*

But instead I said: "I need a cocktail."

"Why do you think sailors drink?" Jeff said with a sigh. "It's the only way they stay sane."

"*What happened out there?!*" I said. "What *was* that?"

"I don't know," Jeff said, scowling. "I found myself in a pretty dark place all of a sudden. I'm sick of things breaking on this boat. I'm sick of having to fix everything by myself. When I realized you had to literally *stop and think* about putting the jib up, that you couldn't do it second nature, I frickin' lost it."

I considered this, how my husband—a kind and extremely competent man who likes a well-oiled machine—was navigating slippery docks right now, how even our beautiful *Heron* could be fickle and infuriating, how frustrating that must be.

"I just thought you'd be better at everything by now," he said with a sigh.

"*You wouldn't even be here if it wasn't for my wanting to be here!*" I hurled back.

"And my getting you here," he countered. "I need you to be more than a passenger. You're a very nice passenger, don't get me wrong. But for now? You're a passenger."

This was crushing. But there was truth in it. Aside from being able to navigate using the chart plotter, and carefully watching our depths, and not getting seasick, and putting in long solo hours at the helm, and considering myself a kick-ass helmswoman . . . I really didn't know what I was doing yet when it came to sailing.

~~~~~~

I sat and stewed. Was this current state of affairs something that required tweaking? I wondered. All long-term relationships have their dark times, their hard passages, their unforeseen difficulties. I got that. What was out of alignment—and unfair—on the boat was that these first seasons afloat, Jeff was the only one aboard with the seafaring skills (not to mention mechanical and electrical) to get us out of tricky spots. And there were a lot of tricky spots. Plus, the farther we went the more infuriating they became.

As in any relationship, though, we each brought our strengths and weaknesses to this rocky vessel. Jeff's superpower was his many aptitudes, shadowed by moodiness and a lovable pessimism. He's the kind of man who approaches most things with Eeyore's point of view. But my superpower was calm inner strength, along with a big soft spot for this particular Eeyore. And this, I hoped, was one of the reasons we'd always worked and would work—even way up here on the slick wooden docks of Hartley Bay, where halyards were clanging, and ravens were cawing, and rain was pounding like battle drums on *Heron*'s cabin roof.

An hour or so later, like a missive from another world, a strange sound echoed through the cabin. *Ping!* Then a few seconds later, *Ping!* A *text*? Here?

"We must be back within cell range!" Jeff exclaimed, brightening. "Or at least, within text range." He picked up the phone.

"Hey—it's James!" he said, handing it over.

"Hey, where are u guys now? How's life on *Heron*?"

It was like a lifeline: this simple text, winging its way from our son in upstate New York to the two of us trying to get used to our new world as well, barely making it through another day.

"Well, we can tell him that at least we haven't killed one another yet," I quipped, raising an eyebrow.

"It's not over till it's over," Jeff said. But just hearing from James back East, adjusting to school at the exact moment we were struggling with realigning our own voluble compass, somehow put everything in perspective. We poured two glasses of pinot and shot back a signal flag.

"Mom still working on the clove hitch," it read.

HEALING

~~~~~~

The rain was incessant on this gray morning in the village of Hartley Bay. Time in the cockpit was wearing on us. We'd started to joke about "tiny hands"—my sneaking up on Jeff during long watery crossings and "accidentally" bumping him overboard. "If you ever feel those tiny hands on your back, don't be surprised!" I'd said.

But despite our frayed nerves, we'd reached the northernmost point of our journey. Here, at least, we could get off the boat and stretch our legs. Sturdy cedar-plank boardwalks snaked across the boggy land, linking the modest dwellings—all of which faced the sea—to the small harbor. Exploring town, we counted sixty or seventy mostly one-story clapboard and aluminum-sided houses connected by the wooden boardwalks. The community was anchored by a whitewashed wooden church topped with a weathered red steeple, a K–12 school clad entirely in cedar, a brand-new cultural center modeled on a cedar longhouse, a First Nations band office, and a two-nurse clinic. Tendrils of wood smoke curled up from the houses in the rain, and small First Nation boys and girls played along the boardwalks, oblivious to the drizzle, as ravens' croaks echoed.

After exploring the village, we hunkered down, waiting for Marven Robinson to return on the ferry that ran every fortnight. We moved *Heron* away from our spot on the fuel dock. It was a good thing we did—at noon a small navy-hulled ferry charged around the corner, sped into the cove, and tied up in the spot we'd just vacated. It seemed half of Hartley Bay was waiting for it; people crowded on the dock: bristly-black-haired men and frizzy-gray-haired women, young First Nations mothers with tiny, round daughters wearing fuchsia parkas.

Younger men and women with olive skin and round faces stepped off the ferry, pulling wheeled duffels, and walked up the gangway into the crowd—a man pushing a small refrigerator; a five-year-old boy in pajama bottoms and a red parka leading a white toy poodle on a leash. "Hi, Nelson!" a woman in the crowd called out to him, and I realized that of course everyone knew everyone in a place as tight-knit as Hartley Bay. We watched while the group formed a chain and unloaded boxes of produce, dry goods, parts, supplies. The rain fell harder. Although a few outliers carried umbrellas, most everyone seemed oblivious to the downpour, motoring ATVs along the wooden boardwalks in jeans and sweatshirts, the men's raven-black hair shiny wet.

~~~~~~~~

Ken, the biologist we'd met in Shearwater, had also printed on a scrap of paper: HARTLEY BAY, WALLY BOLTON.

"Just look him up," he'd said. "He's great."

But in a place like Hartley Bay, where everything revolves around the sea, we didn't have to look far. Moving *Heron* out of the way of the incoming ferry, I'd noticed a man motoring a small skiff toward me. The neon orange floats in his bow were labeled: WALTER BOLTON.

I walked over and introduced myself, saying Ken had told us to look him up. He seemed surprised. Maybe Wally Bolton didn't remember Ken? Topping off his oil on the dock, he appeared robust and forthright, dressed in a Helly Hansen rain slicker and rain pants. He was heading out to pull in halibut, he said with bravado, as Jeff walked up. Then, with a hearty laugh, he raised his eyebrows beneath his orange-brimmed rain hat and said, "Yep, I'm long-lining—twenty-four hundred feet down—and I pull it all in by hand. Sixty-one years old. Not bad, eh?"

"*You pull those lines in by hand?*" Jeff and I both said at once, stunned, trying to picture all that dead weight and the brutal simplicity of fishing the old-fashioned way.

Wally Bolton peered out to sea. "Sure do. This young guy? Six-foot-six. Came out with me last year," he continued. "After ten minutes, he was dead."

~~~~~~

As Jeff and I settled into the pace of Hartley Bay, our raw nerves healed. It was as if the place itself, with its tight-knit community and proud, largely self-sufficient First Nations culture was a balm. We brewed tea, read, caught up on boat chores. We pulled rain jackets and boots on over our jeans and hopped down from the boat to explore. We strolled the boardwalks and peeked in the windows of the school. We walked up the trail to the salmon hatchery, a two-mile-long elevated cedar-plank walkway that wound over thick green devil's club, fern, and salmonberry.

That afternoon there was a knock on the hull. Wally Bolton stood on the dock.

"Want two crabs?" he said, pointing a meaty thumb at his boat.

He'd caught six red snappers, and insisted on handing over two ginormous Dungeness crabs.

"Those are the biggest crabs I've ever seen," Jeff said, grinning.

We slipped Wally twenty bucks. He protested, then showed me how to hold the huge crabs by their pincers. When I lifted one up, its shell was nearly as wide as I was.

An hour later when we were walking the cedar boardwalk, a teenaged boy followed. *What does he want?* we both wondered, looking over our shoulders. He came up behind us.

"Hey, Wally wants you guys to stop by his house later," the boy said.

"He does?"

"Yep, told me to tell you."

We laughed at ourselves, feeling like a team again.

When we found Wally's place, he opened the aluminum-clad door, leaned out, and said almost apologetically, "From my deep freeze." He then handed over a gorgeous ling cod fillet. It was two feet long, had spots like a leopard's, and even encased in plastic wrap, its scales glinted gold in the sun.

"Wow!" we both said, then Jeff stashed the fish under his arm, a touchdown pass of generosity we'd managed to catch in spite of ourselves. And after thanking Wally heartily, we dashed back to the boat.

INTO THE
GREAT BEAR RAINFOREST

"Just look for something yellow," Marven said, when we finally took off in search of the spirit bear. The three of us were speeding past Princess Royal Island in his small aluminum fishing skiff. "The bears sometimes come down to feed here."

I looked and looked. Each white-yellow patch along the rocky shore revealed itself to be something else: a cedar stump, a weathered log, a boulder. But Jeff and I were finally here—here in the epicenter of the Great Bear Rainforest!—home of the legendary Kermode, one of the rarest animals in the world. I smiled. This was what I'd been hoping for. If we didn't understand just how wild and remote and storm battered this stretch of the Pacific Northwest Coast was when we'd first left on our empty-nest adventure, we did now, flying across the water with Marven Robinson in his small boat, cold fresh air streaming off the Pacific.

I want to see a spirit bear, I thought, my mind fixed on our surroundings, *but if I don't, that's all right too*. I glanced over at Jeff and grinned. He looked psyched—his face intent, his eyes lit up.

Maybe it was enough—just being out here together and feeling so alive—searching for a fabled white bear on this far edge of the continent with its rocky shore stretching on and on in a misty gray-green band of forest and island. Maybe it was enough, and would always be enough: just trying to pay attention. That was the thing. Just opening our eyes to this day: its clouds, its mist, its sky.

~~~~~~~~~~

Marven dropped us off on the shore of Princess Royal with a handheld radio and a canister of bear spray.

"Ever use one of these?" he asked, handing over the spray as we scrambled out of the boat onto the mudflats lining one of the island's coves.

"Sorry?"

He raked the bristly hair atop his head. Marven was in his early forties, with a handsome, fleshy face, a direct gaze, and thatch of black hair. "Only use it if the bear is five feet or less from you, and if his ears are back," he said, then shrugged in a fatalistic way. "If his ears are forward, he's just checking you out."

We stood and watched Marven speed off to anchor farther out.

"*I won't be long!*" he hollered, his lichen-colored rain jacket vanishing in the mist.

Jeff and I turned and stared at each other, incredulous. "Yikes, he has to kayak all the way back!" I said after a slightly startled pause. The head of the inlet where we stood, boots on barnacles, looked like a salmon slaughterhouse: fish carcasses strewn everywhere—some ripped and shredded by hungry bears; others intact, only the brains bit out of their heads. ("Wolves," Marven explained later, describing how sea wolves feast on that delicacy.)

"This place is insane!" Jeff said appreciatively as squadrons of white gulls shot past, wave after wave of them, followed by lines of frantic, electrified terns. We took in the raucous scene: salmon leaping, bald eagles soaring, herons squawking. There were more birds than either of us had ever seen in a single place, trees and canyon walls reverberating with crazed caws and cries. A great blue heron swept the length of the inlet like a jumbo jet, its huge wings flapping slowly, neck outstretched, thin yellow legs trailing behind. Before long we were staggering with laughter, blundering around on the mud bank.

"You look mighty tasty there, sir," I quipped, my voice ringing out across the deserted estuary. "Do you even know how to *use that stuff*?" I added, miming a guy with a can of bear spray.

Jeff shrugged. "*Hell* no! Are you kidding me? I'll die of a heart attack before I pull the trigger."

This struck us both as hilarious.

"If a grizzly comes, we're dead," I pointed out.

"Shit, if a *black bear* comes, we're dead!"

"The boys would think we're so lame."

"*Who cares?* They think we're lame already—we're their parents!" Jeff said.

"Well, you've got that right."

~~~~~~~~~

"Are you guys ready?" Marven asked, dragging his kayak onshore and plunging into the forest. "The bears have been gorging themselves here for the past few weeks," he said, over his shoulder. Hearts beating madly, we trailed him toward the head of a copper-colored creek.

And then, none of us said anything. We crept through thickets of thick spongy moss, over fungus-wrapped trunks edged with devil's club, and past thousand-year-old cedars, trying not to snap any twigs. Fortunately, the forest floor was clotted with leaves that dampened our step. There was so much moss cloaking the branches it looked like there'd been a green blizzard. The leaves sucked at our boots. We found a log buried in a bed of wet ferns and crouched down on the bank, waiting for bears.

This was the same spot where after weeks of reconnaissance and hours of waiting, the *National Geographic* team finally found and photographed *Ursus americanus kermodei*, the legendary spirit bear. Thrilled, Jeff and I settled down to wait.

"Spirit bears are shy," Marven said, leaning in close. He smelled like pine needles and mint. "They could be right here and we wouldn't even know."

We made ourselves still. Marven poured coffee from a brown thermos. Slanted late-afternoon light haunted the centuries-old forest. Everything felt verdant and ancient. We waited and waited. Wind breathed through the branches. I tried to watch for movement on the river's opposite bank but instead felt the coffee warm my stomach. Rust- and cinnamon-brown leaves shuttled downriver. Everything seemed to be flowing into the river, except the fish, which were going back up it. In the river salmon were packed so close fin to gill it seemed like you could almost walk across their backs. You could hear them muscling their way upstream, fighting to fling their silver lengths up the gravel streambed—splashing and scraping and then, when they got their energy back, leaping again. The whole thing was so fierce and sad, noble and inevitable. It was Nature and Death, that final dance.

None of us said a word for a long time. The creek hummed with the sound of fish jumping and river stones jostling and spruce needles dripping. A gang of ravens went by croaking and cawing, and flying so low we could hear the *shhh-shhh-shhh* sound of their wings. My joints started to ache and my foot was falling asleep, and it hadn't even been an hour. I crouched and waited some more. Jeff *hates* to wait, but when I snuck a peek at him he was sitting as still as a Gore-Tex statue—until he turned his head and raised his eyebrows in a mock grimace.

"Listen," Marven whispered, his head slightly cocked as he caught my gaze intently. "We never spoke of *mooksgm'ol*—the white bear. My grandmother, Helen, tells the story of Raven. How Raven made one in every ten black bears white to remind people of a time when the world was all snow and ice, so people would be thankful for the lush and bountiful land of today. Many of our people believe *mooskgm'ol* holds supernatural powers—that the white bear is a special creature left to remind us of that earlier time when everything was covered by glaciers . . ."

"You mean like an ice age?" I said.

"Yup . . ." Marven nodded gravely, his voice trailing off.

That's when we saw the bear ambling up the river. The bear was midsize, lovely, but it wasn't a white bear—it was another hungry black bear, *Ursus americanus*. It pawed at a pile of dead salmon it had stashed on the riverbank. Our quest to see the spirit bear, I realized, was just beginning.

MOOKSGM'OL

~~~~~~

"This is the big moment, Brown," my husband said.

Neither of us could believe this was it: I noted our coordinates, N 53° 32' 27", W 129° 00' 7". We'd been up since six, sliding *Heron* out of Hartley Bay on a rising tide before seven. And now, motoring along on a stunning still morning, we'd reached the apex of our trip, having traveled close to seven hundred nearly windless nautical miles. White waterfalls tumbled down Gribbell Island's rocky flanks in the dawn, and a small brown sparrow settled on our halyard, hitching a ride.

That morning the sky was steel blue, the water dark and deep. Islands of mist crowned Gribbell's granite peaks and cloaked its escarpments, scraped smooth by glaciers eons before, and although it was the last day of August, snow patches clung to the highest bowls. I stood in the cockpit, steering *Heron* up a channel called Verney Passage, the northernmost point of our whole trip.

"I'm glad it's not pouring rain today," I said, tilting my face toward the burgeoning light.

"I'm glad it's not pouring rain *any* day," Jeff said. He'd pulled his red foulies over his faded fir-green fleece in the predawn dark, and with his old knit wool ski cap topping his tanned face and silver stubble, he looked like the star of a Norwegian sitcom.

~~~~~~~~~

We were ninety miles south of the Alaska border, close enough to dip a toe across that finish line. But turning south here—at the northernmost range of the spirit bear—made sense. We'd made plans to meet Marven again: this time on Gribbell Island. We'd anchor, hike in to a different spot, and wait for the white bear.

The sea glided along beneath us, spattered with the countless chevrons of tiny waves. The mountains ranged around us illuminated, silent and bright. Everything had a shining edge to it. As the granite cliffs and forested humps of uninhabited Gribbell Island passed to starboard in the new-day sun, I suddenly understood why the Gitga'at people would have been so secretive and protective of their white bears for so many years. Decades. Centuries. How it could be that Marven, now forty-three and a revered bear guide, hadn't even *seen* a white bear until nineteen years ago.

When your world is water, rock, sky . . . When everything else external is stripped away . . . What is left? Cloud. Light. Wind.

Spirit.

I'd come to appreciate out here that the essential truths, the only truths that really matter in the end, are the ones we don't always understand. What's mysterious, nebulous, holy. The things that don't have an easy answer. Patch of dirty white fur in a dark forest. Flash of cream-colored paw fishing for salmon. The space between dreams and wakefulness, the gray between black and white, a line so tenuous it sometimes doesn't exist . . . like a river between a thousand trees.

Jeff and I had pushed ourselves nearly to the breaking point as a couple, and now our world was stripped to that: water, rock, sky. Piloting *Heron* over the lead-blue sea, sharp wind on my face, bright sun warming my bones, I was almost sorry to reach the turning point of our trip. We were in the middle of nowhere, but we hadn't gotten lonely. Instead, being out here in these immense open spaces, we didn't have a sense of ourselves the way most couples do. Sometimes it was almost as if we were the wind, or the weather itself.

I longed to see a Kermode bear because it seemed magical and beautiful. I longed to see a spirit bear because in its rarity it felt, somehow, like the living embodiment of the loneliness that separates every living creature from every other living creature.

But it was going to take time. Yesterday, after hours of waiting in the woods with Marven—after a day packed with gliding humpbacks, dive-bombing birds, and salmon-crazed black bears—finding *mooksgm'ol*, the sacred white bear, seemed about as likely as finding Sasquatch.

~~~~~~~~~

Marven's boat was bobbing in a small forested cove. We saw it flashing in the pale watery light as we neared Gribbell Island. We waved, dropped anchor, pulled on our rain pants, and dinghied ashore.

"Hey, you two—ready?" Marven asked as we lashed the dinghy to a log.

"Yep, can't believe it's already midmorning," I replied.

Marven gathered his things: a radio, a coffee-browned thermos, extra socks in a knapsack. He pulled on his muck boots, fit his backpack over his shoulders. "Let's go find the white bear, then."

We hurried behind him, hiking through thickets, brambles, ferns, fungus-wrapped trunks, and into a sodden ravine where everything smelled of rain. There was the snap of twigs, the crunch of leaves. Even the air emanated wet spruce and dirt and centuries of moss. The leaves pulled at our boots and flung drops of mud onto our rain pants. In the space between our footfalls I could hear the river whispering from the depths of the woods.

The trail got narrower and steeper, winding upward along the side of a deep gulch, when, suddenly, Marven stopped. I looked past his shoulder toward the river, expecting to see some sort of clearing where the bears would magically appear. But there was nothing, just endless forest and the ravine dropping down to the river. We began scrambling down a steep muddy path, backpacks jouncing, boots sliding. And then, when I looked toward the river again, I saw a wooden platform he'd built in the trees on the edge of the river, with a rickety ladder that led up to it and disappeared in the leaves.

Jeff had stopped and was standing behind me, and Marven was saying softly, "Sorry—I've got to hike on and check if there's been any activity upriver"—he nodded in that direction—"so climb up. I'll be back."

What? I mouthed to Jeff as Marven hiked off.

But Marven was already scrambling up the ravine and hiking to the next platform, leaving us alone on the edge of the river.

I turned toward the ladder. Wooden rungs. Wet, leading up. I tugged on Jeff's sleeve.

"Come on," I whispered. "Let's go!" I felt a deep hollow in my core: giddiness.

"This is it!" Jeff said, pushing me toward the first ladder. "Let's do this thing!"

I started up the first slippery rungs. Jeff followed, and together we climbed. The higher we went the wetter it got. We reached Marven's small wooden platform, sat down, and dangled our legs over the side. It started to rain. Suddenly, everything was quiet, and all we could hear was the rain in the trees and the river murmuring. I looked at my backpack on the platform next to me.

It was soaked.

~~~~~~~~

Seeing bears is all about waiting, we were learning. And quiet. There's no talking, no chitchat, no joking around. We hunkered down in the dank tree fort while the rain, which falls ten months of the year here, slipped and slid down the branches and leaves, plumping the mosses and weighing down the ferns.

We poured coffee from the thermos. Adjusted our Gore-Tex. Sat and waited some more. There was the sound of the river threading over the stones and the wind breathing through the moss-coated branches. The splash of the salmon muscling their way upstream to spawn and die. The feel of the wind out of the northwest brushing my left cheekbone.

Sight quickly loses its supremacy, I realized, in dense forest. Hearing, however, is honed. The silence is rich. Even the slightest rustle grew audible, and soon it was as if we could hear for miles and miles, every sound clear and distinct, every murmur announcing itself in a way we'd never heard before. There were the tiny splashes and sucks of the river, the low bass booming of rocks being turned by the river. We heard ravens, trees, leaves falling, stones, fish . . . We both heard a thousand sounds we'd never heard together and would never have noticed. But sitting side by side squeezed onto a five-foot-wide platform secured to a tree—surrounded by the smell of wet stones, and mud, and mulching rotting leaves—we heard everything, the river muttering in a language that lifted through stones, air, and sky on its way to the sea.

I shivered and stood for a while, then sat again and watched the river rushing along, sleek and silver. It felt delicious, the irresistible tug of moving water and my blood coursing with it. I reached for Jeff's hand.

~~~~~~~

It wasn't long, maybe thirty minutes, before a black bear—trailed by two cubs—emerged from the weeds on the opposite bank about forty feet away. She sniffed the air, her coat glistening, and stepped into the creek. Lunged at a salmon. Missed. Grappled with a second fish. Missed again. I felt for her, the pressure to feed her hungry cubs, not half grown into their paws. While the young mother flailed at the fish, her cubs trundled over logs, scaled a tree, got stuck on a limb, unstuck, and forded the river themselves, trailing behind their mom boulder to boulder.

Mom-m-m, you could practically hear them whining while they snorfled up grubs and acorns. *We're* hungry!

Jeff and I rummaged around in our backpacks on the tree platform and, being lucky humans, dug out peanut butter sandwiches. By early afternoon the sun burst through the rain in fast-moving arcs. A Steller's jay flashed through the canopy of spruce and cedar, and a pine marten bustled overhead. On the ground directly beneath us, bear tracks etched the sand. The prints were clear and deep, each individual claw slicing sharply into the grit.

Hours passed. Marven returned. A second black bear trailed by two cubs appeared on the opposite bank, honed in on a salmon, and pounced, holding the fish clenched between her teeth while the first bear, probably a young mother according to Marven, looked on ravenously. When the hungry mom ventured a few feet closer, the older bear bared her teeth. Snarled. Lunged.

"It's like watching two women going after a parking spot at Whole Foods!" I whispered.

"You kidding? Those suburban moms are way more aggressive."

"What if we don't see it?" I said after a while, meaning the white bear.

"Today is your day," Jeff replied with certainty.

~~~~~~~~

Another hour or so crept past. Marven grabbed my elbow. All of a sudden there it was. A giant. He was thickset, probably weighing at least four hundred pounds, alabaster pale. At the sight of him I was paralyzed with happiness; it was the spirit bear, not thirty feet from us, down to the cinnamon-fur stripe tracing its spine; its thick, cream-colored coat seeming to glow.

He stepped out of the shrubs on the opposite bank, stood stock-still, then moved slowly down to the river's edge, milky white, the sun glinting off the tips of his fur. He turned his head left to right, and back again. Sniffed the air. He clambered slowly up onto a moss-cloaked log that stretched across the river and scooped a gigantic paw into the water, trying to snag a fish.

He was so close we could hear him huffing slightly as he crossed the log in slow motion. He was between us and whatever place he'd stepped from, which seemed a landscape beyond. Jeff grabbed the camera. I could hardly breathe. The bear looked to me as old as light, his movement measured. He was both motion and stillness, a deep silence around him. He seemed as surreal as a dream, but with a presence that filled the whole river. Thirty seconds, eternity. It was as if the spirit of the place had become visible, had for an instant taken on material form.

We stood rapt and watched the beautiful bear amble up the river. He had a rare otherness: all the charge and mystery of a singular work of art, the magic of a mythical being that's stepped out of a fairy tale, with late-afternoon light on his back flaring in a copper glow.

I felt luminous. To abide the bear was to feel large. But mostly, I recognized in those moments, that feeling of abundance was about the waiting for the bear, and the journey to the waiting, and doing those things together. It made everything, including the mystery that's always there, even between two people who think they know every-thing about each other, seem whole.

We leaned way out over the railing, trying to make the won-der of those minutes last. The bear crossed a log, stood sniffing the air, head turning back and forth. Then he was past, paws crunching gravel, and we watched him continue up the river until the forest swallowed him.

MORE CANVAS!

An hour after we saw the bear, something totally unexpected happened. Jeff and I were hiking out, weaving between the trees, with Marven following. "A lot of people feel it's really spiritual to see the white bear," he was saying. Darkness was beginning to fall. Just then, Jeff saw a streak of gray, a flash.

"What's that?" He pointed. "Up ahead on that branch?"

It was an owl hunkered in the limbs not ten feet in front of us, watching with huge black eyes. Suddenly, it spread its wings, lifted off, and disappeared into the forest.

We hiked on, scanning trees in search of the thing. Leaves. Darkness. Moss.

And suddenly, there it was again: this enormous owl blocking the trail.

"A northern spotted owl . . . that's a really rare sighting," Marven said, stunned.

Hello, wondrous owl! I felt like shouting into the cold.

"That's only the second one I've seen in the wild," Marven said. "Some tribal people think it's bad luck to see them . . ." he added, his voice trailing off.

But I didn't think so. The northern spotted owl kept drawing us on, flying ahead through the trees, then strangely stopping to wait, as if it had something urgent to say.

What I heard it say when I thought about it later was this: There is both beauty and darkness in nature. And in life. The poles of existence. It's bittersweet, the reality of the passage of time. Don't worry so much about what's going to happen because it's out of your control anyway. Listen. Have faith. Feel. Even pain has its place, so you might as well grab life by the tail and hold on tight, live it well, all of it, eyes wide-open.

~~~~~~~~

Back aboard the boat the rain slackened; the evening's clouds swelled with brightness. Standing on the bow raising the anchor, I could hear the hypnotic voice of the sea tapping against the hull. A wind had picked up: insistent, briny, bright. Over the next days, as we made our way south, from Khutze Inlet to Reserve Bay, down the great length of Princess Royal Channel to Rescue Bay, and finally to Shearwater, I thought about the bear. Could it be my spirit animal? I pictured its powerful jaws, imagined it sleeping in its moss thicket, its fur dirty white.

"'Each of the four directions: North, South, East, and West,'" or the Four Directions of indigenous oral teachings, I read aloud to Jeff as we continued south, "'represents a particular way of perceiving things. No direction is considered superior to another, the point is to seek and explore each one in order to gain a thorough understanding of your own nature over time and in relation to the surrounding world.'"

"*Hmmph*," my husband grunted.

"But hey, listen to this," I went on. "'North represents Wisdom. *Its color is white*, its power animal is the buffalo, and its gift is strength and endurance. West is the world of introspection; its color is black, its gift is rain, *and its power animal is the bear.*'"

I set down the book. "That's cool, don't you think? That we've just spent the last month sailing *North and West* in search of a *white bear?*"

"Maybe. What's South, then?"

I picked up the book, paged ahead. "From the South comes the gift of warmth and growth after winter is over . . . its color is green . . . its power animal, the mouse."

"You're shitting me. Its power animal is the mouse?"

I laughed, smiled. "Well, at least I'll take warmth any day."

<hr>

With the boys leaving, I'd felt adrift in the world—not just the predictable drift of who to be and what to hope for, but the drift of time and space in a calendar unmoored. I thought of all the places I'd been and all the lives you could lead, all of them interconnected in a time that seemed to be moving faster, growing more layered and complex and uncertain by the minute.

The white bear, nearly as great a mystery now as it was eons ago, seemed so fantastic. When I closed my eyes and saw the bear, dreamed about the bear, I saw a white spark sheltered by wild sea: an elusive spirit surrounded by some of the world's most powerful currents. And in that thought was clarity, a point of focus in the haze.

I'd always been led by instinct, which had brought me my husband and my sons, so I trusted it: the idea of our empty-nest trip, to sail north together hoping to find the mythical white bear. Sometimes, you just have to point your heart toward something to move on. I also knew that although I love to get lost, I'd need a true partner in the wilderness—so I kidnapped my husband, talked him into venturing north together, although we had no idea if we'd make it to the Great Bear Rainforest, what we'd find there, or even if our boat would survive . . .

As we journeyed home, some days we awoke to sun, clear blue sky, and a brisk breeze streaming off the walls of the granite fjords. Others, we awoke to rain pummeling the cabin, and peered out to see lead-gray seas. The crisp air signaled September: we imagined Sam, driving home from San Francisco to pick up a rug we'd left for his apartment. We pictured James on his way to class (hopefully) in upstate New York, where the time was always three hours ahead. This awareness of our sons' comings and goings was like a thick thread of feeling, connecting us materially. Jeff and I laughed at ourselves: the anticipation of the boys leaving had been so much worse somehow than their actual leaving.

Each morning we selected a Song of the Day, choosing a track from the iPod and cranking up Radiohead, the Pixies, old Rolling Stones. We danced on the stern deck to stay warm. We savored simple pleasures: mugs of hot tomato soup in the cockpit, crisp green apples, and the sheer dreamy quality of time, sitting in the main cabin reading, the only sound that of the occasional page turning. I found a spare piece of line and, when I was insanely bored, perfected my clove hitch.

Craziest of all? Once we found the spirit bear we managed to find the Northwest's elusive wind as well. After sheets of rain lashing Mathieson Channel—"I can see where the phrase *sheets of rain* comes from!" I yelled from the helm back to Jeff, who was busy securing the dinghy so it wouldn't buck and slap the sea while vertical planes of rain drenched him. We made our way back down Percival Narrows and Reid Passage, threading the rocky entrance to Seaforth Channel.

There, against an angry indigo sky and with twenty knots blowing from the southwest, we caught enough wind to put the sails up.

We raised the staysail first.

Then the big main.

And finally, with both of us yelling "*More canvas!*"—and agreeing for once—the giant white genoa: dazzling, billowing and flapping.

Spanking along, we hurtled downwind like that all the way to Bella Bella, big sails unfurled like wings against the sky.

<hr />

We put the sails up again the next day in Fitz Hugh Sound, but the wind, maybe seven knots, didn't last. We cut the engine anyway. *Heron* moved so slowly across the water, we wondered if we were moving at all. There was the sound of the wind plying the canvas and wave-splash off the bow and just enough breeze to burn away the fog, leaving a thin white band of silver mist above the water.

Neither of us said anything for a long time. Sailing this slowly, moving imperceptibly, it seemed to me as if we were able to see our lives from above, like birds soaring over a landscape, and with a deepening sense of the connection of all its parts. I felt intensely alive, remembering all the people we'd met—Marven and Richard Hunt and Wally Bolton; Ken and Edith, Jill and Richard; Pat Freeny and Captain Brian; the villagers of Klemtu and Hartley Bay. Everything— the schools of fish swimming beneath us and the great flocks of birds floating past; the lone wolf and the white spirit bear; the ancient orcas and humpbacks, each humpback whale's tail as individual as a human thumbprint—felt linked and fragile and worth fighting for.

"Look, humpbacks!" Jeff said after a while, staring off the starboard bow.

We counted four, then seven, then twelve spouts: a whole family of whales feeding lazily, their white spray rising and falling against the dark flanks of Calvert Island.

"Maybe they're migrating south to Mexico," he mused.

"We could just keep going . . . follow them," I suggested.

We floated on through the stillness across the glassy strait.

Then, when it was time to pull in the sails, we secured them easily, wound them fast, and motored the boat into a forested bay called Fury Cove. It was protected and calm this day; warm with late-afternoon light and ringed by shell beaches piled high with gray driftwood worn smooth by weather and time.

We dropped the anchor and shut down the engine.

Silence.

"Want to go exploring?" Jeff said after a few minutes, eyeing the wild beach.

We stood there a moment, savoring the new quiet. There was a feeling of accomplishment and a feeling of pure freedom. We had done this thing together. That was all, and it was enough.

I leaned over to roll up my jeans so we could wade gingerly ashore in this new place.

"Yes," I said, and felt a spark of wonder that we'd made it here. "I do."

ACKNOWLEDGMENTS

This book owes everything to the generosity of author and naturalist Leslie T. Sharpe, who was both safe harbor and sharp-eyed navigator throughout the (very) long process of taking it from first pages to final draft. *Uncharted* exists because a handful of exceptional people, like Leslie, believed in it from the start.

Gratitude is not a big enough word for dream agent Jennifer Lyons, who took a chance on me and continues to grace me with her wisdom, friendship, and straight talk.

I can't imagine a finer editor than Gary Luke or finer home than Sasquatch Books. I am forever grateful to Gary and the entire Sasquatch team, including Jill Saginario, Tony Ong, Robin Cruise, Callie Stoker-Graham, Nikki Sprinkle, and Molly Woolbright.

Sasquatch said yes because the book had already benefited from the goodwill of so many friends who helped nurture it along the way: Kate Riley, whose writing group in Hailey, Idaho, became my first readers; sincere gratitude to Rob Hannon and Holland Williams for early comments. Love and thanks to Kate Janeway for introducing me to Gail Ross, and to Gail for her wise feedback. Enormous thanks to author Iris Graville and author and publisher L. M. Browning at Homebound Publications for sharing their time and advice as well. To Pat Freeny and Paul Nicklen, my deepest gratitude.

Big thanks to everyone at the former NILA writing residency on Whidbey Island for taking such keen interest in my work. A shout-out to Lawrence Cheek, Melissa Hart, and Ana Maria Spagna, especially for your kindness. Thank you to Cynthia Jones for not only being such a loyal writing partner but for hosting such inspiring writers' salons. To Rick Simonson at Elliott Bay Book Company for key publishing advice at exactly the right moment. To Mary Elizabeth Braun at Oregon State University Press for your support. To Ruth Dickey at Seattle Arts & Lectures for morning coffee and inspiration. And to Michael Wiegers at Copper Canyon Press for poetry.

Dream editors Marika Cain, Peter Fish, John Rasmus, Richard Bangs, Nancy Novogrod, Pamela Fiori, Susan Crandell, Melissa Biggs Bradley, Susan Crandell, Ila Stanger, and Tracey Minkin provided writing assignments that sustained my wanderlust. I am indebted to Marika Cain in particular for the privilege of remarkable assignments around the world during years when many iconic publications folded.

Thank you to my dearest friends along the way: Sue Bogin for your smarts and incredible generosity in reading through multiple drafts. Thank you, Anne Barker, Ellen Rubinfeld, Arthur Rubinfeld, Laura Midgley, Pauline and Robbie Bach, Justina Chen, Margot Kahn, Martha Brockenbrough, Nicole Hardy, Byron Ricks, Blaine Harden, Jessica Kowal, Margaret Lane, Stephen Caplow, Lisa and Sam Verhovek, Charlotte Guyman, Elizabeth Turk, Jane and Rick Bernstein, Nicole Raphaelson, Jean Hanff Korelitz, Eileen Delehanty Pearkes, Jan and Bob Whitsitt, Julie and Erik Nordstrom, Susan Potts, Molly Pengra, Sarah Woodward, Jody Cunningham, Sharon Linton, Nancy Gervais, Lauren Davis, and Beth Drayton, for coffee, walks, snowshoes, dinners, books, encouragement, and more inspiration than you'll ever know. Thanks to Geof Barker and David Midgley, sailing friends extraordinaire, and Dan and Amy Nordstrom for good humor, camaraderie, and commenting on portions of the manuscript. Special thanks to Howard Wright and Kate Janeway for Clam Shack heaven on the edge of the Salish Sea. And to Paul LaRussa and Ivan for helping keep *Heron* afloat.

For nuance on indigenous culture and history, I am indebted to First Nation friends: Jess Housty in Bella Bella; Doug Neasloss and Rosie Childs in Klemtu; and Marven Robinson for reading and commenting on portions of the manuscript.

To my parents, Bart and Laurie Brown, there can never be enough thank-yous for being our inspirations in adventure and life. Thank you for not only believing in me and this book, but for both taking the time to read it so carefully—and for your thoughtful comments.

Thank you, Dr. Kristen Brown Golden, for joining me on assignment in Japan and offering much-needed sisterly support at a crucial stage of the book-making process!

And always and in every way, thank you to Sam and James Seely for being the kind, lovely men you've grown up to be and for not only letting me write about you when you were much, much younger, but also for taking the time years later to read the manuscript and make such deft, insightful comments. Thank you to Annie Vaughn and Colleen Sullivan for so gamely joining us aboard *Mighty Heron* in recent summers, and for being such spirited and charming additions to our crew.

And finally, to Jeff Seely, my love, my happiness, my dearest friend and fellow explorer. Thank you for making life fun and always interesting, for reading so many drafts, and for supporting every word. I would literally not be here without you.

ABOUT THE AUTHOR

~~~~~~~~~

Kim Brown Seely is the descendant of a pioneer family that came to California in a covered wagon (or "prairie schooner") in 1864. Her wanderlust was born during summers tromping about the High Sierras and along the remote Lost Coast of Northern California with her parents when she was a girl. Winner of a 2016 Lowell Thomas Journalist of the Year Award and the Lowell Thomas Award in Environmental Journalism, she worked for many years as senior editor at *Travel & Leisure* magazine, contributing editor at *National Geographic Adventure*, travel editor at Microsoft, and travel editor at Amazon.com. A lifelong adventurer, Kim's passion is experiencing—and writing about—remote, wild places. She has traveled to more than thirty countries for *Virtuoso Life* magazine, where she is a contributing writer and has won nearly a dozen writing awards for her work. She lives near Seattle, Washington.

FLAMES OVER TOKYO

FLAMES OVER TOKYO

The U.S. Army Air Forces' Incendiary Campaign Against Japan

1944-1945

BY

E. BARTLETT KERR

DONALD I. FINE, INC.

New York

Library of Congress Cataloging-in-Publication Data
Kerr, E. Bartlett.
    Flames over Tokyo : the U.S. Army Air Force's incendiary campaign
against Japan. 1944–45 / by E. Bartlett Kerr.
      p.   cm.
    Includes bibliographical references and index.
    ISBN: 1-55611-301-3
    1. World War, 1939–1945—Aerial operations, American.   2. Japan—
History—Bombardment, 1944–1945.   I. Title.
D790.K45   1991
940.54'4973—dc20   91-55175
                                                                         CIP

Manufactured in the United States of America

10   9   8   7   6   5   4   3   2   1

Designed by Irving Perkins Associates

This book is dedicated to the men of the Twentieth Air Force,
both living and dead,
who participated in the massive aerial bombardment of Japan,
an assault which led to the country's surrender
and the end of World War II.

ACKNOWLEDGMENTS
AND SOURCES

IN WRITING THIS account of the air war against Japan I made liberal use of historical and operational records of the U.S. Air Force and will comment further on these below. But to breathe life into the story, I drew heavily on the personal experiences of the participants—the Americans and to a somewhat lesser extent the Japanese. For their shared recollections I am most grateful.

These contributions came in the form of personal interviews, correspondence, memoirs, diaries and published works. All of the sources that are directly reflected in the text are recognized in the chapter notes.

To the scores of individuals with whom I had conversations either by phone or in person, or corresponded with to check a fact or pursue a lead, and who do not find their names mentioned—my thanks. Many of their accounts were fascinating and might well have been included but for space limitations and the necessity for selectivity.

I am indebted to the several organizations that a few dedicated men worked hard to form in the years since the end of World War II—the Twentieth Air Force Association and the wing and group associations. These organizations generously provided me with the membership lists I needed to locate the airmen of the Twentieth Air Force. On several occasions I attended their reunions, where I saw and felt the close kinship that these men feel for each other.

The advice and assistance some former airmen gave me deserves particular mention. Soon after I began work on this book I was on a radio talk show and asked any veterans of the air war over Japan who were listening to call in. Among the first to do so was Raymond Halloran. My first interview was with Ray. We stayed in contact throughout the research and writing of the book, and he read and commented on the final draft. Early in the research phase I met Dennis Pidhayney. Denny shared with me the massive listing of documents pertaining to the Twentieth Air Force's role in the war against Japan that he had compiled over the years. He also read and commented on the final draft. Harry Changnon generously loaned me books and documents from his collection on the Twentieth Air Force.

I was not too far into my research before I met James Pattillo. Jim shared unstintingly of his time and knowledge of the B-29 and aerial combat. His detailed comments on many of its chapters and his abiding interest, advice and support were invaluable.

Later I met Walter Sherrell, historian of the 498th Bomb Group, 73rd Bomb Wing. Walt and his crew flew in all of the major incendiary missions over Tokyo, and he and two other members of his crew kept journals. Walt contributed substantially to the chapters describing these missions. Toward the end of my work on the book I was introduced to Jack Catton. Jack, as a major, flew combat missions with the 73rd Bomb Wing and later was an operations planner on Gen. Curtis LeMay's staff. Jack's comments on my final draft were valuable not only because of this dual perspective but also because of his later experience as a general in the U.S. Air Force.

Others besides the Twentieth Air Force veterans contributed to this work. Among them was Anthony Arthur. Tony, a friend and fellow historian, was a continuing source of encouragement and gave the final draft a good "once over." I owe much to Nancy Nixon for sharing with me her personal recollections about her brother Raymond Ewell and documentary material on him. I am grateful, too, for the help my friend Wilmot R. McCutchen gave me in preparing the maps for this book. Finally, my thanks to my agent Tom Wallace for the efforts that led to the publication of this book.

I found the documentation for my account in a number of research centers and libraries. The most important single source was the Office of Air Force History, located at Bolling Field, Washington, D.C. Most of the original copies of Air Force historical documents, held at the Air Force Historical Research Center located at the Air University, Maxwell Air Force Base, Alabama, are also on microfilm at the Office of Air Force History. William S. Heimdahl of this office and his staff were most helpful in accessing this important store of primary documents.

Another major source of information was the National Archives in Washington, D.C. The Archives house a complete set of the U.S. Strategic Bombing Survey Reports on the bombing campaign against Japan. The set includes working documents and draft material used in preparing the final reports. It was also in the National Archives that I found most of the material used in describing how scientists in the National Defense Research Committee developed the M-69 incendiary bomb.

I drew on the Library of Congress Manuscript Division holdings for Gen. H. H. Arnold's papers. Description of the U.S. Army Chemical Corps' important role in developing and producing incendiary bombs came from the Corps' volumes that are part of the *United States Army in World War II series.*

Most of the photographs in this book are from the U.S. Air Force collection, which is stored, 50,000 photos to a disc, at the National Air and Space Museum Library, Washington D.C. Raymond Ewell's photo is courtesy of his wife, Ingeborg Ewell.

My closing word is for my friend, John Harper. As with my previous book, John's commitment was second only to mine. He was, once again, a source of continuing help and encouragement. For this I am grateful.

FOREWORD

THE GENESIS OF this book occurred while I was doing research for another book on the Pacific War. In the official history of the U.S. Army Air Forces in World War II, I found a brief account of the Twentieth Air Force's incendiary raid on Tokyo on the night of 9 March, 1945. The Air Force historians concluded that the bombing, which killed 83,000 people and left over a million homeless, was the most deadly and destructive of World War II. At somewhat greater length, they described how in the next five months American bombers, carrying firebombs, destroyed or damaged more than sixty of Japan's cities. As one who has read much about the Pacific War, I knew of the bombing of Tokyo but was unaware of its magnitude and role in the war against Japan. This caused me to wonder how much the public might know about the Tokyo bombing and the incendiary campaign that resulted.

Looking into this, I found that most people knew little and what they did know was often inaccurate or ill-conceived. Some confused the 1945 bombing with one in 1942 led by Col. James Doolittle. The Doolittle raid, though it boosted American morale, had no effect on the conduct of the war against Japan. Others who had read about the 9 March, 1945 raid believed erroneously that the whole idea of burning Japan's cities originated with Maj. Gen. Curtis LeMay, commander of the bombers that night. Only a small number of people understood the lethal and destructive power of incendiary bombs. On the other hand, nearly everyone was familiar with the tremendous power of the atomic bombs exploded at Hiroshima and Nagasaki; some believed that these two bombs, virtually alone, compelled Japan to surrender.

I looked for published material that would provide more information on this historic raid. I discovered books about the B-29, the Twentieth Air Force and Gen. Curtis LeMay, as well as a number of articles about the raid. I found only one book, *Target Tokyo*, by Martin Caidin, a paperback published in 1960, that described the 9 March fire raid in some detail. Though Caidin's account of the raid is lucid and interesting, it treats lightly, if at all, the factors that led to this fiery cataclysm and the impact it had on the outcome of World War II. I concluded that a number of important elements of the story had not been covered in published works or, if they had, were described inadequately.

So I began my own research. For information on the development of incendiary bombs used by the Army Air Forces and the planning and decisions that led to the adoption of an incendiary strategy, I went to the National Archives and the Library of Congress. For combat operations and the Pentagon involvement, I relied on Air Force records and interviews with airmen who had flown incendiary missions over Japan. I felt that the following items needed amplification:

• How, after Pearl Harbor, even though U.S. policy strictly prohibited its air forces from bombing cities and civilians, a small band of scientists, working under Dr. Vannevar Bush, head of U.S. wartime research, in just six months designed, produced and tested a unique incendiary bomb, the M-69, particularly suited for setting fire to Japanese cities.

• How these scientists, despite lack of interest on the part of the Army Air Forces, continued to advocate incendiary bombing of Japanese cities with a new high-altitude bomber—the B-29—to carry the bombs.

• How the Committee of Operations Analysts (one of the Pentagon's earliest think tanks and advisor to Chief of the Army Air Forces Gen. H. H. Arnold), influenced by test data and studies furnished them by the developers of the M-69, became convinced that the B-29 incendiary raids on Japanese cities should be carried out and recommended this action to Gen. Arnold.

· How Gen. Arnold, though his air forces in Europe were still firmly committed to bombing only industrial and military targets, decided on a dual strategy for attacking Japan—bomb the factories, then burn the cities.

· How Gen. LeMay, after failed attempts to destroy Japan's factories with conventional bombs, from high altitude, in daylight, decided to send his bombers against Tokyo on 9 March at low altitude, at night, loaded with M-69 incendiaries—with terribly destructive results.

· How LeMay mounted a series of fire raids that, by August 1945, destroyed or damaged more than sixty cities, crippled Japan's war production and dashed the hopes of all Japanese, from Emperor to factory worker.

· How the cumulative effect of the fire raids was a major factor in influencing the peace faction in Japan's governmental power structure as well as the Emperor to accept the Allied demand for surrender, thus forestalling an invasion of Japan scheduled for 1 November, 1945 and saving countless human lives.

Integral to these major events were the individual experiences of participants—American scientists, government officials, military commanders, air combat crews and support personnel; Japanese political leaders, military commanders, air defense forces and civilians who had to endure the fiery onslaught—all stories that needed telling.

These are the reasons I decided to write this book. I hope it will illuminate an important but little understood chapter in the history of World War II.

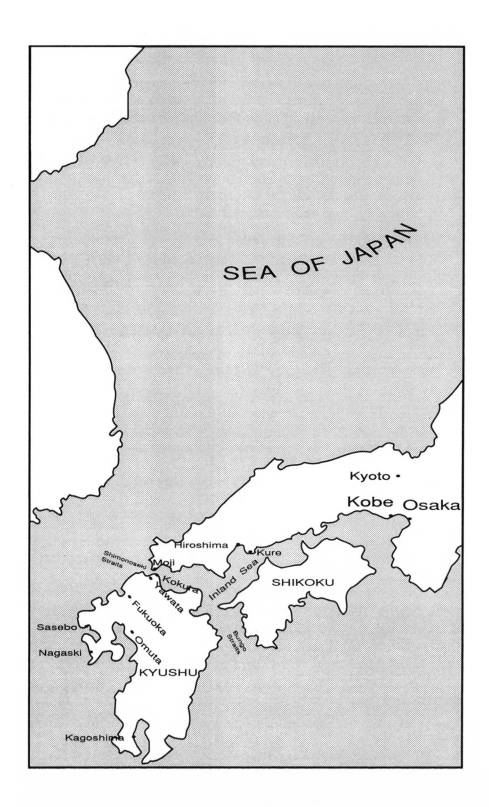

SEA OF JAPAN

Kyoto •

Kobe Osaka

Hiroshima   • Kure

Shimonoseki
Straits   • Moji
           • Kokura
           • Yawata   Inland Sea   SHIKOKU

           • Fukuoka

Sasebo

Nagaski •   • Omuta   Bungo
                            Straits

           KYUSHU

Kagoshima •

CONTENTS

FLAMES
OVER
TOKYO

A Chronology of the Pacific War and Major Events In the B-29 Bombing Campaign Against Japan

1940

JUN · Army Air Corps contracts with Boeing to build first XB-29
SEP · Germans bomb London with incendiary bombs
NOV · Air Corps acquires first incendiary bomb, the 100-lb M-47

1941

MAY · Army Air Corps acquires the 4-lb M-50 incendiary bomb from British
JUN · Army Air Corps redesignated Army Air Forces (AAF)
· Army Air Forces develops air war plan for World War II that includes high-altitude, daylight precision bombing of strategic targets
DEC · Japanese bomb Pearl Harbor

1942

JAN– · National Defense Research Committee (NDRC) develops
MAR   the 6-lb M-69 incendiary bomb
APR · Army Chemical Warfare Service tests M-69 and M-50 at Huntsville, Alabama
APR · American aircraft led by Col. Doolittle bomb Tokyo
MAY · Last troops surrender in the Philippines
JUN · U.S. Navy defeats Japanese fleet at Midway
JUL · After tests at Jefferson Proving Ground, M-69, M-47, and M-50 are accepted for production and operational use by the AAF
AUG · Marines land on Guadalcanal
AUG · U.S. Eighth Air Force flies its first mission (high-altitude precision bombing) against rail yards in France
SEP · Richard Russell and Raymond Ewell go to England to share information on U.S. incendiary tests and review British experience with incendiaries
· First test flight of the B-29

1

1943

MAR   • AAF prepares first list of strategic targets in Japan
       • Committee of Operations Analysts (COA) begins identifying priority targets in Japan
JUN   • First operational B-29s leave the assembly line
MAY–   • M-69 proves best of three incendiaries after intensive testing at Dugway Proving Ground, Utah
SEP
AUG   • British Royal Air Force firebombs Hamburg, killing 45,000
SEP   • First four B-29 bomb groups (later to become the 58th Bomb Wing) begin forming at bases in Kansas
OCT   • AAF Asst. Chief of Staff, Intelligence, recommends use of M-69 bomb to destroy Japanese cities
NOV   • COA recommends six bombing targets in Japan to Gen. Arnold; one is an incendiary target—urban industrial areas
       • Allied leaders at Cairo, Egypt, adopt "Air Plan for Defeat of Japan," code-named "Matterhorn"; the plan calls for initial attacks from bases in China, later attacks from the Marianas
       • Gen. Arnold activates the XX Bomber Command at Smoky Hill Army Air Base, assigning to it the 58th and 73rd Bomb Wings

1944

MAR   • Gen. Arnold orders "Battle of Kansas" to prepare B-29s for combat
       • XXI Bomber Command activated at Smoky Hill Air Base
APR   • Twentieth Air Force activated in Washington, D.C., Gen. Arnold Commanding and Brig. Gen. Hansell, Chief of Staff
       • First B-29s of the XX Bomber Command (58th Bomb Wing) land at bases in India and China
       • AAF conducts highly successful test of M-69 at Eglin Field, Florida
       • Joint Chiefs of Staff list target systems for bombing Japan including incendiary bombing of Japanese cities
JUN   • XX Bomber Command flies first mission against Japan
       • Americans land on Saipan in the Marianas
JUL   • U.S. forces invade Guam and Tinian

AUG • Gen. Hansell assumes command of XXI Bomber Command (73rd Bomb Wing)
     • Gen. LeMay assumes command of the XX Bomber Command

OCT • COA renders final report to Arnold—assuming invasion necessary, bomb aircraft factories, urban areas and shipping
     • Hansell in the first B-29 to land on Saipan

NOV • Saipan-based XXI Bomber Command (73rd Bomb Wing) bombs Tokyo for the first time since the Doolittle raid in 1942

1945

JAN • LeMay replaces Hansell as commander of XXI Bomber Command

FEB • American forces defeat the Japanese Army and Navy in the Philippines
     • Marines invade Iwo Jima

MAR • XXI Bomber Command carries out devastating fire raid on Tokyo, followed by massive incendiary attacks on Nagoya, Osaka, and Kobe
     • B-29s begin aerial mining of Japanese harbors and waterways

APR • American forces invade Okinawa
     • XXI Bomber Command bombs airfields in support of Okinawa invasion

MAY • Germany surrenders
     • In two giant fire raids LeMay's B-29s complete the destruction of Tokyo

JUN– • XXI Bomber Command conducts continuous day and
JUL   night attacks on all Japanese cities and war plants

JUL • Potsdam Declaration calls for Japanese surrender

AUG • B-29s carry out largest one-day mission of the war
     • B-29s drop atomic bombs on Hiroshima and Nagasaki
     • Russia declares war on Japan
     • 1,002 planes fly last mission of the war on 14 August
     • Emperor Hirohito announces Japan's surrender on 15 August
     • B-29s fly POW relief missions

SEP • Japanese representatives sign formal surrender document on 2 September, ending World War II

INTRODUCTION

TOKYO: 9–10 MARCH, 1945

Richard Gerdau's first glimpse of Tokyo—then the third largest city in the world—was one he will never forget. He was a lieutenant in the AAF, copilot of a B-29 bomber, one of more than three hundred flying in darkness from the Mariana Islands toward that city. Gerdau's plane, the *Early Bird*, was near the middle of a bomber stream stretching over three hundred miles of the North Pacific. The first planes had reached the target and released their loads of incendiary bombs shortly after midnight.

About an hour later, Capt. Raymond Tutton, *Early Bird*'s pilot, made a turn to the left that placed the aircraft on its final approach to the target, now thirty miles away. After Tutton completed the turn, Gerdau saw an expanse of flames larger than any he had ever imagined possible. As his aircraft neared the target area, he watched the incendiaries from planes ahead as they struck the unburned areas below—a succession of yellow-orange streaks appearing out of darkness. From several miles away, each streak looked as if a giant match were being slowly drawn across a striking surface in a dark room.

Actually, each streak Gerdau saw was a 2,000-foot-long swath of fire caused by bursts of more than 1,500 6-lb incendiary bombs. Closer, he saw the streaks blend into a mass of billowing flame. Minutes later, the *Early Bird* lurched upward

5

as its load of incendiaries fell free and dropped into the inferno below. Tutton turned around and headed back to base.

Gerdau and his companions released more than 2,000 tons of incendiaries that night. Within hours a gigantic conflagration swept over and beyond the target area, killing 83,000 people, destroying 26,700 buildings, rendering 1,000,000 homeless and changing the course of the war against Japan.

A GERMAN BOMBER pilot, four and a half years before, may have had similar thoughts when he watched flames rise over London. In a series of incendiary raids that began in September 1940 and continued through November, the Germans showered British cities with 2-lb magnesium incendiaries and 50-lb oil bombs, starting many fires and killing and injuring thousands.

The savage raids were the final repudiation of a prediction by two respected American military writers of the thirties, George Fielding Elliot and R. Ernest DuPuy. In a book aptly titled *If War Comes*, they condemned indiscriminate bombing, writing: "No country will consider it worthwhile to start so dreadful a cycle of slaughter." But several had already done so—Spain in its civil war, Russia in Finland, and Japan in its invasion of China.

Both the U.S. government and the American people, expressing feelings of long standing, found these actions unacceptable. During World War I, when bombers were first used, President Woodrow Wilson had said that he did not want the air service of the United States to participate in bombing industry, commerce or populations that were not associated with military needs. As World War II loomed, President Roosevelt, registering his country's objections when the Russians bombed Helsinki and other Finnish cities, stated, "The American government and the American people have for some time pursued a policy of wholeheartedly condemning the unprovoked bombing and machine-gunning of civilian populations from the air." In early 1940, U.S. Secretary of State Cordell Hull protested the Japanese bombing of 35 Chinese cities and denounced particularly the use of incendiary bombs.

The Army Air Corps' (the Air Corps was part of the U.S. Army) position at the time, as expressed by its chief, General H. H. Arnold, was that "the Air Corps is committed to a strategy of high-altitude, precision bombing of military objectives" and "use of incendiaries against cities is contrary to our national policy of attacking only military objectives."

Arnold's statements reflected the concept evolved at the Air Corps Tactical School in Montgomery, Alabama—a school through which most of the Air Corps' World War II leaders passed during the twenties and thirties.

For a while after World War I, the faculty of the Tactical School gave serious consideration to another, very different concept that drew heavily on the theories of an Italian general, Giulio Douhet, and an Air Corps general, Billy Mitchell. Douhet believed that air power—an air force independent of the ground forces—could secure victory at far less cost in time and human lives than the long, drawn-out ground battles of 1914–1918. He envisioned a future war as total, one in which the distinction between combatant and noncombatant would disappear. Douhet foresaw great fleets of war planes that, after securing command of the air, would attack an enemy nation's cities and factories with explosives, incendiaries and poison gas. Under the weight of such an all-out attack, Douhet theorized, the civilian population would become demoralized in a matter of weeks and the nation would surrender. General Mitchell, an outspoken advocate for an air force separate from the Army, had views similar to Douhet's but was unable to voice them publicly until 1926 when he resigned from the service following his court-martial for accusing the War and Navy Departments of incompetent and criminally negligent administration of national defense.

It was during that same year that the Air Corps Tactical School made a drastic change. Its earlier field manuals had reflected the then conventional thinking that the Air Corps' mission was to support the Army's ground forces and to attack the ground forces of potential enemies. In its 1926 manual entitled *Employment of Combined Air Forces*, the Tactical School, influenced by the thinking of Douhet and Mitchell, endorsed the idea of an independent air arm whose

objective, after gaining command of the air, would be to bomb
the enemy population and economic centers, not to defeat
enemy ground forces. Such an attack, the manual stated, was
far preferable to a war of slow attrition.

By the mid-thirties, the school had moved away from this
little-publicized concept to another, under which the Air
Corps would enter World War II. Under the new concept,
aircraft would bomb only the enemy nation's vital centers—
its factories, power sources, transportation, and raw materials. The resultant destruction would undermine the civilian
economy and war production capability, thus causing national
collapse. Several reasons existed for this new concept. Among
them was the belief that the 1926 "Douhetian" thinking, with
its emphasis on destroying whole cities and inflicting great
human casualties, while acceptable for discussion and debate
within the Air Tactical School, would not meet with approval
outside that closed environment. Even if it did, in a time of
extreme military austerity, little chance existed for obtaining
funds to build the huge fleet of bombers necessary to destroy,
in a matter of weeks, all of an enemy nation's cities. Consequently the Air Corps developed a doctrine that would be in
accord with government policy and public opinion and take
full advantage of advanced American technology in aircraft
design.

The B-17 "Flying Fortress" long-range bomber, just coming
into service in 1936, was the instrument around which the Air
Corps built its doctrine of bombing selected targets or "precision bombing" as it came to be called. With relatively limited numbers of this aircraft (and the B-24 "Liberator," another
long-range bomber that entered service a little later), Air
Corps planners believed that they could destroy vital targets
from high altitude and in daylight. The "precision bombers"
would utilize a new bombsight, the Norden—the most advanced device of its type in the world. The sight allowed for
such factors as speed, course, wind direction and distance to
the target. Following its indicators, a pilot could steer a course
to the target and the bombardier could drop the bombs with
great accuracy. Trained crews were able to place bombs within
a few hundred feet of the target from three miles up.

To get the bombs to the target with minimum loss of planes and crews, the Air Corps would depend on the powerful engines, rugged construction and great firepower of the B-17 and B-24. Their turbocharged engines enabled them to climb above many fighters and gave them a speed advantage at 25,000 feet and above. Each plane mounted ten .50-caliber machine guns with which to fend off any fighters that came near.

IN THE LATE 1930s the Air Corps seized two opportunities to demonstrate the long-range bombing capability of the B-17. The first came in August 1937, when the Navy grudgingly allowed the Air Corps to participate in a joint exercise off the California coast. In the exercise, eight B-17s located the battleship *Utah* while 300 miles at sea and dropped water bombs on it. Unfortunately they got no publicity. The Air Corps did better the following year when B-17s, this time with reporters and a radio announcer aboard, intercepted the Italian liner *Rex* 700 miles off the Atlantic coast, dipped their wings in salute and photographically "bombed" the liner. Though these demonstrations, particularly the well-publicized "bombing" of the *Rex*, showed that the United States did have an effective long-range bomber, the validity of the precision-bombing doctrine remained to be proven.

In 1939 the British Royal Air Force (RAF) entered World War II with a bombing philosophy similar to the Air Corps' doctrine. They attacked military targets, flying in formation, during daylight. Losses were so heavy—in a December 1939 strike against German shipping only 7 of the 22 bombers dispatched returned—that they soon abandoned daylight bombing. Meanwhile ruthless German air blitzes of Warsaw, Coventry and Rotterdam loosened British moral standards. Soon after the London bombings began, Prime Minister Winston Churchill ordered reprisal raids against German cities. Heavy losses continued, so the RAF shifted to night bombing and targeted industrial areas in German cities. This resulted in increasingly heavy civilian casualties, which the British at first accepted reluctantly but later made an integral part of their "area-bombing" policy. Both destruction of factories and the breaking down of German morale became bombing objectives. Though night losses continued to be heavy, in September 1941 Churchill approved an RAF proposal for a force of 4,000 heavy bombers to be used for area-bombing of German cities.

In June 1941, the Army Air Corps was redesignated the Army Air Forces (AAF) and submitted its blueprint for air war in the event that the United States became involved in the war against the Axis powers. By this time the political climate had changed and the AAF boldly asked and obtained approval for creating an air force of great size—two million men and more than 60,000 aircraft, of which 11,000 would be bombers. Though American military observers in England were aware of the British experience, the AAF clung firmly to the precision doctrine for bombing Germany, the Axis power against which the United States would direct most of its initial efforts. American strategy would be to bomb specific target systems—aircraft factories, electric power, transportation and oil supplies—and destroy Germany's ability to make war. Meanwhile, defensive strategic air forces would be deployed to defend the Western Hemisphere and United States interests and possessions in the Pacific. Any air offensive against Japan would follow the defeat of Adolf Hitler and employ the same strategic bombing strategy contemplated against Germany.

ONE

FIRE BOMBS: THE M-69

WITH ITS EMPHASIS on dropping high-explosive bombs on selected targets, the Air Corps did not acquire its first incendiary until 1940. That year, munitions experts filled an existing
chemical bomb casing, usually a container for irritant gas,
with a mixture formulated and used by the British—a jellylike
concoction of rubber, lye and coconut oil, blended with gasoline. The resulting incendiary bomb, designated the M-47,
was 4 feet long, 8 inches inches in diameter and weighed
about 100 pounds.

In the spring of 1941, the United States acquired another
incendiary bomb by borrowing from the British not just the
filler but an entire bomb. The Army Chemical Warfare Service (the branch responsible for developing and producing
chemical and incendiary munitions for the Air Corps) took a
British Mark II, 4-lb incendiary, and modified and standard-
ized it as the M-50. Almost 2 feet long and 3 inches in diameter, the M-50's body was made of magnesium and its filler
was powdered aluminum and iron oxide.

Based on their performance characteristics, the two incendiaries would be used for different purposes. The M-47, with
its 100-lb weight, had great penetration capability, making it
suitable for use against large structures. After an M-47 passed

through a building's roof, a burster charge would detonate, blowing the casing apart and dispersing flaming gobs of gasoline gel downward and outward in a conical pattern over a circle of about 60 feet under ideal conditions.

The 4-lb M-50 was designed to set fires in lightly constructed buildings. It was dropped from planes in clusters of 34 bombs held together by metal bands. After a cluster fell free of the plane, an arming wire would release the metal bands that held the bombs, allowing them to separate during descent. After penetrating the roof and coming to rest, the filler mixture would ignite and its intense heat would then ignite the magnesium body. The ensuing fire would burn for about ten minutes at 2400° F and was difficult to extinguish, even by professional firefighters. Both of these incendiary bombs—the M-47 and the M-50—were used during World War II, but American scientists designed and developed a third incendiary that proved to be the most destructive munition in the war.

The scientists who developed this third incendiary were among many who worked as part of the Office of Scientific Research and Development (OSRD), which President Roosevelt established in 1941 to utilize American technology in the event of U.S. involvement in the war in Europe. Roosevelt appointed Vannevar Bush, former dean of engineering at the Massachusetts Institute of Technology, as director of OSRD, in charge of a national program of military and medical research. OSRD had a military research arm, the National Defense Research Committee (NDRC) under Dr. J. B. Conant, president of Harvard University.

Bush and Conant, the latter acting also as Bush's deputy, built the NDRC into a massive research organization. The scientists who headed NDRC's various divisions were recognized leaders in their fields: Karl Compton, president of the Massachusetts Institute of Technology, headed the division conducting research on radar; Richard C. Tolman, dean of the California Institute of Technology, directed research on tanks, vehicles and weapons; Roger Adams, professor of chemistry at the University of Illinois and considered by many as the founder of modern-day organic chemistry, headed the division responsible for explosives and chemicals. By mid-1941, Adams and the other division heads had working under them many of the top scientists and engineers from both industry and academy. NDRC personnel worked closely with their military counterparts, but had independent funding and wide latitude for experimentation.

In September 1941 General Arnold, in a letter to Vannevar Bush, emphasized the shortage of magnesium (used in the manufacture of the M-50) and asked Bush to develop a substitute material for use in incendiary bombs. Because of concern that the supply of rubber from the Far East might be cut off if war broke out with Japan, a team of NDRC chemists at Harvard University, Arthur D. Little (a major scientific consulting firm) and another group at DuPont had already begun work on a substitute for rubber as a filler for incendiaries. Their research resulted in two gasoline gel mixtures that didn't require rubber. One, developed by the Harvard–Arthur D. Little team, became the standard incendiary gel filler. It was called "napalm." [Actually, napalm was the name the team gave a chemical compound that resulted from combining *napht*enic and *palm*itic acids. This compound when combined with gasoline resulted in a thick jelly and, as time passed, the jellied gasoline itself came to be known as napalm.]

NDRC responded to Arnold's request with not only a new filler but a new bomb as well. During the winter of 1941, Richard P. Russell, a vice president of Standard Oil Development Company and head of NDRC incendiary research and development, charged a group of his company's scientists and engineers to develop a prototype bomb that would meet a number of requirements. It could not use scarce materials. It had to be small—the AAF already had the 100-lb M-47 gasoline-gel-filled incendiary. Its small size would greatly increase the number of bombs in a single drop, starting more fires in more places and making fire fighting more difficult. While the designers wanted the bomb to be light, it also had to have enough weight to penetrate the roof of a structure before releasing its incendiary filler. Its casing had to be light and thin but strong enough not to rupture prematurely when striking a roof. After penetration the bomb had to project its contents across a wide portion of the room in which it came to rest.

Both in appearance and function, the 6.2-lb incendiary that resulted from the work through the winter and early spring of 1942 was unique. It did not have the tail fins used for stabilization on other bombs. The steel container, about 3 inches in diameter and 20 inches long, looked more like an elongated tin can than a bomb. Like the M-50, the bombs were held together in an airplane's bomb bay in clusters. When dropped from the airplane and released from their cluster, each bomb separated from the others and fell free. Then, unlike the M-50, a streamer (a 3-foot-long cloth strip resembling the tail of a kite) popped out of one end and caught in the wind. Extended its full length, the streamer stabilized the bomb and controlled the velocity of descent. As the bomb passed through the roof of a house or factory, a delay fuse actuated, which, after 3 to 5 seconds, detonated an ejection-ignition charge. By this time the bomb would have come to rest, lying on its side or with its nose buried in the floor. At detonation, a TNT charge would explode, and magnesium particles would ignite the gasoline gel contained in a cloth sock. Unlike any other bomb, the explosion blew burning gel out of the tail of the casing and— like a miniature cannon—shot it as far as 100 feet. If the gel struck a combustible surface and was not extinguished it started an intense and persistent fire.

During the spring of 1942, the new bomb was subjected to intensive testing. Standard Oil Company and NDRC engineers constructed simulations of attics in residential structures and carried out tests to determine the bomb's ability to penetrate roofs and come to rest in the attic. At Edgewood Arsenal, Maryland, another test team did extensive evaluations of the new bomb in an industrial setting, using typical objects found in factories—workbenches, storage bins, packing cases, etc. Bombs were fired from a mortar downward into arrangements of the items and measurements were taken of the fires started when the positions and distance between the bomb and the target varied. Using these results, engineers constructed a mathematical model of a typical factory with a total area of 2,800 square feet and were able to calculate the probability of a bomb starting a fire when it came to rest in a given area of the factory.

While these tests provided some useful theoretical data, the AAF wanted to be able to calculate the results that might be expected in an actual air raid. These kinds of data could be obtained only by dropping bombs from aircraft and then detonating them in full-scale rooms.

In April 1942, at Huntsville Arsenal, Alabama, the Army Chemical Warfare Service conducted the first tests on actual structures. Static tests of four different incendiaries—the NDRC tail-ejection oil bomb, the M-50 and two others—on a small group of old, abandoned farmhouses yielded inconclusive data on their relative fire-starting capabilities. Poor weather caused most of the air-dropped bombs to miss their targets, so no useful data resulted from that phase of the test. Overall, the tail-ejection bomb seemed a little better than the others.

In July, the Army Chemical Service, not satisfied with the Huntsville tests, located a better test area at Jefferson Proving Ground, Indiana. It contained a number of substantial farmhouses and outbuildings, abandoned but in good condition. During the period 9–22 July 1942, the Army Chemical Warfare Service, in conjunction with the AAF, NDRC and Ordnance Corps conducted extensive tests, both static and air-drop, of different types of incendiary bombs that were under development, among them the M-47, the M-50 and the NDRC 6.2-lb tail-ejection bomb. This time, B-25 medium bombers scored a number of hits on the targets, providing much useful data on stability in flight, penetration and fire-starting ability of each of the incendiaries. Among the observers were Vannevar Bush and Roger Adams, chairman of NDRC's Incendiary and Chemical Division. The tests showed that the new NDRC bomb was an excellent firestarter.

In July 1942, Earl Stevenson, on leave from his position as president of Arthur D. Little and who, with Richard Russell, comanaged NDRC's work on the new incendiary bomb, reported on the results of the Jefferson tests to Roger Adams. Stevenson wrote that based on these tests the NDRC group recommended that the AAF manufacture in quantity a small magnesium bomb (the M-50 or a smaller one, the M-52), a large gasoline gel bomb (the M-47) and "the small, tail-ejection bomb." At the conclusion of his report Stevenson noted that the Jefferson tests brought to a close eight months of intensive work by the NDRC and that "the program for the immediate future will depend largely upon the decisions which now rest with the interested Services." Shortly thereafter the AAF recognized "the tail-ejection bomb" as a standard bomb (designated the M-56 and later changed to the M-69) and ordered it into production along with the M-47 and M-50.

In most research and development projects, the development team ceases to have a significant role, except for technical assistance to the user, after the item goes into production. This did not happen in the case of the M-69. Russell's and Stevenson's interest in and advocacy of the M-69 continued, undiminished, throughout the war.

While Stevenson's interest sprang from his strong feelings of responsibility as a project director, Russell's had deeper roots. As vice president of one of the world's largest oil companies, he was responsible for developing oil-based products and promoting their use. Having had a major role in developing a new "product" for war, he was loath to just turn it over to the Army and go on with other business.

In September Russell went to England to share the results of the Jefferson tests with the British and to review, firsthand, RAF experience with incendiaries. He also hoped to interest the British in using the M-69 in raids against targets in Europe. Russell took with him on this trip a man whom both he and Stevenson held in high regard—Raymond H. Ewell.

Ewell, a 33-year-old chemical engineer, had joined the NDRC incendiary research team six months before and was by now deeply involved in all aspects of the M-69 project. Eldest of four brothers, he was the standout of the family. He became an Eagle Scout and by his example, his three brothers all became Eagles, a unique accomplishment featured in newspapers across the nation. Keen of intellect—his sister recalled his "photographic" memory and that he often made verbatim quotes from the Encyclopedia Brittanica—by age 29 he had earned two masters degrees and a doctorate. Ewell came to NDRC after doing research work at the National Bureau of Standards and teaching at Purdue University. The subject of his doctoral dissertation was the viscosity of fluids, which may account for his early interest and subsequent total dedication to the development of an incendiary bomb whose effectiveness was greatly dependent on the correct viscosity of its gasoline gel filler.

When Russell and Ewell arrived in England, the RAF night-bombing campaign against German cities was capturing world attention. Six months before the two Americans arrived, the RAF high command told its Bomber Command, "It has been decided that the primary objective of your operation should now be focused on the morale of the enemy civil population, and in particular, of the industrial workers." The man who would carry out this directive was the newly appointed head of the Bomber Command, Air Vice Marshal Arthur T. Harris. Harris, a man of strong purpose and great tenacity, was convinced that "a bomber offensive of adequate weight and the right kind of bombs would, if continued long enough, be something that no country in the world could endure." Harris set out to attack Germany's industrial cities and the factories in them, weighing his success not by the number of individual plants destroyed but by the acres of city devastated. If morale was shattered in the process, all the better. But for Harris, the cities were the target, and if enough were destroyed, Germany would be destroyed.

Harris chose as his first target the city of Lubeck, in northern Germany. Though not a major industrial city, its narrow streets and many wooden buildings made it susceptible to rapid fire spread. Harris wanted to see if a mix of bombs—high explosives to blow things apart and incendiaries to set things afire—would accomplish his objective. The raid would also test refinements in RAF night-bombing tactics. On this and other night missions RAF bombers flew one at a time, not in formation. Special crews called "pathfinders" dropped flares on the target areas as beacons for the stream of bombers that followed. Over Lubeck, pathfinders marked the target for 224 bombers. The first 40 carried incendiaries to further light up the city for the main force with its mixture of incendiaries and high-explosive bombs. The test succeeded. The center of Lubeck was wiped out, 1,425 houses destroyed and 312 people killed.

In May 1942, using similar tactics but this time mustering over 1,000 airplanes, Harris hit Cologne, one of Germany's major cities. It was the RAF's ultimate experiment on how to get the maximum number of bombers over the target in minimum time. Normally a raid with this number of aircraft would have lasted seven hours; the raiders finished their job at Cologne in two and a half. The raid did more damage in a single night than had been done in scores of previous attacks on that city—20,000 homes destroyed or damaged, nearly 60 factories knocked out, rail and communications interrupted for as much as two weeks, with only 500 people killed or injured. Churchill sent his congratulations, and the British public applauded the achievements of the Bomber Command.

ALL OF THIS did not change the mind of the Americans who had arrived earlier that year and immediately begun preparations for a bombing campaign of their own—a daylight, precision campaign. Brig. Gen. Ira C. Eaker, commander of the VIII Bomber Command, had hoped to be operating in great numbers by late 1942 but was not able to do so because of the diversion of large numbers of B-17 units to North Africa. On 17 August, Eaker led the VIII Bomber Command's first combat mission against a railroad marshaling yard at Rouen, France. Though the twelve B-17s unloaded only 13 tons of high-explosive bombs on the target area, no aircraft were lost. Eaker and Arnold, in Washington, were delighted. The precision campaign was off to a good start. Over the next few weeks more small missions were flown against precision targets with good bombing accuracy and few losses.

Russell and Ewell were much more impressed by the spectacular RAF night raids than by the AAF small daylight precision missions. After returning to the United States in September 1942, Russell, in a report to Bush (which Ewell probably helped prepare), enthusiastically endorsed British views on bombing and delivered the first of many NDRC appeals for all-out use of incendiaries. He pointed out that "the clue to the successful all-out bombing of Germany lies more in the use of incendiaries than in high explosives." In a direct attack on the USAAF precision bombing doctrine, he added,

> Even more vital, consequently, than the mere temporary dislocation of an industrial target through the use of H.E. [high explosive bombs] is the permanent fire destruction of the homes and essential services for Germany's war workers. These are, therefore, today regarded as the primary target for air attack. If the homes and essential services of Germany's war workers are destroyed through mass incendiary attack there will be realized as an extremely important by-product permanent fire damage to war plants located in or near the urban centers.

He closed with some praise for the NDRC bomb at the expense of the M-50:

> In British opinion, the oil bomb should supplant the magnesium bomb. The British L.C. 30-lb oil bomb per ton of bomb lift is some one to one and a half times as effective as the British or American 4-lb magnesium bomb for attacking German areas. . . . The new U.S. 6.2-lb oil bomb is, the NDRC group believes, several times as effective as the 4-lb magnesium bomb on the same type target.

Though Russell was not successful in making any immediate "sales" of the M-69 to the British, he had kindled their interest. During the winter of 1942–43 the RAF conducted its own trials of the American bomb and, unfortunately for Russell and the NDRC's other M-69 proponents, found it wanting. The British tests raised serious questions about the ability of the M-69 to penetrate typical German roof structures or to set fires to such structures once penetration was effected.

In the United States, some Chemical Warfare Service officers expressed similar doubts to their chief, Maj. Gen. William

N. Porter, along with concerns about the reliability of the M-69—10 percent of the bombs produced had failed to function properly. The critical views of these officers may have been partly due to their personal involvement with the M-69's "competitor," the M-50. The Chemical Warfare Service had done most of the development of the M-50 magnesium bomb after receiving from the British the design specifications for their Mark II 4-lb magnesium bomb.

In February 1943, Gen. Porter called a meeting of NDRC representatives and his staff and listened to differing views on the effectiveness of the M-69. To resolve these differences, he concluded that it would be necessary to construct simulated German structures and test the M-69 on them. The test site would be Dugway Proving Ground, in Utah, and the tests would also include simulated Japanese structures.

Pending the results of these tests, Porter consulted with Dr. Conant of NDRC and decided that M-69 production would be increased. His rationale for this decision was that the M-69 was a "satisfactory" munition, that magnesium to increase M-50 production was lacking, and even if the M-69 proved to be ineffective against German construction, it would probably be effective on Japanese structures.

TWO

TARGET JAPAN

By JANUARY 1943, bombing of Japan had become a matter of interest at the highest level of government. During his meeting with Prime Minister Churchill and the Combined Chiefs of Staff that month, President Roosevelt suggested that bombers based in India could refuel at bases in China and go on to bomb targets in Japan. Gen. George C. Marshall, Army Chief of Staff, cautioned that using bases in China to supply bombers would be a tremendous job that would require transport planes and other equipment needed in the European theater. Despite the problems, Roosevelt remained enthusiastic about the prospect, both for its military potential and for the boost it would give to the morale of America's beleaguered ally, China.

The bombing of Germany and the invasion of Europe, however, were the major concerns of the Allies. Consequently, even with presidential interest, it was not until late in March 1943 that Arnold's Assistant Chief of Air Staff, A-2 (Assistant Chiefs of Air Staff selections were frequently referred to by their short designators, e.g. Personnel: A-1; Intelligence: A-2; Operations: A-3, etc.), completed a preview of potential bombing targets in Japan. After examining nearly 2,000 folders containing information on individual targets, intelligence specialists selected 199 key targets, divided among nine economic groups: aircraft, arms and munitions, steel, machine tools, rail transportation, electric power, petroleum, naval bases and shipyards, and ship concentrations. In response to direction from Arnold's office, they included in their report the distance of targets from Wanan, a base held by Allied forces in China. Among the more important targets in Japan within 1,250 miles of this China base were steel mills and coke ovens on the island of Kyushu.

Determining the most important targets in Japan was one task; identifying, in order of priority, the particular target systems that if destroyed would cripple the Japanese economy was still another. It was to accomplish this second and more important task that General Arnold turned to a small group of men called the Committee of Operations Analysts (COA). Arnold had established the COA about a year before and asked it to analyze the German economy and recommend target groups for precision strikes by American bombers based in England. The Committee did an outstanding job. Its completed report, approved by the Combined Chiefs of Staff, the President, and Mr. Churchill, was a substantial contribution to the American-British combined bombing strategy.

Under Brig. Gen. Byron E. Gates, who was its chairman, the COA brought together civilians with extensive experience in dealing with complex business and industrial problems and military men well-grounded in the field of military intelligence. Its civilian members and consultants included Elihu Root, Jr., New York attorney and director of many corporations; Thomas W. Lamont, chairman of the board of J. P. Morgan & Company; Dr. Edward M. Earle, professor of economics at Princeton University and member of Princeton's Institute of Advanced Study; Edward S. Mason, professor of economics at Harvard University and member of the Office of Strategic Services; Fowler Hamilton, member of the Board of Economic Warfare; Francis Bitter, a Massachusetts Institute of Technology physicist; W. Barton Leach, former professor at Harvard Law School; and Guido R. Perera, a corporate attorney. The latter three held commissions: Perera and Leach in the AAF, and Bitter in the Navy reserves. Most of these civilians worked with the group for the remainder of the war. The military officers, besides General Gates, included Maj. Gen. Clayton Bissell, Assistant Chief to the Air Staff Intelligence; Col. Malcom W. Moss, also of that office; Capt. H. C. Wick, Office of the Deputy Chief of Naval Operations, Air; and colonels Thomas G. Lamphier and Moses W. Pettigrew of Army Intelligence.

As a foundation for beginning their study, the COA had the information on potential targets developed by Arnold's intelligence specialists, as well as a report prepared under the auspices of the Foreign Economic Administration by Seymour Janow. Janow's report, the first to study the possible effects of mass raids on Japanese cities, drew on British damage experience resulting from German incendiary raids and prewar insurance data on property in Japan. The report concluded that incendiary bombing would leave Japanese workers homeless and could profoundly dislocate Japan's economy.

Although the COA had access to data from Army intelligence, the Office of Strategic Services, as well as other government agencies and business and industrial sources, reliable information on the Japanese economy was much more difficult to obtain than on Germany. In 1931 the Japanese had begun to place a veil of secrecy around their industrial activities. Information sources that remained were shut off by the enactment, in 1937, of strict censorship and security laws. Thereafter, foreigners were allowed only limited access to businesses with which they had dealings and companies manufacturing military equipment were off-limits.

By the middle of April 1943, as the COA grappled with the intricacies of bombing Japan, Raymond Ewell had reached some firm conclusions on the subject. Highly self-confident and in awe of no one, Ewell had just completed the first (more would follow) of his incisive personal analyses and recommendations concerning U.S. bombing strategy. His views were continued in a memorandum to Russell and Stevenson in which he warned that possible worsening of the Pacific war situation might lead to the deployment of more airplanes to that theater, to the detriment of the air war against Hitler. To blunt Japanese pressure on our forces with minimum effort,

Ewell advocated that a relatively small-scale bombing offensive be mounted against some large Japanese cities, using the M-69 incendiary bomb. He explained,

The only reason that we, as development people, need be concerned with this matter is that the General Staff probably does not realize the extraordinary potential destructiveness of this bomb on Japanese cities, which puts it almost in the class of the oft-mentioned "secret weapon," and they probably are not taking this weapon into account in their strategy and planning. [It is not possible to state what "secret weapon" Ewell was referring to. Perhaps word of a yet-unidentified weapon of great effectiveness—the atomic bomb, still early in its development—had leaked to some of those like Ewell who worked in the inner circle of the scientific community.]

Anyone familiar with the M-69 and with the construction and layout of Japanese cities can make a few calculations and soon reach a tentative conclusion that even as small amounts as 10 tons of M-69's would have the possibility of wiping out major portions of any of the large Japanese cities. . . .

However, there are not over 20 persons in the country who are sufficiently familiar with the M-69 to form any judgment in this connection and probably not a one of these persons even knows anyone in the strategy and planning circles of the General Staff. It would seem that steps should be taken to bring this weapon and its possibilities to the attention of the General Staff at once.

Ewell did not restrict his comments to advocacy of the M-69 but continued with suggestions for air strategy. He thought the bombing attacks on Japan could best be launched from China and, though a B-17 or B-24 could make the round trip with a small bomb load, the B-29, which he had heard would be in production that spring, would be ideal. (Ewell's "thoughts" indicate that he had access to highly classified AAF plans for the air war against Japan.)

Regarding the supply problem, Ewell stated:

Of course the big problem is one of supply of gasoline, bombs, parts, etc. All of which must be transported by air from India. However, when the strategists dismiss serious bombing from

Chinese bases on this account they are thinking in terms of large-scale bombing with H.E. bombs, involving hundreds of bombers and many thousands of tons of bombs. The key to the situation is just this: that an air offensive could be mounted with the M-69 incendiary bomb as the principal weapon which would require a relatively small number of planes and a small tonnage of gasoline and bombs.

Ewell closed with the concession that not until after the tests on Japanese structures at Dugway Proving Ground were completed could he be absolutely sure of the potential destructiveness of the M-69 in the bombing of Japan. In the meantime, he suggested that "it might be worthwhile getting some thought started along these lines in General Staff circles in advance of the tests, so that quicker action can be taken if the tests give confirmation to the fire-raising possibilities envisioned above."

Russell's and Stevenson's reactions to the memorandum are unknown, but Ewell tried to start others thinking when a few weeks later he wrote Col. Perera in the COA. Perera had been a key participant in developing the bombing objectives for the air war against Germany and would continue to have a major role in planning for the bombing of Japan. Under the guise of asking for copies of a new Air Staff organization chart, Ewell enclosed a copy of his memorandum to Russell (probably the one described above). He told Perera that he was working on the details of a tentative plan for raids on two or three Japanese cities and offered to provide further information if Perera wanted it. Though a seed might have been planted, for some months Ewell would find himself "standing on the outside, looking in," with his ideas on bombing Japan with incendiaries. COA's analysis of Japanese targets was to continue being based on USAAF precision-bombing doctrine.

UNFORTUNATELY, THE B-29 aircraft, which Ewell had suggested as the means for dropping incendiaries on Japan, was not operational at the time of his memorandum to Russell and Stevenson. It would be another month, the end of June, before the first B-29 left the factory and was officially accepted by the

AAF. A little more than three years earlier Arnold had signed the contract for development and testing of what became the world's largest bomber. Its development and testing had been accomplished at an unprecedented cost of $3 billion. By comparison, the development of the atomic bomb, the "Manhattan Project," cost $2 billion.

The high cost reflected the advanced engineering design and innovations built into the aircraft in a comparatively short time. The B-29 was the first American bomber designed for combat operations above 30,000 feet. To permit this, engineers built into the airplane pressurized flight compartments and an air-heating system. At high altitude, crews were free of the necessity of wearing oxygen masks and cumbersome heated flying suits; cruising at 30,000 feet, they worked in an atmospheric pressure equivalent to 8,000 feet. Pressurization had presented a problem because the aircraft had four large midsection bomb bay doors that had to be opened and closed. To allow this, the designers pressurized the forward control cabin and the gunners' compartment to the rear and connected the two with a tube just large enough for an airman to crawl through.

The AAF wanted the plane to have more defensive firepower than any bomber in the world. To meet this requirement, the plane was equipped with five gun turrets—two on top of the fueselage, two on the bottom and one in the tail. The upper forward turret had four .50-caliber machine guns, and the other three turrets each had two guns of the same caliber. In the tail was a 20-mm cannon flanked by two .50-caliber machine guns, bringing the total armaments to twelve machine guns and a cannon. For aiming and firing, a specially designed automatic computer gunsight corrected for range, altitude, temperature and airspeed. A central fire-control mechanism enabled any gunner except the tail gunner simultaneous control of two or more of the five power-driven turrets. A gunner without a target within his field of vision could pass control of his turret to another crewman who could use it. Gunners were also physically removed from manual contact with the guns and, except for the tail gunner, fired them from remote sighting stations. This spared them the jar and vibration of the guns. In their heated compartment they escaped the drafts and bitter, numbing cold endured by the waist, tail and ball turret gunners who flew in B-17s and B-24s.

The B-29 was designed to fly far and fast—3,250 miles at 25,000 feet with a 5,000-lb bombload. To assist in navigating to distant targets the airplane's pilot, navigator, bombardier and radar operator had the latest radar equipment: the APN-9 Loran constant-beam navigation aid and the APQ-13 radar bombing and navigational aid. The aircraft was powered by four Wright R-3350 Cyclone 18-cylinder radial supercharged engines, each developing 2200 horsepower at takeoff, which enabled the B-29 to attain a maximum speed of 375 mph and a cruising speed between 200 and 250 mph.

Designing and building all this new technology into one aircraft was not easy. Problems were encountered in the complex electronics of the central fire-control system. The cumulative weight of over 150 electric motors and generators essential for the B-29's power-driven systems—e.g., landing gear, wing flaps—required substantial weight reduction elsewhere in the aircraft.

By far the most serious problem was with the engines. An engine on each of the first two prototypes overheated and caught fire during test flights. On 18 February 1943, a double engine fire resulted in a crash that killed Boeing's chief test pilot and the expert test crew. It brought the test program to a standstill. Arnold ordered an investigation immediately, which was soon followed by a Senate committee investigation headed by Senator Harry S. Truman. The basic cause was faulty engine design. A number of "fixes" were devised by Wright and Boeing engineers to keep the engines from overheating, but engine fires would remain a problem even after the B-29 went into production and reached combat.

As the engineers were attempting to solve the engine puzzle, Gen. Arnold, impatient with the delay, stepped in to revive a project he considered critical to the success of the AAF's part in the war effort. In April 1943 he set up the "B-29 Special Project," gave it top priority and put it under the command of Brig. Gen. Kenneth B. Wolfe, one of the AAF's most experienced procurement and engineering officers. Wolfe was responsible for the entire program, including flight testing, production and crew training. Arnold wanted B-29s ready for combat by the end of 1943.

EWELL'S CONTENTION THAT the General Staff was not as knowledgeable as they should be about the M-69 could have included all incendiaries and applied to Arnold himself. At about the time he was reorganizing the B-29 program, Arnold heard complaints from General Eaker in England and other air commanders about the ineffectiveness of their incendiary bombs. He responded by sending a memorandum to Maj. Gen. O. P. Echols, Assistant Chief of Staff for Materiel; the memo contained Arnold's views on incendiaries and directions for Echols.

In Arnold's opinion incendiaries had three purposes: to burn down suitable, precise industrial objectives; to start daytime fires to serve as flaming beacons to guide British bombers to targets during hours of darkness; and to burn down densely built-up portions of cities when the occasion warranted. Arnold was particularly interested in the effectiveness of incendiaries against industrial installations and asked Echols to send him a report on this. Finally, he asked if anyone had built German, Italian and Japanese model-structures for testing incendiaries—unaware that construction of German and Japanese dwellings for airborne incendiary tests had been underway for nearly two months.

Echols reported to Arnold that, based on tests against industrial installations by NDRC at Edgewood Arsenal, the incendiaries ranked in the following order: first, the M-50, 4-lb magnesium; second, the M-69, 6.2-lb gasoline gel, base-ejection (though the British, in tests of their own, had found that the M-69 had insufficient penetrating power against German construction); and third, the M-47, 100-lb gasoline gel.

Only the M-47 could be used for precision bombing, but, Echols added, the British preferred to drop incendiaries on lightly constructed areas (homes) near factories while bombing the factories with high explosives in hopes that fire from the burning areas would spread to the factories and result in a lasting degree of destruction. He also told Arnold that when an "aimable cluster," then under development, was put into service, the M-50 and M-69 would have ballistic qualities comparable to high-explosive bombs. Cluster mechanisms then available for the M-50 and M-69 released the bombs only seconds after leaving the bomb bay, so they dispersed widely. The new mechanism, just months away from service, would hold the small bombs in the cluster until released at a preset altitude, usually 3,000 to 5,000 feet. Echols pointed out that of the three bombs, the Eighth Air Force had used only the M-47 against enemy targets. He concluded with a brief description of the planned Dugway tests and recommended that no final conclusions as to the relative capabilities of the three bombs be made until the Dugway tests were complete. What Echols had not made clear was that the Dugway test structures were to be replicas of German and Japanese residential dwellings, not factories, which were Arnold's primary concern.

THE RESIDENTIAL STRUCTURES at Dugway were a vital concern to Stevenson (who had taken over from Russell as chief of NDRC's Chemical Engineering Division in March). Stevenson and the other NDRC M-69 "backers" subscribed to the British concept that Russell and Ewell had brought back with them: if you burn the cities you destroy the factories in them.

Since the tests at Huntsville Arsenal and Jefferson Proving Ground had not produced the quantity of airborne bomb hits necessary for thorough analysis, NDRC had its contractor, Standard Oil Development Company, construct several replicas of German buildings and test the M-69 and M-50. Though these tests yielded useful technical data on penetration and fire-starting characteristics, they were not deemed conclusive. NDRC then knew that the only way to convince the AAF of the efficacy of the M-69 and provide the conclusive data that NDRC needed to make its case for mass incendiary raids on Japan's cities was to conduct the large-scale airborne tests at Dugway.

Planning for the tests had begun in February 1943. The two men from NDRC's Incendiaries and Petroleum Warfare Section who shared responsibility for the planning and construction of the Dugway test facilities were Norval F. Myers and H. C. Hottel. As Myers would later recall, the buildings had to be exactly like those in Berlin and Tokyo—the same construction and furnishings, the same wood, the same dimensions, thicknesses, angles, paints—everything. Through the American Institute of Architects, they found Eric Mendlesohn, a leading German architect who had fled the Nazis. To design the Japanese structures the Institute turned up Antonin Raymond, an architect who had worked in Japan for twenty years, and Philip Sawyer, who had laid out Japanese factories. They also located Alfred Gemperle, a buyer of oriental furniture for a large San Francisco importer. For details, the NDRC team turned to RKO Studios in Hollywood, where they were given access to thousands of photographs of everything from a living-room chair in Berlin to a tatami mat in Osaka.

Surprisingly, tatami mats—the heavy mats of woven straw that serve as a combination of carpet and seat to millions of Japanese—proved to be difficult to reproduce in the large quantity needed using machines in this country. Few were found on the West Coast, so the searchers went to Hawaii and, with help from the Army, gathered up the needed tatamis from Japanese-American homes, stores and clubs throughout the islands.

Another difficult item to procure was sugi. The experts had called for two types of wood for the Japanese structures, hinoki for the structural members and sugi for the framework and trim. Rocky Mountain Douglas fir was a suitable and readily available substitute for hinoki. But the substitute for sugi was Russian spruce, and the supply of that in the United States was zero. NDRC learned of a load of Russian spruce that was being shipped from Siberia for some special purpose in the United States. They never did find out what the special purpose was, but Myers and the NDRC team were able, with their higher priority, to obtain the entire shipment. The spruce was shipped to New Jersey, where it was milled and conditioned to a moisture content comparable to that in Japan. The dwelling structures were then prefabricated, after which they were moved by rail to the Utah site for final assembly.

Construction of the multinational "village" began on 29 March 1943, and was completed six weeks later. It consisted of twelve two-story Japanese row houses and six German houses, all of which had been constructed as authentically as humanly possible. Each Japanese house, with its smooth plastered walls and sliding paper screens, was equipped with carefully placed tatami mats, low tables, sitting pillows, cupboards, charcoal braziers, even cooking utensils and chopsticks. Between the Japanese houses ran typically narrow streets—exactly 8 feet wide—as prescribed by the NDRC consultants.

On the day the tests began, 17 May, the NDRC team must have had some of the same feelings other scientists would have in 1945 at Alamagordo, New Mexico, when the weapon they developed—the atomic bomb—was subjected to its final test. Three bombs—the M-50 4-lb magnesium; the M-52 2-lb magnesium and the M-69 6.2-lb gasoline gel were tested during the period 17 May–1 September 1943. (A fourth bomb, the M-54, was dropped from the program early because of its poor performance.) Bombers flying in formation released the incendiaries from quick-opening clusters at altitudes of 3,500 and 10,000 feet. Detailed and complete records were kept on each bomb hit, including the point at which it entered the building, the path it followed through the structure until it came to rest, the location where the incendiary action occurred and the incendiary result achieved. The evaluators also recorded data on fires caused by the M-69 bombs that missed the target but were near enough to eject gel onto the side of the building.

The relative ratings of the bombs were determined using three classifications:

A. A fire that burned out of control after six minutes of attempt by trained fire guards to put it out;
B. A fire that was ultimately destructive if unattended;
C. A fire that went out when unattended, with no destruction resulting. To preserve the buildings for further testing, the fires were extinguished with full-scale fire-fighting equipment as soon as the evaluators had established the classification of the fire.

Using the classifications above, fires resulting from hits on Japanese and German houses were as follows:

FIRE CLASS	JAPANESE HOUSES			GERMAN HOUSES		
	M-50	*M-52*	*M-69*	*M-50*	*M-52*	*M-69*
A	22%	26%	68%	0%	0%	37%
B	20%	14%	13%	26%	18%	16%
C	58%	60%	19%	74%	82%	47%

The evaluators concluded that

- The M-50 bomb had excessive penetration for Japanese structures, often going through to the ground. In the German dwellings it penetrated to the attic or to the floor below, but caused no rapid fires and was effective only when it burned in a favorable location.
- The M-52 bomb exhibited instability in flight but showed penetrating characteristics and incendiary effectiveness adequate for Japanese construction.
- The M-69 was the most effective of the bombs tested and showed itself to be a very potent weapon against Japanese construction. It also caused more destructive fires in the German buildings and was judged the best of the bombs tested on these structures.

The NDRC team was delighted with the results. Ewell and others began immediately to analyze the data to determine both the vulnerability of Japanese cities to attack with M-69 incendiaries and the bomb tonnages required to start fires of major proportions in these cities. Dr. Conant wrote Bush, telling him of the outcome of the Dugway tests, and asked him to see if he could persuade the British to use the M-69, which the United States was beginning to manufacture in quantity.

★   ★   ★

WHILE AMERICANS WERE testing incendiaries, the British, satisfied with their own heavier (18-, 30-, and 250-lb) gasoline gel bombs, were dropping them on a massive scale. The third of four large incendiary raids on the German city of Hamburg ended on 3 August 1943. The raid caused a fire storm with temperatures of 800°C and powerful air currents that developed as the fire drew in air from surrounding areas like a giant chimney. People in shelters could hear the roar of the wind over the crash of the bombs. Some of those caught in the streets were hurled to the ground or sucked into the conflagration. The wind carried sparks and burning debris and drew all the fires into one vast inferno. The burned-out area was about 13 square miles and the dead numbered close to 45,000.

The 252 American B-17 bombers that attacked in daylight between the first and second British night attacks were not successful. They went after precision targets, a submarine yard and an aircraft engine factory, but the objectives were largely obscured by smoke, and little damage was done.

Earlier that year, in England, the Eighth Air Force had begun to emerge from its fledgling status. At Casablanca, where the China-based bombing of Japan had first been discussed, General Eaker had made an impassioned plea to Churchill for his agreement to a British-American joint air offensive. Eaker explained that daylight precision attacks by the Americans would complement and support the nighttime area raids conducted by Harris's Bomber Command. Daylight bombing could destroy targets missed by the RAF. The B-17s could destroy enemy fighters—the nemesis of both British and American bombers—and light up targets, creating beacons for British night bombers. Churchill remained deeply skeptical of the American approach, but finally agreed to a Combined Bombing Offensive plan that incorporated the set of target objectives developed by the Committee of Operations Analysts.

By late spring of 1943 the Eighth Air Force had graduated from the forays over France to missions aimed at the vitals of Germany. Losses were heavy, but the Americans were gradually beginning to function as true partners in the Combined Bomber Offensive. Allocation of bombers to the Eighth increased so that by August 1943 over 900 bombers were available, which permitted dispatching formations of 300 planes or more. At last, Eaker had sufficient strength to launch a maximum-effort precision attack on two of his top-priority targets—the Messerschmidt fighter plant at Regensburg and the ball bearing plant at Schweinfurt. The attacking forces met ferocious German fighter defense, and the losses on both sides set new records for the air war. Despite heavy losses the two bomber forces reached the two targets, hit them with exceptional accuracy and caused heavy damage. With precision bombing, the Americans were flying missions that approached in size those of the RAF but at a much higher cost. Eighth Air Force losses continued to be heavy for some months until long-range fighter planes were able to accompany the bombers all the way to the deepest targets in Germany.

While General Eaker and his commanders were employing ever larger numbers of B-17 and B-24 bombers in their daylight campaign against precision targets in Germany, General Arnold's staff was working on the deployment of the B-29. At a meeting of Allied leaders in Quebec in August 1943, Arnold presented an "Air Plan for the Defeat of Japan," as prepared by General Wolfe. It called for basing B-29s in central China: with their 1,500 mile operational range, it was expected that they could carry out a sustained bombing campaign against Japan's war-making industries. Final action on the plan was deferred until a meeting scheduled for late November in Cairo, Egypt, where Roosevelt and Churchill were to be present.

AT THIS TIME Wolfe was one of the busiest generals in the AAF. In addition to his responsibilities for planning the bombing of Japan and keeping the B-29 production lines on schedule, he had to develop an air-crew training program. The training was conducted at four airfields in Kansas: Pratt, Great Bend, Walker and Smoky Hill (Salina).

Among the first crewmen to arrive at Smoky Hill in September 1943 was a 23-year-old Texan, Capt. James L. Pattillo. He had jumped at the chance to join a combat outfit and be among the first to fly the superbomber that, though still held secret from the public, was the subject of great interest among airmen. Of the early arrivals at the new B-29 bases, some had had prior combat experience flying bombers in Europe or in the South Pacific. Most were handpicked, experienced pilots who had served as flight instructors in the United States. Pattillo was one of these. He had over 3,000 hours of flying time and had instructed the B-17 Flying Fortress and the B-24 Liberator. Some of his students were flying these bombers over Germany.

Other crewmen—ten besides the pilot for each B-29—arrived from the AAF installations at which they had received individual training for their combat jobs. The pilot, copilot, flight engineer, navigator and bombardier were commissioned officers. Most copilots were selected from among the top graduates of flying schools. Navigators and bombardiers came from schools for their specialties. Flight engineers (the B-29 was the first combat aircraft to have such a crewman) had either had pilot training or had attended engineering courses on the B-29. The remaining combat crew members were enlisted men, most of whom were noncommissioned officers or soon would be. The radiomen and radar operators had completed technical training courses; top gunners had completed a course on the central fire-control system, unique to the armament of the B-29. Right and left gunners, as well as tail gunners, had been cross-trained so they could perform engine and electrical system maintenance as well as operate and fire their weapons. The total number of crewmen to be trained was doubled because of a policy decision to man each B-29 with two crews. This was done in anticipation of extraordinary demands on the crews because of the long hours and enormous distances they would have to fly.

The unit which Pattillo joined, the 468th Bomb Group, consisted of four squadrons. Each squadron was to have ten B-29s and go overseas at double strength—20 combat crews. The 468th was part of the 58th Bomb Wing, which included three other bomb groups. Each group was to have 40 aircraft, so at full strength the 58th Bomb Wing would have 160 B-29s.

It would be months before Pattillo would see B-29s in such large numbers. A single B-29, one of the first 14 production models, was assigned to his squadron. As soon as he could after he arrived, Pattillo walked out to take a look at #26207. All AAF airplanes bore serial numbers but usually weren't "named" until they had an assigned crew and a theater of operations. Bomber #26207 was an exception. It had earned the name *Ramp Queen* because it almost always sat on the ramp while technicians and mechanics swarmed over it to make the changes necessary to comply with a stream of "Red X" technical orders that had to be complied with before a plane could be flown. On the day Pattillo walked out for his first look, the *Ramp Queen* was grounded.

As Pattillo approached the aircraft he noticed first the bulbous glass nose where the bombardier sat and the long, upward sweep of the rudder. (Refer to the cross-section illustrations that appear in the photo gallery section.) To the rear and above the bombardier's position sat the pilot and copilot. With its multiple glass panels the nose resembled a greenhouse. Walking down the side of the airplane, Pattillo subconsciously compared it with the bomber he, and most of the American public, was familiar with—the B-17 Flying Fortress. He noticed that the B-29 had two bomb bays, not just one. Though at the time he could only estimate its actual size, he would soon learn that the B-29 had a wingspan of 141 feet, 3 inches, a length of 99 feet and an empty weight of 74,500 pounds, roughly twice that of the B-17. (The Boeing 727, a commercial airliner in use today, has a wingspan of 108 feet and a length of 153 feet, 2 inches.) To lift this great weight the aircraft had four of the most powerful aviation engines in existence at the time—Wright R-3350s, each with 2200 horsepower that turned a 16-foot, 7-inch, four-bladed propeller. The B-29 was said to be faster than the Flying Fortress and could carry a 6-ton bomb load to a target 1,600 miles distant and return, an impossible mission for a B-17.

Returning to the front of the plane, he climbed up through the opening behind the nosewheel, the normal entry into the forward compartment. The first thing he saw as he came up through the floor was the flight engineer's station with its fixed seat facing a large instrument panel to the rear and an array of powerplant controls. Moving toward the left of the plane (at over 6 feet tall, he had to hunch a bit), he came to the navigator's chair—it looked like a typist's chair bolted to the floor. The navigator had a small, folding table to work on and a little window on his left. Moving rearward, he came to the radioman's position. From here, Pattillo observed only the rounded shapes of the two forward gun turrets; otherwise there were no signs of the sets of twin .50-caliber machine guns he had noticed above and below the fuselage at these locations before entering the plane. In B-17s and B-24s the gunners sat at their hand-held guns. In the B-29 all four gun turrets, the upper and lower forward and the upper and lower rear, were controlled from gun-sighting stations situated some distance from the guns themselves.

Just behind the navigator and radioman's position was a bulkhead that separated the forward crew compartment from the forward bomb bay. (Behind this bomb bay was the center wing section and then the rear bomb bay.) The airtight bulkhead was part of the cabin pressurization system of the B-29, the first ever used in a combat aircraft. Air, compressed by engine-driven compressors, was directed through a system of ducts to the plane's three compartments—the forward (where Pattillo was), the waist (located behind the rear bomb bay) and the tail gunner. With this system, an inside atmosphere equivalent to 8,000 feet could be maintained to altitudes as high as 30,000 feet. Pattillo noticed an opening in the upper part of the bulkhead, which was the entrance to an airtight 29-foot-long tunnel that a crewman could crawl through to reach the pressurized waist compartment. Just inside and on the top of the tunnel was a Plexiglas bubble that the navigator used for celestial navigation.

Next Pattillo went forward to examine the section of the airplane where he would spend the most time—the pilot's cabin. He liked its roominess compared to the B-17. The pilot (later called the airplane commander in the B-29) sat in a large armchair to the left. The bombardier was just ahead of him, so close that most conversations could be carried on without using the interphone. To his right, the copilot sat, with an instrument panel and set of controls similar to those of the pilot. Sitting in the left seat, Pattillo was impressed by the visibility to the front and seeming openness of the pilot's cabin but also noticed a "greenhouse" effect when one looked forward, because of the curved panes of glass enclosing a large part of the aircraft's nose. Rearward vision was another matter. Instrument readings notwithstanding, pilots like to be able to look directly at the engines that keep the aircraft aloft. Unlike the other bombers he had flown, in which he and the copilot could look at all the engines, in the B-29 they could see only the noses of the engines on the side where they sat. Neither could see the rear of the engines—the portion where oil or flames appear when there is a serious engine problem. Looking down across his knee, Pattillo could see the back of the bombardier's seat, the forward gunsight and the mount for the Norden bombsight that gave AAF bombers the accuracy necessary for precision bombing.

Realizing that he would have the opportunity to become more familiar with the pilot's station when he received his checkrides, Pattillo climbed back out the entrance and walked down the airplane's right side to a ladder hanging out of the right side of the fuselage, about halfway between the wing and the tail. This rear entrance was the one regularly used by the gunners and the radar observer to enter the aircraft. At the top of the ladder Pattillo stepped through a door into an unpressurized area. Straight ahead of him was mounted a small engine that drove an electrical generator. This generator (the crews called it the "Putt-Putt") supplied power to start the aircraft's engines. To his immediate left, in the center of the fuselage, was the rack for mounting an aerial camera ordinarily used to take bombing "strike" photos and, at times, for aerial reconnaissance. Behind that was the lower rear gun turret and its ammunition containers and, further toward the rear of the plane, oxygen bottles and a short catwalk to the tailgunner's station. To his right and leading forward was a pressure bulkhead with a round door which he crawled through. Standing up, he moved forward, and felt that he had entered a photographer's darkroom. On his left were metal containers of radar components to assist in navigation and target identification at night and in bad weather. On his right was the radar operator's chair and table, which faced the radarscope and other instruments on his console. Pattillo also noted the aircraft's only toilet, an aluminum container on the left side of the radar room.

He walked farther forward and came next to the gunners' compartment. As he reached the gunners' positions, he could see that the forward "wall" of the radar room was actually a fixed panel on which the electromechanical components of the central fire-control system's computers and power supply were mounted. In the center of the gunners' compartment was a raised, rotating seat that looked much like a barber's chair. The central fire-control gunner sat here with his head in a clear Plexiglas blister on the top of the fuselage that afforded him a 360° view from his rotating seat. At floor level, on either side of him, were the right and left gunners' positions. Each gunner sat next to a shoulder-width circular blister on which an electrically operated, optical gunsight was mounted. Besides his own gunsight, the central-fire-control gunner had a panel of controls with which he could assign control of the four gun turrets to himself, the left or right gunner or the bombardier, who also had a gunsight and served as the forward gunner. Forward of the central-fire-control gunner's seat was the entrance to the tunnel leading to the forward compartment, and just below that entrance was a small pressurized door into the rear bomb bay.

Pattillo finished his inspection by working his way back to the tail of the aircraft into the rear gunner's station. The rear gunner sat facing the rear, surrounded on three sides by bulletproof glass, his guns in a rotating turret just below him. Isolated from the other ten members of the crew except for voice communication, the rear gunner, unlike the other gunners, was responsible for only one turret, his own.

Pattillo left the *Ramp Queen*, hoping that he would be back to fly her soon. With 20 pilots to be trained and only one B-29, which was under modification much of the time, a lot of waiting was anticipated. In the meantime crews would do bombing, navigation and gunnery from B-17s and a B-26 medium bomber, which, with its tricycle landing gear, had takeoff, landing and ground-handling flying characteristics similar to the B-29.

One day in early October 1943, Pattillo finally got his

chance. That day their squadron commander, Lt. Col. James V. Edmundson, a South Pacific veteran, took him and two other pilots, Clarence C. MacPherson and Harold Brown, for their first familiarization ride in the *Ramp Queen*. Pattillo was the last of the three to fly the aircraft. As he settled into the right seat while Edmunson ran up the engines preparatory to takeoff, he noticed with some concern the lack of certain engine instrument gauges on either pilot's panel when compared to the B-17, B-24, or B-26. Then he realized that most of the "missing" gauges were on the flight engineer's panel and that flying with and relying on a flight engineer was something that he would just have to get used to. Landing the plane also took a little getting used to. Pattillo's first landing was fair, and the second so bad that the bombardier's gunsight came loose from its stowed position. The third one was better.

After each pilot had completed three landings, Col. Edmunson told them they were checked out for daylight flying. Night transition would follow. Pattillo flew the *Ramp Queen* whenever possible, but it wasn't until three months later, after a second B-29 arrived, that he was able to fly the airplane with his full crew aboard. He and his crew received ample bombing and gunnery practice in the B-17s but none in the B-29. They, like most crews, would leave for combat never having fired the guns or dropped a single bomb from the aircraft.

As THESE PILOTS were receiving their first checkrides, the M-69 had finally caught the attention of Gen. Arnold's staff. During the week preceding the Dugway tests, Brig. Gen. Orvil A. Anderson, Arnold's planning chief, had asked the Assistant Chief of Air Staff, Intelligence (A-2), to study the vulnerability of Japanese targets to attack. In response, on 15 October 1943, A-2 submitted a study report entitled "Japan, Incendiary Attack Data." This was a highly inaccurate title. The report (hereafter referred to as the "A-2 Incendiary Report") actually contained a comprehensive evaluation of what was required to attack Japanese cities with M-69 bombs and the probable results of these attacks.

The report drew on more than a score of U.S. and British

studies of bombs, incorporated the A-2 target analysis of the previous March, and utilized all available intelligence data on Japan's cities and general economy. The documents exerting the most influence on the report were probably the results of the tests at Dugway Proving Ground (prepared by NDRC's H. C. Hottel and J. R. Adams) and a paper by Ewell entitled "Theory and Tactics of Incendiary Bombing"—an ambitious topic for a man never known to have flown in a bomber and who certainly never piloted one.

NDRC consultants were deeply involved in analysis and preparation of the A-2 Incendiary Report: Ewell wrote over half of the substantive portions of the report, and other major contributors included Boris Laiming and Horatio Bond, both members of the National Fire Protection Association, and N. J. Thompson, director of research of the Factory Mutual Fire Insurance Companies.

The report was bold and explicit. It ignored the M-47 and M-50 bombs in favor of the more efficient M-69. It defined and advocated a wholly new target system—Japanese cities—and offered estimates of the bomb tonnages required to destroy them. It found the most striking aspect of large Japanese cities to be the virtual solid mass of one- and two-story buildings with only a small proportion of multistoried modern buildings. Though revised building regulations and zoning laws aimed at reducing the spread of fire—including parks, wider streets and firebreaks—had been in effect since the great Tokyo earthquake and fire of 1923, most Japanese cities continued to be congested with predominately wooden structures. Over 90 percent of Tokyo consisted of readily flammable wooden buildings—factories, warehouses and dwellings. Other Japanese cities had a similarly high percentage of wooden structures with roofs that could be easily penetrated by the M-69 bomb. Mixed residential/industrial districts, which composed relatively large portions of Tokyo, Osaka, Nagoya and Kobe, were considered especially good targets, since factories of all sizes were located in close proximity to densely clustered houses and were subject to rapid fire spread.

The A-2 Incendiary Report showed that in comparison with

Germany, where the British nighttime raids were causing substantial damage and casualties,

- Japanese residential construction was much more flammable than German,
- Japanese cities were more congested and more susceptible to conflagration than German cities,
- Industrial and military targets in Japanese cities were often surrounded by residential congestion and thus more exposed to sweeping fires than in German cities,
- Japan's war industry was more highly concentrated in a few key cities than was that of Germany.

The report provided estimates of the bomb concentration necessary to start sweeping fires in heavily built-up urban areas. The idea was that the combustible materials in Japanese residential construction would serve as "kindling" for conflagrations that would destroy factories and other military objectives over wide areas.

Ewell and his colleagues selected 20 cities as targets for analysis. The 20 were chosen because of their importance to Japanese war production, military potential and vulnerability to incendiary attack. Estimated incendiary tonnages were developed from (1) a detailed analysis of the combustible qualities of the vulnerable zones of the selected cities and (2) calculations based on test data concerning the M-69 bomb that showed it would take 864 "appliance fires" to overwhelm fire defenses and set a concentration of fires sufficient to ensure complete destruction. (An "appliance fire" is one beyond control by hand equipment such as buckets, stirrup pumps or pump tanks—its suppression requires a pumper fire truck or other major fire appliance.) The tonnage requirements represented the concentration of incendiaries that would have to be placed within the approximate limits of the vulnerable zones in order to ensure their complete destruction.

The report defined three categories or zones of vulnerability to incendiary attack:

ZONE I—Most Vulnerable Zone The commercial center of the city, inner congested area and mixed residential/industrial areas with small factories interspersed among workers' homes with an average population density of 91,000 persons per square mile—25 percent of the total city population. Under average weather conditions, an estimated 6 tons of incendiaries per square mile would be required for complete destruction of the zone.

ZONE II—Less Vulnerable Zone The less congested residential areas (but still very congested by European standards) containing port facilities, warehouses, freight yards, etc., mixed residential/industrial areas and some wholly industrial areas, with a population density of 54,000 persons per square mile—46 percent of the population. Under average weather conditions, an estimated 10 tons of incendiaries per square mile would be required for complete destruction of the zone.

ZONE III—Non-Incendiary Zone The suburban residential, park and wholly industrial areas with factories vulnerable to incendiaries, and modern, fire-resistant business districts, low population density—29 percent of the city population.

Though more vulnerable (requiring less bomb tonnage), Zone I was not considered more important than Zone II because Zone II contained more factories whose destruction would have a greater direct effect on war production. On the other hand, destruction of Zone I, with its higher population density, would have a greater indirect effect on the Japanese war effort by disrupting and dislocating industrial workers.

To start conflagrations of major proportions, it would be necessary to lay down incendiary patterns spaced so as to merge all burning areas into a general conflagration extending over the entire target zone. The report went so far as to suggest the tactical formation and spacing of bomber squadrons to produce the desired incendiary patterns. It appraised the probable Japanese fire-fighting response and concluded that the fire departments of Japan's cities could not contend with a concentrated incendiary attack of the type and weight described. This section of the report concluded by pointing out that any type of attack formation would be satisfactory if it produced the required cluster density and gave adequate protection to the attacking aircraft.

The report evaluated the effect of weather on incendiary attacks and determined that the rate of fire spread is almost directly proportional to wind velocity. The report revealed that gusting winds along Honshu's east coast—where Tokyo and most of the major cities are located—occurred most frequently during the months of December through May, of which March and April were the most favorable for fire spread.

The report included descriptions of 10 of the 20 target cities (Tokyo, Kawasaki, Yokohama, Osaka, Kobe, Nagoya, Hiroshima, Yawata, Fukuoka and Nagasaki) along with incendiary zone maps and photographs.

The final section of the A-2 Incendiary Report contained an analysis of the anticipated effects of incendiary attacks on the Japanese war effort. It showed that 1,690 tons of incendiaries effectively placed on the 20 cities (ranging from 631 tons for Tokyo, 349 tons for Osaka to 14 tons for a small city like Moji) would

- destroy areas totaling 186 square miles,
- reduce the output of 58 percent of the major industrial plants in Japan proper,
- destroy 26,000 small plants in the Tokyo, Osaka and Nagoya areas,
- cause a 30 percent loss of industrial production, which might last from four to six months,
- disrupt public utilities and essential services affecting both industry and the population, and
- dehouse approximately 12 million people (71 percent of the total population of the twenty cities).

The A-2 Incendiary Report of 15 October 1943 did not cause a major shift in AAF thinking away from precision bombing, but its content eventually became the basis for the evolution of the incendiary concept in American air strategy. Its most immediate consequence was its contributions to the ongoing COA effort to develop bombing objectives in Japan. Soon after receiving the report, Brig. Gen. Gates, COA's chairman, asked

Dr. Bush if Dr. Ewell could be loaned to the COA for work on a subcommittee studying the incendiary bombing of Japan. Bush agreed. Ewell now had yet another opportunity to "get the attention of the General Staff."

AT THIS TIME interest in bombing Japan was not confined to the Air Staff, COA, and NDRC. Just prior to the Allied conference at Cairo, which General Chiang Kai-shek attended, Roosevelt advised Churchill that "We have under development a project whereby we can strike a heavy blow at our enemy in the Pacific early next year [1944] with our new heavy bombers. Japanese military-naval and shipping strength is dependent upon the steel industry, which is strained to the limit. Half of the coke for that steel can be reached and destroyed by long-range bombers operating from the Chengtu area of China. The bombers can supply themselves by air from bases to be constructed near Calcutta without disturbing current airlift commitments."

The President's message obviously reflected part of the emerging Air Staff thinking. On 11 November 1943, the COA submitted its report "Economic Objectives in the Far East" to Gen. Arnold. The seventy-page report's summary contained the Committee's conclusions that the six most important strategic targets in Japan—with no order of priority—were merchant shipping, steel, urban industrial area, aircraft plants, anti-friction bearings and electronics. The COA report did not consider the location of bombing forces, but Arnold's operational planners knew that most Japanese steel plants were on Kyushu, westernmost of Japan's home islands. B-29s from China could reach Kyushu, but Honshu, where most of the other target groups were located, was beyond their range.

The most significant difference between the thrust of the A-2 Incendiary Report of 15 October 1943 and the COA's 11 November 1943 report was that the latter, by implication, adhered to the precision-bombing doctrine. To cripple steel production the COA singled out for destruction six coke plants, thirteen aircraft plants, six bearing factories and three electronics plants.

The COA report in describing the "urban industrial area" target system, summarized the A-2 report, but its summary was far less bold and explicit than the A-2 report. In its summation, the COA informed Arnold that a relatively small weight of incendiaries could cause great damage by destroying housing, public services and a significant number of industrial installations, but the report did not contain any of the hard-hitting estimates found in A-2's report. (Top generals like Arnold often only had time to read the summary of a report, though their key staff officers always read the complete report.) Whether deliberately or not, the authors of the COA report did not adequately describe the nature and magnitude of urban industrial targets when they stated: "Japanese war production (aside from heavy industry) is peculiarly vulnerable to incendiary attack of urban areas because of the widespread practice of subcontracting to small handicraft and domestic establishments. Many small houses in Japan are not merely places of residence, but workshops contributing to the production of war materials." The report recommended strong attacks (preferably conducted during the period from December through May) and observed that hitting many urban areas at once might "overwhelm the relief and repair facilities of the country as a whole."

Arnold accepted the COA report, and a synopsis of its recommendations was later sent on to the Joint Chiefs of Staff. (In April 1944 the Joint Chiefs would issue a list of target systems that paralleled those recommended by the COA's report, including the incendiary bombing of urban industrial areas.) Roosevelt, because of his strong interest in beginning the bombing of Japan from the China bases, was told that the first target would the the steel industry on Kyushu. There is no evidence of his reaction, if any, to the recommendations on other target systems—including the one "authorizing" incendiary bombing of Japan's cities. Nor do we know what Secretary of War Henry L. Stimson felt. The AAF and the Joint Chiefs had made the decision and in so doing took the first major step toward destruction by fire of Japan's cities.

In view of the military and political environment at the time, Arnold's decision to accept the urban target system was, for many reasons, a bold one. His air forces in Europe were deeply involved in proving the efficacy of precision bombing in Europe. The AAF had little or no experience in area bombing. Production of incendiary bombs was small. Most of the support for incendiary bombing of cities had come from civilians—the scientists of NDRC and his COA advisors. The new bomb, the M-69, was yet to prove itself under operational conditions. Finally, as a national figure, Arnold was aware that the concept that he had accepted (even though then a military secret) was contrary to the prevailing feelings of the American public.

As NOVEMBER ENDED, Arnold had little time to ponder his decision. He now faced one of a series of crises that would plague him in readying the B-29 for combat. Just a few weeks before, he had learned of the President's disappointment when told by Arnold that it would be March or April 1944—not January—before B-29s would be deployed to China. The President wrote Gen. Marshall of his disgust with the India–China situation and complained that everything was going wrong, saying, "The worst thing is that we are falling down on our promises [to China] every single time."

With this kind of pressure, Arnold and his staff took action to ensure that the AAF would be able to make good on the new target dates that had been given the President. Gen. Wolfe sent an advance party to India to prepare the way for the B-29s. Next, Arnold asked the Joint Chiefs of Staff for top priority for B-29 production. They turned him down because it wasn't a shortage of materials or manpower that was delaying production; rather, it was the complexity of manufacturing such a highly advanced aircraft. In late November Arnold activated the XX Bomber Command at Smoky Hill Army Air Field, Kansas, and assigned to it the two recently activated bomb wings—the 58th and the 73rd. Command of the new XX Bomber Command and the mission of taking it overseas was assigned to the already heavily burdened Gen. Wolfe.

At their Cairo conference of November–December 1943, Roosevelt and Churchill approved a plan for the defeat of Japan. The plan's major strategy was to continue the two mutually supporting advances across the Pacific: Gen. MacArthur's from the southwest and Adm. Nimitz's through the central Pacific. The prior August, Roosevelt and Churchill had discussed but not finalized an "Air Plan for the Defeat of Japan"; at Cairo they adopted a modified version of this plan and made it part of their "Overall Plan for the Defeat of Japan." The Air Plan would later be code-named "Matterhorn" for the famous Alpine peak whose ascent was a great challenge to mountain climbers of the 19th and 20th centuries. Arnold would find the task of bombing Japan from China no less challenging.

Buried deep in the plan was a provision that would create an even greater challenge for Arnold. As first written, the plan called for obtaining sites in the Western Pacific from which to conduct an intensive bombardment of Japan, but didn't name the geographic objectives. A month or so later it was revised to state: "A strategic bombing force will be established in Guam, Tinian and Saipan for a strategic bombing of Japan proper." It was from these islands, not from China, that the AAF would strike at the vitals of Japan.

Finally, the framework for the air war against Japan was in place. Its success would depend, ultimately, on an airplane and a bomb—the B-29 and the M-69—and airmen who could guide the airplane and the bombs to the target. But, as 1943 ended, none of the three were ready.

BY EARLY JANUARY 1944—soon after Arnold had abruptly ordered Wolfe to India to prepare for arrival of his command—ninety-seven B-29s had rolled off the assembly lines. Only sixteen were certified as ready for service. These had been sent to the four B-29 airbases in Kansas, where pilots like Jim Pattillo waited their turn to get checked out. The rest had been sent directly to centers around the country, where military, civil service and contractor technicians attempted to keep up with changes each aircraft required to make it reliable under combat conditions. Flight tests conducted by Boeing at Wright Field, Eglin Field and the air bases disclosed scores of mechanical and electrical defects: engines, flaps, rudders, turrets, fuel tanks, radars and compasses required replacement or modification. The list seemed endless.

In mid-February Arnold flew to one of the modification centers located at Marietta, Georgia, to check on progress. He found the progress slower than he liked. After ordering additional technicians assigned to the center, he was assured that planes would start departing for overseas on 10 March.

In another February inspection trip, this one to the AAF Proving Ground at Eglin Field, Florida, Arnold verbally ordered institution of a program to test incendiaries and high-explosive bombs. Arnold and his immediate staff seemed completely unaware of the Dugway tests, although bombing Japanese cities was certainly on their minds. A follow-up memorandum directed the commander at Eglin to "find a group of buildings such as an abandoned camp in order to test out the various effects of various types of incendiaries with long and short delay fuses to determine the proper type of bombs to drop on Japanese urban objectives." Brig. Gen. E. Montgomery, the Air Chemical Officer, advised Arnold's headquarters that tests had been conducted at Dugway and the M-69 had proven to be the most effective incendiary for use on urban Japanese targets. The Proving Ground, however, had already initiated a project to comply with Arnold's verbal order.

Meanwhile, for Arnold, the most important project in the AAF was sending the first B-29s on their way overseas. Arnold arrived at Smoky Hill Army Airfield, Salina, Kansas, on the afternoon of 9 March to watch the first departures. Not a single airplane was ready. After a quick review, he found the modification program "void of organization, management and leadership." With his pledge to the President in great jeopardy, Arnold ordered an all-out crash effort and gave the B-29 top priority among AAF programs. What followed came to be known as the "Battle of Kansas"—a frenzied effort to complete and deploy 150 bombers to India by mid-April.

All of the planes, personnel and materiel were transferred to the four Kansas air bases. Headquarters for the effort was at Smoky Hill. Men worked around the clock, in snow and subzero weather, much of the time outside, since hangar space was limited. Men from Georgia, particularly affected by the extreme cold, were fitted with sheepskin-lined flying suits. With the program still behind schedule, Boeing voluntarily pulled 600 men off the assembly lines at their Wichita plant and assigned them to the modification project. The massive effort paid off. In late March the first B-29s were certified as combat ready, turned over to the XX Bomber Command and took off, nine or ten per day, for India. By 15 April 1944, 150 had left the United States.

As the first B-29s were leaving for India, the organization under which they and their crews would operate was established. On 4 April, the Twentieth Air Force (not to be confused with the XX Bomber Command, which, along with the XXI Bomber Command, would be major commands under the Twentieth Air Force) was activated in Washington, D.C. Gen. Arnold was named commander. Selected members of Arnold's Headquarters AAF staff were assigned to serve also on the Twentieth Air Force staff. Arnold appointed, as Chief of Staff of the Twentieth, Gen. Haywood S. Hansell, known as "Possum" to his friends.

Possum, a southerner born into a military family, was nicknamed by classmates at Sewannee Military Academy where, according to Hansell, "popular belief was that I bore more than a passing resemblance to the physiognomy of the beast, and also possessed some of his habits." But the similarity ended there—young Hansell was anything but docile and slow moving. Small, light, but aggressive, he tried football at Sewannee but did not excel. Militarily he showed more promise. He became captain of the cadet corps in his senior year, a position he held until demerits brought him down. Hansell graduated from Georgia Tech and then the Air Corps Advanced Flying School, winning his wings and commission in 1929. He soon demonstrated that he was a natural and exceptional pilot. The young lieutenant soon became one of the Air Corps team of the precision acrobatic flyers known as "Three Men on a Flying Trapeze." The team consisted of Capt. Claire L. Chennault (later a major general who gained fame in China as head of the Flying Tigers), Lt. Luke Williamson, and Possum. Chennault, their leader, would conceive a nearly impossible maneuver, explain it to the others, and the next day they would go up and execute it. Hansell later recalled, perhaps half seriously, "If we had kept at it long enough, certainly all would have been killed."

Gifted as he was as a flyer, it was Hansell's analytical and conceptual skills that eventually brought him into the highest councils of the AAF. He had been one of the small group of bright young instructors at the Air Corps Tactical School who developed and taught the strategic bombing concept—high-altitude, daylight precision bombing—with which the Air Corps entered World War II. Just before America entered that conflict, Hansell and several other officers, all former members of the faculty at the Air Corps Tactical School, under Col. (later Lt. Gen.) Harold L. George, produced plan AWPD-1 (named after the Air War Plans Division, in which they worked) describing the Air Corps role in any war that might arise between the United States and Germany or Japan. It emphasized a powerful strategic air offensive based on the precision-bombing doctrine.

Hansell's work in this plan brought him to Arnold's attention. Thereafter he was a key participant in planning the American-British Combined Bomber Offensive in Europe and had a brief stint as commander of the 1st Bomb Wing in England in the early days of the American air offensive against Germany. In December 1943, Arnold returned Hansell to duty in the Pentagon and then took him to Cairo as one of his advisors during the Roosevelt-Churchill Conference. It was Hansell who had steered "Matterhorn" through the planning process and named Guam, Saipan and Tinian as the bases from which the AAF would bomb Japan.

The Twentieth Air Force was a unique command. It operated directly under the Joint Chiefs of Staff, with the Commanding General AAF as executive agent to implement Joint Chiefs' directives for its employment. (The Twentieth was the only AAF air force with only one type of aircraft assigned to it.) But with Gen. Arnold's wide-ranging responsibilities it fell to Hansell to run the Twentieth Air Force Headquarters. He was assisted by an able deputy, Col. Cecil B. Combs, who had fought the Japanese in the Philippines and the southwest Pacific. Hansell inherited all of Gen. Wolfe's former responsibilities—B-29 production, training and supply—and more. He had to plan the bombing of Japan from the Mariana islands, once these islands were captured by U.S. forces, and the role of incendiaries in such attacks.

In mid-April 1944, as a result of Arnold's verbal order in February, the AAF conducted incendiary bombing tests at Eglin Field. Maj. Watkins, an Air Staff observer at one of the tests, sent a report to Combs. Watkins had watched a B-17, flying at 10,000 feet, bomb 18 simulated Japanese dwellings made of pine boards with no ceilings, doors or windows (far cruder construction than the replicas used at Dugway). The B-17 released three aimable clusters of M-69 incendiaries, each cluster containing 38 bombs. The aimable cluster had recently been adopted by the AAF and rushed into production for shipment to China for use by the XX Bomber Command. Unlike the quick-opening cluster, which opened soon after it left the bomb bay, the new cluster held the bombs together as a unit and could be set to release them at about 4,000 feet, allowing them to fall individually. Fifteen M-69s struck the test buildings, and after three and a half minutes fires were burning so intensely that motorized fire equipment and trained firemen were required to extinguish them. Five minutes after bomb impact, the fires were out of control and all structures in the major group were destroyed. A smaller group of structures about 60 feet away were undamaged because the wind blew the fire away from them. Impressed by what he had seen, Watkins reported that if fires like this were kindled in Japanese cities, the civilian casualty rate would be tremendous—"at least 60 percent."

But from another quarter, Hansell heard criticism of the October 1943 A-2 Incendiary Report. In early May, Dr. Edward M. Earle, a member of the COA, had been in England conferring with members of the Ministry of Home Security at Princes Risborough. Earle wrote the COA chairman, Brig. Gen. Gates, informing him that he "had come across some data at Princes Risborough which may be of interest to Colonel Perera and General Hansell . . ." and enclosed copies of

memoranda written by members of R.E. 8 (a British organization that did research and analysis for the RAF) indicating that
Japan might not be the "pushover" for incendiary attack that
the A-2 report suggested. Specifically the British commenters
were concerned that the American study had (1) underesti-
mated the fire-prevention measures taken in the last two decades in Tokyo and other major Japanese cities and (2) taken
too optimistic a view of the weight of incendiaries necessary
to destroy the twenty Japanese cities included in the report.

Though more likely through coincidence than as a reaction
to the British comments, shortly after Earle's letter reached
Washington, Headquarters AAF requested the Air Forces
Board—the most senior of the AAF boards established to review or analyze selected matters—to analyze and determine
the bomb tonnage that would have to be lifted from the ground
to produce the desired concentration on the target under operational conditions. Operational conditions would take into
account such factors as losses of planes enroute, poor target
definition, weather conditions and bombing accuracy.

Perera seemed to be unaffected by the British comments
when, on 9 May, he and W. Barton Leach, a COA colleague,
sent Hansell a memorandum on targets for the operations that
the Twentieth Air Force expected to initiate from Saipan during the coming fall. They gave first priority to the coke plants
in Japan that were not successfully attacked by the China-
based XX Bomber Command. Second priority was aircraft and
radio/radar production on Honshu, Japan's main island. Nine
plants were listed, none of which could be reached from the
China bases.

The remainder of the memorandum was a forecast of how
the incendiary campaign from the Marianas bases might take
shape. It stated that a general incendiary attack on Japanese
urban industrial areas should start in March 1945, provided a
force large enough to accomplish total destruction of the targeted cities was available. A smaller attack might burn parts
of a city, creating firebreaks that would render subsequent
attacks less effective. It listed 13 Japanese cities (from the
20 listed in the October 1943 A-2 Incendiary Report), indicating parenthetically that two—Yawata and Nagasaki—were

"listed" for experimental incendiary attack by the XX Bomber Command from China bases. In closing, the two officers expressed their belief that planning beyond one year was unrealistic and that operational experience over the coming year would show the feasibility of various operations against Japan. In a closing sentence that probably did not sit well with Hansell—an architect and staunch believer in daylight precision bombing—they observed: "If daylight operations prove more costly than expected, it may prove wise to shift to night attacks on areas at a date earlier than March 1945."

While the pros and cons and the future of incendiary bombing were being considered in the Pentagon, NDRC scientists were busy running tests at Eglin Field, Florida. By now NDRC was satisfied the M-69 was very effective against dwellings—particularly Japanese dwellings. But they were also aware that AAF doctrine emphasized precision bombing of *industrial* targets, and they needed more data on incendiary effectiveness against such objectives. With AAF permission, NDRC constructed at Eglin a large industrial-type building with three typical roof types. One section of the building had a wood roof, the middle had a concrete tile roof, and the third was a three-story reinforced concrete structure. NDRC ran tests on the M-69's capability on these types of structures and how well it caused fires, once inside. Using these test data, NDRC concluded that the M-69 was capable of penetrating over 90 percent of the roofs of the listed industrial targets.

THREE

"MATTERHORN"

WHILE TESTS OF the M-69 and speculation on its future continued, the plane that would bomb Japan was undergoing its first test as a long-range bomber. It did not do well.

The trip from Kansas to India was 11,530 miles and included stops at Presque Isle, Maine; Gander, Newfoundland; Marrakech, Morocco; Cairo, Egypt; Karachi, India (now Pakistan); and finally Calcutta. The longest leg was the 2,700-mile flight across the Atlantic from Gander to Marrakech.

On 2 April 1944 Gen. Wolfe, along with American and British dignitaries, met the first B-29 to land in India. It was piloted by Brig. Gen. LaVerne "Blondie" Saunders, an All American football player at West Point and organizer of the B-29 crew training program. A second B-29 arrived four days later after a stopover in England—an unsuccessful attempt to make the Japanese think that B-29s were going to be used in the impending Allied invasion of Europe. Almost immediately, Japanese broadcasts announced the arrival of B-29s in India and construction of airfields near Calcutta and Chengtu, China.

The other 158 planes followed, in daily increments of ten, and had no difficulty on the long leg over the ocean. After that, however, crews began running into problems—engines

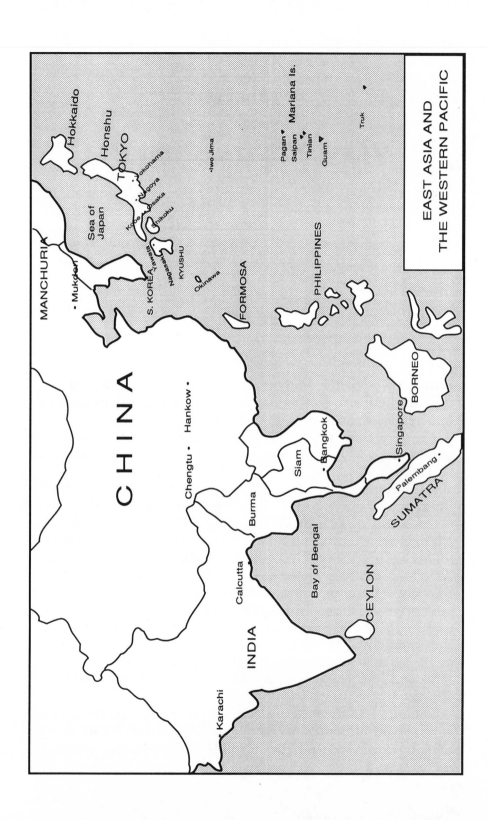

EAST ASIA AND
THE WESTERN PACIFIC

failed, fuel tanks sprung leaks, and starters and generators malfunctioned or broke down completely. Then misfortune set in. On 13 April one airplane crashed at Marrakech; on 15 April, another at Cairo; finally, five crashed at Karachi. From 21–29 April, Wolfe stopped all flights. Later, he attributed the earlier accidents to crew inexperience, but the five at Karachi had resulted from overheated engines due, in part, to the 115°F ground temperatures and inadequate cooling of the B-29's R-3350 engines. It is likely that some of the crews survived these noncombat, mechanically related accidents. However, the number of surviving airmen is unknown. Engine overheating had been a problem since the first B-29 had flown. Though engineers in the United States would work intensively on the problem for months to come, it would be the most serious of many malfunctions that would plague XX Bomber Command operations in India and China. By 8 May, 130 airplanes had arrived at the India bases. The rest would soon follow.

Gen. Wolfe established XX Bomber Command headquarters at a recently completed airfield near the town of Kharagpur, west of Calcutta and north of the Bay of Bengal. There were three other B-29 airfields with "exotic" names—Dudhkundi, Piardoba, and Chakulia—in the vicinity of Kharagpur. For convenience the Americans gave each base a simple designation: Kharagpur was B-1, Chakulia was B-2, etc. Twelve hundred miles away, about a five-and-a-half-hour B-29 flight in a northeasterly direction and over the Himalayas—known to the British and Americans as the "Hump"—lay the Chinese town of Chengtu. To get over the Hump pilots had to climb to more than 24,000 feet and contend with severe weather—violent up- and downdrafts that robbed them of control, 0 to −10°F temperatures that iced their wings and seemingly impenetrable cloud formations that suddenly forced them to rely totally on their instruments. Around Chengtu were the forward airfields from which the B-29s would take off to bomb targets in Manchuria and Japan.

Arnold had ordered Wolfe to mount his first mission by 1 May 1944. Before he could do this, Wolfe had to build up adequate stocks of fuel, bombs, ammunition and other supplies at the Chengtu bases. The materiel all had to be hauled by air. He had a few C-47s to haul personnel, parts and tools, but most of the aviation gasoline, bombs and ammunition had to be carried by B-29s that had been stripped of their armaments and fitted with special fuel tanks. These were called "tankers" and could lift over six tons of fuel per trip, but it was a slow process. Under the best conditions it took two gallons of fuel burned by the B-29 to deliver one gallon to Chengtu. With headwinds and diversions to avoid bad weather it might take twelve gallons for every one delivered. The supply runs were tedious and dangerous. In the early days it was not uncommon to lose three or four B-29s a month, mostly from engine failure. For each round-trip across the Hump a crew would paint a camel on the nose of their aircraft.

While building up supplies at Chengtu, Wolfe received approval from Washington to conduct a "practice" combat mission against the Makasan railway shops at Bangkok, Siam, on 27 May. The mission, originating and using gas and munitions from the Kharagpur bases, would not cut into the Chengtu stores. Operational planners believed the 2,000-mile round-trip and the expected light Japanese air defenses would offer a real but not-too-severe test to the "green" crews, most of whom had neither dropped a bomb nor fired the guns of the B-29. Wolfe ordered a night mission, with planes bombing individually. His reasons were twofold. The combat crews had no B-29 formation-flying experience, and darkness would protect them from enemy fighters.

He may also have been drawing on recommendations made the previous February by the AAF Proving Ground Command and the AAF Board that initial B-29 operations against Japan be conducted at night by single aircraft or small units against concentrated, high-priority targets. These recommendations resulted from tests conducted at Salina, Kansas, that same month (February 1944) to determine the defensive capabilities of the B-29. Experienced fighter pilots in ten P-51B "Mustang" fighter planes, one of the AAF's best, attacked a B-29 from all possible angles and experienced great difficulty.

At the Pentagon, Col. Emmett O'Donnell, Jr., reviewed the test data and sent his own report to Gen. Arnold. O'Donnell was one of a small group of relatively young officers Arnold kept during the war years as "idea men" and troubleshooters. Others who were or would be among this inner council were Charles P. Cabell, Laurence S. Kuter and Lauris Norstad, who were colonels when selected by Arnold but would later all achieve general officer rank.

In his report O'Donnell showed that he was a creative thinker. He was aware that the B-29 had been designed and built as the AAF's most heavily armed bomber and was considered capable of defending itself in formation daylight raids on enemy targets. But after examining the test data he found that the B-29's most outstanding defensive features were its speed and maneuverability. Then, in a radical proposal that the AAF board accepted only in part, he stated:

> As a matter of fact, for use in the specific task of attacking Japanese cities from Chinese bases with incendiary bombs, I believe this airplane could be used with great effect *without any armament by dispatching them singly at night and bombing by radar.* [Italics added] . . . Considering the difficulty our P-51s experienced in pressing home attacks in daylight, I believe that the Japs would be absolutely frustrated in successfully attacking them at night. . . . This single-airplane operation would have the additional advantage of allowing the ships to be used to their absolute maximum range. Great difficulty is to be expected in flying large formations for great distances. The cooling of the engines is a critical item, and wingmen and rear elements are bound to experience mechanical difficulties due to excess throttling.

Neither the Board's recommendations nor O'Donnell's report pleased Arnold. Stripping the airplane of its guns was out of the question, and a night mission was contrary to what he wanted—a daylight precision raid. So Arnold ordered that the Bangkok mission be a daylight raid.

Wolfe postponed the strike for two weeks and conducted as much training as possible. Bombing runs were made at a nearby British practice range, and crews did some formation flying. Even when hauling fuel across the Hump, B-29s flew in formation in an attempt to gain a modicum of experience.

With unrelenting pressure from Washington, Wolfe scheduled the mission for 5 June 1944.

Ninety-eight planes took off for Bangkok that day. One crashed on takeoff, and sixteen did not reach the target area. The field order called for four-plane elements to bomb in diamond formation. Poor visibility and inexperience caused some planes to join the wrong elements; others gave up trying and proceeded to Bangkok singly. Things did not improve. Over the target heavy undercast caused many to bomb by radar, a technique in which few crews had experience. Fortunately, Japanese antiaircraft fire and fighter opposition was relatively light and no bombers were lost to enemy action. On the return trip four planes went down with engine trouble, making a total of five lost.

The XX Bomber Command had been through its shakedown, but on the whole, it was a disappointing start. The three groups carrying high-explosive bombs dropped inaccurately and did little damage. One group carried M-69 incendiaries in 500-lb aimable clusters; this was the first combat drop of the M-69 from B-29s. Again, bombing accuracy was poor. Post-strike photos showed no evidence that fires had been started.

His bombers had no more than returned from Bangkok when Wolfe received an urgent message from Arnold telling him a maximum effort was needed against Japan. The date set was 15 June, and the target was the Imperial Iron and Steel Works at Yawata on Kyushu, the westernmost of the main islands of Japan. The plant produced one-quarter of the nation's rolled steel. The mission would be a 3,200-mile roundtrip. In recognition of this, Washington ordered a night mission so airplanes could proceed to the target singly and bomb individually from relatively low levels—8,000 to 18,000 feet. The bombload was 2 tons of 500-pound general-purpose bombs per mission. The mission was to be led by Brig. Gen. Saunders.

THE JAPANESE, THROUGH their highly effective intelligence network, had been carefully keeping track of the buildup of the B-29 bases in India and China. After the Bangkok mission they knew that an attack on Kyushu, the only home island within range of the American bombers, was imminent. For some months, Japanese air defense planners had had to contend with two deterrent factors—one philosophical and the other operational. Philosophically, Japanese military leaders were imbued with the spirit of the offensive. During the war in China, and in the Pacific after Pearl Harbor, the Japanese Army and Navy Air Forces' primary mission was to take the fight to the enemy and destroy him. Switching to the defensive, particularly over the home islands, was an unwelcome and difficult task.

The basic difficulty lay in the fact that neither the Japanese Army nor Navy had an aircraft designed for intercepting a bomber with the high-altitude capability of the B-29, particularly at night. Fighter aircraft of the Japanese Army Air Force (JAAF), the service branch with primary responsibility for air defense of the home islands, had been designed to operate at altitudes lower than 16,000 feet—about half the cruising altitude of the B-29. Though skilled pilots in the JAAF's most up-to-date airplanes could attain an altitude of 30,000 feet, it took them a long time to do so. Then, having burned most of their fuel to get there, the pilot could spend little time at extreme altitude—usually only enough for one pass at an enemy bomber.

Beginning in early 1944 the Japanese began to transfer fighter aircraft from China and the south and to organize the air defense of Japan. The Tokyo area was the responsibility of the Eastern Army Command's 10th Air Division; most of the rest of the island of Honshu was the responsibility of the Central Command's 11th Air Division; the western end of Honshu and the island of Kyushu fell under the 12th Air Division of the Western Army Command. Though initially only responsible for defending its own naval bases and coastal areas, the Japanese Naval Air Force eventually assigned units in support of the Japanese Army Air Force defensive mission.

The 10th Air Division would eventually consist of over 400 fighters of different types and varying effectiveness; the 11th Air Division, about 200 aircraft; and the 12th, about 150.

Though other fighters would be employed later, from the outset and until the end of the war three aircraft would predominate in fighting off the B-29s. Of the three, the Ki-61, a single-
engine fighter manufactured by Kawasaki Aircraft Company,
mounted both two 20-mm and two 12.7-mm machine guns
and called *Hien* (translated "Swallow") by the Japanese, was
rated as best at attaining and fighting at high altitudes. By this
time the U.S. AAF had adopted the practice of assigning a code
name to each type of military aircraft that had been
identified—male names for fighters, female names for bombers. The AAF gave the Ki-61 "Swallow" the code name
"Tony" soon after it was met in action in 1943. Next in high-
altitude performance was the Ki-44, a single-engine aircraft
manufactured by the Nakajima Aircraft Company, supporting
two 12.7-mm and two 7.7-mm machine guns. The Japanese
called the Ki-44 *Shoki* (translated "Demon") and the Americans code-named it "Tojo" after the then premier and war
minister of Japan. The third Japanese workhorse fighter was
the Ki-45 manufactured by Kawasaki. Called *Toryu* (translated "Dragon Killer"), the Ki-45 was a twin-engine aircraft
with a crew of two, and it carried the heaviest armament—
three machine guns and a 37-mm cannon. Its American code
name was "Nick."

The Japanese Navy Air Force fighter that would fly against
the B-29s in large numbers was the Type-0 A6M carrier
fighter, armed with two 20-mm cannons and two machine
guns and manufactured by the Mitsubishi Company. The
fighter had no Japanese popular name, but after Pearl Harbor
the American public came to know it by its Japanese type
designation—"Zero." However, the official code name for the
aircraft, "Zeke," was the reference commonly used by American airmen. The Japanese Navy had a twin-engined fighter
that the Americans at first took for a naval version of the
Army's "Nick." The fighter J1N1-S, known as the "Gekko"
and classified by the Japanese as a night fighter, was one of the
few Japanese aircraft commonly fitted out with a radar system
for use in targeting enemy bombers at night. Unfortunately
for the Japanese, the radar was primitive and pilots found it
unreliable and ineffective in combat. Like the Army fighters,

the Zero and the Gekko had limited capability for aerial combat at high altitudes.

If the Japanese pilots faced problems, so did the crews of Japanese antiaircraft and searchlight batteries. The antiaircraft gun that the Japanese deployed in large numbers around their military installations and cities was a 75-mm weapon with an effective range of about 22,000 feet, far below the cruising altitude of the B-29. They had, initially in limited numbers, a mobile 88-mm gun that could reach 30,000 feet. Most of these guns were deployed in the Eastern Army Area in defense of the major industrial cities of Tokyo, Yokohama and Nagoya, but as more became available the Army used them in other areas. A third gun, a 120-mm model weighing over 21 tons, first produced in 1943, could easily reach the B-29s, but the supply of these guns was even more limited than the 88-mm model. Because it was not a mobile weapon, the Japanese used them in fixed emplacements around a few of the major cities.

Another deficiency in Japanese air defense was the lack of target acquisition and tracking radar. The British and the Germans had highly developed radar systems. In such systems long-range radar would pick up enemy aircraft miles away from the target city or industrial complex and vector an alerted night fighter to it. When the night fighter got close enough, the pilot could find the target on his own short-range radar screen and close in for a visual sighting and the kill. The small number of radar-equipped units the Japanese possessed were used primarily around Tokyo and other major cities to spot oncoming aircraft for searchlight batteries. Because of the shortage of radar, sound-locating devices were more frequently used for this purpose.

Except for their shortage of acquisition radar, Japanese tactics for using searchlights were much the same as that of the British or the Germans. The Japanese used a searchlight with a diameter of about five feet and an effective range of about 26,000 feet, again falling short of the B-29. A small number of searchlight batteries equipped with sound-locator equipment or radar were stationed around or on the expected approach routes to the area they were protecting. It was the job of these batteries to catch the incoming bomber and hold it just long enough for the manually operated searchlight batteries, usually positioned closer to the target area and in greater numbers than the acquisition batteries, to lock on and hold the aircraft in illumination long enough for antiaircraft batteries to fire on it or fighters to make their attack. Meanwhile the acquisition searchlight batteries were picking up new targets to pass on to the tracking batteries. Successful execution of this sequence required considerable skill and timing. Though batteries throughout Japan had been trained in the techniques, by mid-1944 they had yet to put them into practice.

ON 13 JUNE, Gen. Saunders led his four bomb groups to their forward fields around Chengtu, and late in the afternoon of 15 June, 68 B-29s labored down their gravel runways, headed for Japan. Because of Washington's great expectations for the mission, they carried eight correspondents and three news photographers. A crash on takeoff, "aborts" (turn-backs because of engine trouble) and inability to find the target reduced the number of B-29s arriving in the vicinity of the Imperial Iron and Steel Works to only 47. By then the Yawata area was completely blacked out, making it necessary for two-thirds of the aircraft to bomb by radar.

If the Americans were having difficulties, so were the Japanese defenders. Though alerted long before the arrival of the first B-29s, the Japanese sent up less than 30 fighter planes, of which about eight were heavily armed Ki-45s. Their pilots lacked the radar to locate the bombers and found it difficult to climb rapidly enough to close with the few that they caught sight of. Searchlights lit the sky, and over a hundred Japanese antiaircraft guns of various calibers blazed away, firing thousands of rounds. At 11:38 P.M., the first B-29 gave the "bombs away" signal—Betty—which, because of the historic significance of the mission, was flashed back to Washington. A Japanese broadcast claimed that seven Superfortresses had been destroyed, asserting that the crew of one had been captured and consisted of six lieutenant colonels and a major! The Americans acknowledged only one B-29 shot down over the target, either by a fighter or antiaircraft. Though losses were light, results were poor. Only one bomb hit Imperial Steel's sprawling shops; the rest fell far wide of the target area, causing some damage to the Kokura Arsenal and miscellaneous industrial buildings.

Here and throughout the text that follows, when planes are described as being shot down, lost, missing or seen to crash over Japan or Japanese-held territory, the reader may safely assume that the entire crew, usually eleven men, died. Only a small percentage of those who parachuted to the ground survived as POWs. Consequently, except in a few instances, one will not find in this account the number of airmen who were killed or wounded on a particular combat mission. The total number of aircraft lost and the number of airmen who died during the Twentieth Air Force bombing campaign against Japan is stated at the conclusion of Chapter Twelve.]

Though it did virtually no damage to Japan's steel industry, the mission boosted XX Bomber Command morale and was believed a success by the American public. For the first time since the Doolittle Raid in 1942, American planes were over Japan. Accounts of the Yawata strike, coupled with announcements of the existence of the Twentieth Air Force and descriptions of America's new superbomber, the B-29, shared space on the front pages of U.S. newspapers with reports on the progress of the recent Allied invasion of Europe. Reflecting this publicity, a ground crewman wrote home, "I'm in a B-29 outfit and they're sure great. Read about them in the papers and watch *Life* magazine—you may see a picture of me helping load bombs. I wrote your name on one."

The American raid was also big news in Japan. The government-controlled press minimized the size of the attacking force, lauded the inflated claims of B-29s shot down, and acknowledged damage to some hospitals and schools. Millions of Tokyo residents didn't need their newspapers to know that something had happened. An air-raid alert sounded in that city as the first B-29s arrived over Kyushu, and continued in effect until 17 June. The Japanese people now knew their home islands were vulnerable to attack from the giant new American warplanes.

Arnold wanted to keep the pressure on. In Washington, Twentieth Air Force Headquarters set the following as immediate objectives: a major—100 plane—daylight attack on the Showa Steel Works at Anshan, Manchuria; a strike against the oil refinery at Palembang, Sumatra; and small harassing raids against Kyushu. Wolfe, faced with the harsh realities of inexperienced combat crews, crippling engine problems and supply difficulties, responded with what he considered to be a more realistic plan; it called for only 50 or 60 B-29s for the Anshan attack. In response, on 4 July, Arnold relieved Wolfe of his command and ordered him to Washington where he was put in charge of the Materiel Command at Wright Field and later promoted to major general. "Blondie" Saunders took over at Kharagpur.

On the night of 8 July Saunders sent a small force to Kyushu, where it bombed four cities. The mission did insignificant damage, but no planes were lost and the vulnerability of Kyushu was demonstrated. The size of the force was due, in part, to a desire to conserve his force for the "maximum effort" 100-airplane precision daylight attack that Washington demanded be carried out in July.

Saunders met the deadline, getting 96 aircraft in the air. Though weather prevented 36 of them from reaching Anshan, the others hit alternate targets. Those bombing Anshan maintained tight four-aircraft diamond formations and bombed from altitudes close to the prescribed 25,000 feet. Damage to the steel works was substantial. The command finally had its first major precision daylight strike on the books.

The XX Bomber Command's next two missions were during the night of 10 August. One went to Palembang and the other to Nagasaki.

The Palembang mission, with a stopover on the island of Ceylon, turned out to be the longest flown by the Twentieth Air Force during the war—some aircraft flew a round-trip of 4,030 miles between Ceylon and the target. Despite early reports of huge fires having been started, actual damage was slight. The results fell far short of the tremendous effort the operation required.

For Nagasaki, with its shipyards, docks and military installations, Saunders' plan called for each plane to carry a mixed load of incendiaries and general-purpose bombs, nearly 6,000 lbs per airplane, the heaviest loads yet. If the Twentieth Air Force staff intended this as a "test," which is doubtful considering Hansell's predilection for precision bombing, it failed. No fires of any size were started. The only flames of significance were those of a Japanese fighter that Tech. Sgt. H. C. Edwards shot down. This was the command's first official "kill."

Saunders had intended his seventh mission to be a night incendiary raid on Yawata. Some of his staff favored employing the B-29 at night, and four of the first six missions had been night missions. On night missions, formation flying was impossible, so aircraft flew to the target area and bombed individually. Though the cover of darkness provided some protection from enemy antiaircraft fire, the major advantage of night missions was that heavier bombloads could be delivered by each airplane. The reason for this was that in formation flying each pilot had to constantly adjust his power settings so as to maintain his position in the formation. Such frequent adjustment was not necessary when flying individually and as a result the engine required less fuel. The weight of fuel held in reserve on long missions could be reduced and, in its place, bomb loads could be increased. But, after reviewing the strike and reconnaissance photos of the Anshan mission, Saunders changed his mind and decided to attack the Imperial Iron and Steel Works with a precision daylight attack. Arnold and Twentieth Air Force Headquarters were pleased.

"Yawata Day," as it came to be known (to distinguish it from the XX Bomber Command's first night mission over that city), was costly. It started badly when a runway crash prevented some aircraft from leaving with the main force and made it necessary for them to take off later and attack at night. Over Yawata the 61 planes of the main force encountered heavy antiaircraft fire and determined Japanese fighters. Nakajima Ki-43s and Kawasaki Ki-45s were out in force and pressed their attacks aggressively, although they were not as well-coordinated as those of Luftwaffe fighters over Europe. One pilot accidentally flew into the lead B-29 of a formation, causing both planes to explode. Another B-29, "filling in" the formation, flew into the debris, and it too exploded. Two more B-29s were shot down. One of these was being flown by Col. Richard Carmichael, commander of the 462nd Bomb Group. Carmichael had survived both the Pearl Harbor attack and a tour as group commander in the Southwest Pacific. He and some of his crew parachuted and then spent the rest of the war as prisoners of the Japanese. Ten of the late starters reached Yawata that night and dropped their bombs with no losses over the target. B-29 gunners claimed 17 fighters shot down.

The Americans did only minor damage to the Imperial Iron and Steel Works, but the XX Bomber Command's losses were high. In addition to the four airplanes downed over the target, ten more were lost to crashes caused by fuel exhaustion and other reasons. The total of fourteen would be the highest for any mission during the B-29 campaign out of Chengtu. Though units of the XX Bomber Command were awarded Distinguished Unit Citations for the Yawata mission, its failure to inflict serious damage was a disappointment to advocates of daylight precision bombing.

One of these advocates was Curtis E. LeMay, who at 37 was the AAF's youngest major general. At the time of the second Yawata raid (Yawata Day), LeMay was en route to India to take command of the XX Bomber Command. For Arnold this was none too soon. Arnold didn't know LeMay personally but knew of his outstanding record in the Eighth Air Force while serving under the command of Maj. Gen. Ira Eaker. Based upon Gen. Eaker's recommendation Arnold had decided to give LeMay command of the XX Bomber Command.

LeMay and Saunders had won wings the same year—1929. After seven years as a fighter pilot, LeMay transferred to bombers and earned recognition in the late thirties as one of the Air Corps' best navigators. It was he who, in May of 1938, brought the flight of three B-17s out of the clouds to "bomb" the Italian liner *Rex* in the mid-Atlantic, a feat that gained much favorable publicity for the Air Corps.

But it was in England in 1942, where he was among the first bomb group commanders to arrive, that LeMay demonstrated his exceptional understanding of piloting, navigating and bombing, as well as his outstanding ability as a combat leader. As commander of the 305th Bomb Group he soon earned the reputation for driving his men hard. Taciturn, aloof, seldom showing emotion, LeMay set high standards for his men in all aspects of their training—piloting, navigation, formation and instrument flying, gunnery, bombing, maintenance. Nothing was omitted. Highly innovative, he personally developed and tested the tactic of flying straight and level on the final run to target. Until that time it had been customary to take evasive action during this critical period. With LeMay's implementation of this tactic, bombing accuracy greatly improved. Soon this practice became standard throughout the Eighth Air Force. He was also largely responsible for developing the "combat box" formation, which increased both mobility and defensive strength and also became standard operating procedure. In 1943 he took command of the Third Air Division and led it in a maximum effort against the Messerschmidt fighter aircraft plant at Regensburg. Later that year he was promoted to brigadier general and in March 1944 to major general.

LeMay arrived at Kharagpur on 29 August and rode as an observer on the next mission, on 7 September, another daylight strike against the Showa Steel Works at Anshan. Saunders got 108 planes airborne for this one, damaged more coke ovens at the Showa plant and lost only four aircraft.

Though LeMay may have been encouraged by this improvement, he knew there was much to accomplish if he were to execute effective daylight precision attacks consistently—an objective he and Arnold shared. In the days that followed, LeMay ordered changes that he believed would achieve this objective. He substituted the 12-airplane "combat box" formation for the 4-airplane diamond. This would require many training flights. He would emphasize the concept of "lead crews" that had proven so worthwhile in Europe. Lead crews would lead the daylight precision formations or, on night raids, find and mark the target area for the main force that followed. He set up a lead crew school at Dudhkundi, which the flight crews called "Dudhkundi Tech." There he trained his best crewmen to accomplish what he and his airmen had learned at great expense in Europe. He required radar training and instituted a new technique for bombing, whereby both the bombardier and the radar operator directed the aircraft on the bomb run; responsibility for final directions was the bombardier's if the target was visible and the radar operator's if not.

If these changes in tactics were to be effective, LeMay knew that he had to deliver more airplanes to the target. In XX Bomber Command's first seven missions, 22 percent of the aircraft failed to bomb the target. Pilots turned back, ditched at sea or crashed for a number of reasons. The most common causes were overheated engines, running out of gas and extreme weather. Though he couldn't control the weather he worked on some of the other problems. Again, the answer was training. Pilots and flight engineers went "back to school" on cruise control, the technique for gaining maximum range and performance from their aircraft with minimum fuel consumption. Navigators, gunners and mechanics also attended classes in their specialty fields. To accomplish such intensive training, LeMay obtained approval from Washington to reduce his mission requirements during September to just two. By the end of that month, the XX Bomber command was beginning to measure up to LeMay's high standards.

FOUR

BURN THE CITIES

MEANWHILE, IN WASHINGTON, interest grew in the use of incendiaries against Japan, as did the number of persons analyzing the consequences of their use. In June 1944 the COA (Committee of Operations Analysts) established a subcommittee to study "the question of fire attack upon urban industrial areas in Japan" and named Comdr. John Mitchell, a Navy air intelligence officer, as its head. (During its four-month existence the subcommittee would be referred to by various names. Here, it will be referred to as the Incendiary Committee.) The study had three goals: (1) determine the forces it would take to burn Japanese cities, (2) evaluate the vulnerability of various areas of Japan, and (3) estimate the economic effects of successful attacks. Analysis actually focused on the first and third objectives. The Incendiary Committee's membership consisted of representatives from the COA, the OSRD (Office of Scientific Research and Development), the Army, the Navy, the Air Staff and the British Ministry of Home Security. Much detailed analysis was done by two subgroups—one worked on force requirements and the other on the economic effects.

Early in their deliberations those studying force requirements recognized that the 1943 A-2 Incendiary Report's figure

71

of 6 tons of M-69 incendiaries required per square mile to create total destruction in Zone I—the most vulnerable zone of a Japanese city—was too small. Tests performed in early 1944 had shown that the number of unquenchable fires created by M-69 hits was substantially less than had been determined using the Dugway test data. Committee members made new computations and arrived at a required tonnage of 14–20 tons per square mile. They recognized that these were theoretical figures only. More facts needed to be determined before a commander could dispatch a given number of B-29s with a specific bombload and have reasonable assurance they would destroy the targeted area.

Throughout the summer of 1944 a second group compiled data and evaluated the economic effects of incendiary attacks on Japanese cities. Because of their relative size and importance, the study team gave priority to six cities—Tokyo, Kawasaki, Yokohama, Kobe, Osaka and Nagoya. They reviewed data on the Japanese earthquake and fire of 1923 as well as information on the effects of German air attacks on English cities. Data on production, labor, transportation and housing in each of the six cities was accumulated and analyzed to arrive at the contribution each made to the production of vital war materials and to the general economy. The team did not concern itself with specifying target factories in the cities. These were contained in the Air Target Folders prepared and maintained by Air Intelligence staff. The team's focus—one for which they asked assistance from the Office of Strategic Services (the predecessor of the CIA)—was on the nature and number of factories and workshops contributing to the war effort that were too small for the Air Intelligence personnel to plot on their maps. The OSS reported to the committee that

"... (1) In Tokyo, Osaka and Nagoya between 15 and 20 percent of all manufacturing workers are employed in establishments so small in size that they can hardly be distinguished from dwelling units. These workshops are probably located in quite random fashion through the business, industrial and residential areas. Destruction of residential areas by fire would probably account for many small-scale manufacturing enterprises.

(2) Small-scale units very often serve as feeder plants and parts manufacturers to large factories. There is considerable evidence that small-scale units are producing parts for airplanes, machinery, ordnance items and other war material. Designs, technical advice, credit and equipment are frequently provided by the larger prime contractors. . . .

Meanwhile the AAF Board at Orlando, Florida, in two study reports, one in June and another in August, addressed the questions that the Incendiary Committee's group working on force requirements had left unanswered. The first report discussed whether fragmentation bombs should be mixed with incendiaries to kill, injure or otherwise deter fire fighters. The Board recommended a ratio of 80 percent incendiaries to 20 percent fragmentation bombs. A copy of this report found its way to Raymond Ewell and drew a quick and pointed reaction from the M-69's most vigorous champion. In a letter to Dr. Robert L. Stearns (president of the University of Colorado, on leave to the Air Force), a member of the Incendiary Committee, Ewell contended that the number of fire fighters put out of action by fragmentation bombs did not warrant what would be lost by displacing 20 percent of the total weight from incendiaries.

The AAF Board's second report outlined a hypothetical incendiary raid on Zone I of Kobe, Japan, from the Marianas, once these islands were captured. (Kobe could not be reached by B-29s flying out of Chengtu.) The Board visualized a daylight high-altitude (25,000–30,000 feet) attack by formations of 9 to 12 aircraft, each carrying 4.6 tons of bombs. Using data from the Dugway Proving Ground tests, the Board calculated that a 12-airplane formation using the M-18 aimable cluster opening at 5,000 feet would produce a pattern on the ground approximately ⅓ miles wide and 2½ miles long. The Board assumed 20 percent of the airborne aircraft would fail to reach the target and 15 to 25 percent of those reaching the target would miss because of loss of sight of lead aircraft, failure to identify the target, mechanical trouble and gross bombing errors. Based on these planning factors, the Board concluded that dispatching 153 B-29s (84 of which would drop their bombs in the target area) would have a high probability of destroying Zone I (the most flammable area) of Kobe. It felt that a smaller number of aircraft would be inadvisable because fires started by such a force would create firebreaks that a subsequent attack would have to overcome. The Board found that night bombing or "blind" bombing during daylight with minimum visibility would probably require up to twice as many aircraft to accomplish the same results and recommended that: (1) actual incendiary pattern bombing tests using 12 B-29s in formation be conducted as soon as possible, and (2) if all-out incendiary bombing of Japan was contemplated, the incendiary bomb requirements first be checked by experimental raids on relatively small and lightly defended objectives in Japan.

Ewell was unwilling to wait for the bombing to start from the Marianas. On 9 August he sent to his superiors in OSRD a proposal for a large-scale test of M-69 incendiaries against specified sections of six cities—Yawata, Tobata, Wakamatsu, Kokura, Sasebo and Nagasaki. All were on the island of Kyushu and therefore within range of the XX Bomber Command. (Coincidentally, on that same day, 10 August on the other side of the International Dateline, 29 planes of the XX Bomber Command executed an unsuccessful night raid on Nagasaki, carrying a mixed load of incendiary and general-purpose bombs.) Ewell had studied recent aerial photographs of these cities, selected densely populated areas in each and specified the tonnage of bombs he believed would cause "substantially complete destruction." He specified the number of B-29s that would have to drop their bombs on each city. Nagasaki alone required 52, and the total for the six cities was a hefty 215 airplanes. Though his was an "internal" paper, it probably soon found its way to the intended recipient—the Incendiary Committee. Several weeks later he sent a report entitled "Incendiary Attack of Japanese Cities" directly to the Committee. In it he stated his estimate of the required ground density of M-69s: 20 tons per square mile for all cities except Tokyo and Yokohama; these, he believed, would require 30 tons.

Meanwhile, the AAF Board's recommendation that extensive flight tests be conducted to better define incendiary bomb patterns and ground densities resulted in no immediate action. This was probably because all available B-29s were then destined for either the XX Bomber Command or the 73rd Bomb Wing. The latter was to form the nucleus of the XXI Bomber Command, and was then in training at the same four Kansas bases the 58th Wing of the XX Bomber Command had vacated in April. Early that spring, Gen. Arnold had released Col. O'Donnell from his personal staff for assignment as commander of the 73rd Bomb Wing. O'Donnell, with earlier experience in the war as a B-17 commander in the Philippines and Java and as operations chief of the Tenth Air Force in India, faced some of the same problems as Wolfe had before him—a new aircraft, still with plenty of "bugs," insufficient B-29s for training and limited time to weld the men and machines into a functioning team. O'Donnell would also have to adopt his own bombing tactics in response to a very different set of circumstances—conditions and locations of bases and targets—than those faced by the XX Bomber Command. It would be on these tactics that he would have sharp differences with the new commander of the XXI Bomber Command, Haywood S. Hansell.

Hansell left the post of Chief of Staff, Twentieth Air Force, in the Pentagon on 27 August 1944 to accept one of the choicest combat assignments in the AAF. He took with him—and this was probably a key factor in Arnold's choice of him for the job—a thorough grounding and knowledge of Twentieth Air Force plans and operations and a staunch belief that high-level, daylight precision bombing would be successful in the air war against Japan. This belief had caused disagreements even before he left the Pentagon and would be a source of trouble throughout his tenure as commanding general of the XXI Bomber Command.

When Gen. Wolfe began operations from bases in India and China, largely with night missions, Hansell had prodded him to conduct daylight attacks against the steel plants at Mukden, Manchuria. Wolfe had vigorously denied that his planes were capable of flying to these targets in daylight and, to Hansell's chagrin—since Wolfe was the only air commander at the time with B-29 combat experience—added that B-29s flying in formation from the Marianas bases would be incapable of reaching their targets. Already informed by Arnold of his next assignment, Hansell was so concerned about this "body blow to operational plans of the XXIst" that he directed his deputy, Col. Cecil B. Combs, to conduct test flights to confirm or refute Wolfe's contention. Combs, using three B-29s with a simulated 4-ton bomb load, flew a test run over the Gulf of Mexico equivalent to the distance from the Marianas to Tokyo. Combat-flying procedures were followed throughout. The aircraft returned to their Eglin Field base without mishap, but the reserves of gasoline were very low. The feasibility of such flights had been confirmed, but barely. Hansell knew that much needed to be learned about fuel conservation in the new aircraft if large formations were to hit Japanese targets from the Marianas.

Hansell's second surprise came when he arrived in Kansas and reviewed 73rd Bomb Wing activities with O'Donnell. After the war Hansell would recall: "When I finally took command of the XXIst Bomber Command on 28 August 1944, the units of the 73rd Wing were training for radar bombing at night, along the pattern of the XX Bomber Command in China, of which it was to have been a part." Whether or not 73rd Wing training, limited as it was, concentrated exclusively on night operations is not clear. But in Hansell's view they were not training for long-range daylight bombing and he was so concerned about O'Donnell and the group commanders that he considered relieving them. He did not, but after a frank talk with O'Donnell the 73d began a new training program that, starting in late August, included round-trips from the Kansas bases to Havana, Cuba. The distance to Havana was comparable to that of the trip to Japan from the Marianas, and the approach to the city over water was similar to the approaches to Japan. Airplanes on early missions ran out of gas on the return and landed at airfields all over the southeastern United States. Some of Hansell's concerns were borne out. With the airplanes destined to be flying missions against Japan in a few months, they couldn't complete a similar mission—even with good communications, the best available weather information and no enemy fighters or antiaircraft attacks. But in ensuing weeks, flight engineers and pilots began to master cruise-control techniques and became more proficient in long-range flying. The 73rd had crossed a big hurdle.

In mid-September, in the midst of all this activity to build an effective precision-bombing force, Hansell held a conference at the XXI Bomber Command Headquarters in Colorado Springs, Colorado, attended by his top staff, the commanders and staff of the 73rd Wing, and those of the two other wings—the 313th and the 314th—which would join the XXI Bomber Command in the Marianas. The principal speaker, Dr. Ewell, introduced as "Technical Advisor to Headquarters, Twentieth Air force," discussed "Tactical Employment of Incendiary Bombs Against Japanese Targets." In his talk Ewell described the nature of the targets suitable for incendiary attack, the types and quantities of bombs necessary to destroy these targets and the effects on the Japanese war effort; he concluded with a comparison between bombing German targets and Japanese targets.

AT THE PENTAGON, Brig. Gen. Lauris Norstad had taken Hansell's place as Chief of Staff, Twentieth Air Force. Like O'Donnell, Norstad was one of Arnold's personal advisors and was considered to be one of the best minds in the AAF.

On 4 September, just a week after Norstad took over, the Incendiary Subcommittee completed its study on the "Economic Effects of a Successful Area Attack on Six Japanese Cities" (hereafter referred to as the Incendiary Committee Report). The Committee concluded that destruction of Zones I and II in the six cities—Tokyo, Kawasaki, Yokohama, Osaka, Kobe and Nagoya—would destroy 70 percent of the houses in those cities. It would cause a loss of 20 percent of one year's output in the major war industries that produced "front line equipment" (a term used by the Committee to cover military aircraft components, aircraft engines, tanks and trucks, radio and radar, guns and ammunition). These were the tools of war vital to continuing the fight against Allied forces and the last-ditch defense of the Home Islands contemplated by both the Japanese and the Americans.

While widespread damage would be done, the Committee pointed out that no one industrial category would be so reduced as to substantially affect front-line strength. Precision attacks, they felt, could "knock out" an industry, provided adequate target information were available and operations were conducted effectively. Both provisos were fraught with difficulties and unknowns. To demonstrate openness on the question of area-bombing with incendiaries versus precision-bombing with high explosives the Committee concluded: "Final judgment on the desirability of incendiary attacks requires similar analyses of alternative target systems and estimates of comparative force requirements." While the COA would debate the relative priority of incendiary bombing over the coming weeks, it remained for Ewell and his indefatigable associates to do the straightforward kind of comparative analysis that the Incendiary Committee suggested.

The Incendiary Committee hedged a bit in its views on whether to resort to incendiary bombing but was most positive about timing. Area incendiary attacks should be undertaken only when possible to conduct them in force and destroy all six cities in a period of three weeks.

On 6 September, COA members Elihu Root, Jr., and Fowler Hamilton, along with Dr. Stearns and Col. Combs, met with General Norstad. Norstad had probably read the Incendiary Committee Report by then or would have done so shortly thereafter. At the meeting he expressed a need for an overall appraisal of the target systems in Japan and, in particular, asked COA to advise him on immediate targets for the XX Bomber Command. On the day Norstad met with the COA members, Gen. Laurence S. Kuter, Gen. Arnold's Assistant Chief of Air Staff, Plans, asked for copies of the Incendiary Committee Report and Dr. Ewell's report of 29 August, "Incendiary Attack of Japanese Cities" (with its recommendations for incendiary ground densities of 20 tons per square mile for all cities and 30 tons for Tokyo and Yokohama), which the Incendiary Committee had adopted informally as its basis for estimating force requirements.

On 8 September the COA received two assignments. The first was from Norstad, asking them to let him know by 15

September what the best targets were for the China-based XX Bomber Command in the immediate future. The second, from Kuter, asked the COA to revise its report to General Arnold of 11 November 1943, "Economic Objectives in the Far East," which had named six strategic target systems—merchant shipping, aircraft plants, antifriction bearings, electronics, urban industrial areas and steel plants (with no priorities assigned)—using two assumptions: (1) defeat of Japan by combined aerial and naval blockade and bombardment; (2) defeat of Japan by combined aerial and naval blockade and bombardment and by invasion of the industrial heart of Japan.

The COA held two meetings, one on 13 September, another on the fourteenth, and gave Gen. Norstad his answers after the second meeting. The significance of these meetings, beyond the naming of LeMay's next targets, was twofold. First, they started a dialog that would continue for nearly a month and culminate in a report to Gen. Arnold. Second, Gen. Norstad, who sat in on these meetings, had an opportunity to hear the thought processes, concerns and doubts behind the carefully worded reports that he read. The insights he gained would have considerable influence on his thinking in coming months.

The COA members considered three target groups—aircraft plants, coke and steel plants, and urban industrial areas—in deciding on two specific targets to recommend to Norstad. Col. John F. Turner led off with a description of four aircraft factories located in Manchuria, Kyushu and Formosa. Committee members asked about the location and importance of these targets. Turner was followed by Fowler Hamilton, who reviewed the bombing results against coke and steel plants and the targets remaining.

Next, Navy Lt. Charles Hitch briefed the group on the results of the Incendiary Committee Report. He expressed the view that the force estimates were based on laboratory and field tests and that the only way the size of the bombing force necessary to destroy the six major cities of Japan could be estimated with any degree of accuracy would be to conduct a test mission. He suggested that a 100-airplane mission against Nagasaki or Yawata, loaded with enough incendiaries to create a ground density of 20 tons per square mile, could—with good before and after photographs—provide a sound basis for planning incendiary operations.

The second day was devoted to a discussion of steel, aircraft and urban areas. Aircraft plants were dropped early in the discussions on the basis that their destruction could be accomplished more effectively from the Marianas. That left coke and steel plants and/or the experimental incendiary strike. All agreed to the need for the experiment, but some thought it could be done later from the Marianas and that LeMay should be allowed to "finish the job" on coke and steel. The proponents (and there were a number of them) for carrying out the experimental incendiary raid as soon as practicable from Chengtu argued that it would take time to analyze the data, possibly test it further at Eglin Field and, assuming the results were favorable, transmit them to the air commander who would have the job of burning the cities—Gen. Hansell. Col. Turner probably expressed the feelings of others when he said: "We have been intrigued with the possibilities . . . of complete chaos in six cities killing 584,000 people." He speculated that if the raids were successful the casualties might be far greater. Then he also said, "It may be that our expectations will never be realized." In Turner's opinion the only way to find the answer was to launch an experimental attack soon.

The group then considered whether it would be better to run the experimental attack from Chengtu or Saipan. Most felt the attack should be executed from Saipan. Consequently, the COA recommended that the next two missions of the China-based XX Bomber Command be directed against coke ovens at the steel plants located in Anshan, Manchuria, with two alternative targets for a second mission, if the first took out the target.

The COA next turned to their major assignment—recommendations for the strategic target systems that should be attacked to help achieve the defeat of Japan. The procedure was to review each target system and determine its relative significance to the others in bringing about such a defeat. The emphasis was on plants and facilities in the six major cities and other locations on the island of Honshu. The committee agreed that the aircraft industry—engine plants and final assembly plants—was a concentrated and lucrative target system. Under the first of the two assumptions that they had been given, defeat by blockade and bombardment, they discussed aerial mining of the entries to Japan's Inland Sea. Here they concluded that air operations could be effective in a blockade but should supplement those of the Navy.

Lt. Hitch presented the salient features of the Incendiary Committee Report as they related to the urban-area target system. Hitch could not be accused of overselling the recommendations of the report. Rather, he pointed out what he considered some of the more fragile bases upon which the impressive claims of the report rested. He informed the COA members that the major uncertainty in the whole study effort was the location of Japanese industry in relation to Zones I and II in each city. The study's initial estimate of a 15-percent loss in industrial output was based on the assumption that two-thirds of the plants were in the zones of destruction. Later calculations showed that the number was considerably less than two-thirds of the plants in those zones and the expected production loss would be closer to 11 percent. He also reemphasized that the only industry that would be crippled for six months or longer would be the machine tool industry; others would recover sooner. Then, to reinforce the recommendation for a test attack on Nagasaki, he reminded the committee that "We do not know how effective these available incendiary bombs are in starting fires in Japanese cities. It is possible the force requirements may be as estimated by us, or twice, or half." One member countered that the M-69 had been proven effective against Japanese construction, to which Hitch replied that he was thinking of its effectiveness when Japanese fire fighters were at work.

In its final considerations of urban industrial areas, the COA turned to a subject that had not been treated at all in the Incendiary Committee Report—the psychological effects. To answer questions about the extent to which the population would be demoralized and the administrative machinery break down, the committee called in Comdr. William M. McGovern of the OSS. McGovern was a political scientist, an explorer, a war correspondent and a recognized expert on the Japanese and their language.

McGovern recommended that the attacks not be launched until sufficient strength was available to strike rapid, powerful blows. These blows should be struck at the psychological heart of Japan, the Tokyo-Yokohama and the Osaka areas. He recalled that on one of his lecture tours through small towns in Japan, he had tried time after time to find out what the people thought. Repeatedly they would tell him that they did not know or that the answer would have to come from Tokyo. "Knock out Tokyo," McGovern advised the COA, "and the Japanese throughout the country will say, 'We have been hit.' "

McGovern believed that a series of successful incendiary raids would have serious economic effects beyond the actual damage inflicted. He found that the Japanese were very involved in written orders and paperwork. Loss of records and orders in Tokyo would create administrative chaos in factories outside that city.

On the matter of surrender, McGovern believed that after two or three attacks panic would overtake the people of Tokyo because the Japanese have always been terrified by fire. Once panic started they would demand an extreme nationalist right-wing government. By the third attack they would be so scared that they would demand a complete political reorganization with some kind of surrender and negotiations. He didn't believe Japan would agree to unconditional surrender until American troops arrived.

Even while the Committee members analyzed and argued the merits of incendiary warfare, the Chemical Warfare Service was pushing ahead with production of the M-69. Leaving little to chance, the Service hoped to produce close to 60,000 tons of the bombs by the end of 1944 (a goal it would not achieve until early 1945). Using Ewell's estimates of the M-69's destructive capabilities, 60,000 tons of M-69s was ten times the amount necessary to destroy Japan's six largest cities.

★   ★   ★

On 10 October 1944 the COA submitted its report to Gen. Arnold. It consisted of two parts, Report I and Report II. Report I was premised on defeat of Japan by a combined aerial and naval blockade and bombardment. It recommended, in order of priority, bombing attacks on shipping, the aircraft industry and urban industrial areas. Report II used the same premises but *with invasion* and changed the order of priority to the aircraft industry, urban industrial areas and then shipping. Since the COA knew the Joint Chiefs of Staff were contemplating an invasion, most discussion of the recommendations was placed in Report II. (The description here will be wholly devoted to the content of Report II.)

Beginning with a summary of its recommendations, the Committee briefly explained that the diminished priority for shipping was in anticipation of a cutoff of Japan's southern occupied areas and "the swift progress of the American attack, then well underway, on shipping." After advising Arnold that no strategic targets of importance remained for the Chengtu-based XX Bomber Command (though a few tactical targets existed), the Committee laid out the strategic targets for the Marianas-based XXI Bomber Command.

First priority would be attacks on the aircraft industry. The Committee specified five engine plants to hit first. *Second priority* would be attacks on the urban industrial areas—the six major Japanese cities on Honshu—which were to be delayed until they could be delivered in force and in a brief period of time. *Third priority* was an aerial mining campaign against Japanese shipping. The Committee explained that they had reviewed 17 target systems and found that except for three—aircraft, cities and shipping—none appeared to warrant attack by the XXI Bomber Command.

In contrast to its November 1943 recommendations, the Committee's current recommendations—they would be the last it would make to Gen. Arnold as a formal body—were a powerful endorsement for area incendiary bombing. The six target systems named in the November 1943 report (with no priorities assigned) had been cut to three, only one of which—

aircraft—called for precision bombing. The Committee's statement was clear: once the threat to U.S. control of the air and its invasion forces had been eliminated, the Twentieth Air Force should be loosed on Japan's cities, with a secondary effort devoted to aerial mining.

The COA had not arrived at its position easily. For over a year and a half, against the increasing body of information on the potential destructiveness of the M-69 bomb, it had weighed the criticism of the British, its own doubts as to the bomb's effectiveness in actual use and finally the knowledge that a recommendation for giving area incendiary bombing high priority would be in direct conflict with existing AAF strategic bombing doctrine.

With the submission of its report, the COA ceased to exist. Its functions and some of its members were absorbed by a new organization—the Joint Target Group, working under the Assistant Chief of Air Staff, Intelligence. Like the COA, the Joint Target Group was an interservice organization and drew on many of the same military and civilian agencies for intelligence and expert opinions bearing on air targets in the Pacific.

ABOUT THE TIME he received the COA Report, Arnold received a letter from Vannevar Bush that enclosed a memorandum from Ewell in which Ewell made a personal and final plea for giving all-out area incendiary bombing top priority in the air war against Japan. Ewell began with a sweeping statement that would prove prophetic—tragically for the Japanese, but beneficially for the Allies. He wrote:

> . . . [T]his mode of attack [incendiary bombing] may be the golden opportunity of strategic bombardment in this war—and possibly one of the outstanding opportunities in all history to do the greatest damage to the enemy for a minimum of effort.

After briefly decrying—this time without justification—what he believed to be preoccupation of the Air Staff with precision bombing, Ewell estimated that based on his figures, by applying 30 tons of incendiaries per square mile to Tokyo and Yokohama and 20 tons to the other Japanese cities, the six major cities could be destroyed by approximately 6,000 tons of incendiaries (M-69s in aimable clusters). He believed one wing (180 B-29s) operating out of the Marianas could accomplish all of this in one month. Ewell recapitulated the economic damage that would result from these attacks as it had been stated in the Incendiary Committee Report, adding that, in his opinion, the report's damage estimates were somewhat low.

Ewell contended that area incendiary bombing of Japanese cities could be much more effective than the RAF's area bombing of German cities, because according to his calculations,

> 158,000 tons [dropped by the RAF] on 31 German cities gave 8.4-percent loss of one year's production and dehousing of 5,136,000 persons; 6,000 tons on six Japanese cities is estimated to give 15-percent loss of one year's production and dehousing of about 9 million persons.

The main reason given by Ewell for the potentially greater damage to Japan was the more flammable construction used in that country and the greater concentration of industry and people in its major cities.

Ewell presented figures that he felt showed area incendiary bombing to be more effective than precision bombing. He included an analysis of AAF records of precision bombing of German aircraft factories during the first nine months of 1944 and estimated it would take 40,000 tons of high-explosive bombs to seriously damage the Japanese aircraft industry. The 6,000 tons of high explosives would do only minor damage to the aircraft industry, but the same amount of incendiaries would devastate hundreds of factories (including aircraft plants) and cripple future production by uprooting millions of workers. Additionally Ewell stated:

> The bad weather anticipated in Japan will militate further against the success of precision attacks, but would have relatively little effect on the success of area incendiary attacks.

Though he could not have read the final COA report at the time he prepared his memorandum, Ewell was aware of its

expected content and challenged its conclusion regarding the
timing of incendiary attacks head on:

> It is my impression that the incendiary attack of Japanese cities
> is expected to be brought into the program eventually, but not
> until the precision attacks on one or more selected industries
> have been completed. I believe that this is probably a wrong
> emphasis and that the incendiary attack should be initiated as
> soon as the advance estimates of cost and results can be con-
> firmed and carried through to completion as rapidly as possible
> thereafter, to the exclusion of all other types of strategic attack.

Ewell emphasized to Bush that

> Recognition by the Air Staff, War Department General Staff,
> Joint Chiefs of Staff, the Secretaries of War and Navy, and the
> President that the incendiary attack of Japanese cities may be
> the key to accelerating the defeat of Japan, and if as successful
> as seems probable, it might shorten the war by some months
> and save many thousands of American lives.

After recounting several steps he thought necessary to finally
test the incendiary concept he suggested:

> If results look promising, be prepared to go "all out" on this
> type of attack until the 15 to 30 major cities of Japan have been
> devastated and the incendiary attack on the remaining smaller
> cities has become sufficiently less fruitful that further tonnage
> can better be placed on aircraft or other priority war plants
> unaffected by the incendiary attacks.

Ewell also demonstrated that his thinking was not limited to
the destructive aspects of the strategy he advocated. He raised
an issue that had received scant attention in the COA deliberations and no recognition whatsoever in its final report. He
suggested that a decision be made at the highest level on the
"humanitarian and political question."

No discussion of the morality of area incendiary bombing
appears in the transcripts of the meetings held by the COA, its
subcommittees, or in its final report. At the outset of its study

of the Japanese economy, most of the members of the COA had concluded that within most of Japan's large cities, and within Tokyo in particular, there existed myriad feeder factories and workshops that were vital to war production and were impossible to locate for precision bombing. These shops and small factories could only be destroyed by incendiary-bombing the areas in which the shops and small factories were known to exist. The members of COA accepted the fact that such bombing would cause great human casualties. The Incendiary Committee estimated that deaths might run as high as 584,000.

Bush gave Ewell's paper immediate attention. The day after reading it, he sent it to Arnold. In his transmittal note, Bush blandly said he was enclosing "a paper which gives the line of thought of some of my group." In the bureaucratic world, in which Bush was well-versed, merely transmitting the memorandum indicated his agreement with its content.

While drafters of the COA's final report to Arnold did not find it necessary to comment on the morality of their recommendation for massive area incendiary attacks on Japanese cities, Bush, in transmitting Ewell's paper, did. As Roosevelt's chief scientific advisor on the development of the atomic bomb, a project that was in its final stages, Bush was aware of the great human casualties that the new device could produce if it met expectations. He knew that the decision to produce an atomic weapon had been made by President Roosevelt and that, from the outset, the President expected that the bomb would be used against Germany or Japan. Just a little over two weeks before receiving Ewell's memorandum, Bush had prepared a paper for Secretary of War Stimson to use in informing the President on the status of the bomb and its possible use. In it he had proposed a demonstration of the bomb and subsequent notice to Japan that it would be used against the Japanese mainland if that country failed to surrender. Given this recent experience and sensing that the mass destruction of Japanese cities had similar political and moral ramifications, it is not surprising that Bush would suggest to Arnold that "the decision on the humanitarian aspects will have to be made at a high level if it has not been done already, and that this might as well be settled, since it is bound to come up sooner or later." By "high level," Bush must have been thinking of Secretary Stimson and the President.

ARNOLD READ THE Ewell–Bush communications and asked Gen. Norstad to have his staff study them. At about the same time, he accepted the COA's final report and passed it on to his staff to incorporate in the operations plans for the Twentieth Air Force. There is no record of Arnold having sought to clear the COA report with either Stimson or the President. Apparently, Arnold's acceptance of the COA recommendations amounted to a decision to firebomb Japan's cities, a major change in American air strategy.

Arnold knew, however, that several important tasks remained before adopting this new strategy: the M-69 had to be combat-tested, the B-29 force had to be greatly enlarged, and Japan's air power had to be destroyed at its source—the aircraft manufacturing industry.

FIVE

ASSAULT FROM THE MARIANAS

ON 12 OCTOBER 1944, at about the time Norstad received the COA report on bombing objectives in Japan, the man the report's recommendations would most affect—Haywood Hansell—landed on the unfinished airstrip on the island of Saipan, at the controls of *Joltin Josie–The Pacific Pioneer*. Officers and men of the XXI Bomber Command advance echelon and Army combat engineers lined the runway to watch the first B-29 land on the island.

Saipan is part of a chain of islands formed by the summits of a submerged mountain range that extends about 1,500 miles from Saipan almost to Japan. A little more than four months before Hansell landed it had been in Japanese hands. One of three islands in the Marianas that would be used as air bases for B-29s—the others were Tinian and Guam—Saipan stretches about 12 miles from north to south, with the airfield that became known as Isley Field located at the southern end. Near the center of the island is a 1,500-foot peak, Mount Topatchau. Tinian is so close it can be seen at almost any time, day or night. In prewar days Saipan had a picture-postcard atmosphere with its coconut palm groves, sugarcane fields, quiet sugar mill towns and long white beaches with fringing coral reefs.

Little of this tranquility remained when the Army's aviation engineers and Navy construction battalions arrived to transform the old Japanese airstrip into a runway for the biggest bomber in the world. The engineers began work with stray bullets and shells landing in their work area. Within days they filled 600 craters and made the field usable for fighters. In the weeks that followed they worked on the heavy bomber runway and hardstands. Nearly everything they needed to build with—trucks, bulldozers, fuel, asphalt to surface the runways—had to be shipped over thousands of miles of ocean. One material that didn't have to be shipped was coral—ideal for the runway base. They had plenty of that. They carved out two quarries, working around the clock for weeks. Hundreds of trucks hauled millions of cubic yards of coral, which bulldozers and graders crushed, compacted and smoothed; after that, asphalt from their improvised "plant" was poured and smoothed. When Tinian and Guam were captured by U.S. forces during July and August, more Army and Navy construction units moved in and began constructing three more airfields for the B-29s—two on Tinian and one on Guam.

On the eve of Hansell's departure for Saipan, both Gen. Arnold and Gen. Marshall made it clear that much was expected of him and his new command. In a September letter to "Possum," Arnold reminded him: "As you well know, the original conception of the B-29 was an airplane that would carry tremendous loads for tremendous distances. We have not to date fulfilled this promise." The letter closed with the challenge, "I know that you, in your position as commander of one of our great striking forces, will do your utmost to help accomplish the earliest possible defeat of Japan. This can only be done by making the best possible use of the weapon at your disposal." At a meeting with Hansell in early October, Marshall talked about strategy for the Pacific War and that bombing Japan was an important part of that strategy. He asked Hansell whether the XXI Bomber Command would be prepared to attack Tokyo in November, in a coordinated operation with the Navy's carrier task force. Hansell would later recall: "I couldn't very well tell him that we couldn't do it, so I told him 'Yes, we could.'"

After his first few days on Saipan, Hansell must have wondered how he could make good his commitment. Of the two bases under construction on Saipan, one was unusable for B-29s and the other would not reach its planned length—8,500 feet—until a week after his arrival. He found finished only 40 hardstands, a bomb dump and a small vehicle park. Isley Field was hardly ready to receive the 180 aircraft and 12,000 men of the 73rd Wing. The airfields on Tinian, intended for later use by two more wings of the XXI Bomber Command, had barely been started, and those on Guam where the headquarters of the XXI would be located, along with a fourth wing, were not even laid out. There was no supply depot. When the ship carrying the depot stocks had arrived at Guam, the combat situation was so precarious it dumped its cargo onto a remote jungle beach. The cargo was never recovered.

On 20 October, General O'Donnell arrived on Saipan and established headquarters for his 73rd Wing not far from Hansell's XXI Bomber Command—a top-heavy arrangement until the arrival of the other three wings that were to fill out Hansell's command. After O'Donnell's arrival, B-29s began arriving at the rate of two or three per day. The method for flying the airplanes to the Marianas had been another disappointment to Hansell. He had asked permission to fly the airplanes to the Marianas in formation so as to provide experience for his combat crews. The Air Transport Command, however, denied the request on the grounds that the aircraft lacked the range to fly from Sacramento to Hawaii, 2,400 miles—without a bombload and no opposition. Yet the plane was expected to attack Japan with a round-trip of about 3,000 miles.

From the end of October into early November, Hansell and O'Donnell scheduled a series of six training missions; four were to the bypassed Japanese base at Truk and two were against Iwo Jima, which lay halfway between Saipan and Tokyo. These were modest affairs, ranging from 9 to 36 aircraft, compared with the XX Bomber Command's maiden effort of 98 airplanes the previous June. Hansell's frustrations continued when his airplane was not able to continue to the target on the first mission to Truk. As it turned out this was his last chance to lead a mission. Later, Washington forbade him to do so because his knowledge of U.S. strategic war plans was too extensive to risk his becoming a prisoner of the Japanese. Small as they were in size, the six missions gave the new crews some experience in flying their aircraft moderately long distances over enemy territory.

On 1 November, Hansell had a brief taste of good fortune. He was reasonably certain that he would be ordered to hit a target in Tokyo soon, but had no aerial photographs of that city. On 30 October two F-13 photo reconnaissance aircraft (modified B-29s containing some of the world's most advanced cameras and photographic equipment) arrived at Saipan after flying, with stops only for fuel, from Smoky Hill Army Airfield, Salina, Kansas. Weary as they were, Captain Ralph D. Steakley and his crew took off at 5:50 A.M. on 1 November and flew to Tokyo, arriving over that city a little after noon—the first U.S. plane over Tokyo since the Doolittle raid in 1942.

The skies were absolutely clear, a condition that, unfortunately, XXI Bomber Command B-29s would seldom find thereafter. Following the procedures for combat aerial photography, Steakley held his aircraft on a straight and steady course and, after flying one "line" as prescribed by the navigator, turned and flew back over the city following the next "line." For more than an hour Steakley criss-crossed above Tokyo with three cameras—one pointing straight down, and two, one on each side, pointing toward the horizon—recording everything along the flight path. At its altitude of nearly 6 miles, the plane, with the bright sun's rays reflecting off its polished aluminum surfaces, must have appeared to those Japanese who spotted it as a shining silver speck moving back and forth in the sky. Not until they were finished and turning back toward Saipan did Steakley's crew see any Japanese fighters. The tailgunner had one in his sights and was waiting for it to come within range when the pilot broke away, probably because he lacked the speed and power to press the attack.

The pilot may have been a member of the 47th Air Regiment stationed at Narimasu Air Base, west of Tokyo. The 47th was one of the five Japanese Army Air Force fighter-interceptor air regiments that made up the 10th Air Division. The other four regiments, like the 47th, were based at airfields ringing the capital city—Chofu, also to the west, and Matsudo, Kashiwa and Imba north and northeast of Tokyo. Pilots of the 47th Air Regiment—considered to be the most skilled in the division—flew Ki-44 Tojos. If, in fact, the failed attempt at interception was by a Tojo of the 47th Air Regiment, it must have left the 47th's commander, Maj. Noburu Okuda, frustrated and disappointed.

The source of Japanese disappointment was Hansell's delight. Upon return, the photo lab hurriedly processed Steakley's film rolls and turned out 7,000 prints, which contained excellent coverage of a number of Tokyo's big aircraft plants. Steakley and his crew later received well-deserved decorations for their mission. Also, since their aircraft had not yet been named, they named it *Tokyo Rose* after the Japanese female radio announcer who daily broadcasted propaganda for American consumption.

On 11 November, the Twentieth Air Force sent Hansell the first of a series of target directives. In line with the COA recommendations, first priority was the destruction of Japanese aircraft production facilities. Area incendiary attacks on urban areas and aerial mining, if any, would come later. Hansell's targets, to be attacked using daylight precision methods, were *four* aircraft engine plants, to be hit first, followed by *five* aircraft assembly plants. A Mitsubishi factory was first on the aircraft-engine list. But to achieve the maximum effect from the XXI's first blow from the Marianas, Washington went to the second on the list, the Nakajima plant at Musashino, in the northwest part of Tokyo, about ten miles from the Emperor's Palace. Musashino, Target 357 on the AAF's list, was the single most important military target on the home islands of Japan. Intelligence experts estimated that this plant, along with another Nakajima plant nearby, manufactured 30 to 40 percent of all Japanese combat-aircraft engines.

With the XXI Bomber Command poised for its first strike on Japan, Arnold and Norstad tried in Washington to organize a three-way blast at Japan. This would involve a carrier sweep to coincide with Hansell's attack on the Musashino plant in Tokyo and an attack by LeMay's XX Bomber Command on an aircraft plant located at Omura on the island of Kyushu, Japan. After successive delays, primarily on the part of the carrier force, the joint attack never materialized.

The planned strike against Tokyo, which Arnold had long anticipated, was labeled "San Antonio I." While preparing for the operation, Hansell had to deal with some disturbing views from Arnold and his subordinate, "Rosie" O'Donnell. A letter from Arnold included the comments of Gen. George C. Kenney, Gen. MacArthur's air chief, in which Kenney contended that the B-29s lacked the range to hit Tokyo from Saipan and that those that did make it would suffer severe losses. To Hansell's chagrin, Arnold stated that he shared Kenney's skepticism, but that if Hansell was convinced that the daylight precision attack was feasible he was free to go ahead. Arnold closed his letter by wishing Hansell luck. Hansell understood the reasons for doubt—until this time the XXI had never flown a formation as large as a squadron a distance as far as Tokyo and back, even without enemy opposition. (The flights to Cuba had been smaller than squadron size and many aircraft had failed to make the round-trip.) Years later Hansell would write that Arnold had probably placed the responsibility for the operation on him so that if it failed, the effect on the B-29 program and the AAF would be lessened. Whether his later speculation was accurate or not, at the time Arnold's letter was most disturbing.

Next, Hansell received a handwritten letter from Gen. O'Donnell, who was to lead the strike because Hansell was not permitted to do so. O'Donnell stated that he too doubted the capability of his 73rd Wing to carry out the attack as planned. He recommended a night attack, with aircraft flying individually and bombing an area target. His reasoning was probably largely based on his feeling that his crews were not yet ready to fly the new aircraft at the extreme limits of its range into expected strong enemy defenses. O'Donnell believed that the night attack would not only minimize losses but could also inflict considerable damage.

To Hansell, O'Donnell's thinking was totally unacceptable. The XXI Bomber Command's charge was to destroy the aircraft industry, using daylight precision methods. Any other attack plan would lay the Twentieth Air Force open to serious criticism. He told O'Donnell that if he was unwilling to lead the mission, he would have his (Hansell's) deputy, Col. Roger M. Ramey, lead it. O'Donnell assured Hansell that he would lead the mission but that he had felt obligated to make his views known. Hansell, respecting but strongly disapproving of O'Donnell's views, destroyed the letter and considered the matter closed.

As if this was not enough, a delegation of congressmen paid Hansell a visit. Possibly because of the poor food, comments from men they had talked to and the fact that Hansell did not spend much time with them, the group returned to Washington and wrote a scathing report on XXI Bomber Command's administrative arrangements. Despite these distractions and doubts, Hansell decided to go ahead and scheduled the mission for the morning of 17 November.

On the afternoon of 16 November 1944, crewmen from the XXI Bomber Command's four bomb groups—the 497th, 498th, 499th and 500th—attended mission briefings. Lt. Chester Marshall, a member of the 499th, recalled the briefing he attended, and it was probably typical of the others. (Marshall was pilot of the *Lil Lassie*. The airplane commander was 1st Lt. John Cox.) The assembled crews quieted down when Col. Sam Harris, the group commander, stepped up on a small stage, behind him a large map of Japan, the Marianas and the area between. He told them that they were about to embark on a historic mission, something they all had been waiting for. Success depended on their understanding and adherence to the mission plan. After the colonel finished his remarks, his staff officers explained details of the plan. A red line running almost vertically up the big map showed the route to Tokyo and the Musashino aircraft plant—Target #357. A black line traced the return route. The red line showed the major navigation checkpoints en route: the islands of Pagan, Iwo Jima (to which they had to give wide berth because of enemy fighters based there) and finally Hachijo Jima, about 175 miles south of the Japanese capital. Their initial point (IP) would be the world-famous and highest mountain peak in Japan, Mount Fuji. The IP was the landmark from which the bomb run to the target began. This mission required them to make a 90° turn over Fuji and then fly at an altitude of 30,000 feet on an easterly course to the target. If they could not drop on the Musashino plant, the city and dock areas were designated as secondary targets. The weather officer's announcement that they would probably encounter two fronts between Iwo Jima and Japan brought some groans from the assemblage, as did the statement by the intelligence office that the Japanese had more than 600 fighters in the Tokyo area. Though for most of the crews present it needed no emphasis, the group flight engineer stressed the importance of fuel conservation. Two extra fuel tanks were installed in the forward bomb bay of each aircraft, which, along with the regular wing tanks, provided just enough fuel for the nearly 3,000-mile round-trip. Deviations from the charted course and excessive power settings would mean they would be unable to return to their home base and would have to "ditch." (This would entail bringing their airplanes down on the open sea, taking to their life rafts and, hopefully, being picked up by the U.S. Navy.) The crews were told that they would have breakfast at 4 A.M. and were to be on the flight line an hour ahead of the scheduled takeoff—6 A.M. The group briefing lasted for about an hour and was followed by separate briefings for pilots, navigators, bombardiers and so on. Afterward the crews returned to their Quonset huts, where some discussed and others simply contemplated the big day ahead.

Shortly after dawn, the long line of B-29s converged on the single taxiway that led to the beginning of the runway. Although takeoff time was a widely held secret on the base, still, men from all over the island drove to the field to see the takeoff. Twenty-four war correspondents representing all the major new services were on hand. Flashbulbs illuminated "Rosie" O'Donnell as he climbed into his B-29, the first in line. Then the wind, which had been blowing down the runway, died then reversed direction. When it began to rain and visibility was reduced, any thoughts of changing the direction of takeoff had to be abandoned. Despite the fact that the crews were at a psychological climax, Hansell was forced to postpone the mission for 24 hours to see whether a storm that was sweeping by Saipan would dissipate. The weather, which would prove to be the major problem for the B-29 campaign, was offering an ominous preview. This time it was weather at the base; in the future it would be the weather over the target that would be the XXI's nemesis.

The next day Hansell had to postpone again. For a week it was on-again, off-again. For the entire command it was a period of intense frustration. Three times crews were actually at their stations in their airplanes when the mission was called off. Other units on the island, probably slightly envious of all the attention the B-29s were getting, joked that the Superforts were the best airplane made that never left the ground.

In Washington, it was no joking matter. Arnold, never known for patience, fretted about the delay in launching this crucial mission. Norstad would later write Hansell in reference to the delays: "You were not 'on the pan' at any time. I think that I can best illustrate his [Arnold's] attitude by telling you his reaction to the fourth or fifth postponement. After he indicated he was disturbed, I made a statement to the effect that I didn't think that it would do any good to put any heat on you, under the circumstances. He replied, 'Who said anything about putting the heat on Possum?' in a rather irritated manner."

Finally, during the night of 23 November, the weather broke. At 6:15 the next morning the first aircraft, *Dauntless Dotty*, rolled down the runway. O'Donnell was at the controls, leading a force of 111 B-29s. New arrivals, some on Saipan only a week, had swelled the number of airplanes available for the strike. As it always was with the big aircraft, each takeoff was an ordeal. The maximum allowable takeoff weight for the B-29 was 132,000 pounds. In order to carry every gallon of fuel possible to obtain maximum range, the B-29s on this mission had a ramp weight of 140,000 pounds. A faltering engine could be the end of an airplane and its crew, and, worse

yet, could ruin an entire mission if the aircraft blocked those
that followed. The hundreds of spectators thought *Dauntless
Dotty* would never get off the ground. The airplane ate up
every bit of the blacktopped runway and a portion of the coral
before becoming airborne, just feet above the surface of the
ocean beyond. Spotters directed following airplanes to the runway at the proper time. At the starting point on the runway a
flagman and a timer sent an airplane down the strip every 60
seconds. Each had to take off and climb into the wake turbulence left by the one ahead. In just under two hours the entire
force was airborne.

Marshall and Cox and the rest of the crew of *Lil Lassie*
thought for a few frantic moments they might not make the
mission. Because of a slipup on the part of a crew member,
when their time came to start the engines they found the
batteries drained. By the time they obtained an auxiliary generator, started the engines and got underway, their 499th
Bomb Group had left. North of Pagan Island they decided that
it would not be possible to catch up with their own group, so
they spotted two planes of the 500th Bomb Group and flew in
loose formation with them. By now the first-mission jitters
had subsided a bit, and the crew members went about their
jobs. With the expectation that within hours they would be
confronting enemy fighters, the whole crew drew comfort
from the noise and vibration when the gunners test-fired the
twin .50-caliber machine guns mounted in the five gun turrets
and were joined by the tailgunner firing his 20-mm cannon.
The navigator, 2nd Lt. James R. O'Donnel, not wishing to rely
completely on the leader of the flight they had joined, plotted
Lil Lassie's course himself. Assisting him was Sgt. Robert J.
Slizewski, the radar operator, sitting in his darkened area in
the back of the rear compartment. He watched the blips on his
screen and, over the plane's interphone system, helped the
navigator, who had a radar scope at his station, identify which
was which of the many small islands and large rock formations that lay along the path from Saipan to Japan. Another aid
in navigation was the radio compass which, when tuned to a
Tokyo station, indicated the direction to that station. With
radio silence in force, Cpl. Alvin Torres, the radioman, was

listening for SOS signals from other planes and was ready, in case they had to ditch, to transmit *Lil Lassie*'s position to Navy rescue ships spotted along the way.

Further north *Lil Lassie* encountered the front—a huge, dark cloud mass—the weather officer had predicted. Rather than fly into the blackness and risk collision with other B-29s, Cox and Marshall decided to fly under it. Down they went, leveling off at 500 feet, where they flew alone with no other B-29s in sight until O'Donnel told them that, according to his calculation, they were about 250 miles from the Japanese coast. Cox took the aircraft up through the clouds, hoping to avoid colliding with another B-29. At just over 10,000 feet they broke out of the gray-blackness into the sun and blue sky. Soon they spotted four other B-29s circling, were joined by others and set out in formation for the target area.

At 1:00 P.M., six hours after takeoff from Saipan, the coast of Japan came into view through the haze. Off to the right was the mouth of Tokyo Bay and straight ahead loomed snow-capped Mount Fuji. Having by this time climbed to the assigned bombing altitude, the formation made its turn over Fuji and began the bomb run, with Cox carefully maintaining his position in formation. Meanwhile, Lt. Herbert Feldman, the bombardier, kept his eyes glued on the lead ship and prepared to drop his bombs simultaneously with the bombardier in that airplane. If a Japanese fighter attacked head-on, Feldman was to aim and fire the forward gun turret and pass the release for the bombs (which was on a flexible cable) back to Marshall, who would drop the bombs. Well into their run to target, that is exactly what happened.

At about the same moment, Marshall and Feldman spotted a Kawasaki Ki45 twin-engine fighter coming directly at them. As the Nick passed underneath *Lil Lassie,* Feldman passed the bomb release to Marshall and got off several bursts from the forward turrets. Minutes later, now flying anxiously through antiaircraft fire for the first time, Marshall finally saw the lead B-29 open its bomb bay doors and called for Feldman to open their bomb bay. Moments later Marshall, keying on the leader, toggled off their 5,000 pounds of general-purpose bombs. It was 1:39 P.M., Friday, 24 November 1944 (a standing order

required that the time of bomb release be recorded and reported by coded radio signal to command headquarters) and
Thanksgiving Day in the United States, where, on the calendar, it was the day before—Thursday.

Marshall and the crew were thankful to be rid of their
bombs. In the next few minutes they flew out of the heavy
antiaircraft fire only to be attacked again by fighters. This
time, three single-engine Tonys. Before they broke off, the
tailgunner saw flames coming from the engine of one of the
Tonys as it dove out of control into a cloud bank. Soon they
were out over the Pacific. Conversation on the intercom was
heavy as the men, exhilarated and relieved, shared their experiences with each other. What one gunner saw may not
have been seen by the others; what the pilot saw may not
have been seen by the copilot; what the tailgunner saw may
not have been seen by the others. The flight engineer, radar
operator, navigator and radioman had been at stations and
duties that prevented their seeing anything that occurred outside.

Lt. Sam P. Wagner and his 497th Bomb Group crew did not
have this opportunity. As they left the target area other crews
saw a single fighter, probably a Tony, on Wagner's tail and
fired on it. The fighter began to wobble through the air and
then crashed into the tail of Lt. Wagner's B-29. Both planes
crashed into the sea and no parachutes were sighted. Wagner's
crew were the first combat casualties in the air attacks from
the Marianas.

Tragic as this was for the crew, their next of kin and their
friends in the 497th, mission losses were far less than XXI
Bomber Command had expected. One aircraft had ditched,
but the entire crew was rescued. The intelligence staff had
greatly overestimated the number of fighters the Japanese
would send up against the attacking force. On the other hand,
B-29 crews over Tokyo that day had to contend with an "enemy" to which intelligence and operations briefing officers
had given scant, if any, attention—unbelievably strong winds
aloft.

The field order for "San Antonio I" had assigned bombing
altitudes to the various units ranging from 27,000 to 33,000

feet. As the airplanes assigned to the higher altitudes turned over Mount Fuji, they experienced a tremendous drift in the direction of their turn, caused by a powerful wind coming from the west. Flying toward the target with this wind behind them, aircraft commanders were amazed to find that they had up to a 140-mph tailwind that gave them groundspeeds approaching 445 mph. At such groundspeeds bombardiers found it difficult, if not impossible, to accurately aim their bombs. Bombing tables and bombsight computers were not designed to cope with such high speeds. In large measure these tremendous tailwinds and the inexperience of the crews resulted in only 24 planes dropping bombs in the area of Target 357. The Nakajima plant was damaged only slightly. The other 64 B-29s released their loads on the dock area or overshot the city and dropped in Tokyo Bay.

That day the B-29s "discovered" what today is commonly referred to as the "jetstream," a narrow current of air that originates in northern Siberia and at altitudes of 30,000 to 40,000 feet reaches speeds up to 500 mph as it passes over Japan and continues around the Northern Hemisphere. Up to this time no one, the Japanese included, had reason to be particularly interested in the winds at such altitudes. The Japanese may have been aware of them from observation of weather balloons. But even if they were, such knowledge had no practical value to them, since their own aircraft rarely flew that high and the jetstream's influence on surface weather was not then understood.

The high winds over Japan would plague the precision-bombing campaign for some months. Operational planners could find no solution for the problem. If they routed their bombing force into the powerful wind, the airplanes' groundspeed was so slow that they became easier targets for antiaircraft fire and enemy fighters. Crosswind approaches to the target were ruled out because it would be virtually impossible to achieve any degree of bombing accuracy. The only option left was the downwind approach with the disadvantages encountered on the first Tokyo raid. The high winds often made it impossible for crews to attack at all if a navigation error brought them downwind of the target.

Despite the discouraging bombing results, when *Lil Lassie* and other XXI Bomber Command planes returned to the Marianas their crews were greatly elated. They had bombed Tokyo.

In Washington, Gen. Arnold was pleased. Soon after receiving word that the Tokyo raiders had landed, he went to the White House, briefed the President on the operation and informed him that no part of Japan was out of reach of the Twentieth Air Force. Then he radioed to Hansell, "You have successfully engaged the enemy in the very heart of his empire. This marks the beginning of what I know will be a most distinguished career for the XXI Bomber Command. We are proud of you. Good luck and God bless you." Throughout the nation, newspapers heralded the first attack on Tokyo since the Doolittle raid of 1942.

Hansell must have been gratified. Gen. Kenney's dire predictions had proved unfounded. Compared to the air war over Europe, losses were light—of 111 airplanes airborne only two were destroyed, eight damaged by enemy action and three by fire from other B-29s. Hansell believed he had proved the feasibility of daylight precision raids on Japan, but he knew that he must deliver more bombs to the target. He expected that with training, experience and more aircraft he could do so and thereby achieve his first objective—to destroy the Japanese aircraft industry with daylight precision bombing.

While it caused only slight damage to the Musashino plant, the 24 November strike drew quick reactions from the Japanese. Domei radio announced that any B-29 crewmen who parachuted onto Japanese soil were "enemies of civilization and humanity," outside the protection of international law and would be killed on the spot by angry Japanese. The Japanese Air Force struck back quickly and effectively. In two night attacks on the B-29s' Saipan base, Japanese fighters and bombers flying from Iwo Jima destroyed four B-29s, caused three more to be declared unserviceable and put six more out of service for over a month. The XXI lost more bombers as a result of these Japanese raids than in any mission flown during the remainder of 1944. The attacks continued sporadically for over a month and were damaging enough to cause

Hansell—on 8 December, the third anniversary of the Japanese attack on Pearl Harbor—to divert some of his bombers from their strategic bombing mission to join with other AAF and Navy air units in attacking the airfields on Iwo Jima.

In Washington, on 29 November, Gen. Norstad had proposed to Gen. Arnold a more dramatic way of commemorating the eighth of December—a large-scale attack on the Imperial Palace. Norstad had had discussions with Comdr. McGovern (advisor to the COA during their analysis of Twentieth Air Force bombing objectives) and other experts on the Japanese people. These discussions caused Norstad to believe that even partial destruction of the palace would undermine the Japanese belief that the Emperor was an invulnerable deity. He pointed out to Arnold that such an attack would arouse the Japanese and that they might retaliate by punishing or executing American POWs. Arnold turned the idea down, saying in a note to Norstad, "Not at this time. Our position—bombing factories, docks, etc.—is sound. Later destroy the whole city. HHA." Arnold's reaction strongly suggests that while he was still committed to precision bombing, he had few, if any, reservations about destroying entire cities in the future.

FAR MORE SIGNIFICANT than the immediate reactions by Domei and the Japanese Air Force was the reaction of the Japanese people to the 24 November attack. As Comdr. McGovern had told the COA, when you hit Tokyo you strike the "heart of Japan." The people of Tokyo had experienced two days of air alerts the previous June (1944), when the Americans, from their China bases, first struck Yawata, on the island of Kyushu, far to the south. The sirens had sounded again in early November, this time not falsely, triggered by Capt. Steakley's and other F-13 photoreconnaissance flights, visible to many Tokyo residents. But when, on the afternoon of 24 November, the B-29s came over in force and bombed with relative impunity, people began to fear their capital might soon suffer the ordeals of London and Berlin.

Tokyo was not only the capital but also Japan's preeminent

city in virtually every respect. The Emperor and the Imperial
Court resided there. The armed forces headquarters and the
civil government were located within the city. Tokyo, Osaka,
Nagoya, Kyoto, Yokohama and Kobe were known as the "Six
Great Cities of Japan," but the population of Tokyo equaled
that of all of the other five cities combined. Tokyo was, at
once, the industrial, financial, communications, transportation, commercial and entertainment center of the country. In
addition, the country's most important universities, muse-
ums, hospitals, office buildings and theaters were found there.

Tokyo lies at the northwestern end of Tokyo Bay, on the
edge of the Kanto plain. Except for low foothills, land west of
the bay is at sea level for about 6 miles, then rises to hills of
300 or more feet. Farther west are mountains as high as 8,000
feet. Sixty miles to the southwest is Mount Fuji, at 12,295
feet, the highest mountain in Japan. In 1944 the city proper,
made up of 35 political jurisdictions called wards, occupied
about a quarter of the Tokyo metropolitan district but contained over 90 percent of the population—about 6 million
people.

The Sumida River flows from north to south through Tokyo's most heavily populated areas. On the west side of the
Sumida are the Imperial Palace grounds, the city's largest open
space. The government and commercial districts lay between
the palace grounds and the Sumida. Just to the east of the
palace grounds were the Tokyo Main Railroad Station and the
Maranouchi district, where the offices of Japan's leading commercial and industrial concerns were located. Also to the east
lay the city's mercantile district, which included the Ginza,
with Tokyo's largest stores and shops. The Army and Navy
headquarters, Imperial Diet (Japan's legislative body), and
other public buildings lay just south of the palace grounds.

Extending northward from the palace grounds on the west
side of the Sumida were more stores, offices and highly congested areas of individual dwellings. In the northwestern corner of the city lay Ueno Park, one of the city's largest parks.

East of the Sumida, extending to the Ara River, was the
industrial area of the city. In the northern part was the
Koishikawa arsenal area; to the south could be found steel

mills, machinery, chemical and textile plants; farther south were lumber mills, warehouses and food processing plants. Scattered throughout were hundreds of small factories and workshops that supplied components to the larger plants. Another industrial zone extended along the waterfront in the southernmost part of the city. It contained aircraft, steel, machinery and communications equipment plants.

The most densely populated area of the city lay to the east of Ueno Park and extended across the Sumida River well into the industrial area. The heaviest concentrations of people, mostly industrial workers, lived in two of Tokyo's wards—the Asakusa ward, just to the east of Ueno Park, and the Honjo ward, across the Sumida from the Asakusa ward.

IN 1933 THE first blackout exercise was held in the city, and model bomb shelters and World War I bombs were displayed in department stores. One of a number of measures taken to demonstrate it was a "modern" city; the exercise became an annual event for a number of years. Coincident to the beginning of Japan's expansionism, the government in 1937 passed a National Civilian Air Defense Law. Under it, Tokyo's air-raid defense measures were to be the model for other large cities. But at the time the civilian populace did not see any immediate threat from the air, and the government's basic premise was that if any enemy aircraft did reach Japan they would be very few in number and would not constitute a serious problem. These assurances continued. But in 1940 when the Tokyo Undertakers Association, who for some reason became concerned about their role in the event of an air raid, asked the Army Headquarters how many deaths from air attacks they might expect in one year, they were given an estimate of 30,000. Evidently there were those in the headquarters who did not view Japan as invulnerable to air attack. The ambiguity of national civil defense policy and action went far beyond the Army's reply to the undertakers. Other than bringing into being an effective air-warning system, the national government did little, even after the Doolittle raid on Tokyo in 1942, to prepare for serious air attacks.

The government did stimulate and encourage civil defense activity at the local level. The focus of these efforts was on neighborhood groups, which were, and would continue to be, a major element in civilian air defense. Historically the Japanese, particularly those in the densely populated cities, had been forced to look upon cooperative communal effort as a necessity of life. Informal groups concerned with the health and living conditions of their neighbors had been in existence in Tokyo and other cities for years. Seizing on this, Japan's rulers established, through the prefectural government, the neighborhood group (*tonari gumi*) and the block association (*chokai*) as government-sponsored organizations and began to use them as agencies of air defense, training, rationing and other wartime services.

Usually from 10 to 20 households formed a neighborhood group. Membership was compulsory. Typifying Japanese conformity and respect for authority, members took an "air defense oath of certain victory" and publicly pledged to "follow orders," "refrain from selfish conduct" and "cooperate with one another in air defense." Meetings were held once a month or when necessary. As the war progressed, one of the main purposes of these meetings was dissemination of civil air defense information. The households elected a leader, whose position was similar to an American air raid warden at the time but went much further. The air raid defense leader received training from auxiliary police and fire units. He, in turn, passed this training on to his group, supervised blackout measures and was responsible for organizing and directing fire-fighting activities by members of his group using water buckets, shovels, hand pumps or any other equipment available. Since each of Tokyo's 35 wards contained thousands of neighborhood groups, the block associations, made up of representatives from 10 to 20 neighborhood groups, served as the intermediate organization between the two, passing on information and equipment to the groups as necessary.

It was not until late 1943, as Japan's aura of victory began to fade, that some concerted national action began to occur in three main areas. The first of these was the evacuation of people from the Tokyo area. It is ironic that only after destroying the lions in the Ueno Park Zoo, for fear they might escape during the air raid, did the national government decide to evacuate persons nonessential to war work from the cities to rural areas. The hope was that city leaders and neighborhood groups could persuade the families of soldiers, the elderly and the infirm to resettle in the countryside, preferably with relatives. The announced program was voluntary and, paternalistically, was designed to preserve the family unit as much as possible.

By July 1944, with relatively little response to the program, the government released a short movie, titled *Evacuation*. The film showed whole blocks of houses ablaze from bombing and carried with it an exhortation to move out of harm's way. At about the same time, with no success in their voluntary program, the cabinet announced an obligatory program for evacuating schoolchildren. Early that fall all third- through sixth-graders in Tokyo and other major cities were moved in groups to meeting halls, temples and resorts in rural towns and villages. Though successful, these were only token measures, since by the end of November 1944 less than 4 percent of the urban population had left Tokyo.

The national program for providing bomb shelters to the citizenry was poorly planned, administered and supported. Though the government expressed the desire that some type of shelter be available to everyone, it left the execution of the program largely in the hands of the neighborhood groups and individuals. Early in the war it had directed that open-trench shelters be built. Orders issued in September 1943 called only for construction of covered trench-type shelters. A month later this order was amended to state that each house was to have a shelter beneath it or in a nearby open area—a difficult, sometimes impossible, assignment for the millions who lived in such congested wards as Asakusa or Honjo. Another amendment in June of 1944 directed that the open-trench shelters remaining be covered over and that tunnel-type shelters be dug into the sides of hills. The latter shelter provided the best protection of all but required equipment, materials and construction skills. Little financial support for these shelters was forthcoming; consequently few were built. Despite all of this confusion, by the end of 1944 many Tokyo residents had access to some sort of trench shelter, inadequate as it might be, and derived some sense of security from this fact.

During 1944 the national government ordered the destruction of long lines of buildings through major industrial areas to create firebreaks. Here again, the work was poorly planned and organized. Much of the work was done by the neighborhood groups, who had to tear down houses, a large proportion of which were occupied by low-income workers who were left to find other housing with little or no government help. Shortages of manpower and equipment prevented this program from being carried out on the scale originally intended.

HAVING DONE LITTLE damage to the Musashino plant on 24 November, Gen. Hansell sent 81 airplanes to hit it three days later. Nineteen B-29s aborted the mission. Those arriving at the target found it completely hidden by clouds and had to bomb dock and urban areas by radar. Musashino was intact after 192 airplanes had flown from the Marianas to attack it.

Hansell wanted very much to go back in force a third time, but bad weather and airplanes in need of service prevented this. To keep the pressure on the enemy, on 29–30 November he scheduled a small mission of 29 aircraft—the first night incendiary raid on an industrial area in Tokyo. The field order for the mission, code-named "Brooklyn #1" (probably because "Rosie" O'Donnell, the 73rd Bomb Wing's commander, was from that city), called for an attack by individual aircraft, a necessity at night. As was customary in specifying bombloads, the order directed that the maximum bombload be carried "consistent with fuel requirements," then specified a minimum load along with the type of bomb(s). For "Brooklyn #1" the minimum was 2.5 tons, of which 80 percent would be made up of 500-lb aimable clusters, each holding 38 M-69 bombs, with the remaining 20 percent made up of 500-lb clusters of fragmentation bombs. For reasons that are not clear, three-quarters of the airplanes were to drop on the target area first, with the remainder of the force, divided into two groups, following at two-hour intervals. Bombing was to be by visual methods if possible and by radar if necessary.

Radar proved to be necessary. Once again, during the entire four-hour period, the target area was completely obscured by clouds. Twenty-three B-29s dropped their bombs into the blackness amid sometimes heavy antiaircraft fire. Twenty-eight planes returned. One was never heard from after takeoff. Aerial photos taken on the thirtieth revealed little, but air intelligence officers estimated that approximately one-tenth of a square mile of industrial area had been destroyed. Though Hansell probably did not plan it as a "test," considering that approximately 64 tons of M-69 bombs had been dropped, this mission did little to confirm the favorable test results at Dugway and Eglin Field.

If analysts in Washington found the results of this mission unimpressive, the same could not be said for Robert Guillain, an interned French journalist who spent the war years in Tokyo. He later recalled the raid as a time when Tokyo's millions learned, for the first time, what it was like to awaken to air raid sirens, crawl out from under their padded quilts, rush outdoors into chill rain and huddle in their muddy trenches from midnight until the all-clear siren sounded at 4:20 A.M. Guillain was not in the bombed area, but observed from the terrace of his house. He recalled the deep, powerful pulsation of the engines of the invisible planes as they passed by his house. Minutes later he watched searchlights go on and flashes of antiaircraft fire light the sky. Then, rising from behind a hill to his front, he saw a pink light spread across the horizon and slowly turn to red. Other red splotches appeared in different directions. Feudal Tokyo had been called Edo, and over the years the city's people, always fearful of accidental fires, had christened night fires "Flowers of Edo." That night Tokyo began to blossom.

The next day, perhaps even while American F-13 photoreconnaissance airplanes flew overhead for the same purpose, Guillain rode a streetcar to the bombed area to assess the damage. He found it almost impossible to tell where the streets and alleys had been that ran between the burnt-out squares that were once houses, now evidenced only by blackened pieces of sheet metal and shards of tile lying in a field of gray ash. The homeless moved in with their neighbors. By police count, 2,773 buildings, most of them dwellings, were completely destroyed by fire that night. In the surrounding areas, Guillain noted, life went on as usual.

On 3 December, with most of his airplanes back on line, Hansell decided to hit the Nakajima plant at Ota, 40 miles northwest of Tokyo, with a daylight precision attack. He was foiled by the weather on two counts. First he changed the target because winds as high as 180 mph were forecast over Ota. Then, when his bomber force arrived over the alternate target (for the third time in less than two weeks), Target #357, Musashino, they met even higher winds. This resulted in one bomb group missing the initial point, Mount Fuji. At bombing altitude the observed winds ranged from 170 to 190 mph. Even though the visibility was excellent, bombing results were poor, probably because of the high groundspeeds attained while bombing downwind. Again the Command had little to show for the loss of six B-29s, half of which ditched on the return trip.

Wind speeds over Japan were apparently a matter of some interest in Washington and were the subject of a Teletype request for more information on 9 December. In its reply, XXI Bomber Command reported winds over Tokyo on 3 December to have been 190 mph at 29,000 to 31,000 feet, from 270° (the west), and estimated at other altitudes to have been 155 mph at 25,000 feet, 140 mph at 20,000 feet, 100 mph at 15,000 feet, and 80 mph at 10,000 feet. The reason (provided by the command weather officer) was "tight pressure and temperature gradient aloft caused by the abnormally cold low-pressure center near the ocean-modified air to south and east of Japan." What the weather officers on Saipan did not realize was that whatever the causal factors, the powerful winds at high altitudes over Japan were a normal weather condition, not an infrequent phenomenon. It is not evident what, if any, conclusions either headquarters came to as to the advantage of bombing from a lower altitude. But, a short time later, Hansell would make a change that he thought would counter the adverse effects of the winds on bombing accuracy.

ON 13 DECEMBER, Hansell finally tasted some success. After hitting again at Iwo Jima, he sent 90 airplanes against a new target, the Mitsubishi aircraft factory at Nagoya. In a letter to Arnold on 15 December, Hansell provided insight into the operation. He enclosed aerial photos showing that considerable damage had been done. (The XXI Mission Report, which Arnold had already received, stated that 16 percent of the general-purpose bombs had fallen on the target, with 20 bomb hits on the aircraft assembly buildings.) Hansell's letter stated he thought the winds aloft over Europe had been high, but the 200-mph winds over Japan were something new. He explained that up until the 13 December mission, they had been bombing down wind, but over Nagoya they flew *upwind* to improve bombing accuracy. How much the damage to the Mitsubishi plant was a result of the reversed direction Hansell didn't say. He did note two features of the change, neither of which seemed beneficial. Whereas before they had dropped bombs beyond the target because of the great speed, over Nagoya they had the opposite experience—a great many bombs fell short because of the slow groundspeeds. Most of the "shorts" were 500-lb clusters of M-69 incendiaries (a little less than half of the attacking aircraft carried incendiaries). Because of this poor performance, Hansell informed Arnold that he was going to use the M-76 500-lb napalm-filled incendiary until the M-47 100-pound incendiary became available. Because the tremendous head wind reduced the groundspeed of the attackers to about 130 mph, they were more vulnerable to antiaircraft fire. Japanese gunners damaged at least 31 aircraft over Nagoya, and two were lost to antiaircraft fire. With his total dedication to the B-29 as a high-altitude precision bomber, Hansell seems to have given no serious consideration to lowering the bombing altitude.

He was, however, impressed by some of the ideas of Dr. E. L. Bowles, scientific advisor to Secretary of War Stimson, who had just completed a visit to Hansell's headquarters. Their discussions left Hansell with two convictions: (1) ". . . that we can do radar bombing against our primary targets with improved training" and (2) ". . . that we should have by all means a wing equipped with stripped airplanes (i.e. those from which most, if not all, of the guns, fire direction equipment and ammunition had been removed, thus permitting the aircraft to carry the maximum bombload) to do radar and night bombing, carrying approximately 20,000 lbs per airplane." This stripped wing should be an additional wing and "not at the expense of our present three wings." (Two more wings were scheduled to arrive in the next few months.) Hansell was telling Arnold that he didn't want to strip any of the incoming wings for night radar bombing, a concept "Rosie" O'Donnell had earlier found had considerable merit.

Hansell's letter is more important for what it revealed about his attitude than the effect it might have had on Arnold, which was probably very little. Arnold boldly scrawled across the top of the first page of the slightly more than two-page letter a note: "Gen Norstad. Summarize for me. HHA." At about the same time, Arnold was reading with great interest letters from his other Twentieth Air Force commander, Curtis LeMay.

WHILE HANSELL WAS beginning the aerial assault on Japan from the Marianas, Twentieth Air Force headquarters in Washington had given LeMay's XX Bomber Command a share in the AAF's first priority—the destruction of Japan's aircraft production facilities. From mid-October into December, LeMay's bombers had hit three aircraft plants located at Okayama on the island of Formosa, Omura on Kyushu, and Mukden, Manchuria. While none of them were comparable in size and importance to the big plants in the Tokyo and Nagoya areas, they were within range of the XXth's Chengtu-based B-29s.

On 14 October, 104 airplanes dropped 650 tons of bombs, a mixed load of general-purpose and 500-lb M-76 napalm incendiaries, on the Okayama plant. This, the heaviest bombload carried up to that time, caused considerable damage. After two follow-up strikes on Okayama on 25 October, LeMay sent his planes to hit the Omura aircraft plant, a manufacturer of Navy fighter planes. Carrying the same mixed bombload as on the Okayama strike, the attackers, with excellent visibility, did considerable damage to many of the buildings but only superficial damage to the engine-manufacturing works.

On 17 November Arnold wrote LeMay:

... The progress you have been making in adding to your bomb load is most gratifying. You will recall that at the time you first took command of the XX, one of my greatest concerns was the fact that the B-29 had not yet demonstrated its ability to carry a reasonably large weight of bombs. We haven't completely whipped this to my satisfaction yet, but I am pleased with the improvement. I have seen your bomb strike and PRU photos of Okayama and Omura, but as yet the Rangoon and Singapore pictures have not arrived. Large-scale blowups have been made of the former, and I have proudly displayed them whenever opportunity arose. I don't recall any pictures of the European Theater which surpass those of Okayama for concentration of bombs and damage resulting therefrom. . . .The fine work your people have been doing is providing a standard for the other B-29 units. We are passing to Hansell everything of interest from the XX Bomber command, and he, in a recent letter here, stated that he would have to push his people pretty hard to stay in the same league with your command.

The Rangoon and Singapore strikes were flown out of the India bases and were very successful. In early 1942 the Japanese had taken over the huge British naval base at Singapore, including some of the largest and best dry docks in the world. One of these, the King George VI Graving Dock, was the primary target for the strike. The 40th Bomb Group's Lt. Frank McKinney put a 1,000-lb bomb 50 feet from the caisson gate, and Lt. Bolish McIntyre, moments later, dropped another bomb alongside McKinney's, putting the dry dock out of use for about three months. This was "pinpoint" bombing at its best.

LeMay did not do as well in his strikes against the aircraft plant at Omura. On 21 November, in his third mission against this target, he met bad weather and tough fighter opposition. Because of navigation errors in trying to fly around or through foul weather, only 61 of the 109 B-29s taking off arrived at the target. They found it obscured and, amid determined attacks by enemy fighters, had to bomb by radar. Five airplanes were lost to enemy action, a high for the XX to that date, and no additional damage was done to the factory. Like Hansell with Target #357, Mushashino, in Tokyo, LeMay was finding Omura a hard nut to crack.

On 17 December Arnold wrote LeMay, thanking him for his letter that enclosed a four-page report by W. B. Shockley, a consultant in the Office of the Secretary of War. The report showed that the XX Bomber Command, over the previous six months, had increased the number of flying hours per B-29, had increased the weight of bombs carried and had improved bombing accuracy. Arnold found that it "helped answer some of the questions that are constantly on my mind." Arnold continued:

I follow the work of the XX Bomber Command in far greater detail than you probably think, so I have already deduced most of the points covered in this report. As I told you before you went to India, the B-29 project is important to me because I am convinced that it is vital to the future of the Army Air Forces. I think progress has been made and you have contributed materially to this . . . we will always continue to have problems of one kind or another. None of them, however, are insurmountable and we must not let ourselves use them as an excuse for doing anything less than the best possible under the circumstances. The report you sent me proves that you have the right attitude in this matter.

I have just learned that on the Singapore attack 41 percent of your bombs were within 1,000 feet of the briefed aiming point. I don't have to tell you that I am impressed by this progress. . . . I think we can do better bombing with the B-29 than has been done by any aircraft up to this time and I expect you to be the one to prove this.

On the same day that Arnold sent his letter to LeMay, LeMay dispatched 94 B-29s to the Chinese city of Hankow on the first major incendiary raid of the Pacific War. The target was chosen by Maj. Gen. Claire L. Chennault, commander of the Fourteenth Air Force. In June 1944, with a major Japanese offensive gaining momentum in east China, Chennault asked Wolfe, then in command of the XX Bomber Command, to mount a 100-aircraft incendiary attack on the port and storage facilities at Hankow, which he, at a later date, said would be comparable to attacking similar American facilities in Hawaii. Wolfe declined on the basis that Hankow was a tactical, not a strategic, target and he was supported by Arnold. In a memorandum to Col. Combs, Norstad's deputy, in early August, Major Bowers reported that it might take as much as 2,100 tons of general-purpose bombs to destroy the storage areas at Hankow. (This was triple the largest bombload carried thus far by the XX.) Even if the storage warehouses were destroyed, Bower contended it would have little chance of critically affecting enemy troop operations.

The XX Bomber Command's position remained unchanged after LeMay's arrival in late August. In October, Gen. Albert C. Wedemeyer replaced Gen. Joseph W. Stillwell as commander of the newly formed China Theater and strongly endorsed the idea of the Hankow attack, but LeMay demurred. (Norstad and LeMay had been jointly working on a plan to attack Nagasaki with 100 airplanes, half of them carrying M-69 incendiaries in aimable clusters and the other half carrying M-47 incendiaries. The plan was never carried out because of the later decision to pull the B-29s out of Chengtu and send them to the Marianas.) Wedemeyer referred the matter to the Joint Chiefs of Staff in Washington, who confirmed Wedemeyer's authority to order the attack.

In early December LeMay flew to Kunming to review plans with Chennault. At first LeMay opposed Chennault's position that the bombing altitude should be from below 20,000 feet to obtain maximum accuracy and surprise. Chennault believed the Japanese would expect them at the altitudes they had been flying—in excess of 25,000 feet. After listening to Chennault's arguments, however, LeMay agreed to drop the B-29s to a bombing altitude of 18,000 to 21,000 feet.

The XX's operations planners had divided the dock and storage areas into four sections, three of approximately the same size and the fourth somewhat smaller. Three different incendiaries were to be used: M-76 (500-lb), M-47 (100-lb) and M-50 (4-lb in 500-lb aimable clusters). Formations, consisting of airplanes carrying the same type of incendiary, were assigned to drop on a particular section. Since the prevailing surface winds were from the north, the plan called for the first arriving aircraft to drop on the southern sections of the target area so smoke from the resulting fires would not obscure the northern sections from following formations.

Against light enemy opposition and with unlimited visibility, 84 B-29s in ten formations varying in size from two to thirteen aircraft attacked the dock and storage area. Because of communications problems on the morning of takeoff, the formations that were supposed to bomb the northern sections arrived first. Thirty-three aircraft in these formations dropped 139 tons of M-50s and 57 tons of M-47s on the two northern sections. Within 30 minutes fires in the two sections had merged. Smoke billowed to 20,000 feet, turning day into night for the people of Hankow. Subsequent formations could not see their aiming points and released most of their bombs outside the target area. Even with the mistiming, 40–50 percent of the target area was totally destroyed. The huge fires across the length of Hankow's waterfront gutted the warehouses and dock facilities along three miles of Hankow's waterfront. Military and civilian casualties among the Japanese are not known, nor are those of America's allies, the Chinese, but it is likely that the Japanese death toll was small and that of the Chinese large. Photos taken five days later showed no signs of activity in the devastated area, only two fires still smoldering and thin wisps of smoke rising here and there.

Though Chennault would later infer that LeMay's attitude toward incendiaries was greatly influenced by the successful Hankow strike, LeMay, though obviously pleased with the results, did not make much of it at the time—nor did Headquarters, Twentieth Air Force, because, at least in part, neither LeMay nor Arnold had wanted to bomb Hankow. As his plan for the XX to hit Nagasaki demonstrated, Norstad had an urgent need for data on incendiary bombing of actual targets upon which to plan urban area-bombing of Japan's major cities. Norstad was heavily influenced by the contention of his own staff, the COA and the NDRC, that the M-69 was the best incendiary for use against Japanese cities; he wanted data on that bomb, not on the M-47 or the M-50. Since LeMay knew this, the question arises as to why the M-69 was not used in Hankow. Clearly one reason was that the data Norstad and his target planners needed was the M-69's effect on *Japanese* structures, not Chinese. Consequently, no compelling reason existed for using the M-69 in this particular operation.

As it turned out, LeMay's target operation's planners chose, in addition to M-76s and M-47s, to use clusters of M-50s because they believed this incendiary could do the job and an adequate supply of the bombs was on hand.

Even as the results of the Hankow bombing were coming in to his headquarters, Norstad was dispatching a teleconference message to Hansell:

1. At the earliest practicable date on which you can dispatch a maximum force of approx one hundred aircraft on a visual daylight mission, it is desired that Nagoya be given a full incendiary attack. The purpose of this attack is twofold: first, to destroy as much of the city as possible to reduce its industrial capacity; second, to determine the effectiveness of our incendiary weapons, particularly the M-69, in aimable clusters.

2. The Joint Target Group has prepared a study on this subject and recommends attacking that portion of the city bounded by the following coordinates:
   136°54′ E, 35°06′15″ N
   136°55′ E, 35°06′15″ N
   136°55′ E, 35°09′   N
   136°55′ E, 35°08′30″ N
   They recommend that the entire bombload be M-69 bombs in aimable clusters, and that all of the attack be put into the above area. They also recommend that the duration of the attack be in the minimum time. Strike photos for each formation plus poststrike photography immediately after the attack and on the next succeeding day are required in order to utilize [to] the utmost the information gained from this mission.

3. The performance of this mission is an urgent requirement in order that future operations may be planned with far greater assurance as to our capabilities than we now possess.

4. It is further desired that the provisions of (2) above be followed. Request your detailed plan at the earliest possible date.

Hansell replied within hours:

I have with great difficulty implanted the principle that our mission is the destruction of selected primary targets by sustained and determined attacks using precision bombing methods both visual and radar. We are just beginning to get results on our present primary targets, the Japanese aircraft industry. The last two operations have caused great damage to the two Mitsubishi Hatsudoki plants at Nagoya which produce about 30 to 40 percent of Jap aircraft engines and which we seriously damaged on the 13th. By determined application we can cripple the Japanese aircraft industry, but it will take sustained accurate bombing of primary targets . . . The temptation to abandon our primary targets for secondary area targets is great and I have been under considerable pressure to do so, but I have resisted so far. I am concerned that a change to area bombing of the cities will undermine the progress we have made. However, I am accepting your No. S-18-2 [Message Number] as an order from you and a change in my directive and I will launch this operation next. Designation "Microscope."

Norstad immediately replied that the XXI's primary mission—destruction of the Japanese aircraft industry—was unchanged. The requested strike was a "special requirement resulting from the necessity of future planning." He stated again the need to know "the capabilities of our weapons" and that no tests or experiments had been conclusive to date. Hansell responded that he would run the mission after completing those already scheduled.

The day after his reply to Norstad, on 22 December, Hansell sent his bombers to Nagoya. The mission was not intended as a response to Norstad. The B-29s were loaded with incendiaries—500-lb M-76 bombs, not M-69s—and the target was the Nakajima Aircraft Factory, not an area of the city. Weather over the target was terrible and little damage was done.

On the twenty-seventh the XXI went back to Target #357, Musashino, for the fourth time, with 72 aircraft carrying a mixed load of general-purpose and M-76 incendiaries. Only 39 airplanes bombed the target, with poor accuracy. Once again, no measurable damage was done, but a hospital may have been set afire, giving the Japanese press an opportunity for condemning the inhumanity of the Americans.

On 28 December a lengthy statement by Hansell appeared in U.S. newspapers. A headline in the Honolulu *Advertiser* said, "GENERAL GIVES SOBER REPORT ON BOMBER RESULTS OVER JAPAN." In his statement Hansell summarized the first 30 days of the bombing campaign, revealing that the XXI Bomber Command had dropped more than 3,000,000 lbs of explosives on Japan during the period. He cited raids on Nagoya as examples of the kind of pinpoint strategic bombing he wanted to repeat in the future. He cautioned that though the B-29 had proved to be a magnificent weapon of war, "We are still in our early experimental stages. We have much to learn and many operational and other technical problems to solve."

It was around the time of Hansell's public statement that Arnold decided to relieve Hansell and turn the XXI Bomber Command over to LeMay. On 3 January 1945, Norstad notified Hansell that he was leaving Washington for Guam (now the location of the XXI Bomber Command) and would arrive there on the eighth. Norstad's mission was to notify Hansell of his relief, which would not become official until later that month.

Hansell received Norstad's message (which he assumed was notice of a routine inspection) on the day following completion of the test mission against Nagoya that he had opposed so strongly. It did not turn out well. Of the 97 airplanes that left Saipan, only 57 dropped their loads of M-69s on the designated area. A number of isolated fires were observed throughout the target area, but soon smoke mixed with clouds and obscured the area. Because of the obscuration, the extent of damage could not be determined. The Twentieth Air Force still lacked the kind of data it desperately needed. (Postwar information revealed that the fires had not spread and were quickly brought under control by fire fighters.)

Norstad arrived on the sixth of January and told Hansell of his impending relief. The message was a complete surprise to Hansell. As he would recall later, he was so totally absorbed in the work of getting the bombing campaign to produce satisfactory results that it hadn't occurred to him that Arnold was thinking of replacing him. After receiving the disturbing news, Hansell and Norstad spent time discussing the arrangements for turning over the command to LeMay, who was expected to arrive from India the next day.

Hansell also spent part of that day in discussions with Maj. Gen. James E. Fechet, a retired officer who had been Chief of the Army Air Corps in the late twenties. Arnold, realizing the severity of his action and knowing the shock it would be to Hansell, had decided to send this respected senior officer to help Hansell through the abrupt and painful ending of what had, up to that time, been a brilliant wartime career. Gen. Fechet discussed with Hansell the possibility of Hansell's staying on as LeMay's vice-commander, an option that Hansell declined. It was probably in the course of the conversation with Fechet that Hansell first voiced his desire to become commander of a B-29 training wing in Texas or Arizona. There he hoped to do plenty of flying and spend some time with his family, two important things in his life that had long been denied him.

The day after Hansell's sessions with Norstad and Fechet, LeMay flew in from India and the three young generals—Hansell, 41, LeMay, 39, and Norstad, 38—sat down and discussed the command turnover. It must have been a difficult meeting for each of them. Norstad and Hansell had worked closely together in the Pentagon; LeMay had served under Hansell in England. Despite their personal feelings, they decided on the immediate actions to be taken. LeMay would fly back to India, taking with him Roger M. Ramey, Hansell's Chief of Staff and now a brigadier general, who would take over the XX Bomber Command.

Soon after the meeting, Norstad flew back to Washington. LeMay, with Ramey, flew to Kharagpur, where another command turnover took place. LeMay was to return to Guam and assume command of the XXI Bomber Command on 20 January 1945. Hansell remained in command, with three more missions scheduled before LeMay's return.

The first was another attack on the Nakajima plant at Musashino, the fifth attempt to destroy Target #357. Extremely heavy clouds en route made formation-flying impossible. Eighteen of the 72 airplanes airborne bombed the target individually, but with poor results. Six B-29s (with 66 crewmen) were lost. Next, on the fourteenth, the XXI again attacked the Mitsubishi Aircraft Works at Nagoya. The B-29s damaged three buildings—a poor result for the loss of five more airplanes with their crews.

Ironically Hansell's last mission, flown on 19 January, was highly successful. The target was a "new" one, Kawasaki Aircraft Industries, located near Akashi, a town 12 miles west of Kobe. Although smaller than Nakajima or Mitsubishi, Kawasaki was a substantial producer. In 1944 it had delivered 17 percent of Japan's combat airframes and 12 percent of its combat engines. Hansell sent 77 airplanes on the mission. With 20-mile visibility over the target area, 62 B-29s dropped 152 tons of general-purpose bombs from altitudes of 25,100 to 27,400 feet—about 4,000 feet lower than previous bombing altitudes. The results were excellent. Poststrike assessment indicated that 39 percent of the roof area of the engine and assembly plants had been damaged or destroyed. Actual damage was much greater. Every important building in the entire complex was hit. Production was cut by 90 percent, and the facilities were later used only for limited assembly jobs. These outstanding results were obtained with no aircraft lost—a gratifying achievement for Hansell on the eve of his departure.

On 20 January, LeMay took over the most important combat command in the Army Air Forces. Hansell flew home to a well-deserved leave and command of the 38th Flight Training Wing at Williams Field, Arizona.

SIX

LEMAY: SEARCH FOR A SOLUTION

NEWSPAPERS AND MAGAZINES devoted little space to Hansell's relief, but seemed to sense that the B-29 campaign was not going too well. The New York *Times*, in a mid-January editorial reviewing the Twentieth Air Force's activities since the bombing of Yawata in June 1944, commented:

> . . . There has been no indication from General Arnold as to just what program he has set for his Twentieth Air Force, the global organization that was formed to direct the B-29s. It may be that delay in base construction and difficulties of supply have held the Twentieth's big bombers to a lesser activity than had been hoped for. The Japanese, though, can find small comfort in that. . . . They can look forward only to increasingly heavy and increasingly more frequent attacks until, if need be, every factory and airfield and military installation they possess lies in ruins. They asked for it. They are getting it.

Arnold did not share the *Times* editorial writer's optimism or enthusiasm.

Norstad had barely returned to Washington from Guam when Arnold wrote him:

I am still worried—we have built up ideas in the Army, the Navy, and among civilians of what we can do with our B-29s. We had all realized that in order to do considerable damage, large numbers of B-29s would have to deliver their loads of bombs against Japan continuously and consistently, and yet in spite of the above, really and truly, our average daily delivery rate against Japan is very, very small ... Unless something drastic is done to change this condition soon, it will not be long before the B-29 is just another tactical airplane.

Three days later Arnold suffered his fourth serious heart attack in less than two years and for the next two months would convalesce in Florida, leaving Norstad with the responsibility of making decisions for the Twentieth Air Force at the Washington level.

The New York *Times* was not alone in editorializing on the B-29. With the damage to military plants and civilian casualties still relatively light, the Japanese newspaper *Mainichi*, in January, took the opportunity to tell the people that according to confirmed war results against B-29 raiders, the United States had been losing more aircraft per month than it produced in a like period. According to *Mainichi*, the AAF was depleting its original fleet of B-29s, and although not stated, the implication was that the United States would eventually run out of B-29s. For all this expense and trouble the enemy raiders were only carrying out "blind bombing," dropping their bombs on civilian homes, mountain areas and into the sea. The newspaper's assessment of American bombing proficiency was reflected in a joke told by some Tokyo residents at the time, which accused the Americans of trying to starve the people of the city by killing all of the fish in Tokyo Bay.

Jokes aside, if Tokyo residents wanted proof that B-29s were being shot down they had only to visit Hibiya Park. There, thousands could take their turn at examining a full-scale replica of a B-29 shot down on 3 December, along with remnants of the bomber's tires, machine-gun parts and a fuel tank. The replica included a cutaway view of the nose of the aircraft with painted figures showing the crew stations. Alongside was the fighter that brought the B-29 down.

AT XXI BOMBER Command Headquarters on Guam, LeMay knew of Arnold's deep concern about the B-29 campaign. He was also aware that the American public and the other service chiefs were wondering when the B-29s were going to start dealing the massive blows that they had come to expect. Despite the tremendous pressure on him, LeMay did not attempt to make immediate and radical changes. Instead, he proceeded in the manner he found had worked for him in Europe and in India—take a careful look at the command, note and build on the good features, eliminate the bad ones, and seek and adopt new approaches for achieving bombing effectiveness.

Among the first messages he sent to Norstad after taking the XXI Bomber command was a request for "any available information . . . on evaluation of incendiary bomb damage of targets in the European Theater of Operations with a comparison of . . . types of bombs used." The brief response said that the advice from Europe was that the M-50 (4-lb magnesium) bomb was best "under blind bombing conditions" against marshaling yards and urban areas, the M-47 (100-lb gasoline gel) bomb was the next best, and the M-76 (500-lb gasoline gel) was a relatively ineffective incendiary. Absent was any comment on the M-69, since this bomb was not used in Europe. (LeMay already had test data on the M-69 and was aware of Norstad's strong feeling that it was the bomb to use against Japan's cities.) What immediate use LeMay made of the information from Washington is not known, but his request shows his keen interest in incendiaries.

After a brief look, LeMay gave full support to the centralized maintenance program that Col. C. S. "Bill" Irvine, Hansell's Deputy Chief of Staff for supply and maintenance, had started. The program, designed to boost the number of B-29s available for missions and reduce aborts, was just beginning to show some results. LeMay was pleased to have Irvine, an old friend, continue as his own chief of supply and maintenance.

Another of Hansell's staff who would become one of LeMay's most valuable subordinates was Col. John B. Montgomery. In 1938, Montgomery was copilot of the B-17 that LeMay navigated to intercept the Italian liner *Rex*. He and Montgomery had had their first checkrides in the same B-24 in 1941. In the prewar days, when LeMay was considered to be one of the Air Corps' best navigators, Montgomery was a recognized expert in bombing techniques and also an excellent navigator. As Deputy Chief of Staff for plans and operations, Montgomery had ample opportunity to apply his expertise and assist in bringing the command up to LeMay's high standards of operational efficiency.

Of course, LeMay brought people and ideas of his own to his new command. As his Chief of Staff, LeMay brought in an officer who had served in the same capacity in England, Brig. Gen. August Kissner. As in England, Kissner kept the administrative activities of the command running with machinelike efficiency, leaving LeMay able to devote his attention to combat operations.

Much as he had done in England and India, LeMay immediately ordered intensive training for his bomber crews. Rumors of nine hours a day of ground school caused some alarm. Though the hours weren't that long, crews were required to attend frequent classes in their specialties when they were not on missions. Training flights to improve formation flying, gunnery and bombing proficiency were conducted. For the third time in as many years, LeMay was regarded by most of his men as the toughest commander they had ever worked for.

While LeMay was going about his careful overhaul, the forces and facilities of his command grew rapidly. In January, the 313th Bomb Wing (composed of the 6th, 9th, 504th and 505th Bomb Groups), commanded by Brig. Gen. John H. Davies, arrived in the Marianas. The 313th was assigned to the new North Field on the island of Tinian. North Field, when completed, with its four parallel paved runways—each 8,500 feet long—miles of taxiways and hundreds of hardstands, would be the biggest bomber base ever constructed. The 314th Bomb Wing was en route to the Marianas. Upon arrival it would use another giant airfield (then approaching completion) on Guam. This field, also called North Field, sat on

Guam's north end, about ten miles northeast of XXI Bomber Command Headquarters. Eventually the road between the headquarters and North Field would have four asphalt lanes— wider and more congested than contemporary highways in the United States.

By this time the area around LeMay's headquarters had taken on the appearance of a small city. Thousands of men with their machines and equipment lived and worked there, with more arriving constantly. Like their fellow Americans throughout the Pacific, the men on the Marianas used the Quonset hut, a round-roofed structure made of corrugated sheets of metal laid over semicircular arched ribs, as protection from rain and sun. Named for Quonset Point, Rhode Island, where the first models were built, the Quonset was an adaptation of the British Nissen hut of World War I. Despite its tendency to become unbearably hot inside, the Quonset was widely used because it was highly portable and could withstand severe weather and high winds. The Quonset city on Guam included living quarters (cramped and hot), offices, communications centers, aircraft maintenance areas, classrooms, briefing rooms, food and equipment storage, hospitals and rooms for a variety of other uses. A herd of cows was imported to provide fresh milk for hospitals, and even their "barns" were Quonsets.

In the Pentagon, far from the Quonset city, General Norstad, with the boss out of action, was doing his best to get the lagging B-29 campaign moving. In a January meeting with his staff, Norstad stated that the Twentieth Air Force's two major problems were unsatisfactory maintenance (resulting in too few planes available for missions) and, more important, the inability of those aircraft reaching the target to put their bombs on it.

Lt. Col. Robert S. McNamara, who later became Secretary of Defense under President John F. Kennedy, in charge of the statistical analysis function of the Twentieth Air Force, provided Norstad with a mixed report on the two problems. While radar bombing had not improved, visual bombing had become a little more accurate. He cited the example of the XXI Bomber Command's 19 January mission (Hansell's last) in which 22 percent of the bombs landed within 1,000 feet of the aiming point. McNamara noted that the increased accuracy was achieved after the bombing altitude had been reduced 5,000 feet; he added that, in Europe, the Eighth Air Force had improved bombing accuracy by 50 percent and, in some cases, as much as 150 percent when it had lowered bombing altitudes the same amount. The maintenance picture was less favorable. The number of aircraft of the XXI Bomber Command that failed to bomb primary targets because of mechanical malfunctions had risen from 20 percent in November and December to 25 percent in the first half of January.

On Guam, LeMay, after looking at the results of the 19 January strike, must have come to the same conclusion on bombing altitude as McNamara had. LeMay's experienced eye spotted something else. The intensity of enemy fighter defense over Tokyo and Nagoya was increasing dramatically. The 73rd Bomb Wing had hit targets in each of these cities twice during the period from 27 December to 14 January. During this period Japanese attacks on American aircraft rose from 272 to 583. The number of Japanese fighters shot down did not rise proportionately but averaged an estimated 21 per mission, with American losses due to enemy action averaging about three. The 19 January strike broke the pattern—only 159 attacks, an estimated six Japanese shot down and no loss by the Americans. This was because the target was a new one near the city of Osaka and the Japanese were not expecting an attack there. LeMay knew that if he went back to either Tokyo or Nagoya, particularly at an altitude that made his B-29s more accessible to the fighters and antiaircraft, he was in for a tough fight. But he was not one to avoid risks if the payoff was bombing success and depletion of Japanese Air Force pilots and airplanes. So on 23 January, for the first mission flown under his command, LeMay ordered his aircraft to bomb the Mitsubishi plant at Nagoya from an altitude of 25,000–27,000 feet.

Chester Marshall would note later in his journal that he and the crew of *Lil Lassie II* "were briefed this afternoon for a mission to Nagoya tomorrow, going in at 25,000 feet, and we have started to sweat already." Marshall and his crewmates had some reason to sweat. Enemy fighter opposition on 23 January was, in the language of the official mission summary, "heavy and aggressive." American crews recorded 691 separate attacks on B-29s and claimed destruction of 33 fighters and 22 "probably destroyed" with the loss of only two B-29s. But the crews could not aim their bombs at a factory they couldn't see. With clouds covering the city, only 28 out of 73 airplanes bombed, and they inflicted only minor damage. Though weather persisted in keeping them from destroying the factories that produced enemy fighters, they were beginning to take a heavy toll on those already in service.

LeMay's next mission was against the all-too-familiar Target #357 or, if the weather was better over Nagoya, another try at the Mitsubishi plant. Chester Marshall and his crew "sat this one out" but *Lil Lassie II* went with lieutenants E.G. "Snuffy" Smith and Jim Edwards at the controls. Marshall had trained at Smoky Hill Air Base with Smith and his crew and was delighted when Snuffy and the Rover Boys, as his happy-go-lucky crew were called, had arrived in December. The new crew's move into the Quonset just across from Marshall's was the occasion for a party at which Rover Boys navigator Lt. Ray "Hap" Halloran lead a quintet of lieutenants—Smith, Edwards, William Franz (flight engineer) and Robert Grace (bombardier)—in the barbershop harmonies for which they had become known during the training days in Kansas.

Clear skies over the Marianas had favored *Lil Lassie II* and the 75 other B-29s that took to the air on 27 January. Aircraft of the four bomb groups assembled in formation with little trouble. About two hours out, however, they encountered a moderate front, a prelude to poorer weather ahead. About 400 miles south of Japan some B-29s came under fire from two Japanese Navy vessels that probably notified the air defense forces in Japan of the approach of enemy bombers. Though the Japanese did not yet know which city would contain the target, they had good reason to believe it would be one of the two aircraft factories the Americans were determined to destroy. As the Americans approached the coast of Japan their reconnaissance aircraft reported that weather conditions favored an attack on the Musashino plant, so, according to the attack plan, it became the primary target. If visual bombing was not possible, the airplanes were to bomb the harbor facilities and built-up areas of Tokyo by radar.

FIRST IN THE procession of bombers to catch sight of the Japanese coast just south of Hamamatsu were airplanes of the 497th Bomb Group. Even as they did so, five Japanese fighters made a pass, fired on them and pulled away. This was the beginning of the most intense aerial battle of the B-29 campaign. The Japanese sent about 350 fighters into the air that day, from the five Army airfields ringing Tokyo and the Navy air base at Atsugi, south of Tokyo. They hoped to defeat the Americans decisively.

As the bombers passed over Hamamatsu on their way to Kofu, the point at which they would turn east on their final run to the target area, Japanese fighters attacked in ever increasing numbers. They came from below, shooting at the bellies of the big bombers, from above and the side, strafing the Superforts from wing tip to wing tip. Diving, climbing, turning, fighters of every size and description pressed their attacks. The bulk of the attacks were carried out by Tonys (Ki-61 Swallows) and Tojos (Ki-44 Demons) from the Army bases and Zekes (Type-0) from the Atsugi naval base. In lesser numbers crews identified twin-engined Nicks (Ki-45 Dragon Killers) and Irvings (J1N1 Gekkos), the Navy's night fighter, many painted black. American gunners, becoming more skilled with experience, directed thousands of rounds at the attacking Japanese with whoops of victory when they saw the fighters in their sights veer off and plunge earthward, trailing smoke. It seemed to B-29 crewmen that many of the attacks were unorganized. "Hopped-up" Japanese pilots, firing at random, often got in each other's way. Still others attacked right down a B-29's stream of tracer fire—an action which suited the American gunners just fine.

Some of the better trained Japanese fighter units did not immediately join the fray but waited until the most favorable time. After crossing the coast, American crewmen had sighted to their left a formation of 20 silver Tonys at 24,000 feet, stacked in tiers. The formation, keeping its distance, followed the B-29s as they flew toward Kofu with Mount Fuji looming off to their right. When the American formation, over Kofu, changed course to the east and headed for Tokyo, 100 miles away, the formation of Tonys turned with them. Minutes later the Japanese commander gave the order and his fighters peeled off and soon were maneuvering to get into position for their 20-mm cannons and 12.7-mm machine guns to bring a Superfort down.

Because of its relatively high state of training and location of its base—on the path of the first arriving B-29s—it is highly likely that the Tonys were from the 244th Air Regiment stationed at Chofu, under the command of Capt. Teruhiko Kobayashi, one of the youngest fighter unit commanders in Japan.

Kobayashi and the 244th had fought against the B-29s before. They had attacked primarily from the sides and below. Despite the fact that the B-29s could bring all of their firepower to bear on attacks from these directions, the 244th had downed a number of Superforts. With experience they had found that by attacking frontally they avoided some of the defensive fire from the B-29's machine guns. A frontal attack could kill the pilot and copilot or, lacking that, kill the bombardier and render the airplane's bombing ineffective. Besides these conventional tactics, in the fall of 1944 some of the 10th Air Division units—the 244th Air Regiment was one—organized Special Attack Units, called by the Japanese "Shinten-Tai." Pilots in these units dedicated themselves to ram B-29s whenever possible. Successful ramming required a great deal of daring and a high degree of pilot skill. In some units the pilot was expected to stay with his ship; in others, he bailed out at the last moment.

Kobayashi's Tonys, along with hundreds of other Japanese Army and Navy fighters, pressed their attacks all the way from Kofu to Tokyo. The 497th Bomber Group, in the lead, bore the brunt of the onslaught. Gunners of *Irish Lassie*, piloted by Lt. Lloyd Avery, were holding their own, calling off sightings over the interphones and firing at planes that seemed to be coming from all directions. They destroyed three. Then in rapid succession two fighters rammed the aircraft. One, identified as a Zeke (the Navy also had Special Attack Units), dove almost straight down and sliced off 8 feet of the plane's aileron. Another, a Jack (J2M Raiden, Navy fighter) making his approach from the rear, sheared off the entire left stabilizer. The plane dropped, out of control, 8,000 feet before Avery was able to pull it out of its dive and start for the coast with more fighters following to finish him off.

After Avery's plane dropped out of the formation the others reformed and continued toward the target. As they approached Tokyo thick clouds appeared below at about 20,000 feet. Through the clouds came an increasing amount of antiaircraft fire. Apparently the Japanese gunners were getting better at using their sound detectors, as more and more shells burst around the American formation. Now the Japanese fighters went all out with deadly effect.

Using the tactical numbers assigned each aircraft, returning B-29 crews described the fate of three B-29s during the final run and over Tokyo: A-26 "exploded in mid-air. No one seen to bail out"; A-22 "saw fire coming out of bomb bay, made a sharp turn to the left and was not heard from again"; A-23 was "last seen on bomb run under heavy fighter attack."

The 73rd Wing field order had directed that if the primary target was obscured, the alternate target—harbor and built-up facilities—should be attacked, using radar. This the 497th's crews did, after which the airplanes headed back to Saipan individually or in small groups.

It had been a bad day for the 497th. Of the 17 aircraft that reached the coast of Japan, four did not return. It would have been five except that Avery, on two engines after the rammings, successfully nursed his plane back to a crash landing on Saipan with no loss of life. Of the 211 men who flew on the mission, over 20 percent were lost due to enemy action.

The Japanese had expended most of their fury on the 497th. Though it was anything but easy for the three groups that followed, their losses were not as severe. The 498th lost two aircraft; the 499th, one; and the 500th, none. For Chester Marshall, who "sat out" the mission, the fate of aircraft No. 42-24769 had great impact. The report on this airplane's loss read:

Crashed—due to enemy action. Enemy fighters heavily attacked A/C near target and #4 engine began smoking immediately after "bombs away." [Halloran told me later that fire from
a Japanese fighter hit the nose and electrical controls, preventing them from fully opening the bomb bay doors, so that *Lil
Lassie II* never had a "bombs away."] #1 engine also started
smoking and A/C was seen to go into half roll. It recovered
from the roll but had lost altitude and was attacked by 15 enemy fighters. A/C was seen to crash on land; there was no
visible explosion or fire.

Aircraft 42-24769 was *Lil Lassie II*. Six of the Rover Boys died
in the crash, but five—Snuffy Smith, the airplane commander;
Jim Edwards, pilot; Hap Halloran, navigator; Guy Knoebel,
radio operator; and Monk Nickolson, radarman—escaped
death by parachuting from their stricken aircraft. They were
held captive by the Japanese until war's end.

The 73rd Bomb Wing had lost nine airplanes—the most that
would be lost by a B-29 wing in a single mission during the
war—but had not dropped a single bomb on its primary target,
the Nakajima plant at Musashino. It did little or no damage to
the secondary target, a section of Tokyo's industrial and dock
area. However, the 62 Superforts in combat that day had made
a major contribution in the air war against Japan. In taking on
over 300 enemy fighters in 984 individual attacks, they shot
down 60 airplanes and counted 56 more as probably shot
down. In doing so they had taken a first big step in cracking
Japanese fighter defense of the home islands. The Japanese
would never again send up such a large force against B-29s.

LeMay must have found the losses his bombers had inflicted on the enemy some consolation for the poor bombing
results. But he was also concerned about the cost to his own
airmen. Consequently, on 28 January, he proposed to Norstad
that he send his bombers to another, less heavily defended,
target. He suggested the Mitsubishi plant at Tamashima.
Norstad responded with the recommendation that LeMay run
an incendiary attack on Kobe because he felt that Tamashima
was not an important enough target to make the Japanese
change their air defense deployment. An attack on Kobe, Japan's sixth largest city, its busiest port and a major industrial

producer, might accomplish this and, at the same time, provide information lacking from Hansell's incendiary test raid on Nagoya on 3 January. LeMay agreed and asked Col. Montgomery to plan the mission.

In the attack on Kobe, the XXI Bomber Command, for the first time, sent airplanes from the 313th Bomb Wing over Japan. Two of the 313th's groups (the other two would not be on station until the end of February) had been training and flying from North Field, Tinian, since early January. The 313th was under the command of 41-year-old Brig. Gen. John H. Davies. "Big Jim," as he was called by those who worked directly under him, six foot four, with handsome, youthful features and broad shoulders, looked like a movie version of an Air Force general. Like O'Donnell, Davies distinguished himself as a bomber commander in the Pacific at the outbreak of the war. He returned to the United States in early 1944 and took command of the 313th Bomb Wing in April of that year. In June, while organizing and training the 313th, he flew to India with members of his staff and spent a month observing the operations of the XX Bomber Command. Davies flew to Tinian with advanced units of his Wing at the end of December 1944. During training and in the early days on Tinian, the combat crews of the 313th came to respect Davies' confident leadership, decisiveness and, as they would later learn, his great courage in combat. When the force attacking Kobe took off on 4 February, it included 72 airplanes of the 73rd Bomb Wing and 38 of the 313th Bomb Wing, a total of 110.

Because of heavy winds and navigation errors, only 69 airplanes bombed Kobe. Bombing upwind, they released 159 tons of M-69 incendiaries, losing only one B-29 to enemy action over the target. Poststrike photos showed fire damage covering about .15 square miles of the city, including three important industrial targets. (Postwar information, agreeing roughly with the poststrike estimate of the area burned, disclosed greater damage. Of the dozen factories that accounted for most of the city's war production, five were damaged. One of the two biggest shipyards had to reduce operations by 50 percent.)

Though the results, as known at the time, were somewhat better than those at Nagasaki, they fell far short of Norstad's expectations. With the weight of incendiaries dropped and the high winds (over 160 mph) encountered by the attacking aircraft, he had expected extensive fire spread. Norstad speculated that the lack of spread might have been due to effective firebreaks. This was because he assumed—mistakenly—that there would be high winds at the surface anytime there were 160 mph winds at bombing altitude. Disappointed and frustrated, on 12 February he radioed LeMay:

> We have run two test incendiary attacks [Nagoya and Kobe] the results of which have been inconclusive. It is absolutely necessary for us to know our capability with regard to incendiary attacks in the Japanese urban areas. We believe that the only diversion from the attack on the aircraft engine industry that is justifiable at this time is another major incendiary attack. It is recommended that the center of Zone I of Nagoya be used as the target. The immediate purpose of this attack is to produce a conflagration that is beyond the capacity of fire-fighting control.

Norstad wanted at least 300 tons of M-69s placed on the target—about twice the tonnage delivered in each of the two previous tests. After asking that each aircraft carry a 500-lb GP bomb for marking purposes, he suggested that if the wind direction on the ground could be determined prior to takeoff, the airplanes should bomb perpendicular to this direction. The latter request must have been greeted with some amazement by Montgomery and his assistants on Guam. They were seldom able to predict the wind and weather conditions at bombing altitudes 1,500 miles distant, much less determine wind direction on the ground in the same area.

LeMay was not yet ready to mount an attack of this size but continued to press his attacks on Japan's aircraft industry. Through clear skies 84 aircraft from the 73rd and 313th Bomb Wings dropped 248 tons of bombs on an important Nakajima aircraft plant at Ota, the largest tonnage yet dropped on a target in Japan. Despite the rare visual bombing conditions, only a small proportion of the bombs fell on the target. Aggressive enemy fighter attacks probably contributed to bombing inaccuracy. Even so, considerable damage was done, but at a high cost—12 B-29s lost and 29 damaged.

LeMay's next two strikes continued the precision campaign against aircraft plants, but with an additional purpose—to support the invasion of Iwo Jima scheduled for 19 February.

Navy and Army planners believed that B-29 attacks on the Japanese mainland before and during the amphibious landings on Iwo Jima would draw off some support to forces defending the important Japanese bastion. In addition, the 5-mile-long volcanic island midway between the Marianas and Japan had, from the beginning, been a major impediment to the XXI Bomber Command operations. It was a bomber and fighter base threatening the Marianas bases. B-29s en route to and from targets in Japan had to fly a course avoiding the island, which increased fuel requirements and reduced bombloads. Even so, radar on Iwo could pick them up and give early warning of their approach to Japan's air defenses. In American hands these problems would no longer exist. Iwo could serve as a staging area and emergency landing field for B-29s, be a base for fighters to escort B-29s to Japan and play an important role in air-sea rescue efforts.

The target for LeMay's first strike—scheduled four days before the Iwo landings—was the Mitsubishi engine works at Nagoya—the XXI's fourth trip there. En route 117 aircraft of the 73rd and 313th Wings hit a severe cold front with poor visibility and icing conditions that broke up their formations and hampered navigation. As a result only 33 airplanes bombed the plant, causing only superficial damage; nevertheless, most of the others dropped on Hamamatsu, a rail and industrial center, with considerable effect.

For the next two days, 16–17 February, airplanes from Adm. Marc A. Mitscher's Task Force 58 ranged over the Tokyo area in force. On the first day, in the face of rain and snow squalls, the Navy's fast carriers launched nearly 1,000 sorties, mostly fighters. Their mission was to knock out enemy air opposition. By the end of the two-day attack, the carrier pilots would claim 340 Japanese aircraft shot down and 190 destroyed on the ground. These massive losses, though not a "knockout" blow, on top of the aircraft shot down by LeMay's B-29s severely crippled the Japanese Army and Air Forces. The Japanese could replace some of the planes but not the hundreds of experienced combat pilots lost.

On the second day, Navy Helldiver dive-bombers and Avenger torpedo bombers struck hard at Japanese aircraft factories in the Tokyo area. One of their targets was the B-29 nemesis—Musashino. Loosing their bombs and rockets from low altitude with accuracy, the Navy pilots caused substantial damage to the big engine plant. In the two-day operation the carriers lost 88 aircraft, 60 to enemy action. In successfully attacking the aircraft plants on their first effort through bad weather, the Navy had, at least partially, made good on thoughts the Fifth Fleet Commander, Adm. Raymond A. Spruance expressed to a fellow admiral three months before when he said that it was time to "stop fighting the products of the Jap aircraft factories on the perimeter and take our carrier air into the center to knock out the factories themselves. We cannot afford to await the outcome of bombing with 'precision instruments' from 30,000 feet, often enough through solid overcast [an obvious reference to B-29 bombing]."

The Navy's raids drew headlines in the United States. The New York *Times* called it "the most daring operation of the Pacific war to date."

Gen. Arnold, still recuperating in Florida, wrote on 16 February to his Chief of Staff, Maj. Gen. Barney M. Giles, and expressed concern about two newspaper articles he had seen— one about the one-thousandth B-29 produced by the Wichita plant and the other about the Navy's 1,500 planes having hit the Tokyo area. Arnold estimated that if the Wichita plant had produced a thousand B-29s, the other two B-29 plants together must have produced at least another thousand. That being so, he felt that "if sixty or eighty is a maximum we can put over the Japanese mainland, a change in management is certainly in order." Arnold went on to say that either Nimitz or MacArthur would have every right to claim that if they had command of the B-29s, they could get more airplanes over Japan than the Twentieth Air Force was getting. Arnold counseled Giles that he would hear many reasons for not sending two, three or four hundred B-29s over Japan, but "all of these reasons must be pushed to one side with a grim determination."

Across the Pacific, LeMay didn't need any such reminder from his boss. With the Navy's success just two days old, LeMay sent 150 airplanes, the largest number dispatched against Japan up to that time, against Musashino. Thick clouds blanketed the plant entirely, forcing the attacking force to drop on the secondary target, Tokyo's port and urban area. This was the XXI's seventh try at Musashino, and once again it had resulted in failure.

LeMay AND HIS top commanders were not alone in finding this latest failure in their precision bombing campaign a source of disappointment and frustration. By now the crews, particularly those of the 73rd Bomb Wing, a number of whom had flown over 15 combat missions, were showing the effects of the lackluster bombing campaign to which they were committed. An undated report entitled "Human Elements of the Operations of This Command" reviewed the psychological status of flight personnel of the XXI Bomber Command in late February and thereafter. (Though the report is unsigned, the language strongly suggests that the author was a flight surgeon.) The report stated that even though maintenance had improved, combat crews still lacked confidence in the mechanical reliability of their aircraft. The increased aggressiveness of Japanese fighters and rising number of airplanes shot down was causing concern. But the most disheartening factor was their inability to put their bombs on the target and begin to accomplish their mission, which was to destroy Japan's aircraft factories and urban industrial areas. Morale was low, the writer noted, but he and his professional associates found new cases of individual disintegration from anxiety. What they did find was a dutiful "flying of missions." Most crews tried to do their duty to the best of their ability, but went about it with a dull emotional tone, lacking in enthusiasm and hope for eventual success. They sought a rotation policy (none had been established) so that after a fixed number of combat missions a crew member would be eligible to return to the United States. The report concluded that "Symbolically this 'something to shoot for' was not connected with waging the war or defeating the enemy but with home, security and reward for the dutiful completion of a hopeless task." Only the more visionary individuals were able to maintain a satisfactory emotional tone toward their combat duties.

LeMay was aware of his crews' problems and more. He did not have to see Arnold's letter to Giles to know that in the arena of high command, the B-29's record was becoming a liability to Arnold rather than an example of strategic air power at its best, an example he had hoped to use postwar to help justify a separate air force. Clearly, as the commander in the field, LeMay knew that he alone was in a position to inject success into the faltering air campaign. Just four months before, the AAF had used the recommendations of the COA to set the objectives for the air attack on Japan: first, destroy key aircraft plants; second, attack the cities with incendiaries; third, mine Japanese waters. LeMay had tried to achieve the first objective by using precision bombing and had achieved little. As a seasoned air commander, he reasoned that if he couldn't hit the primary target, he should continue the attack and drop his bombs on his secondary target—the cities.

The XXI Bomber Command was scheduled for another mission in support of the invasion of Iwo Jima. LeMay's original intent was, in coordination with a carrier strike scheduled for 25 February, to hit Musashino with another precision strike. As the date approached, his weather officer predicted that the Tokyo area would, once again, be covered with heavy clouds. Based on this prediction, LeMay ordered a maximum-effort incendiary attack using radar against an urban-industrial area of Tokyo.

On the evening of 24 February, 229 B-29s—a force twice the size of any sent over Japan before—took to the air. In addition to planes of the 73rd and 313th Bomb Wings, for the first time a bomb group from the newly arrived 314th Wing, just establishing itself at North Field on Guam, joined the two wings flying from Saipan and Tinian. With 454 tons of M-69s aboard, this would be a major test for the incendiary.

SEVEN

BLACK SNOW

THE JAPANESE 10TH Air Division was still recovering from the U.S. Navy's onslaught of the week before, when a picket boat, one of a Japanese fleet of about 50, stationed about 500 miles off the coast, sighted and reported an American carrier task force. At about the same time, the division commander learned that B-29s based on the Marianas were preparing for a large-scale attack.

The Japanese air commander obtained this information from a special intelligence unit that had only recently been assigned to his division. Officers and men assigned to this unit were fluent in English and trained in cryptoanalysis. They obtained information on enemy operations by intercepting and deciphering American military radio communications. The American air bases on Guam, Tinian and Saipan were among their prime radio surveillance targets. In this case the unit was able to give notice of preparation activity for an attack; at other times it could tell the commander of the time of takeoff. The unit also tried to intercept American weather reports and, by interpreting them, along with other information, estimate the course of the attacking force and its probable target. How much of this precise information the intelligence team gave the 10th Air Division commander is not known. All he could do was brace for what he expected to be a combined attack by both B-29s and Navy carrier aircraft. Fortunately for the Japanese, the Navy did not attack Honshu but hit the island of Hachijo Jima to the south.

Besides its size and big load of M-69 bombs, the force winging its way to Japan on 25 February had another distinction. Normally, on daylight precision missions, formations were authorized to bomb by radar only if nearing the target they found it obscured. Because a blanket of thick clouds was known to exist over most of the island of Honshu, the field order for this mission called for both radar navigation and radar bombing.

After flying from their bases in loose formation at about 2,500 feet, as was by now customary, the wings were to assemble over the island of Nishino Jima, about 300 miles south of Japan. After assembly the wings were to climb to bombing altitude, 26,000 feet, and were expected to reach this altitude at about the time they made landfall. According to the weather forecast the wings would already have been above the heavy cloud layer by this time. The attacking bombers were given a radar checkpoint for making landfall, Hamana Lake, close to the coast southwest of Tokyo. It was a good checkpoint because the reflection of a radar signal from an area that includes both land and water appears with great clarity on a radar scope. The same could not be said of the initial point, the geographic location from which the bombers were to begin their bomb run to the target. The initial point, a familiar one to veteran crews, was the city of Kofu, due west of Tokyo. Though easy to recognize visually, Kofu was difficult to identify by radar because the terrain there did not give the radar observer the benefit of land-water contrast. After turning at Kofu, with expected 150 mph winds blowing from behind them, they were to fly a course to the aiming point. The aiming point was located in the center of the target area, a section of north Tokyo. The point lay about 3.5 miles up the Sumida River from its mouth on Tokyo Bay, and both the river and the bay were easily distinguishable on radar. In terms of the navigation and bombing, this mission, as planned, would be like one executed at night. The major difference was

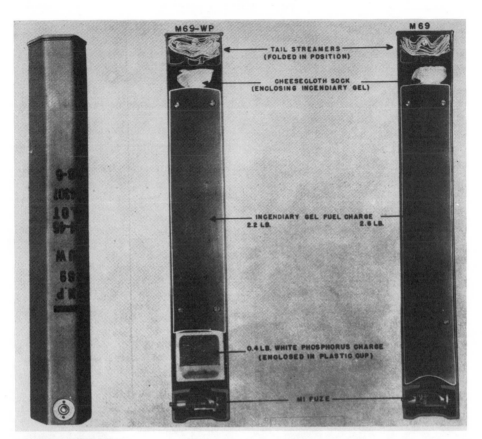

An M-69 incendiary bomb, external and cross-section views. (The M-69-WP, center view, was in production at the end of World War II but was never used.) *(National Archives)*

A 500 lb. aimable cluster of M-69 bombs. Each cluster held 38 bombs. A single B-29 could carry 40 clusters, or about 1,520 fire bombs. *(National Archives)*

A single M-69 test bomb destroys a Japanese-type house. Pictures show the structure before the bomb was fired and at 10, 15 and 20 minutes thereafter. *(National Archives)*

General H. H. Arnold, Commanding General, United States Army Air Forces. *(USAF Photo, National Archives, NASA Museum, Smithsonian Institution)*

Raymond H. Ewell, National Defense Research Committee. Ewell was a key planner and staunch advocate of incendiary warfare. *(Courtesy of Mrs. R. H. Ewell)*

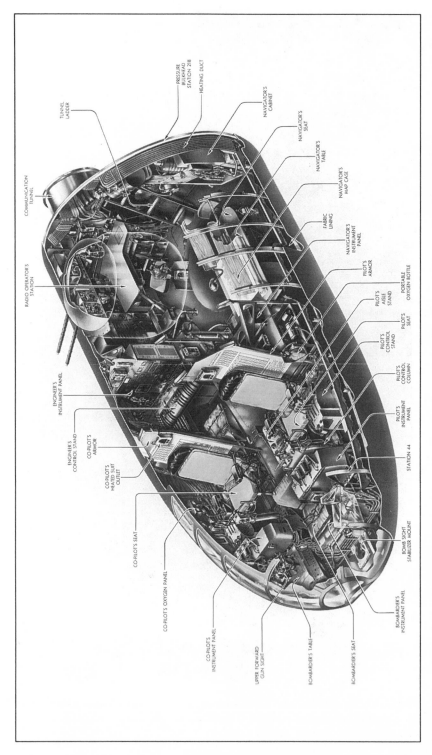

PRESSURE
BULKHEAD
STATION 218

HEATING DUCT

NAVIGATOR'S
CABINET

NAVIGATOR'S
SEAT

NAVIGATOR'S
TABLE

NAVIGATOR'S
MAP CASE

FABRIC
LINING

NAVIGATOR'S
INSTRUMENT
PANEL

PILOT'S ARMOR

PORTABLE
OXYGEN BOTTLE

PILOT'S
AISLE
STAND

PILOT'S SEAT

PILOT'S
CONTROL
STAND

PILOT'S
CONTROL
COLUMN

PILOT'S
INSTRUMENT
PANEL

STATION 44

BOMB SIGHT
STABILIZER MOUNT

BOMBARDIER'S
INSTRUMENT PANEL

BOMBARDIER'S SEAT

BOMBARDIER'S TABLE

UPPER FORWARD
GUN SIGHT

CO-PILOT'S
INSTRUMENT PANEL

CO-PILOT'S OXYGEN PANEL

CO-PILOT'S SEAT

CO-PILOT'S
HEATED SUIT
OUTLET

CO-PILOT'S ARMOR

ENGINEER'S
CONTROL STAND

ENGINEER'S
INSTRUMENT PANEL

RADIO OPERATOR'S
STATION

COMMUNICATION
TUNNEL

TUNNEL
LADDER

A cutaway view of the Forward Crew Compartment (Pressurized) of an early production model of the B-29 shows the crew positions, instrumentation and other features of the aircraft. (*Boeing Company Archives*)

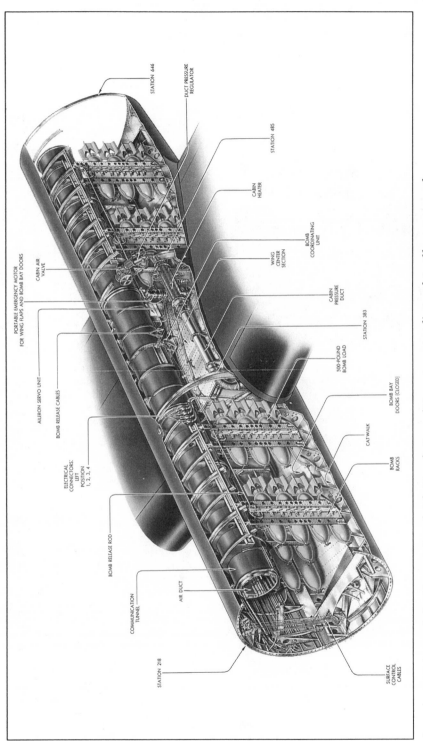

A cutaway view of the Forward and Aft Bomb Bays (Unpressurized). In this illustration the bomb load is made up of 500 lb. high explosive bombs which, for incendiary missions, could be replaced by 500 lb. aimable clusters of M-69 bombs. (*Boeing Company Archives*)

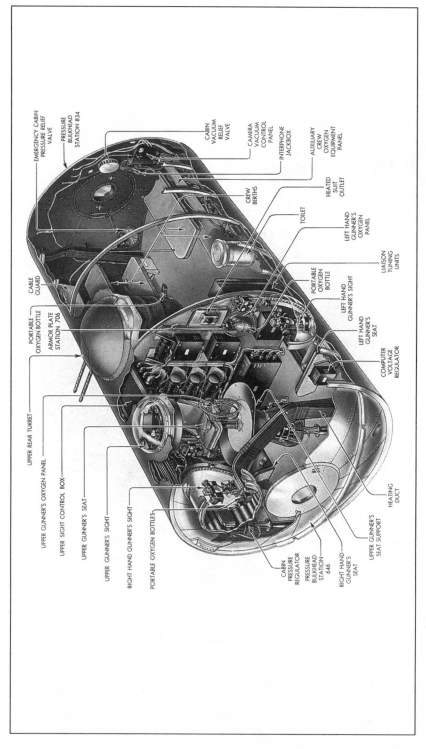

EMERGENCY CABIN PRESSURE RELIEF VALVE

PRESSURE BULKHEAD STATION 834

CABIN VACUUM RELIEF VALVE

CAMERA VACUUM CONTROL PANEL

INTERPHONE JACKBOX

AUXILIARY CREW OXYGEN EQUIPMENT PANEL

HEATED SUIT OUTLET

CREW BERTHS

TOILET

LEFT HAND GUNNER'S OXYGEN PANEL

LIAISON TUNING UNITS

PORTABLE OXYGEN BOTTLE

LEFT HAND GUNNER'S SIGHT

LEFT HAND GUNNER'S SEAT

COMPUTER VOLTAGE REGULATOR

CABLE GUARD

PORTABLE OXYGEN BOTTLE

ARMOR PLATE STATION 706

UPPER REAR TURRET

UPPER GUNNER'S OXYGEN PANEL

UPPER SIGHT CONTROL BOX

UPPER GUNNER'S SEAT

UPPER GUNNER'S SIGHT

RIGHT HAND GUNNER'S SIGHT

PORTABLE OXYGEN BOTTLES

CABIN PRESSURE REGULATOR

PRESSURE BULKHEAD STATION 646

RIGHT HAND GUNNER'S SEAT

UPPER GUNNER'S SEAT SUPPORT

HEATING DUCT

A cutaway view of the Rear Crew Compartment (Pressurized) shows the gunner's positions and their equipment. In all B-29s sent into combat, radar equipment and a position for the radar observer replaced the crew berths shown in this early model. *(Boeing Company Archives)*

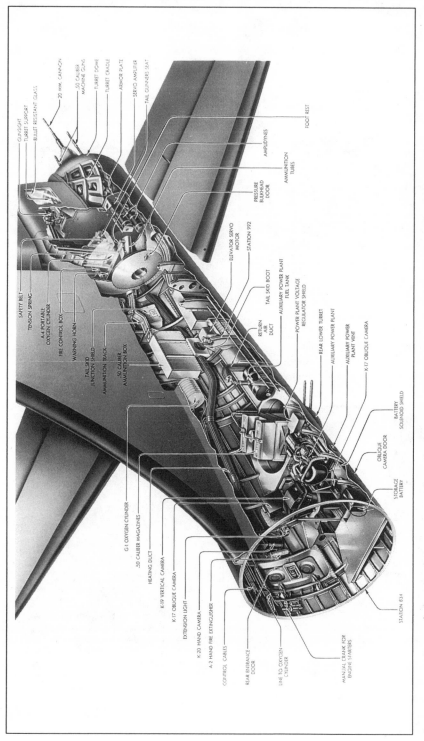

GUNSIGHT
TURRET SUPPORT
BULLET RESISTANT GLASS
20 MM. CANNON
.50 CALIBER MACHINE GUNS
TURRET DOME
TURRET CRADLE
ARMOR PLATE
SERVO AMPLIFIER
TAIL GUNNER'S SEAT
FOOT REST

AMPLIDYNES
AMMUNITION TUBES
PRESSURE BULKHEAD DOOR

SAFETY BELT
TENSION SPRING
A-4 PORTABLE OXYGEN CYLINDER
FIRE CONTROL BOX
WARNING HORN
TAIL SKID JUNCTION SHIELD
AMMUNITION TRACK
.50 CALIBER AMMUNITION BOX

ELEVATOR SERVO MOTOR
STATION 992
TAIL SKID BOOT
AUXILIARY POWER PLANT FUEL TANK
POWER PLANT VOLTAGE REGULATOR SHIELD
RETURN AIR DUCT
REAR LOWER TURRET
AUXILIARY POWER PLANT
AUXILIARY POWER PLANT VENT
K-17 OBLIQUE CAMERA

BATTERY SOLENOID SHIELD

OBLIQUE CAMERA DOOR

STORAGE BATTERY

G-1 OXYGEN CYLINDER
.50 CALIBER MAGAZINES
HEATING DUCT
K-19 VERTICAL CAMERA
K-17 OBLIQUE CAMERA
EXTENSION LIGHT
K-20 HAND CAMERA
A-2 HAND FIRE EXTINGUISHER
CONTROL CABLES
REAR ENTRANCE DOOR
LINE TO OXYGEN CYLINDER
MANUAL CRANK FOR ENGINE STARTERS

STATION 834

A cutaway view of the Tail Section and Tail Gunner's Compartment (Pressurized) shows the B-29's cameras, auxiliary power equipment and the tail gunner's lonely location. (*Boeing Company Archives*)

Brigadier General Haywood S. Hansell, Chief of Staff, Twentieth Air Force (April-August 1944) and Commanding General, XXI Bomber Command (August 1944-January 1945). *(USAF Photo, NASA, Smithsonian Institution)*

Brigadier General Lauris Norstad, Chief of Staff, Twentieth Air Force (August 1944-July 1945). *(USAF Photo, NASA, Smithsonian Institution)*

Brigadier General Emmett O'Donnell, Commanding General, 73rd Bomb Wing. *(USAF Photo, NASA, Smithsonian Institution)*

Brigadier General Roger Ramey, Commanding General, 58th Bomb Wing (from May 1945). *(USAF Photo, NASA, Smithsonian Institution)*

Brigadier General John R. Davies, Commanding General, 313th Bomb Wing. *(USAF Photo, NASA, Smithsonian Institution)*

Brigadier General Thomas S. Power, Commanding General, 314th Bomb Wing. Shown here as SAC Commanding General. *(USAF Photo)*

Major General Curtis LeMay, Commanding General of the XX Bomber Command, Twentieth Air Force (August 1944-January 1945) and the XXI Bomber Command (January-July 1945). *(USAF Photo, NASA, Smithsonian Institution)*

LeMay with the wing commanders who led the March 9-10, 1945 fire raid on Tokyo that burnt out an area of 15.8 square miles and took more than 83,000 lives. (From left to right, Brig. Gens. John H. Davies, Thomas S. Power, Maj. Gen. Curtis E. LeMay, and Brig. Gen. Emmett O'Donnell. *(National Archives)*

Tinian, the Mariana Islands, base for the 313th and 58th Bomb
Wings, as it appeared from a plane directly over neighboring Saipan,
the 73rd Bomb Wing's base of operations. *(USAF Photo courtesy of
H. Willis and H. Changnon)*

Mechanics get one of the
big engines ready for a
combat mission. *(USAF
Photo, NASA, Smithsonian
Institution)*

A ground crewman moves a 500 lb. cluster of M-69 incendiaries into position to load it into the rear bomb bay of a B-29. *(USAF Photo, NASA, Smithsonian Institution)*

B-29s wait their turn to take off for the long trip to Tokyo. *(USAF Photo, NASA, Smithsonian Institution)*

Four B-29s fly past Mount Fuji enroute to Tokyo. *(USAF Photo, NASA, Smithsonian Institution)*

Tokyo, as fires start on the night of March 9-10. *(USAF Photo, NASA, Smithsonian Institution)*

Tokyo burning on the afternoon of March 10, 1945. In the center of the photograph, note the distinctive "Y-mouth" of the Sumida River and the Imperial Palace Grounds, the dark oval space above the Sumida. *(USAF Photo, courtesy of R. F. Halloran)*

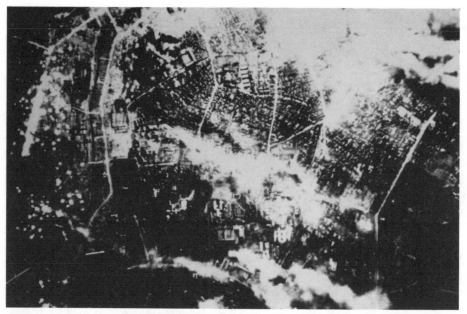

Flames and smoke mark Tokyo in this photograph taken during the last fire raid on the city, May 25-26, 1945. After this raid LeMay's target planners removed Tokyo from the list of productive targets for mass incendiary attacks. *(National Archives)*

Burnt out areas on each side of Tokyo's Sumida River, resulting from the fire raids of March-May 1945. Many of the buildings left standing were gutted by the fires that burned all around them. *(USAF Photo, NASA, Smithsonian Institution)*

A view from a low-flying aircraft of an area of Tokyo, showing the terrible destructiveness of the fire raids. Only a few buildings and smoke stacks survived. *(USAF Photo, courtesy of R. F. Halloran)*

Hundreds of 500 lb. clusters of M-69 bombs rain down from seven B-29s, part of a larger force on a daylight incendiary mission over one of Japan's cities. *(USAF Photo, courtesy of W. J. Sherrell)*

Toyama, Japan, aflame during the predawn hours of August 2, 1945. Virtually all of the city's built-up area was destroyed, making this the most destructive incendiary raid of the war. *(USAF Photo, courtesy of W. J. Sherrell)*

that the bombers were expected to be in 12-ship formations on reaching the coast of Japan and proceed to the target and bomb in formation. This they never accomplished.

As the operations planners would learn, one assembly point is not adequate for three wings. After an uneventful six-hour flight up from the Marianas, airplanes arriving at the assembly point began the always difficult task of locating their squadron mates after the dispersion that inevitably occurred en route. This time it was further complicated by the large number of aircraft circling around in the designated area. The more experienced 73rd and 313th Wings finally assembled, but not without tragedy. Two aircraft of the 73rd Wing's 497th Bomb Group collided and exploded just before reaching the assembly point. The 314th Wing did not attempt to assemble.

The climb to bombing altitude was through dense clouds and freezing temperature. Two airplanes iced up so badly they could not even reach the required altitude. Of those that finally struggled up through the clouds, only one squadron was in formation. After some circling and attempts to gain formations, most of the aircraft gave up. The aircraft, individually or in small groups, next headed for the initial point. A number of airplanes had difficulty locating Kofu on their radar and, failing this, set their own course for the target area. Nearing Tokyo, all of the airplanes had little difficulty identifying the aiming point on their radar. Because of their navigation and weather problems, the aircraft arrived over the target area individually or in small groups, at altitudes from 23,000 to 30,000 feet, from a variety of directions. The attack lasted over an hour and a half. One hundred and seventy airplanes dropped 411 tons of M-69 incendiaries through the clouds on a snow-blanketed Tokyo.

FATHER GUSTAV BITTER, rector of the Jesuit house at Sophia University, a Christian institution located in Tokyo, had watched the snow begin falling about ten o'clock that morning. Earlier he and other Tokyo residents had heard the air raid sirens' three-minute-long warning blast, but later an all-clear sounded. (They expected an attack from Navy carriers that hit the island of Hachijo to the south.) Most people relaxed and went about their business, but Father Bitter didn't. Before entering the priesthood he had been a soldier under the Kaiser and had fought against the French in World War I. He had not lost that sixth sense of impending trouble that some combat soldiers have. He told his secretary, Peter Ito, that he felt a big raid was coming. A short time later sirens sounded again. Ito turned on the radio and heard that enemy planes were nearing the city. Short, successive blasts from the sirens for one minute confirmed that danger was imminent, so Father Bitter put on a helmet and climbed four flights of stairs to the rectory roof. The snow was falling heavily now, and he could not make out the landmarks of Tokyo that were usually visible from his vantage point—the grounds of the Emperor's estate, the white-marbled embassies and legations, the gray stone tower of the Diet building, and the Japanese military's most revered place, the Yasakuni Shrine. As he stood there he heard, very near, and very low, the deep, pulsing rumble of the *Bi-ni-ku-ju*—B-29s—filling the sky. Bitter did not hear any bombs explode, but soon saw, in several directions, areas of orange glowing through falling snow. The orange areas grew in size, and as the fires burned, the smoke, seemingly trapped at roof level, darkened the sky and blackened the falling snow. Father Bitter watched until long after the airplanes had left and finally, in the darkness, descended the stairs.

In the embassy and legation area, Lars Tillitse, Danish Minister to Japan, also heard approaching enemy airplanes. He was in his house with his servants and two Japanese policemen when they heard a loud rattling sound as if something were falling close by. Everyone ducked, but nothing exploded. When they went out and looked down the street, they saw a section of wooden houses burning fiercely. What Tillitse and his companions had heard was the clatter of scores of M-69 bombs striking the roofs of the houses and the paved street between.

Above the city, the B-29s were having an easy time. They dropped their bombs with virtually no opposition, as no fighters rose to meet them. Amazed but pleased, the Americans could only assume that the weather had prevented fighters from taking off. Antiaircraft fire was sporadic and ineffective. The thick clouds obscuring the planes were one reason. The other was that Japanese soldiers manning sound detectors and the few radar sets were used to large formations that nearly always came from the west. This time, the planes were coming over singly or in small formations, and from several different directions. Confused, the Japanese were unable to direct fire accurately against this different method of attack.

Brig. Gen. Thomas S. Power, commander of the 314th Wing, was in one of the 22 aircraft of his 19th Bomb Group, which was returning unscathed from its first mission. Power had earned his commission and wings at Kelly Field, Texas, in 1929, the same year as LeMay. After Pearl Harbor and a series of rapid promotions to the grade of colonel, and operations and training assignments in the United States, he went overseas in January 1944 as deputy commander of the 304th Bomb Wing. He flew B-24 bombers in combat until August of that year, when he was ordered back to the United States to assume command of the 314th Bomb Wing being formed at Peterson Field, Colorado. In January 1945, prior to flying out with the first group of the 314th Wing to Guam, he was promoted to brigadier general.

Power had sought and welcomed positions of responsibility. All business, he expected a lot of himself and those who worked for him. He was direct of manner and not prone to lighthearted banter. Many of his contemporaries had him tagged as a man "on the way up."

On the seven-hour return flight, Power had plenty of time to reflect on the mission just completed. Several of its features must have caught his attention. First, having studied the reports of the XXI Bomber Command's past missions, he was surprised by the almost complete lack of opposition that day. Where, he asked himself, were all the Japanese fighters and antiaircraft guns that had taken such a heavy toll of American aircraft and lives on 27 January? The weather had been bad at the target and nearby fighter bases, but Japan's better pilots had not let this deter them from attacking B-29s before. True, the Japanese had taken some pretty heavy fighter losses in the past month, particularly from Navy carrier planes. What was puzzling was that this time the Japanese had twice as many B-29s for targets as they had ever had before. Could it have been, he pondered, that the pattern of attack—bombing by one and twos—had confounded the Japanese defenders? If so, would a plan which *dictated* that the attacking force approach the target from different directions and bomb individually have a similar effect on Japanese defenses? What's more, since the bomber force had made it all the way to the target by means of radar, why couldn't a mission of this size or larger be carried out at night? He recognized the possibility that the airplanes on the mission had only been "lucky" in their navigation and bombing, and that others trying a similar method of attack might end up being blown way off target by 150-mph crosswinds. However, one way to avoid the wind problem would be to drop the bombing level to lower altitudes. Power was intrigued with these thoughts and decided that after talking them over with his staff he would discuss them with LeMay.

What Power did not know as he flew back toward Guam was that in spite of the disrupted attack plan, the bombers had achieved excellent results. The more than 2,000, 500-lb M-69 clusters they had dropped through the snow had set fires that destroyed more than 26 million square feet of built-up area— roughly one square mile. This was ten times the area burned by the 29 November incendiary raid.

As HE LOOKED over reports of his most successful raid to date, LeMay also read news reports of an RAF raid on a German city just two weeks before. On the night of 13 February, hundreds of British bombers attacked Dresden, a center of art and culture with relatively few military targets within its boundaries, unloading tons of incendiaries and high-explosive bombs that burned out the core of the city. American bombers followed with two attacks on Dresden's rail marshaling yards, dropping 296 tons of incendiaries and 475 tons of high explosives. Physical destruction was widespread. Postwar estimates of the death toll ranged from 30,000 to 60,000.

Press reports on this raid led to questions of whether the

AAF would attack purely civilian targets. A few days after the Dresden raid an Associated Press correspondent, after listening to a British press briefing on the raid, posted a story that reported: "Allied air bosses have made the long-awaited decision to adopt deliberate terror bombing of the great German population centers as a ruthless expedient to hasten Hitler's doom." It had, nonetheless, been the British policy for years to use area bombing to disrupt the social fabric of German society (in Churchill's words, "dehouse" them) as well as to destroy industrial plants and kill workers. American involvement in such a strategy was new and, to some in Washington, disconcerting. In a flurry of activity, AAF headquarters asked Gen. Carl Spaatz, commander of AAF units in England, for his views. He replied that the city did have military significance and that "civilian populations are not suitable military objectives." On 22 February 1945 Secretary of War Stimson announced that "Our policy never has been to inflict terror bombing on civilian populations" and explained that Dresden and other major transportation hubs did have military significance—they helped feed and supply the troops we were fighting. Two weeks later Gen. Arnold, still recuperating in Florida, would downplay concern over the bombing with a marginal notation he put on a report sent to him by Gen. Giles, his Chief of Staff in the Pentagon. Arnold noted: "We must not get soft. War must be destructive and to a certain extent inhuman and ruthless."

Equally undeterred by the furor were the principals in the air war against Japan—Norstad and LeMay. In Washington, Norstad, with evidence that the highly touted M-69 could accomplish what its advocates claimed, was disposed to moving ahead with the long-standing plan to destroy the war-making potential of Japan's major cities.

On Guam, LeMay realized it was not a matter of *whether* to launch the intensive attack on Japan's cities, but *when*. Months before, Arnold had placed the bombing of Japan's urban areas right behind aircraft plants on the XXI Bomber Command's priority list. Washington had established two prerequisites for the initiation of urban attacks: First, the M-69 incendiary bomb, which had been developed and tested exhaustively in the United States, had to be proven efficient against Japanese cities. It had done that. Second, enough B-29s would have to be based in the Marianas to launch a series of powerful incendiary strikes in a short period of time. Within two weeks LeMay would have the capability of sending more than 300 airplanes per mission to Japan. He knew he must attack the cities soon. He also knew that it was his sole responsibility to decide, in a matter of days, how these attacks—perhaps the ultimate test of the B-29's worth in the war against Japan—should be carried out.

This would become one of the most important decisions of the Pacific War, and LeMay was uniquely qualified to make it. Among his great strengths was an extraordinary ability to immerse himself in the details of a complex problem and extract from a number of proposals and divergent views the essential information needed to make his own analysis and arrive at a sound, innovative solution. He could rely on his experience as a bomber commander at virtually every level of combat command in both the European and the Pacific theaters. Also, he could turn to his able Operations and Planning staff headed by Col. Montgomery and his combat-experienced Wing commanders. Except for ordering what proved to be another unsuccessful high-level precision strike against the Nakajima plant at Musashino, LeMay spent the rest of February and the early days of March reviewing information on the command's operations, consulting Montgomery and his Wing commanders, smoking the inevitable cigar and thinking.

The plan that emerged constituted a radical change from the strategic bombing doctrine and the tactics used by the AAF in Europe and the Pacific Theater up to that time. LeMay proposed, and subsequently ordered, an attack in which the B-29—designed as a high-altitude, daylight precision bomber to be used for visual bombing from large formations—would drop incendiary bombs by radar, at night, flying individually at altitudes between 7,000 and 8,000 feet. Each feature of LeMay's plan was a change from the intended use of the big bomber. By far the most radical and daring element of his plan was reducing the bombing altitude from 26,000 to less than 8,000 feet.

This was not the first time the AAF had considered using heavy bombers at low altitudes. Less than three months before, the staff of the United States Strategic Air Force in Europe developed a plan called CLARION; subtitled "General Plan for Maximum Effort Attack Against Transportation Objectives," it called for a series of attacks by small groups of bombers and fighters, at low levels, to bomb and strafe transportation targets all over Germany. Since most transportation centers were in or very close to populated areas the attacks were expected to kill many civilians. General Ira Eaker, Commanding General of U.S. Air Forces in the United Kingdom, in a letter to General Spaatz, objected to the plan; he felt it was an unwise use of heavy bombers and would expose them to unnecessary risks. He added that such an effort would divert the American air effort from its key precision target—oil—and serve as a precedent for those who wanted to use the bomber force for tactical purposes. Despite Eaker's objections CLARION was executed in February 1945 and some heavy bombers participated at low altitudes.

LeMay, unlike Eaker, apparently had little concern about "misusing" the B-29. His intent was to use the airplane in the most effective way; thus far, the major hindrance had been the weather: heavy cloud formations over Tokyo had permitted visual bombing only five days per month during December, January and February. Unrelenting winds at high altitudes had made it difficult to bomb accurately even on those days when the weather cleared. AAF doctrine—bombing visually from high altitude—was based on the assumption that sooner or later there would be favorable weather over an enemy target. Experience to date had shown that with respect to the skies over Japan this assumption was wrong. If LeMay decreased his bombing altitudes he could avoid most of the problems of high winds and poor visibility, but in so doing he would radically depart from AAF doctrine. He chose to do so.

LeMay listened to Power's ideas growing out of the 25 February mission and reasoned that if he dropped below the ferocious winds at the higher altitudes (low-level winds ranged from 10 to 30 mph), his crews would be relieved of the operational straitjacket—always bombing from the west—that those winds imposed. Freed from this constraint, he could use different axes of attack to keep the Japanese from setting up defenses along an expected path as they had done in the past, notably on 27 January when the 73rd Bomb Wing had suffered such heavy losses on the way to its target. He could also choose initial points, clearly identifiable on radar, from which to begin the bomb runs and not be restricted to those lying on a path directly west of target.

As significant as these advantages were, equal or perhaps greater were two others that would result from the low-altitude bomb run. They were, in effect, answers to a bomber commander's prayer—the ability to carry more bombs to the target and to drop them accurately. Elimination of the climb to 26,000 feet saved great amounts of fuel. The weight of the fuel saved could be traded for bomb load. Engines were also under less strain at reduced altitude. This could lead to fewer maintenance problems, so more bombers would be available to carry more bombs to the target. The increased engine efficiency would reduce the number of aircraft lost because of mechanical problems. Bombardiers would no longer have to contend with the effect of the winds at 26,000 feet. Errors in the use of the Norden bombsight decrease with a reduction in altitude, resulting in less dispersion of bombs and improved accuracy.

The advantages of the low-level approach were great but so were the risks that there would be heavy losses from enemy fighters and antiaircraft artillery. To minimize potential losses, LeMay decided to adopt the tactic the British had used since 1941 and that his veteran wing commander "Rosie" O'Donnell had months before felt was an effective means of employing the B-29—strike at night. He carefully surveyed enemy night fighter capabilities with his intelligence staff. His assessment—and it turned out correct—was that the Japanese Army and Navy Air Forces had only a few night fighter units. These were ill-equipped and poorly trained and should not constitute a serious threat. Antiaircraft batteries were another matter. At reduced altitudes the B-29s would be flying within range of most of the Japanese antiaircraft batteries stationed in and around the cities. But experience had shown that these batteries were not effective under low visibility or at night because Japanese target-acquisition and fire-direction radar and their sound detection equipment were inferior in both quality and quantity. Searchlights targeting the B-29s posed the most serious threat. But with the planes flying over the target area individually from different directions and at extremely low altitude, LeMay expected the searchlight batteries would be forced to contend with the elements of surprise and confusion.

Once LeMay had decided to bomb from low altitude at night, the decision for aircraft to attack individually became unavoidable. Formation flying at night with the B-29, even with formation and running lights (blue lights across the top of the wing, green on the right wing tip, red on the left wing tip and white on top of the rudder), was not feasible. An important advantage of having airplanes navigate and attack individually—a concept pioneered by the British with their "bomber streams" at night over Germany—was that it decreased fuel consumption. In formation flying each pilot had to constantly adjust his throttles, engine rpm and fuel mixture controls so as to maintain his position in the formation. This frequent adjustment in power settings was not necessary when flying individually, and as a result the engines functioned more efficiently. In fact, LeMay's planners estimated that the fuel savings would double the bomb load—from about 3 to more than 6 tons.

The method of individual attacks was, however, a major departure from the lead crew principle, which had become the major feature of combat flying in the Command. In daylight bombing, a lead crew, made up of the most experienced pilot, bombardier, navigator and radar observer available in the unit, navigated to the target and made the bomb run. All other airplanes in the formation flew and took their actions based on those of the lead aircraft. One of the unknowns was how well an average crew, accustomed to depending on the lead crew, would perform when sent on its own.

Several factors may have given LeMay and Montgomery a degree of assurance that the crews would perform adequately under the new conditions. One was that on high-altitude formation missions it was customary to fly individually on the return journey, usually at night. Thus many crews had substantial experience in solo night navigation. Another indication of "average crew" competence, when they knew they were on their own, was the 25 February all-radar mission in which all crews performed well and bombed accurately despite the adverse factors encountered. Finally, learning from that mission and his own combat experience, LeMay would have his operations planners select the most clearly defined initial points—with good land-water contrast on the radarscopes—and do the same for the aiming points.

Flying individually at night posed other problems, for which LeMay and his staff had rather innovative solutions. With hundreds of planes converging in the darkness on a target area 1,500 miles from base, there was a risk they might collide or mistakenly shoot at each other. To prevent collisions and for general control, LeMay planned to have the wings and bomb groups fly at different altitudes. To avoid accidentally shooting at each other and to increase the weight of bombs that could be carried, LeMay ordered that no ammunition would be carried on the mission and firing mechanisms would be removed from the guns. He issued this order with the belief that with the advantage of surprise and the ineffectiveness of Japanese night fighters, he would not be putting his crews at undue risk.

If his attack plan was daring and courageous, so was his schedule. Washington's long-standing guidance (based on the COA final report to Gen. Arnold in the fall of 1944) was that Japan's major cities should not be attacked until there was sufficient force to hit them in rapid succession. This would preclude the Japanese from developing methods for opposing these raids or dealing with the fires they started. LeMay planned maximum-effort incendiary attacks on Tokyo, Nagoya, Osaka and Kobe, in that order, all to be accomplished within a week.

With the major features of his plan in place, LeMay continued taking action to confirm its validity. He had O'Donnell conduct a test run sending a group of 12 B-29s to bomb a small island near Saipan at extremely low level. The test was a success. He instituted extra training for radar observers. The aspect of this training given most emphasis was the ability to identify at low level small spits of land of the type that would be used for navigation and aiming points in the upcoming mission. To be sure the points were clear, select crews flew night missions over Tokyo and the other target cities at 5,000 to 7,000 feet, taking radarscope photographs. They came back with excellent photos of landfalls, initial points and targets in each of the cities. They also reported surprisingly little Japanese antiaircraft fire and fighter activity. Leaving no source untapped, LeMay asked the U.S. Navy to give him any low-level radar photos it might have as a result of its forays over Tokyo and other cities, as well as any information it might be able to provide on enemy defenses against its low-level attacks.

As the overall plan took shape, Col. Montgomery had to translate LeMay's decisions into a field order that would carry them out. An early focus in the many grueling hours of detailed planning for the mission was the first target for over 300 B-29s—Tokyo.

The area of that city to be attacked had been specified as Zone I in the intelligence report "Japan–Incendiary Attack Data" of October 1943 on which Raymond Ewell and other experts of the NDRC had worked with members of the Air Staff. Zone I in Tokyo was a highly congested, roughly rectangular area, approximately 3 miles from east to west and 4 miles from north to south. Running diagonally across the rectangular area and roughly dividing it was the Sumida River.

The western side of Zone I ran from the Imperial Palace grounds north to Ueno Park, another prominent open space. The boundary then curved to the northeast along the Joban railroad until it crossed the Sumida River. From here it ran south along the eastern borders of the Honjo and Fukugawa wards for about 4 miles. The boundary then turned due west, crossed the Y-mouth of the Sumida and ended at the Imperial Palace grounds.

Zone I included six important targets contained on the Twentieth Air Force target list, the most important of which was the Hattori Company—in peacetime a watch manufac-

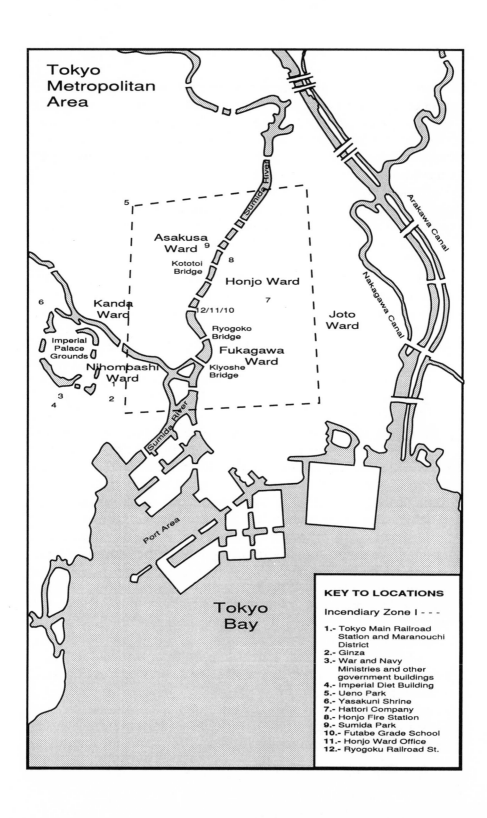

Tokyo
Metropolitan
Area

Sumida River

Arakawa Canal

Nakagawa Canal

5

Asakusa
Ward   9

Kototoi
Bridge

8

Honjo Ward

7

6

Kanda
Ward

Joto
Ward

Imperial
Palace
Grounds

12/11/10

Nihombashi
Ward   1

Ryogoko
Bridge

Fukagawa
Ward

3

2

Kiyoshe
Bridge

4

Sumida River

Port Area

Tokyo
Bay

KEY TO LOCATIONS

Incendiary Zone I - - -

1.- Tokyo Main Railroad
  Station and Maranouchi
  District
2.- Ginza
3.- War and Navy
  Ministries and other
  government buildings
4.- Imperial Diet Building
5.- Ueno Park
6.- Yasakuni Shrine
7.- Hattori Company
8.- Honjo Fire Station
9.- Sumida Park
10.- Futabe Grade School
11.- Honjo Ward Office
12.- Ryogoku Railroad St.

turer and in wartime a maker of fuzes for artillery shells and other precision military instruments. Other targets included railroad yards, stations, markets and storage areas.

Actually, more major targets existed in the area east of Zone I—over 35 plants, manufacturing everything from railroad cars to steel cable, guns to aircraft parts. The reason Zone I was designated to be hit first was that the zone contained a substantial area of industry and commerce intermixed with residences, was heavily populated and would require the least amount of M-69 incendiaries for total destruction.

In addition to its major targets, Office of Strategic Services studies had concluded that Tokyo's Zone I contained a large number of small plants employing 50 persons or less—"shadow factories." While some of these small factories were near (in the "shadow" of the large plants that they served as subcontractors), others were far removed, interspersed among dwelling areas and small shops. Also widespread and invisible from the air were the hundreds of "home industries" that produced small machine parts. Workers would pick up raw materials from a nearby plant and return with the finished product.

The Japanese armament and war material industries had yet other methods of boosting production. School authorities suspended academic work for many young Japanese in their third and fourth years of high school. They put these young people to work in factories, or in their own school buildings, assembling small parts for radios, aircraft and other military equipment.

Within Zone I and on the western side of the Sumida lay the Asakusa ward, the most populous of the 35 wards that made up greater Tokyo. With 135,000 inhabitants per square mile it was one of the most densely populated areas in the world. Most of the remainder of the zone, occupied by the Honjo and Fukugawa wards on the east side of the Sumida, had a population density of between 80,000 to 135,000 persons per square mile. About 1.1 million people—15 percent of Tokyo's population—lived and worked in Zone I.

No other residential area in the world equaled the "built-upness" (a term coined by fire and target evaluation experts of the time, which referred to the percentage of a given area covered by roofs) of Zone I. The roof area of the zone was 40 to 50 percent of the total area, including its streets, parks and rivers. By comparison, the average American residential area of the time was only about 10 percent built up.

Most of the dwellings in Zone I were of two-story wood frame construction, with tile or wood roofs. In many cases the first floor was used for the home workshop. Outside walls were covered with thin boards or bamboo lath and mud plaster. These houses were much the same as those test-bombed with M-69 incendiaries at Dugway Proving Ground in 1943, which had burned to the ground in minutes. Even more flammable were a large number of wooden barracks in the zone. After the great earthquake and fire of 1923 these barracks had been thrown up to meet immediate needs and were to be torn down later as part of the rebuilding of the city. This rebuilding was never accomplished, and the barracks had degenerated into permanent substandard housing.

As Ewell and his fellow scientists had told the AAF for nearly two years, Tokyo was extremely vulnerable to a devastating incendiary attack with all of its effects—great loss of civilian life and housing, as well as destruction and dislocation of war industry. As a bomber commander, LeMay had had to inure himself to civilian casualties in aerial warfare. In Europe his bombers had inflicted such casualties in bombing precision targets, and he was aware of the substantial number of civilians killed in nighttime area bombings conducted by the British. As a human being, but also a soldier, he had to suppress his feelings about killing civilians. After the war he would describe his reaction to German deaths:

> You drop a load of bombs, and if you are cursed with any imagination at all, you have at least one quick horrid glimpse of a child lying in bed with a whole ton of masonry tumbling down on top of him, or a three-year-old girl wailing for *Mutter* . . . *Mutter* . . . because she has burned. Then you have to turn away from the picture if you intend to retain your sanity. And also if you intend to keep doing the work your nation expects of you.

LeMay probably felt much the same about the Japanese civilian casualties his bombers would inflict in the massive incendiary attack he was planning.

Meanwhile, in the Quonset hut that housed LeMay's Target Section, officers were selecting aiming points on a map of Zone I. They chose four with clearly identifiable features, about 4,000 to 6,000 feet apart. One was in the Asakusa ward; another across the Sumida River in the Honjo ward; a third was in Fukugawa ward and the fourth was northeast of Tokyo Station. The planners estimated that about half of the bombs intended for a particular aiming point would fall within a 2,000-foot circle around that point. The rest would fall outside the circle but would overlap and merge with bombs aimed at the other points. The resulting blanket of fire would produce a conflagration.

On 5 March, men of the three wings were surprised at notices on their bulletin boards stating the XXI Bomber Command would not schedule another strike until 9 March. With the unprecedented delay between missions and the inevitable "leaks" from Bomber Command headquarters, these notices set off a whirlwind of speculation. Central to the rumors were the two major features of LeMay's plan—they would bomb from low level and at night. Suspense among the combat crews grew as they passed the time playing cards, making their Quonsets more livable, watching movies and waiting for the inevitable field order that would provide the "real dope."

If the combat crews were idle, most other members of the Command were not. In addition to Montgomery's operations staff, which was working around the clock to put the myriad details of the plan together, hundreds of aircraft maintenance crews were working equally long hours. Ordnance personnel were hauling thousands of tons of incendiary bombs from storage areas to aircraft hardstands because once the planned series of attacks started, they wouldn't have enough men, equipment or time to be traveling to the storage areas for the next load of bombs. In each group, aircraft maintenance officers made sure that all airplanes due for periodic inspections received them and as much other maintenance as could be accomplished. Specialists worked on aircraft that had been unready for combat because of battle damage or serious mechanical problems. Mechanics replaced defective or damaged generators, fuel pumps, drive motors and engines. Sheet-metal workers patched holes in airplanes damaged by antiaircraft fire. Electricians tested, repaired and adjusted electrical components. No effort was spared to prepare the maximum number of aircraft for combat.

Early on 8 March, the XXI Bomber Command issued Field Order #43—"Meetinghouse #2"—with amplifying details to the three wing headquarters. LeMay radioed the content of the order to Twentieth Air Force Headquarters in Washington for information; approval was not required in his command arrangement with Washington. LeMay expected little reaction from Washington, even though the order was a radical departure from AAF doctrine. He knew that neither of his Washington superiors would be there when his message arrived. Arnold was still in Florida recuperating from his heart attack. Norstad was en route to Guam. Even if both had been in the Pentagon, it is doubtful either would have challenged his decision. Both knew the air campaign was faltering. Bold measures were required, and LeMay's plan contained them. If the attack succeeded LeMay would be credited with a brilliant stroke and the lagging B-29 campaign would be given new life. If it failed it would only be a matter of time before Washington would replace him.

Now it was the turn for the bomb group headquarters to translate the order into the detailed information necessary for the flight and ground crews to carry out their assignments. Montgomery and the Bomber Command continued to send down supplementary guidance and information, but the focus of activity was now in the subordinate staff. Throughout the day each wing issued its own field order to its bomb groups. In addition to items in LeMay's field order, it covered such matters as bomb loads, the runways to be used, sequence of take-off, route to target, altitudes to be flown en route, bombing altitudes, and the return route. Takeoff was scheduled for 6:15 P.M. on the ninth for the 73rd Wing on Saipan and the 313th on Tinian, and 40 minutes earlier for the 314th Wing on Guam, to the south, which had to fly about 75 miles more to get to Tokyo. The strategy was to have airplanes from all three wings over the target area at about the same time and for as short a time as possible.

The men who learned the details of the mission earliest were the three or more combat crews in each group designated to hit the target points first. The lead crew's aircraft (later called "pathfinders," a term used by the British in their night bombing tactics) carried M-47 incendiary bombs. This bomb, which weighed 70 lbs, in contrast to the 6.3-lb M-69, was chosen to penetrate the roofs of the larger and more substantial structures and create fires quickly enough to mark the target area for the aircraft that followed with their loads of M-69s. The mission planners expected that fires in the larger buildings would require most of the city's professional fire fighters and motorized equipment to put them out, leaving the neighborhood fire fighters to combat the thousands of fires started by the M-69s.

Early in the afternoon the select lead crews attended special briefings at which they were informed of the plan for the mission and were given detailed target data so that they could study it and do their individual planning before takeoff.

Maj. Jack Catton's crew was one of the lead crews for the 73rd Wing. When Catton entered the small briefing room that afternoon, he was greeted by his bombardier, Lt. Robert Canfield, who said, "Major, wait till you see this. It will kill you!" What Canfield was referring to was the bombing altitude shown on one of the briefing charts. Catton will never forget his amazement at the figure—7,000 feet!

LATER, THE REST of the combat crews learned the mission details. At different times on 9 March, men from the ten bomb groups to fly the mission (the 73rd and 313th Wings had the authorized four groups each, while the entire 314th had not yet arrived from the United States, so it had only two groups) filed into the large, frame buildings used for premission briefings. The setting for group briefings seldom varied—usually rows of wooden benches on which the combat crewmen sat facing a small, raised stage. On the wall behind the stage was

a map (usually covered at the beginning of the briefing) showing the route to Japan, the initial point, the target and return,
charts containing information on the mission or the target
and, sometimes, a lectern for notes. The colonel commanding
the group or his operations officer usually opened the briefing,
outlining the mission's principal points.

When the cover of the map was removed, the men learned,
as some had already suspected, that the target was Tokyo. It
would be a nighttime incendiary raid. Each aircraft would fly
to the target individually. Groans and soft whistles greeted
the announcement that they would be bombing from altitudes between 5,000 and 8,000 feet. Many were shocked and
found this hard to believe. Equally surprising was the revela-
tion that guns and ammunition would be removed from the
airplanes. After the opening description, and while the crews
were absorbing the impact of the radical plan, staff officers
provided more details on the operation—the intelligence officer provided information on expected enemy opposition and
the target; the group bombardiers furnished details on bomb
loadings; the group navigator would go over the navigation
plan; the group flight engineer would review the "flight plan"
for maximum utilization of fuel; other officers would describe
the expected weather and rescue plans for aircraft forced to
ditch.

One intelligence officer was Capt. Gould of the 9th Bomb
Group. After telling 9th Group crews of the importance and
vulnerability of that night's target, he described the route to
their particular target within the city, enemy defenses they
would fly near or over. These excerpts from his briefing notes
are illustrative of the information the crews received that day:

A. Tokyo lies 25 mi. from mountains—60 miles N.E. Fuji on
   coastal plain in the center of Honshu. As you can see from
   this relief of N. Honshu.
B. Your route carries you along the Chiba Peninsula to [word
   omitted in Gould's notes] and across on a heading of 304 to
   Iwaga Pt. at mouth of Goi River. You will be bombing at
   night & will probably see only L.W. Cont. [land-water con-
   trast] & fires.
C. From Iwaga Point 15 miles—passing left of Chiba to center

of Honjo Ward one mile East of Sumida River. Your target to right of arrowhead dock area—just to right of Sunamachi Airfield.

D. Tokyo bounded on south and west by TAMA—east and north by EDO. Don't be confused by 25' extension to south—10 x 10 (100 Sq.)

E. Honjo is west half of the area bounded by Sumida and Naka—1500'. Honjo is 2 x 3 and Delta is 4 x 6.

F. Elevation 183 feet.

G. Your radar Aiming Point is main R.R. bridge crossing Sumida at bulge to west—River here 400 feet. 3 bridges below—7 above.

H. Your visual Aiming Point is 1 mile east of bridge across Sumida.

I. Remember all fires not ours.

J. P.O.W.—Several camps, some locations unknown—none known in target area.

V. ENEMY DEFENSES

A. Flak and balloons covered by flak officer.

B. Many searchlights—wear red goggles.

C. No camouflage, dummies or smoke screens other than our own.

D. Give surface wind and velocity _____ .

E. Experience recently over Empire most encouraging. Without trying to make you apprehensive, it is still our duty to tell you that there are, according to 21 Feb recon. 1. 60 twin 2. 300 single [fighters] 3. 80 airfields (13 combat fighter strips) others building. 4. _____ night fighters 5. Keep lights out 73rd Wing jumped 200 miles out to sea.

F. Radar—you will be picked up but we hope enemy's sets will be confused and saturated.

VI. CAUTION [In case of capture]

A. Japanese money, souvenirs, diaries.

B. Name, rank and serial number only.

At the conclusion of the briefings, the key participants—pilots, navigators, bombardiers, flight engineers and radar observers—gathered separately, and their staff specialists gave them more information on their respective areas of responsibility. Usually during this time navigators accomplished a seemingly minor but actually critically important action:

each would see that the time on his chronometer matched—to the second—that of the group navigator, who had obtained the exact time by radio from the Naval Observatory in Washington, D.C. This was accomplished by countdown "Five, four, three, two, one—HACK." It was because of this procedure that the navigator's chronometer had come to be known as the "Hack Watch" and was one of the most important items carried in the airplane. A difference of seconds between the Hack Watch and the correct time might lead to serious errors in determining an airplane's location when using celestial navigation, the primary method of navigation.

Before leaving the briefing room, each officer was issued typed directions and guidance (called "flimsys"), which he could take with him and study before flight time.

Meanwhile thousands of M-69 incendiary clusters and M-47 incendiary bombs had been removed from their packing cases and hauled to positions near the 325 B-29s slated for the mission. Here, during the previous night and into the day, ordnance men threaded arming wires in the fuses of each cluster and trundled the bombs under one of the two open bomb bays of each B-29 of the main force. Working inside the bomb bay, men winched the 500-lb clusters into place on the racks inside. Into the bomb bays of the pathfinder aircraft they loaded 100-lb M-47 incendiary bombs in racks of six. The average bombload for the mission was 6.6 tons.

WALKING BACK TO the Quonsets, combat crewmen voiced their feelings about what they had been told at the briefing. Reactions varied. The more seasoned officers saw the merit of LeMay's radical plan and accepted it. Many were apprehensive. Some were furious at LeMay—outraged. Others thought he was crazy or plain desperate and that they were the scapegoats. Typical of these would be 314th Wing aircraft commander Van R. Parker's recollection that having completed only two missions, he was being "condemned to a quick demise." Despite the emotional reactions, their mutual combat experience had forged in virtually all the men of the XXI Bomber Command a sense of loyalty to their crew, squadron, group, wing and command, and confidence in their leaders. Apprehensive or not, all expected to fly the mission.

THAT MORNING, GEN. Norstad and a small group of officers from the Pentagon had arrived on Guam. Gen. LeMay met privately with them for about an hour, during which time he must have reviewed his plan for the mission that night. After that, in the XXI Bomber Command mission planning room, LeMay presided as his staff officers briefed the Pentagon visitors on the status of the Command. The meeting took up most of the day and is significant, not so much for what went on during the meeting—lengthy briefings on personnel, operations and logistical status, plans and problems and ways Washington could be of help—but for what it revealed about LeMay's character. Having ordered an attack that placed his own, the B-29's and the AAF's reputations on the line, LeMay spent most of the day on matters having little or no bearing on the upcoming mission. He possessed that rare ability, found only in great leaders, which enabled him, once having made a decision, to put thoughts of it aside, trust the men he had chosen to carry it out, and proceed with other matters.

After the crew briefings, most of the combat crews went to the mess hall and had an early dinner. One crewman would later recall that the cooks, aware that the upcoming mission presented great risks, served the biggest and best meal they could—their contribution to the maximum effort. Back in their Quonsets, according to their individual preferences, men wrote letters, attended religious services, took showers, slept, smoked, talked. Later they went to the equipment room and picked up their parachutes and "Mae West" life-preservers.

BY 6:00 P.M. the crew of the *Southern Belle* had boarded one of the trucks in front of the briefing building and were headed for their airplane. Fifteen minutes later, as Capt. Walter Sherrell, aircraft commander, and his crew arrived at the flight line, M. Sgt. Marcus Allen, *Southern Belle*'s crew chief, and his two assistants were securing cowling and closing access doors after changing a leaking fuel pump and accomplishing other work necessary to give the aircraft its best chance to fly to Tokyo, drop its load and return safely. As the combat crew climbed down from the truck, one remained on it and passed down the equipment—parachutes, Mae Wests, flight jackets, flight lunches, coffee jugs, candy bars and other items. Then each picked up his own gear, boarded the airplane, stowed the gear and checked the equipment at his station to see that it was ready for takeoff.

S. Sgt. Norbert Haskins, radio operator, after securing his radio log and frequency and code book at his station, took the coffee jugs and flight lunches he had been assigned to bring along (typically, two peanut butter and jelly sandwiches, an apple, an orange and a piece of candy for each man) and divided them between the front and rear crew compartments.

Inside the rear compartment, S. Sgt. Leland J. Sawyer, tail-gunner, checked and started a small motor that powered the generator called the "putt-putt." This was used to drive the engine starters and back up the engine-driven generators during takeoffs and landings.

Lt. Edward A. Ososky, bombardier, went into the two bomb bays, counted the bombs and made sure they were securely hung in their racks and the arming wires were in place.

S. Sgt. Richard O. Bowers, radar operator, turned on his set, checked to see that it was functioning properly, then made sure he had the radar navigation and approach charts, scope photos and instructions for the radar bomb run that had been issued to him at the briefing that afternoon.

Outside, Lt. Ernest T. Rasmussen, flight engineer, listened to Marcus Allen tell him about work the ground crew had done on the aircraft since its last flight. After a few questions, Rasmussen climbed into the airplane and checked the readings on his control and instrument panel.

AFTER EACH MAN had completed his individual preflight check at his crew position, most left the aircraft and, along with the ground crew, gathered at the propellers. There, with a lot of good-natured banter, they paired up and started the unpleasant chore of "pulling the props through"—turning an engine's 16-foot propeller around the required number of times—12. If, in doing this, they encountered heavy resistance it indicated oil had accumulated in one of the lower cylinder heads since the previous flight in sufficient quantity to cause a hydraulic lock, which could bend a piston rod and lead to engine failure. When a hydraulic lock was encountered, a mechanic would have to drain the oil out of that cylinder before the engine could be started. This seldom occurred, but despite the many advanced technological features of the B-29, this was still a job that had to be done by hand before each flight on this and other radial-engine aircraft of the time. *Southern Belle*'s prop turners encountered no problems, so with less than fifteen minutes left before takeoff, they climbed back aboard and went to their stations, buckled up and prepared to start the engines.

Rasmussen, at his flight engineer's controls, and Walter Sherrell began the process. As he started each engine, Rasmussen would announce over the interphone to Sherrell (and all the other crew members who by now had put on and checked their individual headsets and throat mikes) that the particular engine had engaged. When each engine achieved the desired rpm and sounded right, Sherrell would call over his shoulder to Rasmussen, "I've got it," after which Rasmussen could start the next engine. The engine start procedure was repeated until all four engines were running. A pleasant by-product of starting the engines was that the rotating propellers caused air movement all around the airplane. As a result, "fresh air" flowed through the windows and other openings into the front cabin and dissipated the intense heat from the sun that always accumulated there.

With the engines running smoothly, Sherrell called down to the bombardier to close the two bomb bay doors and signaled to the ground crewmen to pull the wheel chocks. *Southern Belle* was ready to roll.

It was 7:05 P.M., and Sherrell could see the sun low on the horizon to his left. Already over half of the 43 aircraft of the 498th Bomb Group scheduled for the mission had left their hardstands and were lumbering by on their way to the head of the runways. Sherrell, twenty-fourth on the takeoff list, waited, then, seeing his turn, eased all four throttles forward to get *Southern Belle* moving, then eased the throttle of the left outboard engine a little farther forward and touched the right brake, which caused the airplane to slowly turn right and join the line. It was like a procession of dinosaurs moving slowly, irregularly, nose-to-tail down a trail.

After checking the ignition magnetos on all four engines, Sherrell arrived at the head of the runway and fixed his gaze on the takeoff control officer, "biscuit gun" in hand, standing on top of an old Japanese blockhouse. The biscuit gun was a powerful light whose color could be manually changed from white to green or red. A white light shining on the takeoff control officer's feet told the watching pilot, "Stand by and be prepared to start your takeoff roll in 30 seconds." A green light signaled "Start rolling. Get off the ground or get out of the way!" And a red light meant "Don't move."

Sherrell and the rest of the *Southern Belle* crew seldom approached a takeoff lightheartedly. This one was no exception. *Southern Belle* was carrying the heaviest load of bombs ever and had little reserve engine power. Once under way, the aircraft developed great momentum and needed a long distance to either reach takeoff speed or be braked to a stop. If, during takeoff, an engine failed before the airplane had traveled more than halfway down the runway, the pilot had enough runway left in which to stop and turn off at one of the several taxiways. If the engine failed after he passed the halfway point—literally a point of no return—the pilot had two choices, neither good. He could try to get the aircraft off with three engines and possibly crash because of insufficient power, or he could attempt to stop and probably run off the end of the runway, which on Saipan was a 600-foot cliff.

At the end of the taxiway Sherrell watched some of his squadron mates take off, then he turned *Southern Belle* onto Runway #2 and waited. Moments later, he got the white light from the takeoff control officer. With his feet still on the brake pedals he ran the engines up to fast-idle and watched the progress of the airplane taking off ahead of him. Then, seeing his green light, Sherrell released the brakes, pushed his throttles to full-power and began the takeoff roll. Though he listened to his pilot, Lt. Orlo H. Hall, calling out the increasing airspeed, Sherrell used his own feel and experience to tell him when the airplane was approaching rotation speed. Most pilots in Sherrell's group had learned that with the heavy bomb loads they were carrying, the best way to achieve a margin of safety was to keep the nose down and hold the airplane on the ground until it attained a speed of about 130 mph—far in excess of the takeoff speed listed in the operating manual. Each moment during the takeoff roll Sherrell gauged the amount of runway left against the airspeeds being called out. The constant question was, "If an engine quits, do I stop or keep going? Stop or keep going?" Slowly the airspeeds increased. He felt the elevator controls to sense how near flying speed he was. Still keeping the nose down, he saw the end of the runway looming ahead. When he heard Hall call out, "one-thirty," Sherrell gently lifted *Southern Belle* off the runway—just enough to keep the tires from touching again—and called, "Gear up!" Off the end of the runway, he took advantage of the 600-foot drop to the ocean's surface to gain additional speed. Then he eased the throttles back a little, had Hall retract the wing flaps and set the RPM and manifold pressure for climb power. He turned left, kept climbing on a heading of 346° and, when he reached 3,500 feet, joined the column winging its way to Japan.

On Guam, after the staff meeting, Norstad and his party had visited the nearby 314th Wing and observed final preparations for the upcoming mission. Then, an hour before the first airplanes took off, about 50 newspaper correspondents gathered for a press conference and listened to LeMay and Norstad tell them about the upcoming raid. After the conference most of the correspondents went over to North Field to watch airplanes of the 314th Wing take off and began writing their stories. Norstad also watched the airplanes leaving North Field. Earlier he had sent a message to his staff at Twentieth Air Force Headquarters in Washington:

Operations tonight will be largest yet, if plan can be carried out. Its effect may be significant. If over three hundred aircraft take

off you should release that number. In any event release fact
that largest number participated if that proves to be a fact. In
order to establish foundation for what may be an outstanding
show, you should leave no doubt that this is an important operation. We will give you further details as they may arise.
Results are not certain until they can be seen so hold something back but it should be stressed that this is a big one.

By 8:10 P.M. 325 aircraft of the XXI Bomber Command were
en route to Japan. The first airplane of Gen. Power's 314th
Wing (two bomb groups, 54 aircraft) on Guam had taken off at
5:36 P.M. Davies' 313th Wing on Tinian (four groups, 110
aircraft) began taking off 39 minutes later at 6:15 P.M. as did
O'Donnell's veteran and full-strength 73rd Wing on Saipan
with four bomb groups and 161 aircraft.

LeMay's "outstanding show" was on the road and it certainly was a big one.

EIGHT

"MEETINGHOUSE": IN THE SKY

DESPITE THE FACT that they were part of an armada of more than 300 aircraft stretching over 200 miles, Jim Sherrell and the rest of the *Southern Belle*'s crew, with mile after mile of blackness slipping under them, felt very much alone. Though many pilots kept running lights on to prevent collisions, after an hour in the air Sherrell had not sighted another B-29. He would not see one until he neared the Japanese coast, which the flight plan showed over five hours away.

As did most other pilots, Sherrell flew primarily with the autopilot engaged. This device would keep the aircraft flying on a set course and speed, compensating for winds and other factors. Though watchful for emergencies that might require them to override the autopilot and take control, Sherrell and his copilot, Hall, were relieved of the strain of constantly adjusting the aircraft. All that was necessary was for one of them to "retrim" (make minor adjustments in the aircraft's control devices) about every half hour and, of course, change the course setting when required.

The first occasion for course change came as they approached Iwo Jima, which they had to avoid because the island was not yet fully under U.S. control. To bypass the island required two changes in headings. It was Lt. Ruderman's job to keep track of their flight path and to inform Sherrell or Hall when to make these changes. At frequent intervals, hunched over his little table behind Sherrell, with a pencil, calipers and a "circular slide rule" for his calculations, Ruderman plotted the *Southern Belle*'s position. He used a combination of dead reckoning (charting his position by course, speed, elapsed time and drift caused by wind), celestial navigation (estimating position by sighting on the sun or stars, when the weather permitted) and loran (triangulating position based on difference in time interval between radio signals from loran transmitting stations). In addition, he received reports from Richard Bowers in the rear of the airplane as Bowers spotted islands, rock formations and other checkpoints on his radarscope.

Just forward and across from Ruderman, the flight engineer sat in front of his instrument panel with its array of dials, switches and throttles. With the lights out in the front cabin the radium dials glowed under the UV lamp that shone on them. Lt. Rasmussen had to keep careful track of fuel consumption and try to catch any engine malfunctions as early as possible so that he and the pilot could take the necessary corrective action. By this time—in sharp contrast to the serious problems experienced in bombing from China bases and in early missions from the Marianas—the B-29 engines were becoming quite reliable. The terrible overheating problem had been overcome as a result of engine modifications made by Boeing engineers and increased knowledge of engine performance characteristics on the part of the pilots. Consequently, watching the dials, while still a necessary task, was usually uneventful and tedious. After an hour or two, for some, the glowing dials seemed to burn right into the back of the eyeballs. One way the flight engineer could alleviate this discomfort was to close his eyes for a while and listen to the beat of the engines or catch a misfiring cylinder through the feel of his hand on the four throttles.

Except for Norman Haskins, the radio operator, who had to monitor his receivers and transmitters, and Bowers watching his radarscope, the rest of the crew—the four gunners—had little to do on the long flight except to take a turn watching the engines through their blisters and report any sparks, oil leaks or other abnormalities to the aircraft commander and the flight engineer. Once near the target zone they would keep a lookout for enemy aircraft, spot any engine malfunctions or flak damage and, after the mission, tell the debriefing officer about any unusual sightings. To pass the time until they got to Japan the gunners smoked, played cards and talked. But, even with these distractions, along with the other gunners flying north that night, they couldn't help wondering how their aircraft would survive without the powerful defensive fires of the B-29's 12 machine guns.

UP IN THE pilot's cabin, Sherrell was wondering, too, how this night incendiary raid would compare to others he had flown. While some of the other crewmen flying the mission that night had bombed targets in Germany during the daytime, Sherrell may have been the only pilot in the XXI Bomber Command who had flown on night incendiary raids over Europe.

In 1940 he had left college and his home state, Arkansas, and joined the RAF. He took his pilot's training in Canada, and after receiving his RAF wings he went to England where he flew Spitfires in defense of England's cities against German air attacks. Later he volunteered for multi-engine training, and after a stint of ferrying bombers from England to locations in the Middle East, he was assigned to a bomber squadron. In early 1942, as pilot of a Lancaster bomber, Sherrell flew a number of missions over German cities as part of Air Marshall Harris's night incendiary campaign. Following this he flew fighters and twin-engine bombers against Field Marshal Erwin Rommel's Afrika Korps in North Africa. Then, in the summer of 1943, with his own country now in the war, Sherrell returned to the United States and obtained a transfer to the AAF. After an assignment as a combat flight instructor, he volunteered for the B-29 program, trained with the 73rd Bomb Wing and flew with the wing on its first mission over Japan.

Because of his experience with the RAF, Sherrell believed that night raids might be the way to increase the XXI Bomber Command's bombing effectiveness. When the rumors of LeMay's plan to radically change the command's bombing tactics had started circulating in late February, he had expressed such feelings to his squadron commander. Sherrell's positive views about the mission were not shared by his flight engineer, Ernie Rasmussen. After returning to their Quonset hut from the mission briefing that afternoon, Sherrell had noticed Rasmussen writing in his diary. In response to Sherrell's query as to why he was writing, Rasmussen stated that he was making his final entry because he didn't expect to return from the mission. He planned to turn the diary over to the chaplain to make sure that his wife received it after his death. Sherrell tried vainly to allay his friend's fears. Rasmussen listened but, unconvinced, soon left for the chaplain's office.

As THEY PASSED Iwo Jima, Sherrell changed the *Southern Belle*'s heading to 320°, and an hour later, with a radar fix on the Nanpo Shoto islands (part of the Bonins), turned north to 354°. For the next hour the weather worsened. The *Southern Belle* bucked its way into and out of huge cloud masses where the visibility was zero, rain swirled, thunder sounded and lightning flashed. It was here that Sherrell witnessed the most spectacular display of Saint Elmo's Fire that he had seen in his flying experience. Heavy charges of static electricity formed circles of blue-white light around the tips of the four propellers, and similar charges of light danced eerily across the wings. The phenomena, observed by sailors over the centuries, had been known to damage communications equipment in aircraft. The B-29 had static discharge devices to help prevent this, and on this occasion the *Southern Belle*'s radios were not affected.

It may have been during one of the intervals between the storm cloud-banks or sometime before that Haskins and a few other radio operators in airplanes of the 73rd Wing listened to a set of American popular songs played by Radio Tokyo.

Among the selections which the amazed crewmen recognized were "Smoke Gets in Your Eyes," "My Old Flame" and "I Don't Want to Set the World on Fire." Neither then nor now is there any explanation except coincidence for such a combination of tunes being aired on that night.

ABOUT THE TIME *Southern Belle* was passing Iwo Jima, Capt. George A. Simeral, aircraft commander of *Snatch Blatch*, was about 100 miles south of the southern tip of the Chiba peninsula, the land mass that forms the eastern shore of Tokyo Bay. Six hours earlier, Gen. Power had arrived at the hardstand with a map case tucked under his arm and boarded the awaiting aircraft. With Power were Lt. Col. Besse, the 314th Wing intelligence officer, and two other officers who along with Besse were coming along as observers. The three took the places of Simeral's three gunners in the aft section. Once aboard, Power strapped himself into the copilot's seat to Simeral's right, and shortly thereafter Simeral took off, the first airplane of the 29th Bomb Group to do so.

On the flight up Simeral and Power had some lengthy conversations. Simeral expressed some concern about the radical plan. Power responded with an enthusiastic and highly optimistic description of the major features of the plan, which allayed some of Simeral's worries but still left him a bit edgy about how the operation was going to turn out.

Power explained that the three wings on the way to Japan were following the same route until they made landfall just south of the Chiba peninsula. At this point the 314th Wing's course paralleled the Tokyo Bay coastline to the initial point, a small land mass jutting into the bay that could easily be identified on the radarscope because of its shape and the land-water contrast. From the initial point, aircraft of the 19th and 29th Bomb Groups of the 314th Wing were to bomb Target Area #4, an area north of the Ginza commercial district between the Tokyo Railroad Station and the Sumida River.

The 73rd and 313th Wings used a different route. They were to fly along the eastern side of the Chiba peninsula and then turn to the northwest and fly across the peninsula to their initial point, another jut of land on Tokyo Bay. From there the target assignments were as follows:

497th, 498th, and 499th Bomb Groups, 73rd Bomb Wing— Target Area #1: An area west of the Sumida River near the center of the Asakusa ward, the most densely populated and flammable part of the total target area.
500th Bomb Group, 73rd Wing, and 505th Bomb Group, 313th Wing—Target Area #2: An area east of the Sumida River covering most of the Honjo ward, the center of which lay just south of the Honjo main fire station.
6th, 9th, and 504th Bomb Groups, 313th Wing—Target Area #3: An area east of the Sumida covering most of the Fukugawa ward, the center of which lay about one mile east of the main railroad bridge across the Sumida River.

Power asked Simeral to begin a climb so as to arrive over the city of Tokyo at an altitude of 20,000 feet. Power expected that, with their early time of departure, *Snatch Blatch* would reach the city at about the same time that the first airplanes of the bomber force arrived over their respective target areas. Simeral was to circle the area at altitude. Power would observe and note on his target map the location of the fires as they started. Lt. Col. Besse along with the two other officers in the rear compartment would also record their observations for use in determining the mission's effectiveness and for planning future incendiary missions.

BACK ON GUAM, Lt. Col. St. Clair McKelway, XXI Bomber Command, Public Relations Officer, had gone over to the big operations control room to wait for first reports on the mission. It was McKelway's responsibility to read the first "bombs away" messages and early reports on the mission to be sure that the war correspondents had the right information before giving them permission to radio their stories back to the United States.

When he entered the big room, with its walls covered with charts, maps and graphs showing the strength and condition of the command and the status of the current mission, he saw operations officers, some sergeants and one other person—Curtis LeMay, who was sitting on a bench smoking a cigar. McKelway approached LeMay and asked him why he was up. (Norstad was asleep in LeMay's quarters. He, along with Montgomery and other top staff, had left word to be awakened when the first news came in.) LeMay explained that he usually could sleep but couldn't tonight. "A lot could go wrong," he said.

LeMay was experiencing in full measure the loneliness of a field commander—air or ground—who has planned and launched an attack force in a major battle engagement. He alone bore the total responsibility for its success or failure. Besides this burden, which all commanders share, LeMay must have felt a deep sense of uneasiness because of his inability to influence the outcome until the attack was over. Ground commanders are constantly in contact with their major commanders and can and very often do make adjustments in the attack as it progresses. LeMay's forces were proceeding in radio silence, inalterably committed to carrying out the attack order he had issued the day before.

Despite these feelings, LeMay expressed confidence. "If this raid works the way I think it will, we can shorten the war. We've figured out a punch he's not expecting this time. I don't think he's got the right kind of flak to combat this kind of raid, and I don't think that he can keep his cities from being burned down—wiped right off the map." With some time still left before the expected bombs-away reports, LeMay asked McKelway if he wanted to join him in a Coke. They drove over to LeMay's quarters, and LeMay, careful not to wake up Norstad, went in and brought out the Cokes. They sat facing the tropical growth that surrounded the headquarters area and talked about India, where both had served and which neither had found to his liking.

As LeMay and McKelway were ending their wait, the first of the lead airplanes of the 29th Bomb Group, 314th Wing, were nearing the coast of Japan. The navigator had calculated that they were about 30 minutes away and had informed the pilot and the rest of the crew. Crewmen soon began to don their flak jackets and helmets and check their parachutes. The flak-jacket looked like a baseball catcher's chest protector and was lined with bullet-resistant steel. The helmet had hinged flaps over the ears, so that it would fit over earphones. When body armor was introduced in Europe and first used in the Pacific, many air crewmen still believed that antiaircraft shell fragments came from below and for this reason, and because it was bulky and uncomfortable to wear, chose to sit on their flak-jackets. As experience showed that the fragments could come from any direction and that the armor was really effective, the men's attitude changed. Cumbersome as the jackets were, most men wore them.

Back in the rear of the airplane, the radar observer, hunched over his panel watching the white line on the orange screen of his radarscope sweep round and round, would begin to get a clear (to him, but not necessarily to an untrained eye) image of the outline of the southern tip of the Chiba peninsula. Ten miles north of the tip, at the town of Wada, was the point at which aircraft of his group were supposed to make landfall and turn toward the initial point. In the front section, the navigator, also equipped with a radarscope that displayed the same image as that on the radar observer's instrument, would check his chart and calculations and, after a brief conversation on the interphone with the radar observer, would come on the interphone and inform the aircraft commander that they would make landfall in 15 minutes. The aircraft commander would answer in the way many did to minimize unnecessary conversation on the interphone system: he pushed his microphone button twice. Two clicks on the bomber's interphone meant "I heard and understand you."

(At this time radar was a young technology and the XXI Bomber Command's operations would be a major testing ground for its use in bombing at night or when visibility was poor. New techniques for bombing by radar were being developed and refined as experience increased. Procedures taught to radar men in the United States sometimes differed from those in the classes LeMay had established to improve the skills of his command. The abilities of the individual radar observers

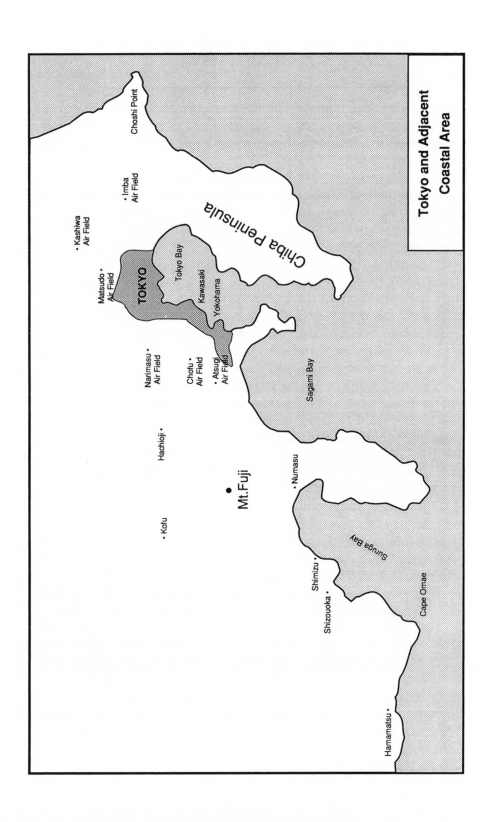

Tokyo and Adjacent Coastal Area

Choshi Point

Imba Air Field

Kashiwa Air Field

Chiba Peninsula

Matsudo Air Field

TOKYO

Tokyo Bay

Kawasaki

Yokohama

Narimasu Air Field

Chofu Air Field

Atsugi Air Field

Sagami Bay

Hachioji

Numasu

Mt.Fuji

Kofu

Suruga Bay

Shimizu

Cape Omae

Shizouoka

Hamamatsu

varied widely, as did pilots' use and reliance on radar bombing techniques. Recognizing this lack of uniformity, following are the actions that probably took place as the first aircraft in the vanguard of LeMay's bomber force approached and made its run on the target.)

The navigator would come on the interphone and tell his aircraft commander that landfall was coming up and to make a turn at the turning point in 30 seconds. Thirty seconds later the aircraft commander would roll into his turn by twisting the autopilot control.

(Though some aircraft commanders chose to fly the approach to the bomb run and the bomb run itself manually, others, as here, used the autopilot because they felt that when properly set up, it would deliver the bombs more accurately than when the airplane was flown manually.)

The aircraft commander would roll out of the turn and make a small correction to attain the proper heading.

They would now be on a northwesterly course heading for their initial point. Flying across the Chiba peninsula at 5,000 feet, all would be dark below. As they crossed the southern end of Tokyo Bay, the radar observer would shift from the 50- to the 20-mile sweep on his scope, making it possible to distinguish features of the shoreline, though Tokyo and its outlying areas would be in a total blackout.

The radar man could pick up the initial point, a jut of land on the bay, and could also see on his scope the direction that the aircraft was flying. He would now take over from the navigator and inform the aircraft commander that the initial point was ahead and to begin a right turn in 30 seconds. After rolling out of the turn on the prescribed heading, the aircraft commander would announce that he was on the run to target.

Next, the bombardier would activate the bomb-bay door release mechanisms and notify the aircraft commander that this had been accomplished. Then one of the rear gunners and the radio operator, each of whom could see down into the bomb bay adjacent to their position, would announce over the interphone that the rear and forward bomb bays were open. Any experienced aircraft commander would have felt the bomb bay doors open, but such vital steps on the run to target had to be confirmed nonetheless.

The entire crew listened over the interphone system. Tension would begin to mount as they began their run to the target, still in total darkness, undetected by the enemy below.

As they approached the city at a distance of less than 15 miles, the radar observer could easily identify the mouth of the Sumida River as it flowed into Tokyo Bay. The docks located in this area were the aiming point for the night's bomb run. The radar observer would place the aiming point under the "track line," a line on his screen describing the course of the airplane. As they flew toward the target, the crosswind might prove to be stronger than predicted. This would cause the track line to move to the left or right of the aiming point on the radarscope. The radar observer would then call a course correction to the aircraft commander, who would make a small adjustment on his autopilot control. This would put the aircraft back on course and the aiming point back under the track line.

With the target less than four minutes away, it remained for the radar observer and the bombardier to jointly see that the bombs were released at the correct moment so that they would follow a trajectory that would place them on the target. In the nose of the airplane, the bombardier would look through the telescope on his Norden bombsight. On his screen, the radar observer would watch the target and warn the bombardier that the aiming point was approaching the "clutch-in" point—a mark on the radarscope that corresponded to a certain sighting angle to the aiming point. Hearing this, the bombardier would verify that the reading on his telescope was at the same angle and, based on previously entered information, was being automatically moved at a rate that would keep it focused on the aiming point. The radar observer would call out successive checkpoints for the bombardier to re-aim his telescope, as necessary. The crew would listen expectantly as the call-out continued, until the moment when the bombsight automatically released the bombs. The bombardier would announce the traditional "Bomb's Away," and the airplane, free of the great weight in its belly, would lurch upward.

*   *   *

IT WAS SEVEN minutes after midnight as the lead airplane of
the 29th Bomb Group dropped 122 M-47 gasoline gel bombs
through the darkness on Target Area #4, the area in the southwest corner of the city between the main railroad station and
the Sumida River.

As the second and third aircraft flew over the target and
released their load of M-47s, searchlights pierced the darkness
and successive aircraft encountered the lights and antiaircraft
fire over both the target and the Bay. One of the lead aircraft
was hit almost immediately and plunged "like a ball of fire"
into the ground at 12:16 A.M. Despite this loss, the first airplanes over target area dropped their M-47 bombloads accurately, creating fires that, in a night of unusually good
visibility, clearly identified Target Area #4 for the airplanes
that would follow. Though the 24 aircraft of the 29th Group
had taken off from their base nearly 1,400 miles to the south
at one-minute intervals, they arrived over Tokyo at irregular
times and it would be more than an hour before all the aircraft
had made their bomb runs. This was because of variations in
weather, wind and navigation over the long distances flown.

AS WAS THE case with the lead aircraft of the 29th Bomb
Group, the first airplanes of the 497th Bomb Group, 73rd
Bomb Wing, found the city completely blacked out upon
reaching their initial point. They too made their bomb run by
radar but at an altitude of 7,500 feet, 2,500 feet higher than the
airplanes of the 29th. The first aircraft, one of the three designated as pathfinders for the group, dropped its load of 184
M-47 bombs on the tinderboxlike Asakusa ward at 12:14 A.M.,
just seven minutes after the first bombs had fallen on Target
Area #4 to the south. (Airplanes of the 73rd and 313th Wings
could carry substantially larger bomb loads than those of the
314th Wing because they were not carrying the extra fuel
tanks mounted in the airplanes flying up from Guam on this
mission.) The next pathfinder dropped six minutes later, and
the third didn't arrive until 48 minutes later. Thereafter aircraft of the 497th, each carrying 40 clusters of M-69 incendiary bombs, each cluster set to release its 38 M-69 bombs at

2,000 feet, flew over the target area just minutes apart. Twenty-nine of the group completed their runs in the next 45 minutes.

Japanese searchlights came on immediately, and many of the early arrivals were picked up by the lights and carried all the way over the target area. One beam would pick up an aircraft and then five or more would converge on it. With the forward compartment brightly lit, pilots found the amber goggles that they had been issued to be a big help in overcoming the glare, making it possible for them to see and keep their aircraft under control during their bomb run.

Lt. Jack Bizanz, bombardier of Capt. Edward W. Cutler's *Texas Doll*, wrote in his journal later that on their approach to Tokyo a huge black cloud obscured the target, but Lt. Don Julin, the navigator, and Sgt. Harold La Plante, the radar observer, did a good job and they hit the target "right on the nose." Despite the fact that airplanes all around them were "getting lots of attention," *Texas Doll* got through without being caught in the searchlights or being hit by flak. Bizanz watched as their bombs hit between two already burning areas. As they passed over, he was able to make out a medium-sized factory burning fiercely. Cutler's major concern was getting the bombs to the target and avoiding a collision with the hundreds of other airplanes converging over Tokyo. He had kept his position lights on all the way up to the initial point, and after leaving the target and passing Choshi Point, he turned them on again—just for good measure.

Maj. James Coats, a squadron operations officer in the 499th Bomb Group, did not have a regularly assigned crew and flew the mission that day in an airplane that had not yet been given a name. He shared Cutler's and other pilots' apprehension about a collision and was on a constant lookout for other airplanes. His attention shifted when, as he crossed Tokyo Bay, he saw Japanese searchlights picking up aircraft and converging in the shape of a giant inverted cone. He lowered his altitude and managed to edge below the level at which the lights seemed to be converging. This maneuver kept his airplane out of the lights for a while, but soon it too was caught and Coats and his crew experienced the helplessness of being illuminated on the final phase of their bomb run. The temptation was to drop the bombs early and take evasive action; however, Coats, who in his job as operations officer was responsible for getting the orders out to flight crews and seeing that they were followed, was hardly one to take such an action. He held his course on the designated aiming point and dropped into an already burning area.

Turning off the target and out of the lights, Coats glimpsed some fighters flying across his path. To avoid the fighters as well as the possibility of being caught in the lights again, he flew into a smoke cloud. It was a poor decision. The aircraft was lifted upward at a terrific rate by thermal action and at one point was almost flipped over by the tremendous forces acting upon it. Seconds later Coats regained control and now, content to take his chances in clearer night skies, headed east toward the Pacific and home.

Over the target most of the fire came from light-caliber automatic weapons with tracers ending in small red and white bursts. The bursts were evenly distributed ahead and behind the airplanes and most occurred below the level that the bombers were flying. As the attack progressed and the spreading fires created billowing smoke, the searchlights became confused. They were unable to pick up airplanes coming into the clear out of the smoke. Aircraft weren't fired on unless illuminated. After the first hour of the mission had passed, the validity of two of the assumptions on which the bold new tactics were based had been proven. The attackers were below the altitudes at which Japanese heavy antiaircraft batteries were designed to operate and, except for the planes of the 314th Wing flying at 5,000 feet, above the effective range of most of their smaller caliber automatic weapons. The inability to track the aircraft when obscured showed that the Japanese had no radar operating, or if they did, neither it nor their sound detection equipment was effective.

Aircraft of the 500th Bomb Group, 73rd Wing, and the 505th Group, 313th Wing, began arriving over Target Area #2, the Honjo ward, at 12:34 A.M., and aircraft of the 6th, 9th and 504th Bomb Groups of the 313th dropped their first loads of M-47 marker incendiaries on Target Area #3, the Fukugawa ward, at 12:26 A.M.

By THE TIME Simeral and Gen. Power had climbed to 20,000 feet over Tokyo, they could see fires beginning on the west side of the Sumida River in the Asakusa ward and to the south near the Tokyo Railroad Station. As Simeral began what was to be a long series of circles to his left, they spotted incendiaries from the early arrivals dropping on the Honjo and Fukugawa wards on the east side of the river. From his vantage point Simeral vividly recalls what appeared to him to be a Fourth of July sparkler effect—a trail of white light followed by a swath of orange. Such a visual effect could have been the result of reflected light from searchlights on the long white tail streamers of more than a thousand M-69 bombs from a single B-29 bursting out of their clusters at 2,000 feet and falling to earth. The swath of orange would appear when the bombs struck and their gasoline gel contents burst into flames over an area one-quarter of a mile long.

After observing for a while from behind Simeral, Power climbed down in the bombardier's compartment in the nose and, using the map that he had brought along, plotted the spread of the fires in each of the four target areas. As the fires spread and he began to enter more and more fire locations, Power would, from time to time, turn to Simeral and tell him how well the attack was progressing. Simeral was also pleased with the way the attack was going, but expressed concern for the pilots below after he saw one of them get hit and go down burning.

Meanwhile the radio operator, S. Sgt. Henry "Red" Erwin, using an extension line to his command set so he could maintain contact, climbed up in the "astrodome," where the navigator took his celestial sightings. From this vantage point, he watched, fascinated, as Simeral flew circle after circle. Erwin recalls how clear it was before the smoke built up. He could make out large sections burning and next to them darkness. Then he would see silver B-29s, glistening in the light, pass over the dark areas and they too would turn orange. (Erwin later earned the Congressional Medal of Honor, the only one awarded to a member of the Twentieth Air Force, for saving the lives of his fellow crewmen when, after a phosphorous flare had ignited prematurely inside the airplane and threatened to set off its load of incendiaries, he succeeded in pushing it out the cockpit window, but only after suffering near fatal burns all over his body.)

As AIRPLANES OF the 73rd Wing's 498th Bomb Group neared Japan the weather cleared somewhat, and Jim Sherrell, behind the controls of the *Southern Belle*, saw a glow out to the north. Curious as to what it was, he asked Rudy Ruderman to estimate their distance to landfall. Rudy told him that it was over 100 miles. Upon hearing this Sherrell guessed that the glow might be the result of a bombload of incendiaries jettisoned by a B-29 to his front and burning on the water. But as minutes passed the glow grew larger, and he and all those in the front cabin knew that what they saw were flames over Tokyo. Soon they were donning their oxygen masks, flakjackets and helmets, and checking their parachutes. Just as they made landfall the *Southern Belle*'s radar went out, so Sherrell guided on the flames. Moments later the radar came back on and they used it to hit the initial point and proceed on their bomb run.

When they neared Target Area #1, much of the Asakusa ward's blocks of highly flammable dwellings and narrow streets was a sea of flames. As Sherrell recalls, the heat had lifted the clouds, and bright red-orange flames billowed hundreds of feet in the air above the city. For the first time he caught sight of other airplanes in his group—two of them illuminated by the light of the burning city. As they flew on with the airplane depressurized, a pungent odor began to permeate the front cabin. To Sherrell it smelled like burning pine or cedar, the material that thousands of structures in Tokyo were made of. To some others recalling the mission in later years, the cabin seemed to reek of burning flesh.

Alone back in his little compartment, tailgunner Leland

Sawyer was relieved to discover that despite the low altitude at which they were flying, they weren't going to be blown out of the sky. Actually, by this time virtually all of the search-lights were out and Sawyer did not observe any antiaircraft fire aimed at *Southern Belle* nor any sign of Japanese fighters. Still on the alert but with most of his apprehensions dissi-pated, Sawyer, with almost limitless vision from his seat, looked down in amazement at the burning city below him.

The scene was far different from any he had viewed on his previous missions over Tokyo, flown at altitudes from 28,000 to 32,000 feet. From those heights (when visibility permitted) he had seen only the outlines of the city and Tokyo Bay. It was a big sprawling city. That was about all he could make out. During the 25 February mission, when they had dropped their bombs through a snowstorm, Sawyer had looked down through the gray swirl and, for a brief time, had been caught up in the realization that men and women were down there going about the everyday activities of working and living. *Southern Belle*'s bombs (along with others) would likely drive many of them out of their factories and homes into the snow. They would be down there freezing while he, in a matter of hours, would be sweating in a hot Quonset.

Now, at 7,500 feet, he could see, outlined in flame, not the whole city, but its streets, factories, large buildings, housing areas, the Sumida River and the canals. As blocks and sections of Tokyo swept into his field of vision—all burning—he real-ized once more that people were down there and that many would not survive the conflagration.

Up in the front cabin, seeing the designated area engulfed in fire, Sherrell decided to drop just outside of that area. He did so and *Southern Belle*, purged of over 7 tons of bombs, surged upward. As he executed his breakaway turn, Sherrell watched his incendiaries hit and start some fires in the unburned area. Satisfied, ten minutes later he was over Choshi Point turning south toward Saipan.

ACROSS THE SUMIDA, between the hours of 12:34 A.M. AND 2:32 A.M., 51 airplanes from the 505th Group of the 313th

Bomb Wing and the 500th Group of the 73rd Wing dropped their incendiaries on Target Area #2, the Honjo ward.

Col. John E. Dougherty, group commander of the 500th, who, along with two of his squadron leaders, had flown the low-level practice runs for LeMay, flew in the lead aircraft of his group with pilot Capt. Austin W. "Shorty" La Marche. Dougherty remembers that on the approach to their target, he saw fires already beginning to burn in several areas, probably those set by the main force of the 73rd Wing and the 314th Wing, the first airplanes of which had arrived 20 minutes before. After "Bombs Away," he was impressed by the number of B-29 propellers he could see through the darkness, spinning and glistening in reflected light from the fire and searchlights.

First Lieutenant John Reeves, a pilot in the 500th Group, flying *Sting Shift*, hit the initial point without any problems after encountering poor visibility, ice and turbulence most of the way up from Saipan. Halfway to the target, searchlights caught *Sting Shift*. Seeing a large smoke cloud ahead, Reeves flew around it and on the other side heard small-caliber antiaircraft fire that "sounded like buckshot" hit the side of his aircraft. He was able to get back on his target run and drop his clusters of M-69s. As he turned off his run, *Sting Shift* caught more antiaircraft fire, heavier caliber this time. A burst broke a 3×7-inch hole in the slide window just to Reeves' left, and glass showered all over the cockpit. Reeves suffered cuts on his left hand and face, but his helmet and flak suit protected him from more extensive injury. Lt. Warren Long, his bombardier, also caught a few splinters. (Results of the hits could have been much worse. Inspection on Saipan disclosed two flak holes in the left wing tip and two 20-mm shell holes in the left flap. Two feet forward and the two shells would have hit a gas tank.) Seconds later, a Japanese fighter swept out of the darkness and missed the left wing by only 100 feet. Leaving the scene, Reeves and his crew counted 18 separate fires in the Tokyo area, and in the glare of the flames they saw more B-29s arriving to drop their loads.

*   *   *

MAJ. DEAN A. FLING, pilot of *God's Will*, was seventh in the takeoff order of his group—the 9th Bomb Group, 313th Bomb Wing. His takeoff time of 6:21 P.M. placed him with the leading aircraft on the way to Tokyo, and if all had gone well, *God's Will* might have been among the B-29s arriving early over Target Area #3, the Fukugawa ward, the southeastern section of the total target zone.

All did not go well. Flying at 4,000 feet through the heavy weather front, Fling, like others, placed reliance on radar to pick up landfall. Apparently *God's Will*'s radar was not operating properly, and Fling flew past the designated landfall, by Choshi Point and on up the coast. Fling and his navigator finally concluded, based on their elapsed time of flight, that they must have missed the designated landfall and were somewhere off the east coast of Japan. After turning west and flying for a few minutes he broke out of the clouds and, with improved visibility, found to his dismay that he was flying down a valley with dark, forbidding mountains towering on each side. Fling lost no time; he climbed out of the valley, flew back out to sea and turned south. By this time the weather had cleared, and he and his pilot, Lt. H. L. Peterson, could see a glow off to their right that they assumed to be Tokyo burning. The extra distance they had flown north of Tokyo made it questionable whether they had enough fuel to make the trip back to Tinian. However, since the first B-29s had landed successfully on Iwo Jima just five days before, Fling figured, if fuel ran short, he could land there. He decided to make the bomb run.

Fortunately, visibility was now good, enabling Fling, flying his nonprescribed route to the target area, to avoid colliding with the aircraft that had completed their bombing and were leaving the burning city. With his attention completely on the run to target, Fling heard Peterson exclaim that fire was coming at them off to right front. As they got closer it became evident to Fling that what Peterson had spotted was actually incendiaries dropping on the city. The reflection of light on the long tails of the thousands of little M-69 bombs as they fell earthward looked to Peterson like tracers coming up at him. Seeing most of his target area burning, Fling dropped on a dark area and turned on his prescribed exit course.

*   *   *

OF THE 325 B-29s taking to the air on 9 March, none had a crew with less combat experience than those aboard the airplane commanded by Lt. Rennie Fontham. They had flown an airplane from the United States and arrived on Guam on 5 March, where they joined the 29th Bomb Group, one of two groups making up Gen. Power's still under-strength 314th Wing (its 39th and 330th Groups had not yet left the United States). Without any of the practice bombing runs on Japanese-held islands that were customary for new units and crews, Fontham and members of his crew were assembled along with others of the 29th on the morning of 9 March and told to get their B-29 ready for a mission. This was their first surprise. The next, more a shock than a surprise, came that afternoon when they were ordered to attend the 29th Bomb Group briefing along with 26 other crews. Here the group commander, Col. Carl R. Storrie, and staff told them of the maximum effort against Tokyo that night. Trained in high-altitude daylight precision bombing, they listened with amazement and concern to their commander and staff describe an attack plan that differed radically from their training and from what they had heard about the missions against Japan up to that time. These concerns they shared with their experienced fellow airmen in the 73rd and 313th Bomb Wings, and in addition they felt the uneasiness of a crew that would be flying into combat for the first time.

Despite their inexperience, Fontham and his crew did an excellent job contending with the weather that gave many of the veteran crews problems on the mission. Thanks to the skill of their navigator, Lt. Alfred K. B. Tsang, they arrived at their initial point without trouble and proceeded on their bomb run toward Target Area #4, the area across the Sumida River from the Fukugawa ward, lying between Tokyo Railroad Station and the river. By this time searchlights were on, but they did not catch Fontham's airplane. As he approached the target area Fontham could see the "strings of flame" made by the M-69s dropped by aircraft to his front. The pathfinders had done a good job with their loads of M-47s, and the target area was already partly burning. Consequently, following the instructions given him at the mission briefing, Fontham would bomb visually on a part of the target area not yet on fire. Not far from his bomb release point, Fontham watched one of his squadron's airplanes catch fire and plunge to earth. Continuing on, Fontham dropped his load of M-69 bombs, kept briefly on the same heading, then broke off sharply to the northeast.

UNLIKE FONTHAM, COL. John A. Roberts, group commander of the 19th Bomb Group, 314th Wing, had flown many bombing missions against the Japanese during his two years of air combat in the southeast Pacific. Seasoned as he was to the destruction that bombs could cause, the veteran pilot was astonished at what he saw happening to Tokyo that night. After his aircraft had dropped its bombs, he spent a period of time flying over the city to survey where the fires were.

The fires were everywhere. High above Tokyo, Power's map was beginning to fill up with fire locations. Not surprisingly, Target Area #1, the Asakusa ward, was the first to become almost completely engulfed in flames. A total of 106 aircraft would drop on this area with its tinderbox construction and closely packed housing. By contrast Target Area #4 just to the south, about the same size but with more substantial construction and less densely populated, was hit by less than half the number—51—as the Asakusa ward. This assignment of forces was not consistent with LeMay's official report on the mission. In the portion of his report describing the aiming points designed to set fires in the four areas of Tokyo's "Incendiary Zone 1," LeMay stated that "Equal force [was] assigned to each point to make certain that the average density of bombs would be greater than the minimum requirement of 60 tons of incendiaries per square mile for the entire zone." Though this may have been the original plan, in the field order for the mission and in the execution of the attack it is apparent that LeMay followed a classic maxim of war—concentrate your most powerful force at the enemy's weakest or most vulnerable point.

Elsewhere in his report, LeMay stated that since the predicted wind was from the west (280°), the bombing sequence planned was from east to west to prevent smoke from obscuring aiming points previously bombed. Strangely, nothing in his field order provided for the bombing on the east side of the Sumida to precede that on the west side. As Power had observed, the first fires started on the west side of the river and incendiaries were falling in all four target areas before 20 minutes had elapsed.

Fortunately, the failure to follow through on this sound planning concept did not have the adverse effects that blowing smoke had had on LeMay's Hankow fire mission three months before. Apparently the intensity and volume of hot air of the extraordinarily fierce fires, at least in the initial periods of the attack, forced the smoke clouds up to the higher altitudes, and the increasingly strong west winds dissipated them. As a result, smoke did not interfere with setting fires in the Honjo and Fukugawa wards, east of the Sumida River. Actually the wind contributed substantially to the spread of fire in these two areas. It drove the flames before it. No natural firebreak existed before the Nakagawa Canal, three to five miles to the east.

As THE ATTACK wore on, smoke began to obscure Power's vision in his airborne observation post. Because of this and because he already had on his map more than enough evidence to show LeMay that the mission was a great success, Power climbed up from his position in the bombardier's compartment, took the pilot's position and told Simeral to head back to Guam.

Once clear of the Tokyo area, Power asked Erwin, the radio operator, to inform the ground station at Guam of their expected time of arrival. Power knew that LeMay would want to be on hand when they landed, to hear his report.

NINE

THE FLOWERS
OF EDO

PLEASED AS HE was with what appeared to him to be a highly successful mission, Gen. Power had no way of knowing the magnitude of what had taken place on the ground below. The series of fires that had plagued Tokyo for centuries and which the Japanese, with their penchant for descriptive names, called the "Flowers of Edo" (the Japanese name for Tokyo), reached their zenith that night. No single act of war, before or since, would exact as great a toll in life and property as was inflicted on Tokyo during the hours between midnight and dawn Saturday, 10 March 1945.

The gravity and nature of the attack surprised and overwhelmed Tokyo's military and fire defenses alike. Two assistants to the Tokyo fire chief went to the roof of City Hall minutes after the first bombs fell near the docks less than a mile away. From their vantage point they saw the fires starting directly north and, across the Sumida River, to the northeast and east. Any confidence Tokyo's professional and neighborhood fire fighters had gained as a result of their success in the incendiary attack of 25 February was quickly erased that night.

Most workers and their families were asleep when the warning siren sounded at 10:30 P.M. The siren signifying that an air attack was imminent or in progress did not come until 12:15 A.M. By then the first B-29s had already released their incendiaries. Soon, in many homes, people heard metal cylinders crash through their roofs, saw them hit the floor and watched helplessly as the long metal containers sprayed flaming globs of gasoline against the walls. Attempts to follow the official dictum—each citizen should stay and protect his own house—failed completely. Occasionally a family was able to put out fires with water buckets, shovels and wet sacks, only to have their house catch fire again, ignited by flames from their neighbor's house. Most citizens, seeing the rapid spread of fires, made no attempt to protect their homes and only sought to save their lives.

Over 6,000 professional fire fighters manning 843 fire engines, along with many auxiliary units, were unable to contend with the onslaught. Fires sprang up so quickly that dispatchers were overwhelmed with calls for help. Many fire fighters found themselves and their equipment surrounded and trapped. Some fire stations were destroyed by fire. In one station all the firemen were burned to death while attempting to get their equipment started and on the way. Months later this equipment was still in the same position that it was on the day of the bombing. Ninety-six fire engines were destroyed and more than 600 firemen were dead or missing after the night was over.

Though the Tokyo firemen were ill-equipped by American standards, it is doubtful whether any fire department in the world could have successfully fought the fires that night. As the bombing progressed, the wind from the northwest, which earlier had been blowing at 12 mph, increased to 28 mph. After an hour or so, as fires in various areas merged and increased in intensity, a fire condition known as a "conflagration" developed. The chief characteristic of a conflagration is a wall of flames moving in the direction of the prevailing wind, preceded by a mass of preheated vapors. In Tokyo's highly combustible areas the heat in front of the wall of flame was so intense that, according to observers, often an entire row of houses would burst into flame before the main body of fire reached them. The same heat and vapors snuffed the life out of those unable to flee before it. The firestorms that had incinerated large areas of Hamburg and Dresden in Germany—terrible in their own right—lacked a prevailing wind. They burned as a huge column of flame that created a massive inrush of air at great velocity. Virtually everything within the area at the base of the fire column was consumed, but the destruction did not extend much beyond this perimeter. The conflagration, considered by experts to be the worst type of mass fire, fed on everything in its path and would continue until it encountered an area in which nothing was burnable.

On the morning of 10 March, on the west side of the Sumida River, the conflagration moved across the Asakusa ward, burning to the ground virtually all of the dwellings in this ward. Then it moved on to burn many of the residences of Kanda, consumed the contents of many of the large businesses and industrial buildings in Nihombashi ward and burnt itself out when it encountered the river.

On the east side of the Sumida, the great wall of fire moving in an easterly to southeasterly direction swept across the Honjo and Fukugawa wards with similar destructive force. It continued to burn well beyond the eastern boundary of the target zone into the Joto ward until it was stopped by open areas, firebreaks or, finally, the Nakagawa Canal.

All that night, for the 1.5 million people living in the target areas, life or death was determined by chance—whether they stayed at home or left immediately, whether they sought safety to the north, south, east or west, whether they stopped or continued to flee, whether they followed the crowd or not. The number of choices were myriad. Any one of them could spell the difference between survival or a fiery death.

In the populous Asakusa ward, hundreds of men, women and children, having abandoned their homes and possessions, joined a large crowd running toward a Buddhist temple, dedicated to Kwan-Yin, Goddess of Mercy. The large, 200-year-old building had survived many Flowers of Edo, including the devastating fire that had followed the Great Earthquake in

1923. Soon hundreds of citizens had run across the small treed park that surrounded the temple and crowded themselves inside. The safety that they had sought was brief. Ignited by either the tremendous heat of the oncoming wall of fire or the flaming gel from M-69 incendiaries, or possibly both, the huge structure caught fire. People trying to leave through the temple doors ran into others who were still trying to enter. As fire and smoke increased, terror-stricken people pushed, shoved and kicked in a desperate attempt to get out. As was the case in individual battles for survival throughout the night, many of the weak, usually the very young or the very old, died, not from the fire, but as a result of being trampled or crushed in crowds crazed by fear and desperation.

AFTER THE FIRST hour or so, most of the population of the Asakusa ward was fleeing eastward, away from the wall of flame. Along the way buildings were burning and collapsing, telephone poles and wires fell in flames on the streets, and the terrible heat and smoke followed no matter how fast people ran. Most wore a heavily padded hood over the head and shoulders, which was supposed to protect the wearer from flying debris resulting from high-explosive bomb blasts. Women wore baggy trousers; men, trousers plus cloth leg wrappings. The "protective" clothing turned out to be a liability. Sparks flying through the air landed on the thick hoods and often ignited them without the person feeling it. In the superheated dry air, the flames traveled rapidly over the rest of the clothing. Unless the flames were extinguished rapidly, and often this was not accomplished, the person would fall and be left behind to die. The same terrible result might occur when sparks landed on the padding enveloping infants, customarily carried on women's backs. Those whose hoods did not catch fire might be burned as a result of a phenomena of the conflagration: the downward thrust of the hot vapors in front of the rolling wall of flame. These vapors created such a layer of tremendous heat on the street surfaces that even the smallest spark or ember could ignite a man's leg wraps or a woman's trousers. People who did not burn from the head down might burn from the feet up.

Some found temporary protection from the fire by dousing themselves with water from water barrels and other containers intended for quelling fires. But the water evaporated in minutes and they were once again in trouble.

MOST OF THE crowds fled toward the Sumida River, hoping to find some protection there or to cross on one of the bridges to the other side. The Kototoi Bridge, one of more than a dozen bridges spanning the river, was the objective many struggled to reach. The long bridge, like most of the others constructed of steel and concrete, could not be damaged by fire. Its wide pavement began at Sumida Park and stretched the length of two football fields to the Honjo ward on the other side.

Some, reaching the Sumida Park, decided to take refuge in its open space. The park, scarcely 100 yards wide, soon filled to overflowing. Those along the riverbank used the water to stay cool and to keep from catching fire. As the mass of fire pushed ever closer, new arrivals forced their way into the park itself. The crowding and heat became oppressive and people began to fight for space. Along the river's edge, some were pushed and others leaped into the water to escape. Oppressive heat was replaced by numbing cold. It was March of the coldest winter that Japan had experienced in nearly 40 years. The water, at 40°F, would only sustain life for a short time. Nearly all of those forced into the river drowned. Those in the park died of burns and asphyxiation.

Thousands did not stop at Sumida Park but pushed on, hoping to find a haven on the bridge itself or cross it and put the river between them and the fires in Asakusa. Again, the frantic quest for safety was, for most, fruitless. Earlier, people living near the river had moved onto the bridge. When the flood of humanity from Asakusa began to arrive, the remaining space on the bridge soon filled. Another battle for survival—with frantic individuals pushing, shoving, beating and stomping on each other—ensued. Some desperate individuals climbed over the bridge rail and jumped, a drop of nearly 100 feet into icy water. Like those in the park who had chosen to jump or had been forced into the river, few survived.

*   *   *

ON THE NIGHT of 9 March, Masae Oshita was in her home in the Honjo ward, a mostly residential area west of the Asakusa ward. Twenty years old, she lived with her father, who was retired, her mother, an older sister, Michiko, and a younger sister, Tomiya. By this time the government had closed schools in Tokyo, so the girls spent their school time sewing robes for hospitalized Japanese soldiers.

The Oshitas' house had two bomb shelters, one under the kitchen and another under the living room floor. Like all Tokyo residents, Masae and her family had often had to retreat to the shelters before that night. So far no bombs had fallen in their area, but Masae was aware of what they could do. After the 25 February daylight incendiary raid she had visited the burnt-out sections a few miles south of where she lived.

When the sirens sounded that night, Masae's mother and her younger sister went to the shelter under the kitchen and Masae and her older sister occupied the one under the living room. Mr. Oshita left the house to join other men who, like himself, had responsibilities for fire and safety in the neighborhood during air raids. Some hours later Masae heard unusual noises and, curious as to what they were, left the shelter with her sister and went outside. The sky to the east was bright with fire and a house not far away was burning. Soon their father appeared. He assembled the family and told them he had to stay but that they should split up and leave the area. Masae's mother and younger sister started walking to the north, and Masae and her older sister went south toward the Kanda ward.

Along the way Masae and her sister, part of a growing crowd, passed people who had fallen, exhausted and stricken by the heat. One prostrate woman grabbed Masae by the leg, begged for water and wouldn't let go. Masae's sister struck the woman with a bucket that was lying nearby. The woman released her hold. The desperation of the crowd increased. More homes and commercial buildings were catching fire, creating smoke, acrid fumes and intense heat. Masae's eyes watered and burned. The hot air burned the inside of her nose. She began to wonder about their decision to go to Kanda.

About then, word spread that there was a church ahead, where they could find shelter. Masae and her sister ran to the church, a substantial structure, and, along with hundreds of others, crowded inside. For a while they found some relief from the conditions outside, but sparks from burning buildings nearby penetrated the building, igniting wood, cloth and other combustibles. Masae and her sister ran out of the church into the street. Buildings all around were on fire. They spotted a water reservoir, about the size of a small swimming pool. The city had built this one and others like it in various parts of the city to provide water for the fire department. It was full of water and almost full of people. Masae and her sister climbed over the side and immersed themselves. They spent the remaining hours of the night in the water, leaving only occasionally to relieve themselves of the crush of humanity in the reservoir and then having to fight for a place to fit back in. The water protected most of the body, but the head had to remain exposed to heat and smoke. At some point, as the night wore on, Masae discovered that she could no longer see.

At dawn Masae's sister determined that the heat was tolerable outside of the reservoir and helped Masae climb over the side onto the street. As they sat collecting themselves, her sister described the scene. Bodies of those killed in the crush floated in the reservoir. Other dead lay around the outside— they had been either unable or unwilling to get in. Grateful for their survival, the two girls decided to go back to their house. They set out, with her sister leading the now sightless Masae.

All along the way they encountered scenes of smoldering desolation. As they approached their own neighborhood, Masae's sister saw many homes destroyed. Closer, she saw that their home had burnt to the ground. Following her family's instructions, Masae's sister found a piece of wood and some charcoal and wrote their names and that they were alive on the wood and left it at the site of their house. Hours later, their father found them wandering around the neighborhood. His pleasure at finding them was diminished by his concern about Masae's inability to see. He took her to a hospital, where, after she had waited in a long line for hours, a doctor washed and bandaged Masae's eyes. The doctor's actions provided some relief from pain but the condition of Masae's eyes was still undetermined. Together, the father and his two daughters trudged wearily to his sister's house, about an hour away, and found it undamaged. The sister welcomed them, and they slept for the first time since the sirens had sounded the night before.

Masae's mother and younger sister had found safety in a temple in Ueno Park. After returning and finding their house destroyed, they, too, made their way to the sister's house.

Later the family returned to their house to survey the damage. Everything had been destroyed. Even the papers and money in their father's steel safe had been reduced to thin black ashes. Masae's sister did find the ceramic head of the first doll that Masae had bought with her own money. Despite the material losses, the family was alive and Masae's sight was returning. They had reason to be thankful. Together, they enjoyed a meal prepared from a small sack of rice and red beans that the resourceful Masae had carried throughout the ordeal.

FATE DID NOT deal so kindly with thousands of families in the Honjo ward across the Sumida River from the Asakusa ward. Many members of these families died in the Futabe Grade School, a large, three-story, reinforced-concrete building, five blocks east of the Honjo ward office. The school basement had been designed as an air raid shelter. Part of the ground floor was a gymnasium, with the rest made up of offices and classrooms. The upper two floors consisted entirely of classrooms. On the east side of the building was a large swimming pool.

When the seriousness of the fires became evident, it occurred to most of the working people who lived in the vicinity to go to a familiar, safe place—the Futabe Grade School. One of those who made such a decision was Hidezo Tsuchikura.

Soon after the first incendiaries fell in the Honjo ward, Hidezo and his two young children (his wife and newborn child were in an outlying area) hastened to the school building. He and his children were among the first to arrive but after going down into the basement shelter he decided not to stay. The shelter was filling rapidly and he feared that in a panic his children would be crushed or, if the building collapsed, buried alive. The latter fear was deep-seated in Hidezo, because as a boy of six he had survived the collapse of a building in the Great Earthquake of 1923.

He went next to the gymnasium. Space was scarce, so he went upstairs to one of the classrooms. Here, again, over-crowding caused him to take the children up to another, less crowded, classroom on the third floor. Once settled, he looked out of a window and was shocked by what he saw. Instead of the occasional fires that he had observed on the way to the school he now saw a wall of fire rolling from the river toward the building they occupied. Houses in its path caught fire, burned and collapsed, spewing sparks and embers high into the air like a fireworks display.

As minutes passed, all the classrooms on the third floor, including the one he was in, filled. People crowded the hall-ways. With the windows kept closed to keep sparks from en-tering, the air became stifling. His children begged him to take them out of there. In desperation he decided, against the ad-vice of others in the classroom, to face the fiery conditions and go up to the roof.

Flaming embers and sparks danced through the air as Hi-dezo emerged from the stairwell and moved across the roof. He spotted a water tank, and he and his children sat down next to it. Frightening and hot as it was, at least a person could breathe. After a while he went to the edge of the roof and looked toward the river. In the reflected light of the massive fires, he could see for many blocks. What he saw appalled him. People running down the streets, running to the school, run-ning away from the school and, worst of all, falling to the ground and dying like human torches.

While he was watching the chaos and death below, he heard his daughter scream; turning, he saw that sparks had landed on her, igniting her clothes. He quickly scooped some water from the tank and put out the fire on his daughter, only to hear his son scream that he was on fire. Hidezo lifted up his son and plunged him into the tank. Then, finding that his own clothing was beginning to burn, he jumped into the tank him-self. For the next hour the little family used the tank to keep from catching fire and to cool off. By three o'clock the flames had passed on to the east.

At dawn Hidezo decided it was safe to leave the roof. Together with his children, he went to the stairs just 30 feet from where they had spent the night. Opening the door and looking down he saw nothing but smoke, fumes and bodies. Aghast, he went to the other two stairwells and found the same conditions. Meanwhile he encountered a dozen others who had spent the night on the roof. They concluded that they were the only survivors of the hundreds, perhaps thousands, who had sought refuge in the school building. While they waited for the smoke to dissipate and lingering fires to burn out in the floors below, one of the men discovered a steel emergency stair on the side of the building. Together they walked down to safety.

WHAT HAD HAPPENED at Futabe Grade School occurred in other "fireproof" buildings that night. Through openings or windows shattered by the intense heat, flaming embers entered the buildings, igniting desks, drapes, cabinets, wood molding, stair rails—anything that could burn. The resulting fires turned the multistoried building into a huge oven, burning or suffocating the occupants.

Other Honjo residents who sought shelter in the Futabe Grade School could not get there or, after arriving, could not get in. One of these was Mrs. Kikue Mizuta. Six months earlier her husband had been drafted into the Navy. She and her five-year-old son lived with her husband's aged parents. Dutifully, she stayed in her house as long as she could, but with many fires starting in the neighborhood she finally was forced to leave. With her son and two aged parents, she headed for the Futabe Grade School. On the way she had to beat out fires that started on her child, and when they finally arrived at the school the grandparents were missing. She tried all of the entrances and could not get in. The building was filled. She gave up and, for no particular reason, started toward the Sumida River. She and her children came to a park that was nearly filled with people. Noticing that on both sides of the park were rows of wooden houses, and with sparks flying through the air, Kikue pressed on. Minutes later they arrived at a large, open plaza in front of the Ryogoku Railroad Station. The station itself was concrete, as were the nearest buildings on the other side of the plaza. Kikue decided to stay there. She, her son and the others on the plaza survived. The bodies of her husband's parents were never recovered.

An even larger haven existed just south of the plaza where Mrs. Mizuta stopped: a firebreak created as part of the government program earlier in the war. It was nearly a block wide and extended underneath and alongside the Sobu Electric Elevated Rail Line, east of the Sumida River, for the equivalent of three blocks. Thousands avoided death after they found their way there.

North of the Fatube Grade School thousands more citizens tried to find refuge along the steep banks of Kikugawa Creek. People crowded along the banks, thinking the embankment would protect them from fire above and that they could use creek water to douse fires and keep cool. They discovered too late they had made a terrible choice. As the houses built along the top of the embankment caught fire and burned furiously, the downward force of the conflagration pushed superheated air down into the creek bed. Thousands died there from suffocation, burns and drowning.

SOUTH OF HONJO ward, the raging conflagration continued to exact its toll as flames swept across the Fukugawa ward. As the fires approached his neighborhood, Imai Hisaki, an office boy at the Kyodo News Service, decided to stay and try to save his house after his mother had left with the younger children. He soon realized that the approaching fires would inevitably consume his house and decided to leave. Only then did he discover that his eight-year-old brother had stayed behind in the confusion. So he grabbed his brother's hand and together they left the house. Unsure at first where to go, he remembered a large vacant lot that he had played in as a child and decided to head for it. Along the way he and his brother dodged falling timbers and sparks from collapsing houses. They passed many persons running in the opposite direction, but Imai and his brother pressed on. When they finally arrived at the big lot Imai had remembered, they found that houses had been built on it. He decided to try to reach Tokyo Bay, still a mile and a half away. With wet cloths over their faces, they finally made their way to a location near the shore and spent the night there. Imai was later reunited with his mother and the rest of his family. She had also made her way to Tokyo Bay and spent the night near the water with her three-year-old son clinging to her back.

The Nihombashi ward, with its mostly commercial and business buildings, did not suffer the extensive damage done in Asakusa, Honjo and Fukugawa, but those who lived or worked there were not spared a share of the horror. Masuko Harino, a young factory worker, stayed in a hostel for volunteers in Nihombashi. When flames began to threaten the hostel, the manager announced that if the building caught fire, he was going to stay and fight. He stayed, but Masuko and a companion, along with most of the hostel occupants, fled. The two ran away from the flames toward the Sumida River. The heat became intense. People fell with their clothing afire, but no one stopped to help. Masuko's eyes burned and every breath was difficult. She saw a broken fire hydrant, soaked her hood in the water and put it back on. It helped. She finally reached the Kiyosu Bridge, across the Sumida. Looking across the river toward the Fukugawa ward she saw a sea of fire on the other side. Still, people continued onto the bridge. Others jumped into the river to escape the heat. Masuko and her companion could go no farther. Exhausted, they fell by the side of the road. They remained there along with others, some conscious, some not, until the flames subsided.

In another part of Nihombashi, police had directed fleeing citizens to a modern theater, the Meiji. It soon filled. When fire neared the building, smoke and hot fumes entered through the ventilating system. Panic ensued, the exits jammed with people, and as flames surrounded the building all of its occupants perished from heat and asphyxiation.

*   *   *

JUST TO THE north of Tokyo lies the town of Kawaguchi. Michiko Kanno lived just outside of the town in a compound owned by the NHK (Radio Corporation of Japan). Her father was in charge of the NHK station with its two giant transmission towers.

On the night of 9 March, Michiko's father, who was also a radio communications officer in the Army, was in Manchuria. Michiko, age 17, her mother and four brothers were in the family home. After they heard the first warning of a possible raid on the radio, they kept their set on. Then shortly after midnight the announcer declared that a raid was in progress. Since night raids were unusual, Michiko, her mother and the older boys took up stations near the windows facing the south so they could see what was taking place. The countryside between their house and the Asakusa and Honjo wards, a distance of less than five miles, was flat, mostly rice fields, so they had a virtually unobstructed view of the city.

At first they saw only an orange glow at one spot on the horizon. Then the spot began to spread until it seemed to cover the entire horizon. The fiery panorama grew to towering proportions. Michiko saw searchlights crisscrossing in the sky and, on one or two occasions, spotted a silver B-29 caught in the lights for a short period then disappear. Fascinated, she watched bombs dropping through the air, trailing flames as they fell earthward. (The trailing flames must have been the reflection of the fires below on the long white streamers of the M-69 bombs.) Then they saw, less than a mile away, a huge pillar of black smoke, illuminated by the bright light from the burning city. A B-29 had crashed and was burning. At this point Michiko's mother became concerned for the safety of the family and decided they should go to the concrete air raid shelter at the base of one of the radio towers. They spent the rest of the night there.

SIRENS SIGNALING THAT the air raid was over sounded at 3:20 A.M., 20 minutes after the last airplane of the 313th Bomb Wing had dropped its load of M-69s on the Fukugawa ward. By 6 A.M. the conflagration that had swept across central Tokyo had expended itself. Isolated fires would burn on, some for days, but the tremendous destruction to life and property had taken place in the hours before dawn.

Dr. Shigenori Kubota headed a military rescue unit of nine physicians and eleven nurses that headed into the burned areas. His team drove through streets, dodging the charred remnants of telephone poles and strands of wire, and arrived at the Ryogoku Bridge at dawn. The scene there—even to the eyes of these medical professionals—was appalling. "In the black Sumida river," he later wrote, "countless bodies were floating, clothed bodies, naked bodies, all as black as charcoal. It was unreal. These were dead people, but you couldn't tell whether they were men or women. You couldn't even tell if the objects floating by were arms and legs or pieces of burnt wood."

After crossing the bridge into the Honjo ward, the team encountered more grim reminders of the terrible chaos of the previous night. Bodies of men, women and children lay in the streets and on the sidewalks in the positions in which they had died. Mothers clutched babies in a last embrace. Families huddled together. Some corpses lay in grotesque positions; others reclined peacefully. Many bodies, like those in the Sumida, were charred beyond recognition. Others bore hardly a mark on them: these had died of suffocation or heat prostration and, by chance, the flames had passed them by.

Besides the human reminders, the streets were littered with material things: burnt-out cars and trucks, charred remainders of carts, baby carriages and wheelbarrows in which people had hoped to carry their belongings to safety; pots, pans and other metal objects blown by the wind after the dwellings in which they had been used were reduced to ashes; and even heavier items that had been swept by the wind at its peak— pieces of galvanized steel, metal window frames, shards of glass, hunks of plaster—mute testimony to the fact that there had once been dwellings where now there was nothing but open space.

As light increased and most of the smoke dissipated, Kubota could look to the east across acres and acres of desertlike landscape broken only occasionally by the shell of a concrete building, a smokestack, a steel lamp post, a stone monument or wall—objects that the flames could neither consume nor melt as they roared through the city.

Dr. Kubota had little time to contemplate the enormity of the disaster. Soon he and his team had set up an emergency aid station in the Honjo National School and, along with Japanese Red Cross teams at other locations, provided as much medical care as they could to an endless stream of injured people. Besides those with burns, which Kubota's staff were able to treat only superficially, many persons had suffered injury to their eyes, throat and lungs. Carbon monoxide poisoning and oxygen deficiency were common. One man had so much pain in breathing that he felt he wanted to cut open his chest and let some clean air in. Countless others, like Masae Oshita, had lost their sight from the effects of ashes and dust blown into their eyes. Unlike Masae, who recovered completely, many others were permanently blinded because of infections that went untreated.

While Dr. Kubota and the limited medical staff available did their best to treat the injured, Japanese soldiers and policemen were assisting those who had lost their homes and property and contending with the massive problem of disposing of the dead.

The great number of human remains created a problem of unprecedented proportions. It took the combined resources of the Army and the police and fire departments to recover, attempt identification of and dispose of the dead. Bodies were found in the ashes of dwellings, rivers, canals, basements, schools, temples, theaters, parks and in the streets—virtually everywhere. The remains were hauled in carts and trucks to schoolyards and parks and there laid out for identification, usually with a white paper tag stating where the body was found. Many were burned beyond recognition, and even those who were recognizable had usually fled from the area in which they resided. Most of the remains were never identified. Individual cremations at established crematoriums—the custom of the Japanese people—were seldom possible. Identified bodies were buried in individual graves, but the bulk of the human remains, the unidentified, were buried in pits in parks and temple grounds in groups of 20 or more.

For survivors, the Army and the ward governments set up relief stations at undamaged schools and other buildings. They provided shelter and distributed limited amounts of food, mainly rice balls, and blankets. Tokyo residents who previously had opposed leaving the city, now homeless, had no choice. Once necessary repairs had been made to the rail system, police and firemen were sent to the main stations in the city to assist the station employees in moving the large number of refugees desiring transportation to the countryside. Initially some citizens were assisted in moving to homes in wards west of the city that had not been affected by the bombing. But in the days that followed, the tremendous number of refugees required the government to arrange for accommodations in schools, temples and other public buildings.

While some Japanese soldiers were burying the dead and assisting refugees, still others were on parade. Saturday, 10 March was Armed Forces Day and despite the havoc of the previous night and the destruction all around, troops marched in downtown Tokyo. A photograph of the parade graphically portrays the striking contrast in attitude of the military hierarchy and the people to the realities of that day. In the center of the photo is an Army band, presumably at the head of the marching troops. The front rank of the band is composed of musicians with bass drums, cymbals and snare drums, followed by ranks of trombonists and other traditional bandsmen. In the background, standing on the curb, people are watching the parade go by, much as others might have watched similar parades for more than four decades. In the foreground, apparently moving down a lane in the street kept clear for them, are refugees, a man pulling a loaded bicycle cart, a woman carrying a single bundle and others carrying nothing, all moving down the street abreast of the marching band. For the Army it was a time for putting on the best front. For the civilians it was a time of loss and sorrow.

In sharp contrast to the mood of the people of Tokyo, the crews making the final turn over Choshi Point and heading to their bases in the Marianas felt more than the usual relief that came after a bomb run was over. They would not need a post-mission report to tell them that they had dealt the enemy a serious blow that night. Looking back to the northwest, even from a distance of 100 miles away, they could still see the fires of the city reflected in the sky. Though most must have harbored a deep-seated awareness of the terrible human toll they had exacted, the overriding feeling, from pilot to tailgunner, was one of elation—a mission accomplished far beyond their expectations.

As their intense emotions subsided, the crews settled down for the usually uneventful trip back to base. Dean Fling and the crew of *God's Will* did not find it uneventful, however. Three hours south of Japan and with fuel low, they again lost their course. Luckily they got a navigation assist from a Dumbo (a rescue plane), made a safe landing on Iwo Jima and picked up 500 gallons of fuel. Grateful, they gave some thankful Marines bottles of Coca Cola and flew on to Tinian.

Others in the more than 300-airplane armada whiled away the time in much the same ways they had on the way up, but now the tension was gone. The crewmen in the rear compartment slept, talked, ate sandwiches, smoked and listened to Armed Forces Radio Network broadcasting from Saipan. Up front it was pretty much the same, with the pilot and copilot taking turns, one watching the controls while the other might climb up in the tunnel and take a nap. North of the Marianas, those that weren't sleeping, particularly those in the nose and on the left side of the ship, might look out and see a beautiful sunrise with variations in light and color characteristic of that part of the Pacific.

LATER THE ISLAND bases come into view, Saipan for the veteran 73rd Wing, Tinian for the 313th, and Guam for the 314th.

As Walter Sherrell, at the controls of the *Southern Belle*, entered the traffic pattern, everyone in the aircraft heard over their earphones the welcome call, "Tower to *Southern Belle*, you are cleared to land." Sherrell adjusted his trim tabs and prop controls while Hall lowered the landing gear and the flaps halfway. The gunners on each side watched as the land-

ing gear and flaps moved down and locked, and reported this
to Sherrell. As the airplane banked toward its final approach
the flaps were lowered all the way and the aircraft lost altitude
rapidly. As the gunners peered out of their plastic windows,
the ground seemed to streak by. Then they heard the engines
cut back and the tires bark as they contacted the runway. The
airplane settled down on its three sets of dual gear. Sherrell
braked down the runway until he was at taxi speed and turned
off on the taxi strip. Ground crews were out there and so was
the chaplain. Brakes squealed as Sherrell maneuvered into his
assigned place on the hardstand. Once stopped, he gunned the
engines to provide power for the bomb bays to be opened, then
ran them up once more before shutting them down for good.
Silence. Mission complete. After swapping a few pleasantries
with the ground crew, the weary combat crewmen grabbed
their personal effects, climbed down and loaded into awaiting
trucks.

The return to base was much the same as Sherrell's for all
the airplanes completing the Tokyo mission except one—the
Snatch Blatch. General Power had taken Simeral's place at
the controls about an hour north of Guam. After he landed
and brought the airplane to a stop, flashbulbs started popping.
Waiting to greet the *Snatch Blatch* were LeMay and Norstad.
As Simeral and the rest of the crew got into a truck and left,
Power, tired but exultant, with a heavy growth of beard, told
LeMay and Norstad that it had been "one hell of a mission."
Then, with more flashbulbs popping, he handed his map folder
to LeMay who, with Norstad looking over his shoulder, studied the marks that Power had made on it. Both LeMay and
Norstad were impressed with the coverage and congratulated
Power. After a few more pictures, Power went to his quarters
for a shower and some rest. Pleased as LeMay was with Power's report, both he and Norstad knew that final evidence of
the success of the mission would not be available until after
the first photo mission had been completed, and that was 24
hours away.

Shortly after noon the last of the airplanes had landed. By
this time most of the crews had completed their postmission
routine. Trucks took them to group headquarters where the
S-2 (intelligence officer) waited to interrogate them. On the

way to their debriefing, many stopped and scanned the status board to see what airplanes had returned, ditched, landed at Iwo or were missing. Over coffee and doughnuts, the intelligence officers plied their trade, asking questions designed to find out as much as possible about the mission—damage inflicted, enemy defenses, tactics, facilities, etc. Some of the detailed information might not seem important to an individual crewman but to a trained interrogator, along with other elements of information, it might prove to be of great value in planning future operations. Group and wing commanders often sat in on some interrogations to get firsthand information on mission results.

As ground crews and maintenance specialists out on the hardstands were swarming all over the aircraft to prepare them for the next mission, in Tokyo the authorities were assessing the effects of the one just completed.

THE JAPANESE DETERMINED that in addition to the Asakusa, Honjo and Fukugawa wards, the Joto and Shitaya wards had been almost totally destroyed by fire. Over a dozen wards suffered partial to substantial fire damage. The Metropolitan Police Bureau records (considered by the U.S. Strategic Bombing Survey to be the most reliable of those turned over to them) showed that 267,171 buildings burned, about 25 percent of the buildings in Tokyo at the time. As a result of this destruction 1,008,000 people were homeless. The police bureau estimated that 83, 793 people died as a direct result of the bombing and 40,918 suffered injuries.

Damage to war production was substantial. The Hattori Company, manufacturer of time fuzes for artillery shells, employed 4,000 people. Plant personnel put out fires from M-69 bombs falling on or around its reinforced concrete buildings, but nearby structures caught fire and burned furiously. The heat from those fires was so great that it melted the wire-glass windows of the main plant. Propelled by the powerful winds, the fire entered the buildings, burned through them and heavily damaged the machinery. The management estimated the damage at 35 percent, and production had to be continued on a reduced scale until the end of the war. Embers and sparks from burning shops and warehouses blew across a canal onto the buildings of the Fujikura Electric Cable Works, a company about the same size as Hattori. The resultant fire caused such serious damage that the entire plant was closed for the rest of the war. Twenty-one other industrial plants were damaged to varying degrees. The number of small suppliers and home workshops destroyed is not known, but it must have been large, since virtually the entire area in which this type of production took place was burned.

In addition to the direct effect that the incendiary bombs had on war production—damage and destruction of plants and machinery—they had an important indirect effect, as exemplified by the Mitsubishi Steel Works, Fukugawa plant. A shower of M-69s fell in the vicinity of the plant, but only one hit an isolated warehouse. Though the steel plant itself suffered no damage whatsoever, it ceased production after the attack because most of its workers had lost their homes and had to leave the city. Of the approximately one million people displaced on 10 March about 25 percent were members of the industrial work force. The impact of the loss of a quarter of a million workers, virtually overnight, on the production capacity of the Tokyo industrial complex was serious.

Though the aerial photographs that Lt. Omer Cox took from an altitude of 30,000 feet during the daylight hours of 10 March did not reveal the impact on Japanese industrial manpower, they did reveal to LeMay, Montgomery and others looking at them on the following morning that the burned out area had exceeded their expectations. The strike had been an overwhelming success. Fires still burning obscured some areas from Cox's camera lenses, but follow-up photo missions disclosed that the attacking force had destroyed an area of 15.8 square miles, in addition to the one square mile destroyed on 25 February. Twenty-two identified AAF industrial targets had been destroyed as well as many other unidentified plants.

JAPAN'S FIRST ACKNOWLEDGMENT of the Tokyo incendiary raid, directed at the world press, came in the form of a war com-

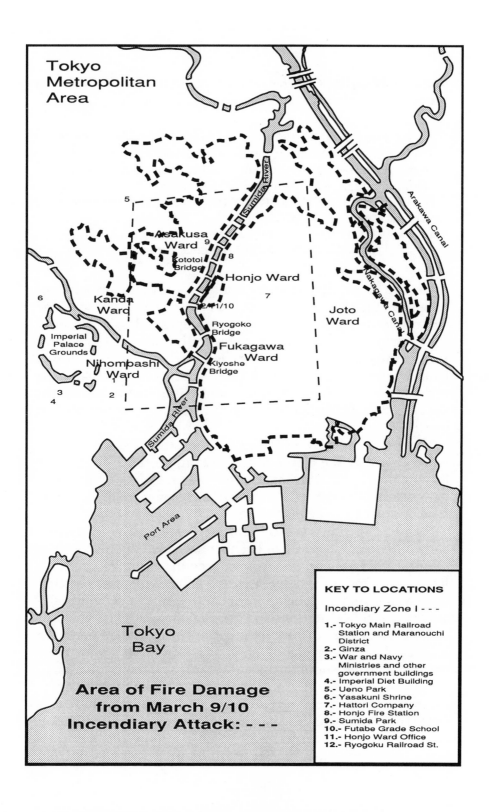

Tokyo
Metropolitan
Area

Sumida River

Arakawa Canal

Nakagawa Canal

5

Asakusa
Ward
9

Kototoi
Bridge

8

Honjo Ward

6

Kanda
Ward

2/11/10

7

Joto
Ward

Imperial
Palace
Grounds

Ryogoko
Bridge

Fukagawa
Ward

Nihombashi
Ward

Kiyoshe
Bridge

1

3

2

4

Sumida River

Port Area

Tokyo
Bay

Area of Fire Damage
from March 9/10
Incendiary Attack: - - -

KEY TO LOCATIONS

Incendiary Zone I - - -

1.- Tokyo Main Railroad
    Station and Maranouchi
    District
2.- Ginza
3.- War and Navy
    Ministries and other
    government buildings
4.- Imperial Diet Building
5.- Ueno Park
6.- Yasakuni Shrine
7.- Hattori Company
8.- Honjo Fire Station
9.- Sumida Park
10.- Futabe Grade School
11.- Honjo Ward Office
12.- Ryogoku Railroad St.

muniqué from Imperial Headquarters, issued on 10 March. In the understated language typical of such documents, it said:

> Today, approximately 130 B-29s, with their main force, raided Tokyo from a little after midnight to 0240 and carried out blind bombing attacks on certain sections. Resulting from this blind bombing attack, various places within the city were set afire. However, fire in the Shime-Ryo of the Imperial Household Ministry was put out at 0235 and others were all extinguished around 0800. The war results thus far confirmed are as follows: 15 planes shot down and about 50 planes damaged.

On the same day, the governor of Tokyo made two announcements to the citizens of his city, one inspirational, the other practical. He called upon the people to be "unafraid of the air raids," to "steel themselves to the great task of guarding the imperial capital" and to "lend support to the unfortunate sufferers." He also decreed that victims of the current air raid could ride municipal trams and buses free of charge for the next four days. (Many buses and streetcars had burned in the fire.)

The first note of the gravity of the situation was an announcement by the Home Ministry that, for those desirous of leaving the capital, the government was speeding up its evacuation plans. Enemy raids, the Ministry cautioned, would be more frequent than ever before.

For most of the war, covering up battle losses in remote parts of the Pacific area had been a relatively easy task for the Japanese government. Newspaper accounts were based on official government news releases and subject to close scrutiny by censors. As the geographic locations in the accounts describing Japanese victories and "negligible losses" grew closer and closer to the Japanese mainland, some readers began to wonder about the accuracy of their government's war information. Though some of the public might wonder, none had information with which to refute the government version of military events. Many accepted the government accounts because they were what the average Japanese wanted to believe. So, even when the Americans began bombing the home islands (an action that the Japanese high command had told

them early in the war would never happen), the official releases played down the importance of the bombings, exaggerated American losses and consistently emphasized that the
damage was "negligible"—as it often was.

But with the destruction of a massive area of the heart of the
Japanese empire, the Japanese high command was faced with
an event that could not be denied. As a consequence, soon
after the Tokyo bombing, the Japanese government allowed
(perhaps encouraged) newspapers and radio stations to reveal
to domestic and worldwide audiences that the Japanese capital had, indeed, suffered a heavy blow.

The major thrust of these articles, while unprecedented in
their admission of Japan's inability to protect its most important city, was to indict the United States. The Tokyo radio
agonized:

The man [Lemay] who invented and carried out the big raids of
Hamburg now directs the attacks on Japan from the Marianas.
A few nights ago he repeated here in Tokyo what he had learned
in Germany. Owing to various unfavorable circumstances the
storm of fire caused by incendiaries swept whole districts,
which were burned to the ground; only here and there were
blackened walls of the rare stone building left standing. That
bright, starlit night will remain in the memory of all who witnessed it. . . .

United States Army Air Forces attacks on Tokyo are known
among Japanese as "blind" bombing or "indiscriminate" air
raids because nonmilitary business and residential districts
have been the targets of these attacks, while noncombatant
civilians have been ruthlessly victimized. "Blind" bombing or
"indiscriminate"—these expressions have appeared in our official communiqués but are now regarded as a gross misnomer in
describing the enemy's savage attacks. It is now thought more
appropriate to call them "slaughter" bombing, a natural reflection of the growing popular indignation against their brutal
bombing attacks.

Tokyo officials did not allow the newspapers or radio to
reveal the actual casualty figures or the fact that nearly 16
square miles of the heart of the city had been burned out. This
did not stop rumors (probably based on information leaking

out of the police or fire departments) from spreading quickly through the city. These rumors often placed the casualties and destruction in excess of the official figures.

STILL RECUPERATING IN Florida, Gen. Arnold radioed Gen. LeMay that he was "exceptionally well pleased" with the 9 March attack on Tokyo. Arnold had good reason for his pleasure. In looking at the results, his experienced eye must have told him that the air war against Japan had taken on a whole new dimension. In a single night, the B-29 had dramatically proved its effectiveness and offered promise of more successes to come. Arnold's deep concern over the B-29 had disappeared.

Apart from Arnold in Florida and the Air Staff in the Pentagon there were others who were gratified by the outstanding results of the Tokyo incendiary mission. Chief among these were Ewell and the other scientists and technical experts working under Dr. Vannevar Bush in the Office of Scientific Research and Development. LeMay had proved what they had contended for months—the AAF could inflict tremendous damage on Japan's cities with incendiary bombs, principally the M-69. True, LeMay had upped the bomb tonnage per square mile substantially from Ewell's earlier estimates and employed the B-29 in a manner not envisioned by the scientists, but ultimately it was the M-69 that set the fires.

ACROSS THE PACIFIC, LeMay, the man who had delivered the blow, relayed Arnold's message to members of his command and, in a message of his own, commended both the combat crews and the maintenance people for their accomplishment and fighting spirit. In a press release on 11 March, after describing the results of the mission, LeMay reiterated the deep-seated feeling he had expressed to McKelway while his airplanes were on the way to Tokyo:

> I believe that all those under my command on these island bases have by their participation in this single operation shortened this war. . . . [T]hey are fighting for a quicker end to this

war and will continue to fight for a quicker end to it with all the brains and strength they have.

This conviction would become LeMay's personal credo for the rest of the war.

THE NEW YORK *Times* Sunday edition of 11 March subordinated the Tokyo bombing to the long-awaited news from Europe. The headlines that day read: "WESEL BRIDGEHEAD COLLAPSES, ENEMY CUT OFF; AMERICANS GAIN MILE ON EAST SIDE OF RHINE; CENTER OF TOKYO DEVASTATED BY FIRE BOMBS." In describing the mission and the damage done to the city, the *Times* drew heavily on LeMay's press release and highlighted LeMay's remark (quoted above) about fighting for a quicker end to the war. A small box to the left of the continuation of the *Times* article contained the following:

SPECIAL FIRE BOMB USED TO SET BLAZES IN JAPAN (Associated Press) San Francisco, March 10
Why flames spread so fast and leaped so high in Tokyo Saturday was made clear today when the Army's Chemical Warfare Service released a limited description of the M-69 incendiary bomb, designed especially for use in Japan.
At about 5,000 feet the 500-pound cluster bomb opens, releasing individual six-pound bombs filled with jellied gasoline. Each small bomb spreads burning gasoline for some thirty yards around upon exploding.

The New York *Times* article glossed over the civilian casualties. "How many perished in the holocaust cannot be estimated," it stated. Top-level Washington officials did not take the death toll lightly. With the uproar over the death toll in the February combined British and American bombing of Dresden still fresh in his mind, Secretary of War Stimson told J. Robert Oppenheimer, civilian director of the atomic bomb project, that he "thought it appalling that there should be no protest in the United States over such wholesale slaughter."

Though the casualty figures would not be known in the United States until after the war, Stimson probably based his conclusion that a wholesale slaughter had occurred on informal estimates furnished to him by the Air Staff. (While no record of such estimates was found, it is reasonable to assume that it would have had to be large, since, of the 15.8 square miles burned out, a large proportion contained population densities of 80,000 per square mile, or more.)

Vannevar Bush would also find the civilian casualties disturbing. Though he made no mention of it in the two books that he later wrote about his wartime experiences, a friend and fellow physicist would recall that "For years after the war Van Bush would wake up screaming in the night because he burned Tokyo. Even the atomic bomb didn't bother him as much as jellied gasoline."

MEANWHILE LeMAY WASTED little time in capitalizing on the night's success. When, four months before, the COA had recommended to Arnold that he launch incendiary strikes against Japan's major cities, they had emphasized that the cities be hit in rapid succession so as to give the enemy minimum time to react to the new form of attack. LeMay's combat experience and instincts told him the same thing. He scheduled incendiary strikes on Nagoya, Osaka and Kobe, to take place with only one-day intervals between the missions. The pace was so rapid that it would later earn the name of "the blitz" (a short version of the then well known German term *blitzkrieg*—"lightning war").

LeMay embarked on his air "blitz" with confidence because he quickly grasped the dramatic change in the attitude and morale of his air crews. They had tasted success beyond their wildest speculation and had achieved this success without the losses that had accompanied previous, mostly failed missions. The Tokyo mission had transformed the entire command— the ground crews too had been caught up in the infectious spirit. LeMay knew that he could send them back again and again.

TEN

CITIES TO THE STRAITS

NAGOYA: 11–12 MARCH

LeMay's bombers had already attacked Nagoya, Japan's third largest city and its major aircraft producer, seven times—six precision strikes and the test incendiary mission—without significant results. This time LeMay targeted a triangular wedge of the city's industrial area for incendiary attack and modified the tactics he had used on the Tokyo mission. Observers returning from the Tokyo mission had reported that despite the mission's great success some of the bombload may have been wasted. Crews were dropping their bombs on areas that were already burning and the incendiary clusters were being released too close together. Based on this information LeMay decided to split the bomber force. The second group of airplanes would follow the first by one hour and drop its bombs on the sections of the target area that the first force had missed. He also had his crews increase the release interval between clusters from 50 to 100 feet.

The tremendous fires that had gutted Tokyo did not occur. Nagoya's fire fighters performed efficiently and the city had more and better firebreaks than Tokyo. The modified attack plan did not work. During the interval between the two waves the fire fighters had a chance to subdue the fires already set and to prepare for the next fires. The 100-foot interval scattered the bombs over too wide an area. Only 2 square miles of the city were destroyed.

Though the damage reports may have been disappointing, the mission had been most successful in another respect. Of the 285 airplanes bombing the target, not a single one was lost to enemy action. LeMay knew now that the Japanese had no effective means for shooting down his low-level, night-flying bombers.

OSAKA: 13–14 MARCH

Japan's second largest city, with its shipyards, steel mills and other heavy industry, was the next target. Because of the heroic efforts of the ground crews, the command was able to put up 301 aircraft for the attack. Fifteen thousand men—mechanics, electricians, sheet metal repairmen and bomb handlers, to name only a few—worked long shifts to keep the maximum number of the Command's aircraft operational. Bomb-loading operations for the mission had started as soon as aircraft returned from Nagoya and, in some cases, were continued as the airplanes were warming up their engines to take off for the new target. Up on their scaffolds, mechanics changed engines in record time. In one wing during the blitz, mechanics changed 17 engines in one day, averaging nine hours per engine change. Sheet metal men worked feverishly to patch the flak damage and repair damaged bomb bay doors. Because of their crucial nature and because no spares were then available in the Marianas, bomb bay doors were removed the minute an aircraft landed, loaded in a truck, rushed to a central repair shop, and after repair rushed back and installed on the waiting bomber.

For Osaka, LeMay dropped the tactical changes he had made for the Nagoya strike and returned to the concept that had worked so well over Tokyo—get as many airplanes over the target as you can in the least amount of time and release your incendiaries so as to achieve maximum density of ground bursts. The attackers wiped out 8.1 square miles in the heart of Osaka. Raging fires killed nearly 4,000 people and destroyed more than 130,000 houses.

DURING EACH MISSION, officers and men in the three wing control rooms kept track on big blackboards of each of the Command's more than 300 airplanes. For each bomb group, a board contained space to enter the status of each airplane crew: takeoff and landing times; whether the aircraft aborted, ditched, was lost to enemy action or was missing. A clerk with a headset was constantly in touch with the operations staff and made the entries as they came in. The man at the boards was always happy to be able to print a big "ALL IN" after a group completed a mission. Fortunately the opportunity came more often during the blitz than it had in past missions.

KOBE: 16–17 MARCH

LeMay gave his crews an extra day's breather before sending 300 aircraft up to bomb Kobe, across the bay from Osaka and Japan's most important overseas port. Stocks of M-69 and M-47 incendiaries were diminishing, so for this attack, the fourth against Japan's major cities, the airplanes carried 500-lb clusters of M-50s, the 4-lb magnesium incendiary. The bombing force quickly set fires that burned furiously, creating big thermal updrafts that gave the following airplanes trouble on their bomb runs. Though aerial photos would show that fire spread was limited to 2.9 square miles, the Japanese counted more than 2,600 dead and 65,000 houses destroyed. More fighters countered than on previous nights but still were unable to down a single B-29.

For those who had flown all four of the blitz missions the physical drain was beginning to show. As 2d Lt. Robert Turkisher, a flight engineer in the 19th Bomb Group, 314th Wing, later recalled, "With three hours of preflight and briefing, plus fifteen hours of actual flying time, then an additional two hours for debriefing and eating, a single mission required us to stay awake for over 20 hours." On the return trip from Kobe, Turkisher's pilot put the airplane on autopilot. As flight engineer, Turkisher had to make an entry in his log every 30 minutes. At 0300 he checked his instruments, made his entry and dozed off. At 0350 he awoke, looked around and saw that both the pilot and copilot were sound asleep, as were the bombardier and navigator. A call over the interphone got no response from the rest of the crew in the back of the airplane. Turkisher shook the pilot and copilot awake and together they woke up the rest of the men. The crew had been asleep for about 45 minutes, but the plane was on course and the air speed and rate of descent were correct. In Turkisher's view, "Needless to say, someone up there had been looking out for us."

ON SUNDAY, 18 March, as ground crews readied airplanes of the XXI Bomber Command for the last mission of the blitz—a return trip to Nagoya—Emperor Hirohito and a small group of his retainers left the palace grounds to inspect the damage inflicted by the B-29s on 9–10 March. The Emperor had spent that night in the Imperial air raid shelter, the "Obunko" (library). Firebrands from the fires to the east of the palace grounds set fire to grass and hedges near the Obunko. Soldiers and guards put the fires out, but not before some smoke and fumes had reached the Emperor and those in the Imperial shelter. On the following morning the Emperor expressed a desire to see the city. Transportation and escorts were hastily assembled.

As the Emperor's motorcade drove north to the Asakusa ward it occasionally passed a man or woman poking in the ashes. Amazed subjects bowed when they recognized the Imperial pennant flying from the car. In the midst of one of Tokyo's hardest hit areas, the cars stopped and the Emperor emerged to survey the destruction—block after block of vacant space where houses and shops used to be, gutted buildings, burned out vehicles, rubble. The Emperor's party next went to a bridge (probably the Kototoi, where so many Japanese were crushed to death or drowned) and viewed the scene from there. The final stop on the Emperor's inspection tour was a police station. Here police told him that almost all of the ward's 12,934 houses had been destroyed and that 10,500 people had been killed or injured. After this briefing the Emperor got back in his car and returned to the Imperial Palace. Having seen for himself the terrible results of the firebombs on Tokyo and having heard by then of the incendiary raids on Nagoya, Osaka and Kobe, the Emperor must have wondered how long his country could survive such destruction.

THAT EVENING, AFTER drawing on the last remaining stocks of incendiaries, 310 B-29s took off for Nagoya. Aircraft arriving over that city dropped 1,858 tons of bombs, burning out an area of 3 square miles for a total of 5 square miles for the two incendiary missions.

By any measure the blitz had been an amazing success. The B-29s had swept across four cities, laying waste to 32 square miles and destroying many important targets. The vulnerability of Japanese cities to incendiaries had been proven conclusively, as had LeMay's tactics for delivering massive bombloads effectively. Morale of combat and ground crews soared. Most shared LeMay's feeling when he concluded a commendation for his men with the statement, "The enemy learned at Tokyo, Nagoya, Osaka and Kobe that nothing can stop you."

Major newspapers in the United States featured LeMay and the Command's missions against the individual cities. In its commentary on the five missions as a whole, *Newsweek*, in an account titled "JAPAN: IN PANIC," called them unprecedented:

> No Jap—and for that matter few Americans—had ever expected that such attacks could be mounted . . . the vital centers of four of Japan's five greatest cities burned out . . . an entirely new technique of bombing for the Army Air Forces . . . The top planning had been done in Washington under Brigadier General Lauris O. ("Swede") Norstad . . . the details were left to Major General Curtis E. ("Old Ironpants") LeMay.

The "new technique" and the bombs must have aroused some interest on the part of Gen. George C. Marshall, Army

Chief of Staff. On 17 March the air chemical officer received a hurry-up call from Gen. Arnold's office asking for materials to show Marshall the bombs being used against Japan. The air chemical officer made available sectionalized M-69 and M-47 bombs, a cluster mechanism and pictures of the Dugway tests on Japanese buildings.

Added to the highly favorable national press coverage and attention from the nation's senior general was a personal letter to LeMay from his boss, Gen. Arnold. Back in Washington after his long convalescence, Arnold wrote that "Your recent incendiary missions were brilliantly planned and executed" and later commented:

> A study of the effect of the Tokyo attack of March 10 and the knowledge that by July 1 you will have nearly a thousand B-29s under your control leads one to conclusions that are impressive even to old hands at bombardment operations. Under reasonably favorable conditions you should then be able to destroy whole industrial cities should that be required.

This was probably one of the few cases in which Arnold's goals were far less than those of one of his subordinates. LeMay expected to destroy many industrial cities long before his boss's target date of 1 July. After the photos from the 9 March Tokyo mission were analyzed, LeMay knew that he had found the key to a successful aerial campaign against the Japanese.

NORSTAD AND THE Joint Target Group (successor to the COA) reached the same conclusion. As they saw it, except for certain aircraft engine plants, Japan's industry as a whole was vulnerable to incendiary attacks on the principal urban areas. With this rationale in mind the Joint Target Group recommended to Norstad that 33 urban areas in Tokyo and six other major industrial cities (on the planners' maps each city was divided into areas or zones, Tokyo with four, Osaka with seven, etc.) be designated as targets as part of a comprehensive plan to destroy Japan's industrial potential. The areas were listed in the order in which the Joint Target Group felt they should be attacked. On 3 April the Twentieth Air Force issued a new directive to LeMay. It targeted the engine plants at Musashino in Tokyo and Mitsubishi in Nagoya, followed by the first seven urban areas from the Joint Target Group's list.

Despite the enthusiasm and confidence in both Washington and on Guam, continuation of the successful incendiary campaign would not be possible for a number of reasons. The most immediate obstacle was the lack of incendiaries in the Marianas. The Command had dropped over 9,000 tons of incendiaries during the blitz, leaving insufficient tonnage for continuing fire-bombing on a large scale. Though large quantities of incendiaries were in the supply lines flowing across the Pacific, LeMay's staff had told him that the five scheduled missions would virtually exhaust the supply of incendiaries on hand, so on 12 March, the day after the Nagoya strike, he had them request an emergency shipment of 36,000 tons of incendiaries. Two days later he was informed that the quantities of M-69s and M-47s requested were available for immediate water shipment, which would take several weeks.

MEANWHILE PLANS FOR the assault on Okinawa, which would turn out to be one of the bloodiest battles of the war, were going forward. The first landings were scheduled for 1 April. LeMay had known for some time that he would be expected to strike enemy airfields on Kyushu in order to prevent Japanese airplanes from attacking the U.S. invasion fleet. These attacks were to be top priority for the XXI Bomber Command before and during the invasion of the island and would continue until Adm. Nimitz agreed to release them to their strategic bombing mission. On 27 and 30 March the command flew the first of a series of 97 support missions, which would continue for a period of over a month. On the first two missions, the largest of the series, 288 airplanes in daylight at medium altitude (14,000–18,000 feet) hit airfield facilities across Kyushu. On 1 April, the first American troops landed on Okinawa. Thereafter bombers, in numbers ranging from 10 to 34, hit individual airfields on an almost daily basis.

*   *   *

ONLY HOURS AFTER the 73rd and 314th Wing bombers took off on their first Okinawa support mission, airplanes of the 313th Wing left Tinian on the first aerial mining mission from the Marianas. It was the beginning of an operation that the U.S. Navy had for some time advocated and the Twentieth Air Force had, until three months before, resisted. Like high explosive bombing, aerial mining would become an integral part of the overall air war against Japan, though LeMay was now dedicated, once freed of his Okinawa support mission and when adequate bomb supplies arrived, to continue the incendiary campaign as his major thrust in defeating Japan.

In the Pacific, since early in the war, U.S. Navy aircraft had been mining harbors used by the Japanese to defend the wide area of the Pacific that they dominated. AAF planes had carried out some mining operations in 1944 and early 1945. AAF bombers had mined Hong Kong harbor and the area around the Bonin Islands. B-29s of the XX Bomber Command had laid mines at Singapore, Saigon, and Palembang, Sumatra. Aware of the great striking range of the B-29 and the huge capacity of its bomb bays, Adm. Nimitz had sought in the fall of 1944 the employment of B-29s of the XXI Bomber Command for large-scale mining of the Shimonoseki Straits and Japan's principal ports. He wanted operations to begin on 1 January 1945. Arnold initially demurred on the basis that such a diversion of effort would undermine the primary mission of the Twentieth Air Force. He later shifted his position and in late December told Hansell that he should plan for mining operations but not begin any mining until 1 April 1945. Shortly after he took over, LeMay ordered the 313th Wing to set up a training program for aerial mining.

During February and throughout March crews of the 313th trained for mine laying. They learned that the mines that they were to drop came in two sizes—1,000 lbs for water up to 15 fathoms deep and 2,000 lbs for deeper water. The mines were attached to a small parachute to control the descent and protect the sensitive mechanisms used to set them off. Once they came to rest on the bottom they became sensitized, ready for the approach of an oncoming ship. Most of the mines dropped by the 313th contained either magnetic or acoustic sensors. Mines with magnetic sensors detected the presence of a ship by the effect of the steel hull on the magnetic field of the sensing device. Those with acoustic sensors (a recent development in underwater mining warfare) were set off by the noise of a ship's propeller or the change in water pressure as a vessel passed.

In addition to these sensors, mines could be equipped with other devices designed to confuse the enemy or make the detection of the mines more difficult. Some had delayed arming mechanisms, which armed the mine after a specified time had elapsed. Others with "ship count" devices would permit a certain number of ships to pass without causing detonation. In anticipation of the end of the war and future use of the waters for peacetime purposes, mines were equipped with a timing mechanism that rendered them inert after a predetermined period of time.

The laying of mines was to be done at night to minimize enemy defenses against the B-29s and also to make it more difficult for the Japanese to determine where the mines were being dropped. Aircraft would fly at low level, permitting them to carry loads of 12 tons—six 2,000-lb mines. Individual aircraft would use initial points and aiming points easily identified by radar, and drop their mines in a string. Together the individual strings formed a broad area hazardous to enemy ships.

The target for the night of 27 March was the Shimonoseki Straits, a narrow body of water between the southern end of Honshu and the north coast of Kyushu. With the East Indies, French Indochina, Malaya and the Philippines partly or totally cut off from Japan, the insular nation had become dependent on Manchuria, Korea and North China for raw materials—coal, iron, oil, etc., for its war industry, and on soybeans and rice for food. Most of the ships carrying these vital supplies had to pass through the Shimonoseki Straits en route to Kobe and other ports along Japan's Inland Sea. Traveling in the opposite direction were Japanese Navy warships and supply vessels destined for Okinawa, the next objective for U.S. forces.

The skies on the night of 27 March were unusually clear, and a bright moon shone as airplanes of the 313th dropped about 571 tons of acoustic and magnetic mines on the Shimonoseki Straits. At a cost of three B-29s lost to heavy anti-aircraft fire, the American airplanes succeeded in closing most of the shipping lanes through the straits. Three nights later the 313th dropped more mines on the straits, completing the mine barrier. On that same night, B-29s mined the harbors of Sasebo, Kure and Hiroshima.

The blockage of the straits, the first phase of an extensive mining effort in support of the Okinawa campaign, achieved the results hoped for. Warships and supply vessels were forced to take other routes. This resulted in a major disaster for the Japanese Navy. On 6 April a naval task force built around the giant battleship *Yamato*, avoiding the mined Shimonoseki Straits, attempted to slip out of the Inland Sea via the Bungo Strait (east of Kyushu). The *Yamato* was detected by U.S. Navy carrier pilots, who sunk it along with several supporting ships.

WITH THE SUCCESS of individual airplanes bombing at night at low level and his supply of incendiaries temporarily exhausted, LeMay decided to launch a series of missions to find out whether the same tactics could be employed against precision targets using high-explosive bombs instead of incendiaries.

On the night of 24 March he sent 248 aircraft against the Mitsubishi plant at Nagoya. Using techniques that the RAF had found successful in recent months, ten B-29s dropped flares to light up the target area. Five minutes later, 10 more pathfinder B-29s arrived and dropped M-50 incendiary clusters to start marker fires. Like the British, LeMay had an observer plane euphemistically called the "Master of Ceremonies" fly above the target area to survey the damage and possibly direct some changes in the attack. The main force attempted to drop their 500-lb general-purpose bombs visually, using their Norden bombsight. Cloud cover obscured Nagoya and the marker fires. Little damage was done to the Mitsubishi plant, but photos showed that several other factories had been heavily damaged. Six days later a smaller force using the same tactics attacked the same target and inflicted no damage. LeMay followed this with an attack by the 73rd Wing on the seemingly invulnerable Musashino plant and attacks on three other aircraft plants, all using tactics modeled after the RAF. Results continued to be poor. Among the reasons was that the XXI Bomber Command lacked the special 1,000-lb marker bombs and the reflex optic bombsights that the British used. LeMay sent an urgent request to Washington to have some of the British marker bombs shipped to him, but meantime he abandoned the new approach.

Tenacious and ever flexible, LeMay watched the weather reports, and when he received a favorable one on 7 April he sent the 313th and the 314th Wings back to hit Mitsubishi–Nagoya and the 73rd to bomb the Musashino plant—in daylight. (By this time LeMay had dropped the prohibition against aircraft carrying fully operational machine guns and ammunition. He anticipated correctly that during daylight opposition would be heavy, and as the surprise of the March blitz wore off, fighter activity would increase, even during night attacks.) To keep the bombloads as high as possible, he ordered his airplanes to fly at relatively low altitudes. For this mission the 73rd Wing would fly altitudes ranging from 11,000 to 16,000 feet and the other two wings from 16,000 to 25,000. With clear weather over both targets the bombing was very accurate. Both plants were heavily damaged, with the Mitsubishi plant experiencing somewhat the worst of it.

On 12 April the 73rd returned to Musashino for what would be a near knockout blow to its old nemesis. In daylight, though the visibility was not as good as on the previous mission, the B-29s bombed accurately and added substantially to the damage done on the seventh. Poststrike photographs showed that together the two strikes had damaged 48 percent of the roof area of the plant. This damage far exceeded the total for the nine previous attacks on this target, the first being Hansell's historic initial mission from the Marianas the previous November. Production dropped to about a third of its normal rate. Ironically, with a combination of luck and skill, LeMay had piled an outstanding set of precision attacks on the very heels of his sensational departure from that very concept.

Fighter opposition over Musashino on 7 April had been exceptionally heavy. The crews of the B-29s over Musashino that day must have been able to do their jobs better because of the 97 P-51 Mustang fighters that for the first time flew cover for bombers over Japan. Fighter airplanes of the VII Fighter Command based on Iwo Jima rendezvoused with waiting B-29s off the coast of Japan. Because they lacked the necessary navigation equipment for the more than 700-mile trip, the fighters were led to the rendezvous area by three B-29s. Flying top cover for the B-29s, the Mustangs dove into the Japanese fighter formations, breaking them up and downing an estimated 21 enemy aircraft. With the B-29s claiming 80 downed fighters (probably some overlap with the P-51 claims) it was the XXI Bomber Command's biggest victory over the Japanese fighters since 27 January and would be one of the largest in the war with Japan.

Next, taking advantage of stocks that had built up since the end of the blitz, LeMay launched three successful night incendiary strikes. On 13 April, 327 B-29s dropped 2,124 tons of incendiaries on the arsenal area of Tokyo, northwest of the Imperial Palace, with a loss of seven of the attacking aircraft. Fires burnt 11.4 square miles, destroying the plants that manufactured and stored machine guns, artillery, bombs and other armament. Two nights later 303 bombers burnt out another 6 square miles in Tokyo and 3.6 miles in Kawasaki, south of Tokyo. Twelve B-29s failed to return. With his incendiary stocks again depleted and his commitment to support the Okinawa invasion, LeMay would not be able to schedule any incendiary missions for nearly a month.

PREVENTING THE JAPANESE from using their airfields on Kyushu for attacks on American forces on Okinawa required frequent B-29 strikes on a large number of targets. During the last two weeks in April, the XXI Bomber Command sent out missions almost daily, ranging in size from 104 to 256 airplanes to hit 14 airfields with a combination of fragmentation

and general-purpose bombs. The "frags" hurled steel fragments over a wide area when they burst and were intended to
destroy or damage aircraft on the ground. The "GPs" blew
holes in runways. Many crew members found the airfield missions "uninteresting"—fly to Kyushu, drop bombs on an airfield, not knowing whether airplanes were there or not, then
fly back to base.

Not all were "milk runs," however. For Ed Cutler and the
Texas Doll crew, veterans of 18 missions including all five of
the blitz, the mission to Tachiarai airfield was their most
harrowing aerial battle of the entire war. As he approached the
field in clear weather with 19 other B-29s, Cutler saw no
aircraft on the ground. Then out to the front and above, he
spotted about 30 or more Japanese fighters in two formations,
one on each side of the path they were flying to bomb the
field. As soon as the American bombers committed to their
bomb run—straight and level, no turns or maneuvers
permitted—the Japanese, one and two at a time, began diving
attacks from both the right and left through the B-29 bombing
formations. The worst occurred right after bombs away. Cutler watched as a fighter, firing on the B-29 to his right front,
like a "gigantic Singer sewing machine" stitched a line of
holes through the airplane's #1 and #2 engines, along the left
wing section and then through the tail. Cutler could see the
fuel spurt out of the engines and, expecting the airplane to
blow up any second, altered his course to avoid the flying
debris. The severely damaged aircraft made it almost to Iwo
Jima before it had to ditch. Only three crewmen survived.

Meanwhile a seemingly endless procession of fighters
pressed their attacks on the *Texas Doll*. As Cutler, one of the
few pilots in his original squadron to survive the war, would
later recall, "This was the only time we ever heard the roar of
battle—screaming, pounding fighter engines, guns and cannon, theirs and ours, all going at the same time." Then, as
Cutler watched, horrified, a twin-engined Japanese fighter
dove through the formation from the right, leveled off, narrowly missed colliding with one airplane, banked vertically
and with one of his wings tore off the tail and #4 engine of the
B-29 piloted by Lt. "Andy" Anderson, Cutler's right wing man.

Spellbound, he watched as the separated engine, with its propellers spinning, briefly struggled upward, then fell away. Anderson's airplane, now uncontrollable, flipped over, spun earthward and was gone. No parachutes. Still the fighters came. Sgt. Elmer Hendershot, central fire-control gunner, shot down one. Finally, *Texas Doll*, with over 300 holes in her but with a crew miraculously unharmed, broke free and headed for the coast, trailed by some Japanese fighters who eventually turned back after having not fired a single shot.

As LeMay's staff studied the photographs and damage assessment reports for the airfield missions in support of the Okinawa invasion it became apparent that they were not very effective. Cratered runways, taxiways and aprons were often repaired and operational in a matter of hours after an attack. By the end of April, only about 3 of the 14 fields that had been targeted were inoperative; however, although airplanes could still take off and land despite hammering by LeMay's B-29s, the destruction of hangars and repair shops limited to some degree the number of airplanes the Japanese could service and have ready for combat missions. In LeMay's view he was carrying out his Okinawa support assignment to the best of his Command's ability but with limited success. He asked Washington to relieve him of his assignment but was told on two occasions, once on 18 April and later on 5 May, that attacks on the airfields continued to be the top priority for his Command.

THOUGH TEMPORARILY SIDETRACKED, LeMay never lost sight of his strategic mission. In a letter to Norstad on 25 April he described in broad terms his view of the role of the Twentieth Air Force in defeating Japan:

> I am influenced by the conviction that the present stage of development of the air war against Japan presents the Army Air Forces for the first time with the opportunity of proving the power of the strategic air arm. I consider that for the first time strategic air bombardment faces a situation in which the strength is proportionate to the magnitude of the task. I feel

that the destruction of Japan's ability to wage war lies within
the capability of this command, provided its maximum capacity is exerted unstintingly during the next six months, which is
considered to be the critical period. Though naturally reluctant
to drive my force at an exorbitant rate, I believe that the opportunity now at hand warrants extraordinary measures on the
part of all sharing it.

LeMay's statement that his Command had the capability to
destroy Japan's ability to wage war and his view that the next
six months was the critical period implied that the XXI
Bomber Command had the power to force Japan's surrender
without the invasion of Kyushu scheduled for November
1945. In anticipation of a massive firebombing campaign,
LeMay had ordered 90,000 tons of incendiaries—ten times the
amount expended in the March blitz. His extraordinary measures would, among other things, require that his crews fly 80
hours a month instead of the 60 hours (already a high rate)
they had been flying. He made the decision to establish such
a policy despite warnings by some of his commanders and his
flight surgeon that such a rate over a period of six months
might burn out his combat crews.

LeMay's views were shared in Washington. Earlier that
month, Col. Cecil Combs, Gen. Norstad's deputy, had written
a memorandum to Norstad in which he, too, anticipated great
opportunities for the Twentieth Air Force. As he saw it,

The effect on the morale of the Japanese people of the burning
of the major cities with the destruction wrought therein and
casualties caused cannot be evaluated statistically but the possibility exists that this alone might break the will of the people
to continue to fight. This may be the thing that will bring home
the futility of continuing the war to the Japanese people as well
as the leaders of Japan. The Japanese industrialists must recognize that recuperation [of a destroyed industrial base] will take
many, many years after the war and that they must depend on
their industry to be a national power in peacetime. . . . Incendiary attacks on Japanese inflammable Zone I areas of her major
cities have been disastrous for the Japanese. It is believed that
no other form of attack can bring home so clearly to the Japa-

nese people the power of the Air Forces to destroy Japan as an industrial nation.

Combs recommended that Norstad issue a directive to LeMay, calling for large-scale incendiary attacks sufficient in size to complete the destruction of the burnable areas of the major cities. He recommended that the massive incendiary assault begin on 1 May or upon the surrender of Germany, whichever was earlier. (Combs apparently expected that the XXI Bomber Command would be released from its Okinawa support mission by then.)

On 1 May, Germany had not yet capitulated and LeMay was continuing with his strikes against the airfields and with aerial mining. By this time LeMay had become convinced that his mining campaign, known by the code name "Starvation," had great potential. The 1,500 mines that the 313th Wing had dropped on the Shimonoseki Straits during April had not only severely hampered Japanese Navy operations aimed at the U.S. forces attacking Okinawa but had reduced overall ship traffic by some 80 percent. During the first two weeks in May, "Starvation" entered a new phase. The purpose of these new attacks was to cut off or seriously impede shipping between the major ports along Japan's Inland Sea. To accomplish this the 313th Wing sowed 1,422 mines of all types at the ports of Tokyo, Nagoya, Kobe and Osaka and along the major shipping lanes of the Inland Sea. Additional mines were dropped on the Shimonoseki Straits to keep that vital avenue choked off. A total of 1,422 mines were laid in this phase and results were soon evident. Traffic at all the ports began to fall off rapidly and ship sinkings and damage increased. Ships that had formerly moved through the Shimonoseki Straits from Korea and Manchuria to the big industrial ports now had to go to smaller ports on the western side of Honshu and to Kyushu.

The continuing success of the mining campaign was a result of both LeMay's aggressive program and lack of effective countermeasures by the Japanese. The sudden introduction into their home waters of mines on a large scale took the Japanese by surprise. Though the United States had been mining Japanese-held ports in parts of the Pacific for over two years, clearing was usually done by subordinate commands. The Japanese high command was unaware of the scope and nature of these activities. As a consequence, they did not take the threat of mines seriously until they suddenly found themselves facing large-scale mining that could have a serious effect on the defense of their homeland.

The basic means for clearing mines were common knowledge among the navies of the world. Magnetic mines were cleared by a sweeper towing either magnetic bars or an electrically charged cable. Acoustic mines were swept by dropping noise bombs in the water. Sometimes divers were used. What was not known by the Japanese was how to contend with the various types and combinations of detonating devices that U.S. scientists built into the mines. As Capt. Kyuzo Tamura, a Japanese Navy expert on mines, would recall:

> It was very effective when you dropped mines with a new device in them. During the period after a mine with something new was used, there would be a period of recovering it, taking it apart, finding a countermeasure and then constructing the machinery and educating personnel in using the equipment. There was a one- or two-month lag during this particular period, when we didn't know what the solution was and would take big losses.

The surrender of Germany was announced on 8 May. Three days later Adm. Nimitz, with a message of thanks, released the XXI Bomber Command from further support of the Okinawa campaign. By this time U.S. Navy ships had delivered large quantities of incendiary bombs to the Marianas, more than enough for LeMay to return to his unfinished business—the aerial assault on Japanese cities.

ELEVEN

"LEAPING TIGERS"

FOR THE FIRST of his renewed incendiary attacks on Japan's major cities, LeMay chose Nagoya, the city that had hitherto resisted his attempts to set major fires. He scheduled the mission for 14 May as a daylight strike to confuse the enemy (who, based on the blitz of a month before, would probably be expecting a night raid) and to possibly increase bombing accuracy. It would be a four-wing mission—the 58th Bomb Wing, which had pioneered bombing of Japan from its China bases, was by this time operating from its new location on the island of Tinian. With this fourth wing, for the first time, more than 500 airplanes would take to the air for a mission. Flying at altitudes between 16,000 and 20,000 feet, the attackers dropped 2,515 tons of incendiaries on the northern area of the city, setting fires which burned an area of a little over 3 square miles. Japanese defense was vigorous. Eleven planes were lost from various causes.

The Command went back to Nagoya two days later, hitting the southern area of the city, this time at night. Pathfinders pinpointed the target zone with M-47 incendiaries for following B-29s loaded with M-50 magnesium bombs, selected because of the heavy structures in the area. Though fewer planes participated in this attack than in the previous one, they were able to drop a much greater tonnage of bombs—about 8 tons per airplane as against 5.3 tons—because of the low-level, individual tactics. The weight of bombs dropped that night, 3,609 tons, surpassed the heaviest attack ever carried out by the Eighth Air Force against Germany. Another area of more than 3 square miles was set afire, for a total of nearly 7 square miles from the two raids. The Mitsubishi Aircraft Works and other industrial plants were severely damaged; many dwellings were destroyed, leaving hundreds of thousands homeless. More than three thousand persons were killed.

Even though his bombers had not started huge fires at Nagoya like those that occurred on 10 March at Tokyo, after four major incendiary attacks and numerous precision strikes LeMay felt the damage was so extensive that no further mass incendiary attacks on the city were warranted.

WITH NAGOYA STRICKEN from the list, LeMay turned again to Japan's most important target—Tokyo. In the previous four mass incendiary raids the XXI Bomber Command had dropped more than 5,000 tons of bombs and destroyed 34.2 square miles. As knockout blows, LeMay planned two maximum-effort incendiary attacks against the city. For the first strike, scheduled for the night of 23 May, he planned to commit a force twice the size of the one that had bombed Tokyo on the night of 9 March. The target area was an industrial and residential area south of the Imperial Palace grounds, along the west side of Tokyo Bay. The area, less densely populated than that bombed in March, contained important targets—aircraft-part, tank, petroleum, and railroad-car plants—and was a major rail hub.

Like the March attack, this one would be at low level and at night, but from a different direction. Instead of having his bomber stream fly across Tokyo Bay and approach the target area from the east, LeMay chose for them to attack from the west. Landfall would be the tip of Cape Omae at the mouth of Suruga Bay—easily identified by radar. Aircraft would continue on a northeasterly course up the bay, then pass to the right of Mount Fuji to the initial point southwest of Hachioji.

The target area lay about six minutes' flying time to the east of the initial point. From the new direction he believed he could avoid some of the heaviest antiaircraft defenses and get more bombers to the target. He directed his pathfinders to drop their M-47 bombloads on the eastern edge of the target area. The main body, with loads of M-69 bombs, would drop their loads short of the fires set by the pathfinders. With expected prevailing winds blowing from behind the attacking bombers, the Command's operations planners hoped that the target area would be less obscured by smoke as successive waves of B-29s unloaded on the burning area. LeMay was intent on achieving the greatest possible concentration of bombs on this attack. To accomplish this (despite the apprehension it caused his pilots) he directed that each wing schedule the timing of their bombers so that the whole bomber command would be compressed over the target in the shortest possible time.

The 558 aircraft that took to the air beginning at 6:14 P.M. on 23 May would be the largest number of B-29s to take part in a single mission during the air war against Japan. The planned route was not successful in avoiding enemy antiaircraft defenses. Enemy batteries at points along Suruga Bay, east of Mount Fuji, and at the initial point fired on passing aircraft. From the initial point to the target area the intensity of fire increased. Over Tokyo a majority of the attackers were caught in the searchlights for varying lengths of time. Thirteen B-29s were lost to enemy action and 69 were damaged. Losses might have been heavier but for the fact that enemy interceptors were, for unknown reasons, late getting into the air and were largely ineffective. In a period of two hours, 520 aircraft, flying at altitudes between 7,000 and 15,000 feet, dropped 3,646 tons of bombs. Considering the high tonnage and concentration of bombs dropped, the area burned out—5.3 square miles—was not as great as expected. Not long after their return the crews learned that they would be going back to Tokyo again on the following day.

LeMay's TARGET FOR the night of 25 May was the very heart of Tokyo. North of the area hit on the twenty-fourth, the new target was a band about 3 miles wide and 4.5 miles long, west of the waterfront and immediately south of the Imperial Palace grounds. The area included industrial and residential districts as well as parts of the financial, governmental and commercial sections of the city. As an incendiary target, it was a difficult one. Its business and industrial sections contained more multistory fire-resistant structures than previous targets. Houses lying south and west of the Imperial Palace were not the tightly packed workers' hives that had burned so readily in the Asakusa, Honjo and Fukugawa wards. Finally, in bombing this target area pilots were reminded that they should not bomb the Imperial Palace. The order had been in force since the first raid on Tokyo and was reinforced when Gen. Arnold turned down Gen. Norstad's proposal to bomb the Palace on Pearl Harbor Day, 8 December 1944. Arnold's veto of the proposal was probably for the same reason the prohibition had been imposed in the first place—it would be politically counterproductive.

The bombing scheme devised by Col. Montgomery and his operational planners utilized all types of incendiaries available and employed them differently from previous missions. The 12 pathfinders from each wing would attack from the east, flying a route similar to the one flown by the force that attacked on the night of 9 March. Though this axis of attack was considered to be better defended and hence more hazardous, it provided the clearest radar checkpoints and thus offered the pathfinder crews the best possible chance of setting their markers on the designated targets. Taking off ten minutes ahead of the main forces, the pathfinders were to attack the two easternmost of the six target points designated for the mission. They would each carry a load of M-76 incendiaries. Buildings in the areas where the pathfinders would drop included 10- and 12-story concrete and brick structures, as well as plants and commercial buildings of relatively heavy construction. The 500-lb M-76 had sufficient weight and striking velocity to penetrate and set fires within such structures.

The main force would follow the same route flown on the night of 23 May. The first third of the main force would drop their bombs on the same points as the pathfinders. They would carry 500-lb clusters of M-17 4-lb magnesium incendiary bombs, used because the large numbers would saturate the area and because they had somewhat greater penetration than the M-69. The remaining two-thirds of the main force were assigned the four other target points. Half of the force would carry clusters of M-69s and the other half would carry 100-lb M-47 incendiaries.

JAPANESE COMMANDERS, AS characterized by their "Banzai" charges, often committed their military force in all-out attacks intended to overwhelm the enemy. Even as LeMay was sending everything he had in his arsenal to knock out Tokyo, the city's defenders, alerted by their intelligence teams to the likelihood of an attack, readied their forces to inflict the highest possible losses on the attacking force.

Both in experience and in equipment, Tokyo's air defenses, particularly its searchlight and antiaircraft units, had achieved their best state of preparedness since the attacks against the Japanese mainland had begun. They had strengthened the antiaircraft units that ringed the city and were capable of firing on attackers coming from any direction. In addition to the 88-mm medium and 120-mm heavy guns in their fixed emplacements, the Japanese had in recent months emplaced near the city two recently manufactured 150-mm guns. These huge pieces, with 29-foot barrels, could fire their big projectiles at a rate of 15 rounds per minute. Other units had, for some time, been positioned across Tokyo Bay on the Chiba peninsula athwart the path of airplanes attacking the city from the east. Still more batteries were positioned eastward all the way to Choshi Point, long a favorite turning landmark for B-29s leaving Tokyo to head back to the Marianas. Apparently Japanese Army planners had anticipated that LeMay might attack from the west as he had on the twenty-fourth, hoping to find it less heavily protected than the eastern approach. They had stationed searchlight and gun batteries at Cape Omae, landfall for the bombers, and at Shizuoka, Shimizu and Numazu on Suruga Bay, all locations that LeMay's airplanes would pass en route to the initial point near Mount Fuji. Still more medium and heavy batteries lay along the bombers' final run from the initial point to the city. Hardly a milk run.

Besides the searchlight and gun batteries, the Japanese Army had recently placed a large number of flare and rocket firing units around the city. The rocket batteries were the latest, and still largely untested, addition to the Japanese defensive fires. The flare units were intended to illuminate the oncoming B-29s as well as to harass them.

Nighttime incendiary raids had lost the surprise and shock effect that had accompanied the 9 March strike. In addition to accurately estimating the routes the bombers would take, the Japanese also expected night attacks to be at low level. Sound detection devices, range finders and ammunition fuzes were all adjusted with this in mind. The Japanese had also learned that focusing 10 to 20 searchlights on a single airplane permitted many B-29s to escape undetected and unfired upon. Antiaircraft commanders had recently emphasized adherence to the basic doctrine of no more than four lights to a single aircraft.

Though late in launching aircraft during the previous night attack and still ill-equipped for radar-directed air attacks on B-29s, the Japanese hoped that with adequate warning and better coordination with the searchlight batteries their night fighters could contribute more to the city's defense. One of the problems faced by the Japanese Army and Navy Air Forces was a shortage of well-trained, experienced fighter pilots capable of intercepting the B-29s at night.

Seeking to employ every possible means to bring down the enemy aircraft, on the night of 23 May the Japanese had introduced what came to be known as the "Baka." The concept of the Baka was patterned after the suicide "Kamikaze" planes used with great success against U.S. naval vessels off the coast of Okinawa. Kamikazes, carrying a large explosive charge, took off from the island of Kyushu with only enough fuel to get to the target area and crash their aircraft into a U.S. ship. The Baka, a small rocket-propelled airplane containing a large explosive charge, was carried by a Japanese medium bomber such as the "Betty." When searchlights illuminated an attacking B-29 the mother airplane released the Baka. The pilot then sought to crash into the B-29 before the rocket's limited fuel supply was exhausted.

*　　*　　*

ABOUT 30 MINUTES before the first pathfinders made landfall the Japanese air defense command concluded that a large force of B-29s flying north from the Marianas was headed for Tokyo. The Tokyo air alert system announced that "The enemy seems to be carrying out a wave of attacks with single planes which will last several hours."

AT 10:27 P.M. Tokyo time, a B-29 from the 58th Bomb Wing dropped its load of 500-lb M-76 incendiaries on blacked-out Tokyo, the first of 44 pathfinders from the four wings assigned to light up the target area for the main force. Alerted, searchlight and gun batteries on the Chiba peninsula and around Tokyo were able to concentrate their fires on the relatively few aircraft that made landfall on the peninsula and from there flew across Tokyo Bay to the target.

Flying one of these aircraft was Capt. Charles C. Fishburne. He and two other pathfinder pilots of the 73rd Bomb Wing were flying their thirtieth mission. (At that time 30 missions were required to complete a combat tour. Later this requirement was raised to 35.) Before departure Fishburne's crew had joked that they were finishing their tour the hard way—losses among the pathfinders on the previous mission had been high.

Fishburne recalls that soon after landfall searchlights picked up his aircraft and, as he flew on, passed him on to other lights ahead. The sky was clear and the moon shone. As he approached the target area he could see fires resulting from bombs dropped by pathfinders who had preceded him. Suddenly, when he was about halfway from the initial point to his drop point, Fishburne saw a B-29 about a quarter of a mile ahead suddenly burst into flame and explode. Minutes later, on his bomb run, with bomb bay doors open and bathed in the light of many searchlights, he prayed that God would let him and his crew get through. Finally—bombs away!

Fishburne was now free to fly the evasive maneuvers that he, as a highly experienced pilot, knew so well. He dove, turned, changed headings, left, then right, slowed down, speeded up. He shook off the searchlights, only to hear a report from his tailgunner that a night fighter was trailing them.

Next came the report that antiaircraft fire, probably from one of the few radar-controlled installations, was bursting not far behind. Finally, to the surprise of all the crew listening in, the tailgunner announced that the Japanese fighter had been hit by his own antiaircraft batteries. As Fishburne climbed rapidly and headed to the sea north of Choshi Point, his gunners, looking back toward Tokyo, reported seeing two more B-29s in flames.

On the long trip back to Saipan, Fishburne and his crew, grateful they'd completed their last mission and would soon be heading home, wondered if any of the airplanes they had seen go down were either of the other two "Thirtieth Mission" crews. Back on the ground, they discovered that both aircraft had returned safely.

Some of the pathfinders from the 58th Wing were less fortunate. Capt. John. E. Siler and his crew were among them. Siler's was one of the original crews of the XX Bomber Command and had participated in most of the missions flown from the India and China bases. One of the best "lead crews" in the group, they had been selected to leave India six weeks before the rest and flew with the 313th Wing until rejoining their own unit after its arrival. Siler named his first airplane after his wife, Eileen; the plane had gone through four "editions." (It was customary for a pilot to transfer the name of his aircraft to another plane if the original plane became unserviceable, was transferred to another crew, or was lost.) *Princess Eileen I*, flown by another pilot, was lost over the Hump a year before. *Princess Eileen II* and *III* were still operational in the squadron. Siler was flying *Princess Eileen IV*. In past months the plane had been featured in newsreels, recruiting posters and bond drives.

Princess Eileen IV was the first pathfinder from the 40th Group to take off, and it was among the first airplanes of the 58th Wing to reach Japan. Another pathfinder, arriving over the mainland soon after, saw a flash and a glow in the sky over Tokyo. It was Siler's airplane exploding. Another pathfinder, Capt. Bright and his crew, also veterans of the air campaign from India and China, who had taken off just after the *Princess Eileen IV*, disappeared without a trace.

*   *   *

CAPT. ARTHUR C. CLAY, 313th Wing, was flying in the first third of the main force that night and had the same target as the pathfinders. Clay flew the prescribed route from landfall at Cape Omae, up Suruga Bay, past Mount Fuji (whose snow-capped peak stood out in the clear skies) and on to the initial point, southeast of Hachioji.

Clay did not encounter searchlights until he neared the initial point. From there to his bomb release point, six or more lights illuminated his aircraft and another B-29 that he saw flying to his left. About two minutes before "bombs away," Clay spotted what appeared to him to be a Baka heading toward his airplane or the airplane to his left. Both B-29s opened fire and blew the Baka up. Clay dropped his load of incendiaries at 11:30 P.M. and turned to the northeast. As he began to throw his propellers out of synchronization to fool Japanese sound detection devices, he had a crew member shove more "rope" out of a hatch behind the radar compartment. ("Rope" was what crewmen called strands of aluminum foil, which, as it fell earthward, reflected emissions from Japanese ground radar, confusing and disrupting Japanese attempts to locate and track the B-29s.)

This time Clay's actions, standard procedure for XXI Bomber Command pilots when at or near the target zone, did not work. Only a few minutes into his breakaway from the target, an antiaircraft battery found his range and laced the aircraft from end to end with shell fragments. Three crew members in the rear compartment were wounded. The central fire-control gunner, Sgt. McAuliffe, and the right gunner, Sgt. Gilliam, were both wounded in the legs. Left gunner Sgt. Neel was seriously wounded. Damage to the aircraft was extensive. The gun turrets were inoperative and the radar compartment was on fire. The fuselage had hundreds of holes in it, some as large as 12 to 18 inches in diameter.

After the barrage the airplane became uncontrollable. Both rudder and elevator controls were severely damaged. Engines #2 and #3 were hit and had to be feathered. Clay and his copilot managed to wrestle the airplane back under partial control and headed toward the sea. Then Clay sent the copilot back through the tunnel to help Sgt. Grow, the radar operator, treat the wounded. (On the premise that during combat they would be the least involved, the Twentieth Air Force training program had required that radar and radio operators take a total of 18 hours of medical training that included bandaging and splinting, administration of hypodermics, control of hemorrhages and plasma administration.)

Meanwhile, the bombardier had climbed up in the copilot's position; someone had put out the fire; the engineer was splicing some of the control wires; the navigator was trying to fix his equipment, and the radio operator had sent out his first distress signal.

Clay reached the coastline, flew out about 40 miles and set a course for Iwo Jima. As if piloting the heavily damaged aircraft were not enough, three Bakas were sighted, but fortunately none caught up with them. Finally free of hostile threats, Clay now hoped he could make it to Iwo Jima.

Lt. Frank Lord, another pilot in the 313th Wing, was flying his twentieth mission that night. He arrived over the target about 30 to 40 minutes after Clay did and, though he didn't lose two engines, found the going the roughest yet. Lord wrote afterward, in his usual laconic style,

> Never again, in lights for about twelve minutes, AA [antiaircraft fire], automatic weapons, rockets, balls of fire, got shot up pretty badly. No. four prop blade hit with 20 mm, stick fist through hole. 20 AA holes, Hutchison really lucky, three holes by his feet. Three salvos of four rockets each across nose, scared half to death. Good bomb run, best results yet observed.

Walt Sherrell's *Southern Belle* was in the last group of the 73rd Wing to head north to Tokyo. When he saw tracers in the sky as he approached Cape Omae, he decided to follow a course to the east up Suruga Bay. In this way he avoided the gauntlet of fire that many airplanes encountered on the way to the initial point. Approaching Tokyo, he saw that large areas of the city were already burning. Sherrell's aiming point was just south of the Imperial Palace, and coming up on the initial point he worried that if a cluster got hung up on a bomb shackle or if he missed the aiming point some of his M-69s might drop on the forbidden area—the Palace. He did not have much time for such thoughts, as the lights finally found him and he and his crew had to concentrate on the lining up on his aiming point.

The bomb run was, in Sherrell's view, a "good one." After "bombs away" (40 clusters of M-69s, weighing almost 10 tons) Sherrell turned his attention to avoiding antiaircraft fire, now becoming heavy, and the threat of Bakas, which he and other pilots in his outfit called "Foo-fighters." He desynchronized his propellers and had a gunner push out chaff. As he turned on his "breakaway" and, in a steep climb, headed toward the sea, he heard his copilot Orlo Hall exclaim, "Oh, my God!" Sherrell turned his head just in time to see a shadowy shape with a fiery tail hit a B-29, after which the B-29 went down flaming. Seeing a thin cloud layer ahead, he flew into it, seeking cover. He had barely emerged on the other side when one of the gunners reported a shadow trailing on the right. Sherrell put *Southern Belle* into a screaming dive and, with his airspeed indicator reading well over 300 mph, pulled out after losing about 3,000 feet of altitude. Another possible Baka was sighted, this time on the left. Sherrell racked the B-29, at full power, into a steep climbing turn to the right and into some clouds. After several more dives and climbs, they saw no more "Foo fighters." Sherrell's aerobatics had lost them. The series of evasive actions had taken a little over 10 minutes. (In the hands of a skilled pilot, with no bombload, the B-29 was exceptionally maneuverable for an aircraft of its size.)

After that they flew through some antiaircraft fire at Choshi Point without damage and headed south. About daylight, Rasmussen, the flight engineer, came up and sat behind Sherrell. Rasmussen confessed that when they had pulled out of one dive he had blacked out. When he came to, his head was down among the throttles and mixture controls. One of the gunners, Sgt. Don P. Valenzuela (he later changed his surname to Thrane), would recall it as the wildest ride he had ever had.

*   *   *

FEW OF THE 464 crews that flew over Tokyo that night will ever forget it. Some who made both the 23–24 May mission and the one on 25–26 May would later find it hard to distinguish between them. But for those who kept journals or whose recollections were sharper, the second mission stood alone for stark drama in the sky—a phantasmagoria of enormous proportions. Observations by returning crewmen, most of whom were veterans of many missions, both daylight and at night, were in some instances blurred by the sheer number of visual images that confronted them in the air over the city.

The number of searchlights—some with their beams, five feet in diameter, sweeping the skies, others "coned" in groups on a single B-29—was unprecedented. One hundred or more were reported in the area of the initial point. More than 150 were estimated to encircle Tokyo itself. Five searchlights with particularly intense green-colored beams were reported northwest of the city. Crews had never seen searchlights so effective in finding and tracking aircraft. In one group, all but 5 of the 22 aircraft flying over the target were held in searchlight beams for varying lengths of time.

Shell bursts—white, black and orange-red—from heavy antiaircraft guns, estimated at over 300 in number, punctuated the sky at altitudes between 10,000 and 11,000 feet. Some of these bursts, resulting from barrage firing, covered broad expanses of sky. Other bursts could be seen exploding around a B-29 as it flew, locked in the beams of searchlights. Hundreds of red-orange trails laced the sky, as tracer bullets from Japanese rapid-fire antiaircraft guns arched through the air before burning out at 8,000 to 10,000 feet.

There were numerous reports of colored, glowing lights or flashes in the Tokyo area, particularly along the bomb run. Intelligence officers later classified most of these lights as different types of aerial flares. Some, after being fired into the air, ignited and burned briefly as they descended. Other flares were suspended under parachutes and remained at higher altitudes until they burned out. The color of one type of flashing light was described as ranging from bluish green to bright green. The flashes were intensely bright and hurt the eyes. The light would flood the sky for about 10 to 15 seconds then die away. At its maximum intensity the greenish light revealed B-29s, which searchlight beams quickly locked onto. Other sightings were variously described: "Twenty orange lights were seen hanging in midair over the target, the light continuing for about 30 seconds"; "Between the IP and the target, a steady red light lasted for two minutes, trailing sparks from 14,000 feet to the ground"; "Balls of fire were apparently suspended by parachutes. When first observed they put forth a bright white light which changed to a dark red. Then after four or five minutes they burst into three separate balls of flame and fell to the ground."

Scores of rockets, with their propulsion fires glowing, rose from batteries located south of Tokyo. Returning crewmen found the rockets to be inaccurate and ineffective, but they added to the nightmare of fire and light over the target area.

THE KALEIDOSCOPE OF colors and cacaphony of sound that set this night apart from others for the airborne American crews made it a memorable one for those viewing it from the ground as well. Yoshio Matsuoka would recall strings of little balls— red, green, blue and white—shoot up into the sky. She also noted horizontal balls of fire that she presumed were Japanese fighters and returning fire from the B-29s. A B-29 caught in the searchlights glowed white, then, after it was hit, bright orange, as it continued eastward, still glowing till it was out of sight. Another bomber exploded with a terrific noise, trailing flames a thousand feet, and fell slowly earthward. All the while, the noise of the airplanes, the booming of antiaircraft batteries and the clatter of rapid-fire guns combined in a continuous roar.

Another viewer, Father Flaujac, a French Catholic priest at Bethanie House, a sanatorium for tubercular patients in Tokyo, though professing difficulty in describing "that fairy scene," nevertheless did so in unrestrained terms. Rockets took off "in cascades of fire and their flashes were like comets." B-29s moved like stars across a sky red with fire. Exploding airplanes were likened to the aurora borealis. To Flaujac it was a scene that no motion picture camera could reproduce.

He could only imagine the fear, desperation and death that was resulting from the dreadful panorama in the sky.

BECAUSE OF THE early warning, the Americans encountered substantially more enemy fighters than they had on the previous night. Of the 60 interceptors sighted, air crews claimed 17 as being shot down. Enemy fighters were believed to have destroyed at least one B-29 and damaged 21 others.

Many enemy aircraft sightings (most of which occurred where Sherrell had had his encounter—the area between Tokyo and Choshi Point) described what observers believed to be Bakas: "One ball of fire came in at aircraft #806 from 9 o'clock level and was fired on at a distance of about 500 yards. The ball of fire was observed to break away and explode on the ground." "An unidentified enemy aircraft launched two Bakas at our plane. One of these came within 500 yards and was hit and exploded. Wings and fuselage were seen." "One Baka followed aircraft #863 out towards land's end, but #863 speeded up to about 300 mph and outdistanced it. The Baka, or ball of fire, was seen to fizzle out before reaching land's end."

Though intelligence analysts believed that a number of the "balls of fire" reported as Bakas were flares or rockets, they acknowledged that some of the small, one-way aircraft were in the air that night. No losses could be attributed directly to Baka attacks. However, the psychological effect on combat crews was substantial. Pilots and crews alike found the Bakas to be new, fearsome and elusive.

WHILE THE BAKAS were a threat and interceptors took a toll of B-29s, it was the Japanese antiaircraft batteries that were responsible for most of the 26 B-29s lost. Returning crews brought back numerous sightings of B-29s going down that night. Typical of these were recorded observations by the 504th Bomb Group, 313th Wing. (Each refers to a single B-29.):

11:40 P.M. Over the target, on fire in a dive, blew up on ground.

12:07 A.M. Seen to blow up 20 miles from coast on route out.

12:11 A.M. Blew up 15 miles east of target.

1:07 A.M. On east edge of target, on fire for 5 minutes. No parachutes seen.

1:20 A.M. Two miles from the coast on the route out. Blew up, 5 chutes observed, probably 2 or 3 more.

1:32 A.M. Small, flickering engine fire for two minutes. Was getting tracer fire from what seemed to be a turret—possibly a B-29. Blew up. [Over-anxious gunners in a B-29 may have thought the flame from the burning engine looked like a Baka.]

1:35 A.M. Five miles south of Choshi Point and on fire. Blew up. No chutes seen.

In addition to the airplanes lost, 100 of the 464 airplanes over the target sustained antiaircraft damage but were able to make it back.

SGT. DALE JOHNSON's aircraft (he was a right gunner in the 40th Bomb Group, 58th Wing) may have been one of the early sightings of a B-29 going down. His pilot, Lt. Ronald Harte, had turned and just begun his run to the target when search-lights picked the plane up. In the crew compartment the light was bright enough to read a newspaper by. Johnson waited, hoping for "bombs away" so that they could break out of the lights, but this did not occur. Then they were hit, he believed by antiaircraft fire. Reacting reflexively, he saw a gaping hole near his position, rolled through it, waited a few seconds and jerked the ripcord of his parachute. He landed uninjured near what appeared to him to be a lake, about a half mile from an antiaircraft battery. As he lay watching, this battery and oth-ers brought down two B-29s. (The next morning Johnson, fear-ing what civilians might do if they found him, surrendered to soldiers of the antiaircraft battery. After interrogation, the Japanese confined him in a special detention camp for air crews. He stayed there until the final days of the war when he was transferred to a regular POW camp where he was later liberated. None of the rest of the 11-man crew survived.)

The *Arkansas Traveler,* piloted by Capt. Richard M. Mansfield of the 314th Wing, was another victim of intense Japanese antiaircraft fire. Mansfield was close to his target, an area just south of the Imperial Palace grounds, when his plane was hit. The left wing and an engine on that side began to burn. When he saw that the fire extinguishers built into the engine nacelles had no effect, he continued on his bomb run and dropped his incendiaries. Then he turned north to clear the burning area, ordered his crew to bail out and jumped himself. As he descended through clear skies, he kept an eye on the *Arkansas Traveler* as it spiraled down and finally crashed. (Mansfield's crew was more fortunate than most of those shot down over Japan. He and eight of his crew were liberated at war's end.)

A Japanese account told of another B-29 that crashed that night. All of its crew except one were killed. The commander of the Japanese military unit that found this airplane, after determining that the man was seriously wounded, ordered one of his sergeants to carry out *kiashaku* (a Bushido term for "a sympathetic and merciful act to stop pain and hasten death"). The act, death by beheading, was carried out on the spot.

As IT HAD in the devastating bombing of 9 March, nature played a major role on the night of 25 May. All that day the weather had been still and muggy. Smoke from the raid of two nights before still hung in a thin haze over parts of the city. Soon after dark, wind began to blow out of the southwest, gently at first, then increasingly stronger.

Father Gustav Bitter, alerted to a possible air attack, was on the roof of his rectory at Sophia University that night, just as he had been three months before during the "Raid of the Black Snow" and again on the night of 9 March. Looking toward the east, he saw the searchlights flash on, search the sky and hold the first arriving B-29s in their beams. Red tracers began to cross the sky, along with flashes of exploding shells. Instead of the silver streamers of M-69s that he had seen falling through the darkened sky previously, he saw big, round cylinders (probably the 500-lb M-76s carried by the pathfinders) caught in the reflected light of the searchlights. Wherever one of these cylinders struck, after a brief time a fountain of fire would rise into the air. As he continued to watch, more B-29s swept across Tokyo south of the Imperial Palace, starting many separate fires. Then, airplanes of the main force swept over the city, releasing their loads of bombs. Whipped by the near gale force winds, the separate fires spread rapidly—house to house, block to block. As the Japanese would say of this raid afterward, the flames "bounded across the rooftops like leaping tigers."

TOMOKO SUZUKI HEARD the first planes of the main force pass over her house at about the same time as the "air raid imminent" siren sounded in her neighborhood. Tomoko, 15, lived with her father and a younger sister in their house in Setagawa ward, an upper-class residential area in southwestern Tokyo. Tomoko's older brother was in Yokohama, and her mother and younger children—two sisters and a brother (born in 1941 and named Katsushisa, which means "Victory Forever")—had left in early 1944 to stay on a farm in the country west of Tokyo. Mr. Suzuki was an executive with an electronics firm and worked in downtown Tokyo. Tomoko did war work at the Meiji Rubber Company in Tokyo, first on tires for Zero fighters and later on aircraft machine guns.

On 10 March, from a distance of nearly 10 miles, she, her father and sister had watched the eastern part of the city burn and had seen the terrible devastation when they went into the city. This night Tomoko was no longer a viewer from afar.

Tomoko recalls the sound of the engines, thunderous and overpowering. She and her sister ran outside (they and most other Tokyo residents slept fully dressed) and, facing the southeast, watched the dark shapes of airplane after airplane fly overhead. Then they heard the sound of guns firing, and colored lights appeared in the sky in the direction of downtown Tokyo.

The girls' father insisted that they go into the family air raid shelter; they did, but not for long. Tomoko, a curious and adventuresome girl, followed by her sister, went out to watch. Occasionally, she could see bombs falling from the B-29s. It looked like the airplanes were releasing them right over her house to set the fires which she could see lighting the sky to the east. Tomoko and her sister prayed that the bombers would not unload their fiery cargo any earlier.

Soon, the fires came closer. Blown by a strong wind, flying embers ignited the fence and hedge of a neighbor's house. While her father remained inside the house praying at the family's Shinto shrine, Tomoko joined a group of neighbors who were carrying water and throwing it on the burning fence. As she passed near her house on one of her trips to fill her bucket she heard the sound of something falling through the air and felt the ground shake. Since no explosion occurred, Tomoko figured it might be one of the "time bombs" she had heard about.

Later the block warden told Tomoko and her sister to leave. Their father stayed in the house. After battling against the wind, which was blowing debris in their faces, the girls turned around and finally found an open field where they felt safe. Later they went back to their neighborhood, where they found their father in a group fighting a fire near their house. Fortunately, a wind shift saved their home from destruction.

They were not allowed to enter the house that night, but after spending about a week in a nearby school, they returned to find their home water-soaked but not seriously damaged. Nearby was a hole in the ground, cordoned off, with a policeman standing by. Tomoko, curious, got permission to look into the hole and saw a capsule with little bombs in it. Each of the bombs looked like a long can with hexagonal sides. The noise she had heard on the night of the bombing was a 500-lb cluster of M-69s whose release mechanism had failed, causing the entire cluster to plunge to earth and narrowly miss Tomoko's house.

AN AMERICAN PRISONER of war, Sgt. Walter Odlin, also witnessed the bombing that night. Odlin, captured in the Philippines, was one of a small group of Allied POWs who had been brought to Japan in December 1943 and coerced into broadcasting messages favorable to the Japanese cause to their relatives in the United States. He and 14 other POWs were quartered in a school building located north of the Imperial Palace grounds.

Standing outside of their bomb shelter, Odlin and his fellows watched the sky to the south, lit up first by searchlights and later by fire. Battle-seasoned, the trained eyes of the POWs distinguished features of the attack that civilians might not have. In the growing area of burning, Odlin recognized the billowing orange and black flames from a burning oil storage area and later a quick succession of explosions from what he presumed to be a munitions dump blowing up.

At first the Americans attempted to keep count of the number of B-29s they sighted, but soon gave up because there were too many and the aerial combat drew their attention. Odlin saw as many as 40 American airplanes damaged or destroyed. He would later write of observing, on two occasions, Japanese fighters crashing into B-29s:

> The tiny planes [Bakas?] flew against the bombers and exploded, shattering into a thousand pieces. The bombers both burst into flame but remained intact while they came slowly down and crashed. The bombers hit by antiaircraft shells and by fire from Zeros [captured in 1942, the Zero was the only fighter widely recognized by American troops at the time] likewise caught on fire, but in a score of instances their crews managed to extinguish the flames and keep on flying.

Unknown to Odlin, another group of Americans, 62 downed airmen held by the Japanese in Tokyo, were burned to death in the spectacular fire he was watching. The Japanese routinely kept captured fliers separate from other POWs. They considered B-29 crews to be war criminals, subject to trial and possible execution if found guilty of inhumane or indiscriminate bombing. They also did not want the recent arrivals to tell long-time POWs how badly the war was going for Japan. This, despite the fact that most POWs had, by this time, already seen ample evidence of the destruction of Japan's cities and its effects on the nation. Airmen were usually subjected to interrogation, often brutal, though there was little that the Japanese could learn from B-29 crewmen that would blunt the overwhelming power of LeMay's bombing campaign. Consequently, though U.S. Army regulations still required that a soldier give only his name, rank and serial number to his captors, informally the policy in the XXI Bomber Command was to let the captured crewman tell the Japanese whatever would keep him from being tortured or killed.

The 62 airmen, many of whom were B-29 crewmen shot down in previous raids, were being held in one section of the Tokyo military prison. Four hundred Japanese military prisoners occupied the other sections of the prison complex. During the bombing most of the prison buildings were consumed by fire, and all of the Americans burned to death.

(At his trial after the war, the commander of the prison, Capt. Tashiro, claimed that the Americans died because the fire spread rapidly and in the confusion the guards got to the American section too late to free them. A major factor in his conviction for maltreatment of POWs was the fact that none of the 400 Japanese prisoners died in the fire.)

FANNED BY THE powerful wind from the south, the "leaping tigers" roamed far and wide. Fire raged across the area south and west of the Imperial Palace and to the northwest as well. As had happened on 9 March, the areas that the bombers left flaming far exceeded what the planners had expected. This time, however, it was not just the industrial and working-class areas that were caught up in the conflagration. By 1:00 A.M. on the twenty-sixth, when the all-clear sounded, virtually all of the buildings that housed the centers of national military, civil and economic power were ablaze. Among these were the War Ministry, the Navy Ministry, the Army General Staff Headquarters, the War Minister's official residence, the Foreign Ministry and the Transportation Ministry. Landmarks that were destroyed or suffered damage included the Imperial Hotel, designed by Frank Lloyd Wright, the Kabuki theater and the Yasakuni Shrine to the war dead. Foreign embassies, hospitals, temples and university buildings burned. The homes of the affluent and the powerful in the western and northwestern suburbs of the city, for the first time, felt the fury of the firebombs. Finally, despite American attempts to prevent it from happening, the Emperor's own residence, the Imperial Palace, caught fire.

Sometime before 1:00 A.M., flaming embers from buildings across the moat from the palace grounds blew across and landed in the eaves and gutters of the front structure of the Imperial Palace. (The palace consisted of two structures, connected by hallways, as well as a number of outbuildings.) Soon flames filled the space between the roof and the ceiling of the building. Attempts to quench the fire with hoses were fruitless; the aged cypress wood burned like tinder. Flames spread rapidly, melted the copper roof shingles and threatened to continue to the rear building of the palace complex. It was in this rear palace building that the Emperor and his family had resided before they moved into Obunko. With Gen. Tanaka, the Eastern Army District Commander, and Gen. Mori, Commander of the Imperial Guard Division, directing their efforts, Army engineers, using demolition charges, tried to blow up the hallways connecting the buildings, hoping to create a firebreak. This attempt failed, whereupon soldiers equipped with crowbars and sledgehammers attempted to demolish the hallways, but with little success. While troops hauled out 20 truckloads of furniture, paintings, books and personal items (including the Crown Prince's toys), firemen poured water on the threatened rear palace.

At the end of four hours, both of the main palace buildings as well as many of the other buildings in the palace complex had been destroyed or seriously damaged by fire or water. Thirty-four Imperial retainers and soldiers died in the blaze. The Emperor and his family remained underground in the Obunko during the fire, but Japan's Prime Minister, Kantaro Suzuki (his own official residence had burned down that night), watched the palace buildings burn from the roof of his air raid shelter.

*   *   *

SHORTLY AFTER SUNRISE, as Tokyo firemen were still fighting fires, the first of the returning B-29s were beginning to land at their bases in the Marianas. In the hours that followed, ground personnel in each wing "sweated out" the safe arrival of airplanes from their unit. The ground crew of Capt. Clay's airplane, struggling south on two engines, would be one of 26 crews who would wait in vain.

Clay made it to Iwo Jima but found zero visibility; it was impossible to land. Clay circled for over three hours, during which time a flight surgeon in the Iwo control tower advised on how to treat the wounded. Finally, with his fuel supply almost exhausted and the outlines of land barely visible, Clay was faced with the choice of abandoning the airplane by "ditching" or by having the crew escape by parachute. He decided to have them jump because the rear bomb bay doors were stuck open and damaged controls would not permit him to control the aircraft at the low speed required to put the plane down on the ocean's surface. Clay made a final pass over the island and ordered his crew to bail out. All ten of his crew landed safely. Clay flew about 2 miles north of the island, jumped, landed safely, and found himself in a thick fog bank. After about an hour of bobbing on waves, Clay heard the sound of a boat's engines (a mine sweeper) but couldn't see it. He blew the whistle attached to his life vest as hard as he could. The mine sweeper heard it, found him and took him aboard and later to Iwo. After a day's rest he flew back to Tinian.

The 25 May bombing marked the end of Tokyo as a target. When LeMay and his top staff examined photographs and the damage assessment analysis, they found that the night's strike had burned an area of 16.8 square miles, greater than any of the previous missions. Together the six fire missions against the Japanese capital that had begun with the one on 25 February had destroyed 56.3 square miles, just over half of the city area. All of the designated target areas had been destroyed. Though a few targets suitable for precision bombing still existed in the city, Tokyo was scratched from the XXI Bomber Command's list of urban areas for incendiary bombing.

*　　*　　*

ARNOLD'S COMMITTEE OF Operations Analysts had justified the urban-area incendiary raids largely on the basis that they would create widespread disruption of the enemy economy by dehousing workers. They had argued that incendiary bombing was the only way to destroy the large numbers of small subcontractors known to be scattered throughout Tokyo and Japan's other major cities. But Ewell and other strong advocates of the M-69 bomb and area incendiary bombing had contended that such bombing would inflict damage far beyond this.

The destruction created by the six incendiary raids on Tokyo validated their contention. Fifty-seven numbered targets were damaged to varying degrees. Seven of these were classified as high-priority targets:

Tokyo Army Arsenal—guns and ammunition
Ordnance Supply Depot—powder magazines
Army Arsenal and Gunpowder Works
Army Central Clothing Depot
Japan Artificial Fertilizer Company—chemicals for munitions
Military Gunpowder Works
Army Branch Powder Company

Examples of other important targets destroyed or seriously damaged were:

Mitsubishi Aircraft, Shibaura Plant
Kokusan Machinery Company—lathes
Physico Chemical Company—piston rings
Japan Service Company—heavy machinery
Mitsubishi Aircraft, Oimachi Plant
Modensha Electric Equipment Company
Tokyo Central Railroad Station

The Japanese made no attempt to downplay the raid. On the following day, Prime Minister Suzuki said in a radio broadcast that he had seen with his own eyes the roaring flames engulf the Imperial Palace, though he assured the public that the royal family was safe. On the extent of the destruction he commented, "Our beautiful capital must be completely re-

THE SEVEN RAIDS THAT DESTROYED TOKYO

Date of Mission	Day or Night	Aircraft Bombing Primary Target	Altitude Range (in feet)	Tons of Incendiary Bombs	Area Destroyed
29 Nov 1944	Night	23	17,500–26,500	64.6	.10 sq. miles
25 Feb 1945	Day	172	23,500	411.4	1 sq. mile
10 March 1945	Night	279	4,900–9,200	1665	15.80 sq miles
14 Apr 1945	Night	327	6,750–11,000	2037.7	11.40 sq. miles
15 Apr 1945	Night	109	8,000–10,100	754.4	5.2 sq. miles
24 May 1945	Night	520	7,800–15,100	3645.7	22.10 sq. miles (for combined
26 May 1945	Night	464	7,915–22,000	3252	missions)

planned from a bare start." Suzuki called the attack an out-rageous act of barbarism.

Despite the wide area burned, the casualties—3,000 killed and 13,000 injured—were small when compared to the hor-rendous totals resulting from the 9 March raid. Except for downtown, most of the area burned had a much lower popu-lation density than the thickly populated Asakusa, Honjo and Fukugawa wards in which so many people had lost their lives in March. Also, nearly 2 million people had fled Tokyo after the big March raid.

Besides the damage and destruction done to war production facilities, much economic and human disruption followed the 26 May raid. Subway and streetcar lines were out of service for some time. All persons except war plant workers and the homeless were prohibited from traveling within the city. Elec-tricity was furnished to essential facilities within about five days after the 25 May raid, but the average citizen would have to wait for a much longer period for electric service to be restored. Railroad service between Tokyo and Yokohama was stopped until 7 June.

The manpower shortage had become critical. A law was passed requiring homeless workers to return to work. Since many had already fled to the country, another provision of the law required them to return and resume work in war industry. The government would provide them with special priority for travel and free train tickets. Back in the city, returning work-ers would have to live in barracks for the rest of the war.

In the United States, *Newsweek* headlined its description of the 24 and 26 May strikes: "BLAZING TOKYO SYMBOL-IZES DOOM THAT AWAITS EVERY BIG JAP CITY." The magazine's account capsuled the attack, its results and Japa-nese reactions to it. The headline probably captured the mood and attitude of the American people toward the event. Amer-icans were exultant. They had little sympathy for the enemy who they felt was only now paying for the treachery of Pearl Harbor and the cruelty of the highly publicized "Bataan Death March." They also had few doubts that the vaunted Twenti-eth Air Force would continue to destroy Japan's cities. When and under what circumstances the Japanese would capitulate was still an open question.

TWELVE

DEFEAT

WITH TOKYO NEUTRALIZED, LeMay scheduled Yokohama, Japan's fifth-largest city, her second-largest port and a producer of ships, vehicles and chemicals, for his next strike. The city had been hit by spillovers from the various raids on Tokyo but had never before been a primary target.

The relatively heavy losses of the last two night missions over Tokyo caused LeMay to shift to a daylight attack against Yokohama. To counter the expected fighter resistance LeMay called on the VII Fighter Command's P-51s flying out of Iwo Jima. On 29 May the P-51s joined the bomber formations as they reached Fujiyama. About 150 Japanese fighters rose to meet the B-29s. In the ensuing aerial battles, 101 P-51s shot down 26 Japanese airplanes. The bombers burned out an area of 8.9 square miles, somewhat more than the planned target area, and an estimated 4,800 Japanese lost their lives. Yokohama was crossed off as an urban area target.

LeMay next aimed west, at the two giant industrial cities along the shores of Osaka Bay—Osaka and Kobe. Osaka's core had been burned out in the incendiary raid of 13 March, but important targets still remained. Because of the location of the undamaged areas, LeMay decided that they could best be attacked in daylight with fighter escort.

★   ★   ★

ON 1 JUNE, on their way to Japan, 148 P-51s flew into a weather front, which they expected to get through quickly. Soon they found themselves flying blind in a huge, dark thunderhead. Twenty-seven airplanes crashed into each other or into the sea before the rest finally broke out of the darkness. The bulk of the force turned back, but some of the P-51s made it to Osaka, where they provided some protection to a force of 458 B-29s that burned out another 3.15 miles but still left some of the city's outlying industrial area untouched.

Four days later the command hit Kobe, again in daylight, this time unescorted. Flying through a determined enemy defense, the attackers lost nine B-29s to Japanese fighters. The attack burned out the rest of the assigned target area and eliminated Kobe as a future incendiary target.

Back over Osaka on 7 June, again in daylight but this time with an escort of 138 fighters, the XXI Bomber Command struck the east-central section of the city. The weather, which less than a week before had spelled disaster for the P-51s, on this occasion rendered them superfluous. Heavy clouds over the city kept enemy fighters out of action. The attackers bombed by radar, burning out another 2.21 square miles of the city without the loss of a single airplane.

After four consecutive maximum-effort incendiary strikes against urban areas, LeMay temporarily changed tactics. During the next week he sent planes from the 58th, 73rd and 314th Wings against precision targets, while 313th Wing bombers resumed sowing mines across the Shimonoseki Straits.

ON THE EVENING of June 13 Gen. Arnold landed on Saipan and had dinner with LeMay, O'Donnell and others. Arnold's reason for journeying to the Marianas was an outgrowth of discussions and decisions made during late May on grand strategy for the future conduct of the war in the Pacific. On May 25, the Joint Chiefs of Staff approved a directive setting 1 November 1945 as the target date for a landing on the island of Kyushu, the first phase of a gigantic land assault on the Japanese home islands. Gen. Marshall was a strong advocate of the invasion strategy and was fully supported by Gen. MacArthur, who would be overall commander of invasion forces. Officially the other members of the Joint Chiefs agreed with Marshall. Privately Arnold and Admirals Ernest J. King and William D. Leahy were not convinced that a land assault was necessary. But with the decision made, Arnold proposed that the AAF's support of the invasion (which would include the XXI Bomber Command and additional forces from the United States and Europe) be under Headquarters AAF. Both Leahy in Washington and MacArthur (who wanted all land-based air forces under him) in the Pacific objected to Arnold's proposal. As a result, Arnold decided to fly across the Pacific and work out command arrangements in person with MacArthur and Nimitz.

On the day following his arrival on Saipan, Arnold flew to Guam, where LeMay and his staff briefed him on plans for continuing the air war against Japan. LeMay explained that the first phase of the urban area bombing program—the destruction of Japan's major cities—was virtually complete. One more maximum-incendiary mission against Osaka, to take place the next day, would finish it.

LeMay told Arnold that while precision strikes and aerial mining would be important components of his attack plan, continued incendiary attacks were its centerpiece. LeMay reviewed for Arnold a bombing program that was the outgrowth of discussions LeMay had recently had with his operations chief, Col. John B. Montgomery, and his intelligence officer, Col. James D. Garcia. They had concluded that the successful night incendiary tactics used against the large cities could be applied to the smaller cities. Earlier in June Garcia had drafted a bombing program listing as potential targets 25 cities with populations ranging from 323,000 (Fukuoka) downward to 62, 280 (Hachioji). Garcia made his selections from cities that were congested and "burnable," contained some war industry, might be part of the transportation network and, finally, were suitable radar targets.

This was the initial plan (the number of cities on the list

would more than double before the war was over) that LeMay and his staff presented to Arnold. LeMay maintained that destruction of virtually all of Japan's cities, along with the aerial sea blockade and precision strikes, had a good chance of forcing Japan to surrender without the invasion planned by the Joint Chiefs of Staff.

Arnold found different views contained in a report forwarded to him from Washington. Just before leaving the Marianas, Arnold had asked members of the U.S. Strategic Bombing Survey (USSBS) in Europe (a group established by the President to study and assess the bombing campaign against Germany) to provide him and the Joint Target Group with recommended targets in the war against Japan. The team arrived in Washington just after Arnold left. After meeting with the Joint Target Group and others, the staff prepared a report reflecting the USSBS views and sent it to Arnold. Based on their analysis of the results of Allied bombing of Germany, the USSBS team recommended precision bombing of Japanese land and water transportation and selected other targets, aimed at immobilizing the nation and wiping out its food supplies. They contended that the continued urban incendiary attacks, favored by Norstad and other AAF officers in Washington, would neither break Japanese morale nor administer a decisive blow to the Japanese economy.

Arnold found LeMay's views more convincing. He was so impressed by LeMay's presentation that he ordered him to fly to Washington immediately and present his plans to the Joint Chiefs. As a consequence, on 15 June, as over 500 of his airplanes were winging their way north for the final incendiary raid on Osaka, LeMay and several of his staff officers were flying a B-29 east to Washington, D.C.

DESPITE THE FACT that their P-51 escort was forced by a towering weather front to turn back, the bomber force went to bomb Osaka and part of a neighboring city, Amagasaki, without losing a single airplane to enemy action. After studying the poststrike photos, LeMay's planners removed Osaka from the target list.

Though delayed by about a month and a half by the necessity to support the Okinawa invasion, with Osaka "finished," LeMay's XXI Bomber Command had completed its incendiary assault on Japan's six major cities. The accomplishments since the night of 9 March, as shown in the table below, were remarkable:

CITY	URBAN AREA (Sq Mi)	TARGET AREA (Sq Mi)	AREA DESTROYED (Sq Mi)
Tokyo	110.8	55	56.3
Nagoya	39.7	16	12.4
Kobe	15.7	7	8.8
Osaka	59.8	20	15.6
Yokohama	20.2	8	8.9
Kawasaki	11.0	6.7	3.6
TOTAL	257.2	112.7	105.6

LeMay's bombers had made real the optimistic projections of those advocating incendiary bombing during the Pentagon planning meetings the previous fall. B-29s had burned down hundreds of thousands of houses and with them the interspersed small workshops that fed the big plants. Millions of workers were left without housing, seriously disrupting war production of all types. Impressive, even to the most zealous advocates of incendiary bombing, was the tremendous destruction of the great factories: munitions, chemicals, railroad cars, vehicles, steel, machine tools, electrical equipment and aircraft manufacturing plants. Few industrial war plants escaped the ravages of the fires burning across the cities.

The starkest reality for the Japanese people was the loss of their homes and loved ones. An estimated 112,000 persons died as a result of the bombing of these six cities. Beyond this personal loss was the realization that their Army and Navy could do little or nothing to stop the destruction. They had found civil defense measures to be largely futile. After years of being fed news of victories in far-off places and Japanese military omnipotence, in the course of a few months millions of people in the burned-out cities had personally witnessed the overwhelming power of their enemy. The morale of the Japanese people was beginning to erode.

After stops in Honolulu and San Francisco, LeMay landed at Washington National Airport just before midnight on 16 June. The next morning he drove to the Pentagon and made his presentation. He got little reaction from either Gen. Marshall or Adm. King. They had already made their recommendation to the President—invasion in November. LeMay's after-the-fact presentation changed nothing. Frustrated, he flew back to Guam, resolved to prove the merit of his case.

Upon his return from Washington LeMay reviewed the results of the first of the multiple attacks against the small cities. Flown against the cities of Kagoshima, Omuta, Hamamatsu and Yokkaichi on the night of 17 June, the missions were run very much like those against the major cities. Each of the four wings was assigned a target city. Pathfinders marked the target and bombers loaded with M-69 and M-47 incendiaries, flying at altitudes between 7,000 and 9,200 feet, attacked using radar. Enemy opposition was almost nil. The 314th Wing lost one airplane to unknown causes. The total area burned out was 6.073 square miles, greater than the average results of the four-wing missions against the major cities.

Pleased with these results, LeMay ordered the missions against the smaller cities continued, with the bulk of the Command's aircraft devoted to this effort. On the night of 19 June, three more cities (one of the cities, Fukuoka, was considered large enough to require a two-wing attack) were hit with incendiaries. Thereafter B-29s were over the cities about twice a week.

Although, from that time on, between 70 and 80 percent of bombs loaded would be expended on incendiary missions, LeMay still kept after precision targets. Whenever his weather officers predicted visibility over priority targets, LeMay would send his airplanes on daylight attacks against aircraft and chemical plants, army and navy arsenals, and other lucrative precision targets. After two smaller strikes earlier in the month, on 22 June 381 B-29s from the Command's four wings hit six targets in southern Honshu—Kure Naval Arsenal and five aircraft factories. Poststrike photos showed heavy damage to the arsenal and varying amounts of destruction to the aircraft plants. Four days later, 426 bombers hit three arsenals, four aircraft plants and two metal factories. Because the predicted good weather failed to materialize, damage to the various targets ranged from slight to heavy. After this series the weather over Japan closed in and a month would pass before any more precision strikes could be mounted.

The weather was no obstacle to aerial mining, since these missions, like the strikes against the secondary cities, were accomplished at night, using radar. While LeMay's original plan had been indefinite as to mining operations after 1 June, the success of the campaign had been such that he not only continued it, but stepped up its pace. By 3 July, Gen. Davies' 313th Wing, considered the aerial mining specialists of the Command, had planted 3,542 mines in ten areas in the Inland Sea and Sea of Japan. During June the vital Shimonoseki Straits was closed completely on five days, and at other times only a few ships could get through. Of all the mined areas, the one at Shimonoseki was the most critical for the Japanese, and they did their best to keep American bombers from replenishing it.

Lt. Frank Lord found ample evidence of this over Shimonoseki on the night of 25 June, his third trip over the straits. On his previous missions he had encountered between 30 and 40 searchlights in the vicinity of the target area and had seen no enemy aircraft. By throwing out "rope" he had been able to keep out of the lights, except for about two minutes on his first mission.

Lord arrived over the straits at about 2 A.M. in clear skies. As he neared the target area a lunar eclipse took place. ("Timed just right," as Lord would later recall.) Except for a close brush with another B-29, unseen in the blackness, the mine run was good, with no lights or antiaircraft fire. But as he left the target, "things went haywire." The Japanese had installed 30 new lights. Rope did no good. He flew, unable to evade the lights, for nearly ten minutes. A night fighter shot at his aircraft, but the searchlights were so blinding that his gunners could not see to shoot back. Luckily the Japanese fighter's accuracy was poor and Lord escaped with little damage.

Another set of specialists not seriously affected by the poor visibility conditions were members of Brig. Gen. Frank A. Armstrong's 315th Wing. The 315th's B-29s differed from those in other wings in two respects. They were equipped with the AN/APQ-7 (Eagle) radar instead of the AN/APQ-13. The Eagle's advanced features made it a much more accurate precision bombing device than the AN/APQ-13, which had been originally designed primarily for navigation. The 315th's airplanes had been stripped of all armament except tail guns, making them capable of carrying a greater bombload than B-29s of the other wings. With the 315th operational by the end of June, LeMay had, besides night area bombing and daylight precision bombing (weather permitting), a third capability—nighttime precision bombing.

The targets selected for combat-testing this new unit were Japan's oil refineries and storage facilities. Although by April 1945 the flow of oil from outside Japan had ceased entirely, LeMay believed that destruction of its dwindling oil reserves could adversely effect the nation's ability to wage war. On 26 June the 315th Wing hit the Utsube Oil Refinery at Yokkaichi. Thereafter missions ranging upward to more than 100 aircraft bombed oil storage and refining facilities on an average of about once a week. Bombing was highly accurate, and poststrike photos showed substantial damage. The strategic effect, however, was probably minimal, since, as was revealed later, many of the heavily damaged storage tanks were empty and refinery production had fallen to about 4 percent of capacity before the bombing had begun.

WHILE B-29s WERE ranging over Japan's cities, factories and inland waterways, decisions made in Washington designed to bring even more powerful forces to bear on the battered island empire were being implemented. A new command, the U.S. Army Strategic Air Command (USASTAF), would be established, with headquarters on Guam. Gen. Carl A. Spaatz, Commander of the United States Strategic Air Force in Europe, was slated to take over the new command. Under USASTAF would be two air force commands—the Twentieth Air Force, consisting of the former XXI Bomber Command and the VII Fighter Command, and the Eighth Air Force, operating from airfields on Okinawa with Gen. James Doolittle in command. The Eighth Air Force was expected to reach its full strength of 720 B-29s in February 1946. While the USASTAF, with an ultimate strength of more than 1,400 B-29s, would carry out the strategic bombing of Japan, the Far East Air Force (FEAF), under Gen. Kenney, would have the tactical air warfare responsibility. The first major step in this reorganization came on 16 July when the new Twentieth Air Force came into being on Guam with LeMay assuming temporary command.

DESPITE THE FEELINGS expressed in June by the USSBS, Arnold, the Air Staff and LeMay still believed that the ongoing overwhelming air assault on the Japanese islands would increasingly undermine the people's morale and will to continue the war. During June and into July, B-29s dropped millions of leaflets aimed at convincing the Japanese that their cause was futile. Some leaflets urged the Japanese to surrender before they died of starvation. This was not a shallow threat. Shipping losses had reduced imports of Japan's food staple—rice—to a trickle. Coupled with this, the 1945 rice crop was a disastrous failure, 6.6 million tons compared with an average for the previous four years of 10.1 million tons. Spring crops of wheat and barley in 1945 were also far below average. The Japanese government had used these grains as substitutes for rice in the food rationing system.

Food was rationed on the basis of age, sex and type of work performed. Japan had started the war with a per capita availability of food equivalent to about 2,000 calories per day. For the same year the average daily consumption of food in the United States was the equivalent of 3,400 calories. By 1945 the food availability in Japan had shrunk to 1,680 calories, and with the disruption of food distribution caused by the bombing of the cities, many city dwellers consumed less than this.

Lack of food caused both physical and psychological problems. Beriberi and other diseases associated with dietary deficiencies were prevalent. Fatigue caused workers to be less productive on their jobs in war plants. The same lack of energy, often coupled with sickness brought on by malnutrition, contributed to a rising rate of absenteeism from work. The latter problem became so serious that in mid-1945 the Japanese government decreed that a portion of an individual's daily food ration could be obtained only at his place of work. Food—or rather the lack of it—was a universal preoccupation. As one Japanese put it after the war, workers were becoming "more concerned with their personal problems, such as food, than with their jobs."

Other leaflets were aimed at destroying public confidence in their leaders. One such leaflet had on one side a montage showing the faces of Japan's long-time Prime Minister Hideki Tojo and eleven other well-known Japanese militarists. Above the photos was the caption "Military leaders of Japan. Can you convince the people that you are able to defend the soil, the waters and the sky of Japan?" On the reverse side, along with a photo of President Truman, was the following text:

> These questions were asked by Harry S. Truman, President of the United States, in a message directed to the people of Japan: "Did you not in the past solemnly declare that you would defend Guam, Tinian, the Philippines, Iwo Jima and Okinawa, the last barricade on the way to Tokyo? Did you not promise in the past that our planes would not violate the skies of Japan? Were you able to keep these promises?
>
> Let me assure you again and again that my country is determined to fight this war to its predestined end, and I cannot find anyone who thinks that our victory will be too hard and too costly to win. Your future lies in your hands. You can choose between a wasteful unclean death for many of your forces or a peace with honor."

Late in July, Twentieth Air Force bombers delivered a third type of leaflet. This one warned 11 cities the day before the attack was to be launched. The theme of the message that accompanied the list of cities was "In accordance with America's well-known humanitarian principles, the American Air Force, which does not wish to injure innocent people, now gives you warning to evacuate the cities named and save your lives." Psychological warfare planners believed that, in addition to its humanitarian aspects, such an operation would provide the most dramatic and convincing evidence that the Japanese nation was defenseless against American air power.

More than 600,000 of the warning leaflets were crammed into M-26 bomb cases, and on the night of 27 July, six B-29s dumped them over 11 cities. The following night, as the airplanes were en route to their targets, radio announcers on Saipan broadcast the names of the cities to the people of Japan, an action that some of the B-29 crewmen thought might increase Japanese defense of the named cities. It did not. American bombers struck six cities on the list. Even with the advance warnings Japanese opposition was feeble. Of the 496 airplanes that took to the air that night, not one was lost.

The stratagem worked so well that Twentieth Air Force operations planners scheduled two more of these missions to take place in the next eight days.

MEANWHILE, ON 26 July, the United States, together with Great Britain and China, issued a formal declaration to Japan to surrender unconditionally and threatened complete destruction of their homeland if they continued to fight. The declaration was issued from Potsdam, Germany, where Truman, Churchill and Stalin were meeting in the last of the great wartime summits. While there, Truman learned the details of the successful test of the first atomic bomb at Alamagordo, New Mexico, on 16 July.

The test, conducted under the direction of J. Robert Oppenheimer, whose team had designed and built the bomb at Los Alamos, was the culmination of intensive research and development that had begun in earnest in the summer of 1941. Code-named the "Manhattan Project," the supersecret activity under the immediate direction of Maj. Gen. Leslie Groves employed over 120,000 people, including some of the country's leading physicists, chemists, metallurgists, mathematicians and engineers. They worked in 37 different facilities in the United States and Canada; the cost of the "Manhattan Project" was over $2 billion.

As research progressed on an atomic explosion device, the scientists leaned heavily toward a weapon that could be transported by air—a bomb. Beginning in the spring of 1943 Oppenheimer's team started designing such a weapon. Because they expected the bomb to be very large, and because it would probably be necessary to carry it long distances, the B-29, then in its final development stage, became a logical choice for the carrier. To deliver the bomb the AAF, in December 1944, activated a special unit, the 509th Cómposite Group, and Arnold named Col. Paul W. Tibbets, Jr., a pilot with a distinguished combat record in North Africa and Europe, to head it.

After training in the United States and Cuba, the first B-29s of the 509th landed in Tinian on 11 June 1945. The unit was attached to the 313th Wing but its orders came from the XXI Bomber Command and later the Twentieth Air Force and USASTAF. By the end of June the combat crews were flying practice missions over nearby islands while their neighbors in the 313th Wing speculated as to why this new unit was there and what its mission was.

While the 509th was training, officials in Washington were deciding on targets for the new and powerful weapon. In May 1945, Secretary of War Stimson had established a committee of eminent civilians to advise the President on atomic matters. On 1 June the so-called Interim Committee recommended that (1) the bomb be used against Japan as soon as possible, (2) it be used against a target with both military and civilian significance and (3) the attack be made without specific warning as to the nature of the weapon.

Meanwhile Arnold and Groves were reviewing specific targets. They felt that to achieve the maximum psychological and destructive impact, the target city should be one that was relatively untouched by previous bombing. This criteria ruled out most of Japan's largest cities and led to the selection of Kyoto, Hiroshima, Niigata and Kokura as potential targets. Later, at Stimson's personal insistence, Kyoto was dropped from the list because of its cultural and religious significance and the city of Nagasaki was added.

On 28 July, as combat crews of the 509th were carrying out a series of 12 simulated atomic bomb strikes at or near a number of Japan's cities, Prime Minister Suzuki met with reporters and announced that the Potsdam Declaration was "of no great value" to his government. This, coupled with other newspaper reports, prompted Truman and other Allied leaders to conclude that Japan had rejected their terms. Actually Suzuki and his Foreign Minister, Shigenori Togo, had hoped to be able to ignore the declaration while they sought better terms through Soviet mediation. But the provisions of the declaration could not be ignored, since Twentieth Air Force B-29s, continuing the war of words, dropped thousands of copies of the Japanese translations of the document on Japan's cities.

ON THE TWENTY-NINTH Gen. Spaatz arrived on Guam, bringing with him a top-secret letter, approved by Marshall and Stimson, addressed to him in his new position as Commanding General of USASTAF. The letter stated:

> ... The 509th Composite Group Twentieth Air Force will deliver its first special bomb as soon as weather will permit visual bombing after about 3 August 1945 on one of the targets: Hiroshima, Kokura, Niigata and Nagasaki. . . . Additional bombs will be delivered on the above targets as soon as made ready by the project staff. Further instructions will be issued concerning targets other than those listed above. . . .

Now all that was needed was a go-ahead from the President and favorable weather.

ON 1 AUGUST, Gen. Arnold, intent on keeping the pressure on the enemy and commemorating Army Air Forces Day, ordered the greatest air raid of the war. On that day 836 B-29s took to the air and dropped over 6,145 tons of incendiaries, demolition bombs and mines on cities and other targets in Japan. This outdid the Eighth Air Force's biggest raid of 4,778 tons on D-Day and the RAF's largest single mission, a 5,433-ton strike on Dortmund, Germany, in March 1945. Of the five cities bombed, four had been warned beforehand by leaflets.

The havoc created that night once more illustrated the terrible destructiveness of the B-29 missions and the futility of Japanese defensive measures. It was a case of giant blows delivered to small targets. Toyama, the largest target, had a population of only 127,000. The other three cities, Hachioji, Mito and Nagaoka, all had populations of less than 70,000 and small built-up areas. As a consequence it was not the area destroyed (the total area destroyed in the four cities was slightly over 6 square miles.) that made these raids so terrible as the percentage of the city's area that was demolished. The most outstanding example was Toyama, where the B-29s' incendiaries created massive fires destroying 99.5 percent of the built-up area of the city—the most devastating incendiary raid of the war.

In another instance, to meet the challenge of the seemingly omnipotent B-29s, the Tokyo fire department sent 50 of its largest fire trucks, along with 300 professional firemen, to nearby Hachioji, one of the forewarned cities. On hand when the bombers arrived was the largest single concentration of fire-fighting equipment ever mustered by the Japanese for fighting incendiary attacks. The great effort turned into a dismal failure. Within 15 minutes of the start of the attack a cluster of bombs set Hachioji's electrical switching station on fire. Without electricity the three big pumps to bring water to the city's main reservoir were inoperative. After the water supply in the reservoir was exhausted, trucks tried pumping water from the river, but this too failed. A number of the trucks caught fire and hoses burned. Meanwhile fire raged, burning over two-thirds of the entire city.

ON 2 AUGUST, with Japan's apparent rejection of the Allies surrender demand and a go-ahead from Washington, the field order for the world's first atomic bomb strike (ironically, its number in the sequence of orders turned out to be 13) was signed by Lt. Gen. Nathan F. Twining, the new commander of the Twentieth Air Force. The primary target was Hiroshima, the secondary, Kokura and the third, Nagasaki. Three weather aircraft were to be dispatched, one to each target. The three B-29s that would fly to the target were Col. Tibbets' *Enola Gay*, with the bomb aboard, and two observation airplanes, Maj. Charles W. Sweeney's *The Great Artiste* and Capt. George W. Marquardt's *No. 91*, both carrying military and civilian observers along with cameras and scientific instruments.

On 4 August, the crews were briefed on the mission and learned for the first time the nature and the power—the equivalent of 20,000 tons of TNT—of the atomic bomb. With everything ready, Spaatz, Twining and LeMay (as Twining's Chief of Staff, LeMay was involved in all aspects of this most important operation) now had to wait for a break in the weather.

On the fifth the forecast for the next day was favorable. At 2:45 the following morning Tibbets took off, followed by the two observation airplanes. Past Iwo Jima and starting his climb to bombing altitude, Tibbets received the report from the weather aircraft over Hiroshima—visual bombing conditions. An hour later, 8:15 A.M. Hiroshima time, after a smooth run to the target, the bombardier toggled the bomb out from 31,600 feet. Tibbets executed a violent turn and dropped the nose to gain speed. When the bomb exploded, about 2,000 feet above the ground, the three B-29s were about 15 minutes away. Crewmen in the *Enola Gay* and the observation airplanes witnessed the initial fireball, then a cloud mass that spawned a rapidly ascending white column which, after it enlarged at the top, looked like a gigantic mushroom. Thereafter, this would be how most of the world would visualize an atomic explosion.

The bomb destroyed an area of about 4.7 square miles of the most densely populated area of the city. Eighty percent of the buildings were destroyed. Among these were many of the city's hospitals, where most of the doctors and nurses perished. Over 70,000 people died, most from the same causes as did those in the incendiary raids—blast effect, flash burns and falling debris. Immediate deaths from radiation, unique to atomic attack, were estimated at from 7 to 20 percent but would probably have been greater had not many of the victims died outright from the bomb's blast or the ensuing fire. Panic-stricken survivors fled soon after the bomb's explosion but returned the next day to search for relatives and possessions. Rehabilitation of the city was slow and was only beginning when the Allies arrived after the war.

THE *Enola Gay* landed on Tinian at 2:58 P.M. Gen. Spaatz was on hand to greet Tibbets and his crew and present them with medals. News of the mission was flashed to President Truman, who was aboard the cruiser *Augusta* returning from the Potsdam conference. The President's announcement of the dropping of the bomb, released in Washington, contained a warning to the Japanese people that if their leaders did not surrender they could "expect a rain of ruin from the air, the like of which has never been seen on earth."

Japanese Army leaders tried to play down the bomb, calling it a bomb of a new sort that did considerable damage. For a time military censors were successful in preventing the press from referring to it as an "atomic bomb." Anticipating such action, the printing presses on Guam rolled once again and soon thereafter B-29s were flying over Japan and dropping leaflets that informed the Japanese people of the nature of the atomic bomb on Hiroshima.

While awaiting the reaction to the first atomic bomb and preparing to drop another, the Twentieth Air Force kept the pressure on. On 7 August a 131-aircraft mission was sent against Toyokawa arsenal. On the following day 245 planes from three wings attacked Yawata in daylight with incendiaries. Twentieth crews had dreaded the time when they might have to hit Yawata, one of the most heavily defended targets in Japan. That the mission was called as expectations for peace were mounting made it even more disturbing. The men's concerns were justified. The loss of four B-29s and their crews exceeded that of any single mission flown by the Command in over two months.

The primary target for the second atomic bomb was Kokura, a city near the northern tip of the island of Kyushu; the secondary was Nagasaki, on Kyushu's west coast. The weather aircraft took off at 2:30 A.M. on 9 August followed about an hour later by the three-airplane strike force. This time Maj. Sweeney, flying *Bock's Car*, carried the bomb. The weather was bad on the way up, but word came that visual conditions existed over both targets. When Sweeney got to Kokura the weather had closed in, so he decided to try for Nagasaki. He found the visibility there also poor but, with fuel running very low, decided to make the drop anyway, by radar. On the bomb run, the bombadier finally found an opening in the cloud cover and released the bomb over Nagasaki at 10:58 A.M.

The area destroyed, 1.45 square miles out of a total of 3.84, was considerably less than at Hiroshima and only about half the average destruction inflicted on incendiary raids. In terms of human toll, however, Nagasaki, with over 13,000 killed, would be exceeded by only two other Japanese cities—Tokyo and Hiroshima. Human casualties might have been considerably less had better air raid procedures been observed. After experiencing a false alarm on the 8th, the citizens of Nagasaki responded on the morning of the ninth to an alert sounded at 7:45 A.M., followed by a "raid in progress" signal five minutes later. (These signals must have been based on sightings of the weather aircraft.) People entered shelters, many of which were tunnels in the sides of the hills and far superior to shelters in most cities. Forty minutes later the all-clear sounded, only to be followed at 10:53 A.M. by a "raid in progress" signal. Few people went for the shelters this time, and minutes later the bomb went off with a dazzling white flash, catching thousands at work, home or on the streets.

NEWS OF THE explosion at Nagasaki of the second atomic bomb reached Tokyo soon after it occurred. Earlier that morning Prime Minister Suzuki had learned that Russia had declared war on Japan. Suzuki met privately with the Emperor, and they agreed that they must seek peace immediately. That afternoon the cabinet convened, but discussions, which went on for hours, ended in a deadlock between those seeking peace and those in the military who wanted to continue the fight in hopes of securing better terms. Suzuki then asked the Emperor to meet that night with the nation's highest governmental body, the Supreme Council. This meeting took place in the Obunko, since the normal meeting rooms in the Imperial Palace had been destroyed. After several hours of discussion the Prime Minister finally asked the Emperor for his views. This was at about 3 A.M. on the morning of the tenth. The Emperor expressed his desire that the terms of the Potsdam Declaration be accepted with the provision that the Imperial institution be preserved. The full cabinet reconvened and decided unanimously to accept the Potsdam terms, subject to the Imperial proviso. This decision was immediately transmitted to the American government. The United States' reply, received on 12 August, was ambivalent on the matter of Imperial office. This precipitated more argument between the war and peace factions in the Japanese government, which continued for several days.

ON 11 AUGUST, believing that continued bombing might adversely affect the negotiation in progress, Washington ordered that USASTAF stop all strategic operations, even to the extent of calling back missions in progress, if necessary. But with no reply from the Japanese, on the fourteenth Spaatz was ordered to resume bombing.

Arnold wanted the next operation to be a massive one and suggested to Spaatz that the Twentieth Air Force, supplemented by planes from Doolittle's Eighth Air Force on Okinawa, might be able to hit the Tokyo area with 1,000 airplanes. (The 1 August Army Air Forces Day missions had fallen short of this.) Spaatz wanted to drop a third atomic bomb, on Tokyo. Washington did not favor this and Spaatz considered the battered city a poor target for conventional bombing. Instead, he suggested, and Arnold approved, hitting seven different targets.

As it turned out, Spaatz had to stage the grand finale without any aircraft from the Eighth Air Force. From the Marianas bases 443 B-29s struck three targets in a daylight strike on the fourteenth. That night, with officers standing by for a last-minute cancellation if necessary, 366 more airplanes headed for two small cities, an oil refinery and a mine field. Counting the 186 fighter escorts for the daylight mission and 7 B-29s from the 509th Group on a special bombing mission, USASTAF barely passed Arnold's goal with a total of 1,002 airplanes. As it turned out, the men flying that day were on their last combat mission. Good fortune was with them—not a single aircraft was lost.

At noon on 15 August, Emperor Hirohito, in an unprecedented radio broadcast to the Japanese people, announced his nation's capitulation. On the same day President Truman told the world that the Japanese had surrendered. The fighting was over.

MANY B-29 CREWMEN, among them Sgt. Joe Keenan, a gunner in the 58th Bomb Wing, would fly two more important missions. The first of these was flying relief supplies to Allied POW camps.

Soon after the surrender announcement, Keenan began to hear talk of flying supplies to POWs. One day men came and painted "PW SUPPLIES" in big black letters on the underside of Keenan's aircraft. Then nothing happened until the night of 30 August when his crew was notified that they would fly to Japan the following morning with 5 tons of food, clothing and medical supplies. They were to find two POW camps located on the northernmost of Japan's home islands, Hokkaido, and drop half of their cargo on each camp.

On the way to Hokkaido, flying at 4,000 feet in clear weather, Keenan had his first chance to see the devastation at the city of Sendai, which his group had hit in a night incendiary strike about two months before. After that he watched mile after mile of green and fertile Japanese countryside pass by below, as if in a movie travelogue. Later they ran into heavy clouds, which would make locating the camps virtually impossible. Fortunately they found a break in the clouds near where the POW camps were supposed to be located.

Descending to about 1,000 feet, they spotted another B-29

and flew with it for a while. (They later learned that this airplane crashed that day, killing all aboard.) For some time they flew down valleys, often flying as low as 500 feet, with 5,000-foot mountains on either side, without spotting their objective. Then, in a field next to a river they saw the letters PW spelled out in white stones. On the other side of the river was the camp. Keenan's pilot made a couple of practice runs over the prison compound while the POWs below ran back and forth, waving at the airplane that had suddenly burst from the clouds. The drop was a good one, and the big packages, with parachutes to slow their descent, fell inside the compound. As they flew away Keenan could see the men running to the boxes. After spending about two hours trying without success to find the other camp, Keenan returned to the camp by the river and dropped the rest of the supplies there.

For Keenan, even after 12 combat missions, this mercy flight would be remembered as "one of the greatest adventures of my life." Many of the others dropping 4,470 tons of supplies to an estimated 63,500 prisoners must have shared Keenan's satisfaction in rendering aid to their comrades.

But the magnificent effort had a cost, both in POWs and airmen. When the stock of parachutes was exhausted the supplies had to be dropped by free fall. In a few instances POWs were killed by the falling containers. During most of the 900 POW supply flights, the B-29s had to fly at dangerously low altitude over mountainous terrain, often with limited visibility. During the POW missions eight aircraft and 77 airmen were lost.

The latter casualties would become part of the Twentieth Air Force's total combat losses in the air war against Japan— 414 B-29s, more than 2,600 crewmen dead, and 433 wounded. (This estimate is based on AAF figures of December 1945, which showed 576 dead, 2406 missing or captured, 433 wounded. Information from former POWs indicate that a maximum of 300 of the missing/captured returned alive at the end of the war.)

On Sunday morning, 2 September 1945, 462 Twentieth Air Force B-29s assembled off the coast of Japan. From the assembly area the airplanes flew in formation over Tokyo, where they were able to see the devastated city for the first time in daylight and at low altitude (2,800 feet). Then the formations turned out over Tokyo Bay, where hundreds of Allied warships were anchored. In a final salute, the procession flew over the battleship *Missouri*, where, shortly before, representatives of the Japanese government had signed the surrender document. World War II was officially over.

THIRTEEN

RETROSPECT

IN THE FOREWORD I set forth a number of aspects of the air war against Japan about which I felt the American public lacked understanding. Most of them have been covered in previous chapters. Two important features of the air war remain to be addressed and are the subject of this chapter. They are:

- How the fire raids on Japan's cities had, by August 1945, crippled Japan's war production and dashed the hopes of all Japanese, from Emperor to factory worker.

- How the cumulative effect of the fire-bombing was a major factor in influencing the peace faction in Japan's governmental power structure and the Emperor to accept the Allied demand to surrender, thus forestalling an invasion of Japan scheduled for 1 November 1945 and saving countless human lives.

The damage done by the American bombing campaign, principally the area incendiary raids, to Japan's military and industrial capability was immense. B-29s destroyed or severely damaged more than 600 of the country's major manufacturing plants, including such giants as Mitsubishi, Kawasaki and Yawata. Aircraft, oil, steel, munitions, chemicals, machinery—

no sector of Japan's war economy was left unscathed. In July 1945 the level of production in 33 bombed Japanese urban areas—those which included the major proportion of industry—was only about one-third of its 1944 peak.

Urban area bombing also exacted an extremely heavy toll on the myriad nameless feeder plants buried in the fabric of Japan's cities. In the years after World War II some people speculated that AAF wartime statements describing home workshops in Tokyo and other Japanese cities were exaggerations used to justify burning the cities and displacing their populations. The U.S. Strategic Bombing Survey found that of more than 25,000 plants destroyed or badly damaged in the bombings of Tokyo, most employed less than 100 workers, many less than 10. Far from exaggeration, AAF intelligence estimates probably understated the importance of subcontractors in Japanese war production, as the following Japanese statements illustrate:

> *G. Aguri, Ministry of Finance:* "Most of the minor aircraft parts were made in small plants which were scattered in large or medium-size cities."
>
> *R. Sugiyama, Naval General Staff:* "Furthermore, owing to the destruction of large factories and the loss of small factories scattered throughout a city in the way of home industries, the production of parts decreased rapidly and thus hindered the entire war program."
>
> *K. Konishi, Ministry of Transportation:* "Aircraft-engine-part makers and subcontractors were mostly destroyed by these raids, which together with the losses incurred by dispersion and evacuation gave a fatal effect on production of aircraft."
>
> *T. Wada, Fuji Denko Seizo (electrical manufacturing company):* "But as regards our subcontracting factories, which numbered about 400, 225 factories were seriously damaged and their reconstruction was considered very difficult. This caused us great difficulty in obtaining finished and semi-worked parts, resulting in a sudden drop in production. The same circumstances prevailed throughout various industries of the whole

country, and therefore it can be concluded that the air
raids had a grave consequence on the resistive power of
Japan."

Plants, large or small, that escaped destruction or severe
damage had to operate with substantially fewer workers, and
production suffered. Men and women found it difficult or impossible to report to work when their home or that of their
neighbors had been burned. After raids, transportation came
to a standstill, food was scarce and confusion reigned. A postwar Japanese survey of 30 Tokyo factories disclosed that at the
conclusion of the mass incendiary raids on that city the average attendance at the factories had dropped by about one-
third and production had been reduced about two-thirds. After
the 17 March raid on Kobe, not a single worker showed up at
the Kawasaki Rolling Stock plant for an entire week. On a
broader scale, total employment in Kobe dropped from
287,000 to 213,000 after this same bombing. By July, after the
5 June raid, employment in Kobe had slumped to 137,000. In
neighboring Osaka total employment dropped from its 1944
peak of 830,000 to 465,000 in July 1945.

As they systematically destroyed the factories, the urban
area attacks made battlefields of Japan's cities. No rampaging
troops pillaged and raped, as many Japanese had come to believe would occur after Allied troops landed. But the terrible
effects of the fire-bombings had as much or more impact on
the civilian population as an actual invasion. In addition to
the heavy loss of life and physical injuries sustained by Japanese civilians, virtually every facet of Japanese day-to-day existence was impacted: where they worked, where they slept,
the transport they rode, the food they ate, the clothing they
wore, the medicine and drugs they required. Nothing escaped.

Among many privations, one of the most hurtful to the
Japanese was the loss of their homes with no prospect of replacement. "Dehousing" of urban populations, one of Britain's major objectives in its four years of area-incendiary-
bombing German cities, reached new heights during the fire
raids on Japan. In only five and a half months about 2.5 million Japanese dwellings were totally destroyed. This

amounted to approximately 20 percent of the number of dwellings existing before the bombings began. By comparison, during four years of bombing German housing losses amounted to 15 percent.

Massive dislocation accompanied dehousing. Over 8.5 million Japanese left the cities as a result of government-ordered evacuation or fleeing of their own accord. Tokyo alone suffered a loss of approximately 3.8 million persons from February 1944 to November 1945—an exodus of 58 percent of its February 1944 population. Osaka, Nagoya and Kobe lost their populations in almost as high a proportion.

The raids depleted clothing and medical supplies. Even before the air attacks began, the Japanese had barely enough cloth to patch their war-worn clothing. During bombings an estimated six-month supply of cloth for consumer purposes, stored in mills, warehouses and homes, literally went up in smoke. Incendiary attacks destroyed about one-third of the drug-producing facilities, creating serious shortages of vaccines and serum. The 1944–45 winter was the coldest in decades, and Japanese families lacked warm clothing and medicines to treat widespread respiratory illnesses.

Besides their threadbare clothing and lack of adequate shelter, the Japanese had to endure an ever-decreasing food supply. Though the fire raids destroyed some rice and other food supplies stored in warehouses in large cities, it was the aerial-mining campaign that choked off food imports and the chemical fertilizers necessary to produce agricultural crops domestically. Then the 1945 rice crop turned out to be the worst in years. Malnutrition led to fatigue, illness and absence from work. At the time of surrender the nation was facing the prospect of widespread starvation.

In sum, by August 1945 the Japanese war economy was bankrupt. Although military stocks were still considerable, the output of aircraft, armament and fuel had dropped to levels that could not have supported more than a few months of full-scale combat. Though a portion of this diminution of output can be attributed to the lack of raw materials (a result of the submarine and aerial mine blockade), the incessant bombing prevented those industries with raw materials from producing at the levels necessary to support the war effort. Japanese war leaders realized, and their plan for the final battle against the expected Allied invasion recognized, that Japan's military capability was limited to one final, all-out effort. They hoped to inflict such heavy losses on the Allies in the initial phases of the invasion that the enemy would be willing to grant Japan more liberal surrender terms rather than continue the bloody conflict.

Though the Twentieth Air Force did not publicize it, after March 1945 one of the objectives of urban area bombing was to weaken the morale of the Japanese people. The fire raids achieved this objective in large measure. Japanese morale, which began its major downturn in late 1944, fell at an increasing rate after the beginning of the urban area bombing. A USSBS study conducted after the war found that air attacks were

- the source of greatest *worry and concern* to the Japanese during the entire war,
- the most important single factor in causing them to have *doubts of victory,*
- the most important single factor in causing them to feel *certain of defeat,* and
- the most important single factor in making them *unwilling to continue the war.*

Despite their faith in the Emperor and the "spiritual" strength of the nation, Japanese morale deteriorated markedly in the final months. The social fabric began to come apart, giving rise to rumor-mongering and black-marketing. National unity, which had been so strong throughout the years, weakened. Though the still-powerful influence of the civil and military police prevented any revolt, antigovernment and antimilitary attitudes became more prevalent. A Home Ministry study conducted late in the war found that

> Criticism of weak air raid defenses, . . . inability of government officials to act, are gaining strength, and the people's distaste for war, which has always existed deep down in their

hearts, is gradually coming to the surface. Scribblings on walls, letters to editors, and people's talk indicate their desire for peace and [sic] defeatism.

If the people were ready for peace, what of their rulers? The supreme ruler was Emperor Hirohito. But the nation was actually governed by a prime minister who presided over a loose coalition of factions. The Army and Navy factions, predominant since the beginning of the war against China, were represented at the cabinet level by the heads of the War and Navy Ministries. Civilian authority was exercised by various cabinet ministers. These posts were often occupied by members of the aristocracy. A small but very important focus of power was the office of the Lord Keeper of the Privy Seal. The Privy Seal was chief personal counselor and adviser to the Emperor and controlled access to the throne. Outside the halls of government, but of considerable influence, was the "Zaibatsu," a group that included heads of the big industrial and commercial combines. The "jushin," elder statesmen, made up of former prime ministers and other high officials of state, constituted yet another group that the Emperor and the prime minister consulted on important matters.

By the spring of 1944, some members of the power factions recognized that Japan and its ally Germany were losing the war. But any suggestions that Japan seek peace had up to that time been squelched by Tojo, who at his peak of power simultaneously occupied the offices of prime minister, war minister and Army Chief of Staff. In July 1944, the fall of Saipan, which brought Tokyo and other major Japanese cities within range of American bombers, brought down the Tojo government. Replacing him was another Army general, Kuniaki Koiso, who (though he would later profess that when he took office he was convinced that the fall of Saipan meant defeat for Japan) carried on the aggressive policies of the military leaders. These men had pledged to fight a final and decisive battle to defeat the American forces in the Philippines. The battle was joined in the fall of 1944, about the same time that the first B-29s began to bomb Japan's factories.

In February 1945 the "decisive battle" was over—the Japanese Army and Navy in the Philippines were soundly defeated. After the 25 February fire raid on Tokyo, former prime minister Tojo told the Emperor not to be concerned, because the Americans lacked the capability to conduct large and sustained aerial attacks from the Marianas. Two weeks later LeMay's fire-bombers laid waste to Tokyo and followed with devastating attacks against Nagoya, Osaka and Kobe. The Emperor, against the advice of his retainers, inspected bombed-out areas of Tokyo, walked through the ashes and saw the great human and material damage that the B-29s had inflicted. As mentioned earlier, he and his family were forced to desert their palace living quarters and reside in the Obunko with its underground bomb shelter. Through personal experience, the Emperor realized that claims by Tojo and the Army that Japan could be defended against air attack were utterly groundless.

The American invasion of Okinawa on 1 April forced the resignation of Koiso and his replacement by Adm. (Baron) Kantaro Suzuki. Instrumental in naming Suzuki prime minister was Marquis Koichi Kido, Lord Keeper of the Privy Seal. Kido, Prince Konoye and other members of the aristocracy were among those who would make up the peace faction, a group whose aims the Emperor shared. Suzuki would write later that he assumed his new post with the clear understanding that the Emperor wanted him to seek ways to conclude the war as soon as possible.

One of Suzuki's first actions after taking office was to assign his cabinet secretary to prepare a report on the nation's ability to continue the war. The secretary's report provided a dismal picture:

> The ominous turn of the war, coupled with increasing tempo of air raids, is bringing about great disruption of land and sea communications and essential war production. The food situation has worsened. It has become increasingly difficult to meet the requirements of total war. Moreover, it has become necessary to pay attention to trends in public sentiment. Morale is high, but there is dissatisfaction with the present regime. Criticism of the government and the military is increasing. The people are losing confidence in their leaders and the gloomy omen of deterioration of public morale is present.

Suzuki accepted the report and presented its findings to the Emperor, who must have found in it much to confirm his growing feeling that his nation was in a desperate state.

The fall of Germany on 6 May caused Suzuki to call a meeting of the Supreme Council for the Direction of the War (hereafter referred to as the Supreme Council), a group of the most powerful men in the government, known in high government circles as the "Big Six." In addition to Suzuki, the Supreme Council included Minister of War Korechika Anami, Navy Minister Mitsumasa Yonai, Foreign Minister Shigenori Togo, Army Chief of Staff Yoshijiro Umezu and Navy Chief of Staff Soemu Toyoda. The Supreme Council concluded that Russia should be offered concessions in order to induce that country to remain neutral and to serve as a mediator between Japan and the Allies. After the meeting Togo sought out former foreign minister Koki Hirota and asked him to begin discussions with the Soviet ambassador in Japan, Jacob Malik, with a view to obtaining Russia's good offices.

Before Hirota could arrange a meeting with Malik, LeMay's B-29s had, on the nights of 23 and 25 May, inflicted so much damage to Tokyo that the city was no longer considered an urban target. Among the buildings burned in these final raids were the pavilions and palaces of the Empress Dowager, the Emperor, the Crown Prince and other princes. The entire royal family had joined their millions of "dehoused" subjects.

On 3 June Hirota met with Malik at a spa near Tokyo. Though the Russian ambassador seemed receptive, nothing substantial was accomplished. Two days later, with Yokohama and Osaka still smoldering from 500-airplane fire raids, the Supreme Council met again, this time to review a document entitled "The Fundamental Policy to be Followed Henceforth in the Conduct of the War." The Army sought to obtain the highest possible endorsement of its battle-to-the-death plan for defending the homeland. Despite opposition voiced by Togo, others who favored peace said nothing, and the military carried the day. On 8 June the document was presented to Emperor Hirohito at an Imperial Conference. Such meetings traditionally were held to obtain the Emperor's endorsement of national policies and decisions already adopted unanimously by the Supreme Council. During the conference the Emperor, as was customary, remained silent but did not appear pleased by what he heard. The "Fundamental Policy" was later adopted by action of the full cabinet.

Lord Keeper of the Privy Seal Kido was not present at the Imperial Conference, but the Emperor told him about it later and showed him the papers that had been discussed. Kido was appalled at the inability of the Big Six to recognize the urgent need for making peace. Within a short time he had drafted his own approach for accelerating the peace movement, "A Tentative Plan to Cope with the Situation." In it he stated that

> ... from his air force at present and the tremendous effectiveness of his mass incendiary bombing, it would be easy [for the enemy] to sweep away by fire, one after the other, all the nation's cities and towns down to the villages. He would not require much time for it either; with the cold season approaching, extreme shortages of provisions and food throughout the country during the latter part of this year and thereafter would cause serious unrest among the people at large. And, in consequence, the situation would be really past saving.

Kido urged that if peace was not sought without delay, "we can't be sure that we won't share Germany's fate and be reduced to such circumstances that we could not even safeguard the Imperial Household and preserve the national structure." He warned that in negotiating peace through a mediating country the government could expect few conditions favorable to Japan. Kido believed it essential that the intermediary know that the negotiations had the approval and backing of the Emperor. Kido's first step was to present his plan to Japan's supreme ruler.

Hirohito was sick of the war. The Army and the Navy ministers could no longer disguise the terrible state of the nation and its defenses. He remembered his inspection tour after the 9 March raid. The fiery destruction of the Imperial Palace buildings in late May was still fresh in his mind. He had recently read a confidential report from an admiral he had appointed to review the status of naval defenses against Allied landing operations. The admiral told the Emperor that the training of special naval attack units was deplorable and their equipment was inferior. The Emperor could only assume that the Army general's claims that the ground troops were combat-ready were as misleading as those he heard from the Navy admirals. The Emperor enthusiastically endorsed Kido's plan.

In the following days, Kido reviewed his peace scheme with Prime Minister Suzuki and Navy Minister Yonai. Both showed interest, but neither suggested that it be acted upon. Only Foreign Minister Togo was enthusiastic. Sensing that his plan was going nowhere, Kido persuaded the Emperor to hold an Imperial Conference with the members of the Supreme Council and express his views to them personally.

The Big Six sat down in the presence of the Emperor on 22 June, the day that the United States announced the end of the battle for Okinawa and a week after LeMay had begun (as Kido had predicted) the systematic fire-bombing of Japan's small cities. Togo reported that Hirota's talks with the Russian ambassador were going slowly but that he hoped some agreement could be reached by early July before the Allied leaders were expected to meet at Potsdam, Germany. Concerned with the lack of progress, the Emperor broke his usual silence and urged Togo to intensify his efforts to get the USSR to act as intermediary.

Togo could do little to speed things up. Early July passed with the Soviet ambassador continuing to shy away from any commitment in his talks with Hirota. By this time B-29s had fire-bombed 21 of Japan's smaller cities. Prodded by the Emperor, Suzuki, in consultation with Togo, raised the stakes in the quest for peace. Prince Konoye was to be dispatched to Moscow as the Emperor's personal emissary. On 10 July, the Emperor appointed Konoye. During the next two weeks, the Japanese ambassador in Moscow attempted to arrange for Konoye to travel to that city, but without success. The Soviets continued to stall.

Then on 26 July, with Truman, Stalin and Churchill still meeting in Potsdam, the United States, Britain and China issued the Potsdam Declaration, in which the Allied leaders announced agreement that ". . . Japan shall be given an opportunity to end this war." The Declaration's stipulations included Allied occupation of the home islands, destruction of Japan's war industry, trial of war criminals and establishment of a government that recognized democratic principles. The Allies called upon Japan "to proclaim now the unconditional surrender of all Japanese armed forces . . . The alternative for Japan is prompt and utter destruction."

Two days later, still hoping that something could be worked out with the Russians and under intense pressure from the military to reject the ultimatum, Suzuki responded. His reply, quoted in the Japanese press, was a clumsy attempt to neither accept nor reject the Allied message. The American press and radio interpreted it as a rejection. A diplomatic lull ensued, during which the Japanese continued attempts to get the USSR to mediate.

During the lull, the aerial onslaught continued unabated. LeMay's bombers, as previously described, began "advance notice" bombing of cities and, in addition to firebombs, rained millions of leaflets, which described Japan's untenable situation and the irresponsibility of its military hierarchy, across the countryside. By 6 August, only five of Japan's smaller cities had not been subjected to night fire-bombing. Two of these were Hiroshima and Nagasaki.

On 6 August the first atomic bomb fell on Hiroshima. Early on the morning of the ninth, even as Japan's leaders were absorbing the shock of the atomic bomb, Suzuki learned that Russia had declared war on Japan. With the door to peace through the Soviets slammed shut, the only remaining alternative was to respond directly to the United States and its allies. Suzuki met privately with the Emperor and they agreed that peace must be sought immediately. Later that morning Suzuki called a meeting of the Big Six, stated his view that Japan should accept the Potsdam Declaration and asked for opinions. (During the meeting news arrived that a second atomic bomb had been dropped on Nagasaki.) Suzuki proposed that the Potsdam terms be accepted with only one condition—that the Imperial family would be allowed to continue to reign. Togo and Navy Minister Yonai supported this proposal. War Minister Anami and the Army and Navy Chiefs of Staff were opposed. They advocated that occupation be limited and that disarmament and war crimes trials be under Japanese control. The meeting ended in a three-to-three deadlock. After an inconclusive meeting of the cabinet that afternoon, Suzuki, in desperation, asked the Emperor to meet that night with members of the Supreme Council.

At the Imperial Conference that night, after still another lengthy debate between the peace and war factions in the presence of the Emperor, Suzuki asked Hirohito to express his opinion. The Emperor stated that he believed that although the terms of the Potsdam Declaration were "unbearable," they must be accepted, since the alternative—to fight on—would lead only to destruction of the nation. The debate was ended. The Supreme Council agreed to accept the Potsdam terms, and soon after the cabinet approved the dispatch to each of the Allies of notes accepting the terms with the understanding that the prerogatives of the Emperor as sovereign ruler would be preserved. On the morning of 10 August, as these messages to the Allied governments were en route through neutral countries, B-29s were dropping bombs on Tokyo Arsenal in what would be their last attack on that city.

Early on the morning of 12 August, the text of the Allied reply to the Japanese notes was heard in Tokyo, as broadcast by a San Francisco shortwave station. Togo read it with disappointment. Though the Allies did not reject the Japanese demand to retain the Emperor outright, the reply left his ultimate fate unclear. Despite this lack of clarity, Togo decided that the best course was to accept the Allied terms. Before he could present his views to the Emperor, Chiefs of Staff Umezu and Toyoda had expressed theirs. In a hastily arranged audience they told the Emperor that they opposed acceptance. The Emperor, already briefed by Kido, told the two military leaders that their conclusion was premature and that the formal reply would be carefully studied after receipt. The Emperor had already decided that the Allied proposal should be accepted and told Togo this when he arrived after Umezu and Toyoda had left.

Later that day Suzuki convened the cabinet, and debate between War Minister Anami's war faction and Togo's peace advocates began anew, with most of the rest of the cabinet looking on. The next morning debate continued, this time confined to the Big Six. The result was another three-to-three split: Suzuki, Togo and Yonai for acceptance; Anami and the two military chiefs against. In the afternoon the discussion resumed in the full cabinet.

While the debate continued, the Emperor, sensing that the war faction might attempt to influence him in any way they could, held talks with a number of members of the royal family, informing them of his strong desire to accept the Allied terms. As a result, when Anami asked Prince Mikasa to use his influence to persuade the Emperor to change his mind and Toyoda made a similar plea to Prince Takamatsu, their requests were summarily rejected. Meanwhile Anami had to keep in check young staff officers who, fearing acceptance of Allied terms, were plotting various actions ranging from martial law for the capital to changing the government and "neutralizing" the peace faction.

Resolution of the impasse began when, on the morning of 14 August, B-29s dropped 5 million blue-hued leaflets on Tokyo, Osaka, Nagoya, Kobe and Kyoto. The leaflets stated:

> To the Japanese People:
> These American planes are not dropping bombs on you today. American planes are dropping these leaflets instead because the Japanese government has offered to surrender and every Japanese has a right to know the terms of the offer and the reply to it by the U.S. Government on behalf of itself, the British, Chinese and Russian governments. Your government now has a chance to end the war immediately. You will see how the war can be ended by reading the two following official statements. [The leaflets carried the full text of the Japanese government's message to the Allies and the Allied reply.]

Fearing that the leaflets might create a violent reaction from the troops and civilians who were heretofore unaware of the peace negotiations, Kido rushed to the Emperor and urged him to call an Imperial Conference immediately to resolve the issue. The Emperor agreed and at 10:30 that morning he took his seat in front of the Big Six and the full cabinet. Suzuki called upon Umezu, Toyoda and Anami to present their views opposing the Allied terms. As he had on 9 August, the Emperor listened and then rose and, in a long and sometimes tearful statement, enjoined his ministers of state to "Accept the Allied reply forthwith. In order that the people may know of my decision, I request that you prepare at once an Imperial rescript to this effect. . . . If it is desirable, I am ready to speak to my people over the radio." The debate was finally at an end.

Later that day Togo finished drafting the Imperial rescript announcing surrender. That night the cabinet ratified it and agreed that the Emperor's radio broadcast should be at noon on the following day. Just before midnight Hirohito finished recording his statement.

The next morning a group of dissident young officers temporarily took over the Imperial Palace grounds and attempted to prevent the Emperor's broadcast. The abortive coup was quickly overcome and at noon the Emperor informed his people of the war's end. That afternoon Suzuki tendered the resignation of his entire cabinet to the Emperor, who appointed Prince Higashikuni to preside over the period of surrender and act as Japan's first postwar prime minister.

On 3 September, Japan signed the final surrender agreement on the American battleship *Missouri.* The war officially ended without necessity for an invasion that would have taken a terrible toll in both American and Japanese lives.

AFTER THE WAR the USSBS in its final report concluded that

> . . . [C]ertainly prior to 31 December 1945, and in all probability prior to 1 November 1945, Japan would have surrendered even if the atomic bombs had not been dropped, even if Russia had not entered the war and even if no invasion had been planned or contemplated.

It is regrettable that, except for historians and other interested individuals, few Americans have read, or even had access to, the numerous separate reports, totaling thousands of pages, on which the Survey's conclusions are based.

I believe that the Survey's conclusion, even though couched in speculative terms, supports the view that continued strategic bombing alone was sufficient to force Japan, already seriously weakened by land and naval defeats, to accept Allied peace terms.

The reality is that the atomic bombs were dropped and Russia did enter the war. How then was the strategic bombing campaign, in which incendiary bombing was predominate, the major factor that forced Japan to surrender? This can best be assessed by summing up the influence the bombing had on that country's political leaders.

Clearly, Emperor Hirohito was the pivotal figure in the path to peace. Without his power to force decision, the debate might have continued indefinitely. Given this premise, the factors that influenced him are the most important. During his inspection of the devastation following the 9 March fire raid on Tokyo he saw clear and indisputable evidence that his military leaders were not giving him the facts. Only weeks before, he had been told that American air power was incapable of seriously damaging Japan's war potential. Then in late May the B-29s, after a diversion to support the U.S. invasion of Okinawa, returned and completed the destruction of Tokyo. Hirohito saw the Imperial family uprooted along with millions of his subjects. The hub of his country's military, economic and spiritual power was reduced to ashes.

By 7 June, in a series of massive fire raids, LeMay's bombers had gutted Nagoya, Yokohama, Osaka and Kobe. War Minister Anami and the war faction chose the next day to get the Emperor's approval of their "Fundamental Policy," the plan for all-out resistance against Allied invasion. They must have found, in the destruction of Japan's major cities, impetus to hasten their preparations for defense.

Lord Keeper of the Privy Seal Kido, the Emperor's closest advisor, reacted differently. He saw in the bombings proof that all of Japan's remaining cities and towns, down to the smallest, would soon be destroyed by incendiaries. He stated this in his hastily prepared "Tentative Plan to Cope with the Situation" and recommended that peace be sought without delay. Hirohito, the first person to see Kido's plan, needed little convincing and for the first time pledged that he would personally give his full support to the theretofore faltering attempts to persuade Russia to serve as intermediary between Japan and the Allies.

Meanwhile, LeMay's B-29s were bombing smaller cities at the rate of eight a week. By the time of the "Potsdam Declaration" on 26 July, 42 cities and towns had been severely damaged by incendiaries, confirming Kido's predictions. Prime Minister Suzuki, under great pressure from the war faction to turn down the Allied offer, bumbled his reply, but personally leaned heavily toward accepting the Allied terms. After the war he stated: "It seemed to me unavoidable that in the long run Japan would be almost destroyed by air attack, so that merely on the basis of the B-29s alone I was convinced that Japan should sue for peace."

By 6 August, B-29s had set fire to all but 4 of the 60 cities on LeMay's list. On that day and the ninth, the atomic bombs fell and Russia entered the war. Russia's entry left Japan no alternative but to meet the Allies' conditions or fight to the bitter end. As for the atomic bombs, Suzuki declared: "On top of the B-29 raids came the atomic bomb[s], immediately after the Potsdam Declaration, which was just one additional reason for giving in and was a very good one and gave us the opportune moment to make open negotiations for peace. I myself, on the basis of the B-29 raids, felt that the cause was hopeless."

Since the night of 9 March, when flames had first billowed over Tokyo, Emperor Hirohito's hopes for his country had continued to wane. Russia's entry and the atomic bombs provided the platform for him to insist to his government leaders that Japan must surrender.

CHAPTER NOTES

In the notes that follow I have identified the sources used in each chapter. Listed under *Quotations* is the page in the text where the quotation is found, the source of the quote and the page number in that document. Listed under *General Sources* are the documents, interviews, et cetera, used as the basis for the narrative. Finally, under *Background Sources* I have listed those references not applicable to a particular chapter.

Some abbreviations frequently used in the Notes are as follow:
NA National Archives, Washington, D.C.
RG Record Group
AFHRC Air Force Historical Research Center, Maxwell Air Force Base, Alabama
AFHO Air Force Historical Office, Bolling Field, Washington, D.C.
USSBS United States Strategic Bombing Survey
MR Microfilm roll

INTRODUCTION

Quotations

For "No country will" (p. 6): Spector, Ronald, *Eagle Against the Sun*, Free Press, New York, 1985, p. 487.
For the "The Air Corps is" (p. 7): Chennault, Gen. Claire, *Way of the Fighter*, G. P. Putnam's Sons, New York, p. 97.

General Sources

Brophy, Leo, and George Fisher, *Organizing for War;* and Brophy, Leo, Wyndham Miles, and Rexmond Cochrane, *From Laboratory to Field*, Vols. I and II, Chemical Warfare Service Series, the United States Army in World War II, Office of the Chief of Military History, Washington, D.C., 1959.

Kennett, Lee, *A History of Strategic Bombing*, Charles Scribner's Sons, New York, 1982.

Kleber, Brooks, and Dale Birdsell, *Chemicals in Combat*, Vol. III, The Chemical Warfare Series, The United States Army in World War II, Office of the Chief of Military History, Washington, D.C., 1966.

Parton, James, *"Air Force Spoken Here": General Ira Eaker and The Command of the Air*, Adler and Adler, Bethesda, MD, 1986.

Schaffer, Ronald, *Wings of Judgment*, Oxford University Press, New York, 1985.

Stokesbury, James, *A Short History of World War II*, William Morrow, New York, 1986.

CHAPTER 1

Quotations

For "The program for the immediate future" (p. 17): Letter from Earl Stevenson to Roger Adams, July 28, 1942, RG 227, NA.

For "It has been decided that" (p. 19): Kennett, Lee, *A History of Strategic Bombing*, Charles Scribner's Sons, New York, 1982, p.129.

For "A bomber offensive of adequate weight," Kennett, Lee, *A History of Strategic Bombing*, Charles Scribner's Sons, New York, 1982 p. 130.

For "The clue to the successful" and following quotations, (p. 21), memorandum from Richard Russell to Roger Adams, 15 September 1942, RG 227, NA.

General Sources

"Fire Warfare: Incendiaries and Flame Throwers," Summary Technical Report of Division 11, NDRC, Washington, D.C., 1946, NA.

Arnold Papers, Box 137, Library of Congress.

Record Group 227, OSRD Files, NA.

Interviews, letters, and newspaper clippings, February–March 1987, with and from Nancy Nixon, sister of Raymond Ewell.

Brophy and Fisher, *Organizing for War;* and Brophy, Leo, Wyndham Miles, and Rexmond Cochrane, *From Laboratory to Field*, Vols. I and II, Chemical Warfare Service Series, the United States Army in World War II, Office of the Chief of Military History, Washington, D.C., 1959.

Bush, Vannevar, *Modern Arms and Free Men,* Simon and Schuster, New York, 1949.

Fieser, Louis, *The Scientific Method: A Personal Account of Unusual Projects in War and Peace,* Reinhold Publishing, New York, 1964.

Kleber and Birdsell, *Chemicals in Combat,* Vol. III, The Chemical Warfare Series, The United States Army in World War II, Office of the Chief of Military History, Washington, D.C., 1966.

CHAPTER 2

Quotations

For "The only reason that we" and following quotations (pp. 26–27): Memorandum from Raymond Ewell to R. Russell and E. Stevenson, 17 April 1943, File 118.01, AFHRC.

For Personal description of B-29 (pp. 40–44): Interviews with James Pattillo.

For "We have under development" (p. 51): Berger, Carl, *B-29—The Superfortress,* Ballantine Books, New York, 1970, p. 45.

For "Japanese War Production (aside from heavy industry)" and following quotations (p. 52): Memorandum from COA to Gen. Arnold "Report of Committee of Operational Analysts on Economic Objectives in the Far East," 11 November 1943, RG 319, ABC 384.5 Japan, NA.

For "The worst thing is that" (p. 53): Craven, W. and J. Cate, *The Pacific—Matterhorn to Nagasaki,* Vol. V, The Army Air Forces in World War II, University of Chicago Press, Chicago, 1953, p. 21.

For "A strategic bombing force" (p. 54): Hansell, Gen. *Strategic Air War Against Japan,* Government Printing Office, Washington, D.C., 1980, p. 19.

For "find a group of buildings" (p. 55): Memorandum from Chief of Air Staff to AC/AS OC&R Requirements Division, 19 February 1944, Arnold Papers, Box 117, Library of Congress.

For "void of organization" (p. 56): Berger, *op. cit.,* p. 55.

For "If we had kept at it" (p. 57): Shalett, "This Possum Is Jap Poison," *Saturday Evening Post,* 25 November 1944, p. 94.

For "At least 60 percent" (p. 59): Memorandum, unsigned, to Commanding General Twentieth Air Force (Attn: Col. Combs), "Incendiary Bombing of Simulated Japanese Dwellings," N.D., RG 18, Box 101, NA.

For "had come across some data" (p. 60): Letter from E. Earle to Gen. Gates, 4 May 1944, File 118.01, AFHRC.

For "If daylight operations prove more costly" (p. 61): Letter from Col. Perera and W. Leach to Gen. Hansell, 9 May 1944, AFHRC.

General Sources

Memorandum from Assistant Chief of Air Staff, Intelligence, "Japan, Incendiary Attack Data," 15 October 1943, microfilm roll 1299, AFHRC.

Memorandum from Gen. Gross to Chief of Air Staff, "Test of Incendiaries," 5 May 1944, Arnold Papers, Box 117, Library of Congress.

Memorandum from President, AAF Board, Orlando, Florida, to Gen. Arnold, "Incendiary Attack of Japanese Cities," 11 May 1944, RG 243, Box 7, NA.

Microfilm rolls 118.04, 118.15, 1298, 1372, AFHRC.

RG 227, OSRD.

Arnold Papers, Boxes 137, 138, Library of Congress.

"Fire Warfare: Incendiaries and Flame Throwers," Summary Technical Report of Division II, NDRC, Washington, D.C., 1946, NA.

Silverman, "Operation Hotfoot," *Saturday Evening Post*, 16 December 1946, p. 20.

Baxter, James, *Scientists Against Time*, Little, Brown, Boston, 1946.

Berger, Carl, *B-29—The Superfortress*, Ballantine Books, New York, 1970, p. 45.

Caidin, Martin, *A Torch to the Enemy*, Simon and Schuster, New York, 1960.

Collison, Thomas, *The Superfortress is Born*, Duell, Sloan, and Pearce, New York, 1945.

Hansell, Gen. *Strategic Air War Against Japan*, Government Printing Office, Washington, D.C., 1980, p. 19.

Kennett, Lee, *A History of Strategic Bombing*, Charles Scribner's Sons, New York, 1982.

Kleber and Birdsell, *Chemicals in Combat*, Vol. III, The Chemical Warfare Series, The United States Army in World War II, Office of the Chief of Military History, Washington, D.C., 1966.

Noyes, W. A., ed., *Chemistry: A History of the Chemistry Components of the National Defense Research Committee*, Little, Brown, Boston, 1948.

Pimlott, John, *B-29 Superfortress*, Chartwell Books, London, 1980.

Schaffer, Ronald, *Wings of Judgment*, Oxford University Press, New York, 1985.

CHAPTER 3

Quotations

For "As a matter of fact" (p. 66): Memorandum from Gen. O'Donnell to Gen. Arnold, "B-29 Defensive Capabilities Against Enemy Fighters," 7 February 1944, RG 18, Box 17, NA.

General Sources

Letters and comments, James Pattillo to author.

Memorandum from Col. Turner to Air Chief of Staff/Plans and Intelligence, "Nite B-29 Operations Against Japan," 24 February 1944, RG 18, NA.

462nd Bomb Group, historical report for June 1944, N.D., AFHRC.

Assistant Chief of Air Staff, *Mission Accomplished—Interrogations of Japanese Industrial, Military, and Civil Leaders of World War II,* Government Printing Office, Washington, D.C., 1946.

Rust, Ken, "Battle of Kansas," *Ex CBI Roundup,* June 1987, pp. 18–20.

Berger, Carl, *B-29—The Superfortress,* Ballantine Books, New York, 1970.

Caidin, Martin, *A Torch to the Enemy,* Simon and Schuster, New York, 1960.

Craven and Cate, *The Pacific—Matterhorn to Nagasaki,* Vol. V, The Army Air Forces in World War II, University of Chicago Press, Chicago, 1953.

Herbert, Kevin, *Maximum Effort—The B-29s Against Japan,* Sunflower University Press, Manhattan, Kansas, 1983.

Morrison, Wilbur, *Point of No Return—The Story of the Twentieth Air Force,* Time Books, New York, 1979.

———, *Hellbirds: The Story of the B-29s in Combat,* Zenger Publishing, Washington, D.C., 1960.

O'Neill, Richard, *Suicide Squads,* Ballantine Books, New York, 1984.

Pimlott, John, *B-29 Superfortress,* Chartwell Books, London, 1980.

Wheeler, Keith, *Bombers Over Japan,* Time-Life Books, Alexandria, Virginia, 1982.

CHAPTER 4

Quotations

For ". . . the question of fire attack" (p. 80): Memorandum for Chief of Staff Twentieth Air Force, "Determination of Optimum Use of

High Explosives-Incendiary Bombs Against Far Eastern Targets,"
N.A., File 118.01, AFHRC.

For "(1) In Tokyo, Osaka and Nagoya" (pp. 81–82): Office of Strategic Services Report, "Japanese Small-Scale Factories in Relation
to Air Bombardment," 30 June 1944, File 118.01, AFHRC.

For "When I finally" (p. 86): Hansell, Gen. *Strategic Air War Against
Japan*, Government Printing Office, Washington, D.C., 1980, p.
31.

For "Final judgment on" (p. 88); Report "Economic Effects of Successful Area Attacks on Six Japanese Cities: Summary of Findings
and Conclusions," 4 September 1944, File 118.01, AFHRC.

For "We have been intrigued" (p. 90), "It may be that " (p. 90), "We
do not know" (p. 92), and "Knock out Tokyo" (p. 92): Minutes of
meeting of COA, 14 September 1944, p. 39, File 118.15, AFHRC.

For ". . . this mode of attack" and following quotations (pp. 95–98):
Memorandum from Dr. Ewell to Dr. Bush, "Incendiary Attacks of
Japanese Cities," 12 October 1944, RG 18, NA.

For "A paper which" (p. 98) and ". . . the decision on" (p. 99): Letter
from Dr. Bush to Gen. Arnold, 13 October 1944, RG 18, NA.

General Sources

Memorandum from Col. Perera, "Compilation of Data for Evaluation of Economic Effects of Incendiary Attacks on Japanese Cities," 1 June 1944, File 118.01, AFHRC.

Report "Recommendations Regarding Incendiary Attacks of Certain
Kyushu Cities—Yawata, Wakamatsu, Tobata, Kokura, Nagasaki,
Sasebo," 9 August 1944, RG 18, NA.

Memorandum from Dr. Ewell to Chief, Operational Analysis Section, Headquarters TAF, "Load Ratio of Incendiaries and Fragmentation Bombs for Attack on Japanese Cities," 11 August 1944, RG
18, Box 101, NA.

Report of the AAF Board, "Incendiary Attacks on Japanese Cities,"
17 August 1944, RG 18, Box 101, NA.

Memorandum from Lt. Hitch, Incendiary Subcommittee, COA, to
Dr. Stearns, "Memorandum by Dr. Ewell 'Incendiary Attack of
Japanese Cities,' dated August 29, 1944," RG 18, Box 101, NA.

Memorandum from Col. Perera to Col. Lindsay, "Status of Studies
on Incendiary Attacks on Japanese Urban Industrial Areas,," 29
August 1944, File 118.01, AFHRC.

Memorandum, unsigned, to Col. Perera, "Report of a Meeting of the
Subcommitte on Incendiaries, COA," undated, but circa 8 September 1944, File 118.01, AFHRC.

Memorandum, unsigned, to members of COA, "Status Report of Results of Two Committee Meetings, September 13 and 14, 1944," 15 September 1944, File 118.15, AFHRC.

Memorandum from Gen. Hansell to Commanding General 313th Bomb Wing, Peterson Field, Colorado, "Conference September 16, 1944," No date, File 762.01, AFHRC.

Minutes of COA meetings of 13, 14, and 27 September 1944, File 118.15, AFHRC.

Memorandum from COA (signed by ten members) to Gen. Arnold, "Revised report of COA on Economic Targets in the Far East," 10 October 1944, Files 118.01 and 118.04–12, AFHRC.

Memorandum from Col. Combs to Gen. Norstad, "Incendiary and Mining Operations Against Japan," 4 November 1944, RG 18, Box 18, NA.

USSBS, Pacific War, Volume 55, *Effects of Air Attack on Japanese Urban Economy (Summary report)*. This and other volumes and reports in this series were published by the U.S. Government Printing Office, Washington D.C. 1946–1947.

Anderton, David, *B-29 Superfortress at War*, Charles Scribner's Sons, New York, 1978.

Hansell, General, *Strategic Air War Against Japan*, Government Printing Office, Washington, D.C., 1980.

Rust, Ken, *Twentieth Air Force Story in World War II*, Historical Aviation Album, Temple City, CA., 1979.

Schaffer, Ronald, *Wings of Judgment*, Oxford University Press, New York, 1985.

CHAPTER 5

Quotations

For "As you well know" (p. 102): Hansell, Gen. *Strategic Air War Against Japan*, Government Printing Office, Washington, D.C., 1980.

For "I couldn't very well" (p. 102): Anderton, David, *B-29 Superfortress at War*, Charles Scribner's Sons, New York, 1978, p. 71.

For "You were not 'on the pan' at any time" and quotation immediately following (p. 110): Craven and Cate, *The Pacific— Matterhorn to Nagasaki*, Vol. V, The Army Air Forces in World War II, University of Chicago Press, Chicago, 1953, p. 567.

For "Not at this time" (p. 117): Memorandum from Gen. Norstad to Gen. Arnold, November 29, 1944, RG 18, Box 18, NA.

For "An air defense oath" and quotations immediately following

(p. 121): Havens, Thomas, *Valley of Darkness, The Japanese People and World War II*, Norton and Company, New York, 1979, p. 157.

For "tight pressure and temperature gradient" (p. 126): Teletype from XXI Bomber Command to Commanding General Twentieth Air Force, 11 December 1944, MR 7728, AFHO.

For ". . . that we can do radar" and quotation immediately following (p. 127): Letter from Gen. Hansell to Gen. Arnold, 16 December 1944, RG 18, NA.

For "The progress you have been making" (pp. 128–129): Letter from Gen. Arnold to Gen. Lemay, 17 November 1944, RG 18, Box 106, NA.

For "helped answer some of the questions" (pp. 130–131): Letter from Gen. Arnold to Gen. Lemay, 17 December, 1944, RG 18, Box 106, NA.

For "At the earliest practicable date" (p. 134): Telecommunication from Gen. Nordstad to Gen. Hansell (marked personal), 18 December 1944, MR A7729, AFHO.

For ". . . I have with great difficulty" (pp. 134–135): Telecommunication from Gen. Hansell to Gen. Norstad, "Incendiary Attack of City of Nogoya," 19 December 1944, MR 7731, AFHO.

For "special requirement" (p. 135): Telecommunication from Gen. Norstad to Gen. Hansell, N.D., MR 7729, AFHO.

For "General Gives Sober Report" (p. 136): *Honolulu Advertiser*, Thursday, 28 December 1944, MR 7812, AFHO.

General Sources

Interview by author with Gen. Hansell, 1985.

Sellz, Edward Diary (unpublished).

Interview and Briefing Sheets. J. M. Kucera.

Letter from Gen. Hansell to Maj. Boyle, 4 January 1967.

Memorandum from Col. Montgomery to Gen. Perrin, 7 March 1944, Box 137, Arnold Papers, Library of Congress.

Tactical Mission Reports for the 497th and 498th Bomb Groups, 73rd Wing, Field Order 21, Mission 7, 24 November 1944, MR C0032, AFHO.

Telecommunication from Gen. Norstad to Gen. Lemay, "Proposed Target for November 24, 1944," N.D., RG 18, NA.

Telecommunication from Commanding General XX Bomb Command to Gen. Arnold, "Incendiary Attack on Nagasaki," 25 November 1944, RG 18, Box 101, NA.

Bomber Command, Field Order "Brooklyn No. 1," 29 November 1944, MR 7728, AFHO.

73rd Bomb Wing, "Consolidated Mission Report," 3 December 1944, MR C0032, NA.

Telecommunication from Gen. Arnold to Commanding General XX Bomber Command, 16 December 1944, NA.

Telecommunication from Gen. Norstad to Gen. Hansell, 3 January 1945, MR 7729, AFHO.

"XX Bomber Command Report of Operations, December 18, 1944," 4 January 1945, MR A7771, AFHO.

73rd Bomb Wing, "Lost Aircraft as of January 7, 1945," N.D., RG 18, Box 18, NA.

Memorandum from Col. McKee to Chief of Air Staff, "Incendiary Bomb M-69," 16 February 1944.

73rd Bomb Wing, Consolidated Mission Reports, Tactical narratives from Missions 14, 17, 18 and 20, N.D., MR C0032, AFHO.

Gen. Hansell's Oral History, 19 April 1967, Air Force Academy.

"Flanders Field," *Time*, p. 66, 11 December 1944.

Isaacs, "Army Weather Eye Covers Asia," *Newsweek*, p. 76, 9 April 1945.

McKelway, "Reporter with the B-29s," *New Yorker*, 9, 16, 23, 30 June 1945.

Morris, " 'Mr. Bee' Goes To Town," *Colliers*, 8 November 1945.

Anderton, *op. cit.*

Beasley, W., ed., *Modern Japan—Aspects of History, Literature, and Society*, University of California Press, Berkeley, CA, 1975.

Caidin, Martin, *A Torch to the Enemy*, Simon and Schuster, New York, 1960.

Chennault, Gen. Claire, *Way of the Fighter*, G.P. Putnam's Sons, New York, p. 97.

Craven and Cate, *op. cit.*

Dod, Karl, *The Corps of Engineers: The War Against Japan* (Vol. II, Corps of Engineers Technical Series, The United States Army in World War II), Office of the Chief of Military History, Washington, D.C., 1966.

Guillain, Robert, *I Saw Tokyo Burning*, Doubleday, Garden City, N.Y., 1981.

Marshall, Chester, *Skygiants over Japan*, Apollo Books, Winona, MN, 1984.

——, *The Global 20th*, Vol. I, Apollo Books, Winona, MN, 1985.

——, *The Global 20th*, Vol. II, Marshall Publications, Memphis, TN, 1987.

Morrison, Wilbur, *Point of No Return—The Story of the Twentieth Air Force*, Time Books, New York, 1979.

USSBS, Pacific War, Vol. 4, *Field Report Covering Air Raid Protection and Allied Subjects, Tokyo, Japan* and Pacific War, Vol. 11, *Final Report Covering Air Raid Protection and Allied Subjects in Japan.*

Wheeler, Keith, *Bombers Over Japan*, Time-Life Books, Alexandria, Virginia, 1982.

CHAPTER 6

Quotations

For ". . . There has been no indication" (p. 140): "B-29s versus Japan," *New York Times*, 19 January 1945.

For "I am still worried" (pp. 140–41): Coffey, Thomas, *Hap: The Story of the U.S. Air Force and the Man Who Built It—General Henry "Hap" Arnold*, Viking Press, New York, 1982, pp. 357–58.

For "any available information" (p. 142): Telecommunication from Hewitt (XXI Bomber Command) to Ankenbrandt (Twentieth Air Force), 20 January 1945.

For "Under blind bombing conditions" (p. 142): Telecommunication from Ankenbrandt to Hewitt, 23 January 1945.

For ". . . were briefed this afternoon" (p. 146): Marshall, Chester, *Skygiants over Japan*, Apollo Books, Winona, MN, 1984, p. 120.

For "exploded in mid-air" and following quotations in same paragraph and "Crashed—due to enemy action" (p. 151), 73rd Bomb Wing, Mission Report, Mission No. 24, 27 January 1945, MR C0032, AFHO.

For "We have run two tests" (pp. 153–54): Telecommunication from Gen. Norstad to Gen. Lemay, "Incendiary Attack," 12 February 1945, RG 18, NA.

For "Stop fighting the products" (p. 156): Spector, Ronald, *Eagle Against the Sun*, Free Press, New York, 1985, p. 496.

For "the most daring" (p. 156): Wheeler, Keith, *Bombers Over Japan*, Time-Life Books, Alexandria, Virginia, 1982, p. 113.

For "if sixty or eighty (p. 156) and ". . . all of these reasons" (p. 18): Coffey *op. cit.*, p. 360.

For "Symbolically this" (p. 158), report, "Human Elements of the Operations of the Command," N.D., MR 7747, AFHO.

General Sources

Memorandum from Maj. Haas to Col. Montgomery, "Incendiary Attack—Kobe," 27 November 1944, RG 18, NA.

Memorandum from Col. McNamara to Col. Combs, "Effectiveness of the Twentieth Air Force as a Strategic Weapon," 16 January 1945, MR A 7737, AFHO.

Memorandum from Maj. Bowes to Col. Posey, "Re-evaluation of Incendiary Attack Program," 16 January 1945, RG 18, NA.

Telecommunication from Gen. LeMay to Gen. Norstad, "Information on Incendiary Damage," 20 January 1945, RG 18, NA.

Memorandum from Col. McNamara to Gen. Norstad, "Twentieth Air Force Statistical Summary," 23 January 1945, RG 18, NA.

Memorandum from Assistant Chief, Air Staff, Intelligence Joint Target Group, to Headquarters Twentieth Air Force, Attention: Col. Combs, 1 February 1945, RG 18, NA.

73rd Bomb Wing, Consolidated Mission Report, Tactical Narrative, Mission No. 29, 10 February 1945, MR A7800, AFHO.

73rd Bomb Wing, Mission Report, Mission No. 25, 15 February 1945, MR A7800, AFHO.

XXI Bomber Command, Tactical Mission Report, Mission No. 37, 19 February 1945, MR A7800, AFHO.

Commanding General Twentieth Air Force, "Report of Operations, February 4, 1945," 15 March 1945, MR A7800, AFHO.

Anderton, David, *B-29 Superfortress at War*, Charles Scribner's Sons, New York, 1978.

Berger, Carl, *B-29—The Superfortress*, Ballantine Books, New York, 1970.

Coffey, Thomas, *Iron Eagle, The Turbulent Life of General Curtis LeMay*, Crown Publishing, New York, 1986.

Craven and Cate, *The Pacific—Matterhorn to Nagasaki*, Vol. V, The Army Air Forces in World War II, University of Chicago Press, Chicago, 1953.

Marshall, Chester, *Skygiants over Japan*, Apollo Books, Winona, MN, 1984.

Morrison, Wilbur, *Point of No Return—The Story of the Twentieth Air Force*, Times Books, New York, 1979.

Pimlott, John, *B-29 Superfortress*, Chartwell Books, London, 1980.

Wheeler, Keith, *Bombers Over Japan*, Time-Life Books, Alexandria, Virginia, 1982.

CHAPTER 7

Quotations

For "Allied air bosses have" (pp. 166–67), "civilian populations are," and "Our policy never has" (p 168): Schaffer, Ronald, *Wings of Judgement*, Oxford University Press, New York, 1985, pp. 99–100.

For "You drop a load of bombs" (p. 177): Schaffer, *op. cit.*, p. 63.

For "A. Tokyo lies 25 mi. from" (p. 182): 313th Wing Field Operations Report No. 10, 8 March 1945, MR A7800, AFHO.

For "Condemned to a quick demise" (p. 184): Marshall, *The Global 20th*, Vol. I, Apollo Books, Winona, MN, 1985, p. 273.

For "Operations tonight will" (p. 190): Telecommunication from Gen. Norstad to Headquarters Twentieth Air Force, "Forthcoming Operation March 9, 1945," MR A7731, AFHO.

General Sources

Interviews with or journals from:
Jack J. Catton
Edward W. Cutler
James Pattillo
Walter Sherrell

XXI Bomber Command, "Report of Operations of February 25, 1945," N.D., MR 7737, AFHO.

73rd Bomb Wing, Consolidated Mission Report, Mission No. 38, 25 February 1945, N.D., MR A7800, AFHO.

497th Bomb Group, Consolidated Mission Report of Mission on 25 February 1945, 27 February 1945, MR A7800, AFHO.

498th Bomb Group, Consolidated Mission Report of Mission on 25 February 1945, 2 March 1945, MR A7800, AFHO.

Telecommunication from Gen. LeMay to Commanders of the 73rd, 313th and 314th Bomb Wings, "Japanese Fighters Expected on March 9, 1945 Raid," 3 March 1945, MR A7731, AFHO.

Telecommunication from Gen. LeMay to Commander Naval Forces, Pacific Area, "Information on Japanese Fighter Reaction to be Expected on March 9, 1945 raid," 5 March 1945, MR A7731, AFHO.

XXI Bomber Command, "Report of Operations of Mission on March 4, 1945, April 12, 1945," MR A7800, AFHO.

XXI Bomber Command, "Analysis of Incendiary Phase of Operations against Japanese Urban Areas," N.D., MR A7800, AFHO.

XXI Bomber Command, "Notes on General Norstad's Visit," N.D., MR 7782, AFHO.

COOX, Memorandum, "B-29 Bombing Campaign Against Japan—the Japanese Dimension," May 1982.

Tillitse, "When Bombs Rained On Us in Tokyo," *Saturday Evening Post*, 12 January 1945.

Martin, "Black Snow and Leaping Tigers," *Harpers*, February 1946.

Anderton, David, *B-29 Superfortress at War*, Charles Scribner's Sons, New York, 1978.

Berger, Carl, *B-29—The Superfortress*, Ballantine Books, New York, 1970.

Birdsall, Steve, *Superfortress—The Boeing B-29*, Squadron/Signal Publications, Carrauton, Texas, 1980.

———, *Saga of the Superfortress*, Doubleday, New York, 1980.

Caidin, Martin, *A Torch to the Enemy*, Simon and Schuster, New York, 1960.

Detwiler, James, and Charles Burdick, eds., *Defense of the Homeland and the End of the War.* (Vol. 12 of *War in Asia and the Pacific 1937–1949*), Garland Publishing, New York, 1980.

Herbert, Kevin, *Maximum Effort—The B-29s Against Japan*, Sunflower University Press, Manhattan, Kansas, 1983.

Marshall, Chester, *Skygiants over Japan*, Apollo Books, Winona, MN, 1984.

Marshall, *The Global 20th* (*op. cit.*)

McKelway, "Reporter with the B-29s," *New Yorker*, 9, 16, 23, 30 June 1945.

Morrison, Wilbur, *Point of No Return—The Story of the Twentieth Air Force*, Time Books, New York, 1979.

Watanabe, Yohji, *Pictorial History of Air War Over Japan*, Japanese Army Air Force/Hara Shobo, Tokyo, 1980.

Wheeler, Keith, *Bombers Over Japan*, Time-Life Books, Alexandria, Virginia, 1982.

CHAPTER 8

Quotations

For "A lot could go wrong" (p. 197): McKelway, "Reporter with the B-29s," *New Yorker*, June 23, 1945, p. 28

For "like a ball of fire" (p. 203): 29th Bomb Group, Consolidated Mission Report, Mission No. 40, 12 March 1945, N.D., MR A7800, AFHO.

For "Equal Force [was]" (p. 214): XXI Bomber Command, Tactical Mission Report, Mission No. 40, 12 March 1945, 15 April 1945, MR A7800, AFHO.

General Sources

Interviews with or journals from:

73rd Bomb Wing

Jack Bizanz
Jack J. Catton

James H. Coats
Edward W. Cutler
John E. Dougherty
James Farrell
Orlo J. Hall
Eugene Horton
Percy Jones
Warren E. Long
Charles O. McAlister
Lisle S. Neher
Ernest T. Rasmussen
John B. Reeves
Walter Sherrell
Wallace I. Sloan
Don Thrane

313th Bomb Wing

William Carter
Arthur C. Clay
Don F. Dwyer
Dean A. Fling
Henry C. Huglin
Frank Lord
H. L. Peterson

314th Bomb Wing

Henry E. Erwin
Harry L. Evans, Jr.
Rennie Fontham
Charles S. Hoster
William Loesch
Harry F. Mitchell
Samuel P. Moose
George W. Mundy
John A. Roberts
George A. Simeral

Letter from Ralph Holton to James Pattillo, 28 January 1988.
XXI Bomber Command, lead crew manual, 2 March 1945, AFHO.
313th Bomb Wing, Field Order No. 10, 8 March 1945, AFHO.
314th Bomb Wing, Field Order No. 12, 8 March 1945, AFHO.
505th Bomb Group, Airplane Commander, Flight Engineer, Naviga-

tor, Bombardier, and Radar Opoerator "Flimsies," 9 March 1945. (Copies provided by J. M. Kucera).

9th Bomb Group, Tactical Narrative, Mission No. 40, 10 March 1945, MR A7800, AFHO.

497th Bomb Group, Consolidated Mission Report, 10 March 1945, RG 18, NA.

498th Bomb Group, Bombing Data Report, 11 March 1945, AFHO.

29th Bomb Group, Consolidated Mission Report, Mission No. 40, 12 March 1945, MR A7800, AFHO.

6th Bomb Group, Field Order No. 10, 15 March 1945, AFHO.

314th Bomb Wing, Consolidated Mission Report, Mission Meeting House No. 2, 18 March 1945, AFHO.

Memorandum from Maj. Salisbury, XXI Bomber Command, to Commanding General Twentieth Air Force, "Radar Bombing," 27 April 1945, AFHO.

73rd Bomb Wing, Consolidated Mission Report, and Tactical Narrative, Mission No. 40, N.D., MR A7800, AFHO.

XXI Bomber Command, Target Information on Sheet-Tokyo Urban Industrial Area, N.D., MR A7800, AFHO.

314th Bomb Wing, Narrative Report "Mission Against the Enemy," N.D., AFHO.

Tregaskis, "Road to Tokyo," *Saturday Evening Post*, 18 August 1945.

Anderton, David, *B-29 Superfortress at War*, Charles Scribner's Sons, New York, 1978.

Birdsall, Steve, *Superfortress—The Boeing B-29*, Squadron/Signal Publications, Carrauton, Texas, 1980.

Caidin, Martin, *A Torch to the Enemy*, Simon and Schuster, New York, 1960

Craven and Cate, *The Pacific—Matterhorn to Nagasaki*, Vol. V, The Army Air Forces in Word War II, University of Chicago Press, Chicago, 1953.

Herbert, Kevin, *Maximum Effort—The B-29s Against Japan*, Sunflower University Press, Manhattan, Kansas, 1983.

Morrison, Wilbur, *Point of No Return—The Story of the Twentieth Air Force*, Times Books, New York, 1979.

CHAPTER 9

Quotations

For "Today, approximately 130 B-29s" (p. 239): Excerpts from Japanese Home Services Broadcasts, RG 618, Box 45, NA.

For "unafraid of the air raids" (p. 239) and quotations following (pp. 240–41): USSBS, Volume 11, *op. cit.*

For "exceptionally well pleased" (p. 241): Telecommunication from Gen. Arnold to Gen. LeMay, N.D., AFHO.

For "I believe that" (p. 242) and quotations following (pp. 242–243): "Center of Tokyo devastated by fire bombs," *New York Times,* pp. 1 and 13, 11 March 1945.

For "thought it was appalling" (p. 243) and "For years after" (p. 29): Wyden, Peter, *Day One, Before Hiroshima and After,* Simon and Schuster, New York, 1984, p. 185.

General Sources

Interviews:

Seiko Kage
Michiko McKnight (Kanno in text)
Masae Oshita
Tomoka Hoffner (Suzuki in text)

XXI Bomber Command, Damage Assessment Report No. 17 for Mission of 9–10 March 1945 (Third Photographic Reconnaissance Squadron flew over Tokyo 10 March 1945, 11 March 1945), MR A7800, AFHO.

Statement by General LeMay on raid of 9–10 March 1945, RG 18, Box 45, NA.

Memorandum from Col. Combs to Gen. Giles, "Incendiary Attack on Tokyo," 12 March 1945, RG 18, Box 18, NA.

Twentieth Air Force Headquarters, Special Report "On the Incendiary Attacks against Japanese Urban Industrial Areas," N.D., File 760.5, AFHRC.

Bond, Horatio, ed., *Fire and the Air War,* National Fire Protection Association, Boston, 1946.

Caidin, Martin, *A Torch to the Enemy,* Simon and Schuster, New York, 1960.

Guillain, Robert, *I Saw Tokyo Burning,* Doubleday, Garden City, N.Y., 1981.

Kato, Masuo, *The Lost War, A Japanese Reporter's Inside Story,* A. A. Knopf, New York, 1946.

Toland, John, *The Rising Sun*, Bantam Books, New York, 1971.

USSBS, Pacific War, Vol. 4, *op, cit.*, Vol. 11, *op. cit.*, Vol. 14, *The Effects of Strategic Bombing on Japanese Morale*, Vol. 55, *op. cit.*, Vol. 90, *Effects of the Incendiary Bomb Attacks on Japan* (*A Report on Eight Cities*) and Vol. 96, *A Report on Physical Damage in Japan* (*Summary Report*).

CHAPTER 10

Quotations

For "With three hours of preflight" (p. 247) and quotations following (p. 4): Marshall, *The Global 20th*, Vol. I, Apollo Books, Winona, MN, 1985.

For "The enemy learned at Tokyo" (p. 249): Keenan, Richard M., *The Twentieth Air Force Album*, Twentieth Air Force Association, Washington, D.C., 1982, p. 242.

For "No Jap—and for that matter" (pp. 249–50): *Newsweek*, p. 41, 26 March 1945.

For "Your recent incendiary missions" (p. 250): Kenan, *op. cit.*, p. 243.

For "Gigantic Singer Sewing machine" and "This was the only time"
(p. 258): Diary of Edward W. Cutler.

For "I am influenced" (p. 260): Craven and Cate, *The Pacific— Matterhorn to Nagasaki*, Vol. V, The Army Air Forces in World War II, University of Chicago Press, Chicago, 1953, pp. 626–27.

For "The effect on the morale" (p. 260): memorandum from James T. Posey (For Col. Combs) to Gen. Norstad, "Recommended Intensification of Attacks on Japan Immediately Following V—E Day," 10 April 1945.

For "It was very effective" (p. 263): USSBS, Pacific War, Vol. 78, *The Offensive Mine Laying Campaign Against Japan*, p. 41.

General Sources

Journal, Diaries, and/or Interviews:

W. C. Dalke
Harry L. Evans
Frank Lord

Memorandum from Commanding General XXI Bomber Command to War Department, "Shortage of Incendiary Bombs," 13 March 1945, RG 18, NA.

Twentieth Air Force Daily Staff meeting reports for 13 March 1945, 2, 6, 12, 18, April 1945, and one undated. Subjects discussed varied, but did cover shortage of incendiary bombs in the Pacific. File 760.1, AFHRC.

Memorandum to XXI Bomber Command "Shortage of Incendiary Bombs and Actions Being Taken to Overcome It," 14 March 1945, RG 18, NA.

Telecommunication from Commanding General Twentieth Air Force to Commanding General XXI Bomber Command, "Shortage of Incendiary Bombs," 17 March 1945, RG 18, NA.

Memorandum from Gen. LeMay (signed McKelway) to Gen. O'Donnell, "Press Coverage on Recent Bombing Missions," 19 March 1945, MR A7800, AFHO.

Memorandum from Lt. Price, by order of Gen. LeMay, to all staff sections, XXI Bomber Command, "Message of Congratulations." Quotes two telegrams received by Gen. LeMay, one from Gen. Norstad, and one from Commander, Naval Task Force 58, congratulating XXI Bomber Command on successful missions; 19 March 1945.

497th Bomb Group Report following fire-bombing missions of March 1945, N.D., MR A7800, AFHO.

Telecommunication from Commanding General XXI Bomber Command to Commanders of the 73rd, 313th, and 314th Bomb Wings, congratulating them on success of first five incendiary raids and notifying them that Imperial Palace not be attacked. March 1945, Keenan, *The Twentieth Air Force Album, op. cit.*

Memorandum from Gen. Kissner to Deputy Commander Twentieth Air Force, "Flight Mess." Discussions of food prepared for crews in flight; 19 March 1945, MR A7811, AFHO.

Letter from Gen. Arnold to Gen. LeMay, congratulating him and staff on successful raid on 9–10 March 1945; 21 March 1945.

Telecommunication from Twentieth Air Force to Commanding General XXI Bomber Command, "Information on a Joint Target Group Study on Selected Urban Industrial Targets to be Attacked in Future," 28 March 1945, MR 7729, AFHO.

XXI Bomber Command Daily Diary for 30 March 1945. Among subjects covered is notice that a shipment of incendiary bombs will be leaving West Coast on 1 April 1945 and will not arrive before 5 May 1945; 31 March 1945, MR A7788, AFHO.

"Battle of the Pacific—Firebird's Flight," *Time*, 19 March 1945, p. 32.

"The biggest bonfire—Tokyo burns hard for 17 hours," *Newsweek*, 19 March 1945, p. 34.

"Japan: In panic. Giant fire rages in homeland after heavy American air blows," *Newsweek*, 26 March 1945, pp. 41–42.

"Battle of the Pacific—Ten Day Wonder," *Time*, 26 March 1945, pp. 29–30.

Berger, Carl, *B-29—The Superfortress*, Ballantine Books, New York, 1970.

Coox, Alvin, *Japan—The Final Agony*, Ballantine Books, New York, 1979.

Cutler Diary, "The Long Haul"—The story of the 497th Bomb Group (VH).

Marshall, *The Global 20th*, Vol. I, Apollo Books, Winona, MN, 1985.

Marshall, Chester, *Skygiants over Japan*, Apollo Books, Winona, MN, 1984.

Rust, Ken, *Twentieth Air Force Story in World War II*, Historical Aviation Album, Temple City, CA., 1979.

USSBS, Pacific War, Volume 54, *The War against Japanese Transportation, 1941–1945*, and Volume 78, *op. cit.*

Wheeler, Keith, *Bombers Over Japan*, Time-Life Books, Alexandria, Virginia, 1982.

CHAPTER 11

Quotations

For "Never again, in lights" (p. 274): Journal of Frank Lord.

For "Twenty orange lights" and following quotations (p. 277): XXI Bomber Command Tactical Mission Report for 25 May 1945 Mission, 14 July 1945, AFHO.

For "That fairy scene" and following quotation (p. 278): "Journal of Father Flaujac," in Detwiler, James, and Charles Burdick, eds., *Defense of the Homeland and the End of the War*, (Vol. 12 of *War in Asia and the Pacific 1937–1949*), Garland Publishing, New York, 1980, p. 6.

For "One ball of fire," "One baka followed," (p. 279), and listing of downed planes (pp. 16–17): 504th Bomb Group, Mission Report of 25 May 1945 Mission, N.D., AFHO.

For "An unidentified enemy aircraft" (p. 279): XXI Bomber Command, Tactical Mission Report, 25 May 1945 Mission (*op. cit.*).

For "Bounded across" (p. 282): Martin, "Black Snow and Leaping Tigers," *Harpers*, February 1946.

For "The tiny planes" (p. 285): Diary of Walter Odlin, pp. 262–263.

For "Our beautiful capital" (p. 290): *Time*, 4 June 1945, p. 31.

For "Blazing Tokyo" (p. 291), *Newsweek*, 4 June 1945, p. 29.

General Sources

Interviews with or journals/diaries from:
Orlo Hall
Tomoko Hoffner (Suzuki in text)
Frank Lord
Walter Odlin
Walter Sherrell

497th Bomb Group, Mission Summary, Mission of 25 May 1945, N.D. RG 18, Box 626, NA.

497th Bomb Group, Mission Report, Mission of 25–26 May 1945, N.D., MR A7800, AFHO.

504th Bomb Group, Mission Report, Mission of 25–26 May 1945, N.D. MR A7800, AFHO.

XXI Bomber Command, Tactical Mission Report, Mission 181, 24 May 1945, 12 July 1945, MR A7800, AFHO.

XXI Bomber Command, Tactical Mission Report, Mission 183, 25 May 1945, 14 July 1945, MR A7800, AFHO.

United States Army Far East Command, "Air Defense of the Homeland," Japanese Monograph No. 23, 5 June 1956.

Matsuoka, "Japanese Tells How It Felt on Receiving End," *Associated Press Release*, 1 October 1945.

Johnson, Dale, "Memories of Dale Johnson," *40th Bomb Group Association Memories*, March 1986.

Caidin, Martin, *A Torch to the Enemy*, Simon and Schuster, New York, 1960.

Coox, Alvin, *Japan—The Final Agony*, Ballantine Books, New York, 1979.

Craven and Cate, *The Pacific—Matterhorn to Nagasaki*, Vol. V, The Army Air Forces in World War II, University of Chicago Press, Chicago, 1953.

Marshall, *The Global 20th*, Vol. I, Apollo Books, Winona, MN, 1985.

Wheeler, Keith, *Bombers Over Japan*, Time-Life Books, Alexandria, Virginia, 1982.

CHAPTER 12

Quotations

For "more concerned with" (p. 302): USSBS, Pacific War, Volume 42, *The Japanese Wartime Standard of Living and Utilization of Manpower*, p. 103.

For "Military Leaders of Japan" and "These questions were"

(pp. 302–303): USPAC/POA, CINCPAC-CINVPOA Bulletin No. 164–45 "Psychological Warfare, Part Two, Supplement No. 1," 14 July 1945, File 760.01, AFHRC.

For "In accordance with" (p. 303): Wheeler, Keith, *Bombers Over Japan*, Time-Life Books, Alexandria, Virginia, 1982, p. 180.

For "of no great value" (p. 305): Spector, Ronald, *Eagle Against the Sun*, Free Press, New York, 1985, p. 549.

For ". . . The 509th Composite Group" (p. 306): Craven and Cate, *The Pacific—Matterhorn to Nagasaki*, Vol. V, The Army Air Forces in World War II, University of Chicago Press, Chicago, 1953, facing p. 697.

General Sources

Interviews with and/or journals/diaries from:
Frank Lord
Richard M. Keenan
Arnold Papers, Boxes 137, 138, Library of Congress.
Caidin, Martin, *A Torch to the Enemy*, Simon and Schuster, New York, 1960.
Herbert, Kevin, *Maximum Effort—The B-29s Against Japan*, Sunflower University Press, Manhattan, Kansas, 1983.
Kerr, E. Bartlett, *Surrender and Survival*, William Morrow, New York, 1985.
LeMay, General, and Bill Yenne, *Superfortress: The B-29 and American Air Power*, McGraw Hill, New York, 1988.
MacIsaac, David, *Strategic Bombing in World War Two—The Story of the United States Strategic Bombing Survey*, Garland Publishing, New York, 1976.
Wheeler, *op. cit.*
Wyden, Peter, *Day One, Before Hiroshima and After*, Simon and Schuster, New York, 1984, p. 185.

CHAPTER 13

Quotations

For "Most of the minor" (p. 316): "Furthermore, owing to" (p. 316): "aircraft engine part" (p. 316) and "But as regards" (pp. 316–317): Assistant Chief of Air Staff, *Mission accomplished* pp. 69, 74, 76, 78.

For "Criticism of weak" (p. 320): USSBS, Pacific War, Volume 14, *op. cit.*, p. 29.

For "The ominous turn of the war" (pp. 322–23): Brooks, Lester,

Behind Japan's Surrender, McGraw Hill, New York, 1968, p. 140.
For ". . . from his air force" (pp. 324–25): Brooks, *op. cit.*, p. 145.
For ". . . Japan shall be given" (pp. 326–27): Brooks, *op. cit.*, p. 158.
For "To the Japanese People" (p. 330) and "accept the Allied" (p. 16):
Brooks *op. cit.*, (pp. 258–59), 267.
For ". . . certainly prior to 31 December" (p. 331): USSBS, Pacific
War, Vol. 1, *Summary Report (Pacific War)*.

General Sources

Toland, John, *The Rising Sun*, Bantam Books, New York, 1971.
USSBS, Pacific War, Volume 14 *op. cit.*, Volume 42, *op. cit.*, Volume
53, *The Effects of Strategic Bombing on Japan's War Economy*,
and Volume 55, *op. cit.*

BACKGROUND SOURCES

Akizuki, Tatuichiro, *Nagasaki, 1945*, Quartet Books, New York,
1981.
Anders, Curt, *Fighting Airmen*, C. P. Putnam's Sons, New York,
1966.
Arnold, H. H., Gen. *Global Missions*, Harper and Brothers, New
York, 1949.
Birdsall, Steve, *B-29 Superfortress*, Squadron/Signal Publications,
Warren, MI, 1977.
Blair, Clay, *Silent Victory: the U.S. Submarine War Against Japan*,
Lippincott, Philadelphia, 1975.
Brodie, Bernard, *Strategy in the Missile Age*, Princeton University
Press, Princeton, NJ, 1959.
Cortesi, Lawrence, *Target Tokyo*, Zebra Books, New York, 1983.
Cotten, Paul, *The Realm of the Submarine*, MacMillan Company,
New York, 1969.
Craig, William, *The Fall of Japan*, Dell Publishing, New York, 1968.
Creswell, John, *Sea Warfare 1930–1945*, University of California
Press, Berkeley, 1967.
Deighton, Len, *Bomber*, Harper and Row, New York, 1970.
Emme, Eugene, *The Impact of Air Power—National Security and
World Politics*, Van Nostrand Company, Princeton, NJ, 1959.
Halberstam, David, *The Reckoning*, William Morrow, New York,
1986.
Hansell, General Haywood, *The Air Plan That Defeated Hitler*, Arno
Press, New York, 1980.

Hashimoto, Mochitsura, *Sunk: The Story of the Japanese Submarine Fleet 1941–1945*, Holt Publishing, New York, 1954.

Hastings, Max, *Bomber Command*, Dial Press, New York, 1979.

Hersey, John, *Hiroshima*, A. A. Knopf, New York, 1965.

Holley, Irving, *Buying Aircraft Material: Procurement for the Army Air Forces* (Volume VI, Special Studies Series, The United States Army in World War II), Office of The Chief of Military History, Washington, D.C., 1964.

Holmes, Wilfred, *Undersea Victory: The Influence of Submarine Operations on the War in the Pacific*, Doubleday, Garden City, NY, 1966.

Hoyt, Edwin, *Closing the Circle, War in the Pacific: 1945*, Van Nostrand Reinhold Company, New York, 1982.

———, *Japan's War*, Van Nostrand Reinhold Company, New York, 1983.

Irving, David, *The Destruction of Dresden*, Transworld, London, 1966.

Kosaka, Masataka, *100 Million Japanese, The Postwar Experience*, Kodansha International, Tokyo, 1972.

Larrabee, Eric, *Commander in Chief*, Harper and Row, New York, 1987.

LeMay, General Haywood, with MacKinlay Kantor, *Mission with LeMay: My Story*, Doubleday, Garden City, NY, 1965.

Manning, Paul, *Hirohito*, Dodd, Mead and Co., New York, 1986.

Maurer, Maurer, ed., *Air Force Combat Units of World War II*, Franklin Watts, New York, 1959.

Middlebrook, Martin, *The Battle of Hamburg*, Charles Scribner's Sons, New York, 1981.

Overy, R. J., *The Air War 1939–1945*, Stein and Day, New York, 1980.

Pacific War Research Society, *The Day Man Lost: Hiroshima, 6 August 1945*, Kodansha International, Palo Alto, CA, 1972.

Parsons, Ian, ed., *The Encyclopedia of Air Warfare*, Thomas Y. Crowell, New York, 1975.

Perera, Guido, *Leaves From My Book of Life*, Volume II, Privately Printed, Boston, 1975.

Rhodes, Richard, *The Making of the Atomic Bomb*, Simon and Schuster, New York, 1986.

Sinclair, William, *The Big Brothers*, Naylor Company, San Antonio, Texas, 1972.

Stockholm International Peace Research Institute, *Incendiary Weapons*, Almquist and Wiksell, Stockholm, 1975.

Sunderman, James, *World War II in the Air: The Pacific*, Franklin Watts, New York, 1962.

Toland, John, *Gods of War*, Doubleday, Garden City, NY, 1985.

Webster, Sir Charles, and Noble Frankland, *The Strategic Air Offensive Against Germany, 1939–1945* (4 volumes), Her Majesty's Stationary Office, London, 1961.

Wolfe, Stephen, ed., *The Story of the "Billy Mitchell" Group, 468th Bomb Group From CBI to the Marianas*, Dayton, Ohio, N.D.

Yass, Marion, *Hiroshima*, Putnam, New York, 1972.

Zanetti, J. Enrique, *Fire From the Air, The ABC's of Incendiaries*, Columbia University Press, New York, 1941.

Zuckerman, Sir Solly, *From Apes to Warlords*, Hamish Hamilton, London, 1978.

APPENDIX A

TWENTIETH AIR FORCE
CHAIN OF COMMAND

April 1944 - July 1945

JOINT CHIEFS OF STAFF

HEADQUARTERS - U.S. ARMY AIR FORCES
General H. H. Arnold

HEADQUARTERS - TWENTIETH AIR FORCE
The Pentagon, Washington, D.C.

HEADQUARTERS - TWENTIETH AIR FORCE
The Pentagon, Washington, D.C.
Commanding General: General H. H. Arnold
Chiefs of Staff
Brig. Gen. Haywood S. Hansell - April - August 1944
Brig. Gen. Lauris Norstad - August 1944 - July 1945

HEADQUARTERS XX BOMBER COMMAND
Kharagphur, India
Commanding Generals
Brig. Gen. Kenneth B. Wolfe - Nov. 1943 - July 1944
Brig. Gen. LaVerne G. Saunders - July - Aug. 1944
Maj. Gen. Curtis E. LeMay - Aug. 1944 - Jan. 1945

58th BOMB WING
Brig. Gen. LaVerne G. Saunders - Apr. 1944 - Feb. 1945
Col. Dwight O. Monteith - Feb. - Apr. - 1945

BOMB GROUPS:
40th 444th 462nd 468th

73rd BOMB WING
Saipan
Brig. Gen. Emmett O'Donnell

BOMB GROUPS:
497th 498th 499th 500th

HEADQUARTERS XXI BOMBER COMMAND
Saipan - Guam
Commanding Generals
Brig. Gen. Haywood S. Hansell - Aug. 1944 - Jan. 1945
Maj. Gen. Curtis E. LeMay - Jan. - July 1945

313th BOMB WING
Tinian
Brig. Gen. John R. Davies

BOMB GROUPS:
6th 9th 504th 505th
509th (Atchd)

314th BOMB WING
Guam
Brig. Gen. Thomas S. Power

BOMB GROUPS:
19th 29th 39th 330th

58th BOMB WING
Tinian (From May 1945)
Brig. Gen. Roger Ramey

BOMB GROUPS:
40th 444th 462nd 468th

315th BOMB WING
Guam
Brig. Gen. Frank Armstrong

BOMB GROUPS:
16th 331th 501st 502nd

319

APPENDIX B

MAJOR XX BOMBER COMMAND MISSIONS, 1944–45

(Training missions and those involving less than 20 aircrafts have been omitted.)

Date*	B-29s Airborne	Target Site	Target Type	Bomb Type
1944				
JUN 5	98	Bangkok, Thailand	Rail Yards	HE
JUN 15	68	Yawata, Japan	Steelworks	HE
JUL 7	18	Sasebo/Omura/ Tobata, Japan	Urban areas	HE
JUL 29	96	Anshan/Taku, Manchuria	Steelworks/harbor	HE
AUG 10	29	Nagasaki, Japan	Urban areas	HE
AUG 10	54	Palembang, Sumatra	Oil refineries	HE
AUG 20	88	Yawata, Japan	Steelworks/assorted targets	HE
SEP 8	108	Anshan, Manchuria	Steelworks	HE
SEP 26	109	Anshan, Manchuria	Steelworks	HE
OCT 14	130	Okayama, Formosa	Aircraft factory	HE
OCT 16	72	Okayama, Formosa	Aircraft factory	HE
OCT 17	30	Okayama, Formosa	Aircraft factory	HE

* Departure from China bases
HE = High Explosives
I = Incendiaries
M = Mines

Based on USAAF records

MAJOR XX BOMBER COMMAND MISSIONS, 1944–45—Continued

Date	B-29s Airborne	Target Site	Target Type	Bomb Type
OCT 25	78	Omura, Japan	Aircraft factory	HE
NOV 3	49	Rangoon	Rail yards	HE
NOV 5	76	Singapore	George VI dry dock	HE
NOV 12	96	Omura, Japan; Nanking, China	Urban areas/assorted targets	HE
NOV 21	109	Omura, Japan	Aircraft factory	HE
NOV 27	60	Bangkok, Thailand	Rail yards/ assorted targets	HE
DEC 7	108	Mukden, Manchuria	Aircraft factory/ rail yards/ arsenal	HE
DEC 14	48	Bangkok, Thailand	Rail bridge/ assorted targets	HE
DEC 18	94	Hankow, China	Docks/assorted targets	I
DEC 19	36	Omura, Japan	Aircraft factory	HE
DEC 21	49	Mukden, Manchuria	Aircraft factory/ arsenal/rail yards	HE
1945				
JAN 2	49	Bangkok, Thailand	Railroad bridge	HE
JAN 6	49	Omura, Japan	Aircraft factory	HE
JAN 9	46	Formosa	Harbor	HE
JAN 11	47	Singapore	Dry docks	HE
JAN 14	82	Kagi, Japan	Airfields	HE
JAN 14	23	Japan	Assorted targets	HE
JAN 17	80	Shinchiku, Japan	Airfield	HE
JAN 17	8	Southeast China	Assorted targets	HE
JAN 25	76	Singapore; Saigon	Channels/harbors	M
JAN 27	25	Saigon	Navy yard/ arsenal	HE
FEB 1	113	Singapore	Dock	HE
FEB 7	67	Saigon	Urban areas	HE

MAJOR XX BOMBER COMMAND MISSIONS, 1944-45—Continued

Date	B-29s Airborne	Target Site	Target Type	Bomb Type
FEB 7	64	Bangkok, Thailand	Railroad bridge	HE
FEB 11	59	Rangoon, Burma	Storage dumps	HE
FEB 19	59	Kuala Lumpur, Malaya/Martaban, Burma	Rail yards/ assorted targets	HE
FEB 24	116	Singapore	Empire docks	I
1945				
MAR 2	64	Singapore	Naval base/ urban areas	HE
MAR 10	29	Kuala Lumpur, Malaya	Rail yards	HE
MAR 12	49	Singapore	Oil storage facilities	HE
MAR 17	77	Rangoon, Burma	Storage facilities/ airfields/ warehouses	HE
MAR 22	78	Rangoon, Burma	Storage facilities	HE
MAR 28	61	Saigon; Singapore	Waterways	M
MAR 29	29	Singapore	Oil storage facilities	HE

APPENDIX C

**PERSONNEL AND EQUIPMENT
TYPICAL BOMB WING
XXI BOMBER COMMAND
(March - July 1945)**

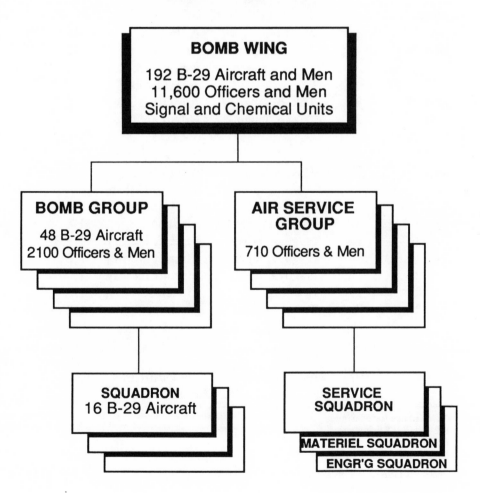

APPENDIX D

XXI BOMBER COMMAND MISSIONS, 1944–45

(Training missions and those involving less than 20 aircrafts have been omitted.)

Date*	B-29s Airborne	Target Site	Target Type	Bomb Type
1944				
NOV 5	36	Iwo Jima	Airfields	HE
NOV 24	111	Tokyo, Japan	Aircraft factory/urban areas/docks	HE
NOV 27	81	Tokyo, Japan	Aircraft factory	HE
NOV 29	29	Tokyo, Japan	Urban areas/ docks/ industrial areas	Incendi- aries
DEC 3	86	Tokyo, Japan	Aircraft factories/urban areas/docks	HE
DEC 8	82	Iwo Jima	Airfields	HE
DEC 13	90	Nagoya, Japan	Aircraft factory	HE, I
DEC 18	89	Nagoya, Japan	Aircraft factory	HE
DEC 22	78	Nagoya, Japan	Aircraft factory	I
DEC 24	29	Iwo Jima	Airfields	HE
DEC 27	72	Tokyo, Japan	Aircraft factories	HE
1945				
JAN 3	97	Nagoya, Japan	Docks/urban areas	HE

* Departure for Marianas
HE = High Explosives
I = Incendiaries
M = Mines

Based on USAAF records

XXI BOMBER COMMAND MISSIONS, 1944–45—Continued

Date	B-29s Airborne	Target Site	Target Type	Bomb Type
JAN 9	72	Tokyo, Japan	Aircraft factory/urban areas	HE
JAN 14	73	Nagoya, Japan	Aircraft factory	HE
JAN 19	77	Akashi, Japan	Aircraft factories	HE
JAN 21	33	Truk	Airfield	HE
JAN 23	73	Nagoya, Japan	Aircraft factory	HE
JAN 24	28	Iwo Jima	Airfields	HE
JAN 27	76	Tokyo, Japan	Aircraft factory/urban areas	HE
JAN 29	33	Iwo Jima	Airfields	HE
FEB 4	110	Kobe, Japan	Urban areas	I
FEB 8	31	Truk	Airfield	HE
FEB 9	30	Truk	Airfield	HE
FEB 10	118	Ota, Japan	Aircraft factory	HE
FEB 12	21	Iwo Jima	Defensive fortifications	HE
FEB 15	117	Nagoya, Japan	Aircraft factory	HE
FEB 18	36	Moen Island	Airfields	HE
FEB 19	150	Tokyo, Japan	Aircraft factory/port/ urban areas	HE
1945				
FEB 24	229	Tokyo, Japan	Urban areas	I
MAR 4	192	Tokyo, Japan	Urban areas/assorted targets	HE
MAR 9	325	Tokyo, Japan	Urban areas	I
MAR 11	310	Nagoya, Japan	Urban areas	I
MAR 13	301	Osaka, Japan	Urban areas	I
MAR 16	330	Kobe, Japan	Urban areas	I
MAR 18	310	Nagoya, Japan	Urban areas	I
MAR 24	248	Nagoya, Japan	Aircraft factory	HE

XXI BOMBER COMMAND MISSIONS, 1944–45—Continued

Date	B-29s Airborne	Target Site	Target Type	Bomb Type
MAR 27	161	Kyushu Island, Japan	Aircraft factory/airfields	HE
MAR 27	102	Shimonoseki Straits, Japan	Waterway	M
MAR 30	94	Shimonoseki Straits/Sasebo/ Kure/Hiroshima, Japan	Waterway/harbors	M
MAR 31	149	Kyushu Island	Factory/airfield	HE
APR 1	121	Tokyo, Japan	Aircraft factory	HE
APR 3	49	Shizuoka, Japan	Aircraft factory/industrial	HE
APR 3	68	Koizumi, Japan	Aircraft factory/industrial	HE
APR 3	115	Tachikawa/ Kawasaki, Japan	Aircraft factory/industrial	HE
APR 7	107	Tokyo, Japan	Aircraft factory	HE
APR 7	30	Japan	Assorted targets	HE
APR 8	53	Kanoya, Japan	Airfields	HE
APR 12	114	Tokyo, Japan	Aircraft factory	HE
APR 12	167	Koriyama, Japan	Chemical plants	HE
APR 13	348	Tokyo, Japan	Arsenal	I
APR 15	219	Kawasaki, Japan	Urban areas	I
APR 15	118	Tokyo, Japan	Urban areas	I
APR 17	132	Kyushu and Shikoku Islands, Japan	Airfields	HE
APR 18	132	Kyushu and Shikoku Islands, Japan	Airfields	HE
APR 21	252	Kyushu and Shikoku Islands, Japan	Airfields	HE

XXI BOMBER COMMAND MISSIONS, 1944–45—Continued

Date	B-29s Airborne	Target Site	Target Type	Bomb Type
APR 22	104	Kyushu and Shikoku Islands, Japan	Airfields	HE
APR 24	131	Tachikawa, Japan	Aircraft factory	HE
1945				
APR 26	256	Kyushu and Shikoku Islands, Japan	Airfields	HE
APR 27	123	Kyushu and Shikoku Islands, Japan	Airfields	HE
APR 28	129	Kyushu and Shikoku Islands, Japan	Airfields	HE
APR 29	121	Kyushu and Shikoku Islands, Japan	Airfields	HE
APR 30	106	Tachikawa, Japan	Aircraft factory	HE
APR 30	66	Kyushu and Shikoku Islands, Japan	Airfields	HE
MAY 3	66	Kyushu and Shikoku Islands, Japan	Airfields	HE
MAY 3	97	Shimonoseki Straits, Japan	Waterway	M
MAY 4	62	Kyushu and Shikoku Islands, Japan	Airfields	HE
MAY 5	60	Kyushu and Shikoku Islands, Japan	Airfields	HE

XXI BOMBER COMMAND MISSIONS, 1944–45—Continued

Date	B-29s Airborne	Target Site	Target Type	Bomb Type
MAY 5	170	Kure, Japan	Aircraft factory	HE
MAY 5	96	Japan	Sea approaches	M
MAY 7	42	Kyushu and Shikoku Islands, Japan	Airfields	HE
MAY 8	44	Kyushu and Shikoku Islands, Japan	Airfields	HE
MAY 10	343	Tokuyama/ Otake/Amami-O- Shima, Japan	Industrial sites/naval fuel storage facilities	I, HE
MAY 10	67	Kyushu and Shikoku Islands, Japan	Airfields	HE
MAY 11	63	Kyushu and Shikoku Islands, Japan	Airfields	HE
MAY 14	102	Kobe, Japan	Aircraft factory	HE
	524	Nagoya, Japan	Urban area	I
MAY 16	31	Shimonoseki Straits, Japan	Waterways	M
MAY 17	516	Nagoya, Japan	Urban area	I
1945				
MAY 18	34	Shimonoseki Straits/Tsuruga Harbor, Japan	Waterways	M
MAY 19	309	Tachikawa, Japan	Urban areas	I
MAY 20	30	Shimonoseki Starits, Japan	Waterways	M
MAY 22	32	Shimonoseki Straits, Japan	Waterways	M

XXI BOMBER COMMAND MISSIONS, 1944–45—Continued

Date	B-29s Airborne	Target Site	Target Type	Bomb Type
MAY 23	558	Tokyo, Japan	Urban and industrial areas	I
MAY 24	30	Shimonoseki Straits, Japan	Waterways	M
MAY 25	498	Tokyo, Japan	Urban areas	I
MAY 26	30	Shimonoseki Straits, Japan	Waterways	M
MAY 29	510	Yokohama, Japan	Urban areas	I
JUN 1	509	Osaka, Japan	Urban areas	I
JUN 5	530	Kobe, Japan	Urban areas	I
JUN 7	449	Osaka, Japan	Urban areas/industrial areas/transportation targets	I, HE
JUN 7	31	Shimonoseki Straits/Fukuoka/Kamatsu, Japan	Waterways	M
JUN 9	116	Nagoya/Akashi/Narao, Japan	Aircraft factories	HE
JUN 10	282	Central Japan	Industrial sites/aircraft factories/seaplane base/army air arsenal/engineering works	HE
JUN 11	28	Shimonoseki Straits/Tsuruga Bay, Japan	Waterways	M
JUN 13	30	Shimonoseki Straits/Niigata, Japan	Waterways	M
JUN 15	511	Osaka and Amagasaki, Japan	Urban areas	I

XXI BOMBER COMMAND MISSIONS, 1944–45—Continued

Date	B-29s Airborne	Target Site	Target Type	Bomb Type
JUN 15	30	Shimonoseki Straits/Fukuoka/ Karatsu/Fushiki, Japan	Waterways	M
1945				
JUN 17	477	Kagoshima/ Omuta/ Hamamatsu/ Yokkaichi, Japan	Urban areas	I
JUN 17	28	Shimonoseki Straits, Japan	Waterways	M
JUN 19	515	Toyohashi/ Fukuoka/ Shizuoka, Japan	Urban areas	I
JUN 19	28	Shimonoseki Straits/Niigata/ Miyazu/Maizuru, Japan	Waterways	M
JUN 21	30	Fushiki/Senzaki/ Nanao/Yuya Bay, Japan	Sea approaches	M
JUN 22	455	Himeji/ Kagamigahara/ Akashi/Tamashima Japan	Aircraft factories	HE
JUN 22	195	Kure, Japan	Naval arsenal	HE
JUN 23	27	Fukuoka/Karatsu/ Sakai/Niigata, Japan	Harbors	M
JUN 25	27	Shimonoseki Straits/Maizuru/ Obama Island, Japan	Waterways	M

XXI BOMBER COMMAND MISSIONS, 1944–45—Continued

Date	B-29s Airborne	Target Site	Target Type	Bomb Type
JUN 26	508	Nagoya/ Kagamigahara/ Akashi/Osaka/ Yokkaichi, Japan	Industrial targets	HE
JUN 26	35	Yokkaichi, Japan	Oil Refinery	HE
JUN 27	30	Hagi/Kobe/ Niigata, Japan	Harbors	M
JUN 28	509	Okayama/Sasebo/ Moji/Nobeoka, Japan	Urban areas	I
JUN 29	36	Kudamatsu, Japan	Oil refinery	HE
JUN 29	29	Shimonoseki Straits/Maizuru/ Sakata, Japan	Waterways	M
JUL 1	575	Ube/Kure/ Shimonoseki/ Kumamoto, Japan	Urban areas	I
1945				
JUL 1	31	Shimonoseki Straits/Nanao/ Fushiki, Japan	Waterways	M
JUL 2	40	Minoshima, Japan	Oil refinery	HE
JUL 3	499	Kochi/Himeji/ Takamatsu/ Tokushima, Japan	Urban areas	I
JUL 3	31	Shimonoseki Straits/Funakawa/ Maizuru, Japan	Waterways	M

XXI BOMBER COMMAND MISSIONS, 1944–45—Continued

Date	B-29s Airborne	Target Site	Target Type	Bomb Type
JUL 6	534	Chiba/Akashi/ Shimizu/Kofu, Japan	Urban areas	I
JUL 6	60	Osaka, Japan	Oil refinery	HE
JUL 9	499	Sendai/Sakai/ Gifu/Wakayama, Japan	Urban areas	I
JUL 9	64	Yokkaichi, Japan	Oil refinery	HE
JUL 9	30	Shimonoseki Strait/Niigata/ Nonao, Japan	Waterways	M
JUL 11	30	Shimonoseki Straits/Maizuru, Japan; Pusan/Najin, Korea	Waterways	M
JUL 12	488	Utsonomiya/ Ichinomiya/ Tsuruga/Uwajima, Japan	Urban areas	I
JUL 12	60	Kawasaki, Japan	Petroleum center	HE
JUL 13	31	Shimonoseki Straits/Fukuoka, Japan; Seishi/Masan/ Reisui, Korea	Waterways/ports	M
JUL 15	28	Naoetsu/Niigata, Japan; Najin/Pusan/ Wonsan, Korea	Waterways	M

XXI BOMBER COMMAND MISSIONS, 1944–45—Continued

Date	B-29s Airborne	Target Site	Target Type	Bomb Type
1945				
JUL 15	69	Kudamatsu, Japan	Petroleum center	HE
JUL 16	488	Numazu/Oita/ Kuwana/ Hiratsuka, Japan	Urban areas	I
JUL 17	30	Shimonoseki Straits/Nanao-Fushiki/Cape Henashi/Iwase, Japan; Seishin, Korea	Waterways	M
JUL 19	487	Fukui/Hitachi/ Chosi/Okazaki, Japan	Urban areas	I
JUL 19	84	Amagasaki	Petroleum center	HE
JUL 19	31	Oyama/Niigata Miyazu/Maizuru/ Tsuruga/ Nezugaseki/ Obama Island/ Kobe—Osaka areas, Japan; Wonsan, Korea	Waterways	M
JUL 23	80	Ube, Japan	Petroleum center	HE
JUL 23	29	Shimonoseki Straits, Japan; Najin/Pusan/ Masan, Korea	Waterways	M

XXI BOMBER COMMAND MISSIONS, 1944–45—Continued

Date	B-29s Airborne	Target Site	Target Type	Bomb Type
JUL 24	625	Handa/Nagoya/ Takarazuka/ Osaka/ Tsu/Kawana, Japan	Aircraft factories/ industrial sites/ urban areas	HE, I
JUL 25	83	Kawasaki, Japan	Petroleum center	HE
JUL 25	30	Nanao/Fushiki/ Obama Island/ Tsuruga, Japan; Seishin/Pusan, Korea	Waterways	M
1945				
JUL 26	361	Matsuyama/ Tokuyama/ Omuta, Japan	Urban areas	I
JUL 27	30	Shimonoseki Straits/ Fukuoka/Niigata/ Maizuru/Senzaki/ Fukawa Bay, Japan	Waterways	M
JUL 28	496	Tsu/Aomori/ Ichinomiya/ Ujiyamada/ Ogaki/Uwajima, Japan	Urban areas	I
JUL 28	82	Shimotsu, Japan	Oil refinery	HE
JUL 29	29	Shimonseki Straits/Fukuoka Karatsu, Japan; Najin, Korea	Waterways	M

XXI BOMBER COMMAND MISSIONS, 1944–45—Continued

Date	*B-29s Airborne*	*Target Site*	*Target Type*	*Bomb Type*
AUG 1	665	Hachioji/Toyama/ Nagaoka/Mito, Japan	Urban areas	I
AUG 1	128	Kawasaki, Japan	Petroleum center	HE
AUG 1	43	Shimonoseki Straits/Nakaumi Lagoon/Hamada/ Sakai/Yonago, Japan; Najin/Seishin, Korea	Waterways	M
AUG 5	494	Saga/Mae Bashi/ Imabari/ Nishinomiya-Mikage, Japan	Urban areas	I
AUG 5	111	Ube, Japan	Petroleum center	HE
AUG 5	30	Sakai/Yonago/ Nakaumi Lagoon/ Miyazu/Maizuru/ Tsuruga/Obama, Japan; Najin, Korea	Waterways	M
AUG 6	3	Hiroshima, Japan	Urban area	Nuclear
AUG 7	131	Toyokawa, Japan	Naval arsenal	HE

XXI BOMBER COMMAND MISSIONS, 1944–45—Continued

Date	B-29s Airborne	Target Site	Target Type	Bomb Type
1945				
AUG 7	32	Shimonoseki Straits/Miyazu/ Maizuru/Tsurua/ Obama, Japan; Najin, Korea	Waterways	M
AUG 8	245	Yawata, Japan	Urban area	I
AUG 8	98	Fukuyama, Japan	Urban area	I
AUG 8	69	Tokyo, Japan	Aircraft factory/arsenal complex	HE
AUG 9	107	Amagasaki, Japan	Oil refinery	HE
AUG 9	3	Nagasaki, Japan	Urban area	Nuclear
AUG 14	328	Hikari/Osaka, Japan	Arsenals	HE
AUG 14	115	Marifu, Japan	Rail yards	HE
AUG 14	186	Kumagaya/ Isezaki, Japan	Urban areas	I
AUG 14	141	Tsuchizakimi- nato, Japan	Oil refinery	HE
AUG 14	39	Shiminoseki Straits/Nanao/ Miyazu/Hamada, Japan	Waterways	M
AUG 27- SEP 20	900	Far East	POW camps containing Allied personnel	Supplies

APPENDIX E

DESTRUCTION INFLICTED ON 67 JAPANESE CITIES 1944–45

The list below shows the percentage destruction inflicted by the B-29 aerial campaign on 67 Japanese cities and pairs a U.S. city with each Japanese city of approximately the same population.

United States	Japan	% Destroyed
San Diego	Shimonoseki	37.6
Spokane	Moji	23.3
San Antonio	Yawata	21.2
Rochester	Fukuoka	24.1
Nashville	Sasebo	41.4
Waterloo	Saga	44.2
Santa Fe	Omura	33.1
Miami	Omuta	35.9
Grand Rapids	Kumamoto	31.2
Saint Joseph	Oita	28.2
Augusta	Nobeoka	25.2
Richmond	Kagoshima	63.4
Greensboro	Miyakonojo	26.5
Davenport	Miyazaki	26.1
Utica	Ube	20.7
no counterpart	Uwajima	54.2
Duluth	Matsuyama	64.0
Sacramento	Kochi	55.2
Butte	Tokuyama	48.3
Toledo	Kure	41.9
Stockton	Imabari	63.9
Macon	Fukuyama	80.9
Knoxville	Takamatsu	67.5
Long Beach	Okayama	68.9
Peoria	Himeji	49.4
Jacksonville	Amagasaki	18.9

United States	Japan	% Destroyed
Baltimore	Kobe	55.7
Chicago	Osaka	35.1
Fort Worth	Sakai	48.2
Lexington	Akashi	50.2
Salt Lake City	Wakayama	50.0
Cambridge	Nishinomiya	11.9
Ft. Wayne	Tokushima	85.2
Columbus	Ujiyamada	41.3
Topeka	Tsu	59.3
Portland	Kawasaki	35.2
Savannah	Chiba	41.0
Battle Creek	Hiratsuka	48.4
Waco	Numazu	42.3
San Jose	Shimizu	42.1
Oklahoma City	Shizuoka	66.1
Wheeling	Chosi	44.2
New York	Tokyo	50.8
Cleveland	Yokohama	57.6
Middletown	Tsuriga	65.1
Evansville	Fukui	86.0
Tucson	Kuwana	75.0
Springfield	Ichinomiya	56.3
Des Moines	Gifu	69.9
Corpus Christi	Ogaki	39.5
Chattanooga	Toyama	98.6
Los Angeles	Nagoya	40.0
Charlotte	Yokkaichi	33.6
Lincoln	Okazaki	32.2
Montgomery	Aomori	30.0
Madison	Nagaoka	64.9
Tulsa	Toyohashi	67.9
Hartford	Hamamatsu	60.3
Wilkes-Barre	Mabashi	64.2
Omaha	Sendai	21.9
South Bend	Kofu	78.6
Sioux Falls	Isezaki	56.1

United States	Japan	% Destroyed
Kenosha	Kumagaya	55.1
Sioux City	Utsunomiya	43.7
Little Rock	Hitachi	72.0
Galveston	Hachioji	65.0
Pontiac	Mito	68.9

APPENDIX F

CHARACTERISTICS OF THE M-69 AND OTHER INCENDIARY BOMBS

	AN-50A2 AN-M50xA3	AN-M69	M47A2	M76
Filling and weight (lbs)	Mg. 1.3 Th. 0.62 Tetryl 38g (in M50xA3)	IM 2.8 or NP 2.8	IM 40 lbs or NP 40 lbs	PT-1 180 lbs
Method of functioning	Intensive: Filling stays near bomb	Tail ejection: Burning sock of mixture is ejected up to 75 yrds	Scatters over a 50' radius	Scatters over a 150' radius
Bomb fuze		M1	AN-M126 AN-M126A1	AN-M103 nose AN-M101A2 tail
Burning time	5–7 min	4–5 min	10 min (approx)	20 min (approx)
Bomb weight (lbs)	3.7 (4-lb type)	6.2 (6-lb type)	69 (100-lb type)	473 (500-lb type)
Terminal velocity	420'/sec	225'/sec	825'/sec	1000'/sec
Penetration at T.V.	4" reinforced concrete (heavy construction)	2"–3" concrete (light to medium construction)	5" concrete from 25,000'	15" concrete from 25,000'
Aimable 500-lb clusters (symbol, weight, contents, adapter, fuzes, burster)	AN-M17A1: 490 lbs 110 bombs M10 adapter T55 nose fuze Primacord	M18: 350 lbs 38 bombs M9 adapter T55 nose fuze T53 tail fuze Primacord	M12 or M13	M14 Adapter-Booster M115
Altitude recommendations	Quick-Opening: from 8000' or less Aimable: Medium to high, with cluster burst set for 5000'	Quick-Opening: from 1000' to 8000' Aimable: Medium to high, with cluster burst set for 5000'	Min safe release: 200' Penetration good from 15,000' and higher	Min safe release: 300' Penetration good from 15,000' and higher

INDEX